# Lecture Notes in Computer Science    12429

More information about this series at http://www.springer.com/series/7409

Constantine Stephanidis ·
Vincent G. Duffy · Norbert Streitz ·
Shin'ichi Konomi · Heidi Krömker (Eds.)

# HCI International 2020 – Late Breaking Papers

## Digital Human Modeling and Ergonomics, Mobility and Intelligent Environments

22nd HCI International Conference, HCII 2020
Copenhagen, Denmark, July 19–24, 2020
Proceedings

 Springer

*Editors*
Constantine Stephanidis
University of Crete and Foundation
for Research and Technology – Hellas
(FORTH)
Heraklion, Crete, Greece

Norbert Streitz ⓘ
Smart Future Initiative
Frankfurt am Main, Germany

Heidi Krömker
Ilmenau University of Technology
Ilmenau, Germany

Vincent G. Duffy
Purdue University
West Lafayette, IN, USA

Shin'ichi Konomi
Kyushu University
Fukuoka, Japan

ISSN 0302-9743                ISSN 1611-3349   (electronic)
Lecture Notes in Computer Science
ISBN 978-3-030-59986-7        ISBN 978-3-030-59987-4   (eBook)
https://doi.org/10.1007/978-3-030-59987-4

LNCS Sublibrary: SL3 – Information Systems and Applications, incl. Internet/Web, and HCI

This Springer imprint is published by the registered company Springer Nature Switzerland AG
The registered company address is: Gewerbestrasse 11, 6330 Cham, Switzerland

# Foreword

The 22nd International Conference on Human-Computer Interaction, HCI International 2020 (HCII 2020), was planned to be held at the AC Bella Sky Hotel and Bella Center, Copenhagen, Denmark, during July 19–24, 2020. Due to the COVID-19 pandemic and the resolution of the Danish government not to allow events larger than 500 people to be hosted until September 1, 2020, HCII 2020 had to be held virtually. It incorporated the 21 thematic areas and affiliated conferences listed on the following page.

A total of 6,326 individuals from academia, research institutes, industry, and governmental agencies from 97 countries submitted contributions, and 1,439 papers and 238 posters were included in the volumes of the proceedings published before the conference. Additionally, 333 papers and 144 posters are included in the volumes of the proceedings published after the conference, as "Late Breaking Work" (papers and posters). These contributions address the latest research and development efforts in the field and highlight the human aspects of design and use of computing systems.

The volumes comprising the full set of the HCII 2020 conference proceedings are listed in the following pages and together they broadly cover the entire field of human-computer interaction, addressing major advances in knowledge and effective use of computers in a variety of application areas.

I would like to thank the Program Board Chairs and the members of the Program Boards of all Thematic Areas and Affiliated Conferences for their valuable contributions towards the highest scientific quality and the overall success of the HCI International 2020 conference.

This conference would not have been possible without the continuous and unwavering support and advice of the founder, conference general chair emeritus and conference scientific advisor, Prof. Gavriel Salvendy. For his outstanding efforts, I would like to express my appreciation to the communications chair and editor of HCI International News, Dr. Abbas Moallem.

July 2020                                                            Constantine Stephanidis

# HCI International 2020 Thematic Areas
# and Affiliated Conferences

Thematic Areas:

- HCI 2020: Human-Computer Interaction
- HIMI 2020: Human Interface and the Management of Information

Affiliated Conferences:

- EPCE: 17th International Conference on Engineering Psychology and Cognitive Ergonomics
- UAHCI: 14th International Conference on Universal Access in Human-Computer Interaction
- VAMR: 12th International Conference on Virtual, Augmented and Mixed Reality
- CCD: 12th International Conference on Cross-Cultural Design
- SCSM: 12th International Conference on Social Computing and Social Media
- AC: 14th International Conference on Augmented Cognition
- DHM: 11th International Conference on Digital Human Modeling & Applications in Health, Safety, Ergonomics & Risk Management
- DUXU: 9th International Conference on Design, User Experience and Usability
- DAPI: 8th International Conference on Distributed, Ambient and Pervasive Interactions
- HCIBGO: 7th International Conference on HCI in Business, Government and Organizations
- LCT: 7th International Conference on Learning and Collaboration Technologies
- ITAP: 6th International Conference on Human Aspects of IT for the Aged Population
- HCI-CPT: Second International Conference on HCI for Cybersecurity, Privacy and Trust
- HCI-Games: Second International Conference on HCI in Games
- MobiTAS: Second International Conference on HCI in Mobility, Transport and Automotive Systems
- AIS: Second International Conference on Adaptive Instructional Systems
- C&C: 8th International Conference on Culture and Computing
- MOBILE: First International Conference on Design, Operation and Evaluation of Mobile Communications
- AI-HCI: First International Conference on Artificial Intelligence in HCI

# Conference Proceedings – Full List of Volumes

**http://2020.hci.international/proceedings**

# HCI International 2020 (HCII 2020)

The full list with the Program Board Chairs and the members of the Program Boards of all thematic areas and affiliated conferences is available online at:

**http://www.hci.international/board-members-2020.php**

# HCI International 2021

The 23rd International Conference on Human-Computer Interaction, HCI International 2021 (HCII 2021), will be held jointly with the affiliated conferences in Washington DC, USA, at the Washington Hilton Hotel, July 24–29, 2021. It will cover a broad spectrum of themes related to human-computer interaction (HCI), including theoretical issues, methods, tools, processes, and case studies in HCI design, as well as novel interaction techniques, interfaces, and applications. The proceedings will be published by Springer. More information will be available on the conference website: http://2021.hci.international/

General Chair
Prof. Constantine Stephanidis
University of Crete and ICS-FORTH
Heraklion, Crete, Greece
Email: general_chair@hcii2021.org

**http://2021.hci.international/**

# Contents

**Interaction in Intelligent Environments**

## Digital Human Modelling and Ergonomics

# HCI in Automotive

# User Preference for Vehicle Warning Sounds to Develop AUI Guideline Focusing on Differences Between Sex and Among Age Groups

Jun Young An[1], Young Jin Kim[2], and Hoon Sik Yoo[2(✉)]

[1] Graduate School of Konkuk University, Seoul, South Korea
jyan.konkuk@gmail.com
[2] Seoul Media Institute of Technology, Seoul, South Korea
dogzone276@gmail.com, hsyoo@smit.ac.kr

**Abstract.** Currently, a car is an essential element for individuals to travel around. As a result, people spend long hours in cars and are exposed to possible dangers. Drivers need to recognize dangers safely and quickly. There are visual and auditory ways of recognizing risks while driving. Also, with the increasing functions of cars, there are various types of warning sounds that drivers should identify. These sounds should not cause confusion or discomfort to the drivers. In this study, a total of 500 participants (male 250, female 250) were surveyed to identify the preference of the warning sounds. The age groups of the participants were separated into the 20s, 30s, 40s, 50s, and over 60s. Each age group consists of 100 participants. They listened to nine sound samples and chose the sounds they preferred for ten given situations. There was only one difference in the preference between sex. However, there was no significant difference among age groups. This study is to give a guideline for the Auditory User Interface design of vehicle warning sounds.

**Keywords:** Sound design · Auditory User Interface · Guideline · Warning sounds of vehicles

## 1 Introduction

A car is a very practical and essential element that allows people to move quickly and conveniently to a destination for daily bases or during business hours. However, the driver and passengers are exposed to all kinds of dangerous situations. It is very important to make drivers aware of factors that are difficult to detect and to provide warning that minimize the workload of the driver while inducing the most efficient response. As a result, there are a variety of alarm systems that help drivers to recognize dangers. Typical methods include visual and auditory information. A warning through auditory devices is faster to detect dangers than other senses and useful when someone needs to keep an eye on the front. However, the sounds should not cause any confusion or discomfort which would affect while driving (Choi et al. 2009; Wiese and Lee 2004; Han and Lee 2017; Park et al. 2011; Song 2009; Parizet et al. 2013).

C. Stephanidis et al. (Eds.): HCII 2020, LNCS 12429, pp. 3–13, 2020.
https://doi.org/10.1007/978-3-030-59987-4_1

The warning sound of a vehicle is considered to be both pleasing and annoying to the consumer. Therefore, it is necessary to develop a way to improve the emotional satisfaction of consumers when developing warning sounds. Accordingly, the importance of the development of warning sounds is increasing in the development of the interior sound of the vehicle. For luxury car brands, the trend is to differentiate their brand identity by implementing a unique sound quality of warning sounds. Also, as vehicle functions are diversified and enhanced, the type of warning sounds is gradually increasing (Park et al. 2011).

Previous research focused on the design of warning sounds, the driver's response to them, and the preference and urgency of the sounds (Edworthy and Stanton 1995; Wiese and Lee 2004; Marshall et al. 2007). Recently, researches on warning sounds of electric cars have been actively carried out. Nevertheless, there were limitations, such as not having enough samples by sex and age groups, and not having comparative analyses of the suitability of warning sounds by sex and age groups (Han and Lee 2017; Kim et al. 2009; Kim et al. 2016; Wiese and Lee 2004).

In this study, 500 samples were obtained to determine the suitability of the ten different contextual car warning sounds and analyzed. Survey data were collected to investigate preferences for user experience to identify the suitability of ten contextual situations of vehicle warning sounds. In order to obtain objective results and compare them, the sex of the participants and the proportion of each age group were recruited equally. All participants are required to have a driver's license and classified according to the driving experience, sex, age, and consumer type. The purposes of this research are to analyze the suitability of warning sounds for specified situations and establish a guideline to support the design of Auditory User Interface (AUI) of adequate warning sounds of vehicles for enhancing user experience. The detailed purpose is to analyze sound patterns appropriate for each function among AUI aspects.

## 2 Previous Work

### 2.1 Vehicle Warning Sound

Electric vehicles generally have lower sound pressure than internal combustion engine vehicles, making it impossible for pedestrians to recognize that the vehicle is approaching. With pedestrians exposed to danger, the need for additional warning tones is increasing (Han and Lee 2017). Han and Lee (2017) made the warning sounds based on the theory of harmonics and signal processing. The detectability of the warning sounds was measured by subjective evaluation by adding the background noise measured on the road to the synthesized signal. Psychoacoustics indicators such as loudness, sharpness, and roughness had a low correlation with detectability, but they found a high correlation between the duration of the sounds. Parizet et al. (2013) found that the sound level of an electric vehicle would be much lower than a conventional car, but it can be detected by pedestrians.

Other issue of the vehicle warning sounds is the sounds provided to drivers. Drivers should detect the danger as fast as possible without annoyance. So, research and development on the characteristics of warning sounds are actively carried out as the auditory information presented by cars increases. Among them are suitability, urgency, and discomfort (Marshall et al. 2007; Choi et al. 2009; Kim et al. 2009; Kim et al. 2016; Parizet et al. 2013). Larsson (2010) tried to investigate emotional dimensions of AUI by designing the sounds using EarconSampler and SoundMoulder. Generated sounds were played to the participants to see the emotional response.

Another issue is warning sirens. Maddern et al. (2011) suggested recommendations to improve effectiveness and the audibility of warning sirens. It also deals with physical and psychological issues, along with considering the position of siren speakers.

## 2.2 AUI (Auditory User Interface)

The way the user interface transmits information is physical, visual, auditory, olfactory, and gustatory senses. Auditory User Interface (AUI) connects humans to sound experience of a product and used as a concept corresponding to the visual user interface (GUI; Graphic User Interface). AUI is a concept that encompasses all auditory experiences to remember the image of brands. It even includes not only digital sounds but also the physical sounds of products. The integration and use of both auditory and visual interfaces can have complementary effects. This is because vision can acquire information in a limited area of sight, while hearing can recognize information that sounds convey even in a space where visual information does not exist. AUI may serve to relieve the amount of information that the visual interface must bear when lots of information to convey (Lee et al. 2015) (Fig. 1).

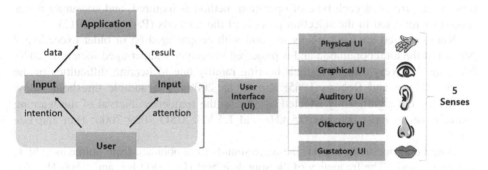

**Fig. 1.** Concept of User Interface (UI) and classification of the interfaces to the five senses (Lee et al. 2015)

## 3 Experiment

### 3.1 Questionnaires and Samples

Participants listened to nine vehicle warning sound samples in ten given situations and scored on a five-point scale to suit their suitability.

Ten given situations are listed below:

1) Suitability of the warning sound when the driver does not fasten a seatbelt.
2) Suitability of the warning sound when the vehicle door is not fully closed.

3) Suitability of the warning sound when the brake hydraulic pressure is insufficient.
4) Suitability of the warning sound when the key is locked in the car.
5) Suitability of the warning sound when the headlamp is switched on.
6) Suitability of the warning sound when the event of a vehicle system failure.
7) Suitability of the warning sound when battery voltage is low.
8) Suitability of the warning sound when the vehicle is off the lane without direction indicators.
9) Suitability of the warning sound when the gear is not on "P", while starting the vehicle.
10) Suitability of the warning sound when the pressures of tires are low.

The first survey question says that "Please listen to nine different vehicle warning sounds and score between one through five how appropriate it is when not fastening a seat belt." The frame of the following questions is the same, only different situations. The preference data were analyzed. To be more specific, the preference value for each sample is the mean value of the Likert Scale. When all values of each sample are defined, analysis based on preferences for sex and age groups was conducted to determine whether differences between groups existed for each question.

### Vehicle Warning Sound Design

The factors that determine the emotional satisfaction of the vehicle warning sounds include volume (sound pressure level), tone (frequency), and duration. Warning sounds of vehicles have been developed individually for each vehicle type and are used in a mix of operating methods (logic). Therefore, to ensure consistent sound implementation, a uniformity of each type of operation method is required, and consumer needs should be reflected in the selection process of the methods (Park et al. 2011).

Korea entered an aged society in 2000 with people aged 65 or older exceeding 7 percent of the total population and is projected to become a super-aged society in 2026. More aged drivers often lose their hearing rapidly due to hearing difficulties of the elderly (Glorig and Roberts 1965; Kim et al. 2009). The audible threshold below 1.5 kHz is not significantly affected by age, so the frequency interval of the warning sound is set to exist between 0.5 kHz and 1.5 kHz (ISO 7029 2000; Han and Lee 2007).

Based on prior studies, nine sine wave sounds were obtained from online as vehicle warning sounds. The frequency of the sounds is 500 Hz, 1,000 Hz, and 1,500 Hz. The duration of the sounds is 300 ms, 900 ms, and 1,500 ms (Choi et al. 2009) (Table 1).

**Table 1.** Elements of vehicle warning sound samples (Choi et al. 2009)

| Elements | 300 ms | 900 ms | 1,500 ms |
|---|---|---|---|
| 500 Hz | Sample 1 | Sample 2 | Sample 3 |
| 1,000 Hz | Sample 4 | Sample 5 | Sample 6 |
| 1,500 Hz | Sample 7 | Sample 8 | Sample 9 |

## 3.2  Methodology

The survey was conducted on online. Participants listened to nine samples for ten given situations and scored one to five points of each sample. Ten situations were selected according to the prior study. The sound samples obtained from the online were most representative frequencies and durations. The preference value for each sample in each question is the mean of scores. For example, the mean value for sample 1 in question 1, 'Safety belt not fastened', was obtained and defined as the preference value. Other values were defined in the same way. The survey ends with demographic characteristics asking their sex, age, whether they have a driver's license or not, and consumer type.

There were total of 500 participants (male 250, female 250). Stata 14.0 MP was used for statistical analysis. First, descriptive statistics on demographic characteristics were conducted, and T-test and ANOVA to analyze differences between sex and age groups.

# 4  Result and Analysis

**Demographic Characteristics**

A total of 500 samples were taken to determine the suitability of the vehicle warning sound in ten situations and used to compare differences between sex and age groups. The number of male and female samples is 250 each, evenly distributed to people in their 20s, 30s, 40s, 50s and over 60s, respectively. The requirement of the participants was the possession of a driver's license. Their driving experiences were divided from less than a year to more than 31 years. In particular, 173 participants (34.6%) had a driving experience of "1-year to 10-year". And the driving experience of "11-year to 20-year" was 121 participants (24.2%). And "21-year to 30-year", 113 participants (22.3%). The survey respondents had 186 early adopters (37.2%), 151 late majorities (30.2%), and 89 innovators (17.8%) (Table 2).

**Result and Analysis**

500 participants scored each sample according to the 5-point Likert Scale. Table 3 is the results of the t-test to determine if there are difference by sex in participants' preferences for the vehicle warning sounds suitable for each situation. In most of situations and samples, there were no significant difference except for sample 7 of situation 2 that the vehicle door is not fully closed. It means that in most samples, the preference of the vehicle warning sounds is identical between men and women. But for sample 7 of situation 2, there is a significant difference between the sex that men thought the sample was appropriate at the situation (M = 3.068); however, women did not think it was suitable (M = 2.840).

One-way ANOVA was conducted to determine if there is a difference among age groups. All samples had no significant difference that the null hypothesis is adopted. The most preferred warning sounds of the samples for each situation is the same. Although there were no significant differences, the results may be used to see the preference in each situation. Mostly, sample 1 or sample 4 is preferred the most

**Table 2.**  User profile

| Elements | | Contents | Percentage (%) |
|---|---|---|---|
| Number of participants | | 500 | 100.0 |
| Sex | Male | 250 | 50.0 |
| | Female | 250 | 50.0 |
| Age groups | 20s | 100 | 20.0 |
| | 30s | 100 | 20.0 |
| | 40s | 100 | 20.0 |
| | 50s | 100 | 20.0 |
| | Over 60 | 100 | 20.0 |
| Driver's license possession | Yes | 500 | 100.0 |
| | No | 0 | 0.0 |
| Driving experience | Less than a year | 40 | 8.0 |
| | Between 1–10 years | 173 | 34.6 |
| | Between 11–20 years | 121 | 24.2 |
| | Between 21–30 years | 113 | 22.6 |
| | More than 31 years | 53 | 10.6 |
| Consumer type | Innovators | 89 | 17.8 |
| | Early adopters | 63 | 12.6 |
| | Early majorities | 186 | 37.2 |
| | Late majorities | 151 | 30.2 |
| | Laggards | 11 | 2.2 |

comparing to other samples (see Table 4). The warning sound, which is 500 Hz and 300 ms, is preferred the most. It shows that people tend to prefer low pitch and fast repetition of sound.

**Table 3.**  T-test

| | Sample type | Freq. | Mean | Std. dev. | t-value |
|---|---|---|---|---|---|
| Situation 1 | Sample 1 | 500 | 3.232 | .869 | −0.926 |
| | Sample 2 | 500 | 2.968 | .943 | −1.807* |
| | Sample 3 | 500 | 2.750 | .939 | −0.714 |
| | Sample 4 | 500 | 3.094 | 1.164 | 0.806 |
| | Sample 5 | 500 | 2.852 | 1.032 | 0.607 |
| | Sample 6 | 500 | 2.636 | .991 | 0.180 |
| | Sample 7 | 500 | 2.850 | 1.218 | 0.698 |
| | Sample 8 | 500 | 2.692 | 1.079 | 0.580 |
| | Sample 9 | 500 | 2.588 | 1.092 | 0.901 |

(*continued*)

**Table 3.** (*continued*)

|  | Sample type | Freq. | Mean | Std. dev. | t-value |
|---|---|---|---|---|---|
| Situation 2 | Sample 1 | 500 | 3.336 | .890 | 0.301 |
|  | Sample 2 | 500 | 3.058 | .897 | −0.848 |
|  | Sample 3 | 500 | 2.778 | . 989 | 0.407 |
|  | Sample 4 | 500 | 3.230 | 1.050 | 1.235 |
|  | Sample 5 | 500 | 2.964 | 1.000 | −0.536 |
|  | Sample 6 | 500 | 2.736 | .980 | 0.547 |
|  | Sample 7 | 500 | 2.954 | 1.186 | 2.157** |
|  | Sample 8 | 500 | 2.780 | 1.053 | 1.104 |
|  | Sample 9 | 500 | 2.572 | 1.031 | 1.041 |
| Situation 3 | Sample 1 | 500 | 3.274 | .934 | 0.814 |
|  | Sample 2 | 500 | 3.088 | .924 | −1.259 |
|  | Sample 3 | 500 | 2.854 | .958 | −0.233 |
|  | Sample 4 | 500 | 3.218 | 1.057 | −0.211 |
|  | Sample 5 | 500 | 2.978 | .984 | 0.136 |
|  | Sample 6 | 500 | 2.812 | .985 | 1.637 |
|  | Sample 7 | 500 | 3.026 | 1.190 | 0.563 |
|  | Sample 8 | 500 | 2.822 | 1.047 | 0.982 |
|  | Sample 9 | 500 | 2.712 | 1.066 | 0.755 |
| Situation 4 | Sample 1 | 500 | 3.188 | .958 | −0.933 |
|  | Sample 2 | 500 | 3.000 | .997 | −0.807 |
|  | Sample 3 | 500 | 2.824 | .987 | 0.181 |
|  | Sample 4 | 500 | 3.236 | 1.075 | −0.832 |
|  | Sample 5 | 500 | 2.984 | 1.021 | −0.788 |
|  | Sample 6 | 500 | 2.874 | 1.034 | 0.043 |
|  | Sample 7 | 500 | 3.188 | 1.157 | 0.154 |
|  | Sample 8 | 500 | 2.878 | 1.022 | −0.306 |
|  | Sample 9 | 500 | 2.724 | 1.023 | 1.401 |
| Situation 5 | Sample 1 | 500 | 3.248 | 1.008 | −0.621 |
|  | Sample 2 | 500 | 3.026 | .961 | −0.698 |
|  | Sample 3 | 500 | 2.870 | .979 | 0.319 |
|  | Sample 4 | 500 | 3.044 | 1.085 | −0.577 |
|  | Sample 5 | 500 | 2.960 | 1.022 | 0.175 |
|  | Sample 6 | 500 | 2.788 | .980 | −0.091 |
|  | Sample 7 | 500 | 2.848 | 1.145 | 0.468 |
|  | Sample 8 | 500 | 2.760 | 1.047 | 1.111 |
|  | Sample 9 | 500 | 2.608 | .976 | 1.653* |

(*continued*)

**Table 3.** (*continued*)

|  | Sample type | Freq. | Mean | Std. dev. | t-value |
|---|---|---|---|---|---|
| Situation 6 | Sample 1 | 500 | 3.220 | 1.050 | −0.426 |
|  | Sample 2 | 500 | 2.846 | 1.014 | 0.749 |
|  | Sample 3 | 500 | 2.696 | 1.048 | 1.110 |
|  | Sample 4 | 500 | 3.308 | 1.062 | −0.505 |
|  | Sample 5 | 500 | 3.036 | 1.010 | 0.885 |
|  | Sample 6 | 500 | 2.794 | 1.011 | 0.575 |
|  | Sample 7 | 500 | 3.296 | 1.200 | 0.000 |
|  | Sample 8 | 500 | 2.978 | 1.051 | 0.894 |
|  | Sample 9 | 500 | 2.794 | 1.082 | 0.041 |
| Situation 7 | Sample 1 | 500 | 3.232 | .986 | −0.363 |
|  | Sample 2 | 500 | 3.034 | .963 | −0.046 |
|  | Sample 3 | 500 | 2.924 | 1.004 | 0.445 |
|  | Sample 4 | 500 | 3.114 | 1.075 | 1.877* |
|  | Sample 5 | 500 | 2.980 | .997 | 1.618 |
|  | Sample 6 | 500 | 2.848 | .985 | −0.454 |
|  | Sample 7 | 500 | 2.978 | 1.178 | −0.038 |
|  | Sample 8 | 500 | 2.798 | 1.081 | 1.035 |
|  | Sample 9 | 500 | 2.692 | 1.104 | 1.134 |
| Situation 8 | Sample 1 | 500 | 3.228 | 1.044 | −0.599 |
|  | Sample 2 | 500 | 2.910 | .984 | 1.228 |
|  | Sample 3 | 500 | 2.768 | 1.022 | 0.963 |
|  | Sample 4 | 500 | 3.244 | 1.115 | 0.241 |
|  | Sample 5 | 500 | 2.900 | .984 | −0.818 |
|  | Sample 6 | 500 | 2.746 | 1.008 | 0.577 |
|  | Sample 7 | 500 | 3.148 | 1.251 | 0.286 |
|  | Sample 8 | 500 | 2.888 | 1.063 | −0.673 |
|  | Sample 9 | 500 | 2.720 | 1.105 | −0.405 |
| Situation 9 | Sample 1 | 500 | 3.210 | 1.020 | −0.921 |
|  | Sample 2 | 500 | 2.964 | .982 | 0.364 |
|  | Sample 3 | 500 | 2.768 | .982 | 0.455 |
|  | Sample 4 | 500 | 3.162 | 1.115 | −1.245 |
|  | Sample 5 | 500 | 2.938 | 1.018 | −0.395 |
|  | Sample 6 | 500 | 2.730 | 1.004 | −0.223 |
|  | Sample 7 | 500 | 2.990 | 1.210 | −0.850 |
|  | Sample 8 | 500 | 2.772 | 1.102 | −0.893 |
|  | Sample 9 | 500 | 2.664 | 1.076 | 0.249 |

(*continued*)

**Table 3.** (*continued*)

| | Sample type | Freq. | Mean | Std. dev. | t-value |
|---|---|---|---|---|---|
| Situation 10 | Sample 1 | 500 | 3.154 | 1.006 | 0.044 |
| | Sample 2 | 500 | 3.046 | .966 | 0.879 |
| | Sample 3 | 500 | 2.932 | .983 | 0.273 |
| | Sample 4 | 500 | 3.092 | 1.118 | −0.240 |
| | Sample 5 | 500 | 2.930 | .996 | −0.763 |
| | Sample 6 | 500 | 2.792 | .991 | −0.812 |
| | Sample 7 | 500 | 2.832 | 1.186 | −0.452 |
| | Sample 8 | 500 | 2.770 | 1.113 | −0.843 |
| | Sample 9 | 500 | 2.688 | 1.100 | −1.384 |

*** $p < 0.01$, ** $p < 0.05$, * $p < 0.1$

**Table 4.** Preferred vehicle warning sounds of situations

| | Sample 1 | Sample 2 | Sample 3 | Sample 4 | Sample 5 | Sample 6 | Sample 7 | Sample 8 | Sample 9 |
|---|---|---|---|---|---|---|---|---|---|
| Situation 1 | 3.232 | 2.968 | 2.750 | 3.094 | 2.852 | 2.636 | 2.850 | 2.692 | 2.588 |
| Situation 2 | 3.336 | 3.058 | 2.778 | 3.230 | 2.964 | 2.736 | 2.954 | 2.780 | 2.572 |
| Situation 3 | 3.274 | 3.088 | 2.854 | 3.218 | 2.978 | 2.812 | 3.026 | 2.822 | 2.712 |
| Situation 4 | 3.188 | 3.000 | 2.824 | 3.236 | 2.984 | 2.874 | 3.188 | 2.878 | 2.724 |
| Situation 5 | 3.248 | 3.026 | 2.870 | 3.044 | 2.960 | 2.788 | 2.848 | 2.760 | 2.608 |
| Situation 6 | 3.220 | 2.846 | 2.696 | 3.308 | 3.036 | 2.794 | 3.296 | 2.978 | 2.794 |
| Situation 7 | 3.232 | 3.034 | 2.924 | 3.114 | 2.980 | 2.848 | 2.978 | 2.798 | 2.692 |
| Situation 8 | 3.228 | 2.910 | 2.768 | 3.244 | 2.900 | 2.746 | 3.148 | 2.888 | 2.720 |
| Situation 9 | 3.210 | 2.964 | 2.768 | 3.162 | 2.938 | 2.730 | 2.990 | 2.772 | 2.664 |
| Situation 10 | 3.154 | 3.046 | 2.932 | 3.092 | 2.930 | 2.792 | 2.832 | 2.770 | 2.688 |

* Orange color is preferred the most. And yellow color is second preferred

# 5 Conclusion

The purpose of this study is to develop guidelines to utilize the warning sounds to support AUI sound designs. As a result, the companies are aware that which characteristics of warning sounds are more appropriate for a specific situation. The analyses, between sex and among age groups, were conducted. According to the results, there was only one significant difference between sex, except for sample 7 of situation 2. The preference for men was higher than that of women. There is no significant difference among age groups; however, the results may be still utilized depending on target users. Since there is not much difference in the results, it is necessary to provide uniformly, rather than to make a difference for sex or age groups, but to present the frequency and duration at the most preferred 500 Hz and 300 ms.

Larsson (2010) made an effort to show an emotional dimension of the drivers by generated sounds with sampler and moulder; however, it does not show what kind of sounds trigger each emotion. Parizet et al. (2013) found that the warning sounds from an electric vehicle can be relatively lower than that of internal combustion engine cars. However, it does not give an exact number. Unlike previous studies, the differentiation of this study is that the person designing warning sounds could refer to the samples as a guideline since the preferences, frequencies, and durations of the sound samples are provided.

The limitation of this study is that the elements other than the frequency (Hz), duration (ms), and the tone or timbre of the sounds were not consider. If later works deal with other elements, further studies of warning sounds could be conducted. The patterns of the sounds were also too simple. It would be better to have more variations for future work. Also, the position of the speakers would affect the quality and tone; however, the actual environments were not considered at all since the survey was conducted online (Park et al. 2011).

In the future, research related to the preferred futuristic sound samples and warning sounds will be performed. Although the sound samples of this research are kind of simple and cliché, it will be one of the footprints to the future research. The results will be useful and may provide sound design guidelines for innovative products.

## References

Choi, K.I., Lee, H., Choe, J.H., Jung, E.S.: Ergonomic design of warning sounds used in cars. J. Korean Inst. Ind. Eng. **35**(1), 101–108 (2009)

Edworthy, J., Stanton, N.A.: A user-centered approach to the design and evaluation of auditory warning signals: methodology. Ergonomics **38**, 2262–2280 (1995)

Glorig, A., Roberts, J.: Hearing levels of adults by age and sex. United States. 1960–1962. Vital Health Stat., vol. 11, pp. 1–34 (1965)

Han, M.U., Lee, S.K.: Detectability evaluation for alert sound in an electric vehicle. Trans. Korean Soc. Mech. Eng.-A **41**(10), 923–929 (2017)

Kim, M.H., Lee, Y.T., Son, J.W., Jang, C.H.: Age-related deficits in response characteristics on safety warning of intelligent vehicle. Korean Soc. Precis. Eng. **26**(12), 131–137 (2009)

Kim, W., Park, D., Shin, J., Oh, J., You, N., Yun, M.H.: Development of in-vehicle auditory display using sound quality metrics. In: Proceedings of the Ergonomics Society of Korea Conference, pp. 93–99 (2016)

Larsson, P.: Tools for designing emotional auditory driver-vehicle interfaces. In: Ystad, S., Aramaki, M., Kronland-Martinet, R., Jensen, K. (eds.) CMMR/ICAD -2009. LNCS, vol. 5954, pp. 1–11. Springer, Heidelberg (2010). https://doi.org/10.1007/978-3-642-12439-6_1

Lee, S.R., Lee, Y.J., Park, S.H.: A study of functional auditory user interface (AUI) design of smartphone. Int. J. Asia Digit. Art Des. 384–389 (2015)

Maddern, A., Privopoulos, E., Howard, C.: Emergency vehicle auditory warning signals: physical and psychoacoustic considerations. In: Proceedings of Acoustics 2011 - Breaking New Ground (2011)

Marshall, D.C., Lee, J.D., Austria, P.A.: Alerts for in-vehicle information systems: annoyance, urgency, and appropriateness. Hum. Factors **49**, 145–157 (2007)

Park, D.C., Hong, S.G., Jung, H.Y.: The study on the development of vehicle warning sounds for improving emotional quality. In: Korean Society for Noise and Vibration Engineering (KSNVE), pp 540–543 (2011)

Parizet, E., et al.: Detectability and annoyance of warning sounds for electric vehicles. In: Proceedings of Meetings on Acoustics, vol. 26, no. 1 (2013)

Song, T.J., Oh, C., Oh, J.T., Lee, C.W.: Effects of in-vehicle warning information on drivers' responsive behavior. J. Korean Soc. Transp. 27(5), 63–74 (2009)

Wiese, E.E., Lee, J.D.: Auditory alerts for in-vehicle information systems: the effects of temporal conflict and sound parameters on driver attitudes and performance. Ergonomics 47(9), 965–986 (2004). https://doi.org/10.1080/00140130410001686294

# Advantages of Using Runtime Procedural Generation of Virtual Environments Based on Real World Data for Conducting Empirical Automotive Research

Arthur Barz[✉], Jan Conrad, and Dieter Wallach

HCI2B Group, Faculty of Computer Science and Micro Systems Technology,
Hochschule Kaiserslautern – University of Applied Sciences, Zweibruecken,
Germany
{arthur.barz,jan.conrad,dieter.wallach}@hs-kl.de

**Abstract.** Driving simulations have become important research tools for improving the in-car user experience. Simulations are especially indispensable when conducting empirical studies in a human-centered development process, where iterative testing in real-world environments is very time-consuming, expensive and potentially dangerous. Constantly advancing possibilities offered by new generations of driving simulations increase the demands and expectations of simulation systems. While the implementation of many components such as simulation hardware or driving physics is very mature by now, the realization of virtual driving environments and scenarios is still a challenging endeavor. A partially automated, algorithmic generation of virtual environments based on real world data provides a possible solution to simplify set-up and execution of research scenarios. The data formats used for this purpose are digital elevation models and map data that can be iteratively processed, improved and expanded for the use in a concrete study. This approach usually requires additional manual steps after the procedural generation is completed. This paper outlines an automated, algorithmic generation of virtual environments based on real-world data, realized at runtime and without subsequent manual post-processing. Significant benefits in automotive research enabled by this approach such as rapid prototyping of study scenarios, support for large-scale virtual environments and the analysis of driving behavior in familiar environments are described.

**Keywords:** Driving simulation · Automotive research · OpenStreetMap · OpenDRIVE · VR

## 1  Introduction

Empirical studies using driving simulations are conducted to evaluate new technologies, interfaces and assistance systems in early development stages and before testing in the real world. Depending on the type of study, different qualitative requirements are imposed on the hardware and software of simulation systems. A range of research questions can be investigated using simplified, abstracted representations and

© Springer Nature Switzerland AG 2020
C. Stephanidis et al. (Eds.): HCII 2020, LNCS 12429, pp. 14–23, 2020.
https://doi.org/10.1007/978-3-030-59987-4_2

interactions that focus on the essential features of the driving task under consideration. Regarding the evaluation of driving performance, Havighurst, Fields, and Fields have argued that the fidelity of the simulation does not yield significant differences for most driving tasks [11]. In select cases investigations on driving performance conducted using low- and high-fidelity driving simulators have not shown significant differences [16]. Some research questions, however, require a certain fidelity to yield valid results. The simulated virtual environment can be directly related to the question, for example, if the visibility of concrete elements such as traffic signs plays a role, or a deeper immersion in the simulation is required.

The use of real vehicles and sophisticated simulation hardware already delivers a highly immersive user experience at several sites [15, 18]. There are also accurate solutions that reproduce vehicle physics or computer-controlled traffic in simulated worlds. Through constant improvements in computer hardware and 3D computer graphics it is possible to recreate almost photorealistic virtual environments. Driving simulation software usually offers different, pre-built scenarios for use in automotive studies. However, depending on the study to be conducted, it may be necessary to create a virtual environment tailored to the requirements of a study.

The conventional approach to overcome this challenge is to manually model the environment using different modeling software packages. Individual objects in a visual scene can be created separately and then combined into a comprehensive scenario. In this way, adjustments on different levels of complexity can be made to meet the respective requirements of the research question that is to be addressed. However, this approach requires profound knowledge of 3D graphics and the associated tool chain.

In [8], Evans discusses the importance of real-world road design to ensure that driving experiences correspond to the real world. The effort involved in creating such real-world experiences can be reduced by recreating real environments. The simulation software Skyline from Intel Labs offers an urban scenario modeled after San Francisco [2]. Some software solutions help to ease or partially automate the creation process. SILAB [12] and SCANeR [5] offer tools specifically designed for creating road networks while CARLA utilizes Vector Zero's software RoadRunner [6]. Nevertheless, the manual creation of scenarios remains a laborious process.

A different approach is taken in the National Advanced Driving Simulator (NADS) at the University of Iowa. A software called Tile Mosaic Tool allows to build environments from a collection of premade square tiles [17]. Using this system is much simpler, but for special requirements it is possible to encounter limitations. If an exact replica of a real environment is required, environments can be scanned three-dimensionally using LiDAR sensors to produce an almost photo-realistic digital representation [1, 19].

The respective approaches offer various advantages and disadvantages and have already been successfully used in several studies. For the approach discussed in this paper, however, there are still no mature solutions. Due to several advantages, which are presented here, this approach should be further elaborated.

## 2   Runtime Procedural Generation

In computer graphics, the term *procedural generation* refers to the creation of graphical content based on algorithms using manually or automatically generated data. Procedural generation can be applied in advance or at simulation runtime. The approach described in this paper highlights the use of procedural generation at runtime.

### 2.1   Database

The choice of suitable data formats is particularly important for procedural generation. On the one hand, data formats need to provide the means for defining virtual environments precisely and efficiently. On the other hand, they need to contain all information for the generation of complex virtual environments. Different formats describe the environment with varying degrees of accuracy and missing information must be supplemented by reasonable assumptions, algorithms, or random distributions. Formats can be evaluated according to several criteria, including:

- How suitable is the data description for driving simulation?
- How time-consuming is the creation of data sets?
- Do data sets already exist that can be used as a basis?
- Do editors already exist for modifying the data?

While different formats for geographic data exist, two specific formats proved to be most useful in this context.

**OpenStreetMap.** OpenStreetMap (OSM) is an open and collaborative project that provides free access to extensive geodata [10]. The file format of the same name is an XML-based markup language focusing on the description of road networks but can also be used for general purposes. Data of the project can be freely obtained via various APIs and edited in accordance with the license conditions. A large variety of existing editors facilitate the work with the data. The OSM editor iD shown in Fig. 1 is particularly user friendly, other editors such as JOSM offer tools for advanced users [3].

Compared to other standards like CityGML [4] and LandInfra [13], OSM data has a simpler design. All required features like defining complex road networks and their surroundings are provided, but an exact description of details in a virtual scene or a hierarchical definition in several layers is difficult (or even impossible). The advantage of a simple description is that the handling of the data is easy. Rather than modelling environments by exact features like explicitly defining precise road geometry, OSM heavily focusses on higher level properties. This approach allows the creation of environments without knowledge of road traffic regulations or geometry. OSM data serve as the standard format for the solution presented in this paper.

**OpenDRIVE.** Just like OSM, OpenDRIVE is an XML file format for the description of geographical data. This format, however, is limited to the description of road networks. As such, it cannot be used as a sole format for complete scenarios. Compared to OSM, OpenDRIVE allows a much more accurate creation of any kind of roads. The format is mature and due to steadily increasing use declared as a de facto standard [7].

**Fig. 1.** User-friendly, web based OSM editor iD

It is practical to convert road networks from OSM data to OpenDRIVE when importing OSM files at the start of each simulation.

## 2.2 Digital Terrain Model

OSM contains mostly no information about the terrain or elevation of individual objects. Therefore, another data source has to supplement OSM. Digital elevation models (DEM) are digital models for representing a planet's surface. DEMs are categorized into point, triangular, grid based and hybrid models [14]. For grid-based models, terrain is defined by a latticed pattern of height samples at constant distances. The height at any point can be determined by bilinear or bicubic interpolation of the surrounding height samples. These models are interesting because of their comparatively simple and efficient algorithmic use.

Another distinction is made between digital terrain models (DTM) and digital surface models (DSM). While DTMs only describe the height of the ground, DSMs include other objects such as buildings and vegetation. Since only information about the terrain is required, DTMs are used in our approach.

Elevation models are created using different measuring techniques. They can be created, for example, from LiDAR data recorded from aircraft or from satellite data. Both variants can be used for procedural generation, but each has its advantages and disadvantages. Satellite images are freely available and cover a wide area, e.g. via NASA's Shuttle Radar Topography Mission [9], LiDAR recordings, however, provide more precise models.

## 2.3 Internal Data Structure

In its original form, OSM data and digital elevation models cannot be used optimally at runtime. Some preprocessing steps are performed at the start of a simulation. The information of all loaded files is imported, enriched and transferred into a model optimized for this application. One of the main optimizations is the distribution of all objects into tiles. This allows to generate only those tiles that are in range of vision and actually needed during runtime. Figure 2 illustrates the layout of the data structure as well as all required inputs. In addition to the elevation model and OSM files, a geographic coordinate marks the origin of a scenario. This is needed for conversions between geographic coordinates in the data formats and the Cartesian coordinates common in computer graphics. After this initialization, a list of all tiles required for a scene is created. Object descriptions are generated from the information in the OSM files and assigned to tiles according to their location. Objects that are too large for a single tile (e.g. forests, lakes) are first divided and then assigned. This step is necessary because large objects like forests can easily exceed what can be generated as a single entity at runtime.

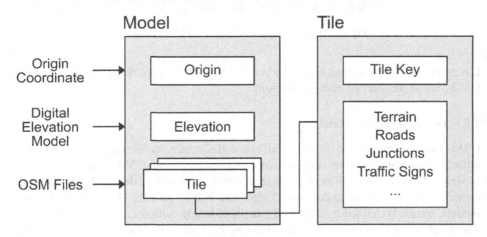

**Fig. 2.** Layout of the internal data structure and required inputs

### 2.4    Implementation of Runtime Generation

After loading and pre-processing all data, an actor—in empirical studies usually the virtual vehicle driven by a participant—is created. In each frame of a simulation, the position of the vehicle is used to determine which tiles are visible, in which order these are created and how far each individual tile is away from the driver. Since the generation of objects is partially synchronous with the rendering of simulation images, time restrictions are imposed by the frame rate. In each frame, procedural generation may only take a few milliseconds on the main execution thread. If calculations take significantly longer, the frame rate will drop. Full tiles usually cannot be generated in this time window, so individual objects are generated in each frame until a defined time limit is exceeded. Procedural generation is then interrupted and continued in the next frame. Some types of objects, e.g. objects consisting of many components (such as forests or buildings), cannot be generated in the given time window. Therefore, they are each broken down into several subtasks that are performed independently.

When implementing multithreading for procedural generation, a common limitation of the underlying software is that operations creating new objects in the virtual world must generally be performed on the main thread synchronously with other computations. This is problematic because the main thread load is constantly high and procedural generation is an additional computationally intensive process. However, by dividing each object generation into individual subtasks, it is possible to separate substeps that can be executed on separate threads. To shift the computational load on multiple threads, a system has been implemented that maps synchronous and parallelized tasks in a directed, cycle-free graph. Each task has dependencies in the form of predecessors in the graph that are completed beforehand. For the generation of e.g. a road section, computationally intensive operations such as the calculation of the geometric shape, the adjustment of the underlying terrain and the creation of road markings can be outsourced, only the placement of objects, such as delineators and road signs, remains on the main thread.

Another significant optimization that we made is the grouping of tasks according to visibility and relevance in levels of detail (layer). Based on the distance between the driver and the tile the object is assigned to, tiles are generated for the layers *Ground*, *Major*, *Minor* und *Detail*. This way overall generation workload is reduced and rendering performance is increased. Figure 3 shows an example scenario in which detail levels are highlighted in different colors. Tiles marked red are at the highest level of detail, tiles marked white are at the lowest level of detail.

**Fig. 3.** Runtime generated scenario with tiles in different levels of detail (Color figure online)

## 3 Scenario Scale

A common requirement that studies impose on driving simulation software is the ability to provide longer test tracks. Studies that include professional drivers or long-term attention studies may require simulated drives that can last over several hours. However, with increasing graphical fidelity this can become a problem: Software frameworks for 3D applications are typically not optimized for such usage. The increasing number of required graphical assets used to create the virtual scenario raises two challenges. First, assets take up a significant amount of memory and second, the calculation effort for rendering single images increases considerably. To ensure high frame rates in a 3D application, it is common practice to create as few assets as possible and to use them repeatedly in a scene. This alleviates both problems, because asset instances do not require additional memory and can be rendered much faster by the graphics hardware. To reduce visible repetition, transformations such as rotations and scaling can be applied to object instances.

For many types of objects in a driving simulation this optimization can be used without problems. The repetition of plants, components of larger objects (e.g. windows, doors and facades of buildings) and small objects are typically not noticeable even after frequent reoccurrences. However, objects of variable shape and especially streets pose problems. If these are modelled according to reality, it is not suitable to use repeated instances. Using procedural generation at runtime eliminates these problems, since graphical assets only exist at runtime and are only generated when needed. This has several additional advantages:

- Little hard drive space is required. Depending on the size of the scenario, OSM files and digital elevation models take up a few dozens to a few hundred megabytes.
- Loading times of simulations are reduced to a few seconds due to the small amount of data and selective generation.
- Since only a minimum of objects is visible at any given time, a high frame rate (a minimum of 30 Hz for a standard setup and 90 + Hz for virtual reality) can be maintained.

## 4   Rapid Scenario Adaption and Expansion

To carry out more specific and advanced studies, automatically generated scenarios often need to be extended by additional elements or triggers. The ability to directly edit many aspects of the virtual environment and to see the effects of the changes within seconds allows improvements in rapid iterations while preparing a study. This can also be done using a custom-made integrated development environment as shown in Fig. 4.

Using the proposed rapid prototyping approach to generate study scenarios allows to detect weaknesses and unexpected errors in early stages. During an exploration period of the approach, we conducted several example studies that took advantage of the aforementioned benefits. Lane highlighting, for example, is the content of an exploratory study that examined a mixed reality driver assistance system. In one condition of a study the middle of the lane was highlighted by a green line, in a second condition the curbside of the lane was highlighted. In both conditions road visibility was reduced by fog in a defined way. Figure 5 shows an example of a test run with a highlighted lane center. This example shows how different experimental conditions can be created to empirically investigate effects on driving performance.

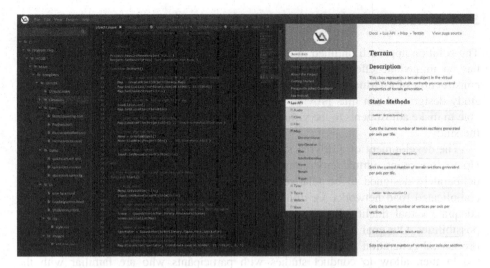

**Fig. 4.** Current implementation of integrated development environment

**Fig. 5.** Driving in poor visibility with augmentation of the lane center (Color figure online)

The scenario in our study was on based on real world data that was created at runtime by procedural generation. Only the highlighting of the center and curbside of the highway was added to complete our test setup.

## 5   Conclusion

The solution approach outlined in this paper provides a high degree of flexibility, that has an immediate effect on the workflow when preparing a simulation study. The construction of a virtual environment including various tests can be performed during study design and can thus provide useful information. In our example case we were able to make adjustments to the virtual environment to follow the exact requirements of the study.

The development of a driving simulation system is a difficult and long-term task. Up to this point, virtual environments as components of such systems have been deliberately designed to be relatively simple, as complex objects like buildings or complicated road networks are difficult to generate in an error-free manner and with adequate visual fidelity. Progressive improvements of our software will yield more possibilities. Our goal is to use data from real environments to create scenarios through procedural generation that are recognizable close to the modeled original scene. This would then allow to conduct studies with participants who are familiar with the "original environment" in order to examine behavior in familiar surroundings.

Regarding the implementation of the system, it has become apparent that procedural generation has limitations in some respects. Many visual details or irregularities in complex road networks, as well as the sheer number of unique objects makes it difficult to reproduce reality with sufficient accuracy. Procedural generation shares some of these problems with file formats that model real-world environments at a data level. However, the results so far already show a considerable benefit for scientific work in the field of empirical research using automotive simulation systems.

**Acknowledgement.** We gratefully acknowledge constructive feedback of the anonymous reviewers. This work has been partially funded by the German Federal Ministry of Education and Research (under grant titles 03IHS075A&B) and by the German Federal Ministry for Economic Affairs and Energy (under grant title 01MF1170113D).

## References

1. Ahlberg, S., Söderman, U., Elmqvist, M.: On modelling and visualisation of high resolution virtual environments using lidar data. In: Proceedings of the 12th International Conference on Geoinformatics, New York, USA, pp. 299–306. ACM Press (2004)
2. Alvarez, I., Rumbel, L., Adams, R.: Skyline: a rapid prototyping driving simulator for user experience. In: Proceedings of the 7th International Conference on Automotive User Interfaces and Interactive Vehicular Applications, New York, USA, pp. 101–108. ACM Press (2015). https://doi.org/10.1145/2799250.2799290
3. Behrens, J., van Elzakker, C.P.J.M., Schmidt, M.: Testing the usability of OpenStreetMap's iD tool. Cartographic J. **52**(2), 177–184 (2015). https://doi.org/10.1080/00087041.2015.1119457
4. Beil, C., Kolbe, T.H.: CityGML and the streets of New York - a proposal for detailed street space modelling. In: Proceedings of the 12th 3D GeoInfoconference, pp. 9–16. ISPRS Annals of the Photogrammetry, Remote Sensing and Spatial Information Sciences, Melbourne, Australia (2017)

5. Champion, A., Mandiau, R., Kolski, C., Heidet, A., Kemeny, A.: Traffic generation with the SCANeR simulator: towards a multi-agent architecture. In: Proceedings of the Driving Simulation Conference, Paris, France, pp. 311–324 (1999)
6. Dosovitskiy, A., Ros, G., Codevilla, F., Lopez, A., Koltun, V.: CARLA: An Open Urban Driving Simulator (2017)
7. Dupuis, M., Strobl, M., Grezlikowski, H.: OpenDRIVE 2010 and Beyond-Status and future of the de facto standard for the description of road networks. In: Proceedings of the Driving Simulation Conference, Paris, France (2010)
8. Evans, D.: The importance of proper roadway design in virtual environments. In: Handbook of Driving Simulation for Engineering, Medicine, and Psychology, pp. 1–6, chap. 33. CRC Press, Boca Raton (2011)
9. Farr, T.G., et al.: The shuttle radar topography mission. Rev. Geophys. 45 (2007). https://doi.org/10.1029/2005rg000183
10. Haklay, M., Weber, P.: OpenStreetMap: user-generated street maps. IEEE Pervasive Comput. 7(4), 12–18 (2008). https://doi.org/10.1109/MPRV.2008.80
11. Havighurst, L.C., Fields, L.E., Fields, C.L.: High versus low fidelity simulations: does the type of format affect candidates' performance or perceptions? In: Proceedings of the 7th International Conference on Automotive User Interfaces and Interactive Vehicular Applications. ACM Press, New York (2015)
12. Krueger, H.-P., Grein, M., Kaussner, A., Mark, C.: SILAB—a task oriented driving simulation. In: Proceedings of the Driving Simulation Conference, Orlando, USA (2005)
13. Kumar, K., Labetski, A., Ohori, K.A., Ledoux, H., Stoter, J.: The LandInfra standard and its role in solving the BIM-GIS quagmire. Open Geospatial Data Softw. Stand. 4(1), 1–16 (2019). https://doi.org/10.1186/s40965-019-0065-z
14. Li, Z., Zhu, C., Gold, C.: Digital Terrain Modeling: Principles and Methodology. CRC Press, Boca Raton (2004)
15. Murano, T., Yonekawa, T., Aga, M., Nagiri, S.: Development of high-performance driving simulator. SAE Int. J. Passenger Cars Mech. Syst. 2(1), 661–669 (2009). https://doi.org/10.4271/2009-01-0450
16. Reed, M.P., Green, P.A.: Comparison of driving performance on-road and in a low-cost simulator using a concurrent telephone dialling task. Ergonomics 42(8), 1015–1037 (1999). https://doi.org/10.1080/001401399185117
17. University of Iowa: miniSim Driving Simulator Technical Description (2018). https://www.nads-sc.uiowa.edu/userweb/veit/NADSMiniSim_TechnicalDescription.pdf
18. Wilkinson, M., Leo Brown, T., Ahmad, O.: The national advanced driving simulator (NADS) description and capabilities in vision-related research. Optometry J. Am. Optom. Assoc. 83(6), 79–84 (2012)
19. Yue, X., Wu, B., Seshia, S.A., Keutzer, K., Sangiovanni-Vincentelli, A.L.: A LiDAR point cloud generator. In: Proceedings of the International Conference on Multimedia Retrieval, pp. 458–464. ACM Press, New York (2018). https://doi.org/10.1145/3206025.3206080

# Improving Emergency Vehicles' Response Times with the Use of Augmented Reality and Artificial Intelligence

K. F. Bram-Larbi¹, V. Charissis¹⁽✉⁾ 🆔, S. Khan¹, D. K. Harrison², and D. Drikakis³ 🆔

¹ Virtual Reality Driving Simulator Laboratory,
School of Computing, Engineering and Built Environment,
Glasgow Caledonian University, Glasgow, UK
Kweku.BramLarbi@gcu.ac.uk, v.charissis@gmail.com
² Department of Mechanical Engineering, School of Computing, Engineering and Built Environment, Glasgow Caledonian University, Glasgow, UK
³ Defence and Security Research Institute,
University of Nicosia, CY-2417 Nicosia, Cyprus

**Abstract.** The rapid mobilization of Emergency Services (ES) could be particularly challenging for ES drivers and staff that have to navigate and manoeuvre through various traffic and weather conditions. Driving, in high speeds through dense traffic is a particularly demanding psychomotor task for the ES drivers and could result in collisions and even fatalities. Current attempts to support the driver and reduce the potential driving hazards had limited success. The paper presents the design rationale of a prototype system that utilises Augmented Reality (AR) in the form of a Head-Up Display (HUD) to superimpose guidance information in the real-life environment. The paper will discuss also the requirements for an Artificial Intelligence (AI) system that could analyse the driving conditions and present the best manoeuvring options whilst maintain the road users' safety. Finally, the paper presents the requirements' framework for the development of the proposed AR/AI system based on the feedback and suggestions of ten ES drivers. Their feedback will be presented and discussed in detail as it provided essential insight into the everyday challenges of ES operations.

**Keywords:** Augmented Reality · Emergency Services · Artificial Intelligence · Collision avoidance · Head-up display · Smart cities · Simulation

## 1 Introduction

Emergency Services (ES) utilise a large and diverse fleet of customized vehicles, offering multiple solutions for ambulance, police and fire brigade services. The main objective of these services is to ensure that citizens in-need receive support efficiently and in a timely manner. The latter parameter requires high-speed manoeuvring through dense traffic, in various adverse weather conditions and road networks. These requirements increase greatly the collision probability [1].

© Springer Nature Switzerland AG 2020
C. Stephanidis et al. (Eds.): HCII 2020, LNCS 12429, pp. 24–39, 2020.
https://doi.org/10.1007/978-3-030-59987-4_3

Current technological advances in computing and telecommunications enable modern vehicular systems to assist the driver's decision-making process. Existing solutions to alleviate this issue are based on the acquisition of information, usually attained by vehicular sensors, GPS and/or Vehicular Ad hoc Network Systems (VANETS). In turn, the data is presented to the driver through several in-vehicle screens and projection conduits with mixed results.

The demanding operating environment of the ES and the constant provision of traffic, incident and patient information through a plethora of screens, interfaces and buttons burden further the driver's cognitive load. Typically a co-driver is required, in order to split the incoming information load and support the driver in the main task. Yet, the co-driver has to reiterate the received information both verbally and gesturally in some cases, dividing further the driver's attention.

Emerging technologies such as Augmented Reality (AR) are well placed for superimposing crucial information on the real environment aiming to improve human responses. Previous work with AR systems aiming to reduce collision probability under adverse conditions has successfully demonstrated the efficiency of AR in the automotive field [2, 3].

The utilization of such technology on inherently more hazardous situations, like fast police pursue or ambulance emergency, however, requires additional support for the driver, beyond the visual guidance. In such cases, the provision of visual guidance should be updated rapidly and offer alternative options following the traffic patterns. Such requirements could only be provided by an Artificial Intelligence Co-Driver which could receive, distil and present crucial information at a swift pace following the driving conditions and traffic patterns [4].

Adhering to the above observations, the proposed work investigates the use of AR in the form of a prototype Head-Up Display (HUD) interface designed for the enhancement of safety, improvement of response times and navigation through traffic for emergency vehicles. In addition, a prototype AI Co-driver aiming to enhance the quality and timing provision of the crucial navigation data to the driver is presented.

Initial system designs and preliminary evaluations in a full-scale VR driving Simulator have been promising as the AR-AI system provides manoeuvring and navigation information promptly and superimposed in scale 1-1 on the external environment.

The paper will present the framework of requirements for the development of the proposed AR/AI system based on the feedback and suggestions of ten ambulance drivers. Their feedback will be presented and discussed in detail as it provides essential insight into the everyday challenges of ES operations. Based on analysis of specialist input, the latest AR/AI HUD interface development will be discussed and will explore the usability benefits and issues in accident scenarios acquired by the local traffic police department. In conclusion, the paper will present a tentative plan of future work aiming to optimize the proposed system and reduce routing collisions through traffic.

## 2 Current ES Driving Issues

A multitude of hazards is potentially faced by ES professionals, contributing to the degree of risk associated with such professions. Inherent hazards such as exposure to infections or hazardous materials are well mitigated for by the use of personal protective equipment, whilst others such as exposure to public violence or traffic-related hazards are somewhat difficult to mitigate for and still remain amongst the highest risks faced by emergency personnel. In particular, high-speed emergency driving in challenging traffic or weather conditions accounts for the majority of fatal ES accidents.

### 2.1 Speed Related Issues

In many countries, including the United Kingdom, ambulances are granted several exceptions to road traffic laws that are mandatory for civilian drivers. No statutory provision imposing a speed limit on motor vehicles shall apply to any vehicle on an occasion when it is being used for fire and rescue authority purposes or for or in connection with the exercise of any function of a relevant authority as defined in Sect. 6 of the Fire (Scotland) Act 2005, for ambulance or police purposes [5].

Thus the law does not set a defined speed limit during an emergency call to facilitate an unrestricted mobilisation speed. In turn, the ambulance driver is tasked to perform the required manoeuvring and to adapt the appropriate speed, taking into account the relations among speed, crash risk and the patient's need for a fast response [6]. Notably, speed is an important factor in traffic accidents, and there are an exponential function and a power function between speed and crash rate [7]. The above reference tends to be valid for ambulance drivers, thus the risk of road accidents increases with increased driving speed. However, speed itself is not the determining factor of a potential collision. Selection of appropriate routes and manoeuvring choices within different traffic and weather conditions could affect significantly the collision probabilities [3, 8].

Traffic accidents also occur during ambulance transportation, both in emergency use and non-emergency use, and several studies reveal that emergency driving at high speed is riskier and causes more accidents than non-emergency driving [7, 9, 10]. This has sparked a worldwide discussion about the advantages versus the disadvantages of ambulance emergency high-speed driving. Several investigations suggest that the time saved is marginal in emergency driving compared to non-emergency driving. Sometimes these manoeuvres cause accidents without involving the ambulance, i.e. wake-effect accidents [11, 12]. This is a major issue, as these accidents occur with a greater frequency and many of these accidents result in damage, serious injury or death [11].

The mean time saved is in the order of 1–4 min, including both urban and rural environments [13]. The benefits when driving ambulances at high speed using lights and sirens are supposed to be rather limited, as this kind of transportation is dangerous for patients, personnel and fellow road users due to inadequate siren direction localization [9, 14]. Therefore, the use of warning lights and sirens has become a controversial issue [13].

## 2.2    Spatial and Situational Awareness

Emergency driving at high speeds is not only a major key point to be taken note of, but it is also a stressful situation for patients and personnel, as well for the driver. These situations result in unsafe vehicle operation to a greater extent, especially among less experienced drivers [9]. The urgency of transporting patients, personnel or equipment in various locations and encountering different traffic and weather conditions can increase dramatically the cognitive workload of the ES drivers. The spatial and situational awareness of the driver can be challenged by the required multitasking and attention division between map-navigation, suggested route, fast-paced manoeuvring and a plethora of additional incoming information presented through other Head-Down Displays (HDD).

Driver's attention can be further challenged by adverse weather conditions that could diminish spatial awareness or could affect the external environment visibility (i.e. fog, heavy rain, glare and snowfall). As such the distance misconception and obstacle masking could occur, resulting in a reduced situational awareness. In this case, the provision of map and route information through contemporary methods (i.e. HDD) is inefficient as it cannot be correlated to the external scene [15]. Current provision of information within the ES vehicles could distract the driver particularity in occasions that require rapid driving and manoeuvring in condensed traffic flow. The majority of the ES in-vehicle systems are engulfing the driver's position with several screens that deliver various information.

## 2.3    Driver Distraction

Besides the navigation and POI information presented to the driver by the in-vehicle screens, the nature of the emergency response is distracting in itself. Rear seat passengers can be un-restrained so as to be able to medically intervene whilst the vehicle is in transit and on multiple occasions a patient may not remain stable throughout the journey to a centralized facility. Thus, action occurring in the rear compartment of an emergency vehicle, especially an ambulance, can have a hugely distracting effect on the driver.

Previous studies have demonstrated the impact of rear-seat passengers' activity on driver distraction [16, 17], but this issue is amplified, in most ES situations, as the co-driver, normally assisting in navigation, is often required to aid a patient and thus cannot offer assistance with the multitude of tasks in the driver's cabin.

Adhering to suggestions and observations by the ES staff, the proposed systems aim to embed an AI Co-Driver that could take over from the human co-driver and assist the driver in the main task of arriving promptly and safely to the required destination. This element of the system will be further discussed in the following sections.

## 3  Current Solutions

Several emerging technologies have been employed to curb the collision occurrences in vehicles such as Vehicular Adhoc Network systems (VANETS), small-estate HUDs, visible (i.e. side mirrors), auditory (i.e. RDS broadcasting method) and haptic warnings amongst others [18–21].

The use of VANETs and Vehicle to Vehicle (V2V) communication could provide the exchange of a multitude of information between vehicles and Vehicle to Infrastructure (V2I) that could warn well in advance traffic flow issues or for other potentially hazardous situations. As such the promptly provided information could prevent a collision and consequently alleviate the driver's anxiety [19, 20].

Yet the real-time acquisition of data requires a fast and efficient conduit for transferring the information to the driver in a meaningful and simplified fashion. To tackle the data presentation and visualisation issue, new interfaces have been devised which utilise audio related and haptic methodologies to decrease the driver's cognitive workload and consequently expand safety while driving [21, 22].

The driver's decision-making process could be further enhanced with the provision of variable speed limits and open/close lanes as required. This is typically offered by smart motorways infrastructure.

Another system based on V2I is the direct communication of the ES in-vehicle system to the Urban Traffic Management Control (UTMC) centres, requesting for adaptation of traffic lights and routes to support the swift movement through urban and motorway traffic [23, 24]. These systems offer a useful addition for the support of the driver as they could reduce the traffic or create alternative routes. However, these systems cannot support the decision-making process for the correct manoeuvring through traffic.

Some contemporary attempts to reduce this infobesity issue has been through the combination of different sources in one in-vehicle data terminal screen. This offers a cost-efficient solution by reducing the multiple providers, interfaces and aftermarket services.

Yet, combining the majority of the incoming information in one system tends to have an impact in the Human-Machine Interface (HMI) design. The latter, increases in complexity and as with the previous systems that attempt to reduce the driver's cognitive workload, they still cannot guide directly and efficiently the driver or support the split-second decision-making process.

Additionally, siren localization has been highlighted as another area that could be improved to warn efficiently the passenger vehicles in the ES vehicle's path. Previous studies have shown that current siren systems do not offer a clear localization of the incoming ES vehicles. As such drivers are not aware of the ES vehicle position and direction or speed of movement [14, 25].

Thus far, such attempts although in theory alleviating partially the driver's cognitive workload had limited success and lack correlation with input from real-time ES vehicle drivers.

## 4  Proposed Solution: AR/AI System

The design of the proposed AR system employs design elements from previous work related to AR HUD and collision avoidance system. However, the previous systems were predominantly developed to assist drivers under adverse weather conditions by presenting in real-time the positions of the neighbouring vehicles [3, 15, 26].

In the ES case, the high-speed manoeuvring and navigation through different states of traffic required, necessitate the use of calculation of relative speeds between the neighbouring vehicles, close-proximity obstacles ahead and road changes/closures amongst other to propose in real-time potential paths of vacant road spaces (see Fig. 1).

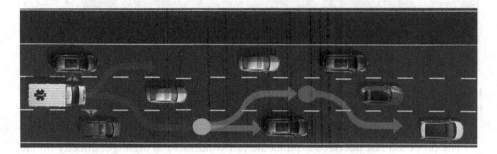

**Fig. 1.** Selection of alternative routes, in dense traffic on motorway environment.

Yet, the information provided in real-time to the driver should be stripped down to the bare minimum, maintaining only the proposed manoeuvring information and speed required to utilise the traffic-flow gaps (see Fig. 2). Due to the unpredictable pattern of traffic flow gaps requiring the instant provision of options to the driver, any other information is irrelevant to the main task. For this reason, the primary function of this proposed interface is to enhance the driver's response times by enhancing the spatial and situational awareness through a simple and clear guidance interface. The utilisation of AR to superimpose the fastest and safest route at any given moment could improve human responses and consequently reduce collision probability as previously demonstrated [8, 15, 20]. To achieve this, the project currently is in the process of embedding an Artificial Intelligence Co-Driver for analysing current conditions both in micro and macro traffic flow [27]. In turn, the AI will utilise the AR interface to highlight directly on the driver's Field Of View (FOV) the suggested options and desired speed to utilise the traffic gap without jeopardizing road users' safety.

This "*slalom driving approach*", will be employed by the human driver and AI only if there is no alternative option available and only if the sirens and blue lights are activated. In different countries, the regulations regarding the ES vehicles movement on the road vary and as such, this project examines a holistic approach without developing the system for one country explicitly [28]. The proposed system intends to enable the driver to maintain a consistent speed and navigate safely through traffic, rather than providing peak-to-peak speed fluctuations and abrupt manoeuvring options. The latter would put additional strain on the ES driver and the vehicle whilst create unnecessary stress to the neighbouring vehicle's' drivers.

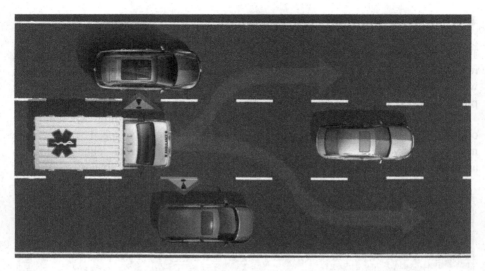

**Fig. 2.** Close up in the selection of alternative routes, whilst ES vehicle is circumventing dense traffic on motorway environment.

The proposed AR interface exploits the full windshield to highlight directly on the existing environment the optimal manoeuvre option (see Fig. 3). Previous work has indicated that the small-estate AR projections through HUDs might confuse drivers' as they attempt in real-time to mentally position the small HUD information to the real-life and scale environment [27, 29].

**Fig. 3.** Close up in the selection of alternative routes, whilst ES vehicle is circumventing dense traffic on motorway environment.

This human-machine collaboration could improve the speed of the vehicle whilst able to identify potential collision obstacles and occurrences. By only displaying pertinent information on a HUD system, faster response times have been demonstrated in previous studies [3, 15, 26].

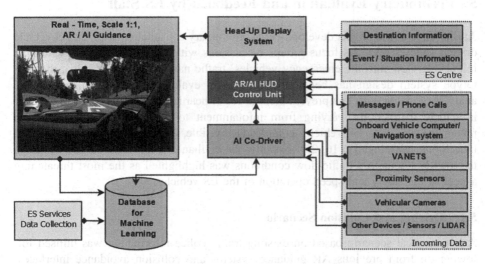

**Fig. 4.** Block diagram of the proposed system's operational framework.

On the proposed system the AR/AI Guidance is projected directly on the real-life environment through a full-windshield HUD (see Fig. 4). The incoming plethora of information (VANETS, proximity sensors, vehicular cameras, and other devices and sensors) feed directly into the AI CoDriver which in turn, updates the provided guidance to the driver (see Fig. 4). Notably, the onus is always on the ES driver to utilise the proposed information and execute the suggested manoeuvre in a safe manner.

However, if the AI assistance is not required, the HUD Control Unit could present other collision avoidance and navigation information as per previous work [2, 3, 8, 20]. In case that both the AI and the AR HUD systems are not required, they could be deactivated.

At the current stage of the proposed system development, a fully autonomous capability is not included as concurrent studies have presented a hesitance from the majority of the drivers to relieve the command of their vehicles completely to an AI system [30].

This tendency and feeling are reinforced by the lack of any high-level Autonomous Vehicles (AV) available on the market. Also, a typical human trait is the preference to continue using familiar systems and technologies rather than explore new options. By increasing the market penetration, the AVs and AI would gradually become more acceptable.

However, the responses of the survey that follows support this notion of hesitance and the hybrid option of human-machine collaboration is currently a more acceptable choice. By training the AI system and updating the road network with the required infrastructure, fully autonomous versions could be required in the near future and will be further investigated [31].

## 5   Preliminary Evaluation and Feedback by ES Staff

At this stage of the project development, a preliminary consultation with ten ES vehicle drivers follows previous focus groups discussions with ES staff which presented an initial overview into the emergency vehicles' traffic navigation issues. Also, the prototype system design has benefited by previous evaluation of 50 civilian drivers' analysis of distractions that prevent them to see or hear incoming ES vehicles [25]. The in-vehicle distractions, varying from infotainment to passenger interferences, can render the incoming ES vehicles completely invisible, despite the activated siren and blue lights' warnings [2, 16, 25]. Notably, the civilian drivers' reduced attendance to the swiftly fluctuating traffic-flow conditions was highlighted as the most threatening aspect of the safety and speed operation of the ES vehicles.

### 5.1   Driving and Collision Scenario

A hypothetical scenario based on existing traffic police information was utilised following on from previous AR guidance systems and collision avoidance interfaces' evaluations [2, 3, 15, 17]. This was considered necessary for maintaining consistency in the future evaluation process of the proposed full-windscreen AR/AI HUD interface. The proposed system's rationale, design and functionality were presented to the 10 volunteers currently working as ES drivers.

### 5.2   Survey Rationale and Structure

Firstly, a two-fold questionnaire was presented to the users. The first arm of the questionnaire was concerned with the demographic information of the group and their current experience and beliefs related to navigation and guidance systems as presented in Table 1. Secondly, a mock-up interface in action acted as a visual aid for explaining the system's functionality to the drivers before conducting the survey (see Fig. 5).

Finally, the third arm of the survey aimed to acquire drivers' subjective feedback that could inform the development of the final version of the proposed interface presented in Table 2.

Table 1 Questions 1–2 were concerned with basic demographics and demonstrated a wide range of sampled ages. Gender distribution was to some extent skewed with 7 male and 3 female drivers. Yet due to the small sample, these variations did not correlate with any significant pattern related to the given responses on the post-assessment questionnaire. Questions 3 and 9 related to the previous driving experience in ES and captured the drivers' prior collision history. Responses to both questions demonstrate a fairly uniform sample of drivers with no significant association between driving experience and incidences of collision.

**Table 1.** Pre-questionnaire for the ES staff.

| Pre-Questionnaire |
| --- |
| Q1. What age group are you in?<br>☐18-24    ☐25-34    ☐35-44    ☐45-50    ☐50+ |
| Q2. What is your gender?<br>☐ Female    ☐ Male |
| Q3. How many years do you work in the ES?<br>☐ 0-5    ☐ 5-10    ☐ 10-15    ☐ 15+ |
| Q4. Do you think that the information provided by EV contemporary navigation systems can *guide you safely in dense traffic*?<br>☐ Yes    ☐ No |
| Q5. Do you think that the information provided by contemporary EV navigation systems can guide you safely in *adverse weather conditions*?<br>☐ Yes    ☐ No |
| Q6. Do you think that the information provided by contemporary EV navigation systems can guide you safely and provide the *fastest route* available?<br>☐ Yes    ☐ No |
| Q7. Do you think that the information provided by contemporary EV navigation systems can provide you with *real-time manoeuvring options through traffic*?<br>☐ Yes    ☐ No |
| Q8. Would you be interested to have real-time guidance suggestions by an AI system?<br>☐ Yes    ☐ No |
| Q9. Have you ever had any collisions (minor or major)?<br>☐ Yes    ☐ No |
| Q10. Do you find the in-vehicle provided information distracting?<br>☐ Yes    ☐ No |

Questions 4–10 presented the views of the staff regarding the current equipment and future expectations (see Fig. 5). Responses to Question 4, in particular, highlighted the potential guidance issue of current systems, as 70% of the drivers suggested that the current systems can provide navigation but cannot guide them. Similarly, the vast majority of the group responded that the current systems could not guide them safely under challenging traffic and weather conditions (Questions 5 and 7). In Question 6, 60% of the drivers felt that the contemporary EV navigation systems can guide them safely and provide the *fastest route* available. However, a significant percentage (40%) questioned the efficiency of the current systems to fulfil this role.

Question 8, identified a potential appetite and requirement for a new technology that could employ AI to suggest guidance options in real-time, as 80% of the drivers were keen to experience such a system.

**Table 2.** Post-questionnaire for the ES staff.

| Post-Questionnaire |
| --- |
| Q11. Did you find the *interface design simple and clear*?<br>□ 1   □ 2   □ 3   □ 4   □ 5   (1 Very Simple – 5 Very Difficult) |
| Q12. Do you think that *interface design and colour coding* would be useful to convey the manoeuvring information?<br>□ 1   □ 2   □ 3   □ 4   □ 5   (1 Very Useful – 5 Not Useful at all) |
| Q13. Would you be interested to have *AR navigation/guidance system in the **ES vehicle***?<br>□ 1   □ 2   □ 3   □ 4   □ 5   (1 Very Interested – 5 Not Interested at all) |
| Q14. Would you be interested to have *AI navigation/guidance system in the **ES vehicle***?<br>□ 1   □ 2   □ 3   □ 4   □ 5   (1 Very Interested – 5 Not Interested at all) |
| Q15. Would you be interested to have *AR navigation/guidance system in the **civilian vehicles***?<br>□ 1   □ 2   □ 3   □ 4   □ 5   (1 Very Interested – 5 Not Interested at all) |
| Q16. Would you be interested to have *AI navigation/guidance system in the **civilian vehicles***?<br>□ 1   □ 2   □ 3   □ 4   □ 5   (1 Very Interested – 5 Not Interested at all) |
| Q17. Would you be interested to have *real-time guidance suggestions by an AI/AR system*?<br>□ 1   □ 2   □ 3   □ 4   □ 5   (1 Very Interested – 5 Not Interested at all) |
| Q18. Do you think that the *AR/AI proposed system could replace other guidance systems*?<br>□ Yes     □ No |
| Q19. Do you think it would be a helpful system (AI/AR) to *integrate into future ES vehicles*?<br>□ Yes     □ No |
| Q20. Do you think it would be a helpful system (AI/AR) to *integrate into future civilian vehicles*?<br>□ Yes     □ No |
| Q21. Do you have *any other suggestions, comments or thoughts* regarding the proposed AR/AI system? If yes please use the space below to write your comments.<br>□ Yes     □ No |

However the majority of them stated in the feedback section that the AI suggestions would be welcomed, however, they would be sceptical to use a full AV option (Question 21).

This confirmed previous focus group discussions in which the participants were reluctant to use full AV capabilities, particularly in busy urban environments. As such the hybrid option of AI/AR on the supportive role of the human driver was in par to the current expectations and was perceived as a more acceptable option. Finally, Question 10, highlighted the fact, that the current navigation systems are distracting the drivers, particularly in stressful situations as the ones encountered by the ES personnel.

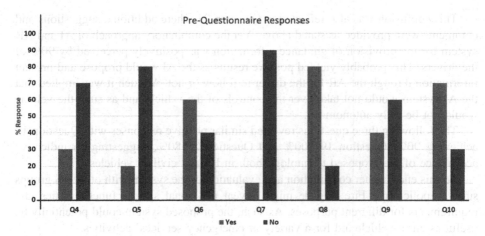

**Fig. 5.** Pre-Questionnaire Results for Questions 4–10.

The post questionnaire results presented some intriguing findings (see Fig. 6). In particular, the interface had encouraging scores with regards to the design and potentially functionality within the frantic situations encountered by the ES staff as illustrated in the responses of Questions 11 and 12. Question 13 revealed that 80% would be very interested and 20% interested to have an AR navigation/guidance system in the ES vehicles. Similarly, the same responses were provided on Question 15 for the civilian vehicles.

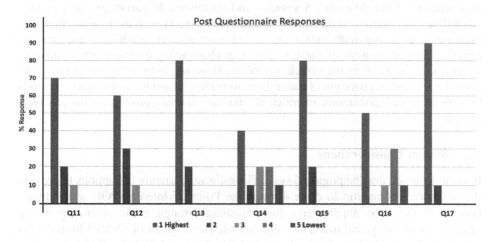

**Fig. 6.** Post Questionnaire Results for Questions 11–17.

However, the provision of AI for guidance and navigation, although overall positive, produced mixed results in the responses of Questions 14 and 16. Notably, the particular emerging technology is typically confused with full autonomous vehicle (AV) which has left unconvinced a large segment of drivers.

This confusion was also reflected in Question 21 where additional suggestions and comments were provided as stated above. Yet the combinatory approach of AI and AR system for the provision of guidance information was positively perceived by 90% of the drivers. This probably yielded positive results as the AI would propose and present information through the AR for the driver to follow or not. As such it was implied that the AI system would not take over the controls of the vehicle and as such the vehicle would not be fully autonomous.

The following three questions revealed similar positive responses with Question 18 achieving 90%, Question 19 100% and Question 20 80%, suggesting an indicative acceptance of the proposed technology both in ES and civilian vehicles.

To this end, further consultation and evaluation of the system with other ES groups such as police and Fire brigade might reveal additional system functionalities and requirements for different purposes. As such, the proposed system could potentially be useful as an in-vehicle aid for a variety of emergency services' activities.

## 6   Discussion

### 6.1   AR/AI for ES Vehicles

The design rationale of the proposed system and the prototype demonstration has proven to be a desirable new aspect for the ES drivers. Notably, the system will have to be evaluated by a larger cohort of ES drivers to acquire statistically significant results and support future commercialization. The system's functionality will require further exploration and the development of different versions to correspond to the diverse requirements of the different ES vehicles and operations. In particular, the guidance capabilities and options of the AI/AR should cover aspects such as, how to efficiently manoeuvre in heavy traffic situations in adverse weather conditions and how to effectively regain control of the ES vehicle in challenging situations where adverse weather conditions affect the vehicle's stability. However, both of these situations will need the significant provision of data related to vehicle dynamics and drivers' methods to respond in such conditions, to enrich the machine learning process for the proposed system.

### 6.2   System Considerations

It has to be noted that the proposed system investigates currently the options to provide the guidance information to drive towards the Point Of Interest (POI) whilst maintaining all the legal requirements for navigating through traffic according to the instructions of the typical motorway legislations. The dispatch of ES staff from the ES vehicle to the accident scene is not a part of this work and there is official documentation which describes the correct process of staff and equipment deployment [28]. Also, the proposed system aims to support the driver in the decision-making process by calculating and presenting the optimal manoeuvres available. However, the manoeuvring process should be performed cautiously by the user according to the relevant motorway laws and regulations of each country.

## 6.3    Future Implications for Passenger Vehicles

Adhering to the survey results and comments related to the different future usage of an AI/AR HUD guidance system, presented an indicative, yet interesting view. The ES drivers were keen to have the system embedded on their work and civilian vehicles, but only if the system provides suggestions regarding the potential manoeuvring and speed options. In contrast, the misconception that the AI would enable a full AV mode was not perceived as a favourable possibility. However, as mentioned previously this view will gradually change given the market penetration and volume of new and used vehicles with AI/AR capabilities, available in the near future. Currently, these emerging technologies might be considered odd or not required. Yet the complexity of the road network on large urban environments and other infotainment technologies will deem these technologies necessary and part of the new smart cities ecosystem.

# 7    Conclusions

The paper presented the background rationale for the development of a prototype AI/AR system that will utilise a full windshield HUD system to superimpose guidance information in a real-life environment and real-scale, opposed to small estate HUDs.

Also, the paper presented current attempts to resolve collision issues and delay factors currently hindering the rapid mobilization of ES vehicles. In turn, this work described a preliminary yet informative appraisal of the prototype systems' functionalities by ten ES drivers. Their suggestions are in accordance with previous consultations with a focus group and civilian drivers' responses on fast approaching ES vehicles.

Furthermore, the paper analysed and discussed the findings of the aforementioned qualitative study, offering suggestions for further system development. In conclusion, the tentative plan of future work will include the finalising of the proposed system, based on the previous and current specialists' feedback and commence a large scale evaluation that will provide clear indications to the benefits and drawbacks of such systems. The evaluation of the proposed system in an urban environment and particularly in road intersections that tend to result in the majority of ES accidents will be pursued. Finally, an analysis of future introduction to passenger vehicles will be also commenced.

# References

1. Hsiao, H., Chang, J., Simeonov, P.: Preventing emergency vehicle crashes: status and challenges of human factors issues. Hum. Factors 60(7), 1048–1072 (2018). https://doi.org/10.1177/0018720818786132
2. Lagoo, R., Charissis, V., Harrison, D.K.: Mitigating driver's distraction: automotive head-up display and gesture recognition system. IEEE Consum. Electron. Mag. 8(5), 79–85 (2019). https://doi.org/10.1109/mce.2019.2923896

3. Charissis, V., Papanastasiou, S.: Human–machine collaboration through vehicle head up display interface. Cogn. Technol. Work **12**(1), 41–50 (2010). https://doi.org/10.1007/s10111-008-0117-0

4. Frank, M., Drikakis, D., Charissis, V.: Machine learning methods for computational science and engineering. Computation **8**(1), 15 (2020). https://doi.org/10.3390/computation8010015 . ISSN 2079-3197

5. Fire (Scotland) Act 2005 - Scottish Parliament Bill, Legislation.gov.uk (2005)

6. Albertsson, P., Sundström, A.: Evaluation of insight training of ambulance drivers in Sweden using DART, a new e-learning tool. Traffic Injury Prev. **12**(6), 621–629 (2011)

7. Smith, N.: A National Perspective on Ambulance Crashes and Safety: Guidance from the National Highway Traffic Safety Administration on ambulance safety for patients and providers, NHTSA Report, EMS World, pp. 91–94 (2015)

8. Charissis, V., Papanastasiou, S., Vlachos, G.: Interface development for early notification warning system: full windshield head-up display case study. In: Jacko, J.A. (ed.) HCI 2009. LNCS, vol. 5613, pp. 683–692. Springer, Heidelberg (2009). https://doi.org/10.1007/978-3-642-02583-9_74

9. Kahn, C.A., Pirrallo, R.G., Kuhn, E.M.: Characteristics of fatal ambulance crashes in the United States: an 11-year retrospective study. Prehosp. Emerg. Care **5**, 261–269 (2001)

10. Maguire, B.J., Huntin, K.L., Smith, G.S., Levick, N.R.: Occupational fatalities in emergency medical services: a hidden crisis. Ann. Emerg. Med. **40**(6), 625–632 (2002)

11. Clawson, J.J., Martin, R.L., Cady, G.A., Maio, R.F.: The wake-effect—emergency vehicle-related collisions. Prehospital Disaster Med. **12**(4), 274–277 (1997)

12. Petzäll, K.: Trafiksäkerhet vid ambulanstransporter (Traffic Safety at Emergency Vehicle Transportation). Report 2005/94/90. The Department of Health and Social Sciences, Dalarna University, Falun, Sweden (2006)

13. Ho, J., Lindquist, M.: Time saved with use of emergency warning lights and siren while responding to requests for emergency medical aid in a rural environment. Prehosp. Emerg. Care **5**, 159–162 (2001)

14. Boslem, S., Moore, J.D., Charissis, V.: Investigating the improvement of the localisation propensity and impact of the emergency vehicle sirens. In: Proceedings of the Society of Automotive Engineers (SAE) World Congress 2011, 12–14 April, Detroit, Michigan, USA (2011)

15. Charissis, V., Papanastasiou, S., Mackenzie, L., Arafat, S.: Evaluation of collision avoidance prototype head-up display interface for older drivers. In: Jacko, J.A. (ed.) HCI 2011. LNCS, vol. 6763, pp. 367–375. Springer, Heidelberg (2011). https://doi.org/10.1007/978-3-642-21616-9_41

16. Wang, S., Charissis, V., Harrison, D.K.: Augmented reality prototype HUD for passenger infotainment in a vehicular environment. Adv. Sci. Technol. Eng. Syst. J. **2**(3), 634–641 (2017)

17. Wang, S., Charissis, V., Campbell, J., Chan, W., Moore, D.J., Harrison, D.K.: An investigation into the use of Virtual Reality technology for passenger infotainment in a vehicular environment. In: International Conference on Advanced Materials for Science and Engineering (IEEE - ICAMSE), Beijing, China, pp. 404–407 (2016). https://doi.org/10.1109/icamse.2016.7840359

18. Kianfar, R., et al.: Design and experimental validation of a cooperative driving system in the grand cooperative driving challenge. IEEE Trans. Intell. Transp. Syst. **13**(3), 994–1007 (2012). https://doi.org/10.1109/tits.2012.2186513

19. Flanagan, S.K., He, J., Peng, X.: Improving emergency collision avoidance with vehicle to vehicle communications. In: 2018 IEEE 20th International Conference on High-Performance Computing and Communications; IEEE 16th International Conference on Smart City; IEEE 4th International Conference on Data Science and Systems (HPCC/SmartCity/DSS), Exeter, United Kingdom, pp. 1322–1329 (2018). https://doi.org/10.1109/hpcc/smartcity/dss.2018. 00220

20. Charissis, V., Papanastasiou, S., Chan, W., Peytchev, E.: Evolution of a full-windshield HUD designed for current VANET communication standards. In: IEEE Intelligent Transportation Systems International Conference (IEEE ITS), The Hague, Netherlands, pp. 1637–1643 (2013). https://doi.org/10.1109/itsc.2013.6728464

21. Lagoo, R., Charissis, V., Chan, W., Khan, S., Harrison, D.: Prototype gesture recognition interface for vehicular head-up display system. In: IEEE International Conference on Consumer Electronics, Las Vegas, USA, pp. 1–6 (2018)

22. Grane, C., Bengtsson, P.: Driving performance during visual and haptic menu selection with the in-vehicle rotary device. Transp. Res. Part F: Traffic Psychol. Behav. **18**, 123–135 (2013)

23. Hui, C., Xianghui, W., Xiqiang, Z., Shaoli, Z.: The evaluation of chinese urban traffic management system application based on intelligent traffic control technology. In: 2014 7th International Conference on Intelligent Computation Technology and Automation, Changsha, pp. 791–795 (2014). https://doi.org/10.1109/icicta.2014.191

24. Li, N., Zhao, G.: Adaptive signal control for urban traffic network gridlock. In: 2016 UKACC 11th International Conference on Control (CONTROL), Belfast, pp. 1–6 (2016). https://doi.org/10.1109/control.2016.7737520

25. Bram-Larbi, K.F., Charissis, V., Khan, S., Lagoo, R., Harrison, D.K., Drikakis, D.: Collision avoidance head-up display: design considerations for emergency services' vehicles. In: IEEE International Conference on Consumer Electronics (ICCE), Las Vegas, USA (2020)

26. Charissis, V., Naef, M.: Evaluation of prototype automotive head-up display interface: testing driver's focusing ability through a VR simulation. In: IEEE Intelligent Vehicle Symposium, (IV 2007), Istanbul, Turkey (2007)

27. Charissis, V., Papanastasiou, S.: Artificial intelligence rationale for autonomous vehicle agents behaviour in driving simulation environment. In: Aramburo, J., Trevino, A.R. (eds.) Robotics, Automation and Control, pp. 314–332. I-Tech Education and Publishing KG, Vienna (2008). ISBN 953761916-8I

28. Aehlert, B.: Paramedic Practice Today: Above and Beyond, ECC Guidelines (2010)

29. Okumura, H., Hotta, A., Sasaki, T., Horiuchi, K., Okada, N.: Wide field of view optical combiner for augmented reality head-up displays. In: 2018 IEEE International Conference on Consumer Electronics (IEEE ICCE) (2018)

30. Li, J., Cheng, H., Guo, H., Qiu, S.: Survey on artificial intelligence for vehicles. Autom. Innov. **1**(1), 2–14 (2018). https://doi.org/10.1007/s42154-018-0009-9

31. Jing, P., Xu, G., Chen, Y., Shi, Y., Zhan, F.: The determinants behind the acceptance of autonomous vehicles: a systematic review. Sustainability **12**, 1719 (2020)

# A Framework for Modeling Knowledge Graphs via Processing Natural Descriptions of Vehicle-Pedestrian Interactions

Md Fazle Elahi🆔, Xiao Luo🆔, and Renran Tian(✉)🆔

IUPUI, Indianapolis, IN 46202, USA
{melahi,luo25,rtian}@iupui.edu
https://et.iupui.edu/departments/cigt/about/

**Abstract.** The full-scale deployment of autonomous driving demands successful interaction with pedestrians and other vulnerable road users, which requires an understanding of their dynamic behavior and intention. Current research achieves this by estimating pedestrian's trajectory mainly based on the gait and movement information in the past as well as other relevant scene information. However, the autonomous vehicles still struggle with such interactions since the visual features alone may not supply subtle details required to attain a superior understanding. The decision-making ability of the system can improve by incorporating human knowledge to guide the vision-based algorithms. In this paper, we adopt a novel approach to retrieve human knowledge from the natural text descriptions about the pedestrian-vehicle encounters, which is crucial to anticipate the pedestrian intention and is difficult for computer vision (CV) algorithms to capture automatically. We applied natural language processing (NLP) techniques on the aggregated description from different annotators to generate a temporal knowledge graph, which can achieve the changes of intention and the corresponding reasoning processes in a better resolution. In future work, we plan to show that in combination with video processing algorithms, the knowledge graph has the potential to aid the decision-making process to be more accurate by passively integrating the reasoning ability of humans.

**Keywords:** Knowledge graph · Pedestrian behavior · Natural language processing

## 1 Introduction

According to road safety status report from World Health Organization (WHO), almost 1.35 million deaths occur due to road accidents, and 54% of them include pedestrians, cyclists, and motorcyclists [1]. For the successful deployment of autonomous vehicles, the Artificial Intelligence (AI) system for decision making is required to interact with not only its passengers but also with diverse on-road

© Springer Nature Switzerland AG 2020
C. Stephanidis et al. (Eds.): HCII 2020, LNCS 12429, pp. 40–50, 2020.
https://doi.org/10.1007/978-3-030-59987-4_4

entities, including the human-driven vehicles, pedestrians, and traffic signals [3, 9]. Although they are adept at navigating on the road among other vehicles, not surprisingly, those vehicles struggle while communicating with pedestrians and cyclists due to the complexity of the interaction [4–6,19]. As stated in [5], unlike human drivers, the autonomous vehicles are unable to communicate through human gestures, for example, 'hand waving' or 'eye gaze' for negotiating the right of way. Also, the car needs to know when to stop before starting the negotiation with the pedestrian in non-designated areas. Furthermore, the crossing behavior articulated by the pedestrians varies across contextual factors, for instance, age-groups [10]. In contrast, the decision-making system treats them almost equally and determines the right of way based on their trajectory.

Most of the state-of-the-art AI systems are trained with end-to-end learning by mapping the features (head pose, current position, distance from the curb) extracted from the scenes to decisions [11,14,18]. These features extracted from the scene alone are insufficient to identify pedestrian crossing intention since it is usually affected by factors from experiences, e.g., traffic density, speed of the oncoming vehicle, type of the road, and the weather [12,13]. Arguably, the research focus needs to be shifted so that the AI system can capture these dynamic, subtle details of human behavior. In this work, we propose a novel method for mining those details that can aid to passively integrate the reasoning ability into the AI by augmenting scene based features with natural text-based features.

## 2   Research Proposal

This study analyzes the descriptions from the drivers about the pedestrian-crossing scenes to support AI development. We organize our research work based on the assumptions that:

- The description of the scenes from drivers will contain the contextual information that can complement the feature-set obtained through image processing algorithms;
- The descriptions can approximate the change of pedestrian's intention across the time when aggregated;
- The aggregated contextual information, along with visual features, can be used to guide the decision-making process.

The text description of the scene is obtained through annotation by the experienced drivers. The subjects watch the pre-selected video clips meeting suitable criteria and express the whole scenario in terms of words in their own way. They are guided to describe the interactions among the relevant objects (referred to as cue/description) followed by the intention of the pedestrian (referred to as intention), and lastly, the reasoning mechanism (referred to as reasoning) for anticipating that intention. In this study, annotations by human subjects are considered more practical instead of using automatic scene captioning algorithms [2,20] for multiple reasons: (1) the natural description embeds the perspective of the reasoning from the drivers who AI will be taking over; (2) no study has been done yet building the knowledge-base relying on which the automatic scene captioning can work reliably; (3) current state-of-the-art automatic scene captioning is too naive to capture the complicated interaction among objects in such scenarios which may not yield the desired result.

The study continues by summarizing the text information in terms of knowledge graphs with temporal data. This implementation helps capture the dynamic changes in pedestrian intention. It is indicative of aggregation of the contextual information as well as the presence of non-verbal behaviors in finer resolution. We expect that if merged with visual features, the natural description of the scenes can not only capture the subtle details but also can enhance decision-making ability to some extent by capturing contextual information.

## 3   Methodology

### 3.1   Data Collection

The video clips used for annotation in this study are a part of the TASI large-scale naturalistic driving data set. Naturalistic data means the video data were recorded from everyday life of the drivers where pedestrians were completely unaware of the recording and interacted as usual. Throughout one year, from a total of 110 drivers, more than 40 thousand hours of driving video were recorded at (1280 * 720) resolution. From this data, 62,000 pedestrian-vehicle encounters are identified through applying advanced image processing algorithms to automatically detect human pedestrians, cyclists, and vehicles [15–17]. Two experts at vehicle-pedestrian interactions selected 100 random video clips with possible pedestrian-vehicle collision cases with varying levels of complexity. Among them, 30 video clips with 15 s of duration are selected for this study, which captures various combinations of pedestrian, vehicle, road types, weather conditions, as illustrated in Fig. 1.

**Fig. 1.** Sample frames from different video clips

All the selected videos contain non-verbal negotiation between the pedestrian and the vehicle, which were later described by the annotators in their own language. Additionally, there are balanced amounts of cases in which the pedestrians either crossed or did not cross the road eventually. In total, 13 people aged between 18 and 67 years with driving experiences in the US were recruited for video annotation. Before the video annotation, the aim of this study and the requirements of text descriptions were explained to them. For data annotation, the subjects used a web-app based interface capable of playing the selected videos. While watching the video, the subjects could navigate back and forth through the video time frame and recorded their timestamped description in three designated text-input boxes used for 'Description of the Scene' 'Pedestrian Decision,' and 'Reasoning' entries.

The annotation goal is to understand how the non-verbal communication propagates and affects the decision making between the pedestrian and the vehicle along time. Thus, the annotators first watch the video for a certain period and then pause the playback when the pedestrian is first seen. Then the annotators describe the scene in the 'Description of the Scene' entry and guess a 'Pedestrian Decision' about pedestrian's crossing intention for that moment. At the same time, the annotator also explains their reasoning process supporting their observation. The interface automatically saved these text entries along with the timestamp of the video for time-based analysis on the same video. The subjects were instructed to include the details they feel important about the relevant entities but not limited to 'pedestrians,' 'vehicles,' 'road and traffic condition,' 'other people,' and 'weather' in the description. Few examples of raw annotations from different annotators for a certain video clip are shown in Table 1. In this way, the subjects keep annotating the video until they can determine the final intention of the pedestrian for crossing. In the cases where annotators were uncertain of the pedestrian's intention due to the complexity of the pedestrian-vehicle encounter, they entered the decision as 'not sure' or 'not enough information.' For each annotator, on average, it took around 6–7 h for labeling all the 30 video clips.

## 3.2  Data Analysis

As shown in Table 1, the raw data of one video acquired from a single annotator contains timestamped text entries of description of the scene, pedestrian decision, and reasoning. Likewise, 13 annotators have 13 similar raw data files for a particular video, which are merged into a single data file containing the text entries with their corresponding timestamps to conduct scene-based analysis along time. Consequently, for each of the 30 videos, there are 30 such aggregated data files containing the text entries from all the annotators associated with various frames with the timestamp.

This study applied several pre-processing steps to transform the observed natural text into structured data, as illustrated in Fig. 2. First, the raw data were formatted, removing white-space characters, and keeping the original meaning unchanged. Then, the descriptions containing the observation were split into

**Table 1.** Raw annotation data for second video clip from an annotator

| Time(s) | Description of the scene | Pedestrian decision | Reasoning |
|---|---|---|---|
| 0 | The driver is in front of a shopping center on a two-lane road going in both directions. The pedestrian is standing on the opposite side of the street to the driver. The driver is behind a motorcycle | The pedestrian will not cross | The motorcycle and the driver are about to pass in front of the pedestrian so it is not safe for them to cross |
| 3.47 | The motorcycle turned left before crossing in front of the pedestrian. The pedestrian stepped out into the road in front of the driver | The pedestrian will cross | The pedestrian has started walking in front of the driver |
| 5.38 | The pedestrian looks back at the driver, and the driver slows down. The pedestrian has walked further into the street | The final intention of the pedestrian is to cross | The pedestrian is crossing the street, and the driver slowed down to let the pedestrian cross |

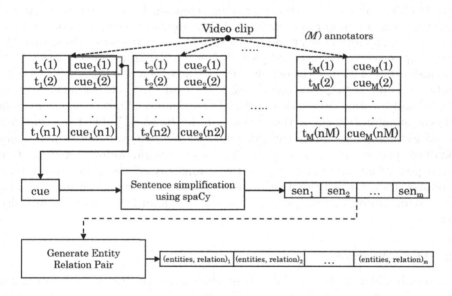

**Fig. 2.** Flowchart to produce entity-relation for a video clip

individual sentences based on period, comma, and semicolon. As expected, in many cases these individual sentences have the form of compound and complex sentences for describing the events. To generate the knowledge graph, another step needs to capture the information of those complex sentences. Instead of working directly with these complex structured sentences, they are further split into simple sentences such that the overall meaning is preserved.

**Table 2.** Decomposition into simple sentences

| Compound or complex sentence | Simple sentences |
|---|---|
| The pedestrian crossed the road and slowed down | (The pedestrian crossed the road, The pedestrian slowed down) |
| The pedestrian is attempting to cross the street when traffic is traveling with a green light | (The pedestrian is attempting to cross the street, traffic is traveling with a green light) |
| A driver approaching an intersection with traffic present and pedestrian running across drivers lane | (driver approaching the intersection with traffic present, pedestrian running across drivers lane) |
| The position of the pedestrian looks as though the pedestrian is in a hurry and is aware of the traffic lights and that the pedestrian should not be crossing at this time and thus why the pedestrian is moving in a fast pace | (The position of the pedestrian looks as though, the pedestrian is in a hurry, the pedestrian is aware of the traffic lights, that the pedestrian should not be crossing at this time, why the pedestrian is moving in a fast pace) |

Generally, a complex sentence comprises a *principal clause* and one or more *subordinate clauses*, which usually shares the same subject. On the other hand, two or more independent clauses linked through conjunctions compose a compound sentence. To simplify these convoluted sentences, an NLP library, namely **spaCy** [7,8] is used for identifying the parts of speech (POS) tags and their dependency (relationship) with other words in the context. spaCy uses convolutional-neural-network-based architecture with residual connections for POS tagging, dependency parsing, and entity recognition within the sentences. The pre-trained models known as *parsers* are trained on the texts found on blogs, news, webpages at various scales. For the purpose of this study, a small-sized off-the-shelf model of spaCy, *'en_core_web_sm'*, trained on English written texts in the web was used for parsing and POS tagging. The POS tags and the dependency information obtained through the parser is used to identify the parent subjects, main verbs, and predicates in the clauses of original long sentences. This information can then infer simple sentences. Again, the naturalistic property of the texts has a range of patterns that often do not follow grammatical structures. Hence, custom rule-based algorithms are developed to capture the wide variety of patterns for identifying the clauses for deriving the simple sentences from the parent sentence. The construction of this rule-based algorithm is an iterative domain-oriented process (pedestrian-vehicle encounter) that can capture these patterns adequately when it is developed based on larger text data set. Then, the child sentences inherit the timestamps of the parent sentence and replace their parent sentences to make the data viable for further processing. Table 2 demonstrates a few representative samples of the compound and complex sentences from the data set that are automatically split into simple sentences.

The knowledge graph is often used to gist embedded representation in a coherent paragraph through interconnected nodes and edges relating them. The

**Table 3.** Entity-relation pairs

| Simple sentence | Entity1, Relation, Entity2 |
| --- | --- |
| The pedestrian does not enter the crosswalk | (pedestrian, does not enter, crosswalk) |
| The driver is still maintaining speed coming up to a walkway | (driver, maintaining, speed) |
| There doesn't seem to be a traffic light | (there, doesn't seem, traffic light) |
| Weather is overcast | (weather, is, overcast) |
| The car is right in front of the pedestrian | (car, is, right front of pedestrian) |
| The crosswalk area already has some pedestrians crossing through | (crosswalk area already, has, some pedestrians) |

nodes in the graph usually represent the objects or entities that are correlated while the edges represent the relation between them. Usually, the relation represents some actions or characteristics of the entity. In this study, the subject-object pairs are used as entity pairs and the verb as relation to creating the knowledge graph. In the cases of the sentences lacking objects, the 'adjective' modifying the 'subject' often can take the place of the 'object' in entity-pair. Naturally the entities include interaction related objects like 'pedestrian', 'driver', 'road', 'cross-walk', 'curb', 'weather condition', 'traffic light', and 'road condition,' whereas relations include the verb forms of 'stop', 'run', 'walk', 'wave,' and so on. Table 3 shows some examples of simple sentences and their corresponding entity-relation pairs.

After extracting the entity relation pairs from the simple sentences, they are grouped by the timestamps with 1 s of interval. All the grouped pairs are further categorized into cues and reasoning along the time axis of the video. For the main interests of this study, the text entries containing the entity: 'pedestrian' and their interaction with other entities from every annotator are aggregated for generating the time-sequential knowledge graph.

## 4   Results

Following the data analysis described above, there are 30 time-sequential knowledge graphs generated for the 30 videos. Two of them, one for the pedestrian decision of 'cross' and the other for 'not cross,' are discussed in detail.

The knowledge graph for the case where a pedestrian's decision is to cross the road without using a crosswalk is shown in Fig. 3, and the 'not cross' scene in Fig. 4. Each graph is split into two sections above and below the time-axis, which mainly portrays the evolution of pedestrian activities along time. The text entries under the category 'Description of the scene (cue)' contribute the upper portion while the lower part contains the 'reasoning.' The snapshots of the video within the corresponding time window also accompany the graph for better comprehension of the pedestrian's behavior alongside the texts. Although each video has a duration of 15 s, only the time-frame containing the text-entries from all the annotators are included in the graph.

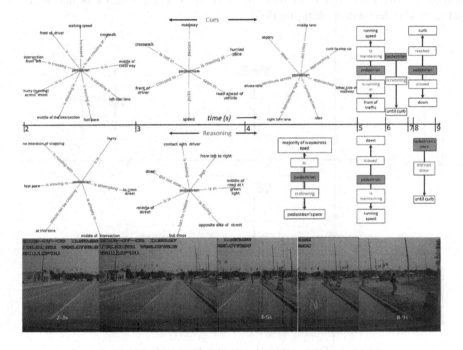

**Fig. 3.** Time-sequential knowledge graph: cross

Evidently, within this time-frame, the uneven distribution of data throughout the time conveys the idea that key information from certain moments may encode the pedestrian's crossing intention during a pedestrian-vehicle encounter. The knowledge graph of the pedestrian-crossing case shows that most drivers have already estimated the pedestrian intention in the first 1–4 s. On the contrary, it took most people a long time to complete the negotiation with the pedestrians in this not-crossing case.

Annotators reached the conclusions based on the current situation as well as their experience and background knowledge with remarkably superior reasoning ability than a CV based algorithm. The repeated mention of 'hastiness' in the pedestrian's movement points towards the final intention, which will be difficult for a CV algorithm to capture. Moreover, the graph also demonstrates the strength of the subtle variation of activities of the pedestrian. For example, the cue of 'is moving at a fast pace' instead of simply 'is moving,' is used to determine the final intention.

Furthermore, some entries, like pedestrian ('is running with no intention of stopping', 'should not be crossing at this time', 'has no choice but to cross', 'is

majority of way across road') from the reasoning part also shows what leads
the subject to estimate the pedestrian's decision. This logic can help to train
intermediate layers of the deep neural network to improve the accuracy and
explainability of AI algorithms. The balanced integration of the subtleties supported by the past beliefs of humans into the CV algorithms is necessary to
enhance the decision-making models.

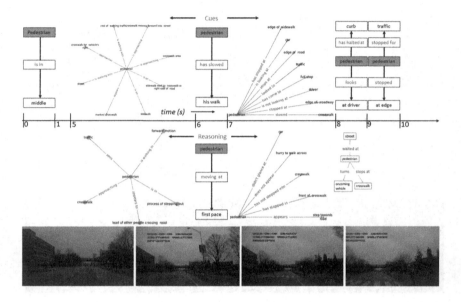

**Fig. 4.** Time-sequential knowledge graph: not cross

## 5   Conclusions and Discussions

In this study, we have presented that the natural scene description of pedestrian-
vehicle encounter by the human can be processed applying NLP algorithms to
generate the knowledge graphs with temporal information. The work also demonstrates that these knowledge graphs aggregated from multiple subjects contain
features critical for modeling pedestrian behavior, which may not be present in
visual features. The experimental analysis shows how the subtle variation of the
pedestrian activity can dramatically influence the pedestrian's crossing intention. The finding in the study suggests that the AI system can be enhanced by
fusing information from visual cues and textual descriptions. Additionally, the
detailed information correlated with reasoning encoded within the scene description can help to transfer the human background knowledge into the AI to attain
a higher level of intelligence.

# References

1. Global status report on road safety 2018: summary (2018). https://www.who.int/violence_injury_prevention/road_safety_status/2018/en/
2. Antol, S., et al.: VQA: visual question answering. CoRR abs/1505.00468 (2015). http://arxiv.org/abs/1505.00468
3. Ezzati Amini, R., Katrakazas, C., Antoniou, C.: Negotiation and decision-making for a pedestrian roadway crossing: a literature review. Sustainability **11**, 6713 (2019). https://doi.org/10.3390/su11236713
4. Faerber, B.: Communication and Communication Problems Between Autonomous Vehicles and Human Drivers, pp. 125–144 (2016). https://doi.org/10.1007/978-3-662-48847-8_7
5. Gupta, S., Vasardani, M., Winter, S.: Negotiation between vehicles and pedestrians for the right of way at intersections. IEEE Trans. Intell. Transp. Syst. **20**(3), 888–899 (2019). https://doi.org/10.1109/TITS.2018.2836957
6. Hagenzieker, M., et al.: Interactions between cyclists and automated vehicles: results of a photo experiment*. J. Transp. Saf. Secur. 1–22 (2019). https://doi.org/10.1080/19439962.2019.1591556
7. Honnibal, M., Johnson, M.: An improved non-monotonic transition system for dependency parsing. In: Proceedings of the 2015 Conference on Empirical Methods in Natural Language Processing, Lisbon, Portugal, pp. 1373–1378. Association for Computational Linguistics, September 2015. https://aclweb.org/anthology/D/D15/D15-1162
8. Honnibal, M., Montani, I.: spaCy 2: natural language understanding with Bloom embeddings, convolutional neural networks and incremental parsing (2017, to appear)
9. Müller, L., Risto, M., Emmenegger, C.: The social behavior of autonomous vehicles, pp. 686–689 (2016). https://doi.org/10.1145/2968219.2968561
10. Oxley, J., Fildes, B., Ihsen, E., Charlton, J., Day, R.: Differences in traffic judgements between young and old adult pedestrians. Accid. Anal. Prev. **29**(6), 839 – 847 (1997). https://doi.org/10.1016/S0001-4575(97)00053-5. http://www.sciencedirect.com/science/article/pii/S0001457597000535
11. Quintero Mínguez, R., Alonso, I., Ferníndez-Llorca, D., Sotelo, M.: Pedestrian path, pose, and intention prediction through gaussian process dynamical models and pedestrian activity recognition. IEEE Trans. Intell. Transp. Syste. 1–12 (2018). https://doi.org/10.1109/TITS.2018.2836305
12. Rasouli, A., Kotseruba, Y., Tsotsos, J.: Understanding pedestrian behavior in complex traffic scenes. IEEE Trans. Intell. Veh. 1 (2017). https://doi.org/10.1109/TIV.2017.2788193
13. Razmi Rad, S., Homem de Almeida Correia, G., Hagenzieker, M.: Pedestrians' road crossing behaviour in front of automated vehicles: results from a pedestrian simulation experiment using agent-based modelling. Transp. Res. Part F Traffic Psychol. Behav. **69** (2020). https://doi.org/10.1016/j.trf.2020.01.014
14. Schmidt, S., Faerber, B.: Pedestrians at the kerb - recognising the action intentions of humans. Transp. Res. Part F-Traffic Psychol. Behav. **12**, 300–310 (2009). https://doi.org/10.1016/j.trf.2009.02.003
15. Sherony, R., Tian, R., Chien, S., Fu, L., Chen, Y., Takahashi, H.: Pedestrian/bicyclist limb motion analysis from 110-car TASI video data for autonomous emergency braking testing surrogate development. SAE Int. J. Transp. Saf. **4**(1), 113–120 (2016)

16. Tian, R., et al.: Pilot study on pedestrian step frequency in naturalistic driving environment. In: 2013 IEEE Intelligent Vehicles Symposium (IV), pp. 1215–1220. IEEE (2013)
17. Tian, R., Li, L., Yang, K., Chien, S., Chen, Y., Sherony, R.: Estimation of the vehicle-pedestrian encounter/conflict risk on the road based on TASI 110-car naturalistic driving data collection. In: 2014 IEEE Intelligent Vehicles Symposium Proceedings, pp. 623–629. IEEE (2014)
18. Volz, B., Behrendt, K., Mielenz, H., Gilitschenski, I., Siegwart, R., Nieto, J.: A data-driven approach for pedestrian intention estimation, pp. 2607–2612 (2016). https://doi.org/10.1109/ITSC.2016.7795975
19. Wolf, I.: The interaction between humans and autonomous agents. In: Maurer, M., Gerdes, J.C., Lenz, B., Winner, H. (eds.) Autonomous Driving, pp. 103–124. Springer, Heidelberg (2016). https://doi.org/10.1007/978-3-662-48847-8_6
20. Yang, X., Tang, K., Zhang, H., Cai, J.: Auto-encoding scene graphs for image captioning. CoRR abs/1812.02378 (2018). http://arxiv.org/abs/1812.02378

# Privacy by Design: Analysis of Capacitive Proximity Sensing as System of Choice for Driver Vehicle Interfaces

Sebastian Frank[1]([⊠]) and Arjan Kuijper[2]

[1] Technische Universität Darmstadt, Darmstadt, Germany
sebastian.frank@gris.tu-darmstadt.de
[2] Technische Universität Darmstadt/Fraunhofer IGD, Darmstadt, Germany
arjan.kuijper@igd.fraunhofer.de

**Abstract.** Data collection is beneficial. Therefore, automotive manufacturers start including data collection services. At the same time, manufacturers install cameras for human machine interfaces in vehicles. But those systems may disclose further information than needed for gesture recognition. Thus, they may cause privacy issues.

The law (GDPR) enforces privacy by default and design. Research often states that capacitive proximity sensing is better to serve privacy by design than cameras. Furthermore, it is unclear if customers value privacy preserving features. Nonetheless, manufacturers value the customer's voice.

Therefore, several vehicular human machine interface systems, with camera or capacitive proximity sensing, are analyzed. Especially concerning gesture recognition, capacitive proximity sensing systems provide similar features like camera-based systems. The analysis is based on the GDPR privacy definition. Due to the analysis, it is revealed that capacitive proximity sensing systems have less privacy concerns causing features. Subsequently, three hypotheses are formulated to capture the customer's voice.

Due to analysis results, it is questionable if gesture recognition systems, which utilize cameras, are compliant with privacy by design. Especially since well-known systems like capacitive proximity sensing are available. A survey concerning the hypotheses will give further insights in future work.

**Keywords:** Privacy · Capacitive proximity sensing · GDPR · Automotive · Human machine interface

## 1 Introduction

Enterprises which include data collection services rank under the most valuable enterprises. For example, Touryalay et al. [52] list Amazon.com on rank two, Alphabet on rank three and Facebook on position five concerning market value. As shown by Alexa Internet [4], websites of those companies, as "google.com" or

© Springer Nature Switzerland AG 2020
C. Stephanidis et al. (Eds.): HCII 2020, LNCS 12429, pp. 51–66, 2020.
https://doi.org/10.1007/978-3-030-59987-4_5

"Youtube.com", are on the top of the most frequently visited. Thus, they play a significant role in the daily life of people.

The collection of private data, like pictures, can cause privacy issues. The European Union (EU) faced this fact by adopting the "General Data Protection Regulation" (GDPR) [19]. Subsequently, the personal data transfer from the EU to foreign countries is under regulation. Paradigms like "privacy by design" and "privacy by default" play a major role (GDPR Article 25: "Data protection by design and by default"). Privacy by design means that product development shall prevent privacy issues causing features. Privacy by default means that the initial settings of data collection should provide the most privacy protecting mode of conduct.

Due to for example smartphones, 26% of United States citizens are almost constantly online [43]. Applications for mobile phones (Apps) facilitate enterprises' data collection. Users exchange sensitive information, enhanced by additional sensors. Therefore, companies are able to derive detailed user profiles [55]. Plenty of sensor systems are provided by vehicles. Originally, those sensors are used to increase safety, comfort and route optimization. Subsequently, primary web service-based enterprises like Alphabet head into the automotive domain. Mobile phone to vehicle interfaces, like Android Auto [1] or Apple CarPlay [2], are already available [42].

New automotive business models are enabled by the collection of driving behavior and passenger data. Positive examples are safety features or comfort features. For example, navigation can be optimized by using traffic information. Heart rate monitoring can inform the driver concerning his abilities to drive. Nonetheless, there are examples which induce data collection, which is not in favor of the driver [49]. For example, insurance companies could buy information about collected driving behavior. This can result in non-insurable drivers. Additionally, some driver monitoring systems include cameras pointing towards the driver. Therefore, health insurance companies could gather more sensitive information about people's health constitution. The health constitution could be derived of identified smokers, frequent meals while driving or corpulence.

Customers may make choices about systems to include into their cars with prudence. Nonetheless, research has shown that there is even a difference between security and privacy aware thinking customers [20]. A customer who has privacy concerns about the product may tempt to buy it while a customer who has concerns about the security of his information may decline. Concerning systems like driver fatigue detection, the consequences of data collection and security issues of vehicle systems may not be obvious. Due to the privacy-security knowledge gap [20], potential vehicle customers may behave different at system selection. This can influence vehicle manufacturers decision about system development. If the product target group is focused on privacy and security conserving technology, manufacturers should concern privacy by design. A target group that favors functionality over privacy may select the best cost system with the highest functionality.

Individuals make decisions frequently based on incomplete knowledge due to the complexity of systems [3]. The decision becomes even more complex due to upcoming security issues at connected vehicles. As indicated by Volkswagen [50], software complexity is growing. Naturally, this enables future exploits. Therefore, currently secure software may become vulnerable in the future. Research already recognized the demand for frequent updates in the future [32,35]. Thus, European law orders privacy by design. Automotive business models, which require data collection, may rely on sensor systems which cause privacy concerns. Furthermore, it is unclear if vehicle customers concern privacy issues at technology package selection. Therefore, we provide an investigation that consists of the following contributions:

– Analysis of vehicular human machine interfaces (VHMI) concerning privacy by design
  • Concerning interior sensor systems
  • Comparison of design intention and inexpedient usage concerning similar sensor system usage (cross usage)
– Overview of the potential of capacitive proximity sensors in VHMI
– Definition of hypotheses with regard to the privacy awareness of vehicle customers.

## 2   Related Work

### 2.1   Influence of Data Protection on the Design of Data Collection Services

The effect of privacy concerns on social network formation is investigated by Gaudeul et al. [30]. The investigation is based on a study with 125 subjects. The subjects are equally distributed in five groups. A social network game, with two phases, is designed as experiment. Sensitive personal information is collected in phase one. Then, in phase two, participants can select a level for the disclosure of confidential information. Subsequently, they can select other individuals to form a network.

In the investigation of Gaudeul et al., a link is established if both participants have selected each other. Further, they can choose to pay a fee for the service. The aim of the study is to find out how the possibility of different data disclosure options affects the formation of individual networks. Several hypotheses are checked: Preference for social approval should increase the willingness to disclose in hypothesis one. A metric for privacy concerns is presented: Privacy cost (PC). Greater PC is shown by disclosure of real name and information than of name only.

Gaudeul et al. shows that PC for disclosure of real name only is greater than PC for fake names. High PC should lower the willingness to disclose information in phase two. This is covered by hypothesis two. These hypotheses shall contribute to the paper's main hypothesis: The absence of past interactions of one individual takes influence on another individual's choice of information disclosure. Five results are captured by the analysis of the study. Subjects contribute less to the network if privacy concerns arose due to the revelation of name and subject information. Result three is of special interest. It concludes that PC is more important to individuals than social approval.

Bloom et al. [12] investigate privacy concerns caused by networked, autonomous vehicles. A study with 302 participants is conducted. To gain significance, they ask subjects in cities with and without autonomous vehicles from the transportation network company Uber. People's knowledge about used sensor systems of automated driving is captured. Furthermore, they check whether people would spend extra time restricting data collection. Diverge knowledge about possible tracking scenarios and the actual tracking application is discovered. Although discomfort is caused by privacy concerns, Uber/Lyft is used by 172 (57%) participants. 54% of the participants would invest more than five minutes to check options which deactivate data collection.

### 2.2 How Research Addresses Privacy Concerns

Martin et al. [37] state that driver monitoring systems may use camera systems to capture images of the driver. Furthermore, the captured image of the driver is often unprocessed. This can include more information than needed. For example, a system which recognizes driver gazing in images could enable driver identification. Thus, an image filter is developed by Martin et al. The filter disables driver identification from the captured image. However, gaze recognition is preserved. 20 people participated in an evaluation under laboratory conditions.

A gaze recognition rate of 71% is resulted by using filtered images as shown by Martin et al. They state that this recognition rate indicates no significant information loss due to the image filter. This approach conserves driver identity at full system function using camera.

### 2.3 Analysis of Privacy Concerns Caused by In-vehicle Sensor Systems

An overview of privacy concerns of vehicle owners, caused by emerging technologies, is given by McDonald et al. [39]. The awareness of people, concerning privacy issues causing technologies, is examined. At first, showcase systems, initially not used for tracking, are presented. As those systems mature, they become of interest to people tracking. For example, New York's MetroCard is introduced as metro usage system. But then, the police used it to persecute subjects. This is enabled by data collection, which is not required for the original system usage.

McDonald et al. state that even though systems are not designed for privacy concerning usage, privacy concerns causing patterns may be captured. Six technologies are investigated: Black boxes (event data recorders), traffic cameras, GPS transponders, OnStar, E-ZPass and Highway Use Tax. Although those systems were not defined to capture privacy relevant information, their evaluation changed to reveal sensitive information about the driver's behavior.

# 3 Contribution

## 3.1 Definition of Privacy

The question is how vehicular human machine interfaces (VHMI) may interfere with personal privacy. Thus, the terminus privacy must be clarified. Privacy is often introduced with the definition of Warren and Brandeis dated 1890: *"The right to be let alone"* [53].

The definition of privacy varies with publications. Nonetheless, states enact laws that define privacy violations. The European Union agreed to the General Data Protection Regulation (GDPR) [19]. Selected processes which can cause violation of GDPR are presented in the following list.

*'biometric data'* *means personal data resulting from specific technical processing relating to the physical, physiological or behavioural characteristics of a natural person, which allow or confirm the unique identification of that natural person, such as facial images or dactyloscopic data* (GDPR, Article 4, Paragraph 14)

*'profiling'* *means any form of automated processing of personal data consisting of the use of personal data to evaluate certain personal aspects relating to a natural person, in particular to analyse or predict aspects concerning that natural person's performance at work, economic situation, health, personal preferences, interests, reliability, behaviour, location or movements* (GDPR, Article 4, Paragraph 4)

*'genetic data'* *means personal data relating to the inherited or acquired genetic characteristics of a natural person which give unique information about the physiology or the health of that natural person and which result, in particular, from an analysis of a biological sample from the natural person in question*(GDPR, Article 4, Paragraph 13)

In summary, the concerned privacy interfering entities are biometric data: feasibility of people identification, profiling: tracking and prediction of people behavior and genetic data: the derivation of people's physiology or health (health also interferes with GDPR, Article 4, Paragraph 15). Subsequent references to privacy refer to this definition.

Additionally, GDPR demands privacy by design and default (GDPR, Article 25: *"Data protection by design and by default"*). Therefore, the difference between system tasks and opportunities is captured as privacy interfering entity (Subsequently called Dedication - Opportunity - Difference). For example, human machine interfaces are dedicated to a specific task, accomplished through sensor data processing. If opportunities to derive more information from data as needed are present, Dedication - Opportunity - Difference is given. This difference is analyzed by comparing VHMI with systems with data protection concerns. Both systems have to rely on similar sensors.

**Explanatory Example:** An interior camera is used by Rezaei et al. [45]. Driver attentiveness, in particular nodding due to fatigue (Fig. 1, left) shall be captured. A similar sensor system, which captures the same region of interest (driver head) is used by Su et al. [51]. Driver behavior like smoking and mobile phone usage is recognized by Su et al. While the system of Rezaei et al. is dedicated to measure head nodding, the captured data provides opportunities for profiling or health estimation, as used by Su et al. Due to this Dedication - Opportunity - Difference, profiling may become an issue questioning privacy by design.

Nod detection           Smoking and mobile usage detection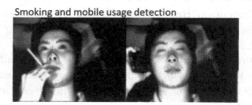

**Fig. 1.** Left: Nod detection [45], Right: Smoking recognition [51]

## 3.2 Selected Driver Vehicle Interfaces

Vehicular human machine interfaces (VHMI) are designed on specific purpose. As presented in Sects. 2.2 and 2.3, research already recognized that the original design intentions often require less information than captured.

Selected VHMI without capacitive proximity sensing (CAPS) are presented in Table 1. Driver movements or conditions are captured. Presented attentiveness systems (# 1, 3, 5, 6), dedicated to detect attentiveness or fatigue, rely on cameras (which may be infrared cameras). Images of the driver's head are captured. These images are used to derive head position and eye opening. Sample camera positions and captures are shown in Fig. 2, *B, C.*

Systems # 2, 4 and 10 of Table 1 are dedicated to capture gestures. Cameras are used to capture hands (Fig. 2, *A*), the upper body or the whole driver body. Additionally, a microphone is required in system # 10. It is used to capture driver voice commands. Gestures like pointing (one finger), swipe and circular hand movement are derived.

Next domain is driver recognition and identification. This is covered by systems # 7, 8, 9 and 11 in Table 1. System # 7 includes a fingerprint sensor. The other systems rely at least on a camera. Additionally, # 8 and 9 require a microphone. The cameras region of interest is diverging. While # 8 and 9 capture images of the driver face, # 11 captures images of driver feet. All of those processes are dedicated to measure driver identity.

A summary of those systems, their domains and the captured driver regions is shown in Fig. 4, left. Most of the required information is captured via cameras. Additionally, driver voice is captured by three systems.

**Table 1.** Vehicular human machine interfaces without capacitive proximity sensing

| # | **Enterprise** Application | System focus | Sensors |
|---|---|---|---|
| 1 | **BMW** [44] <br> Attentiveness assistant | Head position <br> eye opening | Camera |
| 2 | **BMW** [44] <br> Gesture control | Hand <br> movement | Camera |
| 3 | **DS** [9] <br> Driver attention warning | Head position <br> eye opening | Infrared camera |
| 4 | **PSA** [24,31,34] <br> Gesture control | Hand <br> movement <br> Upper body | (Time of flight) <br> camera infrared <br> sensors |
| 5 | **Continental** [38] <br> Adaptive emergency brake and steer <br> assist systems based on driver focus | Head position | Camera (monocular, <br> binocular, array) |
| 6 | **Continental** [48] <br> Adaptive driver assist | Driver face | Camera |
| 7 | **Visteon** [47] <br> Vehicle personalization via biometric <br> identification | Fingertips | Fingerprint sensor |
| 8 | **General Motors** [18] <br> Hierarchical recognition of vehicle <br> driver and select activation of vehicle <br> settings based on the recognition | Driver face, <br> voice | Microphone, camera |
| 9 | **Volvo** [36] <br> Method for performing driver identity <br> verification | Voice, face | Camera, microphone <br> fingertips |
| 10 | **Honda** [21] <br> System and method for controlling a <br> vehicle user interface based on gesture <br> angle | Whole body | Camera, microphone |
| 11 | **Hyundai** [33] <br> Driver recognition system and <br> recognition method for vehicle | Driver feet | Camera |

**Selected Driver Vehicle Interfaces Based on Capacitive Proximity Sensing.** Alternatives to systems in Table 1 are presented in Table 2. In contrast to Table 1, systems in Table 2 are based on capacitive proximity sensing (CAPS).

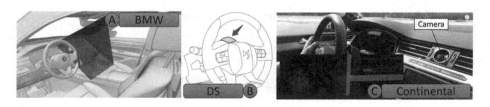

**Fig. 2.** Table 1 sample systems [5, 9, 44]

**Table 2.** Vehicular human machine interfaces based on capacitive proximity sensing

| # | Publication | Application | System focus |
|---|---|---|---|
| 1 | AuthentiCap - A Touchless Vehicle Authentication and Personalization System [26] | Authentication | Hands Fingers |
| 2 | A method for determining a person's identity on a seat of a vehicle [17] | Identification | Head Upper body Legs |
| 3 | CapSeat: Capacitive Proximity Sensing for Automotive Activity Recognition [13] | Fatigue | Head Back Arms |
| 4 | CapSeat: Capacitive Proximity Sensing for Automotive Activity Recognition [13] | Comfort | Head, Back Arms Legs |
| 5 | Towards Interactive Car Interiors: The Active Armrest [15] | Gestures | Arm Fingers |
| 6 | Enabling Driver Feet Gestures Using Capacitive Proximity Sensing [25, 28] | Gestures | Feet |
| 7 | HUDConCap - Automotive Head-Up Display Controlled with Capacitive Proximity Sensing [27] | Gestures | Hands Fingers |
| 8 | Vehicle Occupant Head Position Position Quantification Using an Array of Capacitive Proximity Sensors [57] | Comfort | Head |
| 9 | Distributed sensor for steering wheel grip force measurement in driver fatigue detection [10] | Fatigue | Hands |
| 10 | Developing a multi sensors system to detect sleepiness to drivers to drivers from transport systems [22] | Fatigue | Head |

Two authentication/identification systems (# 1 and 2) are shown in Table 2. Both are based on different processes. System # 1 uses password like gestures, defined by authenticated users themselves. The observed area is around the steering wheel. An array of CAPS electrodes, integrated into the steering wheel, captures free air hand positions.

In contrast to system # 1, system # 2 integrates CAPS electrodes into the driver seat (Fig. 3, A). Under the condition that drivers take a predefined position, drivers are identified by their CAPS profile. The system focus is on the area between seat and head, upper body and legs. A similar electrode setup as in system # 1 is used in system # 3. The dedicated use, fatigue detection, is enabled by head position tracking and steering wheel movement frequency analysis. The system focus is on the area between seat and head, upper arms.

Due to information about head position, driver fatigue is derived by System # 10. The head restraint is used as CAPS sensor mount for fatigue detection. Thus, the system focus is on the area between seat and head. Similar to system # 1, system # 9 integrates CAPS into the steering wheel. Signs for fatigue are derived by variations in driver grip force. Thus, the system focus is on the contact between hands and steering wheel.

Aside of fatigue detection, gesture recognition is provided by CAPS systems # 5, 6 and 7. Hand and finger gestures are provided using a CAPS equipped driver armrest (Fig. 3, B) in system # 5. Thus, driver arm and fingers are in focus of the system. Contrary to system # 5, hand movement is tracked using a CAPS equipped steering wheel in system # 7. The system focus is on driver hands in the area of the steering wheel. Driver foot gestures are enabled by system # 6 (Fig. 3, C). Capacitive proximity sensors (CAPS) are integrated into the vehicle legroom. Therefore, the system focus is on the driver feet.

Aside of identification and fatigue detection, comfort features are provided by systems # 4 and 8 (Fig. 3, E). System # 8 automatically adjusts the driver head restraint based on the output of head restraint CAPS. Thus, the system focus is on the area between seat and head. Similar topology, as of system # 4, is also implemented in ordinary office furniture [14,16].

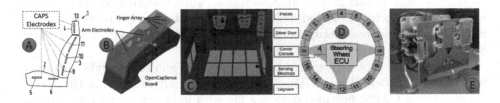

**Fig. 3.** Table 2 sample systems

**Dedication - Opportunity - Difference.** Dedication - Opportunity - Difference aims to reveal conflicts with privacy by design, based on the privacy concepts presented in Sect. 3.1.

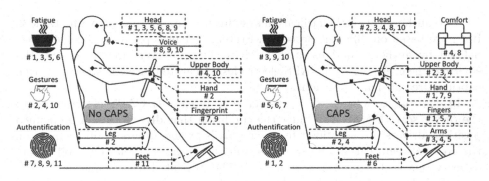

**Fig. 4.** System overview: Left - Table 1; right - Table 2 (CAPS)

Systems # 2, 4, 10 of Table 1 are dedicated to gesture recognition. Recording more information than just gestures could therefore violate the privacy-by-design paradigm. Nonetheless, their sensor systems partly capture images of the whole driver body (# 10). The captured images provide further opportunities. Vehicle manufacturers already use those images to identify the driver (Table 1: # 8, 9). This interferes with privacy concern "biometric data". Furthermore, captured data is used to derive driver attention (Table 1: # 1, 3, 5, 6). Since this may be a person's performance indicator, interfere with privacy concern "profiling" may be given.

Already patented systems like [6,23,54] derive information as texting, smoking or eating. All of those are based on driver image processing. Patent [54] already points to remote state evaluation by third parties. Therefore, opportunity to profile and identify subjects, based on the sensor output, is provided by camera-based systems.

Aside of systems without capacitive proximity sensing (CAPS), CAPS based systems may provide gesture recognition which does not conflict with privacy. Nonetheless, CAPS based systems are used to authenticate/identify users (Table 2: # 1, 2). Both systems sensor setup is similar to gesture recognition or comfort systems (Table 2: # 7, 8). Nonetheless, authentication/identification is not provided due to the sensed data itself. Both systems rely on previous user interaction. Therefore, identity cannot be derived by the data output of # 7 and 8 directly.

Furthermore, captured images or the voice of a subject provide all target information for identification. Thus, data and labels are included in the sensor output. Using CAPS, provided data is a list with unknown target correlations. CAPS require further information as sensing topology and subject information for identity mapping.

### 3.3 Hypotheses About Privacy Concerns of Driver Monitoring Systems

Even though capacitive proximity sensing (CAPS) seems to provide privacy preserving features, we have to check if people take this into account at product selection. Public regulations for privacy by design may be bypassed by automotive manufacturers. But the customers decision about privacy concerns causing systems cannot be bypassed. Three hypotheses are formulated to support the need for further integration of CAPS into automobiles. The hypotheses are based on literature review and the analysis of camera systems versus CAPS. Due to the found privacy concerns of video surveillance, we state that the video surveillance of drivers in vehicles causes privacy concerns. This leads to the first hypothesis:

**Hypothesis I**: *If a vehicular human machine interface (VHMI) contains a camera which captures images of passengers, then people have privacy concerns about the VHMI.*

Furthermore, CAPS is a technology which enables similar features for VHMI like camera systems. Moreover, no image of passengers is captured by CAPS. Therefore, we state the second hypothesis:

**Hypothesis II**: *If a VHMI is based on CAPS and does therefore not capture an image of passengers, then people have less privacy concerns about the VHMI compared to camera-based systems*

Yet we have no connection between the preference of CAPS over camera-based systems. Therefore, we have to check the third hypothesis:

**Hypothesis III**: *If a vehicle customer has to choose between camera-based VHMI and CAPS based VHMI, then he will prefer the CAPS based system*

## 4 Discussion

Capacitive proximity sensing (CAPS) is often attributed to be privacy preserving or more privacy preserving compared to camera-based systems [7,8,11,29, 40,41,46,56]. Some researchers even state CAPS systems do not interfere with privacy at all. Due to Sect. 3.2, the assignment of this attribute to CAPS in vehicles can be confirmed to a limited extent. Information within a driver image or a microphone recording can reveal plenty of targets. A system, initially designed to capture gestures or driver fatigue, may provide information for profiling, biometric or health data extraction.

Nonetheless, CAPS-based systems show the ability to identify people. Therefore, they can interfere with privacy. Yet, CAPS data without further information can barely be used to derive information. Even though target information, like the identity, may be encoded within data, extraction is deemed cumbersome. For example, CAPS data is shown in Fig. 5, left. The corresponding image of this sample is shown on the right of Fig. 5. The system is designed to track child movement in a baby seat. Plenty of privacy interfering information is disclosed on the captured image. For example, biometric information could be extracted. Nonetheless, the provided CAPS information is pretty useless without sensing topology and additional labels.

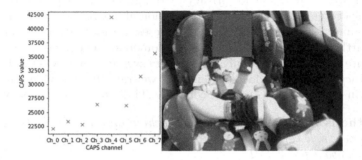

**Fig. 5.** CAPS and related video data

Due to the Dedication - Opportunity - Difference of camera-based systems, it is questionable if they still follow paradigm privacy by design. Nonetheless, this is an issue of regulations. A further impact on design decisions would be the customer's voice. If customers value privacy by design, manufacturers would be encouraged to rethink camera or microphone usage. Therefore, hypotheses for following tests are defined in Sect. 3.3. The hypotheses are strictly designed to reveal customer preferences concerning CAPS and camera. Further comparisons to other sensor systems are not included.

## 5   Conclusion and Future Work

The necessity of privacy preserving systems is presented in Sect. 1 and reviewed in related work (Sect. 2). If vehicular human machine interfaces (VHMI) capture more information as needed, the spillover can cause privacy issues. A system could be hacked or the manufacturers may disclose information to data collection based third party enterprises. Examination of privacy concerns is enabled by the selection of a general definition of causes for privacy concerns: The GDPR. The selection is presented in Sect. 3.1.

Several VHMI systems are presented and analyzed. They are comprised of camera- and/or microphone-based sensors. Furthermore, similar systems based on capacitive proximity sensing (CAPS) are presented. This makes it possible to question the paradigm "privacy-by-design" as required by the GDPR. Due to the Dedication - Opportunity - Difference, especially of camera-based gesture recognition systems, CAPS-based systems seem to preserve privacy better. As presented in Sect. 4, CAPS systems are able to identify people or derive profiles. Nonetheless, the captured information at the running system does not reveal privacy interfering data, directly. A series of CAPS data, sensor topology and labels for comparative evaluation would be required.

Since CAPS usage results in less privacy concerns than cameras, they seem to be a more compliant choice following "privacy-by-design". Therefore, in future work, the selection of manufacturers sensor choice has to be tracked. Furthermore, CAPS is an already applied sensor system in automotive applications. Therefore, manufacturers VHMI sensor selection process has to be examined. Because of this discrepancy, three hypotheses are defined in Sect. 3.3. A subsequent test in future work shall clarify if these are correct. Subsequently, one could rate the manufacturers decision to choose privacy concerns causing sensor systems for gesture recognition.

# References

1. Android Auto. https://www.android.com/auto/. Accessed 25 May 2020
2. iOS 13 - Apple. https://www.apple.com/ios/ios-13/. Accessed 25 May 2020
3. Acquisti, A., Grossklags, J.: Privacy and rationality in individual decision making. IEEE Secur. Priv. **3**(1), 26–33 (2005). https://doi.org/10.1109/MSP.2005.22
4. Alexa Internet: The top 500 sites on the web, February 2019. https://www.alexa.com/topsites#
5. Ang, B.: This car can detect if the driver is paying attention or not. https://www.youtube.com/watch?v=0FUqSOi76UU
6. Aoi, H., Kawade, M., Hamabashiri, H.: Automated driving assistance apparatus, automated driving assistance system, automated driving assistance method and automated driving assistance program (2019). https://patents.google.com/patent/US20190056732A1
7. Arshad, A., Kadir, K.A., Khan, S., Alam, A.H.M.Z., Tasnim, R.: A low cost capacitive sensing system for identifying and detecting falls of senior citizens. In: 2015 IEEE 3rd International Conference on Smart Instrumentation, Measurement and Applications (ICSIMA), pp. 1–5 (2015)
8. Arshad, A., Khan, S., Zahirul Alam, A.H.M., Abdul Kadir, K., Tasnim, R., Fadzil Ismail, A.: A capacitive proximity sensing scheme for human motion detection. In: 2017 IEEE International Instrumentation and Measurement Technology Conference (I2MTC), pp. 1–5 (2017)
9. Automobiles, D.: Handbooks: Ds 7 crossback, January 2019. http://service.citroen.com/DSddb/
10. Baronti, F., Lenzi, F., Roncella, R., Saletti, R.: Distributed sensor for steering wheel rip force measurement in driver fatigue detection. In: 2009 Design, Automation Test in Europe Conference Exhibition, pp. 894–897, April 2009. https://doi.org/10.1109/DATE.2009.5090790
11. Bin Tariq, O., Lazarescu, M.T., Iqbal, J., Lavagno, L.: Performance of machine learning classifiers for indoor person localization with capacitive sensors. IEEE Access **5**, 12913–12926 (2017)
12. Bloom, C., Tan, J., Ramjohn, J., Bauer, L.: Self-driving cars and data collection: privacy perceptions of networked autonomous vehicles. In: Thirteenth Symposium on Usable Privacy and Security (SOUPS 2017), Santa Clara, CA, pp. 357–375. USENIX Association (2017). https://www.usenix.org/conference/soups2017/technical-sessions/presentation/bloom

13. Braun, A., Frank, S., Majewski, M., Wang, X.: Capseat: capacitive proximity sensing for automotive activity recognition. In: Proceedings of the 7th International Conference on Automotive User Interfaces and Interactive Vehicular Applications, AutomotiveUI 2015, pp. 225–232. ACM, New York (2015). https://doi.org/10.1145/2799250.2799263. http://doi.acm.org/10.1145/2799250.2799263
14. Braun, A., Frank, S., Wichert, R.: The capacitive chair. In: Streitz, N., Markopoulos, P. (eds.) DAPI 2015. LNCS, vol. 9189, pp. 397–407. Springer, Cham (2015). https://doi.org/10.1007/978-3-319-20804-6_36
15. Braun, A., Neumann, S., Schmidt, S., Wichert, R., Kuijper, A.: Towards interactive car interiors: the active armrest. In: Proceedings of the 8th Nordic Conference on Human-Computer Interaction: Fun, Fast, Foundational, NordiCHI 2014, pp. 911–914. ACM, New York (2014). https://doi.org/10.1145/2639189.2670191. http://doi.acm.org/10.1145/2639189.2670191
16. Braun, A., Schembri, I., Frank, S.: ExerSeat - sensor-supported exercise system for ergonomic microbreaks. In: De Ruyter, B., Kameas, A., Chatzimisios, P., Mavrommati, I. (eds.) AmI 2015. LNCS, vol. 9425, pp. 236–251. Springer, Cham (2015). https://doi.org/10.1007/978-3-319-26005-1_16
17. Braun, A., Wichert, R., Frank, S.: Verfahren zur feststellung der identität einer person auf einem sitz eines fahrzeugs (2016). https://patents.google.com/patent/DE102014214978B4
18. Chen, S.K., Litkouhi, B.B.: Hierarchical recognition of vehicle driver and select activation of vehicle settings based on the recognition (2014). https://patents.google.com/patent/US8761998B2
19. Council of European Union: Regulation (EU) 2016/679 of the European parliament and of the council of 27 April 2016 on the protection of natural persons with regard to the processing of personal data and on the free movement of such data, and repealing directive 95/46/EC (general data protection regulation). Official Journal of the European Union L 119/1, April 2016. https://eur-lex.europa.eu/legal-content/EN/TXT/?uri=CELEX:32016R0679
20. Crossler, R.E., Bélanger, F.: The mobile privacy-security knowledge gap model: understanding behaviors. In: 50th Hawaii International Conference on System Sciences, HICSS 2017, Hilton Waikoloa Village, Hawaii, USA, 4–7 January 2017 (2017). http://aisel.aisnet.org/hicss-50/in/behavioral_is_security/9
21. Dokor, T.A.E., Cluster, J., Holmes, J.E., Vaghefinazari, P., Yamamoto, S.M.: System and method for controlling a vehicle user interface based on gesture angle (2014). https://patents.google.com/patent/US8886399B2
22. Dumitrescu, C., Costea, I.M., Nemtanu, F., Badescu, I., Banica, A.: Developing a multi sensors system to detect sleepiness to drivers from transport systems. In: 2016 IEEE 22nd International Symposium for Design and Technology in Electronic Packaging (SIITME), pp. 175–178, October 2016. https://doi.org/10.1109/SIITME.2016.7777271
23. Duncan, W.D., Hyde, R.A., Kare, J.T., Pan, T.S.: System and method for monitoring driving to determine an insurance property (2017). https://patents.google.com/patent/US20170132710A1
24. Etcheverry, C., Layerle, J.F.: Man interface/machine and method for controlling functions of a vehicle by detecting motion and/or expressing the conductor (2016). https://patents.google.com/patent/FR3028221A1/en
25. Frank, S., Kuijper, A.: Enabling driver feet gestures using capacitive proximity sensing. In: 2018 14th International Conference on Intelligent Environments (IE), pp. 25–31, June 2018. https://doi.org/10.1109/IE.2018.00012

26. Frank, S., Kuijper, A.: AuthentiCap - a touchless vehicle authentication and personalization system. In: Braun, A., Wichert, R., Maña, A. (eds.) AmI 2017. LNCS, vol. 10217, pp. 46–63. Springer, Cham (2017). https://doi.org/10.1007/978-3-319-56997-0_4

27. Frank, S., Kuijper, A.: HUDConCap - automotive head-up display controlled with capacitive proximity sensing. In: Braun, A., Wichert, R., Maña, A. (eds.) AmI 2017. LNCS, vol. 10217, pp. 197–213. Springer, Cham (2017). https://doi.org/10.1007/978-3-319-56997-0_16

28. Frank, S., Kuijper, A.: Robust driver foot tracking and foot gesture recognition using capacitive proximity sensing. J. Ambient Intell. Smart Environ. 11(3), 221–235 (2019). https://doi.org/10.3233/AIS-190522. https://content.iospress.com/articles/journal-of-ambient-intelligence-and-smart-environments/ais190522

29. Fu, B., Damer, N., Kirchbuchner, F., Kuijper, A.: Sensing technology for human activity recognition: a comprehensive survey. IEEE Access 8, 83791–83820 (2020)

30. Gaudeul, A., Giannetti, C.: The effect of privacy concerns on social network formation. J. Econ. Behav. Organ. 141, 233–253 (2017). https://doi.org/10.1016/j.jebo.2017.07.007. http://www.sciencedirect.com/science/article/pii/S0167268117301853

31. Groupe, P.: Gesture control: effective and intuitive man-machine interaction, August 2016. https://www.groupe-psa.com/en/newsroom/automotive-innovation/car-gesture-control/

32. Herberth, R., Körper, S., Stiesch, T., Gauterin, F., Bringmann, O.: Automated scheduling for optimal parallelization to reduce the duration of vehicle software updates. IEEE Trans. Veh. Technol. 68(3), 2921–2933 (2019)

33. Hong, G.B., Kim, S.U., Oh, K.M., Min, J.: Driver recognition system and recognition method for vehicle (2016). https://patents.google.com/patent/US9245179B2

34. Jacob, Y., Manitsaris, S., Moutarde, F., Lele, G., Pradere, L.: Hand gesture recognition for driver vehicle interaction. In: CVPR 2015 (2015)

35. Kuppusamy, T.K., DeLong, L.A., Cappos, J.: Uptane: Security and customizability of software updates for vehicles. IEEE Veh. Technol. Mag. 13(1), 66–73 (2018)

36. Larsson, P., Hagemann, A., Björk, H.: Method for performing driver identity verification (2013). https://patents.google.com/patent/US8344849B2

37. Martin, S., Tawari, A., Trivedi, M.M.: Toward privacy-protecting safety systems for naturalistic driving videos. IEEE Trans. Intell. Transp. Syst. 15(4), 1811–1822 (2014). https://doi.org/10.1109/TITS.2014.2308543

38. McClain, J.J., Bolton, Z.J.: Adaptive emergency brake and steer assist systems based on driver focus, July 2014. https://patents.google.com/patent/US20140195120A1

39. McDonald, A.M., Cranor, L.F.: How technology drives vehicular privacy. ISJLP 2, 981 (2005)

40. Mühlbacher-Karrer, S., et al.: A driver state detection system-combining a capacitive hand detection sensor with physiological sensors. IEEE Trans. Instrum. Meas. 66(4), 624–636 (2017)

41. Nelson, A., Singh, G., Robucci, R., Patel, C., Banerjee, N.: Adaptive and personalized gesture recognition using textile capacitive sensor arrays. IEEE Trans. Multi-Scale Comput. Syst. 1(2), 62–75 (2015)

42. Perrin, A., Jiang, J.: Apple and android are finally shouldering their way into cars, July 2015. https://spectrum.ieee.org/cars-that-think/transportation/advanced-cars/apple-and-android-are-coming-to-carsfinally

43. Perrin, A., Jiang, J.: About a quarter of U.S. adults say they are almost constantly online, March 2018. http://www.pewresearch.org/fact-tank/2018/03/14/about-a-quarter-of-americans-report-going-online-almost-constantly/
44. Bayerische Motoren Werke Aktiengesellschaft: Owner's Handbook. The BMW 8 Series Coupé. BMW, Munich (2018)
45. Rezaei, M., Klette, R.: Look at the driver, look at the road: no distraction! no accident! In: 2014 IEEE Conference on Computer Vision and Pattern Recognition, pp. 129–136 (2014)
46. Rus, S., Joshi, D., Braun, A., Kuijper, A.: The emotive couch - learning emotions by capacitively sensed movements. Procedia Comput. Sci. **130**, 263–270 (2018). https://doi.org/10.1016/j.procs.2018.04.038. http://www.sciencedirect.com/science/article/pii/S1877050918303892. The 9th International Conference on Ambient Systems, Networks and Technologies (ANT 2018)/The 8th International Conference on Sustainable Energy Information Technology (SEIT-2018)/Affiliated Workshops
47. Sadler, J.G., Madau, A., Gioia, T.A., Heussner, E.M., Chi, D.D., Templeton, R.L.: Vehicle personalization via biometric identification, October 2004. https://patents.google.com/patent/US6810309B2
48. Schanz, H., et al.: Adaptive driver assist, March 2016. https://patents.google.com/patent/US20160068143A1
49. Seiberth, G., Gruendinger, W.: Data-driven business models in connected cars, mobility services & beyond. BVDW Res. **18**(01) (2018). https://bvdw.org/datadrivenbusinessmodels/
50. Stackmann, J., Zöller, R., Hartung, C.: Webcast wirelesscar. https://www.volkswagen-newsroom.com/en/publications/speeches/webcast-wirelesscar-statements-160/download
51. Su, C., Chen, W.: Design and implementation for an automotive DMS system. In: 2019 IEEE International Conference on Consumer Electronics - Taiwan (ICCE-TW), pp. 1–2 (2019)
52. Touryalay, H., Stoller, K., Murphy, A.: The world's largest public companies, June 2018. https://www.forbes.com/global2000/list/#header:marketValue_sortreverse:true
53. Warren, S.D., Brandeis, L.D.: The right to privacy. Harvard Law Rev. **4**(5), 193–220 (1890). http://www.jstor.org/stable/1321160
54. Durie, W.E., et al.: Vehicle safety and driver condition monitoring, and geographic information based road safety systems (2018). https://patents.google.com/patent/US10127810B2
55. Yalcin, H.: Extracting user profiles from mobile data. In: 2017 IEEE International Black Sea Conference on Communications and Networking (BlackSeaCom), pp. 1–5, June 2017. https://doi.org/10.1109/BlackSeaCom.2017.8277701
56. Ye, Y., Zhang, C., He, C., Wang, X., Huang, J., Deng, J.: A review on applications of capacitive displacement sensing for capacitive proximity sensor. IEEE Access **8**, 45325–45342 (2020)
57. Ziraknejad, N., Lawrence, P.D., Romilly, D.P.: Vehicle occupant head position quantification using an array of capacitive proximity sensors. IEEE Trans. Veh. Technol. **64**(6), 2274–2287 (2015). https://doi.org/10.1109/TVT.2014.2344026

# NannyCaps - Monitoring Child Conditions and Activity in Automotive Applications Using Capacitive Proximity Sensing

Sebastian Frank[1]([✉]) and Arjan Kuijper[2]

[1] Technische Universität Darmstadt, Darmstadt, Germany
sebastian.frank@gris.tu-darmstadt.de
[2] Technische Universität Darmstadt/Fraunhofer IGD, Darmstadt, Germany
arjan.kuijper@igd.fraunhofer.de

**Abstract.** Children have to be transported safely. Securing children in a child seat is indicated. Due to structure and restraint systems, children are secured in case of an accident. Children require our attention to keep them healthy and at good mood. Nonetheless, attention must be payed to driving, too. This discrepancy leads to unattended children. Furthermore, responsible must decide to leave their children alone in the vehicle in case of emergencies. This may lead to heat strokes.

Aside of limiting effects of an accident, it would be helpful to assist ambulance after an emergency and to detect injuries even without accident. Besides safety features, preserving good mood of children is an exquisite comfort feature. This can be achieved without privacy issues as they would occur using camera-based systems.

The proposed solution, NannyCaps, is designed to contribute to safety and comfort. An invisible array of capacitive proximity sensors enables head position recognition, sleep state recognition, heart rate recognition and occupancy recognition. The system is included into the child seat, only.

In this paper, we present the design and implementation of Nanny-Caps. By conducting ten test runs under real world conditions, more than 600 km of data is collected. Using this data, NannyCaps is trained and evaluated. Reasonable results are shown in evaluation. Thus, following the development of NannyCaps will likely improve the situation for children in transportation systems.

**Keywords:** Child seat · Capacitive proximity sensing · Active safety · Automotive · Human machine interface

## 1 Introduction

Children have to be transported safely. Securing children in a child seat is indicated. Due to structure and restraint systems, children are secured in case of an

© Springer Nature Switzerland AG 2020
C. Stephanidis et al. (Eds.): HCII 2020, LNCS 12429, pp. 67–82, 2020.
https://doi.org/10.1007/978-3-030-59987-4_6

accident. Nonetheless, attention must be payed to children while driving conditions must be monitored.

A child seat can do more than just prevent injuries passively. Equipped with the right technology, injuries can be avoided, ambulance can be assisted and child's positive mood can be preserved. Those processes are shown on the right of Fig. 1.

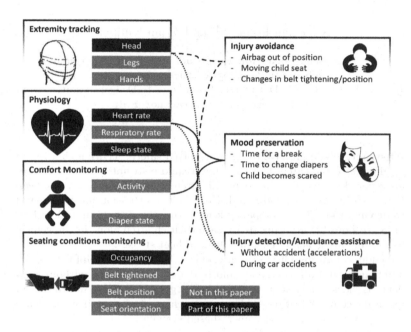

**Fig. 1.** NannyCaps features

While everybody wants to keep its child's mood in good state, driving over long distances may lead to unnoticed conditions. On the one hand, comfort monitoring like the recognition of activity or diaper state may be a hint for a break. On the other hand, changing heart rate and respiratory rate may indicate that the child becomes scared by driving situations or multimedia systems.

Children may be left alone in the vehicle. This results in dangerous situations. The car may heat up and children suffer heat stroke [20]. If someone arrives at an accident, first aid must be provided. Subsequently, the child may be left alone in the car. Therefore, people may have to intentionally leave their child unattended [20].

All boxes on the right of Fig. 1 will likely improve the situation for children in transportation systems. By recognizing injuries and preventing injuries, supervisors can react to the child's condition. Concerning mood preservation, a parent who intentionally left his child in the car may return early. Subsequently, an unintentionally left behind child may get attention if an occupancy recognition system alerts.

Further injuries may be caused by wrongly mounted children on child seats. For example, improper belt tightening and position changes while driving. Therefore, injury avoidance features may help. Similar to passenger out of position detection, child head position recognition may enable enhanced child seat airbags which detect out of position, too.

While injury avoidance aims to prevent injuries, injury detection shall assist medical therapy selection. Especially head acceleration may point to injuries. To assist as fast as possible, physiological conditions and extremity accelerations shall be detected by NannyCaps.

Extremity tracking may point to image processing. Nonetheless, cameras require a line of sight and distance between child and lens. Therefore, manufacturers would have to include them into their vehicles. But the system shall be a child seat which can be used in any vehicle. Furthermore, cameras can lead to privacy issues.

Physiological conditions may be measured using wristband sensors. Since people tend to forget putting on a wristband, this is fault-prone. NannyCaps is seat integrated. Hence, this problem is not present using NannyCaps.

Each of the measures on the left of Fig. 1 shall be enabled by NannyCaps. To enable an autonomous child seat, the system shall integrate all sensors into the seat. Capacitive proximity sensing (CAPS) can measure through non-conductive material. In addition, it can measure object position without touch. This enables autonomous integration.

Those measures are not directly provided by CAPS. All measures require a proper sensing electrode setup and a specific processing algorithm. As indicated in Fig. 1, not all measures are part of this paper. Focus is set on development and evaluation of head position recognition, heart rate recognition, sleep state recognition and occupancy recognition.

A concept for CAPS in child's seat has to be designed for all those measures. Afterwards, a prototype is built following the design. Using this prototype, data of ten real world test rides (child's seat with sensors mounted in vehicle while driving) is captured. Using this data, the designed algorithms are trained and validated. In summary, contributions are stated in the following list:

- Determine proper sensing electrode topology to measure
  - Child seat occupancy
  - Head position
  - Heart rate
- Design algorithms to measure occupancy, heart rate and head position
- Prototype
  - Ordinary child seat
  - Include child seat into vehicle
  - Implementation of sensing topology and algorithms
- Evaluation of designed systems using prototype in ten test runs

## 2 Related Work

### 2.1 Children Seat Safety Systems

As described in Sect. 1, children left behind in vehicles can lead to heat strokes [20]. Thus, a lot of research is conducted on child occupancy recognition [2,6,17, 23] to avoid children being left behind in the car. This shall prevent temperature induced heat strokes. Ranjan et al. [23] even use capacitive proximity sensing (CAPS) inside of a child seat.

Aneiros et al. [2] include a controller into the vehicle. The controller is capable of controlling lights, ignition switch, alarm and further vehicle components. Due to the controller, the system can inform the driver in case of a child left behind in the car. Furthermore, it can open doors and windows to decrease in-car temperature. To do so, the system requires child presence sensors. If those sensors detect an occupied child seat, an alert is started until the driver is seated. Moreover, if the delay between child seated and driver seated is greater than two minutes, the system starts the vehicle's air condition.

Lusso et al. [17] include two force sensors and a wireless video camera into the vehicle. The force sensors detect an occupied child seat. Additionally, the video camera is directed to the child face. It shall monitor child conditions. All sensors are contained within the vehicle electrical system. Similar to Aneiros et al., Lusso et al. alert if a child is left behind. The system is tested in a real vehicle. Two temperature sensors are used to check the system behavior at different temperatures.

### 2.2 Capacitive Proximity Sensing Supported Children Seat Safety Concepts

Besides child conditions, a child seat position recognition system is developed by Smith [25]. Four sensing electrodes are integrated into a vehicle passenger seat. Those are used to produce 16 individual measurements. The seat may be equipped with an additional child seat. Due to the measurements, four classes of child seat position can be distinguished. Those classes are "empty", the passenger seat is empty, "person", there is a person on the seat, "FFCS", there is a front facing child seat on the passenger seat and "RFCS", there is a rear facing child seat on the passenger seat. Smith states that the system success lead to cooperation with automotive supplier NEC Automotive Electronics. NEC Automotive Electronics [16] patented a similar system.

## 3 Contribution

Subsections 3.1, 3.2, 3.3 and 3.4 show design and required topology for addressed measures as shown on the left in Fig. 1. Subsequently, a sensor topology is derived from those measures. The emerging topology is shown in Sect. 3.5.

## 3.1    Occupancy Recognition

Occupancy recognition aims to prevent heat strokes or forgotten children in child seats. Occupancy consists of two classes. The subject can be sitting on the seat which is classified as OnSeat or the seat may be empty. This is classified as NotOnSeat. This is a binary classification problem. Therefore, a decision tree classifier is used.

Since the distance between sensing electrodes and subject is assumed to take the main influence on capacitive proximity sensing (CAPS) measurement data, the feature vector of the decision tree classifier consists of the raw output of the CAPS data.

As provided by existing passenger seat occupancy systems [14], sensors below subject pelvis are required. Nonetheless, this is a minimum constraint. If further detection models require more electrodes, these are also integrated into the feature vector.

## 3.2    Heart Rate Recognition

As shown in Fig. 1, heart rate recognition is an essential task for emergency assistance. Moreover, changes in heart rate are induced by emotions [1]. Thus, heart rate information is helpful for mood preservation, too.

The human body consists of mostly water. Furthermore, the heart is embedded into the human body. Thus, capacitive proximity sensing (CAPS) may not enable to measure heart contraction directly. Nonetheless, measurable body displacement due to heartbeat can be discovered [18]. Body displacement affects the output value of CAPS. Therefore, NannyCaps ought to be able to measure those displacements.

Heart rate measurement is enabled if the subject is on the child seat (class OnSeat in Sect. 3.1). Therefore, heart rate recognition is only active in OnSeat state. Heart rate results from the frequency of heart contraction. Frequency becomes measurable in time series. Therefore, time series of CAPS data is deemed mandatory. Furthermore, subject back movement is expected to be low while subject is OnSeat. Thus, CAPS data of sensing electrodes in the child seat back rest is included. Even though, subject pelvis movement may not contribute to heart rate, since it is not close to subject heart, pelvis sensors may indicate vehicle vibrations. Therefore, pelvis sensors are included.

The heart rate at time t is considered as a result of a previously analyzed heart movement analysis. Thus, frequency magnitudes of ten second time intervals CAPS data is used as basis for model features. Due to the continuous nature of the heart rate, a regression model is chosen: a neural network (MLP) with one hidden layer. The hidden layer consists of ten neurons.

## 3.3    Head Position Recognition

As shown in [7], head injuries can be estimated from head acceleration and exposure time. Acceleration and exposure time can be derived directly from head position. Therefore, child head position recognition shall be enabled by NannyCaps.

The face center (nose) is used as target variable. Head position ought mainly to be based on sensors included in child seat head restraint. Those sensors will point to translational positions of the subject head. Different load variations in pelvis and back rest sensors are expected by different head postures. Therefore, additional sensors in child seat shall enable head rotation estimation.

Head restraint capacitive proximity sensing (CAPS) value difference is expected to be the main indicator for head displacement. Thus, the feature vector for the regression model is based on the difference between each CAPS output. For example, this would mean that a feature vector entry is formed by the difference between left and right head restraint sensor output. Due to the continuous nature of head position, a random forest regression model is selected. Head position recognition shall be enabled by training a model. Subsequently, the model is tested with unseen data.

### 3.4   Sleep State Recognition

Actigraphy is used to distinguish between sleep phases [19]. It is a measure for mapping subject movement to sleep phases. Furthermore, respiratory rate monitoring is included in sleep analysis. Capacitive proximity sensing (CAPS) is applied to track respiratory rate in office furniture in [4]. Furthermore, it is used to track subject activity in [4,5,13] or extremities in [9–12]. Since those two measures point to sleep phases, CAPS is used in child seat to distinguish between asleep and awake child in child seat.

Similar to heart rate recognition in Sect. 3.2, frequencies of CAPS data are used. Therefore, the frequency magnitudes of a time window of ten seconds CAPS data is used. Thus, comparability between heart rate recognition and SR performance shall be enabled. Subsequently, the same CAPS topology as in Sect. 3.2 is deemed appropriate. Nonetheless, to increase activity recognition, leg restraint included CAPS sensing electrodes shall be mounted.

### 3.5   Sensor Topology

Sections 3.1, 3.2, 3.3 and 3.4 name several mandatory sensing electrode positions. Measurement at subject pelvis is required for occupancy recognition, measurement at back rest is required for heart rate recognition, measurement at head restraint is required for head position recognition and additional sensors at leg restraint are required for sleep state recognition.

The spatial electrode topology is derived of those requirements as shown in Fig. 2. Sensing electrode positions are marked by blue circles. All sensors shall be included under child seat cushion. If the provided cushion is not sufficient for placing electrodes, the electrodes shall be mounted under non-conductive parts of the seat structure.

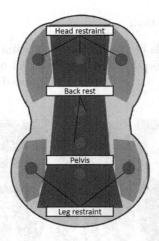

**Fig. 2.** Designed sensor topology

## 4    Implementation

In advance of putting designed sensing topology as shown in Sect. 3.5 into practice in Sect. 4.2, an appropriate sensor system is selected in Sect. 4.1. Furthermore, additional sensors are added to generate labeled data. The measurement setup to monitor test rides and generate labels for capacitive proximity sensing data is presented in Subsect. 4.3.

### 4.1    Capacitive Proximity Sensor Selection

Following design in Sect. 3.5, eight capacitive proximity sensing (CAPS) electrodes are required to map NannyCaps concept to a prototype. Since real systems provide discrete data, an appropriate sampling rate has to be determined. Obviously, heart rate is a frequency based biometric characteristic. Hence, CAPS sampling rate selection is based on heart rate recognition.

Test ride subject age is about 1.5 years. Therefore, the heart rate range is in an interval between 98 to 140 beats per minute (bpm) while awake and 80 to 120 bpm while asleep [8]. Mapped to beats per second (bps), heart rate should be between 1.33 and 2.33 bps ($HR_{max}$). This has to be covered by the heart rate recognition application.

The selected CAPS device is capable to monitor eight sensing electrodes [15]. Each sensing channel output is sampled 25 Hz. This results in an oversampling factor of 10.7 compared to $HR_{max}$. Therefore, the Nyquist Rate is exceeded [22]. Unprocessed circuit boards (copper, epoxy) are used as CAPS electrodes and shielding. Each electrode is of 10 cm length and 16 cm width. This results in an area of 0.016 m$^2$. An equal electrode layout is selected to minimize deviating temperature effects. Due to the setup of circuit boards, CAPS electrodes and shielding area are congruent in sensing direction.

## 4.2  Child Seat Integration

The provided eight channels of the capacitive proximity sensing (CAPS) device and the attached circuit boards are mounted on an ordinary child seat, shown in Fig. 3. As shown in Fig. 3, seat cushion is removed completely.

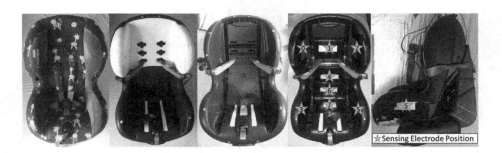

**Fig. 3.** Used child seat with sensors (Color figure online)

Afterwards, the sensing electrodes are placed according to Sect. 3.5 (Fig. 3, yellow stars). The available space at the leg restraint was not sufficient for electrode mounting. As shown in Fig. 3 (right), leg related electrodes are placed under seat skeleton. Then the seat cushion is reinstalled on the seat (Fig. 4).

## 4.3  Test Ride Surveillance System

The test ride surveillance system must capture the activity, occupancy and heart rate of the subject. Concerning heart rate measurement, an optical heart rate sensor [24] is used. The sensor is labeled in Fig. 4 with OH1. Occupancy recognition, head position recognition and sleep state recognition are labeled by using image processing. Images are provided by a camera. The camera is attached to the vehicle interior roof. It points towards the child seat. Figure 4 shows the camera view.

# 5  Evaluation

## 5.1  Captured Data

Captured data is comprised of ten test rides including a heart rate sensor, capacitive proximity sensing and a camera. More than nine hours and more than 600 km are recorded. Video data is analyzed manually to label occupancy and sleep state. Figure 5 shows the distribution of those states among test rides. Awake and asleep state show approximately balanced duration. An imbalanced duration for on seat and not on seat is indicated by a ratio of approximately 36 to one.

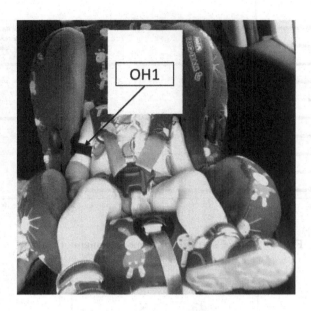

**Fig. 4.** Test setup camera view cut out

## 5.2 Occupancy Recognition

Transition from subject sitting on seat (OnSeat) and not on seat (NotOnSeat) is fuzzy. Therefore, a buffer of ten seconds before and after each transition is excluded. 8.6 h OnSeat and 16.5 min NotOnSeat data is collected. As described in Sect. 3.1, all eight channels raw data is used as model input vector. The complete dataset consists of 776000 OnSeat and 25000 NotOnSeat samples.

Those samples are split randomly into 50% training and 50% test data. Afterwards, a decision tree classifier is trained using training data to distinguish between OnSeat and NotOnSeat. Subsequently, labels for test data are predicted by the classifier. The evaluation of test data results in a true (T) positive (P) rate of $\approx$1 (P: 387057, TP: 387047) and a true negative (N) rate of $\approx$1 (N: 12457, TN: 12444).

## 5.3 Heart Rate Recognition

Heart rate recognition shall be facilitated using data of child seat integrated capacitive proximity sensing (CAPS). Thus, the data of each test ride is filtered for the subject being on the seat. Subsequently, CAPS data with label OnSeat, as shown in Sect. 5.2 is concerned. Except test ride one, all test rides have one single OnSeat phase. As shown in Fig. 5, test ride one hast two OnSeat phases. Since the first phase covers less than four minutes, this phase is omitted. Captured heart rate data are synchronized with CAPS data via time stamp information.

CAPS data is processed according to Sect. 3.2. Thus, a frequency spectrum remains. Figure 6 visualizes the complete dataset. It is grouped by heart rate

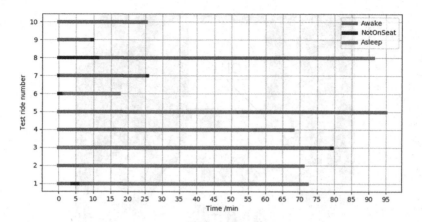

**Fig. 5.** Subject states during measurements diagram

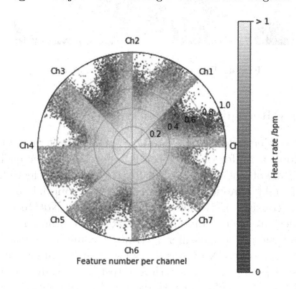

**Fig. 6.** Heart rate recognition feature vector data

data. Afterwards, frequency magnitudes of each group are averaged. This is repeated for all channels. Each circular sector represents one channel beginning from the channel label to the next label in counterclockwise direction. The angle of each sector represents the frequency. For example, frequencies of channel one range from zero Hz at label "Ch1" (angle = 45°) to 12.5 Hz at label "Ch2" (angle = 90°). Colors represent the MinMax normalized heart rate value.

According to Sect. 3.2, a neural network regression model is trained and evaluated. Data is split into 75% training and 25% test data. Subsequently, training data is resampled to show equal value distribution. A mean absolute

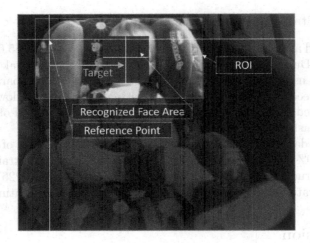

**Fig. 7.** Head position labeling

error of 6.2 bpm is measured. A high difference between training performance ($R^2 \approx 0.85$) and test performance ($R^2 \approx 0.55$) points to overfitting.

## 5.4 Head Position Recognition

Image processing, in particular, face recognition is used to retrieve horizontal head position [21]. A sample recognized face area is shown in Fig. 7. Since relative position of camera and child seat is not fixed, a child seat fixed reference point is added. A label on the child seat is used as stable reference point. Reference points are collected from random image samples. Therefore, influence by child seat movement due to test ride progress (subject movements, vehicle vibrations, rotation due to winding road) ought to be minimized compared to one single reference point.

The used face recognition algorithm is not robust during the whole measurement. Therefore, recognized face position is filtered. Only recognized face areas, within region of interest (Fig. 7: "ROI"), are used. The remaining detected faces are then filtered according to their area. Only areas between 35th and 65th percentile of all areas remain. Recognized horizontal face position is subtracted from reference point position. Afterwards, half of the face areas width is added to retrieve face center point. This results in the target label as shown in Fig. 7.

The used face recognition algorithm does not work during all lighting conditions. Furthermore, only frontal faces are detected and face profile is not tracked. To include more labels, especially from positions at the seating limits, manual labels are added. Those manual labels consist of the subject's nose position.

The labeled data is processed as described in Sect. 3.3. Using this dataset, a random forest regression model is trained and tested. Training and testing are conducted by use of tenfold cross validation. A mean coefficient of determination ($R^2$) of 0.95 is measured. Furthermore, the mean absolute error (MAE) is 3.87 pixels.

## 5.5   Sleep State Recognition

Data is labeled as presented in Sect. 5.1. 261.61 min asleep and 185.62 min awake
are recorded. Due to the fuzzy transition between asleep and awake, a buffer of
20 s at each transition is extracted. As presented in Sect. 3.4, comparable features
to heart rate recognition are generated. In particular, a time window of 10 s (250
samples) is used. Thus, the resulting model dataset is comprised of 1235 awake
(P) and 1737 asleep (N) samples.

Using this dataset, a random forest classifier is trained. Data of all test runs
is split into 80% training and 20% test data. Prior to training, training data is
balanced. A true (T) positive (P) rate of $\approx$0.93 (P: 242, TP: 226) and a true
negative (N) rate of $\approx$0.91 (N: 319, TN: 291) is measured evaluating test data.

# 6   Discussion

NannyCaps capabilities enabled due to sensor topology and integration are covered in Sect. 6.1. A view on data preprocessing and statistical model fitting
and possible dependencies between model targets is presented in Sect. 6.2. In
Sect. 6.3, the significance of exercised measurements and the prototype setup is
discussed.

## 6.1   Sensor Topology and Invisible Integration

Due to the capabilities of capacitive proximity sensing (CAPS), invisible integration into the child seat pan is enabled. CAPS electrodes are mounted under
the seat cushion. This is enabled by non-conductive materials. Hence, the system can be embedded autonomously into child seats. Additionally, the subject is
always closest to sensing electrodes. Thus, the system is not affected by objects
between subject and sensing electrodes. Hence, robustness of sensing is increased
compared to systems which require line of sight.

While there may be no object between sensing electrodes and subject (except
child seat cushion), changing temperature and moisture conditions take influence
on system robustness. Moisture may shadow the subject or at least change the
sensors offset. Recognition models, which rely on static sensor data, could be
affected. NannyCaps occupancy recognition relies on static data. Wet cushion
or changing temperature could lead to false predictions.

## 6.2   Model Performance and Data Interdependence

A violin plot is shown in Fig. 8. A violin plot has similarities with a box plot.
The occurrence of data points for the respective label is shown as outlined areas
in blue and red. Median values are represented by a white point in the middle of
each violin. Furthermore, inter-quartile range (IQR) is plotted as a black thick
vertical bar. Values within first quartile have a value less than IQR. Values which
are not within third quartile are greater than IQR. A range between first quartile

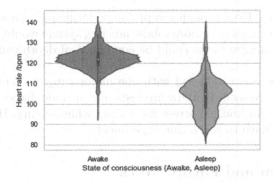

**Fig. 8.** Heart rate and sleep state distribution

minus 1.5 times IQR and third quartile plus 1.5 times IQR is presented by the thin vertical lines. Outliers may be indicated by values greater or less than this line.

As shown in Fig. 8, the median heart rate values are: Awake about 122 beats per minute (bpm), Asleep about 105 bpm. Furthermore, no heart rate intersection is shown within IQR. Nonetheless, data intersections between asleep and awake are indicated. Those intersections are not considered to be outliers.

Due to the data distribution in Fig. 8, heart rate recognition may be based on similar model observations like sleep state recognition. Although sleep state recognition results imply further observations which distinguish between awake and asleep at the same heart rate.

A correlation between sleep state recognition and heart rate seems plausible for healthy humans. Therefore, the correlation in Fig. 8 seems to be valid. Thus, the assumption that heart rate recognition is mainly based on sleep state recognition cannot be discarded. Nonetheless, heart rate recognition could be improved by additional sleep state recognition data. Still, sleep state recognition could be improved by additional heart rate recognition data. In both cases, models could benefit from the respective observations. Contrary to heart rate recognition, head position recognition, occupancy recognition and sleep state recognition show good performance.

### 6.3 Implementation and Measurements

A prototype is successfully built based on design in Sect. 3.5. Furthermore, environmental measurement systems were installed in an ordinary vehicle. The conduct of ten test runs shows plenty of variations in environmental conditions like lighting and interior temperature. Due to conduct in summer, the measurements show large interior temperature ranges. Nonetheless, system evaluation would benefit of winter measurements or moisture simulation as well.

Labels for head position recognition are derived from captured images. Those images are partially captured automatically. Thus, the labels themselves show measurement errors. Even though acceptable performance is shown in head position recognition evaluation, a more robust labeling system would improve performance. Those labeling systems could be comprised of depth cameras or special hat markers.

The test series was conducted with one minor subject. While parents provided a letter of agreement here, future tests may include diaper checking. Thus this could lead to an unusual stress for minors while testing. Hence, an ethics committee would have to check this experiment.

## 7   Conclusion and Future Work

Considering selected measures as shown on the left of Fig. 1, concepts for head position recognition, heart rate recognition, sleep state recognition and occupancy recognition are defined (Sect. 3). The built prototype (Sect. 4) is based on those concepts. An ordinary child seat is used. Within this child seat, all capacitive proximity sensing (CAPS) electrodes are included enabling invisible integration into an autonomous system. Nonetheless, system autonomy is just an idea, yet. Thus, in the future, concepts for an autonomous system have to be defined. A cellular module could be included for communication.

The built prototype and additional sensors are used to collect data in ten real world test rides. Using this data, the defined concepts are trained and evaluated (Sect. 5). Even though environmental conditions vary within those test runs, more data of different subjects, different vehicles and different child seats has to be collected. This shall refine evaluation findings.

*Heart Rate Recognition.* The designed heart rate recognition model shows a mean absolute error of approximately $\approx 6.2$ bpm. Even though an error of $\approx 6.2$ bpm seems to be acceptable for an almost not tuned model, an inconclusive verdict about heart rate recognition is shown in evaluation and argued in discussion. This is enhanced by a coefficient of determination $\approx 0.5$.

Two processes could evaluate heart rate recognition with certainty. On the one hand, the measurement has to be extended to different subjects. More subjects may have different heart rates at rest and during activity. Different heart rate characteristics in similar movement may eliminate direct sleep state to heart rate correlation. This may also improve model performance. On the other hand, the sensing topology could be extended to include sensing electrodes into the seat belt. This configuration would enable shunt or transmit mode sensing [25]. Sensing electrodes close to subjects' breast and back could enable to filter body movement from micro-movements as shown by Michahelles et al. [18].

*Respiratory Rate Recognition.* Those sensing electrodes within seat belt could enable respiratory rate recognition. Similar to heart rate recognition, respiratory rate recognition is assumed to be important for a child seat monitoring system. Thus, it is included in intended NannyCaps measures (as shown in Fig. 1). CAPS systems are already used for respiratory rate checking in office furniture

[4]. Additionally, respiratory emissions like yawning are detected in automotive seats [3]. Therefore, this feature seems to be practicable in a child seat. To get the ground truth, a respiratory rate monitoring system, like a face mask, would have to be included in future measurements.

*Diaper State Checking.* One useful feature for a smart child seat would be diaper state checking. While this may lead to delicate topics, information about diaper state could help parents to protect their children skin and interpret baby's articulations. To tackle this feature, measurements with diaper moisture sensors would have to be included in future measurements.

# References

1. Andreassi, J.L.: Psychophysiology: Human Behavior & Physiological Response. Psychology Press, London (2013)
2. Aneiros, D., Garcia, M.: Vehicle child seat safety system. AKAM LLC, United States. US8232874B1 (2012). https://patents.google.com/patent/US8232874B1
3. Braun, A., Frank, S., Majewski, M., Wang, X.: Capseat: capacitive proximity sensing for automotive activity recognition. In: Proceedings of the 7th International Conference on Automotive User Interfaces and Interactive Vehicular Applications, AutomotiveUI 2015, pp. 225–232. Association for Computing Machinery, New York (2015). https://doi.org/10.1145/2799250.2799263
4. Braun, A., Frank, S., Wichert, R.: The capacitive chair. In: Streitz, N., Markopoulos, P. (eds.) DAPI 2015. LNCS, vol. 9189, pp. 397–407. Springer, Cham (2015). https://doi.org/10.1007/978-3-319-20804-6_36
5. Braun, A., Schembri, I., Frank, S.: ExerSeat - sensor-supported exercise system for ergonomic microbreaks. In: De Ruyter, B., Kameas, A., Chatzimisios, P., Mavrommati, I. (eds.) AmI 2015. LNCS, vol. 9425, pp. 236–251. Springer, Cham (2015). https://doi.org/10.1007/978-3-319-26005-1_16
6. Diewald, A.R., et al.: RF-based child occupation detection in the vehicle interior. In: 2016 17th International Radar Symposium (IRS), pp. 1–4 (2016)
7. Eppinger, R., et al.: Development of improved injury criteria for the assessment of advanced automotive restraint systems - ii. Technical report, National Highway Traffic Safety Administration (1999)
8. Fleming, S., et al.: Normal ranges of heart rate and respiratory rate in children from birth to 18 years of age: a systematic review of observational studies. The Lancet **377**(9770), 1011–1018 (2011). https://doi.org/10.1016/S0140-6736(10)62226-X. http://www.sciencedirect.com/science/article/pii/S014067361062226X
9. Frank, S., Kuijper, A.: AuthentiCap - a touchless vehicle authentication and personalization system. In: Braun, A., Wichert, R., Maña, A. (eds.) AmI 2017. LNCS, vol. 10217, pp. 46–63. Springer, Cham (2017). https://doi.org/10.1007/978-3-319-56997-0_4
10. Frank, S., Kuijper, A.: HUDConCap - automotive head-up display controlled with capacitive proximity sensing. In: Braun, A., Wichert, R., Maña, A. (eds.) AmI 2017. LNCS, vol. 10217, pp. 197–213. Springer, Cham (2017). https://doi.org/10.1007/978-3-319-56997-0_16
11. Frank, S., Kuijper, A.: Enabling driver feet gestures using capacitive proximity sensing. In: 2018 14th International Conference on Intelligent Environments (IE), pp. 25–31 (2018)

12. Frank, S., Kuijper, A.: Robust driver foot tracking and foot gesture recognition using capacitive proximity sensing. J. Ambient Intell. Smart Environ. **11**(3), 221–235 (2019). https://doi.org/10.3233/AIS-190522. https://content.iospress.com/articles/journal-of-ambient-intelligence-and-smart-environments/ais190522

13. Fu, B., Damer, N., Kirchbuchner, F., Kuijper, A.: Sensing technology for human activity recognition: a comprehensive survey. IEEE Access **8**, 83791–83820 (2020)

14. George, B., Zangl, H., Bretterklieber, T., Brasseur, G.: Seat occupancy detection based on capacitive sensing. IEEE Trans. Instrum. Meas. **58**(5), 1487–1494 (2009)

15. Grosse-Puppendahl, T., Berghoefer, Y., Braun, A., Wimmer, R., Kuijper, A.: Opencapsense: a rapid prototyping toolkit for pervasive interaction using capacitive sensing. In: IEEE International Conference on Pervasive Computing and Communications (PerCom 2013), pp. 151–158 (2013)

16. Jinno, K., Ofuji, M., Oka, Y., Saitou, T.: Passenger detection system with electrodes in the seat and detection method. NEC Corp, European Patent Office. EP1080994A1 (2001). https://patents.google.com/patent/EP1080994A1

17. Lusso, R., Jensen, M., Walters, E., Wagner, J., Alexander, K.: Automobile safety - child seat entrapment and mechatronic warning system. IFAC Proc. **40**(10), 287–294 (2007). https://doi.org/10.3182/20070820-3-US-2918.00040. http://www.sciencedirect.com/science/article/pii/S1474667015319388. 5thIFAC Symposium on Advances in Automotive Control

18. Michahelles, F., Wicki, R., Schiele, B.: Less contact: heart-rate detection without even touching the user. In: Eighth International Symposium on Wearable Computers, vol. 1, pp. 4–7 (2004)

19. Morgenthaler, T., et al.: Practice parameters for the use of actigraphy in the assessment of sleep and sleep disorders: an update for 2007. Sleep **30**(4), 519–529 (2007). https://doi.org/10.1093/sleep/30.4.519

20. Null, J.: Trends and patterns in pediatric vehicular heatstroke deaths, 1998–2018 (2019). http://noheatstroke.org/Heatstroke_Trends_2018.pdf

21. OpenCV: OpenCV online documentation: Cascade Classifier, 4.3.0 edn. (2020). https://docs.opencv.org/4.3.0/db/d28/tutorial_cascade_classifier.html

22. Parthier, R.: Messsignale. In: Parthier, R. (ed.) Messtechnik, pp. 9–19. Springer, Wiesbaden (2016). https://doi.org/10.1007/978-3-658-13598-0_2

23. Ranjan, A., George, B.: A child-left-behind warning system based on capacitive sensing principle. In: 2013 IEEE International Instrumentation and Measurement Technology Conference (I2MTC), pp. 702–706 (2013)

24. Polar Electro Inc.: Polar oh1: User manual (2019). https://support.polar.com/e-manuals/OH1/Polar_OH1_user_manual_English/manual.pdf

25. Smith, J.R.: Electric field imaging. Ph.D. thesis, Center for Bits and Atoms, Cambridge, MA, USA (1999). aAI0800637

# Potentializing on Haptic Feedback Mechanism for Developing Interactive Components for Driver Seat

Mannan Ghanizadehgrayli[1], Hoda Eskandar Nia[2],
Sahar Asgari Tappeh[3], Mahdi Najafi[4(✉)], and Nashid Nabian[4]

[1] Young Researcher and Elite Club, Islamic Azad University, Babol, Iran
mannangrayli97@gmail.com
[2] The Bartlett School of Architecture, University College London (UCL),
London, UK
hoda.nia.16@alumni.ucl.ac.uk
[3] Pars University, Tehran, Iran
saharasgari62@gmail.com
[4] Tehran Urban Innovation Center (TUIC), Tehran, Iran
{mahdinajafi,nashidnabian}@tuic.ir

**Abstract.** Semi-autonomous vehicles might be able to transport the driver autonomously on sections of a journey. However, the driver is required to take control occasionally between different levels of autonomy when needed to complete an end-to-end journey. The transitions between autonomy levels cause safety concerns, as the drivers might not be fully aware or focused on distracting situations, precisely when they are overwhelmed with audio/visual signals. The Poking Seat project aims at redefining the function of a driver seat, approaching an interface offering interactive haptic communications. Since the driver seat is in touch with most of the driver's body, it seems to be capable of hosting haptic feedback mechanisms as an alternative for frequent audio/visual interactions. This article sheds light on what the haptic feedback mechanisms can add to the interaction between the driver and the car. The investigation starts with a literature review on topics that supports the theoretical dimensions of Poking Seat, such as human-computer interaction, ubiquitous computing, haptics and feedback mechanisms, and soft robotics. Following this literature review, a short report of Poking Seat is crafted with a focus on its multi-dimensional design-research process.

**Keywords:** Semi-autonomous vehicles · Haptic feedback mechanism · Interactive driver seat · Soft robotics

## 1 Introduction

Bringing real-world problems and challenges to the academic and innovation-oriented research/practice environments can open up various possibilities, other than assumingly early-stage solutions. The main issue that is actually recognized as the focal point of this article is how to overcome distracting situations in semi-autonomous vehicles,

© Springer Nature Switzerland AG 2020
C. Stephanidis et al. (Eds.): HCII 2020, LNCS 12429, pp. 83–95, 2020.
https://doi.org/10.1007/978-3-030-59987-4_7

capitalizing on the haptic feedback mechanisms. Poking Seat is a project exploring a couple of fields to bring solutions to the above mentioned. However, what seems to be more crucial here is how to give a solution rather than the solution itself.

As the legendary technologist Elon Musk famously said, "People are mistaken when they think that technology just automatically improves." The problem-solving approach taken in Poking Seat was mainly about how can we can consider small issues as playgrounds to examine the related technologies and try to develop them. The following lines have tried to situate Poking Seat in a greater landscape of academic discourse and research-oriented practice, followed by more focused design aspects.

## 2  Literature Review

### 2.1  Marrying Bits and Atoms Through HCI

The advent of Internet-based technologies has allowed humans to go beyond the physical environment, shaping an ever-growing overwhelming ubiquitous cyberspace. Despite our dual citizenship in the physical and cyber world, the absence of seamless couplings between these parallel existences leaves a great division between the worlds of bits and atoms. At present, we are torn between these parallel but disjoint spaces [1]. Human-Computer Interaction (HCI) studies the interactions and relationships between humans and computers [2]. For a long time, research on human-computer interaction has been restricted to techniques usually based on a graphical display, a keyboard, and a mouse. This paradigm has transitionally changed. Technologies such as speech recognition, projective displays, and context-aware devices allow for a much more fruitful, multimodal interaction between humans and machines [3]. Graphical user interfaces represent information (bits) through pixels on bit-mapped displays. These graphical representations can be manipulated through generic remote controllers, such as a mouse, touchscreens, and keyboards [4]. Tangible user interfaces (TUIs) are often compared to graphical user interfaces (GUIs) [5]. Tangible bits allow users to "grasp & manipulate" bits in the center of users' attention by coupling the bits with everyday physical objects and architectural surfaces. Also, tangible bits enable users to be aware of background bits at the periphery of human perception using ambient display media such as light, sound, airflow, and water movement in an augmented space. The goal of Tangible Bits is to bridge the gap between both cyberspace and the physical environment, as well as the foreground and background of human activities [1] (Fig. 1).

**Fig. 1.** Iceberg metaphor—from (a) GUI (painted bits) to (b) TUI (tangible bits) to (c) radical atoms (Source: https://www.media.mit.edu/courses/MAS834/) a) A graphical user interface only lets users see digital information through a screen, as if looking through the surface of the water. We interact with the forms below through remote controls such as a mouse, a keyboard, or a touchscreen. b) A tangible user interface is like an iceberg: There is a portion of the digital that emerges beyond the surface of the water – into the physical realm – that acts as physical manifestations of computation, allowing us to directly interact with the "tip of the iceberg." c) Radical Atoms is our vision for the future of interaction with hypothetical dynamic materials, in which all digital information has physical manifestation so that we can interact directly with it – as if the iceberg had risen from the depths to reveal its sunken mass.

## 2.2 Ubiquitous Computing and Marginal Perception

Just as with the rapid advancement of the Internet and web-based technologies, many applications of ubiquitous computing cannot be predicted today and rely on these technologies reaching a critical mass. Mark Weiser saw three waves of computing: the mainframe age when many people shared a computer; the personal computer wave when one person has one computer (the focus of many initiatives); moving to the ubiquitous computing wave when each person shares many computers. The current Internet age is seen as a transitional phase between the personal computer and ubiquitous waves [6] (Fig. 2).

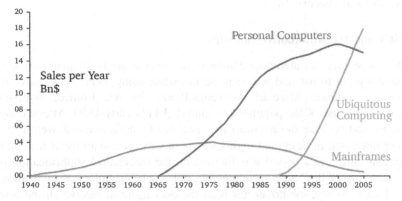

**Fig. 2.** The three waves of computing, Mark Weiser, 1990 (Source: https://www.slideshare.net/gumption/situated-computing-u-korea-forum-20080924-draft-presentation)

In more detail, ubiquitous computing is the method of enhancing computer use by making many computers available throughout the physical environment, but making them effectively invisible to the user [7]. It is a vision of computing power 'invisibly' embedded in the world around us and accessed through intelligent interfaces: 'Its highest ideal is to make a computer so embedded, so fitting, so natural, that we use it without even thinking about it. This is about a shift to human-centered computing, where technology is no longer a barrier, but works for us, adapting to our needs and preferences and remaining in the background until required [6]. In terms of human-computer interaction, ubiquitous computing allows the users to immerse themselves within the overwhelming atmosphere of daily life, and at the same time, keep interacting with a computer. It leverages a situation in which the user is able to get actively engaged and marginally perceive what is to receive as various types of data. This is the evolved form of data perception, from the time when the user merely focuses on the screen to interact with the computer.

Ubiquitous computing and marginal perception have much in common with other human experiences in immersive contexts such as nature or the city. The human body has been trained to some extent to get immersed in the environments that are disseminating massive amount of data in various qualities, and interact with what is being sensed.

### 2.3 Cybernetic and Feedback Mechanism

Putting human-computer interaction, ubiquitous computing, and marginal perception into practice, understanding feedback mechanisms is a key. The feedback mechanism is a term that derives from cybernetics, a field of science that was famously mentioned in detail in Norbert Wiener's book in 1948 [8], and developed in various directions.

It could be claimed that cybernetic implies the adoption of a systematic understanding of communication between subject and object. This meant that by associating control with a communication feedback loop, in which information is delivered into the system as input, and system behavior identified as output. Then the output is functionally steered the injected information as new input back into the system and recognized as feedback. Then by redirecting its next operation, the system redefines its functions towards success [9].

### 2.4 HCI and the Automotive Industry

Over the last century, the automotive industry has seen a variety of changes in terms of the technology put to use and user experiences while using a car. Automotive manufacturers, for instance, Maserati, Mercedes-Benz, and Alfa-Romeo, involved the technology in the use of the populated Formula1 (F1) in early 1950. After a couple of decades, F1 had become the realm of the specialist manufacturers as well as experts who were interested in designing high-speed road cars. The majority of technological development during this period was focused on the mechanical sophistication of the car, yet in terms of the levels of autonomy, not much technological innovation was applied. That is to say, the driver has been the only agent to receive all the essential input from the road and analyze it while using a car.

Today, F1 represents the latest advancements in the technology of the automotive industry. A majority of new cars are equipped with several hundreds of sensors and electronic control units (ECUs) [10]. The progress in designing cars could facilitate the vehicle to maximize the functioning of the engine. This can affect the human driver behavior by providing a controllable environment with more safety for a driver. Fully autonomous systems can make the car to be self-aware. Therefore, today's car can be represented as a sentient platform that, through real-time data, can communicate with the user as well as the surrounding environment. Similarly, in the recent F1 races, not only the driver could receive the input of the road, but all the received data could be analyzed for steering the car in the most efficient and effective way.

In this context, the study on Human-machine interaction is crucial in many aspects, mostly since a large proportion of car accidents are caused by human mishandling [11]. By understanding driver behavior, potentially dangerous habits such as driver inactivity and distracted driving can be identified, leading to the corrective actions at the right time and place. In collaboration with MIT's Senseable City Laboratory, Audi created the Road Frustration Index (RFI) [12], to investigate driver frustration in various road conditions, traffic, incidents, weather, and driver sentiment. To calibrate the frustration algorithm, the team designed a series of experiments to measure stress and frustration during real-world driving tasks using physiological sensors as well as an array of face/body tracking technologies. In such operations, the interaction is conducted between driver and machine as a data platform through visual or audio feedback, while this could drag a driver's attention due to their verbal content as well as visual recognition from a driver. Drivers are expected to maintain their focus on the act of driving and the road; However, using visual and audio feedback could cause information overflow that adds cognitive load to the user; for instance, with tuning the music, interacting with an automatic voice portal or virtual augmented screen. This would suggest the use of haptic information in a vehicle environment to achieve optimal interaction between machine and user.

Some other work, have been conceived in developing driver alcohol detection system for safety (DADSS) [13]. This program is conducted by the National Highway Traffic Safety Administration (NHTSA) and the Automotive Coalition for Traffic Safety (ACTS) to explore the potential benefits and the public policy challenges associated with utilizing technology to prevent alcohol-impaired driving in a non-invasive way. DADSS measures the blood alcohol concentration (BAC) in various ways, including the driver's breath and from a touch-based system utilizing spectroscopy to measure alcohol levels in skin tissue [13], and more recent work uses data coming from mobile phone sensors [14]. This technology aimed to develop an integrated system to prevent a drunk user from driving and save lives. This raises a fundamental question on challenges regarding the overall quality of interaction in the car environment that enables the driver to control the vehicle.

## 2.5   HCI and Haptics

The term haptic from the Greek háptō/haptesthai (touch, relative to tact) is the adjective used to describe everything related to or based on the sense of touch. It also makes reference to the science of all that is relative to tact and its sensations as a means of control and interaction with machines and computers [15]. In general, for manipulation of an object, tactility refers to the static aspects and the information received from the nerve terminals of the skin. Kinesthetic, meanwhile, refers to the dynamic aspects of said interaction with the object [15].

A Haptic Interface (HI) is a system that allows a human to interact with a computer through bodily sensations and movements. Haptics refers to a type of human-computer interaction technology that encompasses tactile feedback or other bodily sensations to perform actions or processes on a computing device [16].

Analogously, HI scan is divided into two main groups through the lens of the sensation they can produce at the moment of contact with some part of the body: those which produce kinesthetic stimuli and those which produce tactile stimuli.

The tactile type of HI, also known as a touch screen, is a device that is in charge of stimulating the nerve receptors of touch to display, in the interaction with the human skin, parameters such as temperature, coarseness, shape, and texture. The mechanical receptors, which are commonly stimulated in touch screens and achieve contact simulation in the skin, are those of vibration and pressure since Merkel disks are activated with pressure and Meissner and Pacini corpuscles are activated with low vibration or high frequency, respectively [15].

## 2.6  Soft Robotics

Soft robots are primarily composed of easily deformable matter such as fluids, gels, and elastomers that enable compliance matching with the environing materials. Compliance matching proposes that materials that come into contact with each other should share similar mechanical rigidity in order to evenly distribute the internal load and minimize interfacial stress concentrations [17]. However, this principle does not apply to rigid robots (E = 109 Pa) interacting with soft materials (E = 102–106 Pa), causing damage or mechanical immobilization (where E is the Young's Modulus, which gives a measure of the stiffness of a solid material). These types of interactions with soft materials are widely spread, as for instance with natural skin, muscle tissue, delicate internal organs, but also organisms, artificial replications of biological functionalities, etc. Due to this

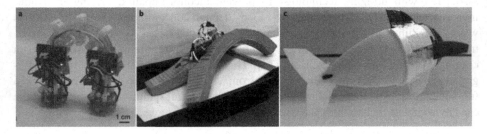

**Fig. 3.** Samples of Soft Robots a. Climbing robot powered by a motor-cable system. b. Robust walking robot powered by on-board pneumatics (65 cm long). c. Biomimetic swimming robot powered by a hydraulic actuation system (35 cm long). (Source: https://www.researchgate.net/figure/Fully-untethered-robotic-systems-a-Climbing-robot-powered-by-a-motor-cable-system-b_fig5_323060353)

dramatic mismatch in mechanical compliance, it is easy to conclude that rigid robots are not adapted and even dangerous for intimate human interaction. Therefore, there is a need for robots that match the elastic properties of materials and organisms found in nature, and this is where soft robots could provide the solution (Fig. 3).

Designing soft robots calls for completely new models in their mechanics, power supply, and control [18]. However, rethinking materials, design methods, and fabrication techniques should open up new areas of soft robotics in macro and micro length scales; since the use of soft material with high deformability and conformability promises various applications, ranging from surgical and wearable robotics to safe human-robot interaction and robot locomotion.

## 3 "Poking Seat": The Project Report

### 3.1 The Scope of the Project

The field of interaction design aims to facilitate and promote the way people work, communicate, and interact. It has been developed at a high pace, mainly since the cost of innovation in both physical and digital product design has been falling down following the digital revolution. With the advancements in Computer-Aided Design (CAD) and Computer-Aided Manufacturing (CAM), the concept of marrying bits and atoms transited into reality at a massive scale, shaping a community of designers and researchers working on developing various prototypes and products.

Poking Seat project and its associated suite of applied knowledge, tools, techniques, and technologies demonstrate and point toward design possibilities that lie at the intersection of human-computer interaction design, product design, and soft robotics in a vehicle environment. The project aimed to design an interactive interface embedded in a car seat to facilitate the functionality of the driving experience, especially in distracting and overwhelming situations, in semi-autonomous cars. But what do we exactly mean when we are speaking about applying a function in the context of semi-autonomous cars?

The concept of autonomy levels for self-driving vehicles was first published by the Society of Automotive Engineers (SAE International) in 2014. The report defines six levels of autonomy that automakers would need to achieve on their way to building the no-steering-wheel self-driving bubble pods of the future, reaching from the fully-manual Level 0 to the fully-autonomous Level 5, where there is no interference required by the human. These semi-autonomous cars might be able to transport the driver autonomously on sections of a journey. However, the driver is required to take control occasionally between different levels of autonomy when needed to complete an end-to-end journey. These transitions between autonomy levels cause safety concerns, as the driver might not be fully aware of the surrounding situation and the enabled autonomy features instantly.

The initial idea of Poking Seat posits a seat as a tangible interface that can interact with the user. In general, a seat is in touch with the majority of the user's body, making it admin to the faculty of tactility in relation to the object. The design approach accounts for using tactile and haptic feedback from an interactive interface in a vehicle environment. Considering a haptic interface, it provides two-way generated input, from the user's body to the seat and the inputs received to the user from the seat. Therefore, it permits the seat to properly function as an input and output device at the same time. This approach is taken to use a haptic feedback mechanism as a means of communication with the driver through an experience of being poked. Haptic feedback provides additional freedom for a driver in processing the data [19]. It can improve the performance of the driver that enables the user to focus on the act of driving. While interacting with automobile voice data and visual data can be distractive for a driver that affects the sensitivity of the user, tactile feedback perceived to be more effective by the driver [20].

This work attempts to define haptic communication in a vehicle environment through the study on the inactive performance of a driver in a single position on a seat for a while. Such constant inaction can be usually considered as a sign for a variety of unusual situations/conditions of the user that can affect driver health and well-being. Poking Seat takes the advantages of haptic and shape-changing interfaces to avoid any mishandling behavior for the drivers through interacting with them in a non-distractive way. This interaction takes place by an integrated, responsive system embedded into a seat that can respond to the user's inactions. We believe this work can contribute to expanding the application of interaction design in the context of the automotive industry.

### 3.2   Design-Research Dimensions

**Material Investigation and Experiment.** In order to reach the maximum effect for the act of poking based on soft-robotic actuation, an array of materials such as plexi, silicon, metal wire, PLA, and wood were examined as the skin and also the supporting structure of the poach robots. In this phase, the fabrication was done by primary tools through primitive crafting techniques. This experiment led to understanding the behaviours of different material with their various qualities and properties (Fig. 4).

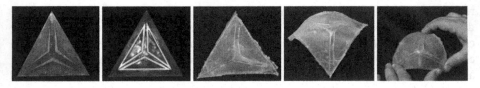

**Fig. 4.** Compressed wood, PLA, and metal bar embedded in silicon skins while casting.

Considering the added values of additive manufacturing in the advancement of digital prototyping, we also examined Thermoplastic Polyurethane (TPU), a foldable material that can be 3d-printed (Fig. 5).

**Fig. 5.** Early 3D-printed TPU prototypes and their folding behaviour

**Origami and Geometric Studies.** Following early stage material investigation and confirming the potentials of TPU, the design capacities of various geometric origami models, and their capability to basically poke the driver as a means of communication were explored (Fig. 6).

**Fig. 6.** 3D-printed TPU surfaces, being examined in terms of the depth and severity of poking

These alternatives got 3D-printed with different thicknesses in mountains and valleys; and were subject to further measurements to reach the optimum stiffness for folding behaviour to poke (Fig. 7).

**Pneumatic-Actuated Interface.** Soft actuator has a unique capability of deformation, flexibility and movement that provide real perception for the user by creating soft changes. However, this soft behaviour is not quite functioning when it is about to alert the driver in distracting situations. That is why the proposed interface in Poking Seat consisted of two main layers: pneumatic actuation mechanism, and poking mechanism. Putting pneumatic actuation into practice, several silicon casting experiments were carried out with variations in thickness and material properties, aiming to fabricate silicon bags that can actuate the upper layer, TPU foldable skin.

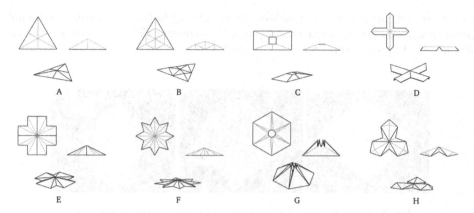

**Fig. 7.** Geometric studies, simulated and fabricated based on the material properties of TPU in folding behaviour inward (_____) and outward (_____)

## 3.3   The Final Design

**The Interaction Scenario.** Asingle cycle of interaction scenario in Poking Seat takes place within the following six steps:

A. The vehicle sensors receive environmental data regarding the situation in which the vehicle and the driver are.
B. The microprocessors and microcontrollers verify the sensed data, and condition it to switch on the air compressor to actuate the silicon bags that are embedded in the driver seat.
C. The silicon bags get inflated softly.
D. The inflation of silicon bags continues to the moment in which they touch the TPU skin.
E. The poking behaviour takes place through the minimum early touch by silicon bags.
F. The driver gets poked, and becomes aware of the environmental alert (Fig. 8).

**Fig. 8.** The transition of the driver's seating position during the process of poking

**The Minimum Working Prototype.** All the prototyping experiments led to craft an integrated one-to-one scale minimum working prototype, to demonstrate the functionality and viability of various aspects of the project. The prototype basically consists of three main categories of components and elements: supportive structure, electronics, and performative skins (made out of TPU and silicon) (Figs. 9, 10, 11 and 12).

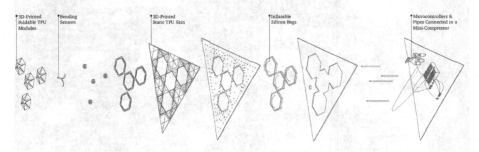

**Fig. 9.** Components of the minimum working prototype, exploded in assembling order

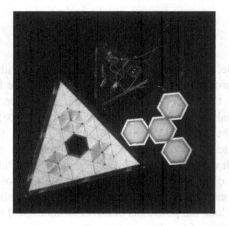

**Fig. 10.** Main components of the prototype

**Fig. 11.** The act of poking, happening through one of the four poking components in the prototype

**Fig. 12.** Materials, early prototypes, electronics, and crafting tools, all to make the final prototype on one table

## 4   Conclusion

As stated in this article, Poking Seat responded to an issue within the context of the automotive industry through leveraging the potentials of haptic feedback mechanisms and some supportive technologies and techniques. However, with the synergetic orchestration of materials, electronics, data and the end user's behaviour, the project is capable of going beyond its defined context. In a future world where dynamic/responsive/interactive conditions will substitute the static ones, interdisciplinary design-research experiments pave the ground for innovative products. To this end, taking advantage of relevantly less commercialised technologies is what we recommend to academic institutions, research labs and design studios to invest on. On a mass scale, this will unlock the potentials of novel technological trends, precisely when the projects have a degree of freedom to adapt themselves to emerging contexts.

**Acknowledgments.** Poking Seat is a project defined and developed by Tehran Urban Innovation Centre (TUIC), 2018, in principal collaboration with Soft Haptics and Robotics Lab at the Department of Mechanical Engineering, University College London (UCL). The detailed credit of the project is, as stated in the following:

Project Coordination: Nashid Nabian Academic Support: Helge Wurdemann, Bani Anvari Project Lead: Raha Ashrafi, Mahdi Najafi Design and Research: Sahar Asgari, Hoda Eskandar Nia, Mannan Ghanizadehgerayli, Mohammadreza Hedayati (part-time) The authors would like to especially thank Helge Wurdemann and Bani Anvari for their constant contribution to the project from the beginning.

# References

1. Ishii, H., Ullmer, B.: The grid: tangible bits: towards seamless interfaces between people, bits and atoms. In: Proceedings of CHI 1997, 22–27 March 1997
2. Fischer, G.: User modeling in human-computer interaction. User Model. User-Adap. Interact. **11**, 65–86 (2001)
3. Hardenberg, Ch., Berard, F.: The grid: bare-hand human-computer interaction. In: PUI 2001, Orlando, FL USA (2001)
4. Ishii, H., Lakatos, D., Bonanni, L., Labrune, J.: Radical Atoms: Beyond Tangible Bits, Toward Transformable Materials (2012). https://doi.org/10.1145/2065327.2065337
5. Zuckerman, O., Gal-Oz, A.: To TUI or not to TUI: evaluating performance and preference in tangible vs. graphical user interfaces. Int. J. Hum.-Comput. Stud. **71**, 803–820 (2013). http://dx.doi.org/10.1016/j.ijhcs.2013.04.003
6. British Educational Communications and technology agency. Http://www.becta.org.uk/research
7. Weiser, M.: Some computer science issues in ubiquitous computing. Commun. ACM **36**(7), 75–84 (1993)
8. Wiener, N.: Cybernetics: Or Control and Communication in the Animal and the Machine. Hermann, and MIT Press, Paris and Cambridge (1961 [1948])
9. Luli, C.: Information, communication, systems: cybernetic aesthetics in 1960s cultures. In: Kosc, G., Juncker, C., Monteith, S., Waldschmidt-Nelson, B. (eds.) The Transatlantic Sixties: Europe and the United States in the Counterculture. Transcript Verlag (2013). https://www.jstor.org/stable/j.ctv1wxt2b.12
10. Fugiglando, U., Massaro, E., Santi, P., et al.: Driving behavior analysis through CAN bus data in an uncontrolled environment. IEEE Trans. Intell. Transp. Syst. **20**(2), 737–748 (2019). https://doi.org/10.1109/TITS.2018.2836308
11. European Commission. Mobility and Transport: Road safety, Mobility and Transport: Road safety. http://ec.europa.eu/transport/roadsafety/indexen.html. Accessed 12 Oct 2015
12. Ratti, C., Biderman, A., Greco, K.: Road Frustartion Index (RFI), MIT Senseable city lab in collaboration with Audi (2013). http://senseable.mit.edu/rfi/
13. The Driver Alcohol Detection System for Safety (DADSS). https://www.rdmag.com/article/2017/08/promising-vehicle-tech-will-detect-drunk-drivers-they-hit-road. Accessed 16 Aug 2017
14. Dai, J., Teng, J., Bai, X., Shen, Z., Xuan, D.: Mobile phone-based drunk driving detection. In: Proceedings of 4th International Conference on Pervasive Comput. Technol. Healthcare, pp. 1–8 (2010)
15. Ariza, V., Santís-Chaves, M.: Haptic interfaces: kinesthetic vs. tactile systems. Revista EIA **13**(26), 13–29 (2016)
16. Definition What does Haptic Interface mean? https://www.techopedia.com/definition/3638/haptic-interface
17. Majidi, C.: Soft robotics: a perspective—current trends and prospects for the future. Soft Robot. **1**(1), 5–11 (2014)
18. Rogóż, M., Zeng, H., Xuan, C., Wiersma, D., Wasylczyk, P.: Soft robotics: light-driven soft robot mimics caterpillar locomotion in natural scale (advanced optical materials 11/2016). Adv. Opt. Mater. **4**(11), 1902 (2016)
19. Gaffary, Y., Lécuyer, A.: The use of haptic and tactile information in the car to improve driving safety: a review of current technologies. Front. ICT **5**, 5 (2018). https://doi.org/10.3389/fict.2018.00005
20. Scott, J.J., Gray, R.: A comparison of tactile, visual, and auditory warnings for rear-end collision prevention in simulated driving. Hum. Factors **50**, 264–275 (2008). https://doi.org/10.1518/001872008X250674

# Automotive HMI Guidelines for China Based on Culture Dimensions Interpretation

Zaiyan Gong[1], Jun Ma[1,2(✉)], Qianwen Zhang[2], Yining Ding[1], and Lu Liu[1]

[1] School of Automotive Studies, Tongji University, Shanghai, China
majun.tongji@ammi.cn
[2] College of Design and Innovation, Tongji University, Shanghai, China

**Abstract.** The in-vehicle HMI system has become a significant part of automotive research and development. When Chinese customers choose cars, they consider the performance of HMI to be one of the deciding factors. Many global car manufacturers have tried to understand the special demand of HMI in the Chinese market. This study developed a method to define the automotive HMI guidelines based on Hofstede's cultural dimension since culture is a basic impetus. Five cultural dimensions were selected: power distance, individualism versus collectivism, long-term orientation versus short-term orientation, uncertain avoidance, and restraint versus indulgence. Chinese customers' special position on the dimensions drives nine internal demands that can be presented as various UX designs for the in-vehicle HMI system, which are defined as UX guidelines for China. Sixteen HMI key guidelines were developed based on this method, which can be a strong reference for product definition and HMI design for the Chinese market.

**Keywords:** In-vehicle HMI system · UX · Hofstede cross-culture research

## 1 Introduction

The in-vehicle human-machine interface (HMI) system is a flourishing topic in automotive research and development. Consumers in China pay more attention to the HMI system than the traditional evaluation standards, such as power and acceleration. German car brands have gained the trust of global users in terms of safety and stability. However, the HMI systems of German car brands do not always meet Chinese customers' tastes. For example, the in-vehicle HMI system of German brands generally tends to list all classified functions in a hierarchical structure, while Chinese customers prefer task - or scenario-oriented design.

Many automobile manufacturers have tried to investigate Chinese consumers' demands. Customer research and market analysis are popular methodologies for understanding consumers [1]. These methods are capable of examining the user awareness of in-vehicle HMI systems, but it is difficult to determine the behavioral motivation beyond consciousness. Yu's study shows that user demand awareness is very uncertain [2]. This could lead to product failure if the product definition is directly affected by customer feedback. In fact, customers are initially influenced by culture, but they are not consciously aware of that.

© Springer Nature Switzerland AG 2020
C. Stephanidis et al. (Eds.): HCII 2020, LNCS 12429, pp. 96–110, 2020.
https://doi.org/10.1007/978-3-030-59987-4_8

Culture has a great influence on people's behaviors and values. According to Hofstede's theory, everyone has their own thinking mode, emotional mode, and potential behavior mode, which they learn from their life experience and are relatively hard to change [3]. Thus, the study of culture can help us to understand the preferences and behaviors of people from different cultures, which has great reference value for cross-cultural designers.

Culture also influences the user experience domain. Aaron Marcus mapped the cultural dimension of Hofstede to the global web design and explained the differences in web design in different countries from the perspective of culture [4]. However, few researchers have explained and deduced automotive HMI design from the perspective of culture. Based on Hofstede's research results and cultural dimensions, this paper summarizes the trends and internal needs of Chinese users and deduces the UX design direction and suggestions suitable for in-vehicle HMI system.

## 2 Theory and Method

### 2.1 Cultural Influence on HMI Experience

HMI experience is a branch of user experience. At the very beginning, the evaluation of the electronic system comes from the TAM (Technology Acceptance Model). Davis proposed the evaluation dimensions of usefulness and usability [5]. In addition, user satisfaction is a new evaluation dimension introduced by IOS [6]. However, it is a subjective index that is influenced by many factors. Thüring found that the user experience components are usefulness, ease of use, symbolic value, aesthetics, and motivation, which are relatively comprehensive in refining the user experience elements [7].

Culture has a limited impact on the utility of user experience but has a certain impact on usefulness and aesthetics. Furthermore, culture has a great influence on symbols and motivation. In China, automobiles are not only a means of transportation but also a symbol of social identity. Therefore, motivation and symbol values are the most culturally influenced parts of the user experience.

### 2.2 Culture Analysis Theories and Hofstede Model

To understand cultural differences, several models have been developed, such as the Hofstede cross-cultural model [8–10], Schwartz and Bilsky [11], Trompenaars [12], and GLOBE Model [13]. Among these studies, both the cultural model developed by Hofstede and the comparatively recent GLOBE Model have provided scholars with much-needed insights into the structure of national cultures. The Hofstede model is the most widely used cultural analysis theory [14]. Studies by Manuela Aparicio prove the influence of collectivism versus individualism, one of the cultural dimensions according to the Hofstede model, on the satisfaction of e-learning products [15]. Studies by Kurt Matzler indicate that individualism and uncertainty avoidance are the most relevant dimensions for brand-self congruity [16].

Hofstede's theory is a framework to measure cultural differences between different countries. Culture is a psychological process shared by people in one environment, which can distinguish one group of people from others.

This theory was originally the result of Hofstede's research on the cultural values of employees of IBM multinational companies in his article published in 1980 [17]. In the initial study, four dimensions of culture were found and defined as follows:

1) Power distance (PDI): acceptance of class differences in a particular culture.
2) Individualism (IDV): the degree to which individuals feel they are "on their own" rather than part of a larger group identity.
3) Masculinity (MAS): the degree to which a culture emphasizes competition, achievement, and "getting ahead".
4) Uncertainty avoidance (UAI): tolerance for ambiguity and risk.

In the follow-up work, Hofstede added two more dimensions [8, 10]:

5) Long-term orientation (LTO): the degree to which a culture focuses on the future.
6) Indulgence versus restraint: the extent to which people try to control their desires and impulses. Relatively weak control is called "Indulgence" and relatively strong control is called "Restraint".

In this study, five dimensions related to HMI are selected: power distance (PDI), individualism (IDV), uncertainty avoidance (UAI), long-term orientation (LTO, and indulgence versus restraint.

The exclusion of Masculinity (MAS) results from its weak relevance with automotive HMI scenarios as well as the small differentiation of Chinese scores compared with the major Western countries.

### 2.3   Research Method

In Hofstede's study, China's scores and explanations can be examined in every cultural dimension. Based on this analysis, this paper summarizes the trend of people's behavior and their internal demands in the Chinese context (see Fig. 1). The internal demands could explain which types of UX designs are approved in China.

Through a comprehensive analysis of cultural dimensions, combined with the actual situation in the automotive consumer field, a series of UX design suggestions has been summarized in the following chapters.

**Fig. 1.** Research model.

# 3   Culture-Derived HMI Guidelines

China's special position on the five selected cultural dimensions drives customers' internal demands. These internal demands can be presented as various UX designs for the in-vehicle HMI system, which are defined as UX guidelines for China.

## 3.1   Power Distance

Power Distance is the extent to which the less powerful members of institutions and organizations within a country expect and accept that power is distributed unequally [10]. China (score of 80) has a higher PDI – it is a society that believes that inequalities amongst people are acceptable. Highly decentralized and supported by a strong middle class, Germany is among the lower power distant countries (score 35). For example, in Chinese classes, students stand up to greet their teachers, while in Germany, teacher-student relations tend to be more equal. In Chinese families, children are still subject to parental authority even after growing up, while German children treat their parents as friends.

**Building Prestige.** In a high PDI society, class gap and privilege are regarded as honors, and people often hope to obtain spiritual or material enjoyment by expanding the power distance. Building prestige is a tendency to expand the power distance, which establishes an unequal relationship in a certain field. The internal demand for building prestige is honor and award.

*Honor and Award.* Honor and award mean the improvement of social status, increase of wealth, recognition of skills, and thus, establishing inequality in a certain field. In China, honors and awards are common: "merit student" certificates are the school's affirmation of students' performance, and "the most beautiful village teacher" is society's affirmation of an individual's work. By comparing and analyzing different products in high and low PDI societies, we found two UX design orientations to meet the internal demand and provide some HMI guidelines accordingly.

Scoring or ranking is a way to create a sense of honor. One of the reasons WeRun (a pedometer with ranking) is so popular in China is that it gives us honor in the sense of exercise and health. Baidu map of China (see Fig. 2, left), after each trip, will rate the driving behavior of drivers and set up a "driver score". The Google map (see Fig. 2, right) only provides the satisfaction score for the map service. For car HMI design, a score can be rated after one journey of navigation to evaluate the time efficiency, eco-friendliness, and law abidingness during the trip. This score can also be shared and ranked among the user's friends. The rating method can be used not only for driving but also for in-car entertainment.

**Fig. 2.** Baidu map rates driving behavior while Google map rates navigation service

Point rules are used by various Chinese apps to increase user stickiness, but this phenomenon is rare in low PDI society. Take video software, for example, IQIYI and Youku use point rules, but YouTube does not. For car HMI design, a point mall can be built in a car for users to redeem the car data packages or skins for the AI avatar (see Fig. 3.).

**Fig. 3.** Points mall in Chinese brand car HMI system.

**Showing Prestige.** Another tendency to expand power distance is to show prestige, which makes authority better felt by others. Showoff is its internal demand.

*Showing Off.* Offering power and wealth is seen as a sign of success and an effective way to show prestige. There are two UX design orientations to meet the internal demand and provide some HMI guidelines accordingly.

Perceived by others. Configurations that are easy to perceive by others are a good way to show wealth and status. Chinese consumers tend to buy cars with splendid configurations such as big wheel hubs, panoramic sunroofs, and big bodies. With the development of the smart cockpit, Chinese consumers' choices are no longer limited to the appearance of cars. For car HMI design, we recommend using narrow-bezel and large-size screens, fancy ambient lighting, and brand-new elements (such as physical AI voice assistant, holographic AI image, AR navigation, etc.). These interior elements, while full of advanced sense and innovation, are feasible for car owners to show off, and Chinese consumers will be willing to pay for it.

Online sharing. Online sharing by electronic devices such as phones is very popular. With access to the Internet, car entertainment functions such as query and sharing become increasingly abundant. At the same time, timely updates can be obtained through wireless OTA technology, so that the devices are always up to date and the users can enjoy the full experience. For car HMI design, we can use online sharing such as in-car karaoke score, driven behavior/mileage, new skin, and UI theme. We recommend an interesting push (see Fig. 4.), like "holiday skin, romantic mode, games" by OTA update. These will provide users with new content and the chance to show off advanced technology.

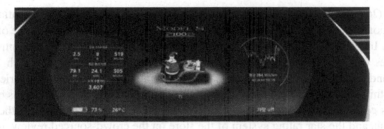

**Fig. 4.** A certain American brand car provides an interesting push on some special days.

According to the above analysis, the following guidelines should be considered for car HMI in the Chinese market:

1) Scoring or ranking for driving behavior and entertainment to meet the demands of honor and award.
2) Points mall in a car to meet the demand of honor and award.
3) Use easy perceived design such as brand-new elements and big screen for showing off.
4) Online sharing design such as location/device sharing, interesting content push for showing off.

### 3.2    Individualism versus Collectivism

The high side of this dimension, called individualism, can be defined as a preference for a loosely-knit social framework in which individuals are expected to take care of only themselves and their immediate families. In contrast, collectivism represents a preference for a tightly-knit framework in society in which individuals can expect their relatives or members of a particular group to look after them in exchange for unquestioning loyalty. A society's position on this dimension is reflected in whether people's self-image is defined in terms of "I" or "we" [10]. China has a culture of collectivism with individualism score only at 20, while Germany has obvious individualism features with a score of 67. In China, three-generation and four-generation cohabitation families are very common. Chinese people usually stay in touch with distant relatives. In Germany, children often do not choose to live with their parents when they grow up, and only immediate family members are closely connected.

**Building Collectivity.** Chinese people often work in "collective" units, and even in their personal life and entertainment, they prefer to work in a collective form. They value the power of identification brought by the collective. The Chinese also have a strong symbiosis that emotionally generates a tendency to be dependent on others, which is reflected in family and social relationships. Due to the collective nature, the Chinese people often do not place much emphasis on the sense of the boundary between the individual and the collective. Whether it is organizational work or personal life, the boundary between the individual and the collective is often blurred. People living under this collectivist culture have three internal demands: following other's opinions, being accompanied, and national pride.

*Follow Other's Opinions.* It is easier for the Chinese to form an organization or a group spontaneously to generate comments, exchange values, and find a sense of group identity. In personal life, Chinese people tend to find or create their own communities or circles around various dimensions. In these groups, they actively search for the voices and opinions of others and are happy to adopt them. The UX design orientation to meet this demand will be to introduce other's comments and scores. Designs of other people's comments and scores can be easily found in China's apps, such as the users' comments and the star rating system of the store on the crowd-sourced review app. For car HMI guidelines, when the car navigation system recommends POI to the owner, similar design logic can be introduced, which shows the scores or real comments of others for the owner's reference (see Fig. 5).

**Fig. 5.** Review crowd-sourced score for POI in the car HMI.

*Being Accompanied.* The collectivism of the Chinese is also more manifested in the importance of "accompaniment" to maintain the emotional link between people. This psychology is largely derived from traditional Chinese culture. For example, Chinese traditional festivals mostly emphasize "reunion" and "getting together". As for UX orientation, the human-like design is an effective way to cater to this internal demand. In UX design, it is common to use a solid, personified, or materialized design to create a virtual spiritual companion atmosphere. Common intelligent assistant images in China, such as Tmall Elf, Xiao Ai, Xiao Du, have adopted similar designs to utilize the image of a human or object to open the emotional channel with users. For in-car HMI guidelines, when considering the design of in-car voice assistants, a certain anthropomorphic or quasi-physical image, coupled with vivid expressions is widely preferred by the Chinese (see Fig. 6).

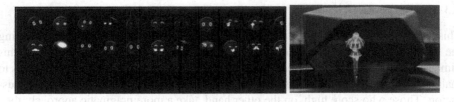

**Fig. 6.** Human-like AI avatar and emotional design in the car HMI.

**Maintaining Collectivity.** Another tendency to show collectivism is to maintain collectivity. For the Chinese, the spirit of collectivism permeates all stages of education, and they always emphasize "collective honor first" and "maintaining the collective". At the primary education stage, Chinese schools will set up similar collective titles of "Excellent Class" and organize group project competitions to cultivate students' collective sense of honor. Chinese college students are generally required to participate in collective military training in the first year of enrollment, and all aspects of military training will repeatedly emphasize that college students establish a collective consciousness.

*National Pride.* The internal demand for maintaining collectivism is national pride. The Chinese are more likely to develop national pride and to spontaneously safeguard national images. This is reflected in UX design orientation, which is highly sought after by national tide design and traditional cultural elements. For example, the national tide series of Li Ning clothing and the IP of the Forbidden City are both a reflection of national pride and cultural self-confidence. For car HMI guidelines, Chinese traditional cultural elements can be appropriately used to form an effective combination with the in-car UI design (see Fig. 7).

**Fig. 7.** Chinese-style UI design.

According to the above analysis, the following guidelines should be considered for car HMI in the Chinese market:

1) Providing another's score and comments when recommending POI to include other suggestions.
2) Human-like AI avatar and giving them different expressions to make Chinese people feel accompanied.
3) Chinese-style UI designs like including popular Chinese icons to develop national pride for Chinese customers.

### 3.3 Long-Term Orientation versus Short-Term Orientation

This dimension measures the acceptance extent of society members towards delaying the material, emotional, and social satisfaction. Societies who score low on this dimension are defined as short-term orientation [10]. For example, this culture prefers to maintain time-honored traditions and norms while viewing societal change with suspicion. Those who score high, on the other hand, take a more pragmatic approach; they encourage thrift and efforts in modern education as a way to prepare for the future. China is a long-term orientation culture with a high score at 87, which shows the features of emphasis on interpersonal relationships, overtime-working culture, etc. However, the USA is at the other end with a low score at 26, which shows that Americans are very practical and business performance is measured on a short-term basis.

**Focus on Long-Term Interest.** China has a strong long-term orientation at present. Chinese people believe that truth depends very much on the situation, context, and time. They show an ability to adapt traditions easily to changed conditions, a strong propensity to save and invest, thriftiness, and perseverance in achieving results. For many young people, the ownership of real estate is still the most important goal of life and they will sacrifice their current living quality to achieve this. Virtue education plays an important role in family, school, and society, which emphasizes the quality of thriftiness and perseverance to obtain future success. In total, Chinese people tend to focus on long-term interests instead of the life they are living at present. Accordingly, Chinese people living in this culture shows two internal demands: interpersonal relationship and efficiency.

*Interpersonal Beneficial Relationships.* Chinese people greatly value interpersonal relationships because they believe that maintaining a good relationship, or Guanxi, can benefit future paths. In China, drinking culture is regarded as a good way to talk about business and people follow the principle of making friends before doing business. Alumni associations are common in China, and people have a great passion to attend these activities to provide and gain resources. In this way, the UX design orientation will provide mutual benefit design for Chinese. For example, it is often difficult to buy a train ticket during peak travel season, and some ticket-buying Apps allow users to enhance the chance to buy tickets by asking for their friends' help (see Fig. 8). For car HMI guidelines, it is suggested to create mutual-help applications or games for friends in the car or owner App to provide Chinese people with chances of enjoying mutual interest.

*Efficiency.* In China, there is a special culture called "996 working schedules", which refers to people working from 9 am to 9 pm for 6 days a week. Chinese people are used to living a fast-paced life to enjoy happiness in their later lives. In this way, Chinese people always emphasize efficiency to make better use of time. The internal demand for efficiency has helped develop a UX design orientation with fewer operation steps. For example, intelligent speakers are popular in Chinese homes and have higher efficiency. Moreover, the short cut design is necessary for mobile phones. Accordingly, for car HMI guideline, on the one hand, the short cut should be provided (see Fig. 9, left); on the other hand, there should be fewer steps required when completing an operating task, such as defining map as the homepage of the HMI (see Fig. 9, right).

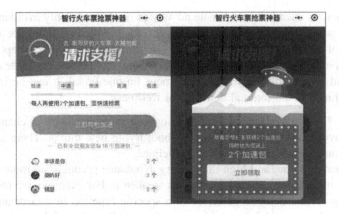

**Fig. 8.** TheChinese will ask for friends' help in the app to buy a train ticket.

**Fig. 9.** Short-cut menu in the car HMI and set map as the homepage to achieve high efficiency.

According to the above analysis, the following guidelines should be considered for the car HMI in the Chinese market:

1) Friend-mutual-help applications in the car HMI or owner App to help them develop the owner relationship.
2) Short cut cards to operate more conveniently and improve efficiency.
3) Decreasing the operating steps like defining a map as a homepage to improve efficiency.

### 3.4 Uncertainty Avoidance

Uncertainty avoidance is defined as the extent to which the members of a culture feel threatened by ambiguous or unknown situations and have created beliefs and institutions that try to avoid these [10]. At 30, China had a low score on uncertainty avoidance, while Germany scored 65, which is at the higher end. For example, the Chinese language is full of ambiguous meanings that can be difficult for Western people to follow. German has a strong preference for deductive rather than inductive approaches to Chinese.

**Novelty.** There is a tendency to pursue novelty in weak uncertainty avoidance society. The idea of weak uncertainty can be summarized as follows: difference encourages curiosity, that is, the desire for novelty. On the contrary, the concept of strong uncertainty avoidance holds that differences are dangerous. Chinese people collect cars from different brands, but German people focus on one brand. It can be inferred that trying new things is the internal demand for freshness.

*Trying New Things.* Trying new things can be a replacement or a change. In low uncertainty avoidance, people are excited about trying new things. There are two UX orientations and some car HMI design guidelines.

One is creative logic, and high uncertainty avoidance products set more strict logic whereas low uncertainty avoidance products weaken it. For example, we found a step-by-step category and detailed guidance to a specific function in a German brand car HMI, but in a low uncertainty avoidance society such as the USA (score of 46), we found many popup windows appear in different sizes and positions according to different tasks in an American brand car HMI. For car HMI design, on a Chinese brand car's navigation interface, the entrance of the foodie map is unusual but can still be accepted by Chinese users (see Fig. 10). We need to come up with better creative interfaces such as touching the navigation arrow and letting it generate several secondary buttons.

**Fig. 10.** Foodie map's entrance.

Another UX orientation is frequent UI updates. The Arena of Valor is the most popular mobile game in China; it has fast version iteration, and the UI style is updated with every version. For car HMI design, UI updates also frequently work in China.

**Accepting Ambiguity and Variety.** The second tendency of weak uncertainty avoidance society is the acceptance of ambiguity and variety. Compared with the strong uncertainty society, the weak uncertainty society can face an ambiguous situation and an unusual risk more calmly. We divide the resulting internal demands into two parts: various information and choices, and no simplicity.

*Various Information and Choices.* In low uncertainty avoidance societies, people are accustomed to dealing with rich information. These societies' products integrate more content while those of high uncertainty avoidance societies have less content. We found JD (see Fig. 11, left) website follows "more is better" strategy that integrates various functions, while the Amazon (see Fig. 11, right) website follows "less is more" strategy and focuses on a single function. For car HMI design, Chinese people tend to put rich information in display media such as digital clusters or HUDs. This is always helpful in reducing the operating step.

**Fig. 11.** The JD website integrates more content than the Amazon website.

*No Simplicity.* People pursue delicacy, not simplicity, in low uncertainty avoidance societies. Delicate details in UX, like dynamic elements, are preferred in low uncertainty avoidance societies. China's ACG website Bilibili (see Fig. 12, left) has more dynamic animation than Niconico (see Fig. 12, right), Japan's ACG website, which has no dynamic animation. For car HMI design, an appropriate dynamic effect is welcome in the Chinese market. It is great to imply dynamic music wave and dynamic icon effect when designing UI.

**Fig. 12.** The Bilibili website has more dynamic animation than the Niconico website.

According to the above analysis, the following guidelines should be considered for the car HMI in the Chinese market:

1) Creative logic to interactions or layouts to build novelty
2) Updating UI frequently to maintain a sense of freshness.
3) Display rich information on the screen because Chinese think "more is better"
4) Use delicate details like the appropriate dynamic effect in UI, instead of the simplicity style.

## 3.5    Restraint Versus Indulgence

Restraint/indulgence is defined as the extent to which people try to control their desires and impulses. Relatively weak control is called "Indulgence" and relatively strong control is called "Restraint" [10]. China is a restrained society, as can be seen in its low score of 24 in this dimension, whereas Germany has a score of 40. In contrast to indulgent societies such as the USA (score of 68), restrained societies do not place much emphasis on leisure time and control the gratification of their desires. People with this orientation perceive that their actions are restrained by social norms and feel that indulging themselves is somewhat wrong.

**Consistency and Balance.** In a restrained society, people always act in a consistent and balanced way. In China, many high schools require girls to keep short hair to suppress their desire to be unique. However, there is usually no such requirement in the USA school system. Consistency and balance create a sense of harmony, which is an internal demand; people in restraint society emphasize the feeling of harmony.

*Harmony.* In UX design, using moderate contrast color to create a sense of harmony is common in restrained society products. For example, the USA website Rotten Tomatoes (see Fig. 13, left) tend to use high saturation and high color contrast, while Chinese apps iQIYI/Youku (see Fig. 13, middle, right) use moderate color contrast. For car HMI design, Chinese brands tend to use low-contrast color blocks; it desaturates color but maintains the differentiation of color blocks at the same time (see Fig. 14).

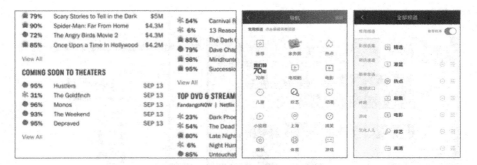

**Fig. 13.** The Rotten Tomatoes website uses a high color contrast while iQIYI/Youku uses a moderate color contrast.

**Fig. 14.** Low contrast color block in Chinese brand car HMI.

**Intuitive Sense.** In restrained societies, people think intuitive expressions are more secure. They prefer figurativeness because things with concrete meanings are easier to understand and accept. Figurativeness is the internal demand when making an intuitive sense of something.

*Figurativeness.* For UX design, figurative images will be better in China. For example, China Airlines' logo shows an almost bird-like figure while those of both American Airlines and British Airways show abstract design ideas, respectively. We can easily find figurative designs such as the deliveryman icon in the take-out app or materialized design car shape icon in the car-hailing app. For car HMI design, the figurative design is enlightening. We can display car simulation in the ADAS (see Fig. 15, left), give animation guidance like informing driver to put the card to start the car, make operation visible (see Fig. 15, right) when adjusting air conditioner or sound, changing the car's color in UI according to the car's real color.

**Fig. 15.** Car simulation in the ADAS and visible operation such as air conditioner adjustment.

According to the above analysis, the following guidelines should be considered for the car HMI in the Chinese market:

1) Moderate color contrast of UI design to create a sense of harmony.
2) Figurative UI design to cater for intuitive expression.

## 4 Conclusion

This study explored a method to define the UX of in-vehicle HMI systems derived by culture. Five of Hofstede's cultural dimensions were selected, including power distance, individualism versus collectivism, long-term orientation versus short-term orientation, uncertain avoidance, and restraint versus indulgence. Chinese customers' special position on the dimensions drives nine internal demands that can be presented with sixteen HMI key guidelines. The result is a structural system that discovers UX differentiation among markets, especially for the Chinese car market.

# References

1. Burns, A.C., Bush, R.F.: Marketing research. Globalization **1**(7), 76–93 (2000)
2. Yu, W.: Insight: let marketing direct to people. Electronic Industry (2018)
3. Hofstede, G.: Cultures and organizations: software of the mind. Adm. Sci. Q. **23**(1), 113–119 (1991)
4. Marcus, A., Gould, E.W.: Crosscurrents: cultural dimensions and global web user-interface design. Interactions **7**(4), 32–46 (2000)
5. Davis, F.D.: Perceived usefulness, perceived ease of use, and user acceptance of information technology. MIS Q. **13**(3), 319–340 (1989)
6. ISO 9241-210:2010: Ergonomics of human-system interaction—Part 210: human-centred design for interactive systems (2010)
7. Thüring, M., Mahlke, S.: Usability, aesthetics and emotions in human–technology interaction. Int. J. Psychol. **42**(4), 253–264 (2007)
8. Hofstede, G.: Cultured Consequences, 2nd edn. Sage, Thousand Oaks (2001)
9. Hofstede, G.: A European in Asia. Asian J. Soc. Psychol. **10**, 16–21 (2007)
10. Hofstede, G., Hofstede, G.J.: Cultures and Organizations. Software of the Mind, 3rd edn. McGraw-Hill, New York (2010)
11. Schwartz, S.H., Bilsky, W.: Toward a universal psychological structure of human values. J. Pers. Soc. Psychol. **53**, 550–562 (1987)
12. Trompenaars, K.: Riding the Waves of Culture: Understanding Cultural Diversity in Btisiness. Nicholas Brealey, London (1993)
13. House, R.J., Hanges, P.J., Javidan, M., Dorfman, P.W., Gupta, V.: Culture, Leadership, and Organizations. The GLOBE Study of 62 Societies. Sage, Thousand Oaks (2004)
14. Mooij, M., Hofstede, G.: The hofstede model applications to global branding and advertising strategy and research. Int. J. Advert. **29**, 85–110 (2010)
15. Aparicio, M., Bacao, F., Oliveira, T.: Cultural impacts on e-learning systems' success. Internet High. Educ. **31**, 58–70 (2016)
16. Matzler, K., Strobl, A., Stokburger-Sauer, N., et al.: Brand personality and culture: the role of cultural differences on the impact of brand personality perceptions on tourists' visit intentions. Tour. Manag. **52**, 507–520 (2016)
17. Hofstede, G.: Culture's Consequences: International Differences in Work-Related Values. Sage, Thousand Oaks (1980)

# User Requirement? Travel Mode Choice Routines Across Different Trip Types

Dorothea Langer[✉] and Angelika C. Bullinger

Ergonomics and Innovation, Chemnitz University of Technology,
09107 Chemnitz, Germany
dorothea.langer@mb.tu-chemnitz.de

**Abstract.** The new concept of Mobility as a Service (MaaS) contains providing access to different travel options such as public transport, car sharing and bike rental by one common digital platform. MaaS development often lacks to take a user-centered view. This can be achieved by aiming to make cognitive user effort as low as possible which is the case in routine behavior. Hence, this study examines how travel mode routines relate to travel mode choice in different situations and what can be derived from that relationship with regard to service design of MaaS. This goal is addressed by a secondary data analysis of 80 questionnaires and mobility diaries from a corporate MaaS pilot study at Chemnitz University of Technology, Germany in 2014. In total, 4198 trips became part of analysis. For these trips, mode choice prediction was done by generalized hierarchical regression modeling with routine measures and trip purposes as predictors. Results showed that in business and leisure situations, car routine strength doesn't predict car use as much as in other situations. Interaction effects imply that even users with high car routine could be susceptible to propositions of alternative transport modes in those situations. With the goal of overcoming car de-pendent routines, this suggests that chances of success are highest in corporate MaaS or tourism services. It could be shown that knowledge about travel mode routines can provide useful information for designing MaaS as genuine alternative or complement to private car usage.

**Keywords:** Travel mode choice routine · User requirement · Mobility as a Service

## 1 Introduction

In recent years, the concept of Mobility as a Service (MaaS) has emerged. It contains providing access to different travel options such as public transport, car sharing, bike rental and others by one common digital platform. Increasing digitalization together with availability of information system solutions enable MaaS and it is regarded as potentially alleviating recent mobility challenges of cities such as traffic congestion, limited parking space, air pollution or noise by providing more efficient usage of means of transport [26].

In contrast to this high expectations, to date few such mobility services actually came into operation and a considerable amount of them are only pilot projects [11, 22]. Furthermore, MaaS literature is often shaped by a questionable optimistic expectation,

© Springer Nature Switzerland AG 2020
C. Stephanidis et al. (Eds.): HCII 2020, LNCS 12429, pp. 111–129, 2020.
https://doi.org/10.1007/978-3-030-59987-4_9

indicating that an operating MaaS will automatically lead to sustainable mobility behavior [19]. A user-centered view on MaaS is rare [17], but there has been psychological research on travel behavior for many years preceding MaaS concept.

## 1.1 Determinants of Travel Mode Choice

Especially travel mode choice has been examined for a long time, often in context of promoting sustainable mobility such as using public transport or active travel modes like walking and cycling [e.g. 2, 9]. Travel behavior is complex, influenced by a wide range of factors, e.g. Gardner and Abraham [7] are listing in their meta-analysis ten determining constructs, Lanzini and Khan [16] even 13 constructs. As this complexity isn't manageable for practical use like service design or policy measures, integrated models of pro-environmental behavior cluster and structure existing knowledge on influencing factors and their interdependencies. The comprehensive action determination model (CADM) was proposed and successfully applied to travel mode choice by Klöckner and Blöbaum [14]. It proposes three classes of processes directly influencing ecological behavior: habitual processes (schemata, heuristics, and associations), intentional processes (intentions and attitudes) and situational influences (objective and subjective constraints). Normative processes (e.g. social and personal norms and values) exert indirect influence on ecological behavior by affecting both habitual and intentional processes. Situational influences impact not only on ecological behavior but also the other three process classes in the model.

## 1.2 The Role of Travel Mode Choice Routine

Habitual processes refer to decisions occurring very often in everyday life, usually under stable conditions, which is also the case with travel mode choice [1]. For a long time, it is well known that in such situations past behavior is the best predictor of future behavior [18]. Verplanken [25, p. 14] define habit as "cue-response associations in memory that are acquired slowly through repetition of an action in a stable circumstance". That makes habitual behavior automated, without binding many cognitive resources, sometimes even exerted unconsciously. Nevertheless, the term 'habit' isn't used consistently, sometimes containing automated behavior and sometimes simply referring to past behavior [16]. Travel mode choice routine is a broader concept which doesn't include automation and repetition assumption but decisions based on prior knowledge which could also be collected in few experiences [4]. Of course, this concept covers automated, habitual choices as well. Therefore, in this paper the term "mode choice routine" is used instead of habit, and is based on past behavior.

In everyday life, many mobility situations are recurring and from user perspective, the mobility problem is already solved with the solution he or she chose last time. Routine behavior is a learned reaction to a well-known situation, resulting in low cognitive effort [4]. Users tend to choose mobility alternatives with cognitive effort as low as possible [17] making routine behavior in stable environments hard to change. Consequently, habit is seen as one of the most crucial obstacles for wide adoption of new mobility services that needs to be overcome [13, 26].

But is it helpful to regard a mechanism beneficial to the individual as an obstacle to be worked against? Maybe a new perspective on travel routines needs to be taken. Schikofsky, Dannewald and Kowald [20] propose the concept of heuristic habitual schemas that people form based on typical usage patterns in familiar domains: If there are new services people don't have experience with, habitual schemas are transferred if service characteristics fit the learned schema (habit schema congruence). Taking new mobility services like MaaS into account, the more applicable an already established schema such as travel mode choice routine is, the more easily it can be deployed to MaaS. For example, designing MaaS features along existing routines could possibly address habitual car users to see MaaS as feasible complement to private car use. As a result, if applicability of travel routine was regarded as a highly important user requirement, it could be used for designing mobility services better fitting to actual processes of travel mode choice decisions.

### 1.3   The Role of Situational Influences

A second class of processes directly influencing ecological behavior in CADM is situational influence. Klöckner and Blöbaum [14] include objective and subjective situational constraints into their CADM model. From a design perspective objective situational factors are interesting primarily, because those are the factors a MaaS provider can adapt to or influence to some extent. Unfortunately, situational influences are most commonly represented indirectly in psychological travel mode choice research. As so, it is usually measured by perceived behavioral control, which is a subjective evaluation of situational possibilities and limitations, rather than objective circumstances [7, 16].

On an aggregated level, national mobility surveys provide knowledge on relationships between objective situational characteristics and resulting travel mode chosen, for example by comparing trip purposes as classes of similar situational characteristics. For example, the German mobility survey MiD [10] shows that approximately 63% of trips to work or business trips are travelled by car or motorbike, whereas this is the case only on 47% of leisure trips. On the contrary, 13% of trips to work are travelled by cycling which is comparable to the proportion of leisure trips (12%), but only 5% of business trips are travelled by bicycle. Hydén et al. [9] report differences in people's statements regarding possibilities for replacing car by walking or cycling for different trip purposes. Respondents stated that commuting to work and leisure trips can be easiest replaced by bicycle whereas shopping trips are easiest replaceable by walking. The car is seen as most necessary on transport trips to pick up or drop-off someone. This indicates that overall situational characteristics of different trip purposes exert considerable influence on travel mode choice.

There are also investigations explicitly addressing the trip purpose commuting, which according to MiD [10] constitutes 20% of all trips. They also report objective constraints that influence mode choice for commuting to work. For example, physical structure of residence area substantially shapes mode choice at commuting trips [21]. Clark, Chatterjee and Melia [5] showed that commute mode is very stable over time, especially with car commuters, but when altering residence or job, changed objective conditions such as trip length, high-quality public transport infrastructure and mixed land use support mode switches away from car.

### 1.4 Routine as a User Requirement Across Different Trip Purposes?

However, it remains unclear whether average situational determinants are applicable to all users equally. People with strong car routines could require a car in every situation whereas people with weaker routine act more flexible depending on trip purpose. It is therefore crucial for MaaS operators to know which options should be offered to meet users' requirements. For example, when providing mobility service for tourists, users' travel mode choice might depend less on routine processes because leisure travel situations are more new and few routine responses have been established. On the other hand, services targeting on commuters might heavily depend on knowledge about users' routine patterns because trips to job or education site occur often and in stable circumstances, fostering establishment of routine behavior. Indeed, in stable commuting contexts, habits moderate how change intentions effect travel mode choice behavior, with strong habits preventing mode change [6].

Therefore, analyzing the interaction between routine patterns and trip purposes should allow testing the following research question: Can travel mode choice routine be used as user requirement for designing mobility services fitting to actual processes of travel mode choice decisions? Hence, this study examines how travel mode routines relate to travel mode choice in different situations and what can be derived from that relationship with regard to service design of MaaS.

## 2   Methods

Research question was addressed by a secondary data analysis of questionnaires and mobility diaries of a corporate MaaS pilot study at Chemnitz University of Technology, Germany in 2014.

### 2.1  Procedure

This MaaS was conceptualized to provide different travel modes to university employees for business travel. Employees could apply for participation in the pilot study via online questionnaire. This screening questionnaire assessed information regarding demographics, mobility, and participation requirements such as driver license, active employment relationship as well as consent with data collection.

Afterwards, applicants fulfilling the participation requirements were asked to fill in travel diaries over the course of two weeks approximately one month apart. Recorded weeks needed to contain at least three regular working days to include part-time workers as well. Diary assessment was splitted to compensate for differences in situational circumstances as for instance weather extremes, holidays or sickness absence. According to application time of participants recorded diary weeks spread over the course of April to October. But data collection was finished before 300th calendar day (on October 26th) where a decrease of leisure travel in autumn could be expected [27].

Only a relevant excerpt of screening and diary questions is reported here. More details can be found in [15].

## 2.2    Participants

Ninety-eight individuals submitted complete application information for participating in the pilot study, with eleven not meeting the participation requirements (two lacking an active employment relationship and two giving no consent of data collection). From the remaining participants, seven didn't submit a travel diary and were therefore excluded from analysis. The remaining sample consisted of eighty university employees with an average age of 32.6 years ($SD = 7.8$), 25 (31%) participants were female. This sample was not representative for general population in Germany but rather a more homogenous sample of higher education and middle age. The smaller amount of woman in the sample corresponded roughly to the amount of female employees at Chemnitz University of Technology at this time which was 38%.

Due to participation requirements for the pilot study, all participants owned a driver license. At least one bicycle was available in households of 75 participants (94%) and at least one car in households of 68 participants (85%). These amounts were somewhat higher than in average households in Germany of the same year with 65,8% and 77.5% (77.2% when owning driver license) respectively [27]. This discrepancy was maybe due to socio-economic status of the sample. A season ticket for public transport was owned by 17 participants, which equals 21.3% versus 20.1% in Germany [27].

## 2.3    Measures

The Screening questionnaire asked for participants' customary usage of travel modes car, bicycle and public transport. Questions regarded the average amount of kilometers per month driven by car and bicycle. As in test trials beforehand kilometers per public transport were difficult to estimate, average number of occasions per month using public transport were asked. Additionally, participants were asked to estimate the number of days within an average week they normally use each of the transport modes. Answers to the latter questions were restricted to numbers between zero and seven. Moreover, an open question asked for extraordinary characteristics of participants' mobility relevant for their statements in the questionnaire.

Travel diaries were designed according to the travel diary of the annual German mobility survey MOP in its version of 2013 [12]. They assessed information on each trip of the participants, including trip purposes, modes used, start and arrival times as well as trip distances. Notwithstanding the MOP diary, trip purpose/destination "education site" was combined with "job site", because this would be identical for present sample of university employees. Therefore, trip purposes collected were job/education site (denoted as *office* hereinafter), *business, errands/shopping, leisure, transport* (pickup, drop-off), *home*, and *other* (with field to specify). Additionally, means of public transport in MOP diary bus, tram, metro and train were combined to category "public transport". Thus travel modes were assessed via the categories walking, bicycle, motorcycle, car as driver, car as passenger, public transport, and other (with field to specify). Collection of trip distances was divided into sequential stages with different modes used within a single trip, and main transportation mode was assigned according to mode of the longest sequential trip stage.

## 2.4    Data Preparation and Analysis

Participants' statements of kilometers per month by car and bicycle (which constituted one of two routine measures) were cross-validated using answers on questions in screening questionnaire for extraordinary characteristics in participants' mobility as well as data of corresponding travel diaries. For doing so, distance of daily commute trips was estimated from participants' residential address and job site via Google Maps (shortest route per car). Furthermore, distances of participants' trips by car and by bicycle over the course of the diary weeks were summed up and divided by two to get an average week estimate. Both measures were plotted against abovementioned routine measures and looked for considerable discrepancies. In two cases stated routine km per month by car were higher than 10000 km, exceeding explainable distances massively and probably representing kilometers per year. Hence they were divided by twelve.

Trip data from travel diaries were cleaned due to some missing values regarding trip purpose and mode used. In total, 47 trips had to be excluded from analysis due to missing data. Travel modes car as driver, car as passenger and motorcycle were combined to one mode, hereafter denoted as motorized. Moreover, trip purposes denoted *other* were assigned to one of the prescribed categories, drawing on specification notes of participants. For example, hiking, playground, sports, and choir were assigned with *leisure* category, whereas supermarket, visit to the doctor or to the authorities, and refueling were assigned with *errands/shopping* category. In total, 403 trip purposes were assigned this way. For 47 trips participants marked more than one purpose. To achieve distinct trip categories, office and home were handled superior to transport followed by errands/shopping and leisure as lowest in hierarchy. This resulted in 4198 trips in total.

Due to hierarchical data structure with trip data (purposes) nested within person data (travel mode routine), prediction of mode choice was done by hierarchical regression modeling. Because mode choice is a categorical outcome, generalized linear models were applied, specified as binomial with logit link function. All routine measures were grand-mean-centered, so that mean routine builds the reference point of analysis. As routine measures referred to single travel modes, probability estimation of their corresponding usage was conducted in three hierarchical regression models separately. E.g. for estimating the effect of car routine across different trip purposes the outcome variable car usage coded with 1 for a trip done by car and 0 for a trip traveled by another mode was used. This allowed for analyzing the information gained through the respective routine measure separately. All analyses were done using IBM SPSS Statistics.

Only fifty-five of the participants delivered travel-diaries for two weeks with the remaining participants just covering one. In multilevel analyses of nested data, number of clusters (in this case participants) is more important than number of observations within those clusters [24]. To achieve sufficient sample size, it was decided to include all participants with corresponding diary data into multilevel modelling.

# 3 Results

## 3.1 Properties of Trip Purpose, Mode Choice Routine Measures, and Modal Split

**Trip Purpose.** Frequencies of different trip purposes in the sample are depicted in Fig. 1. *Home* (28%) and *leisure* (26.1%) were the most frequent trips in the sample. They were followed by trips to *office* (17.8%, including daily commute as well as other trips like way back from lunch break), and by trips for *errands and shopping* (12.1%). Very specialized purposes like *business* (9%) and *transport* trips (7.1%) occurred least often.

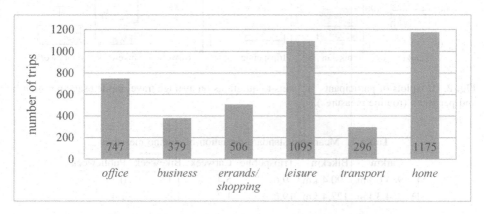

**Fig. 1.** Number of trips per purpose (total$_N$ = 4198)

**Travel Mode Choice Routine.** Routine measures of past behavior were chosen for simplicity of assessment. Statistical properties regarding distribution and relationships between them help evaluating their applicability as user requirements and interpreting their predictive value to travel mode choice later on. Therefore, they are considered in more detail.

Distribution information are shown in Fig. 2. None of the routine measures followed a normal distribution. Most of them were right-skewed, except carweek, which was the number of days within an average week participants normally use a car. Besides, on all routine measures a couple of outliers could be found. All of this should be taken into account when interpreting results of multilevel regressions later on. In regression models, routine measures were grand-mean centered with values presented in Table 1, to create a reference point of average routine. Due to skewness of distribution, average routine actually lay considerably above (and in carweek below, respectively) the most frequent value of routine measures. Spoken in terms of content, regression estimation of 'average' routine referred to a relatively high (carweek: low) routine manifestation in the sample.

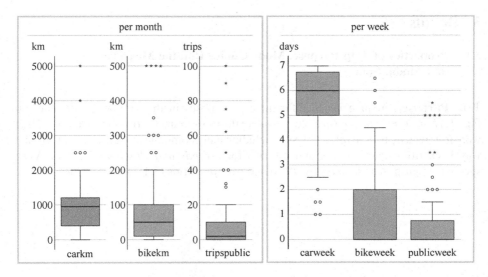

**Fig. 2.** Boxplots of participants' answers to questions on average travel mode usage per month and per week (routine measures).

**Table 1.** Mean and standard deviation of routine measures

|    | Carkm | Bikekm | Tripspublic | Carweek | Bikeweek | Publicweek |
|----|-------|--------|-------------|---------|----------|------------|
| M  | 984.0 km | 90.4 km | 9.6 | 5.4 | 1.1 | 0.7 |
| SD | 864.3 km | 127.4 km | 19.6 | 1.7 | 1.7 | 1.4 |

Furthermore, relationships between the several routine measures were calculated. Due to variables' skewness, assumption of linearity could be violated. Hence, locally weighted scatterplot smoothing (loess) was applied to achieve linearity and, when necessary, variables were transformed accordingly to calculate valid correlations. Car routine measures ln(carkm) and carweek^3 showed the smoothing line closest to linearity and resulted in Pearson's correlation coefficient of r = .519 (p < .001). Relationship of bicycle as well as public transport routine measures didn't require smoothing resulting in r = .634 (p < .001) and r = .740 (p < .001), respectively.

**Travel Mode Choice.** Modal split in the sample is depicted in Fig. 3, in comparison to German population in 2014 according to MOP data [27]. A visual check suggested higher amount of motorized trips in the sample at the expense of trips by public transport. Chi-square testing was used to compare modal split in sample to the one in population. No expected cell frequencies were below 5. Results showed that difference between sample and population modal split was significant, although effect size was small ($\chi^2$(4, N = 4198) = 214.89, $p < .001$, $\varphi_{Cramer}$ = 0.16).

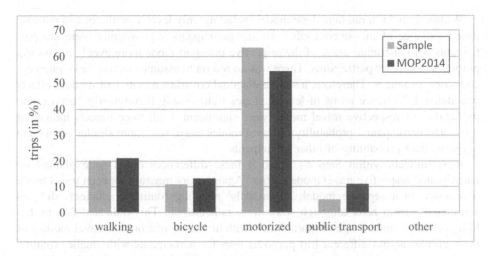

**Fig. 3.** Modal split in recent sample and German population according to MOP2014

## 3.2 Multilevel Modelling of Mode Usage Probability by Trip Purpose and Travel Mode Choice Routine

Informative quality of routine measures introduced previously was tested by predicting probability of corresponding mode choice regarding different trip purposes. Modeling was done for the modes motorized, bicycle and public transport separately, and each time in a stepwise procedure as recommended by Heck, Thomas and Tabata [8]. Fit indices of the subsequent models weren't compared directly because logit multilevel modelling involves rescaling of level-1 variance each time variables are added to the model. Therefore, comparisons between models based on resulting pseudolikelihood values to estimate reduction in variance may not be accurate [8]. Instead, individual parameters and residuals were examined to determine possible sources of misfits. Parameter estimates did not change much over subsequent models. Thus, only result values of final models are reported. Yet, the appendix exemplarily illustrates whole model history (except empty model) with all results for motorized travel mode.

**Model History.** Within Step #1, an empty model was run without predictors to test for sufficient variance in probabilities of travel mode usage between participants for each travel mode separately. In case of sufficient variance multilevel modelling is justified. All three empty models resulted in significant random intercept variance terms ($p < .001$) and considerable intra-class correlation (ICC) with $ICC_{motorized} = .470$, $ICC_{bicycle} = .608$, and $ICC_{publictransport} = .500$.

Within Step #2, a random intercept model including only level-1 predictor trip purpose was run. It tested the overall effect, whether different situation parameters of trip purposes gave rise to differences in participants' mode use. Purpose *office* was chosen as reference category because literature review testified situational conditions influencing mode choice behavior on commuting trips. Unfortunately, only probability of motorized travel modes for *transport* purposes compared to *office* purpose differed significantly.

Within Step #3, a random slope model including only level-1 predictor trip purpose tested variance of this overall effect among participants, e.g. whether there are participants who distribute usage of the respective transport mode more evenly across trip purposes than other participants. There was no reason to assume covariance of intercept and slope variances. Therefore, a simple diagonal covariance matrix of random effects was defined. Variance terms of level-1 slopes (relationship between trip purpose and probability of respective travel mode) were significant in all three models indicating that some participants' probability of travel modes usage was more similar across trip purposes than probability of other participants.

Next, models within Step #4 tested if these differences could be explained by participants' respective travel mode routine. Again, every measure for each travel mode was tested in a separate model. All models' resulting routine coefficients differed significantly from zero, although some were rather small. This indicated that probability of travel mode usage for participants with higher routine on that travel mode was more similar across different trip purposes than for participants with smaller routine. Furthermore, level-1 slope variance values again differed from zero significantly.

Hence, within a last Step #5, cross-level interaction between purpose and routine measures were added to the models. Those final models tested the assumption that routine intensity moderates the relationship just found in the step before. Results of those final models can be found in Table 2 (month-related routine measures carkm, bikekm and tripspublic) and Table 3 (week-related routine measures carweek, bikeweek and publicweek).

**Predicting Motorized Transport Modes.** Odds ratio intercepts indicated that for an average participant using motorized transport for a trip was approximately 2.5 times more probable than using another travel mode on that trip (with holding other predictors and the random effects constant at Zero, e.g. participants, with mean routine regarding motorized transport modes, on *office* trips).

Considering trip purposes in both models, only coefficients for *transport* trips were significant, which means *transport* purposes increased probability of using motorized modes, compared to *office* trips. Spoken in odds ratios, for an average participant using motorized travel modes at a *transport* trip was almost four times more probable than at an *office* trip (again with other predictors and random effects being Zero). Trip purposes *errands/shopping* and *home* seemed to slightly increase probability of motorized transport modes too, whereas trips for *business* and *leisure* purposes seemed to decrease this probability. However, coefficient standard errors for those purposes were almost as large as coefficient values, making those tendencies unreliable.

Regression coefficients for routine measures carkm and carweek were both significant. Nevertheless, for variable carkm, coefficient and consequently odds ratio were infinitesimal providing no practical information. Odds ratio of the other car-related routine measure carweek suggested that increasing one standard deviation (SD) in terms of days per week using a car increased probability of using motorized travel modes by 1.120 log odds units compared with participants of average car routine (holding other effects constant). In terms of odds ratios, as routine measure carweek was increased by one standard deviation, the odds of using a car were multiplied by 3.066 (an increase of 306.6%).

**Table 2.** Multilevel logit regression results predicting use of transport modes motorized, bicycle and public transport respectively, by trip purpose on level 1 and corresponding month-related habit measures on level 2 with cross-level interaction; bold: significant coefficients (B, u) with $p < .05$; standard errors (SE); odds ratios (OR)

| Model: | carkm | | | bikekm | | | tripspublic | | |
|---|---|---|---|---|---|---|---|---|---|
| Fixed effects | B | SE | OR | B | SE | OR | B | SE | OR |
| Constant | **.915** | .274 | 2.498 | **-3.515** | .360 | .030 | **-.4671** | .430 | .009 |
| routine | **.001** | .000 | 1.001 | **.011** | .002 | 1.011 | **.080** | .019 | 1.083 |
| purpose | | | | | | | | | |
| business | -.297 | .311 | .743 | -.737 | .498 | .479 | **1.796** | .497 | 6.028 |
| errands | .159 | .226 | 1.172 | .107 | .355 | 1.113 | -.090 | .591 | .914 |
| leisure | -.329 | .220 | .720 | -.399 | .352 | .671 | .541 | .511 | 1.718 |
| transport | **1.309** | .318 | 3.703 | -1.108 | .563 | 0.33 | .319 | .634 | 1.375 |
| home | .265 | .180 | 1.303 | .067 | .218 | 1.070 | .312 | .445 | 1.366 |
| base = *office* | | | | | | | | | |
| routine*purpose | | | | | | | | | |
| ...*business | -.001 | .000 | .999 | .000 | .003 | 1.000 | **-.051** | .016 | .950 |
| ...*errands | .000 | .000 | 1.000 | .001 | .002 | 1.001 | -.021 | .016 | .980 |
| ...*leisure | **-.001** | .000 | .999 | -.001 | .002 | .999 | -.034 | .013 | .967 |
| ...*transport | .000 | .000 | 1.000 | .003 | .003 | 1.003 | -.061 | .029 | .941 |
| ...*home | .000 | .000 | 1.000 | .000 | .001 | 1.000 | -.017 | .011 | .983 |
| base = ...*office | | | | | | | | | |
| Random effects | u | SE | . | u | SE | . | u | SE | . |
| Constant | **2.614** | .519 | . | **3.238** | .737 | . | **2.024** | .528 | . |
| purpose | **.741** | .128 | . | **.730** | .193 | . | .353 | .207 | . |
| -2Log-Likelihood | 20 661.347 | | | 26 420.812 | | | 28 025.187 | | |
| Classification accuracy | 80.9 % | | | 91.7 % | | | 95.3 % | | |
| guess probability | 63.3 % | | | 89.3 % | | | 94.9 % | | |

Variance of purpose slopes was significant suggesting a moderating effect, in other words, some participants distributed use of motorized travel modes more evenly across trip purposes than other participants.

Cross-level interaction estimates for routine measure carkm again were negligible. Regarding carweek, cross-level interaction indicated a moderating effect, which showed that the effect of car routine varied with levels of trip purpose. Cross-level interactions were significant for trip purposes *business* and *leisure*. As stated above, main effects of those two trip purposes were slightly negative (although not significant). Significant negative interaction terms indicated that increases in car routine intensified the negative effect of *business* and *leisure* trips on the probability of using motorized

**Table 3.** Multilevel logit regression results predicting use of transport modes motorized and bicycle respectively, by trip purpose on level 1 and corresponding week-related habit measures on level 2 with cross-level interaction; model for public transport failed to converge; bold: significant coefficients (B, u) with p < .05; standard errors (SE); odds ratios (OR)

| Model: | carweek | | | bikeweek | | |
| Variable | B | SE | OR | B | SE | OR |
| --- | --- | --- | --- | --- | --- | --- |
| Constant | **.804** | .224 | 2.235 | **-3.589** | .348 | .028 |
| routine | **1.120** | .142 | 3.066 | **1.208** | .154 | 3.345 |
| purpose | | | | | | |
| business | -.316 | .291 | .729 | .222 | .479 | 1.249 |
| errands | .179 | .236 | 1.196 | .310 | .444 | 1.364 |
| leisure | -.293 | .225 | .746 | -.080 | .464 | .923 |
| transport | **1.390** | .336 | 4.016 | -2.894 | 1.554 | .055 |
| home | .315 | .190 | 1.370 | .075 | .302 | 1.078 |
| base = office | | | | | | |
| routine*purpose | | | | | | |
| ...*business | **-.630** | .180 | .533 | **-.564** | .147 | .569 |
| ...*errands | -.232 | .167 | .793 | -.092 | .209 | .912 |
| ...*leisure | **-.564** | .146 | .569 | -.222 | .146 | .801 |
| ...*transport | -.003 | .240 | .997 | .662 | .486 | 1.939 |
| ...*home | -.153 | .131 | .858 | .055 | .140 | 1.057 |
| base = ...*office | | | | | | |
| Random effects | u | SE | . | u | SE | . |
| Constant | **.936** | .231 | . | .295 | .184 | . |
| purpose | **.732** | .125 | . | **.669** | .187 | . |
| -2Log-Likelihood | 20 522.180 | | | 26 355.875 | | |
| Classification accuracy | 81.0 % | | | 91.7 % | | |
| guess probability | 63.3 % | | | 89.3 % | | |

travel modes. More specifically, for a 1-SD increase in car routine above the grand mean, the average log odds of motorized travel were increased by 0.630 units on *business* trips and 0.564 on *leisure* trips respectively.

Again, odds ratios were calculated. For *business* trips of people with strong car routine (one standard deviation above grand mean in carweek measure), the odds were multiplied by 0.729 (or reduced by 27.1%). So, people with strong car routine showed lower probability of traveling motorized on *business* trips compared to *business* trips by people of more average car routine, adjusted for other predictors in the model. Results were the same for *leisure* trips, with odds being multiplied by 0.569 (reduced by 43.1%). This was against the expectation that high routine intensifies usage of motorized travel modes across all trip purposes. However, the result should be regarded with some caution, since main effects of business and leisure trips were unreliable due to high standard errors.

Classification accuracy exceeded guess probability (proportion of motorized trips) considerably, indicating gain of predictive quality with the models.

**Predicting Cycling.** Odds ratio intercepts indicated that for an average participant cycling at a trip is approximately as probable as using another travel mode on that trip (with holding other predictors and the random effects constant at Zere, e.g. participants, with mean routine regarding cycling, on *office* trips).

Considering trip purposes in both models, no coefficients were significant, which means the compared purposes didn't differ in probability of cycling from *office* trips. Regression coefficients for routine measures bikekm and bikeweek were both significant. Nevertheless, like with carkm before, for variable bikekm coefficient and odds ratio were very small, providing no practical information. Odds ratio of the other bicycle-related routine measure bikeweek suggested that increasing one standard deviation (SD) in terms of days per week using a bicycle increased probability of cycling by 1.208 log odds units compared with participants of average bicycle routine (holding other effects constant). In terms of odds ratios, as routine measure bikeweek was increased by one standard deviation, the odds of cycling were multiplied by 3.345 (an increase of 334.5%).

Variance of purpose slopes were significant suggesting a moderating effect, in other words, some participants distributed cycling probability more evenly across trip purposes than other participants.

Cross-level interaction estimates for routine measure bikekm again were negligible. Regarding bikeweek, cross-level interaction was significant for trip purpose *business*, indicating a moderating effect. Main effect of business trips was slightly positive (although not significant). The significant negative interaction term indicated that increases in bicycle routine decreased the positive effect of *business* trips on the probability of cycling. More specifically, for a 1-SD increase in bicycle routine above the grand mean, the average log odds of cycling were diminished by 0.564 units on *business* trips. Again, odds ratios were calculated. For business trips of people with strong bicycle routine (one standard deviation above grand mean in bikeweek measure) the odds were multiplied by 0.569 (or reduced by 43.1%). So, people with strong bicycle routine showed lower probability of cycling on *business* trips, compared to business trips by people of more average bicycle routine, adjusted for other predictors in the model. This was against the expectation, that high routine intensifies cycling across all trip purposes. However, the result should be regarded with some caution, since main effect of *business* wasn't significant.

Classification accuracy mirrored findings of mainly insignificant coefficients, exceeding guess probability (proportion cycling trips) only marginally. However, guess probability was very high due to relatively few trips by bicycle in the sample. Therefore, power to detect effects could be too small because of insufficient sample size.

**Predicting use of Public Transport.** Only final model with level-2 variable tripspublic did converge. Calculating probability of public transport use shared the problem found with cycling models before. In relation to total trip number, trips with public transport were few, causing small sample sizes especially for trip purposes occurring less frequently. Consequently, even if the model converged with routine variable tripspublic, it is very likely that power to detect effects was limited.

Odds ratio intercepts indicated that for an average participant using public transport at a given trip was approximately as probable as using another travel mode on that trip (again holding other predictors and the random effects constant).

Considering trip purposes, a very large effect was found regarding *business* trips, which means *business* purposes increased probability of using public transport, compared to *office* trips. Spoken in odds ratios, for an average participant using public transport at a *business* trip was approximately six times more probable than on a trip to the *office* (again with other predictors and random effects being Zero). All other trip purposes except *errands/shopping* seemed to slightly increase probability of using public transport too. However, coefficient standard errors for those purposes were almost as large as coefficient values, making those tendencies unreliable.

Regression coefficient for routine measure tripspublic was significant, but rather small. Odds ratio of tripspublic suggested, that increasing one standard deviation (SD) in terms of days per week one uses public transport, odds travelling with public transport increased by the factor 1.083 (an increase of 8.3%).

Variance of purpose slopes was not significant, suggesting moderating effect unlikely or too small to detect. However, cross-level interaction of tripspublic was significant for trip purpose *business*, indicating a moderating effect. As stated above, main effect of *business* trips was large. The significant negative interaction term indicated that increases in public transport routine slightly decreased the positive effect of *business* trips on the probability of public transport use. Odds ratios showed that this effect was very small with odds multiplied by 0.950 (or reduced by 5%) as public transport routine increased by one SD. Classification accuracy was high, but due to small overall proportion of trips by public transport means, guess probability was high too, leaving not much variance to be explained by model variables.

## 4 Discussion

The present study shows that travel mode choice routine improves predicting travel mode choice across several trip purposes. This is promising for using them as user requirements when designing new mobility services.

Results regarding motorized transport were most informative. The largest proportion of trips was traveled by motorized means of transport and odds ratio intercepts indicate that for an average participant using motorized transport for a trip is more probable than using another travel mode. Odds ratio of car-related routine measures suggest that increasing them increases probability of using motorized travel modes, compared with participants of average car routine. Cross-level interactions indicate a moderating effect of car routine on travel mode choice in different situations, more precisely, for business and leisure trips. This suggests that in different situations, travel mode choice follows corresponding routine to a varying extend, which should be considered for MaaS design. At sites where frequent transport trips are expectable, e.g. at shopping malls or public transport hubs, high car demand is expectable, independent of users' travel routine. Therefore, such sites need to be equipped by a relatively high proportion of cars to meet users' requirements.

Designing MaaS that way along user' routines could reduce cognitive effort needed for using. From a users' perspective this would ease switching from private car use to MaaS use [17]. In consequence, users with strong car routine can be expected to first and foremost use car-based MaaS offers, potentially diminishing environmental gain [19]. But also shared cars save space and reduce pollution, especially when hybrid or electric cars are used [3]. Furthermore, beginning MaaS car usage could bridge usage toward more flexible mode choice behavior. This is in line with findings of Sochor et al. [23], who found that even mode choice of MaaS users keeping their car shifted towards a more sustainable direction and their share of public transport trips increased. Moreover, results of the present study show that in *business* and *leisure* situations, routine strength doesn't predict car usage as much as in other situations. With the goal of overcoming car dependent routines, this suggests that chances of success are highest in corporate or tourism MaaS offers. Interaction effects imply that even users with high car routine could be susceptible to propositions of alternative transport modes in those situations.

However, regression models regarding bike and public transport were less informative, mainly due to small proportion of those trips raising guess probability to 89% and 95% respectively. Hence, findings are limited and open questions regarding choice of bicycle and public transport remain.

Considering trip purposes, *transport* increases probability of using motorized modes, compared to reference *office* trips. But for other trip purposes and travel modes, effects were small with large coefficient standard errors making tendencies unreliable. Hence, trip purposes alone are not sufficient to differentiate mode usage in all situations from one another and some amount of unexplained variance remains.

## 4.1 Limitations and Future Research

To examine how travel mode routines relate to travel mode choice in different situations, and what can be derived from that relationship with regard to service design of MaaS, CADM [14] is applied incompletely in this study. In a next step, the other influencing factors of CADM, namely intentional and normative processes including mutual interactions, should be included as well. Additionally, with trip purposes only very broad categories of situational conditions are considered. This can only be a starting point to evaluate whether seeing travel mode choice as a user requirement can be useful to derive information for designing MaaS. Further research should include more precise situation information on trips and how they are perceived by the user.

Furthermore, a very broad routine conceptualization is applied here based on previous travel mode use. Frequency-based routine measures performed better in prediction than distance based measures, at least for car and bicycle. Public transport routine was operationalized only with frequency-based measures, but results weren't interpretable. Perhaps distance based measures are more dependent on strongly varying situation conditions like distance between home and frequent goals of participants, whereas frequency-based routine measures may be closer to the previous goal behavior forming a routine. But all included measures showed skewed distributions and limited variance due to ceiling effects. Moreover, two values of routine variable carkm had to be corrected due to cross-validation of data, presuming erroneous statement of participants' kilometers per year. Therefore, future research should aim to use more elaborate routine measures, preferably differentiating between automated habitual processes and situational stability based routines. This would allow a better understanding of determining situational characteristics and support deducting more detailed MaaS design recommendations.

Questions with respect to travel mode routines regarding cycling and public transport use cannot be answered in the present study. This is unsatisfying, because if there were cycling or public transport routines that could be used successfully as user requirements for designing MaaS and facilitating sustainable mode usage, this could help to unfold environmental potential of MaaS most effectively. Hence, larger samples with higher share of cycling and public transport trips, possibly also containing more detailed situational information, should be investigated.

Last but not least, in this study examination of routine processes is limited to everyday mobility behavior. Transferability and effects on mode choice behavior in MaaS should be examined in real MaaS applications.

## 4.2    Conclusion

This study examined how travel mode routines relate to travel mode choice in different situations and what can be derived from that relationship with regard to service design of MaaS. Development of MaaS needs to take the user perspective into account. This aim can be achieved by making cognitive user effort as low as possible which is the case in routine behavior. Hence, this goal was addressed by a secondary data analysis of questionnaires and mobility diaries from a corporate MaaS pilot study. Mode choice prediction was done by generalized hierarchical regression modeling with routine measures and trip purposes as predictors. Results show that in business and leisure situations, car routine strength doesn't predict car use as much as in other situations. Interaction effects imply that even users with high car routine could be susceptible to propositions of alternative transport modes in those situations. With the goal of overcoming car dependent routines, this suggests that chances of success are highest in corporate MaaS or tourism services. It could be shown that regarding travel mode routines as a user requirement can provide useful information for designing MaaS as genuine alternative or complement to private car usage.

# Appendix

**Appendix:** Model history for travel mode car. Coefficients (B) **bold**, when p < .05; Standard Error (SE); Odds Ratio (OR); variance terms (u)

| Model: | Lvl-1-Intercept | | | Level-1-Slope | | | Level-2-Intercept carkm | | | X-Lvl-interaction carkm | | | Level-2-Intercept carweek | | | X-Lvl-interaction carweek | | |
|---|---|---|---|---|---|---|---|---|---|---|---|---|---|---|---|---|---|---|
| Fixed effects: | B | SE | OR | B | SE | OR | B | SE | OR | B | SE | OR | B | SE | OR | B | SE | OR |
| Constant | **.859** | .259 | 2.360 | **.912** | .285 | 2.489 | **.906** | .271 | 2.474 | **.915** | .274 | 2.498 | **.821** | .271 | 2.274 | **.804** | .224 | 2.235 |
| routine | | | | | | | **.001** | .000 | 1.001 | **.001** | .000 | 1.001 | **.810** | .000 | 2.248 | **1.120** | .142 | 3.066 |
| *purpose* | | | | | | | | | | | | | | | | | | |
| business | -.350 | .300 | .704 | -.309 | .317 | .734 | -.316 | .317 | .729 | -.297 | .311 | .743 | -.307 | .317 | .736 | -.316 | .291 | .729 |
| errands | .212 | .202 | 1.236 | .141 | .218 | 1.152 | .147 | .217 | 1.158 | .159 | .226 | 1.172 | .157 | .217 | 1.170 | .179 | .236 | 1.196 |
| leisure | -.292 | .223 | .747 | -.324 | .231 | .723 | -.324 | .232 | .724 | -.329 | .220 | .720 | -.322 | .232 | .725 | -.293 | .225 | .746 |
| transport | **1.285** | .295 | 3.616 | **1.295** | .309 | 3.653 | **1.298** | .310 | 3.662 | **1.309** | .318 | 3.703 | **1.296** | .310 | 3.653 | **1.390** | .336 | 4.016 |
| home | .277 | .158 | 1.319 | .260 | .171 | 1.297 | .260 | .171 | 1.297 | .265 | .180 | 1.303 | .280 | .171 | 1.323 | .315 | .190 | 1.370 |
| base = *office* | | | | | | | | | | | | | | | | | | |
| *routine*purpose* | | | | | | | | | | | | | | | | | | |
| ...*business | | | | | | | | | | **-.001** | .000 | .999 | | | | **-.630** | .180 | .533 |
| ...*errands | | | | | | | | | | .000 | .000 | 1.000 | | | | -.232 | .167 | .793 |
| ...*leisure | | | | | | | | | | **-.001** | .000 | .999 | | | | **-.564** | .146 | .569 |
| ...*transport | | | | | | | | | | .000 | .000 | 1.000 | | | | -.003 | .240 | .997 |
| ...*home | | | | | | | | | | .000 | .000 | 1.000 | | | | -.153 | .131 | .858 |
| base = ...*office | | | | | | | | | | | | | | | | | | |
| **Random effects** | u | SE | | u | SE | | u | SE | | u | SE | | u | SE | | u | SE | |
| Constant | **2.888** | .533 | | **2.900** | .567 | | **2.596** | .519 | | **2.614** | .519 | | **2.874** | .519 | | **2.936** | .231 | |
| purpose | | | | **.830** | .133 | | **.834** | .133 | | **.741** | .128 | | **.835** | .133 | | **.835** | .125 | |
| Classification accuracy | 78.3 % | | | 81.0 % | | | 81.0 % | | | 80.9 % | | | 80.9 % | | | 81.0 % | | |
| **Model fit** | | | | | | | | | | | | | | | | | | |
| -2 Log-Likelihood | 20 368.148 | | | 20 464.177 | | | 20 479.452 | | | 20 661.347 | | | 20 348.619 | | | 20 522.180 | | |
| Akaike (corrected) | 20 370.149 | | | 20 468.179 | | | 20 483.455 | | | 20 665.350 | | | 20 352.622 | | | 20 526.183 | | |
| Bayes | 20 376.489 | | | 20 480.858 | | | 20 496.134 | | | 20 678.026 | | | 20 365.301 | | | 20 538.859 | | |

# References

1. Bamberg, S.: Alltagsmobilität und Verkehrsmittelwahl. In: Lantermann, E.-D. (ed.) Serie IX. Enzyklopädie der Psychologie. Grundlagen, Paradigmen und Methoden der Umweltpsychologie, vol. 2, pp. 549–592. Hogrefe, Göttingen (2010)
2. Bamberg, S., Schmidt, P.: Changing travel-mode choice as rational choice: Results from a longitudinal intervention study. Rational. Soc. 10(2), 223–252 (1998). https://doi.org/10.1177/104346398010002005
3. Baptista, P., Melo, S., Rolim, C.: Energy, environmental and mobility impacts of car-sharing systems. empirical results from Lisbon, Portugal. Proc. – Soc. Behav. Sci. 111, 28–37 (2014). https://doi.org/10.1016/j.sbspro.2014.01.035
4. Betsch, T.: Wie beeinflussen Routinen das Entscheidungsverhalten? Psychol. Rundschau 56(4), 261–270 (2005). https://doi.org/10.1026/0033-3042.56.4.261
5. Clark, B., Chatterjee, K., Melia, S.: Changes to commute mode: the role of life events, spatial context and environmental attitude. Transp. Res. Part A: Policy Pract. 89, 89–105 (2016). https://doi.org/10.1016/j.tra.2016.05.005
6. Gardner, B.: Modelling motivation and habit in stable travel mode contexts. Transp. Res. Part F: Traff. Psychol. Behav. 12(1), 68–76 (2009). https://doi.org/10.1016/j.trf.2008.08.001
7. Gardner, B., Abraham, C.: Psychological correlates of car use: a meta-analysis. Transp. Res. Part F: Traff. Psychol. Behav. 11(4), 300–311 (2008). https://doi.org/10.1016/j.trf.2008.01.004
8. Heck, R.H., Thomas, S.L., Tabata, L.N.: Multilevel Modeling of Categorical Outcomes Using IBM SPSS. Quantitative Methodology Series. Routledge, London (2012)
9. Hydén, C., Nilsson, A., Risser, R.: WALCYNG: How to enhance WALking and CYcliNG instead of shorter car trips and to make these modes safer. Transport research: vol. 75. Office for Official Publications of the European Communities (1998). http://safety.fhwa.dot.gov/ped_bike/docs/walcyng.pdf
10. Infas Institut für angewandte Sozialwissenschaft GmbH. Mobilität in Deutschland: Tabellarische Grundauswertung, Bonn (2018)
11. Jittrapirom, P., Caiati, V., Feneri, A.-M., Ebrahimigharehbaghi, S., González, M.J.A., Narayan, J.: Mobility as a service: a critical review of definitions, assessments of schemes, and key challenges. Urban Plann. 2(2), 13 (2017). https://doi.org/10.17645/up.v2i2.931
12. Karlsruhe Institute of Technology: Wegetagebuch. Deutsches Mobilitätspanel (MOP) (2013). http://mobilitaetspanel.ifv.kit.edu/downloads/Wegetagebuch_2013.pdf. Accessed 05 July 2013
13. Karlsson, I.C.M., et al.: Development and implementation of mobility-as-a-service – a qualitative study of barriers and enabling factors. Transp. Res. Part A: Policy Pract. 131, 283–295 (2020). https://doi.org/10.1016/j.tra.2019.09.028
14. Klöckner, C.A., Blöbaum, A.: A comprehensive action determination model: toward a broader understanding of ecological behaviour using the example of travel mode choice. J. Environ. Psychol. 30(4), 574–586 (2010). https://doi.org/10.1016/j.jenvp.2010.03.001
15. Langer, D., Dettmann, A., Kühnert, D., Bauer, S.: Nachwuchsforschergruppe fahrE - Konzepte für multimodale Mikromobilität unter Nutzung lokaler regenerativer Energien: Abschlussbericht. Technische Universität Chemnitz, Chemnitz (2015)
16. Lanzini, P., Khan, S.A.: Shedding light on the psychological and behavioral determinants of travel mode choice: a meta-analysis. Transp. Res. Part F: Traff. Psychol. Behav. 48, 13–27 (2017). https://doi.org/10.1016/j.trf.2017.04.020

17. Lyons, G., Hammond, P., Mackay, K.: The importance of user perspective in the evolution of MaaS. Transp. Res. Part A: Policy Pract. **121**, 22–36 (2019). https://doi.org/10.1016/j.tra. 2018.12.010

18. Ouellette, J.A., Wood, W.: Habit and intention in everyday life: the multiple processes by which past behavior predicts future behavior. Psychol. Bull. **124**(1), 54–74 (1998). https://doi.org/10.1037/0033-2909.124.1.54

19. Pangbourne, K., Stead, D., Mladenović, M., Milakis, D.: The case of mobility as a service: a critical reflection on challenges for urban transport and mobility governance. In: Marsden, G. Reardon, L. (eds.) Governance of the Smart Mobility Transition, pp. 33–48. Emerald Publishing Limited (2018). https://doi.org/10.1108/978-1-78754-317-120181003

20. Schikofsky, J., Dannewald, T., Kowald, M.: Exploring motivational mechanisms behind the intention to adopt mobility as a service (MaaS): insights from Germany. Transp. Res. Part A: Policy Pract. **131**, 296–312 (2020). https://doi.org/10.1016/j.tra.2019.09.022

21. Schwanen, T., Mokhtarian, P.L.: What affects commute mode choice: neighborhood physical structure or preferences toward neighborhoods? J. Transp. Geogr. **13**(1), 83–99 (2005). https://doi.org/10.1016/j.jtrangeo.2004.11.001

22. Smith, G., Sochor, J., Karlsson, I.M.: Mobility as a service: development scenarios and implications for public transport. Res. Transp. Econ. **69**, 592–599 (2018). https://doi.org/10. 1016/j.retrec.2018.04.001

23. Sochor, J., Strömberg, H., Karlsson, M.: An innovative mobility service to facilitate changes in travel behavior and mode choice. In: Proceedings of 22nd ITS World Congress, Bordeaux, France (2015). http://publications.lib.chalmers.se/records/fulltext/215086/local_215086.pdf

24. Swaminathan, H., Rogers, H.J., Sen, R.: Research methodology for decision-making in school psychology. In: Bray, M.A., Kehle, T.J. (eds.) The Oxford Handbook of School Psychology, pp. 103–139. Oxford University Press, New York (2011). https://doi.org/10. 1093/oxfordhb/9780195369809.013.0038

25. Verplanken, B.: The Psychology of Habit. Springer, Cham (2018). https://doi.org/10.1007/978-3-319-97529-0

26. Willing, C., Brandt, T., Neumann, D.: Intermodal mobility. Bus. Inf. Syst. Eng. **60**, 1–17 (2017). https://doi.org/10.1007/s12599-017-0471-7

27. Weiß, C., Chlond, B., Hilgert, T., Vortisch, P.: Deutsches Mobilitätspanel (MOP) - Wissenschaftliche Begleitung und Auswertungen, Bericht 2014/2015: Alltagsmobilität und Fahrleistung (2015). http://mobilitaetspanel.ifv.kit.edu/downloads/Bericht_MOP_14_15.pdf. Accessed 03 Feb 2020

# User Engagement with Driving Simulators: An Analysis of Physiological Signals

Ying-Hsang Liu[1,3]([✉]) [iD], Moritz Spiller[2] [iD], Jinshuai Ma[3], Tom Gedeon[3] [iD],
Md Zakir Hossain[3] [iD], Atiqul Islam[3], and Ralf Bierig[4] [iD]

[1] Department of Design and Communication, University of Southern Denmark,
Kolding, Denmark
yingliu@sdu.dk
[2] Medical Faculty/ University Clinic A.ö.R. (FME/UKMD),
Otto-von-Guericke-University Magdeburg, Magdeburg, Germany
moritz.spiller@ovgu.de
[3] Research School of Computer Science, The Australian National University,
Canberra, Australia
{ying-hsang.liu,jinshuai.ma,tom.gedeon,zakir.hossain,
atiqul.islam}@anu.edu.au
[4] Department of Computer Science, Maynooth University, Maynooth, Ireland
ralf.bierig@mu.ie

**Abstract.** Research on driving simulation has increasingly been concerned with the user's experience of immersion and realism in mixed reality environments. One of the key issues is to determine whether people perceive and respond differently in these environments. Physiological signals provide objective indicators of people's cognitive load, mental stress, and emotional state. Such data can be used to develop effective computational models and improve future systems. This study was designed to investigate the relationship between the verisimilitude of simple driving simulators and people's physiological signals, specifically GSR (galvanic skin response), BVP (blood volume pulse) and PR (pupillary response). A within-subject design user experiment with 24 participants for five different driving simulation environments was conducted. Our results reveal that there is a significant difference in the mean of GSR among the conditions of different configurations of simple driving simulators, but this is not the case for BVP and PR. The individual differences of gender, whether people wear glasses and previous experiences of driving a car or using a driving simulator are correlated with some physiological signals. The data is classified using a hybrid GA-SVM (genetic algorithm-support vector machine) and GA-ANN (artificial neural network) approach. The evaluation of the classification performance using 10-fold cross-validation shows that the choice of the feature subset has minor impact on the classification performance, while the choice of the classifier can improve the accuracy for some classification tasks. The results further indicate that the SVM is more sensitive to the selection of training and test data than the ANN. Our findings inform about the verisimilitude of simple driving

© Springer Nature Switzerland AG 2020
C. Stephanidis et al. (Eds.): HCII 2020, LNCS 12429, pp. 130–149, 2020.
https://doi.org/10.1007/978-3-030-59987-4_10

simulators on the driver's perceived fidelity and physiological responses. Implications for the design of driving simulators in support of training are discussed.

**Keywords:** Driving simulation · Virtual reality · Sensor · Eye tracking · User study

# 1    Introduction

Research on driving simulation is becoming increasingly interested in the user's experience of immersion and realism when these simulations are moved to virtual reality (VR) environments [32,37]. One of the key issues regarding realism in intelligent VR system design is to determine whether people perceive and respond differently in VR. In addition to subjective user-perceived measures that are extensively used in VR studies, physiological signals provide objective indicators of people's cognitive load, mental stress, and emotional state. Such data can be used to develop effective computational models and improve future systems. Some studies have used the physiological signals in VR environments [16,27], but the relationship between the features of user interfaces in VR environments and the physiological responses remains unclear.

Research on driving and flight simulation has been concerned with the issue of realism in virtual reality (VR) environments. Since the objective is to seek maximum realism, user perception issues, such as people's sense of presence (i.e., the feelings of being there) has been extensively studied [32,37]. Specifically, researchers have attempted to develop a driving simulator with an intelligent tutoring system, enhanced by a motion platform to improve presence [33]. However, in the context of flight simulation, the operator's perceived fidelity is not necessarily induced by the exact simulation of physical environments [32], and graphical fidelity alone is not correlated with galvanic skin responses (GSR) in the context of gaming [27]. One of the key issues regarding realism in intelligent VR system design is to determine whether people have different responses to the VR environments given user perceptions and physiological signals.

The use of physiological signals for building up computational models that can detect cognitive load, mental stress and emotional state for VR environments has the potentials for further development of user-adaptive interfaces. From user-centered design perspectives, the issues of user experience and physiological responses in VR environments have been emerging [11,29]. However, the issue of individual differences in cognitive processing and perception, which is important for developing user-adaptive interfaces, has received scant attention in driving and flight simulation studies [12,36]. More research on the effect of individual differences in cognitive processing and user perception will provide insights into the user-adaptive interface design in VR environments.

In our previous work we tried to establish a relationship between driving intervention task with simulator driving performance [14]. In this study we intend to address the issue of simulation validity by investigating the relationship between the verisimilitude of simple driving simulators and the physiological signals of GSR, blood volume pulse (BVP) and pupillary response (PR). We construct computational models to detect physiological responses from an observer perspective and determine the relationship between the individual differences, user perceptions and the physiological responses in driving simulation. The specific research questions are as follows:

- Is there any difference in physiological responses for driving simulation environments?
- What is the relationship between the individual differences, user perceptions and the physiological responses in a driving simulation?
- To what extent computational models can detect different driving situations with high levels of accuracy?

Our key findings reveal that participants have significantly different GSR responses using a combination of the monitor, keyboard, driving set and VR headset of driving simulation environments. Individual differences such as gender, previous experiences of driving and using a simulator and user perceptions are correlated with some physiological responses. Our classification of the physiological data using a hybrid GA-SVM and GA-ANN approach can achieve a high level of accuracy, close to 90% for the driving situations of normal and emergency.

## 2    Related Work

### 2.1    User Issues in VR Environments

Research on driving and flight simulation in virtual reality environments has been concerned with user perception issues, such as people's sense of presence and simulation sickness. To evaluate user experience in VR, the concept of presence (i.e., the feelings of being there) has been proposed and extensively used in the research literature [22,32]. For instance, the operator's perceived fidelity (i.e., "the degree to which visual features in the virtual environment (VE) conform to visual features in the real environment" [32, p. 115]) is not necessarily induced by the exact simulation of physical environments and a sense of presence can be included in the formal assessment of fidelity. These user perception issues are important considerations for the design of user interfaces in VR environments.

In driving simulation environments vehicle velocity has been identified as a significant factor affecting driving simulation sickness and discomfort [25,34]. To provide driving skills training with the goal of improving presence and immersion in VR environments, a driving simulator with an intelligent tutoring system has been developed and evaluated [33]. These studies suggest that mental workload and user perception issues need further considerations for developing interfaces in VR environments.

## 2.2 User Perceptions and Physiological Responses

In addition to the use of questionnaires for assessing user perceptions, research has also been concerned with the user's cognitive and emotional states using physiological signals, such as skin conductance, heart rate and pupillary response. More specifically, physiological signals of skin conductance and heart rate have been suggested to assess emotional states as objectives measures for people's responses in virtual environments [15]. Using a GSR sensor to measure physiological arousal, it was found that graphical fidelity is not correlated with GSR response [27]. To consider the effect of changes in scene brightness on the pupillary response for 2D screens and VR HMDs (head-mounted displays), an individual calibration procedure and constriction-based models of pupil diameter have been proposed [16]. However, the relationship between the features of user interfaces in VR environments and the responses measured by user-perceived data or physiological signals remains unclear.

From user-centered design perspectives, issues of usability of visualization systems, user experience and physiological responses in VR environments have received more attention in the research literature. For example, the user-centred design principles have been further applied to immersive 3D environments [11]. Besides, researchers have attempted to make connections between presence ratings and usability score [29], and between being present and levels of stress, measured by skin conductance response [37]. Overall, research has adopted the user-centered design principles and techniques for system design in VR environments.

## 2.3 Individual Differences

Aside from user perception issues, research on user experience in VR environments have touched on the issue of individual differences in cognitive processing and perception. For instance, it was found that there are gender differences in simulator sickness [25]. Females experience more simulator sickness than males. In the setting of a driving simulator, it was found that age makes a difference in user ratings for assistive technology [36], but there is no difference in attentional performance [6].

# 3  User Experiment

This study was designed to investigate the relationship between the verisimilitude of simple driving simulators and people's physiological signals, specifically galvanic skin response (GSR), blood volume pulse (BVP) and pupillary response (PR). A within-subject design user experiment with twenty-four participants was conducted for five configurations of driving simulation environment (See Fig. 1) that used a combination of monitor(s), keyboard, driving set, and VR headset. The order of presentation was randomized by a Latin-squared design to minimize possible effects of learning and fatigue [19].

## 3.1 Apparatus

We used five configurations for our driving simulation as shown in Fig. 1 and applied the driving simulator software, CCD[1] for driving environments.

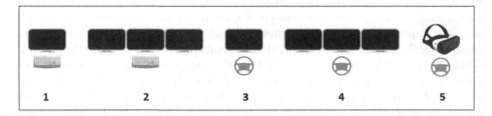

**Fig. 1.** The driving simulation environments include 1) single monitor and keyboard; 2) triple monitors and keyboard; 3) single monitor and driving set; 4) triple monitors and driving set; and 5) VR headset and driving set.

Since we were interested in people's reactions to different driving environments, we chose to provide simple setups, steering, accelerating, braking and switching gears between forward and backward in automatic gear style. To collect data from both normal driving and emergency situations, the traffic and emergency levels in the CCD software were set to 70% that increased the likelihood of emergency situations like 'Hit a car'. This was done based on our pilot study results for stimulating experiences without getting bored or annoyed. While normal driving consisted of basic driving activity like moving forward and stopping, emergency situations included accidents or near-accidents involving objects, other vehicles and pedestrians as listed in Table 1. We implemented a manual labeling program for identifying these driving events that we describe in Sect. 4).

**Table 1.** Driving event with corresponding situations.

|   | Event | Situation |
|---|---|---|
| 1 | Hit a pedestrian | Emergency |
| 2 | Almost hit a pedestrian | |
| 3 | Hit an object | |
| 4 | Almost hit an object | |
| 5 | Hit a car | |
| 6 | Almost hit a car | |
| 7 | Normal driving | Normal |
| 8 | Stopping | |

---

[1] https://citycardriving.com.

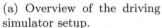

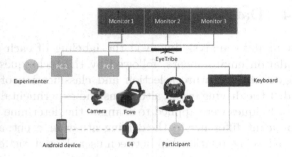

(a) Overview of the driving simulator setup.

(b) Apparatus for collecting physiological signals in driving simulation.

**Fig. 2.** Overview of the driving simulator setup.

We used the E4 wristband[2] to collect real-time signals of GSR and BVP. A customized client program based on the E4 wristband API was developed for recording data, with a millisecond timestamp accuracy. We used the EyeTribe eye tracker[3] for acquiring pupil diameters with timestamps. To create realistic VR environments, we used Fove VR headset[4] with an integrated eye tracker. The main CCD was displayed inside the Fove VR headset, with a duplicated CCD window displayed in the central monitor for mouse operation. A customized client program based on Fove API was developed to record the pupillary response data. The user interface of the sensor program was displayed on the right monitor. All the physiological signals data were synchronised for data analysis (See Fig. 2b).

## 3.2 Procedure

After a brief introduction and after consenting to the study[5] the participant was instructed to wear the sensors that where then initialization and calibrated. A three-minute practice senssion allows the participant to become familar with the devices, including the keyboard and steering wheel driving set. Then the participant was instructed to do free virtual driving for six minutes in each configuration using different devices, with two minutes breaks in-between. The experimenter ensured the proper setup at the beginning of each condition. Participants finished a total of five configurations of driving simulation environments (See Fig. 1 and Fig. 2), followed by a questionnaire regarding demographic information, previous driving experiences and perceptions about the simulator.

---

[2] https://www.empatica.com/en-gb/research/e4/.
[3] http://theeyetribe.com.
[4] https://www.getfove.com.
[5] The study has been approved by the University Human Research Ethics Committee.

# 4    Data Analysis

Our data analysis involved the labeling of each driving event in driving simulation environments, followed by the techniques of signal processing, feature extraction, feature selection and classification of physiological signals to predict the driving event, situations and experimental condition. Statistical analysis techniques were applied to examine the determine if there is any statistically significant difference by the driving situation, event, and experimental condition, as well as the relationship between user characteristics and physiological responses.

## 4.1    Labelling

During the experiment eight different driving events from two different categories can occur, as presented in Table 1. The CCD software logged each event that occurred during an experiment along with the related timestamp. By matching these log files with the files containing the recorded signals a labeled dataset as illustrated in Fig. 3 was generated. Conclusively, the dataset is labeled by configuration, driving event and driving situation.

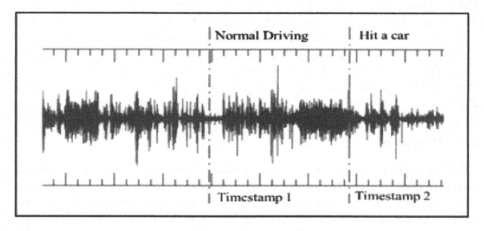

**Fig. 3.** Example of a labelled signal. The dashed lines mark an event and where obtained by matching the log files for the driving simulator software to the physiological signals using their timestamps.

## 4.2    Signal Preprocessing

The synchronized data was filtered to remove noise, which is consistently present in physiological signals recorded during user studies. This is caused by the external environment or movements of the participant. The Butterworth band-pass filter has been applied to both GSR and BVP signals [26]. The used bandpass for GSR signals was 0.1 Hz to 0.5 Hz [4], while the bandpass for BVP signals was 0.5 to 8 Hz [3,24]. The signal of the pupillary responses contains noise in the form of eye blinks, which cause a recorded pupil diameter of 0. To remove those values linear interpolation was applied to the data [23], followed by the application of an S-G filter to smooth out the signal [35].

The individual participants may have different baselines in their physiological signals, which have to be removed by normalizing the measured data [5]. Max-Min Normalisation has been used to do that.

## 4.3   Feature Extraction

**Segmentation.** In order to extract meaningful features from the recorded data, these data need to be segmented into subsegments of length —n—. This is done utilizing the event by which the data has been labeled and which have been introduced in Table 1. Figure 3 shows an example of a labeled GSR signal, where the red dotted lines correspond to that point in time when an event was logged. When an event was logged at time $t_0$ the interval $[t_0-1, t_0+2]$ has been extracted. This three-second data represent stimuli from which the features are calculated as described in Sect. 4.3. We chose this segmentation method according to the results of many preliminary studies where we observed the participant's reaction to an event. On average, after two seconds, the participant's physiological signal recovered from the stimuli. Due to a time delay between the actual stimuli and the point in time when the event is logged, we extract the data one second before the timestamp listed in the log.

Figure 4 illustrates a segmented GSR signal. While each red dotted line represents an event, the solid lines comprise the extracted time segment.

**Feature Calculation.** Features were calculated from the time and the frequency domain [1,30]. To transform the time series data into the frequency domain, Fast Fourier Transform [10] was applied. We calculated mean absolute value (MAV), arithmetic mean (AM), root mean square (RMS), standard deviation (SD), waveform length (WL), zero crossing (ZC), skewness and kurtosis. Additionally, the absolute values of the recorded were summed up and the first and second difference between adjacent measurements were calculated for all signals. Zero crossing was calculated only for BVP signal since GSR and pupillary responses are not zero-mean. Waveform length was calculated for GSR and BVP signal. The skewness and the kurtosis are calculated on the frequency domain signal.

Since the classifier described in Sect. 4.5 are not scale invariant, the feature set was standardised to $[-1, 1]$.

## 4.4   Statistical Analysis

We construct mixed-effects models for determining the effects of driving simulators (condition) and events on physiological responses. Mixed-effects distinguish

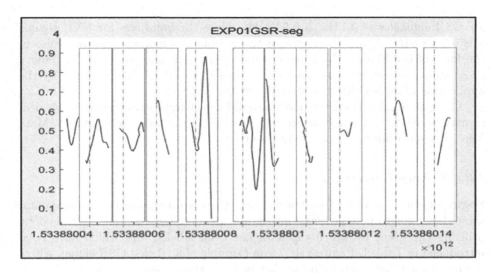

**Fig. 4.** Example of a segmented GSR signal. The solid lines comprehend one time segment of 3 s length, the dashed lines mark an event.

between fixed effects due to experimental condition and random effects due to individual differences in a sample. We choose the mixed-effects models because they are useful for the analysis of individual differences, with subjects and driving simulators as crossed random effects [2]. We use a logarithmic cross-ratio analysis [9] to determine if there is any significant relationship between individual differences and physiological responses.

### 4.5    Feature Selection and Classification

**Genetic Algorithm.** The Genetic Algorithm (GA) is a commonly used feature selection method in machine learning applications [28] to optimize the performance of a classifier. GA is based on the "survival of the fittest" from Darwinian's evolution theory. It iteratively selects random feature subsets organized in populations and evaluates them on some fitness function. We used the classification accuracy of the respective classifier as the fitness function for the GA.

The size of a population has been set to ten, while the maximum number of generations was 1000. The four fittest feature combinations formed the next population by performing six mutations among them.

The termination criteria of the GA was the overall change in accuracy over the last ten iterations as presented in Eq. 1.

$$AccChange = x_n - \frac{\sum_{i=n-10}^{n} x_i}{n} \tag{1}$$

where $x \in X$ and $n = |X|$. X denotes the set of all calculated accuracies obtained from the respective classifier.

**Support Vector Machine.** Support Vector Machines (SVMs) are a broadly used supervised classification algorithm [13,38]. A SVM classifies the data points by finding the best separating hyperplane in the n-dimensional feature space, which separates the data with the greatest margin possible.

For the experiments described in this paper an SVM model with a sigmoid kernel and an error rate of 5.0 has been used. These hyperparameters have been set after tuning the model using Grid Search.

**Artificial Neural Network.** Artificial Neural Networks (ANNs) are supervised learning algorithms that are inspired by the working principle of the human brain and have been used successfully on physiological data [13]. ANNs consist of artificial neurons that are connected and are organized in layers. Each neuron can process received information and transmit it to the neurons connected to it. The signal is processed through the input layer, possibly followed by multiple hidden layers, to the output layer, which computes the final classification result.

The ANN used in our study consisted of one hidden layer with eight neurons, which used a Scaled Exponential Linear Unit (SELU) as activation function [20]. The output layer utilized the Softmax activation function and the weights were optimized using the Adam optimiser [18].

## 5 Results

This section reports the results and findings from the analysis of physiological responses in different situations, event and conditions, followed by the relationship between individual differences and the physiological responses. We then report the accuracy of classifying the physiological data, using a hybrid GA-SVM and GA-ANN approach for driving simulation environments.

### 5.1 Relationships Among Event, Condition, and Physiological Signals

Our strategy for model fitting follows the approach by Baayen et al. [2]. Our null model initially includes random intercepts for condition and subject. To fit the data, we perform an automatic backward model selection of fixed and random parts of the linear mixed model [21]. Since the random intercepts for the subject are significant for both GSR and BVP, we choose a mixed-effects model with subject controlled as random effects.

Table 2 presents the constructed fixed and random effects models for both GSR and BVP. Model 1 is the baseline model with subject as random effects, whereas Models 2, 3, and 4 specify the fixed effects of the condition, event, a combination of both, as well as random effects.

Table 3 shows that Model 4 with condition and event as fixed effects accounts for 31.8% of variances, whereas Model 2 with the condition as fixed effects accounts for 21.4% of variances. Model 3 indicates that event as fixed effects

**Table 2.** Model construction of fixed and random effects for measures of physiological responses by GSR and BVP.

|  | Fixed and random effects model |
|---|---|
| Model 1 | (1\|subject) |
| Model 2 | condition + (1\|event) + (1\|subject) |
| Model 3 | event + (1\|condition) + (1\|subject) |
| Model 4 | condition + event + (1\|subject) |

only explain 0.6% of variances, though the effect of the event is statistically significant. Judging from the AIC value, Models 2, 3 and 4 are significantly better than our baseline Model 1. However, we cannot select the best model based on AIC alone since the values are close for Models 2, 3 and 4. Nonetheless, the results demonstrate that the event has significant but small effects on the mean of GSR. Condition, i.e. different configurations of the driving simulator has very significant effects on the mean of GSR.

**Table 3.** Model selection for effect of condition and event on mean of GSR.

|  | Mean of GSR | | | |
|---|---|---|---|---|
|  | Model 1 | Model 2 | Model 3 | Model 4 |
| Condition |  | 0.015*** |  | 0.015*** |
|  |  | (0.001) |  | (0.001) |
| Event |  |  | −0.002* | −0.002* |
|  |  |  | (0.001) | (0.001) |
| Constant | 0.041*** | −0.003 | 0.051*** | 0.006 |
|  | (0.003) | (0.004) | (0.012) | (0.006) |
| $N$ | 593 | 593 | 593 | 593 |
| Log likelihood | 977.035 | 1,046.232 | 1,044.777 | 1,042.606 |
| AIC | −1,948.069 | −2,082.464 | −2,079.554 | −2,075.213 |
| Marginal $R^2$ | 0.000 | 0.214 | 0.006 | 0.318 |
| Conditional $R^2$ | 0.037 | 0.273 | 0.318 | 0.277 |

Note: *p < .05; **p < .01; ***p < .001; AIC: Akaike Information Criterion.

Further analysis reveals that condition, i.e. different configurations of driving simulator has significant effect on GSR, a measure of mental stress. Event has significant but small effect on GSR. Specifically, a configuration of the driving set and VR headset induces a higher level of stress than other configurations.

Table 4 reveals that there is a very small effect of condition and event on the mean of BVP, a measure of cognitive load and emotional state. The fixed effects of condition only account for 3.2% of variances, whereas the effects of the event explain 3.8% of variances. The results suggest that the level of cognitive load

**Table 4.** Model selection for effect of condition and event on mean of BVP.

| | Mean of BVP | | | |
| --- | --- | --- | --- | --- |
| | Model 1 | Model 2 | Model 3 | Model 4 |
| Condition | | 0.003*** | | 0.003*** |
| | | (0.001) | | (0.001) |
| Event | | | −0.001* | −0.001* |
| | | | (0.0004) | (0.0004) |
| Constant | 0.044*** | 0.035*** | 0.049*** | 0.040*** |
| | (0.003) | (0.003) | (0.004) | (0.004) |
| N | 593 | 593 | 593 | 593 |
| Log likelihood | 1,458.390 | 1,466.051 | 1,466.051 | 1,461.387 |
| AIC | −2,910.781 | −2,922.102 | −2,922.102 | −2,912.773 |
| Marginal $R^2$ | 0.000 | 0.032 | 0.006 | 0.038 |
| Conditional $R^2$ | 0.315 | 0.351 | 0.367 | 0.353 |

*Note:* *p $<$ .05; **p $<$ .01; ***p $<$ .001; AIC: Akaike Information Criterion.

measured by BVP does not change by condition and event. And we do not find statistically significant results for pupillary responses.

Overall, we find that participants have different levels of mental stress measured by GSR in different configurations of the driving simulator. The high level of stress is correlated with a configuration of the driving set and VR headset. The results suggest that the level of stress measured by GSR varies in different configurations. Therefore, our results confirm the validity of driving simulation in the simple setup with monitors and driving set. The use of VR headset has increased the level of stress, as observed in the significant differences in GSR signals.

## 5.2 Relationships Among Individual Differences and Physiological Responses

To determine whether there is any correlation between the individual differences and the physiological signals, a logarithmic odds ratio analysis was conducted. Both dependent and independent variables were broken into "high" and "low" cases with the mean as cut point. Table 5 is a summary of the results. Overall, we find that the individual differences of gender, whether people wear glasses, user perceptions of devices affecting driving performance and whether people can see everything clearly through VR headset were correlated with the mean of GSR and BVP. That is, demographics, previous experience, and user perceptions are correlated with the GSR and BVP signals.

Specifically, female participants were more likely to have a higher mean of GSR and BVP than male participants. People who wear glasses were more likely to have a lower mean of GSR and BVP than people who didn't wear glasses. People who feel that devices affecting driving performance were more likely to

**Table 5.** Summary of the relationship between individual differences and physiological signals. User characteristics N = 593, Statistical significance at 95%.

| | CPm | OR | LO | SE | t | CPm | OR | LO | SE | t |
|---|---|---|---|---|---|---|---|---|---|---|---|
| *Gender* | | | | | | *Driving simulator* | | | | |
| GSR mean | 0.04 | 1.71 | 0.54 | 0.18 | 2.92* | 0.04 | 0.48 | −0.74 | 0.31 | −2.39* |
| BVP mean | 0.04 | 1.75 | 0.56 | 0.17 | 3.26* | 0.04 | 1.02 | 0.02 | 0.25 | 0.08 |
| Left eye PR | 0.89 | 1.13 | 0.12 | 0.17 | 0.68 | 0.89 | 0.95 | −0.05 | 0.26 | −0.21 |
| Right eye PR | 4.32 | 1.87 | 0.63 | 0.17 | 3.65* | 4.32 | 0.68 | −0.39 | 0.26 | −1.49 |
| *Wear glasses* | | | | | | *Devices performance* | | | | |
| GSR mean | 0.04 | 0.59 | −0.53 | 0.20 | −2.73* | 0.04 | 0.69 | −0.37 | 0.18 | −2.07* |
| BVP mean | 0.04 | 0.70 | −0.36 | 0.18 | −2.04* | 0.04 | 0.51 | −0.68 | 0.17 | −3.93* |
| Left eye PR | 0.89 | 1.07 | 0.07 | 0.18 | 0.40 | 0.89 | 0.92 | −0.08 | 0.17 | −0.47 |
| Right eye PR | 4.32 | 1.35 | 0.30 | 0.18 | 1.70 | 4.33 | 0.87 | −0.14 | 0.17 | −0.82 |
| *Driving license* | | | | | | *VR clearly* | | | | |
| GSR mean | 0.04 | 0.45 | −0.80 | 0.29 | −2.72* | 0.04 | 1.66 | 0.51 | 0.18 | 2.88* |
| BVP mean | 0.04 | 0.79 | −0.24 | 0.29 | −0.83 | 0.04 | 1.63 | 0.49 | 0.17 | 2.96* |
| Left eye PR | 0.89 | 1.17 | 0.16 | 0.30 | 0.53 | 0.89 | 1.22 | 0.20 | 0.17 | 1.18 |
| Right eye PR | 4.33 | 0.44 | −0.82 | 0.30 | −2.70* | 4.33 | 1.23 | 0.21 | 0.16 | 1.26 |
| *Steering wheel* | | | | | | | | | | |
| GSR mean | 0.04 | 1.15 | 0.14 | 0.21 | 0.66 | | | | | |
| BVP mean | 0.04 | 1.01 | 0.01 | 0.20 | 0.07 | | | | | |
| Left eye PR | 0.89 | 0.97 | −0.03 | 0.20 | −0.16 | | | | | |
| Right eye PR | 4.33 | 1.60 | 0.47 | 0.20 | 2.36* | | | | | |

*Note:* CPm: Cut Points (Mean); OR: Odds Ratio; LO: Log Odds; SE: Standard Error; t: t-Value marked with asterisk (*) when statistically significant.

have a lower mean of GSR and BVP. People who feel that they can see everything clearly through VR headset were more likely to have a higher mean of GSR and BVP. People who have more experiences using a driving simulator were more likely to have a lower mean of GSR, a measure of mental stress.

In other words, female participants were more likely to have higher levels of stress. Participants with more previous experiences (i.e., wearing glasses, driving license, driving simulator) were more likely to have lower levels of stress. The gender differences were also found in the BVP signals, a measure of cognitive load and emotional state. Female participants were more likely to have a higher mean of BVP by a factor of 1.75, or 75% than male participants.

Concerning the pupillary responses, female participants and those who have more left steering wheel experiences were more likely to have a higher mean of right eye pupillary response by a factor of 1.87 (or 87%) and 1.60 (or 60%) respectively. By contrast, people who have a driving license were more likely to have a lower mean of GSR by a factor of 0.45 (or 55%), and have a lower mean of right eye pupillary response by a factor of 0.44 (or 56%).

These results suggest that gender is an important demographic factor affecting participants' physiological responses to different environments in driving simulation. It is more likely that female participants are more stressed and use more cognitive resources in the simulation environment. Participants with previous experiences in real-life driving and exposure to driving simulators are more likely to have a lower level of stress. Participants' perceptions about whether the devices affect their performance and whether they can see clearly through the VR headset are correlated with GSR and BVP in opposite directions.

## 5.3   Classification

The ANN and SVM described in the Sect. 4.5 were trained on the the 34 features described in Sect. 4.3. Additionally, we included the participants' gender in the feature set because our results suggest that gender is correlated with physiological responses in this study (See Table 5). Consequently, the final dataset included 35 features.

Tables 6a and 6b describe the accuracy (Acc) and standard deviation (SD) obtained by applying 10-fold cross-validation. Iterations correspond to the number of necessary iterations the GA required until the optimal performance was reached. The presented number of iterations corresponds to the total number of iterations until the GA terminated. The termination criteria were the overall change in accuracy over the last 10 iterations as presented in Eq. 1.

Tables 6a and 6b summarize the classification performance of the GA-SVM and GA-ANN approach. The high standard deviation using GA-SVM suggests, that the SVM is more sensitive to the distribution of the data samples in the training and test set.

The SVM shows significantly better performance when classifying the condition (5 classes, e.g. "VR headset") in which the participant is driving. However, since its standard deviation is much higher than the ANN's standard deviation, this result largely depends on the distribution of the data samples.

The ANN outperforms the SVM when classifying the event (8 classes, e.g. "hit a pedestrian" or "stopping"). As again indicated by the standard deviation of the SVM, it might be able to match the ANNs performance at this classification task.

Both classifiers perform similarly when classifying the driving situation (2 classes, "normal" or "emergency").

**Table 6.** Classification results.

| | Acc [%] | SD | Iterations | | Acc [%] | SD | Iterations |
|---|---|---|---|---|---|---|---|
| Condition | 59.33 | 12.25 | 26 | Condition | 47.09 | 0.16 | 10 |
| Event | 65.87 | 6.46 | 10 | Event | 71.24 | 1.87 | 12 |
| Situation | 87.49 | 2.28 | 11 | Situation | 87.75 | 1.02 | 10 |
| | (a) GA-SVM | | | | (b) GA-ANN method | | |

The GA required only a few iterations to find the optimal feature subset on both classification approaches. This indicates that the selection of a feature subset has only a minor impact on the classification performance of the used classifiers. However, both classifiers pursued to reduce the feature set, which initially included 35 features. The GA-ANN approach selected 22 features for the condition, 18 features for the event and 16 features for the situation classification task. The GA-SVM selected 20, 14 and 17 features respectively.

# 6  Discussion

## 6.1  Is There Any Difference in Physiological Responses for Driving Simulation Environments?

Our findings indicate that there is no significant difference in participants' BVP and pupillary responses in the configurations of driving environments. However, there are significant differences in GSR. Since the environmental simulations can be validated by the ability to replicate human responses in physical environments [22], our study suggests that people do not have different responses to the driving simulations by BVP signals and pupillary responses. Our results partially support the use of simple driving simulators as empirical tools in user behavior research. Our finding that there are significant differences in GSR for different driving simulators, however, shows that the use of VR headset induces a higher level of physiological arousal. In the context of virtual environments intended to create the feeling of presence in immersive environments, research shows that increased graphical quality alone is not correlated with GSR responses in the gaming context [15]. Therefore, our findings suggest that participants do not have different BVP and pupillary responses, while the use of a VR headset and a steering wheel driving set induces a higher level of physiological arousal in driving simulation environments.

## 6.2  What Is the Relationship Between the Individual Differences, User Perceptions and the Physiological Responses in a Driving Simulation?

Our findings show that gender is an important factor affecting physiological responses to different environments in driving simulation. Previous research on the role of gender in simulator sickness has been inconclusive [25,36]. Our results support that females experience more simulator sickness than males [25], and females are more likely to feel stressed and use more cognitive resources in the simulation environment. Participants with previous experiences in real-life driving and exposure to driving simulators are found to have a lower level of stress. These findings correspond to the results on driving style familiarity and driving comfort [12], showing that driving style familiarity interacts with driving comfort by different age groups. Therefore, the demographic variables of gender, previous driving experience and age and their effects on physiological responses and user perceptions need further research.

Concerning user perceptions, we find that there are discrepancies between the perceived feelings and physiological responses. Specifically, whether the devices affect participants' performance and whether they can see clearly through the VR headset are correlated with GSR and BVP responses in opposite directions. We speculate that since the use of a VR headset induces a higher level of physiological arousal and participants are engaged with the experiment, they are more likely to have higher GSR and BVP responses when prompted with the question of whether they can see clearly through VR headset. On the other hand, user perceptions about their performance might be explained by the new simulation environments introduced in our user experiment. Nonetheless, future research needs to consider user perceptions of speed and distance in simulated environments [17,22,33].

### 6.3    To What Extent Can Computational Models Detect Different Driving Situations with High Levels of Accuracy?

Our findings suggest that classifying the physiological data using a hybrid GA-SVM and GA-ANN approach can achieve a high level of accuracy, close to 90% for driving situations. Our performance evaluation using 10-fold cross-validation shows that the choice of the feature subset has minor impact on the classification performance, while the choice of the classifier can improve the accuracy for some classification tasks.

The results described in Sect. 5.3 and shown in the Tables 6 suggest the Genetic Algorithm mainly converged after few iterations. Therefore, it seems that the choice of a specific feature subset has a minor impact on the performance of the classifier. Nevertheless, the SVM classifier required more iterations and shows higher standard deviation, which corroborates the observations of other researchers [28] that the SVM is more sensitive to the features used for training.

Our research shows that it is possible to detect what kind of peripheral devices the user applies during the usage of a driving simulator or similar software. That contributes to the development of user adapted simulator software or games. By detecting the type of peripheral device that is used to visualize the software, the resolution or the layout of the user interface can be adapted to the specific device like a VR-Headset. In the case of a driving simulator, the configuration of the driving parameters can be adapted to a keyboard or a driving set. Among others, the latency and accuracy of how the steering impulses of the user are processed by the software can be altered.

### 6.4    Limitations and Future Research

Since this user experiment was conducted in a laboratory setting, one should be cautious about the generalisability of the results to the general population.

Our segmentation method described in Sect. 4.3 works based on the labels that have been matched with logged events from physiological signals. Due to the nature of the domain and the driving simulator experiment in particular as normal driving situations will always occur much more frequently than emergencies. This leads to multiple subsequent labels for normal driving compared to other labels in the dataset, resulting in the trained model to be biased towards normal driving with good classification results for this class and reduced results for less frequent driving events. Researchers [8,31] have proposed two approaches for minority oversampling to improve learning from imbalanced datasets that we will apply in future work.

For the feature selection of eye gaze data, we hypothesise that the number of fixations, as well as the average fixation duration, are higher during an emergency event like "Hit a pedestrian" than in a normal driving situation. At the same time, saccades are expected to occur more frequently during normal driving situations. We suggest future research on additional features (e.g. fixations and saccades) and user-perceived sensory fidelity in different simulation environments for enhancing the user experience of presence [27,29] to make different driving situations more distinctive.

The analysis of pupillary responses could be enhanced by further considering scene brightness caused by the changes in driving scenes in VR environments [16]. To validate the use of the simulated environment for driving skills training purposes, future research can use new driving scenarios in automated driving simulators and simulation of tactile or audio feedback of the real driving environment, with particular emphasis on the usability issues through the analysis of physiological signals [7,29]. Additionally, the sensitivity of the SVM to physiological signal processing can be further investigated.

Our findings inform about the verisimilitude of simple driving simulators on the driver's perceived fidelity and physiological responses. This can be used to inform on the design of driving simulators in support of training. We suggest that individual differences such as prior driving experiences need to be considered in the design of a driving simulator (e.g. by offering difficulty-levels). Virtual environments can increase immersion while also increasing stress levels that should be considered in design (e.g. by leveraging realism through adjusting the likelihood of potentially dangerous situations).

## 7   Conclusion

We investigated the relationship between the verisimilitude of simple driving simulators and people's physiological signals, specifically galvanic skin response (GSR), blood volume pulse (BVP) and pupillary response (PR). We found that participants do not have different BVP and PR in driving simulation environments, which supports the use of steering wheel driving set as empirical tools in user behavior research. Individual differences such as previous experiences of driving should be considered in the design of driving simulators since they are correlated with physiological responses. In terms of predictability, our results further suggest that classifying the physiological data using a hybrid GA-SVM and GA-ANN approach can achieve a high level of accuracy, close to 90% for driving situations while showing that the choice of the feature subset only has a minor impact on the classification performance. Our findings inform about the verisimilitude of simple driving simulators on the driver's perceived fidelity and physiological responses and provide implications for the design of future driving simulators.

# References

1. Ayata, D., Yaslan, Y., Kamasak, M.: Emotion recognition via galvanic skin response: comparison of machine learning algorithms and feature extraction methods. Istanbul Uni. - J. Electr. Electron. Eng. 17(1), 3129–3136 (2017)
2. Baayen, R.H., Davidson, D.J., Bates, D.M.: Mixed-effects modeling with crossed random effects for subjects and items. J. Mem. Lang. 59(4), 390–412 (2008). https://doi.org/10.1016/j.jml.2007.12.005
3. Bagha, S., Hills, S., Bhubaneswar, P., Shaw, L.: A real time analysis of PPG signal for measurement of SpO 2 and pulse rate. Int. J. Comput. Appl. 36(11), 975–8887 (2011). https://doi.org/10.5120/4537-6461
4. Boucsein, W.: Electrodermal Activity, 2nd edn. Springer, New York (2012). https://doi.org/10.1007/978-1-4614-1126-0
5. Cacioppo, J.T., Rourke, P.A., Marshall-Goodell, B.S., Tassinary, L.G., Baron, R.S.: Rudimentary physiological effects of mere observation. Psychophysiology 27(2), 177–186 (1990). https://doi.org/10.1111/j.1469-8986.1990.tb00368.x
6. Cassarino, M., Maisto, M., Esposito, Y., Guerrero, D., Chan, J.S., Setti, A.: Testing attention restoration in a virtual reality driving simulator. Front. Psychol. 10, 250 (2019). https://doi.org/10.3389/fpsyg.2019.00250
7. Dols, J.F., Molina, J., Camacho, F.J., Marín-Morales, J., Pérez-Zuriaga, A.M., Garcia, A.: Design and development of driving simulator scenarios for road validation studies. Transp. Res. Proc. 18, 289–296 (2016). https://doi.org/10.1016/j.trpro.2016.12.038
8. Douzas, G., Bacao, F.: Effective data generation for imbalanced learning using conditional generative adversarial networks. Expert Syst. Appl. 91, 464–471 (2018). https://doi.org/10.1016/j.eswa.2017.09.030
9. Fleiss, J.L., Levin, B., Paik, M.C.: Assessing Significance in a Fourfold Table, 3rd edn. Wiley, Hoboken (2003). https://doi.org/10.1002/0471445428.ch3
10. Frigo, M., Johnson, S.G.: FFTW: an adaptive software architecture for the FFT. In: Proceedings of the 1998 IEEE International Conference on Acoustics, Speech and Signal Processing, ICASSP 1998 (Cat. No. 98CG36181), pp. 1381–1384 (1998)
11. Gerjets, P., Lachmair, M., Butz, M.V., Lohmann, J.: Knowledge spaces in VR: intuitive interfacing with a multiperspective hypermedia environment. In: 2018 IEEE Conference on Virtual Reality and 3D User Interfaces (VR), pp. 555–556 (2018). https://doi.org/10.1109/VR.2018.8446137
12. Hartwich, F., Beggiato, M., Krems, J.F.: Driving comfort, enjoyment and acceptance of automated driving-effects of drivers' age and driving style familiarity. Ergonomics 61(8), 1017–1032 (2018). https://doi.org/10.1080/00140139.2018.1441448
13. Hossain, M.Z., Gedeon, T.: Observers' physiological measures in response to videos can be used to detect genuine smiles. Int. J. Hum.-Comput. Stud. 122(November 2017), 232–241 (2019). https://doi.org/10.1016/j.ijhcs.2018.10.003
14. Islam, A., Ma, J., Gedeon, T., Hossain, M.Z., Liu, Y.H.: Measuring user responses to driving simulators: a galvanic skin response based study. In: 2019 IEEE International Conference on Artificial Intelligence and Virtual Reality (AIVR), pp. 33–40 (2019). https://doi.org/10.1109/AIVR46125.2019.00015

15. Jang, D.P., Kim, I.Y., Nam, S.W., Wiederhold, B.K., Wiederhold, M.D., Kim, S.I.: Analysis of physiological response to two virtual environments: driving and flying simulation. CyberPsychol. Behav. 5(1), 11–18 (2002). https://doi.org/10.1089/109493102753685845

16. John, B., Raiturkar, P., Banerjee, A., Jain, E.: An evaluation of pupillary light response models for 2D screens and VR HMDs. In: Proceedings of the 24th ACM Symposium on Virtual Reality Software and Technology, VRST 2018, pp. 19:1–19:11. ACM, New York (2018). https://doi.org/10.1145/3281505.3281538

17. Kemeny, A., Panerai, F.: Evaluating perception in driving simulation experiments. Trends Cogn. Sci. 7(1), 31–37 (2003). https://doi.org/10.1016/S1364-6613(02)00011-6

18. Kingma, D.P., Ba, J.: Adam: a method for stochastic optimization. In: Proceedings of the 3rd International Conference for Learning Representations (2015)

19. Kirk, R.E.: Experimental Design: Procedures for the Behavioral Sciences, 4th edn. Brooks/Cole, Pacific Grove (2013). https://doi.org/10.4135/9781483384733

20. Klambauer, G., Unterthiner, T., Mayr, A., Hochreiter, S.: Self-normalizing neural networks. In: Guyon, I., et al. (eds.) Advances in Neural Information Processing Systems, vol. 30, pp. 971–980. Curran Associates, Inc. (2017)

21. Kuznetsova, A., Brockhoff, P.B., Christensen, R.H.B.: lmerTest package: tests in linear mixed effects models. J. Stat. Softw. 82(13), 1–26 (2017). https://doi.org/10.18637/jss.v082.i13

22. Marín-Morales, J., et al.: Navigation comparison between a real and a virtual museum: time-dependent differences using a head mounted display. Interact. Comput. (2019). https://doi.org/10.1093/iwc/iwz018

23. Mathôt, S., Dalmaijer, E., Grainger, J., Van der Stigchel, S.: The pupillary light response reflects exogenous attention and inhibition of return. J. Vis. 14(14), 7 (2014). https://doi.org/10.1167/14.14.7

24. Mohd-Yasin, F., Yap, M.T., Reaz, M.B.I.: CMOS instrumentation amplifier with offset cancellation circuitry for biomedical application. WSEAS Trans. Circ. Syst. 6(1), 171–174 (2007)

25. Mourant, R.R., Thattacherry, T.R.: Simulator sickness in a virtual environments driving simulator. Proc. Hum. Factors Ergon. Soc. Ann. Meet. 44(5), 534–537 (2000). https://doi.org/10.1177/154193120004400513

26. Nabian, M., Yin, Y., Wormwood, J., Quigley, K.S., Barrett, L.F., Ostadabbas, S.: An open-source feature extraction tool for the analysis of peripheral physiological data. IEEE J. Transl. Eng. Health Med. 6, 2800711 (2018). https://doi.org/10.1109/JTEHM.2018.2878000

27. Ocasio-De Jesús, V., Kennedy, A., Whittinghill, D.: Impact of graphical fidelity on physiological responses in virtual environments. In: Proceedings of the 19th ACM Symposium on Virtual Reality Software and Technology, VRST 2013, pp. 73–76. ACM, New York (2013). https://doi.org/10.1145/2503713.2503751

28. Paiva, J.S., Cardoso, J., Pereira, T.: Supervised learning methods for pathological arterial pulse wave differentiation: a SVM and neural networks approach. Int. J. Med. Inf. 109, 30–38 (2018). https://doi.org/10.1016/j.ijmedinf.2017.10.011

29. Pettersson, I., Karlsson, M., Ghiurau, F.T.: Virtually the same experience?: Learning from User experience evaluation of in-vehicle systems in VR and in the field. In: Proceedings of the 2019 on Designing Interactive Systems Conference, DIS 2019, pp. 463–473. ACM, New York (2019). https://doi.org/10.1145/3322276.3322288

30. Phinyomark, A., Limsakul, C., Phukpattaranont, P.: A novel feature extraction for robust EMG pattern recognition. J. Med. Eng. Technol. 1(1), 71–80 (2009). https://doi.org/10.3109/03091902.2016.1153739

31. Piri, S., Delen, D., Liu, T.: A synthetic informative minority over-sampling (SIMO) algorithm leveraging support vector machine to enhance learning from imbalanced datasets. Decis. Support Syst. **106**, 15–29 (2018). https://doi.org/10.1016/j.dss. 2017.11.006

32. Robinson, A., Mania, K.: Technological research challenges of flight simulation and flight instructor assessments of perceived fidelity. Simul. Gaming **38**(1), 112–135 (2007). https://doi.org/10.1177/1046878106299035

33. Ropelato, S., Zund, F., Magnenat, S., Menozzi, M., Summer, R.W.: Adaptive tutoring on a virtual reality driving simulator. In: International SERIES on Information Systems and Management in Creative eMedia (CreMedia), pp. 12–17 (2018)

34. Sakamura, Y., et al.: A virtual boarding system of an autonomous vehicle for investigating the effect of an AR display on passenger comfort. In: 2018 IEEE International Symposium on Mixed and Augmented Reality Adjunct (ISMAR-Adjunct), pp. 344–349 (2018). https://doi.org/10.1109/ISMAR-Adjunct.2018.00101

35. Schafer, R.: What is a savitzky-golay filter? [Lecture Notes]. IEEE Signal Process. Mag. **28**(4), 111–117 (2011). https://doi.org/10.1109/MSP.2011.941097

36. Schultheis, M.T., Rebimbas, J., Mourant, R., Millis, S.R.: Examining the usability of a virtual reality driving simulator. Assist. Technol. **19**(1), 1–10 (2007). https:// doi.org/10.1080/10400435.2007.10131860

37. Skarbez, R., Brooks Jr., F.P., Whitton, M.C.: Immersion and coherence in a stressful virtual environment. In: Proceedings of the 24th ACM Symposium on Virtual Reality Software and Technology, VRST 2018, pp. 24:1–24:11. ACM, New York (2018). https://doi.org/10.1145/3281505.3281530

38. Wu, Y., Liu, Y., Tsai, Y.H.R., Yau, S.T.: Investigating the role of eye movements and physiological signals in search satisfaction prediction using geometric analysis. J. Assoc. Inf. Sci. Technol. (2019). https://doi.org/10.1002/asi.24240

# From the Parking Lot to Your Gate: A Need-Centered Approach for Optimizing User Experience in Automated Valet Parking System

Jun Ma[1], Xuejing Feng[1(✉)], Zaiyan Gong[2], and Qianwen Zhang[1]

[1] College of Design and Innovation, Tongji University, Shanghai, China
feng.xuejing@foxmail.com
[2] School of Automotive Studies, Tongji University, Shanghai, China

**Abstract.** Major improvements in autonomous driving allow the realization of automated valet parking. However, parking is known to be a challenging and complex task with high cognitive demand, and many challenges remain within the area of human factors, for example, whether the user trust automated driving vehicle systems and whether the system is understandable and safe. Therefore, we present a need-centered approach and the involved "UX framework", which can optimize user experience in the automated valet parking system. We create Persona models through surveys and interviews to explore pain points and users' needs, and use Kano model to categorize and prioritize these needs from three levels: security, understandability, and controllability, then reflect them in each function of the system to build the information architecture. Meanwhile, we also consider the corresponding services about One-dimensional and Attractive quality. Furthermore, we put forward the "UX framework" and 5 principles for the interaction design of the automated valet parking system, which will provide references for designers and practitioners.

**Keywords:** Automated valet parking system · A need-centered approach · User experience

## 1 Introduction

### 1.1 Background

Autonomous driving is on the horizon. Recent predictions state that in 2030, 20–30% of all vehicles might be capable of fully automated driving [1], so automated driving systems will increasingly pervade traffic systems over the next decades [2], which contributes to increased traffic safety as well as improved comfort for users [3–6]. However, many challenges remain within the area of human factors following human-technology symbiosis. On the one hand, a large number of potential customers express skepticism towards highly or fully automated driving [1] and hardly imagine to own a vehicle without traditional driving controls [7]. Such opinions often go hand in hand with a fear of safety issues and mistrust. Thus, reliable and safe autonomous driving systems are crucial for creating a good user experience. On the other hand, with

© Springer Nature Switzerland AG 2020
C. Stephanidis et al. (Eds.): HCII 2020, LNCS 12429, pp. 150–165, 2020.
https://doi.org/10.1007/978-3-030-59987-4_11

increasing driving automation, the role of the driver is fundamentally changing. Although autonomous driving has the potential to make automatic inferences and decisions, human should still keep monitor and supervisory control on the intelligent autonomous systems, and the active role of the driver changes gradually to a passive one [8]. Thus, we need to reconsider the relationship between the driver and automated vehicle, and a key element is identifying the psychological needs of drivers and cognitive processes that influence how drivers use these technologies [9], which will serve the users to create a better experience.

## 1.2   The User Experience of the Automated Valet Parking System

**Automated Valet Parking System.** Related functions of autonomous driving have been gradually applied in the market. For example, BMW offers a system that lets the car drive in and out of the garage by itself, and Tesla offers a summon function. However, automation is not only technological progress but poses complex questions about how people will interact with and experience future automated vehicles in everyday life [10]. To date, most of the research focuses on the interaction of drivers with automated vehicles when controlling and monitoring driving maneuvers [11–13]. Only a few studies extend this scope to the information interaction between automated vehicles and users who are not sitting in the car [10]. Even less is known about how people experience automated parking [14, 15], especially valet parking a scenario where the car parks itself in a remote parking garage. Moreover, most studies focus on questions of usability and only a few explore users' subjective experiences of particular forms of automation [16]. Automated valet parking is a high-frequency scenario for autonomous driving, potentially leading to a safer and more efficient traffic environment. Users can summon the vehicle on the smartphone, also the vehicle can drive to a parking spot and park itself without people's participation. The automated valet parking system is a typical automated driving scenario in a limited area, and itself appears to be an example of fully automated driving. It means how automation technology so deeply embedded into many people's everyday lives impacts experience as well as practices and habits. Therefore, its user experience will be significant.

**The User Experience of Autonomous Driving.** Some studies indicate that the different levels of automation come with different challenges for UX design in automated driving [17, 18]. Anna-Katharina Frison, Philipp Wintersberger, et al. summarize UX goals according to the role of the driver-passenger in the different levels of automation [8]. They also reveal that in highly and fully automated driving (SAE L4/L5), existing a tension between the wish to engage in non-driving related tasks (as main benefit of automated driving) and distrust into the system [19]. Distler, C. Lallemand, et al. apply a psychological need-based approach, and their results indicate safety as a prerequisite for good user experience [20], and pragmatic quality (including perceived usefulness, effectiveness, etc.) to become a "hygienic factor" [21]. Automated valet parking system is included in the higher level of automation (SAE L4), and parking is known to be a challenging and complex task with high cognitive demand [22]. Hence, compared with building a user experience with non-driving-related tasks with hedonic quality on an automated driving system, many challenges within the area of human factors we need to be more concerned, such as the user trust for automated driving vehicle systems, understandability and safety of the system. It is crucial to consider how to ensure that technology serves users' needs in the best possible way. We should meet the user's expectations of autonomous driving through appropriate design and create a human-machine interaction with a good experience, which will be supported by users and social recognition.

### 1.3    Research Direction

We present a need-centered approach and the involved "UX framework" from a systematic perspective. We create Persona models through surveys and interview drivers who have autonomous driving or auto-parking experiences, exploring users' needs and pain points. Next, we use Kano model to categorize and prioritize these needs, reflecting them in each function of the automated valet parking system to build the information architecture model. Finally, we verify the effectiveness of the design method through experiments and summarize some design principles.

## 2    Method and Analysis

The research methods we used are (1) survey and interview, (2) Persona model, (3) Kano model. We initially got the data of user preference and performance and created Persona Model to segment users into groups to probe the need. Then we established Kano model to prioritize the user need. The result presents some inspiration of design guidelines for the design automated valet parking system.

### 2.1    Survey and Interview

Nowadays, there is no mature system of automated valet parking working in China owing to the traffic laws compared with the development of automated parking system, such as the parallel auto parking system from the beginning to the vertical parking system recently which is one of the advanced driving assistance system (ADAS) function gradually accepted by users. As a result, the criteria for us to choose the respondents in our survey stress on their using experience on automated parking system or autonomous driving vehicle from which we can learn user focus on the automated system design. In the user interviews, we introduced the automated valet parking system and collected user expectations and views on the system. Based on the feedback, we synthesized their demands. We invited 4 typical users to participate in our interview. Their basic information is listed in Table 1.

Respondents shared their experience on automated parking systems and autonomous driving systems including the advances of the automated technology they think as well as the pain points and worries about the automated valet parking system. The following examples are respondents' quotes.

**Table 1.** Basic information of the respondents.

| # | Age | Gender | Profession | Usage frequency |
|---|-----|--------|------------|-----------------|
| 1 | 24 | Male | Student | 2–3 times/month |
| 2 | 26 | Male | Engineer | 2–5 times/week |
| 3 | 35 | Male | Programmer | 3–4 times/week |
| 4 | 42 | Female | Manager | 2–5 times/week |

- "Sometimes the automated parking system is not so intelligent in the scenario of parking space recognition. When there are multiple parking spaces, it cannot park a specific parking space according to my wishes. It is a little bit unpredictable and inconvenient to a certain extent, which I would rather park the car by myself".
- "If the automated valet parking system is put in use in the future, I would worry about the safety issue. I am worried that the car will rub on the way to the parking space. Even if it helps me park it, I would like to know the brand of cars which are parked around me because it is troublesome crashing a premium car".
- "I am quite optimistic about autonomous driving. From the current experience of parking, the whole process is quite smooth. It takes about 1 min which is acceptable for me. The position and the angle of the parked vehicle are pretty good".
- "I am not too worried about the technology of automated parking actually, but when I drive a self-driving car, I worry about accidents. After all, I cannot control the machine, so I feel a little uncontrolled".

We downloaded the scripts of user interviews, recapped user feedback, and listed the important pain points in Table 2.

### 2.2   Persona Model

We dived deeply into the user information such as age, gender, job, domain, and interest to probe the main user characteristics. The analysis included user mental demands and the expecting scenario of the system. Based on these, we divided the users into 4 groups and established Persona Models.

**Persona A.** Business people who travel a lot. They are time sensibility. They have a high frequency of business travel and they are used to park their car in the underground parking lot in the airport or train station.

*User Needs:* They focus on the time efficiency of the solution. They want to get rid of the unnecessary step of the parking progress. In addition, it would be better if they can get real-time vehicle and traffic information to ease their anxiety of uncertainty. They also welcome personalized service. For instance, the autonomous vehicle can recognize the driver's luggage and open the trunk automatically.

**Persona B.** White-collar. They need to commute to and from work with their private electric vehicles. Therefore, they prefer the efficient and stable service progress to save their time and guarantee charging pile supply.

**Table 2.** Summary of main pain points.

| Pain points | Insights | Opportunities |
|---|---|---|
| Worry about the crash | Desire for more running information and feedback | Real-time video and vehicle status feedback |
| Hard to find charging parking space (the charging position is occupied by ICE) | The parking resource is not distributed effectively | If the charging parking space is not accessible at that time, the car can be parked in the normal parking space. When the charging position is available, the car can move to it automatically |
| Lack of confidence and sense of safety of autonomous driving system | Safety is essential to influence the user experience | Add the function of vehicle self-diagnosis, vehicle safety precaution |
| Hard to understand some functions | Complex system may confuse users | Design the user interface based on user cognition |
| Feeling of uncontrolled in the self-driving car | Controllability is the obvious difference between self-driving and manual driving and is the source of users' safety feeling | Add manual mode in the self-driving experience |
| Worry about the vehicle cybersecurity | Doubt on the privacy safety is companied with the development of digital intelligence | Add step of user security verification |

*User Needs:* They hope to have enough charging infrastructure for their cars. They also worried about their privacy safety issues for their knowledge of cybersecurity in vehicles, so they want a superior information safety system to protect their privacy. Real-time feedback information about the automated valet parking progress is nice to have for them to check.

**Persona C.** Students. They are willing to try new things and have a huge interest in intelligent products. They say it takes a long time to park cars during peak hours. The automated valet parking can tackle the problem well.

*User Needs:* Vehicles with intelligent service are able to bring superior experiences, such as voice interaction and artistic interface design.

**Persona D.** Middle-aged people. They have rich driving experience and they are not antipathy to autonomous driving while they enjoy manual driving.

*User Needs:* Safety plays the most important role in their view of autonomous driving. They hope the vehicle is not only flexible but controllable. They want the system to fit their habits. Moreover, there can be more guidance for users at their first time using the system.

## 2.3  Kano Model

Kano model [22] developed by Professor Noriaki Kano is a theory for product development and customer satisfaction, which classifies customer preferences into five categories: must-be quality, one-dimensional quality, attractive quality, indifferent quality, and reverse quality (see Fig. 1).

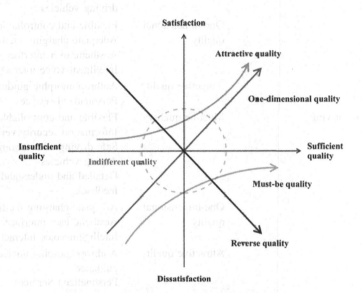

**Fig. 1.**  Kano model of user satisfaction [23].

- Must-be quality. Must-be quality contains attributes of service quality that must be met for customer satisfaction. Therefore, when these necessities are not fulfilled, customers are strongly dissatisfied or even will give up using the product or service.
- One-dimensional quality. One-dimensional quality attributes influence customer satisfaction linearly. Customer satisfaction increases with increasing quality and vice versa. If such needs are not met, user satisfaction will also decline significantly.
- Attractive quality. The attractive quality generates high levels of customer satisfaction when fulfilled, but it does not cause customer dissatisfaction when absent. Since customers are not aware of these product features, they do not expect their provision.
- Indifferent quality. The indifferent quality refers to a quality element that does not affect customer satisfaction whether it is present or not.
- Reverse quality. Reverse quality refers to a quality attribute that leads to customer dissatisfaction when it is provided; if not, customers are satisfied.

We use Kano model to classify and prioritize consumer needs, and in the research, we mainly consider must-be quality, one-dimensional quality, and attractive quality. The results are shown in Table 3.

**Table 3.** Summary of user's needs in each stage.

| Usage scenario | Quality | User's needs |
|---|---|---|
| Summon the vehicle and autonomous parking | Must-be quality | Detailed and understandable feedback<br>Information security verification<br>Safe driving of autonomous driving vehicles |
| | One-dimensional quality | Flexible and controllable travel<br>Adequate charging facilities<br>Aesthetic user interface<br>Intelligent voice interaction |
| | Attractive quality | Anthropomorphic guidance<br>Personalized services |
| Autonomous driving | Must-be quality | Flexible and controllable travel<br>Information security verification<br>Safe driving of autonomous driving vehicles<br>Detailed and understandable feedback |
| | One-dimensional quality | Adequate charging facilities<br>Aesthetic user interface<br>Intelligent voice interaction |
| | Attractive quality | Anthropomorphic novice guidance<br>Personalized Services |

We found that the priority of user needs changes under different scenarios. Taking the scenario of self-driving as an example, passengers are more concerned about their safety. Therefore, they consider controllability and safety as a high priority. But in the scenario of summoning the vehicle and autonomous parking, it will improve the anxiety experience for users with a transparent system that has appropriate feedback with comprehensible information. We focus on Must-be quality and One-dimensional quality to guide the interaction design of the automated valet parking system, which can improve user experience and satisfaction. We also consider Attractive quality to explore more possibilities, which can provide personalized service for different users.

## 3  Design Practice

### 3.1  Information Architecture

In general, we categorize users' needs in Kano model from three levels: security, understandability, and controllability, then reflect them in each function of the auto-mated valet parking system to build the information architecture model (shown in Table 4).

**Table 4.** The information architecture model.

| Hierarchy of needs | Summon the vehicle | Autonomous driving | Autonomous parking | Dynamic parking | Vehicle control |
|---|---|---|---|---|---|
| Security | Vehicle self-diagnosis Fingerprint verification | Driving safety precaution Information security monitoring | Vehicle Safety precaution | Vehicle self-diagnosis | One click to rescue |
| Understandability | Vehicle status and working progress Real-time video monitoring Arrival notice | Travel information Arrival notice | Real-time video monitoring Outdoor and indoor navigation Vehicle status and working progress Feedback about parking completed | Real-time video monitoring Indoor navigation Vehicle status and working progress Feedback about parking completed | Vehicle status |
| Controllability | Startup confirmation Select a pick-up point Change or cancel a pick-up point | Select a destination Manual driving-Autonomous driving switch | Autonomous parking confirmation Change a parking lot | Change a parking lot Cancel dynamic parking | Vehicle control Emergency control |
| The corresponding services of One-dimensional and Attractive quality | Novice guidance | The customized welcome page Voice reminder Reserve an EV parking lot approaching destination | Customized travel summary | Change a normal parking lot to an EV parking lot for charging | N/A |

In order to establish a sense of security for users, we add the function of Vehicle self-diagnosis before starting service; Fingerprint verification before boarding; Safety precaution during driving; One click to rescue to be ready for whatever happens. At the same time, in order to improve the understandability of the system, in the scenario of summoning the vehicle and autonomous parking, we not only use indoor and outdoor navigation to reflect the vehicle status but also have the real-time video to better track the vehicle. Besides, some updated status of the vehicle can promptly push to users. Furthermore, we also focus on the controllability of the system, hoping that the whole process is flexible and controllable. Therefore, in the scenario of automated driving, users can switch automated driving to manual driving, and the itinerary can be changed or canceled at any time. It is also crucial to ensure the adjusted itinerary still transparent and complete in the system. For example, when canceling summon the vehicle, the vehicle can automatically return to the original parking lot after confirmation. In addition, we also consider the corresponding services about One-dimensional and Attractive quality, such as customized travel summary and reserve an EV parking lot.

## 3.2 Visual Communication

We mainly apply two variables (anthropomorphism and system transparency) in user interfaces to meet users' needs. For instance, considering the psychological processes during the initial encounters in the system, we use a corresponding degree of anthropomorphic guidance in the Graphical User Interface (GUI) which matching characteristics of potential users (e.g., age, gender, culture). It can make system features interact with personality factors in building up beliefs and attitudes about a system affecting the further usage of the system, which will build user trust and understandability of the system(see Fig. 2).

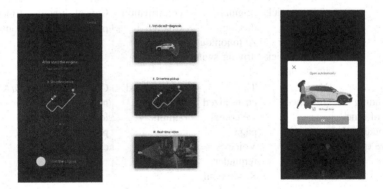

**Fig. 2.** Anthropomorphic guidance in the Graphical User Interface.

Considering the important features of intelligent systems are transparency, we explain and present information in a manner understandable by humans(as shown in Fig. 3). For example, when the vehicle leaves the garage, the user can see the pop-up reminding the vehicle passing through the gate; In the user interface of parking payment, we use a similar visual expression with mobile phones; When approaching the destination, the user can drop his car in the target area which is effectively expressed in the pop-up; The notification page of starting AutoParking has an easy-to-understand illustration to express. Therefore, the operation process and feedback of the system are visible, and using a visual expression based on the user's mental model will not make it difficult for the user to understand the system.

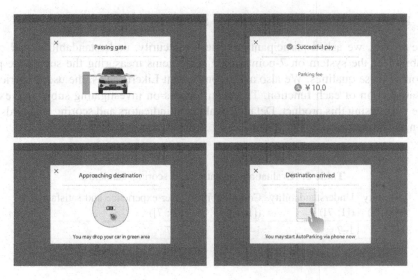

**Fig. 3.** Present information in a manner understandable by humans.

# 4 Experiment

## 4.1 Participants

Four subjects participated in the study, of which two were female, all were between 20 and 40 years old. All of them had more than one-year driving experience, and they were not experts in the automotive field and interaction design.

## 4.2 Procedure

Before the test, researchers described the main functions of the system to participants and they were shown the concept video of automated valet parking to understand. Participants had to complete a questionnaire before and after the test which can evaluate the subjective perception about security, understandability, and controllability and satisfaction of functions. Since there was no actual self-driving car, we used a Wizard of Oz setup in the experiment. In the scenario of autonomous driving, participants were sitting in the rental car, and the central prop was an interactive prototype on the iPad. In the stage of summoning the vehicle, autonomous parking and dynamic parking, participants were asked to sit in the office and image the real context of use, and they performed the interactive prototype on the smartphone to complete specific tasks. During the experience, participants were asked questions about the current function when used, about how much security is perceived, whether the current function can be understood, and whether the system is controllable. At the end of the experiments, subjects were interviewed in the conference room and rated their experience satisfaction, and interfaces were displayed on the desk to help them recall their feelings during the operation.

### 4.3   Evaluation Indicators and Scoring Standards

In the survey, we asked participants to rate the security, understandability, and controllability of the system on 7-point Likert scale items measuring the subjective perception of these qualities. We also asked, on 7-point Likert scales, the user experience and satisfaction of each function. This item focuses on investigating subjective experience when using this product. Detailed evaluation indicators and scoring standards are shown in Table 5.

**Table 5.** Evaluation indicators and scoring standards.

| Security ([1; 7]) | Understandability ([1; 7]) | Controllability ([1; 7]) | User experience and satisfaction ([1; 7]) |
| --- | --- | --- | --- |
| 1–7 | 1–7 | 1–7 | 1–7 |

### 4.4   Results

Results related to the experiment and questionnaires are presented, evaluating the subjective perception about security, understandability, and controllability and user experience before and after the test.

Overall, as shown in Fig. 4, the experimental results showed that users had more enjoyable experiences (with an average of 6.6 points) than the expectation (with an average of 4.9 points) before the test, and it proves that the need-centered research approach is effective. More specifically, in the scenario of summoning the vehicle and autonomous driving, because of the high degree of user perception of system security, intelligibility, and controllability, the user experience also had a comparatively higher score(see Fig. 5).

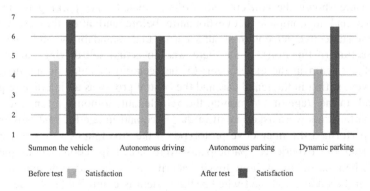

Before test ▮ Satisfaction          After test ▮ Satisfaction

**Fig. 4.** User satisfaction before and after the test.

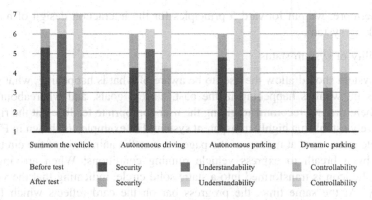

**Fig. 5.** The subjective perception about designed features before and after the test.

In the scenarios of summoning the vehicle, autonomous parking and dynamic parking, their satisfaction scores were relatively close, and it revealed significant correlations between the psychological needs of users and the context of use. Moreover, most users indicated that because dynamic parking was parking within a local range, and they had a high sense of security in this scenario. It means that we should focus on the demand differentiation in different scenarios, which can improve the user experience more effectively. Significantly, although users had lower expectations about the controllability of autonomous driving, they gave a higher score after the experience, and it can explain that some users had a sense of trust and peace of mind when they found the system is controllable. Therefore, we can build controllability of the system through interaction design, giving users more choices to improve the user's subjective perception of the system, which indirectly affects the user experience. According to the usage scenario, we also considered the corresponding services about One-dimensional and Attractive quality in the stage of summoning the vehicle and autonomous parking, such as customized travel summary, recognize driver's luggage and open the trunk automatically and so on. Both of these functions were highly evaluated in user feedback, which effectively improved the user experience. Therefore, in the system design, we need to consider personalized services to meet the user's expectations and preferences.

## 5 UX Framework and Design Principles

Based on the experimental results, we summarize an "UX framework" in the automated valet parking system: (a) Define user characteristics to create Persona models (b) identify different psychological needs and prioritize them by Kano model (c) Consider these needs involved behavioral, product, and experience-oriented aspects, reflecting them in the interaction design. At the same time, we need to pay attention to the dynamic priority of user needs in different scenarios. (d) Rate a product and its aspects as good or bad (e.g., standardized questionnaires like AttrakDiff) and have particular feelings while usage (e.g., standardized questionnaires like PANAS).

Furthermore, we put forward 5 principles for the interaction design of automated valet parking system,

1. Visibility of system status

The system should allow the user to be aware of what is happening, what state the vehicle is in, what is happening in the past, current goals, and whereabouts in the future. Therefore, we recommend giving the user appropriate feedback at the right time to effectively establish a highly transparent system. For example, as shown in Fig. 6, on the vehicle status card at the top of the page, we use the animation of the circular icon inspired by a breath to express vehicle running conditions; When arriving at the location, the icon is transformed into a static solid circle, indicating that the vehicle is stationary. At the same time, the progress bar on the card reflects which floor the vehicle is currently on and which action it has performed.

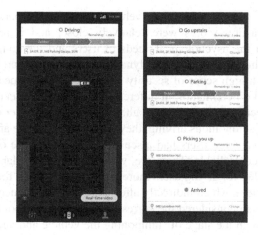

**Fig. 6.** Different vehicle status cards at the top of the page.

2. Present information in a way that understanding user cognition

Since the functions of the automated valet parking system are relatively novel to most users. Therefore, the information in the software should be as close as possible to the real world, using the language and visual expressions familiar to the user, which makes the information more natural and logically easier to understand by the user.

3. User control

In highly automated vehicles, the controllability of the system is critical for the user experience. Importantly, the loss of control will make users feel a sense of distance to the vehicle, and the subjective need for security is not fulfilled. Therefore, we emphasize the importance of collaborative control services (such as users can switch autonomous driving to manual driving in the vehicle), which can optimize the collaborative experience between the user and the vehicle. Furthermore, allowing the user to make adjustments to the itinerary at any time will also improve the user experience.

4. The balance of transparency and user cognition

In the automated valet parking system, people often play an observer role who need superfluous feedback to feel more in control, but it will add cognitive (attentional) load. Therefore, the system should display important information following appropriate feedback, and it is significant to establish the balance between transparent system and user cognition.

5. User-friendly help with an anthropomorphic way

Appropriate anthropomorphic GUI expressions can be used in the system, which is necessary to establish a subjective sense of security affecting the further usage of the system. It can make the system features resonate with the user's personality factors, thereby optimizing the user experience.

## 6  Conclusion

In this paper, we have discussed user experience concepts relevant in the automated valet parking system, highlight the importance of human factor research (such as trust-in-technology, cooperative control, and a sense of security) and consider the psychological processes during the initial encounters with a system. We present a need-centered approach discussing the priority of users' needs to be changed according to different situations, and reflect them in each function of the automated valet parking system to build the information architecture, then mainly apply two variables (anthropomorphism and system transparency) in user interfaces to meet users' needs. Finally, our experiment proves the effectiveness of the research method, indicating that building an automated valet parking system with safety, understandability, and controllability is essential to the user experience.

This research concludes the UX framework suitable for the automated valet parking system and proposes five design principles from the perspective of the combination of system functions and user cognition, which can provide some references for designers.

## References

1. Frison, A.-K., Wintersberger, P., Liu, T., Riener, A.: Why do you like to drive automated? A context-dependent analysis of highly automated driving to elaborate requirements for intelligent user interfaces. In: Proceedings of the 24th International Conference on Intelligent User Interfaces (IUI 2019), pp. 528–537. Association for Computing Machinery, New York (2019)
2. Litman, T.: Autonomous vehicle implementation predictions. Victoria Transport Policy Institute Victoria, Canada (2014)
3. Gold, C., Körber, M., Hohenberger, C., Lechner, D., Bengler, K.: Trust in automation – before and after the experience of take-over scenarios in a highly automated vehicle. Proc. Manuf. **3**, 3025–3032 (2015)

4. Merat, C.N., Jamson, A.H., Lai, F.C., Carsten, O.: Highly automated driving, secondary task performance, and driver state. Hum. Factors **54**(5), 762–771 (2012). https://doi.org/10.1177/0018720812442087
5. Naujoks, F., Mai, C., Neukum: A. The effect of urgency of take-over requests during highly automated driving under distraction conditions. In: Ahram, T., Karkowski, E., Marek, T. (eds.) Proceedings of the 5th International Conference on Applied Human Factors and Ergonomics, AHFE 2014, vol. 7, pp. 2099–2106 (2014)
6. Payre, W., Cestac, J., Delhomme, P.: Fully automated driving: impact of trust and practice onmanual control recovery. Hum. Factors **58**(2), 229–241 (2016). https://doi.org/10.1177/0018720815612319
7. Wintersberger, P., Riener, A., Frison, A.-K.: Automated driving system, male, or female driver: who'd you prefer? Comparative analysis of passengers' mental conditions, emotional states & qualitative feedback. In: Proceedings of the 8th International Conference on Automotive User Interfaces and Interactive Vehicular Applications (Automotive'UI 22016), pp. 51–58. ACM, New York (2016). https://doi.org/10.1145/3003715.3005410
8. Frison, K., Wintersberger, P., Riener, A.: Resurrecting the ghost in the shell: a need-centered development approach for optimizing user experience in highly automated vehicles. Transp. Res. Part F: Traff. Psychol. Behav. **65**, 439–456 (2019)
9. Dikmen, M., Burns, C.: Trust in autonomous vehicles: the case of tesla autopilot and summon. In: 2017 IEEE International Conference on Systems, Man, and Cybernetics (SMC), Banff, AB, pp. 1093–1098 (2017). https://doi.org/10.1109/smc.2017.8122757
10. Neuhaus, R., Lenz, E., Borojeni, S.S., Hassenzahl, M.: Exploring the future experience of automated "valet parking" - a user enactment. In: Proceedings of the 11th International Conference on Automotive User Interfaces and Interactive Vehicular Applications (AutomotiveUI 2019), pp. 24–34. Association for Computing Machinery, New York (2019). https://doi.org/10.1145/3342197.3344518
11. Borojeni, S.S., Boll, S.C.J., Heuten, W., Bülthoff, H.H., Chuang, L.: Feel the movement: real motion influences responses to take-over requests in highly automated vehicles. In: Proceedings of the 2018 CHI Conference on Human Factors in Computing Systems (CHI 2018), article 246, pp. 1–13. ACM, New York (2018). https://doi.org/10.1145/3173574.3173820
12. Borojeni, S.S., Weber, L., Heuten, W., Boll, S.: From reading to driving: priming mobile users for take- over situations in highly automated driving. In: Proceedings of the 20th International Conference on Human-Computer Interaction with Mobile Devices and Services (MobileHCI 2018), article 14, pp. 1–12. ACM, New York (2018). https://doi.org/10.1145/3229434.3229464
13. Wintersberger, P., Riener, A., Schartmüller, C., Frison, A.-K., Weigl, K.: Let me finish before i take over: towards attention aware device integration in highly automated vehicles. In: Proceedings of the 10th International Conference on Automotive User Interfaces and Interactive Vehicular Applications (AutomotiveUI 2018), pp. 53–65. ACM, New York (2018). https://doi.org/10.1145/3239060.3239085
14. Suppé, A., Navarro-Serment, L.E., Steinfeld, A.: Semi-autonomous virtual valet parking. In: Proceedings of the 2nd International Conference on Automotive User Interfaces and Interactive Vehicular Applications (AutomotiveUI 2010), pp. 139–145. ACM, New York (2010). https://doi.org/10.1145/1969773.1969798
15. Trösterer, S., Wurhofer, D., Rödel, C., Tscheligi, M.: Using a parking assist system over time: insights on acceptance and experiences. In: Proceedings of the 6th International Conference on Automotive User Interfaces and Interactive Vehicular Applications, pp. 1–8. ACM, New York (2014). https://doi.org/10.1145/2667317.2667327

16. Frison, A.-K., Wintersberger, P., Riener, A., Schartmüller, C.: Driving Hotzenplotz: a hybrid interface for vehicle control aiming to maximize pleasure in highway driving. In: Proceedings of the 9th International Conference on Automotive User Interfaces and Interactive Vehicular Applications (AutomotiveUI 2017), pp. 236–244. Association for Computing Machinery, New York (2017). https://doi.org/10.1145/3122986.3123016

17. Pettersson, I., Ju, W.: Design techniques for exploring automotive interaction in the drive towards automation. In: Proceedings of the 2017 Conference on Designing Interactive Systems, pp. 147–160. ACM (2017)

18. Rödel, C., Stadler, S., Meschtscherjakov, A., Tscheligi, M.: Towards autonomous cars: the effect of autonomy levels on acceptance and user experience. In: Proceedings of the 6th International Conference on Automotive User Interfaces and Interactive Vehicular Applications, pp. 1–8. ACM (2014)

19. Pettersson, I., Karlsson, M.-A.: Setting the stage for autonomous cars: a pilot study of future autonomous driving experiences. IET Intell. Transp. Syst. 9(7), 694–701 (2015). https://doi.org/10.1049/iet-its.2014.0168

20. Distler, V., Lallemand, C., Bellet, T.: Acceptability and acceptance of autonomous mobility on demand: the impact of an immersive experience. In: Proceedings of the 2018 CHI Conference on Human Factors in Computing Systems (CHI 2018), paper 612. pp. 1–10. Association for Computing Machinery, New York (2018)

21. Tuch, A.N., Hornbæk, K.: Does Herzberg's notion of hygienes and motivators apply to user experience? ACM Trans. Comput.-Hum. 22(4), 1–24 (2015)

22. Krome, S., Beaurepaire, J., Grani, F., Liu, A., Bosdelekidis, V.: Design-led exploration of indoor parking: an industry perspective. In: Proceedings of the 20th International Conference on Human-Computer Interaction with Mobile Devices and Services Adjunct (MobileHCI 2018), pp. 385–394. ACM, New York (2018) https://doi.org/10.1145/3236112.3236172

23. Kano, N., Seraku, N., Takahashi, F., Tsuji, S.: Attractive quality and must-be quality. J. Jpn. Soc. Qual. Control 14(2), 39–48 (1984)

# Optimization of the Method of Maintaining Arousal Level by Inducing Intrinsic Motivation: Using Presentation of Information in Autonomous Driving

Yuki Mekata[1]([⊠]), Shuhei Takeuchi[2], Tsuneyuki Yamamoto[2], Naoki Kamiya[2], Takashi Suzuki[2], and Miwa Nakanishi[1]

[1] Keio University, 3-14-1 Hiyoshi, Kohoku-ku, Yokohama, Kanagawa, Japan
wyume7921@gmail.com
[2] Tokai Rika Co., Ltd., 3-260 Toyota, Oguchi-cho, Niwa-gun, Aichi, Japan

**Abstract.** In recent years, the use of automation has been promoted in various systems such as automobiles, and the interaction between the system and user tends to decrease and be monotonous. Consequently, there is a concern that the arousal level of the user may decrease during work. In a semi-automatic system that requires user intervention in an emergency, performance degradation or accidents may occur because of the driver falling asleep. Therefore, an effective method of maintaining the arousal level must be established. Currently, the methods of stimulating the driver such as the presentation of siren sounds and injection of the scent of mint are being studied as the methods of maintaining the arousal level for automobile drivers. However, these methods of maintaining the arousal level via external stimulation have also suffered with challenges such as discomfort with the stimulation. In our previously conducted study, we proposed a method of maintaining the arousal level by presenting information that induced intrinsic motivation for maintaining the driving behavior in the driver; such a presentation might help maintain the arousal level. We aim to make such a method more applicable by optimizing the timing of the induction of intrinsic motivation.

**Keywords:** Arousal level · Intrinsic motivation · AI agent

## 1 Introduction

In recent years, automation has been promoted in various systems such as automobiles, and the interaction between the system and user tends to decrease and be monotonous. Consequently, there is a concern that the arousal level of a user might decrease during work. In a semi-automatic system that requires user intervention in an emergency, accidents might occur because of degrading performance or falling asleep of the driver. Therefore, an effective method of maintaining the arousal level must be established. Currently, the methods of stimulating such as the presentation of siren sounds and injection of the scent of mint are being studied as the methods of maintaining the arousal level of automobile drivers [1]. However, these methods of maintaining the

C. Stephanidis et al. (Eds.): HCII 2020, LNCS 12429, pp. 166–178, 2020.
https://doi.org/10.1007/978-3-030-59987-4_12

arousal level via external stimulation also encounter challenges such as sleep rebound, discomfort, and familiarity with the stimulations [1, 2].

However, as automobiles become more intelligent, there is growing interest in the possibility of assistance by AI agents. An AI agent can perform various interactions with the driver, and, therefore, by using AI agents to maintain the arousal level, it becomes possible to apply a method of maintaining the arousal level using an approach different from the previous method, which uses external stimulation. A study by Ibe et al. [3] exemplifies a method of maintaining the arousal level using an approach different from external stimulation; it is shown that the effect of maintaining the arousal level is expected compared to passive stimulation such as beeps, by giving the driver the active action. Furthermore, in our previously conducted study [4], we proposed a method of maintaining the arousal level by presenting information that induced intrinsic motivation for maintaining the driving behavior in the driver; in the study, the information to satisfy the needs of competence, autonomy, and relatedness was presented as the presentation to induce intrinsic motivation; it was suggested that such a presentation could provide an effect of maintaining the arousal level in both manual and autonomous driving. Furthermore, in this study, we aim to make such method more applicable by optimizing the timing of the induction of intrinsic motivation. Specifically, after establishing a model that estimates the arousal level of each person in real time, the experiment in which intrinsic motivation is induced when the arousal level drops to a specific level was conducted. We examined the effect of maintaining the arousal level after inducing intrinsic motivation.

## 2   Construction of Arousal-Level-Estimation Model

### 2.1   Experiment to Acquire Learning Data for Model Construction

To construct a model that estimates the arousal level in real time via machine learning, we conducted experiments to acquire learning data. The experimental task followed our previously conducted study and was set as follows. Several participants performed a task to monitor the progress of a course of a certain width for 30 min, and they subjectively evaluated the sleepiness during that duration for every minute. The subjective assessment was answered using a scale presented at the upper right portion of the experiment screen. With the leftmost end, i.e., 0, as the state of minimal sleepiness and the rightmost end, i.e., 100, the state of maximum sleepiness, the participants answered by moving the bar on the scale by pressing the left and right buttons continuously.

Figure 1 shows the experimental screen during the presentation of sleepiness assessment.

As a method for evaluating the arousal level of a driver, a method using facial images has been proposed [5]. Therefore, to evaluate the arousal level using facial images, the video of the face of a participant during the task was recorded at 60 Hz. Considering the experiments that measure multiple physiological responses while estimating the arousal level in real time, as described in the following chapter, the measuring devices that are supposed to be worn on the face at that time were also worn

**Fig. 1.** Example of experimental screen presenting sleepiness assessment.

during this experiment. The participants comprised 9 men aged from 22 to 25 years. Among the nine participants, six participants repeated the task for acquiring the learning data three times; one participant repeated the same task six times; one participant repeated seven times; one participant repeated eight times. Each participant performed the task only once a day; however, the repetition was performed on different dates.

## 2.2    Derivation of Model Estimating Arousal Level in Real Time

The model was created using the local binary patterns histogram (LBPH), which is the OpenCV face-estimation algorithm [6]. The face images of the participants were converted into images for each frame, and they corresponded to the sleepiness assessment at that time. The sleepiness assessment was obtained on a scale ranging from 0 to 100, and this scale was divided into 5 levels (each level comprising 20 increments) as labels 1–5. Notably, label 1 is the state wherein the sleepiness is minimum, and label 5 is the state wherein the sleepiness is maximum. Figure 2 shows an example of a face image for each of the five labels. For each participant, 3000 images were randomly extracted from each label, and, subsequently, LBPH was applied using 15000 images as learning data.

Sleepiness label1    Sleepiness label2    Sleepiness label3    Sleepiness label4    Sleepiness label5

**Fig. 2.** Examples of face images for each sleepiness label.

Employing the model derived for each participant using the above-mentioned method, the estimation accuracy was examined by comparing the sleepiness assessment (after five-step conversion) with the average value of the sleepiness label estimated using the face image for 10 s. Figure 3 shows an example of the sleepiness assessment and the above-mentioned estimated label for a task of a participant. From the results of other participants and other task times, it was confirmed that the sleepiness perceived by the participants subjectively could be correctly estimated from the facial images.

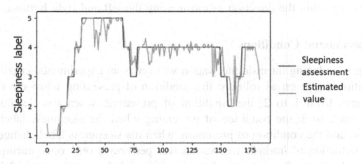

**Fig. 3.** Example of values of sleepiness assessment and estimated sleepiness label.

Figure 4 shows the histogram of the average throughout the task of the absolute value of the difference between the subjective assessment of sleepiness after the five-step conversion and the average value of the arousal level estimated using the face image for 10 s. Except for the two pieces of data, the estimated deviation was 1 or less, and no large deviation was observed exceeding the scale of one step in the five levels of the subjective assessment of sleepiness.

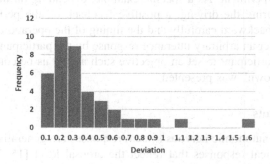

**Fig. 4.** Distribution of deviation between sleepiness assessment and estimated sleepiness label.

# 3 Examination of Timing of Induction of Intrinsic Motivation and Effect of Maintaining Arousal Level

## 3.1 Method

Using the arousal level-estimation model described in the previous chapter, an experiment was conducted to determine the optimal timing of inducing intrinsic motivation.

The participants performed a task to monitor the progress of a course of a certain width for 30 min. During the task, other vehicles may travel in front of the lane, behind the lane, or in other lanes. Although the vehicle was driving automatically, the participants were informed that they could change the lane, if necessary, to drive their vehicle smoothly and not to prevent other vehicles from driving. The lane could be changed by inputting the direction to move using the left and right buttons.

## 3.2   Experimental Conditions

The timing of inducing intrinsic motivation was set as an experimental condition. The four conditions were set as follows: the condition of presenting when the sleepiness label changes from 1 to 2, the condition of presenting when the sleepiness label changes from 2 to 3, the condition of presenting when the sleepiness label changes from 3 to 4, and the condition of presenting when the sleepiness label changes from 4 to 5. The induction of intrinsic motivation was performed only once during the task upon first calculating the corresponding sleepiness label as an estimated label under each condition.

Regarding the induction of intrinsic motivation, in our previously conducted study [4], we devised the presentation after organizing the factors of intrinsic motivation. As in our previously conducted study, the induction of intrinsic motivation was devised on the basis of the factors of intrinsic motivation. To satisfy the needs of competence, autonomy, and relatedness, all of which are the main factors of intrinsic motivation [7–14], we devised both the information that users obtain and information presented to users, following which we decided to give a voice message of feedback on the driving behavior in this experiment. As a specific example, depending on the performance of the participants during the driving, a positive feedback on the performance such as "you checked the backward carefully and the timing of the operation was appropriate" was presented. After an arbitrary utterance response by the participant, the information that prompts the participant to set an objective such as "let us be conscious of driving without slowing down" was presented.

## 3.3   Measurements

Brain activity and autonomic nervous-system responses are generally well known and used as physiological responses that reflect the arousal level [15–27]. Therefore, to measure the arousal level during the task, electroencephalograms, skin conductance level, respiration, electrocardiograms, and skin temperature were recorded using MP150, EEG100C, EDA100C, RSP100C, ECG100C, and SKT100C (BIOPAC). To evaluate the motivation during the task, the change in the cerebral blood volume was recorded using OEG-16 (Spectratech), which works on the concept of functional near-infrared spectroscopy.

Table 1 lists the measurements parameters of the above-mentioned physiological indices.

In addition, the log of performance, gaze transition using EMR-ACTUS (NAC), and face images of the participants during the task were recorded.

To evaluate the arousal level, the alpha-wave content of electroencephalogram, skin conductance level, respiration rate, heart rate, RSA component of heart-rate variability, and skin temperature were calculated. The arousal level was higher as the alpha-wave

Table 1. Measurement parameters of physiological indices.

| Index | Position of electrode | Filter |
|---|---|---|
| Electroencephalogram | A1, A2, C3, Cz, and C4 of the 10–20 system | 0.5–35 Hz |
| Electrodermal | Index finger and middle finger of left hand | 1.0 Hz |
| Respiration | Wear a band on the abdomen | 0.05–10 Hz |
| Electro-cardiogram | Left and right clavicle and abdomen | 0.5–35 Hz |
| Skin temperature | Nose tip | 1.0 Hz |
| Cerebral blood volume change | Wear a band on the forehead | – |

content of electroencephalogram, respiration rate, RSA component of heart-rate variability, and skin temperature were lower, and it was higher as the skin-conductance level and heart rate were higher [27–29].

Both dorsolateral prefrontal cortex (DLPFC) [30] and orbitofrontal cortex (OFC) [31] might be associated with motivation and reward system. To evaluate the motivation, we calculated the oxygenated-hemoglobin concentration in the channels corresponding to each site of DLPFC and OFC. Notably, the motivation is higher if these values are higher.

### 3.4 Experimental Procedure

The participants closed their eyes for 10 min after attaching the measuring devices. To suppress the variation in the arousal level at the start of the task, a pre-task was performed to increase the arousal level immediately before the start of the task. In the pre-task, the participants memorized 9 numbers presented on the screen for 3 s and, subsequently, answered the positions the numbers in the ascending after hiding numbers. In addition, three sets were constructed with five repetitions comprising one set. Each participant spent one day on one task, and each condition was performed on different dates.

### 3.5 Experimental Systems and Environment

The experimental system was created using Unity 2017.1.0f3. The participants performed experiments while sitting facing the desk on which a 50-in display device (NEC) and gaze-measuring device (EMR-AT ACTUS, NAC) were installed. Figure 5 shows the details of the experimental system.

### 3.6 Participants

The participants comprised 9 men aged from 22 to 25 years; they had previously acquired the learning data described in the previous chapter. They did not consume alcohol or caffeine, and they had adequate sleep the night before the experiment.

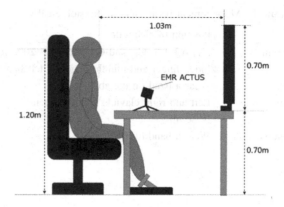

**Fig. 5.** Experimental environment.

This research was conducted after receiving approval from the Research Ethics Review Committee, Faculty of Science and Technology, Keio University.

## 4    Results and Discussion

### 4.1    Effect of Induction of Intrinsic Motivation

During the task, intrinsic motivation was induced at the timing when the estimated sleepiness label changed on the basis of the experimental conditions described in Sect. 3.2. As the estimated sleepiness label, a value smoothed by rounding the 10-s average of the estimated sleepiness label calculated using the estimation model was employed. The estimated sleepiness label change significantly in short time; further-more, in some instances, the timing of inducing intrinsic motivation was different from the intended time. Therefore, the experimental data were assigned to each condition on the basis of the average value of the sleepiness label for 30 s immediately before inducing intrinsic motivation. Upon including the data from the same participant in the same conditions, only one piece of the data was used. Consequently, 7 pieces of the data were assigned to conditions 1 and 2, 7 pieces of the data to conditions 2 and 3, 8 pieces of the data to conditions 3 and 4, and 6 pieces of the data to conditions 4 and 5.

From the results of the change in the oxygenated-hemoglobin concentration at each site of DLPFC and OFC, the average values were calculated for 10 s before the presentation and for 3 min after the presentation, following which they were compared with the average values at rest. Figure 6 shows the results including all the assigned data. The results meant that the intrinsic motivation increased after the presentation in both the sites. Therefore, it was confirmed that the induction of intrinsic motivation had an effect of inducing intrinsic motivation.

**Condition 1 → 2.** From the results of physiological indices, the change in the value of each index after inducing intrinsic motivation was classified into following three patterns: increasing arousal level, maintaining arousal level, and decreasing arousal

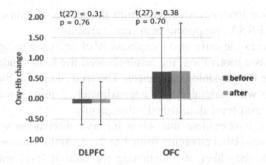

**Fig. 6.** Oxy-Hb change before and after inducing intrinsic motivation on DLPFC and OFC.

level. The change in the arousal level was evaluated on the basis of the average value and standard deviation for 10 s immediately before inducing intrinsic motivation and the change amount after inducing intrinsic motivation. Figure 7 shows the rate of change of patterns in the arousal level after inducing intrinsic motivation on heart rate.

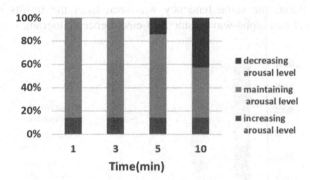

**Fig. 7.** Rate of patterns of arousal level evaluated using heart rate after inducing intrinsic motivation in condition 1 → 2.

The difference between the average value for 10 s immediately before inducing intrinsic motivation, and the average value for each minute for 0–1 min, 2–3 min, 4–5 min, and 9–10 min after inducing intrinsic motivation was calculated. If the absolute value of the difference was smaller than the standard deviation for 10 s immediately before inducing intrinsic motivation, the pattern indicated maintaining arousal level. However, if the difference was greater than the standard deviation for 10 s immediately before inducing intrinsic motivation, the pattern indicated increasing arousal level. In addition, if the difference was smaller than the negative value of standard deviation for 10 s immediately before inducing intrinsic motivation, the pattern indicated decreasing arousal level. From the result, approximately 5 min after inducing intrinsic motivation, the rate of improvement or maintenance of the arousal level was significantly high; however, the effect of maintaining the arousal level diminished subsequently.

In addition, the same tendency was seen from the results of skin-conductance level, respiration rate, and RSA component heart-rate variability.

From the change in the estimated sleepiness label analyzed using the facial image after inducing intrinsic motivation, the result showed the same tendency as shown by the evaluation using the physiological indices. The arousal level at the time of inducing intrinsic motivation was maintained for approximately 3 min; however, the effect of maintaining the arousal level diminished subsequently.

From the results, it is evident that when intrinsic motivation was induced at the timing of the sleepiness label changing from 1 to 2, i.e., at the state at which the arousal level was still high, the effect of maintaining the arousal level was observed up to approximately 3–5 min, and the effect diminished over time.

**Condition 2 → 3.** From the results of physiological indices, the change in the arousal level after inducing intrinsic motivation was examined using the above-mentioned analysis method. Figure 8 shows the rate of change of patterns in the arousal level after inducing intrinsic motivation on the heart rate. Approximately 3 min after inducing intrinsic motivation, the rate of improvement or maintenance of the arousal level was considerable. However, the effect of maintaining the arousal level diminished subsequently. In addition, the same tendency was seen from the results of both skin-conductance level and alpha-wave content of electroencephalogram.

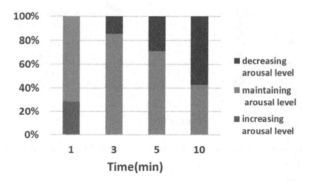

**Fig. 8.** Rate of patterns of arousal level evaluated using heart rate after inducing intrinsic motivation in condition 2 → 3.

From the change in the estimated sleepiness label after inducing intrinsic motivation, the result showed the same tendency as that shown by the evaluation using the physiological indices. The arousal level at the time of inducing intrinsic motivation was maintained for approximately 3 min. However, the effect of maintaining the arousal level diminished subsequently.

From the results, it is evident that when the presentation was performed at the timing of the sleepiness label changing from 2 to 3, i.e., at the timing of experiencing approximately the sleepiness of 50 on a scale of 0–100, the effect of maintaining the arousal level was temporarily seen. The duration of the effect was approximately 3 min, and the arousal level decreased subsequently.

**Condition 3 → 4.** From the results derived using the physiological indices, the change in the arousal level after inducing intrinsic motivation was examined using the above-mentioned analysis method. Figure 9 shows the rate of change of patterns in the arousal level after inducing intrinsic motivation on heart rate. The rate of improvement or maintenance of the arousal level was significantly high. It was observed that the effect of maintaining the arousal level continued after 10 min and more. In addition, the same tendency was seen from the results of skin-conductance level, respiration rate, and alpha-wave content of electroencephalogram.

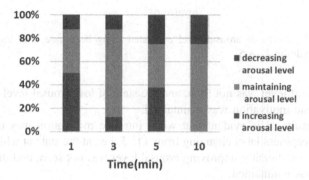

**Fig. 9.** Rate of patterns of arousal level evaluated using heart rate after inducing intrinsic motivation in condition 3 → 4.

From the change in the estimated sleepiness label analyzed using the facial image after inducing intrinsic motivation, the result showed the same tendency as shown by the evaluation using the physiological indices. The arousal level at the time of inducing intrinsic motivation was maintained for approximately 10 min or more in the majority of data.

From the results, it is evident that when intrinsic motivation was induced at the timing of the sleepiness label changing from 3 to 4, i.e., at the timing of experiencing the sleepiness of more than 60 on a scale of 0–100, further reduction in arousal level was arrested, and the effect of maintaining the arousal level continued for at least 10 min.

**Condition 4 → 5.** From the results derived using the physiological indices, the change in the arousal level after inducing intrinsic motivation was examined using the above-mentioned analysis method. Figure 10 shows the rate of change of patterns in the arousal level after inducing intrinsic motivation on heart rate. The rate of the pattern of increasing arousal level was relatively small, and the pattern of decreasing arousal level was seen from immediately after inducing intrinsic motivation. In addition, the same tendency was seen from the results of respiration rate and alpha-wave content of electroencephalogram.

From the change in the estimated sleepiness label analyzed using the facial image after inducing intrinsic motivation, the result showed the same tendency as shown by the evaluation using the physiological indices. Furthermore, the case of significantly

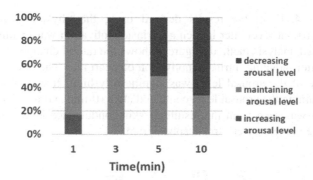

**Fig. 10.** Rate of patterns of arousal level evaluated using heart rate after inducing intrinsic motivation in condition 4 → 5.

improving arousal level was not seen, and the state of low arousal level at the time of inducing intrinsic motivation was maintained.

From the results, it is evident that when intrinsic motivation was induced at the timing of the sleepiness label changing from 4 to 5, i.e., at the state at which the arousal level was low, significantly improving arousal level was not seen, and the state of low arousal level was maintained.

## 4.2    Relationship Between the Timing of Induction of Intrinsic Motivation and the Effect of Maintaining Arousal Level

From the above-mentioned results, it might be appropriate to maintain the arousal level and performance via the induction of intrinsic motivation at the latest the timing of the sleepiness label changing from 3 to 4, i.e., at the timing of experiencing the sleepiness of more than 60 on a scale of 0–100. Upon inducing intrinsic motivation before this timing, the effect of maintaining the arousal level might be maintained for at least approximately 3 min.

## 5    Conclusion

In this study, the relationship between the timing of the induction of intrinsic motivation and effect of maintaining the arousal level was examined experimentally to establish a practical method of maintaining the arousal level via the induction of intrinsic motivation.

From the results, it might be appropriate to maintain the arousal level and performance via the induction of intrinsic motivation at the latest the timing of the sleepiness label changing from 3 to 4, i.e., at the timing of experiencing the sleepiness of more than 60 on a scale of 0–100. Upon inducing intrinsic motivation before this timing, the effect of maintaining the arousal level might be maintained for at least approximately 3 min.

By setting the timing and frequency of the induction of intrinsic motivation on the basis of such knowledge, a practical method of maintaining the arousal level might be obtained without considerable annoyance.

# References

1. Mohri, Y., Kawaguchi, M., Kojima, S., Yamada, M., Nakano, T., Mohri, K.: Arousal retention effect of magnetic stimulation to car drivers preventing drowsy driving without sleep rebound. IEEJ Trans. Electron. Inf. Syst. **136**(3), 383–389 (2016)
2. Hirata, Y.: A study on the effective method of aroma release program for keeping alertness. Proc. JSAE Annu. Congr. (61–00), 9–12 (2000)
3. Ibe, T., Hiraoka, T., Abe, E., Fujiwara, K., Yamakawa, T.: Wakefulness-keeping effect and driving safety by active action while driving. Trans. Soc. Autom. Eng. Jpn. **48**(2), 463–469 (2017)
4. Mekata, Y., Takeuchi, S., Yamamoto, T., Kamiya, N., Suzuki, T., Nakanishi, M.: Proposal of a method for maintaining arousal by inducing intrinsic motivation and verification of the effect. Trans. Soc. Autom. Eng. Jpn. **50**(4), 1138–1144 (2019)
5. Kitajima, H.: Prediction of automobile driver sleepiness: 1st report, rating of sleepiness based on facial expression and examination of effective predictor indexes of sleepiness. Trans. Jpn. Soc. Mech. Eng. Ser. C **63**(613), 3059–3066 (1997)
6. Face Recognition with OpenCV. https://docs.opencv.org/2.4/modules/contrib/doc/facerec/facerec_tutorial.html. Accessed 4 August 2019
7. Uebuchi, H.: The forefront of researches of motivation. Kitaohji, Kyoto, Japan (2004)
8. Deci, E.L., Ryan, R.M.: Handbook of Self-determination Research. University of Rochester Press, New York (2002)
9. Deci, E.L., Ryan, R.M.: Intrinsic Motivation and Self-determination in Human Behavior. Springer, US, New York (1985). https://doi.org/10.1007/978-1-4899-2271-7
10. Usui, M.: The effects of perceived competence and self-determination on intrinsic motivation. Jpn. J. Soc. Psychol. **7**(2), 85–91 (1992)
11. Sakurai, S.: The comparison of the effects of language and token rewards on intrinsic motivation. Jpn. J. Educ. Psychol. **32**(4), 286–295 (1984)
12. Lepper, R.M., Hodell, M.: Intrinsic motivation in the classroom. Res. Motivat. Educ. **3**, 73–105 (1989)
13. Kitamura, R., et al.: Intrinsically motivated cooperation: merits and demerits of monetary reward in social survey. Infrastr. Plann. Rev. **19**, 137–143 (2002)
14. Deci, E.L., Ryan, R.M.: Self-determination theory and the facilitation of intrinsic motivation, social development, and well-being. Am. Psychol. **55**(1), 68–78 (2000)
15. Santamaria, J., Chiappa, K.H.: The EEG of drowsiness in normal adults. J. Clin. Neurophysiol. **4**(4), 327–382 (1987)
16. Makeig, S., Inlow, M.: Lapses in alertness: coherence of fluctuations in performance and EEG spectrum. Electroencephalogr. Clin. Neurophysiol. **86**(1), 23–35 (1993)
17. Lal, S.K., Craig, A.: A critical review of the psychophysiology of driver fatigue. Biol. Psychol. **55**, 173–194 (2001)
18. Japanese society of sleep research: Handbook of sleep science and sleep medicine. Asakura Publishing Co., Ltd., Chapter V-2, pp. 519–532 (1994)
19. Pressman, M.R., Fry, J.M.: Relationship of autonomic nervous system activity to daytime sleepiness and prior sleep. Sleep **12**(3), 239–245 (1983)

20. Horner, R.L.: Autonomic consequences of arousal from sleep: mechanisms and implications. Sleep **19**(10), 193–195 (1996)
21. Japanese society of sleep research:. Handbook of sleep science and sleep medicine. Asakura Publishing Co., Ltd., Chapter I-2, pp. 42–52 (1994)
22. Ishida, K., Hachisuka, S., Kimura, T., Kamijo, M.: Comparing trends of sleepiness expressions appearance with performance and physiological change caused by arousal level declining. Trans. Soc. Autom. Eng. Jpn. **40**(3), 885–890 (2008)
23. Nishimura, C.: Traffic safety from a viewpoint of car drivers' arousal level. Int. Assoc. Traff. Saf. Sci. Rev. **19**(4), 19–28 (1993)
24. Yamakoshi, T., et al.: Physiological investigation of automobile driver's activation index using simulated monotonous driving. Trans. Soc. Autom. Eng. Jpn. **36**(6), 205–212 (2005)
25. Yanagidaira, M., Yasushi, M.: Development of driver's condition monitor. Pioneer R&D **13**(2), 75–82 (2003)
26. Sakamoto, R., Nozawa, A., Tanaka, H., Mizuno, T., Ide, H.: Evaluation of the driver's temporary arousal level by facial skin thermogram-effect of surrounding temperature and wind on the thermogram. Trans. Jpn. Soc. Mech. Eng. Ser. C **126**(7), 804–809 (2006)
27. Technical Information Institute Co. Ltd.: Technology of detection and estimation of driver status and application to autonomous driving and driving support system. Technical Information Institute Co., Ltd., Chapter 2, pp. 11–120 (2017)
28. Society of automotive engineers of Japan: Automotive engineering handbook 3. Soc. Autom. Eng. Jpn. **5**, 371–435 (2016)
29. Japan society of physiological anthropology: Encyclopedia of Human Sciences. MARUZEN Publishing, Tokyo (2015)
30. Ono, T., et al.: Single neuron activity in dorsolateral prefrontal cortex of monkey during operant behavior sustained by food reward. Brain Res. **311**(2), 323–332 (1984)
31. Rolls, E.T.: The functions of the orbitofrontal cortex. Brain Cogn. **55**(1), 11–29 (2004)

# Global Implications of Human Tendencies Towards Automated Driving and Human Driver Availability in Autonomous Vehicles

Ankit R. Patel[1]([✉])[iD], Flora Ferreira[2][iD], Sergio Monteiro[1][iD],
and Estela Bicho[1][iD]

[1] Department of Industrial Electronics, ALGORITMI Research Center,
University of Minho, Guimaraes, Portugal
majorankit@gmail.com, {sergio,estela.bicho}@dei.uminho.pt
[2] Center of Mathematics, University of Minho, Guimaraes, Portugal
flora.ferreira@gmail.com

**Abstract.** In the era of industrial revolution 4.0, an automotive industry flourished in a way that was never before. As different features added in the driver assistance systems time-to-time, hence, nowadays the driving process is not so much tedious as it seems before. This ensures the operation of hassle-free driving, which leads towards autonomous vehicles. Overall, it opens up many opportunities for researchers and business communities, but at the same time, raises concerns and issues for discussion that need to be analyzed before put the final product (here, in the sense of fully automated vehicle) on the road. We conducted an online-survey (N = 3139) with participants from 146 nations was participated and assembled their valuable feedback on the automated driving and human presence in the autonomous vehicles considering all the levels of driving automation. This paper explores the results in terms of useful implications, which highlights and implied us to re-examine the present regulations and policies in automated driving and autonomous vehicles.

**Keywords:** Automated driving · Autonomous vehicle · Implications · Survey

## 1 Introduction

Driving is a decision-making process by the humans and factors like stress can cause changes in decisions, reactions, and concentration capabilities [1–3]. And hence, it is substantial to know the people's opinions about what they are thinking about new technologies. We are fortunate enough that the 21st century is coming up with new advanced technology in the automobile sector, widely known as advanced driver assistance systems (ADAS), which has mainly four cognitive decision making tasks [4]: (a) assess the situation, (b) identify the available

© Springer Nature Switzerland AG 2020
C. Stephanidis et al. (Eds.): HCII 2020, LNCS 12429, pp. 179–192, 2020.
https://doi.org/10.1007/978-3-030-59987-4_13

options, (c) determine the costs and benefits (relative value) of each, and (d) select the option of the lowest costs and highest benefits. The vehicles for today are equipped with these new technologies, and owing to that the stress on a human driver is reduced [5]. The levels of driving automation were provided for the first time in 2014 by the National Highway Traffic Safety Administration (NHTSA) [6], which is an operating body of the US Department of Transportation (DoT). It is quite obvious that with the continuous change in the various driving related operations, NHTSA published new driving automation levels in 2016 [7] and 2018 [8].

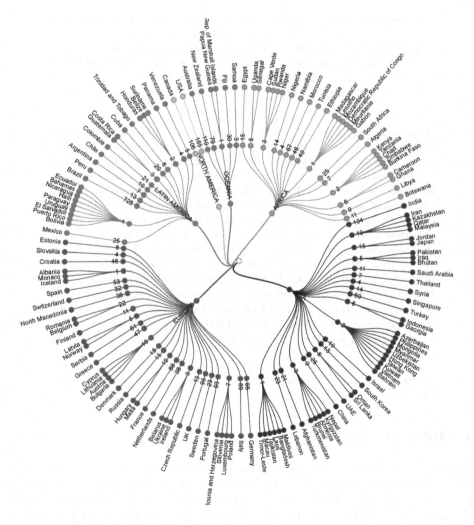

**Fig. 1.** Continent and nation-wise information of respondents.

This progressive rise of introducing new innovations in the automotive industry was more empowered when the first autonomous vehicle event held in California, USA in the year 2007 [9]. This opened up wings for the new development in the sector, especially as the autonomous vehicle has features like useful in traffic control (e.g. Management of traffic control in an effective way), manage the costs of congestion in urban areas, improve fuel economy, provide a new direction in the future city planning, a boon for people who are physically impaired, among others. The success of the autonomous vehicles will depend on the various factors of social-demographic environment, how the way people are accepted or rejected, whether the regulatory policies are enough to protect the rights of human or not. We should discuss such kinds of many obstacles on the way before putting autonomous vehicles on the road for common use and public transportation.

To date, there is no fully autonomous vehicle available on-road for the service, although the technology level reached a stage where the initial test is carried out by several OEMs. However, there are different acceptance criteria by the people around the globe, as it depends on the various factors. Considering all these modalities, we carried out an online survey (N = 3139, 146 nations worldwide (see Fig. 1)) from 14 February 2019 to 10 July 2019 with two key research questions, and to the best of our knowledge this kind of work is the first time combines the parameters of both automated driving and human driver presence in the autonomous vehicle (for the results of the survey, see Fig. 2).

 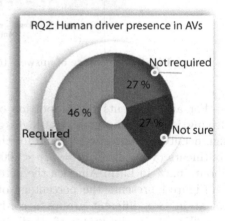

**Fig. 2.** Results of RQ1 and RQ2.

- **RQ1:** Whether automated driving is good or bad (in terms of reducing the driver stress, technological advantage, etc.) for mankind in a long run?
- **RQ2:** Whether the presence of a human driver is required (considering all levels of driving automation) in autonomous vehicles?

## 2   Data Analysis

As it is very clear that to investigate the research questions asked, the age and driving experience plays a key role. Hence, in this study we just consider the answers of people with driving experience and with age higher than 18 years old. Furthermore, double responses and in some cases the responses not appropriate (e.g. the difference between age and years of driving experience less than 18) were excluded. Hence, we only consider 2080 responses as useful for further analysis. The data were cross-tabulated and chi-square ($\chi^2$) analyzes were performed to estimate the statistical strength of association between continents, and answers to the research questions. The level of statistical significance is set at *p-value* < .05.

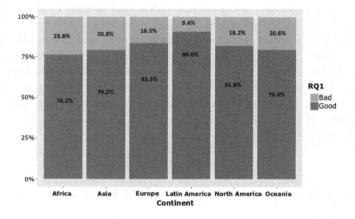

**Fig. 3.** Percentage of answers to each RQ1 option per continent.

For all continents the proportion of people who answered that automated driving is something good was high (greater than 76%, see Fig. 3). However, significant differences were found for the percentage of answers between the six continents ($\chi^2 = 32.79, df = 5, p < .0001$). While in Africa the percentage was about 76.2% in Latin America the percentage goes up to 90.6%.

Figure 4 presents the percentage of answers to each RQ2 option per continent in two different groups according to the answer in the RQ1("Good" and "Bad"). In the group of 'Bad' answers in RQ1, no evidence of the relationship between continents and RQ2 answer was bound ($\chi^2 = 10.97, df = 10, p = .360$). However, amongst the group of 'Good' answers in RQ1 significant evidence of the relationship between continents and RQ2 answer was bound ($\chi^2 = 60.56, df = 10, p < .0001$). While in Africa 64.9% answer 'Required' and just 14.9% answer 'Not Required', in Europe and Latin America the percentage of 'Required' and 'Not Required' were less than 40% and more than 30%, respectively. Comparing the percentage of answers to each RQ2 option between the group that answer 'Good' in RQ1 and the group that answer 'Bad' in RQ1

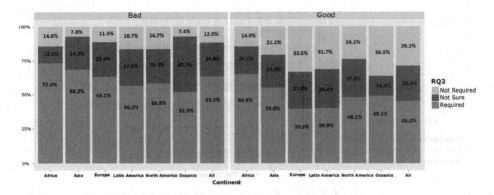

**Fig. 4.** Percentage of answers to each RQ2 option per continent in two different groups according to the answer in the RQ1 ('Good' and 'Bad').

for all answers, strong evidence of the relationship between RQ1 and RQ2 was found ($\chi^2 = 51.79, df = 2, p < .0001$). In fact, while 63.2% of the group that answer 'Bad' in RQ1 answer 'Required' in RQ2, just 45.2% of the group that answer 'Good' in RQ1 answer 'Required' in RQ2.

## 3   Implications

The focus of this paper is to explore the new avenues besides the RQ1 and RQ2 in terms of participant's implications (see Fig. 5). It is quite clear how these factors helpful in defining and developing new human-vehicle based technologies for the upcoming intelligent vehicles (or even future 'cognitive vehicles') that cope up with every situation. They also indicate knowledge gaps between diverse areas where future efforts should be carried out.

Our methodology was developed and adopted involving two steps. First, during the survey period, it is based on the discussion with the participants through online platforms, for example, LinkedIn, Facebook, WhatsApp, etc. And secondly, as a collection of viable feedback from the participants. We are quite conscious about not including any policy reports on automated driving and autonomous vehicles produced by the governments or any other organizations as a part of implication.

### 3.1   Infrastructure

Infrastructure is the entity where physical and digital worlds meet together. For the successful deployment of autonomous vehicles on the road, a dedicated infrastructure facility is needed, which also supports the levels of automated driving [10]. It is split into two categories: (a) physical infrastructure and (b) Information and Communication Technology (ICT) enabled infrastructure.

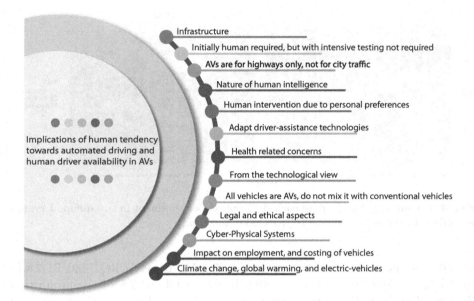

**Fig. 5.** Implications based on human tendencies towards automated driving and human driver presence in autonomous vehicles.

**Physical Infrastructure:** Currently available physical infrastructure is designed based on the conventional (non-autonomous) vehicles and somehow considering the human drivers' cognitive abilities. Also noted that building a new infrastructure that will support autonomous vehicles on the road is a little easy about the developing and undeveloped nations as they have to start with scratch compared to developed nations were already having heavy traffic on the road. The pace at which the autonomous vehicle technology developed and achieve the level of penetration will clearly indicate more investment to be needed in the physical infrastructure. Despite the fact that the nature of this infrastructure will be complex, who and how will maintain the infrastructure under which conditions? This means that whether the infrastructure will be maintained by the government agencies or by the vehicle manufacturers or by the other private organizations. A reformed infrastructure includes road markings and signs, enough charging stations in case of electric autonomous mobility, crash barriers, speed signs are among the others. It is also taking care that the visibility of the said steps has to be maintained in all the seasons.

Physical infrastructure must enable and support not only autonomous vehicles, but also different players including pedestrians and cyclists. A key challenge is to have dedicated areas for walking and cycling that will create a liveability, especially in urban spaces. By doing so, guarantees that the infrastructure will cope with the other traffic players and hence allow fleets more efficient along with socially acceptable and safer.

**Information and Communication Technology (ICT) Enabled Infrastructure:** In addition to physical infrastructure, we have to look after ICT based infrastructure owing to its features including to provide an accurate vehicle localization during the journey, assist a lane-keeping in the case of connected and automated vehicles (CAVs), managing traffic information flows between the traffic management center are among others.

To meet the requirements of rapid improvement and expansion of the current autonomous vehicle technology, a future ICT based infrastructure will be enabled by consistent connectivity between the vehicles and outside partners (e.g. Pedestrians, cyclists, other vehicles, etc.). With the emergence of 5G technology, which assures high-speed data connectivity and downloading facilities, is expected to resolve all the issues of connectivity in the ages of intelligent transportation.

## 3.2  Initially, Human Required, but with Intensive Testing Not Required

Autonomous vehicles will be a game changer in redefining mobility, at the same time requires a lot of development which ensures the safety at all levels and in all conditions. Just to switch from manual to an autonomous vehicle will solve all the current road problems related to safety is not yet guaranteed profoundly with the present development of technology, for example, the latest fatalities by Tesla [11], and Uber [12]. This will come with a new discussion, whether the reliability of autonomous vehicles defined by the number of miles traveled, and if so, how to calculate it [13].

Considering these situations, currently, a human driver is required for testing and safety point of view, however, as the technology grows up the need for a human driver will subside. A completely cloud controlled traffic system would be much safer and more efficient than any system involving human control. The hard part is the transition phase, in which human drivers are inevitable, but autonomous vehicles need to be able to cope with these factors. It is common knowledge that more than 90% of accidents have been occurring today due to human error. The push for autonomy is to focus on the reduction in the number of Killed and Seriously Injured (KSI) and reduce road-related fatalities. There are multiple other benefits such as reduction or elimination of driver fatigue, freeing up of time spent driving, which could increase productivity or free time, more efficient traffic flows through the cities and optimization of the use of road infrastructure. It is also true that correctly developed and deployed autonomous vehicles could reduce the number of vehicles required if shared use and ride-sharing is promoted in an effective way.

When looking at autonomous vehicles, where we are still in the phases of adapting and learning. Before adopting this vehicle to be a part of our routine life, the software and hardware are well-tested for many levels to avoid any malfunctions. However, in the short-term, there may be a need to build trust, which is one of the challenging parts for the successful deployment of vehicles on the road in a mass volume. Thus, human presence may be seen as a good way to win trust. Still, how long a human driver required is not cleared yet, and hence it is quite early to tell about the absence of the human driver in the AVs in the near future. Altogether, in the coming time, it is a challenge for the vehicle manufacturers to develop layouts that support both human driver and driverless configurations at least for the next few decades.

### 3.3    AVs are for (Motorways) Highways Only, Not for City Traffic

The key question with respect to autonomous vehicles is that they occupy the same space as today's conventional vehicles. If so, then it is highly recommended that autonomous vehicles are deployed firstly only on motorways with stronger rules, for example, no human driver car quickly coming on the motorways. This is because of future city centers might be very limited with vehicular transportation in order to give more space for pedestrians and other road users. In these limited-access centers, AVs can be used as a complementary service to some specific areas and tasks. The implementation of fully autonomous vehicles in an urban environment is highly unlikely to occur to a wide scale because of the complexity which lies in the interactions between vehicles for busy city streets, pedestrians, other modes of transport as well as unpredictable behavior of different road users.

### 3.4    Nature of Human Intelligence

There is no doubt that technological innovations increase productivity, but are they enough mature to compete with human intelligence in all conditions, especially, in the case of road accidents. Despite numerous similarities between accidents, it is not possible to find even two identical events (accidents) in which their parameters are exactly the same. Human intelligence should never be replaced by machines, as there are situations where algorithms are not capable of learning as a human can. Hence, automation is great progress and opportunity to improve drivers' skills, however, that has to enhance the drivers' capabilities not to replace them.

### 3.5    Human Intervention Due to Personal Preferences

Apart from other technical modalities, people want the control of a vehicle for their hands and not to the machine (here, an autonomous vehicle). This is due to their mentality, routine habits, and at the same time raise questioning the current regulatory and infrastructure concerns. If the system is totally automated and works as a boss, but in some uncertain situations where machines are not capable to anticipate the situation correctly, hence human intervention is necessary to regain the smooth and safe travel as a supervisory agent.

### 3.6   Adapt Driver-Assistance Technologies

While autonomous vehicles have enormous potential to benefit society, care will need to be taken to optimize these benefits of the whole transport system. Nowadays, automotive majors are rushing into filling the streets with autonomous vehicles predicted to be in the near future, where they compete with each other to prove their technological superiority, rather than cooperating to overcome the existing challenges that still lay ahead. Effort should be spent on driver-assistive technologies, where there is a huge potential to improve and save human lives. We have seen in the last decade that the rapid development and the speed of deployment of different driver-assist technologies in the vehicles is astonishing. This is not only due to only safety concerns, but provide comfort to the driver in day-to-day driving operation, and control the vehicle in an indeterminate state. Today drivers use more than 90% of automatic technologies, in the case of in-vehicle infotainment systems (IVIS) to automatic lane changing and braking systems, while driving to manage the conscious and unconscious state. This way one can travel through quite long periods of time for minimal risk and an optimal amount of mental workloads. It is also observed that the accessibility of the driver-assist systems is increasing day by day, and will continue until the fully automatic vehicles developed which will work in all conditions. We should give surety to make a balance between automation and human intelligence with the effective integration of human factors in the process of design and development of such systems.

### 3.7   Health Related Concerns

In light of the transition to conventional to autonomous mobility, we should have to take care of health-related issues while and after deployment of the system. If a driver is in a passive role or having no role in active driving due to automated driving, especially considering SAE Level 3–5, over the time he/she forget how to drive a vehicle and will cause numerous health-related issues. The use of autonomous vehicles by very ill people along with their pets will increase illness in the cities. Individual autonomous vehicles are not solutions to all these kinds of social trouble, the solution is to aware people to use more and more public transport, which is autonomous in nature.

### 3.8   From the Technology Point of View

If we explore the autonomous vehicles for the technological advancement point of view, of course, there are two sides of the coin, (a) Trust in technology, and (b) Is the technology mature enough to trust?

**Trust in Technology:** In the era of the fourth industrial revolution where the growth of computational power and sensor data is tremendous, hence, automation and artificial intelligence (AI) are inevitable. Where manpower has to be used for other productive purposes to make society more livable and responsible. A person is smarter than a machine, but it depends on a case by case basis. When we are doing repetitive tasks, we generally tend to become easily distracted or tired. Autonomous vehicles are able to maintain the same level of alertness all the time, if well designed. For example, in the military application, it is proven that automation and artificial intelligence-based weaponry system works well, with or without human presence for a long time. Altogether, machines are definitely behaving better than a human if we trained to learn them in all the situations as well as improve them to take the foolproof decision providing the design are trustworthy.

**Is the Technology Mature Enough to Trust?** No machine can rival human judgment, especially if it is based on emotions and values. The judgment on an autonomous vehicle is only based on data given by sensors that are not comparable to human senses in terms of quality, reliability, trust, and self-assessment. There will always be an indistinct case which will be vague to interpret. For example, a fully autonomous system may get troubled or even failed by wrong inputs and create dangerous situations. Artificial intelligence is still in the learning phase (e.g. To recognize road signs, obstacles, the difference from a bike rider and a pedestrian crossing the road, etc.) and mistakes may still be made. The technology is not yet matured enough to work in case of heavy fog, snowfall, bad weather, and hence to adhere to all these will take time depends on how the automation and AI develop over the years.

### 3.9   All Vehicles are AVs, Not Mix It with Conventional Vehicles

It is a nightmare to give a 100% guarantee that no accident will occur with adopting autonomous vehicles for the roads of the future having mixed traffic conditions. Therefore, if all the vehicles on the road are autonomous (considering SAE Level 5) then there is no human driver really necessary. In such a condition, there will be no interaction of driver behaviors (as no human driver presence on the road in any of the vehicle) and the autonomous vehicle will remedy all the safety and operational issues. And hence, great potential for passengers to use their time productively, as all the AVs on the network can produce system having optimal solutions with regard to travel time and energy consumption too.

### 3.10   Legal and Ethical Point of View

**Legal Matters:** In the realm of safety and digitization of the transportation system, for example, intelligent traffic management systems and effective tracking systems, require the establishment of specific legal backgrounds and strict regulations. As of now, the deployment of autonomous vehicles for mixed traffic systems is not studied well due to a lack of legal framework. There are still, some open questions that pointing out legal liability include, (a) Who will be accountable in case of malfunctions? Be a software provider? Be the manufacturer? Be the owner of the vehicle? (b) How to handle different contexts? Are manufacturers enabling to develop a different vehicle for different countries owing to infrastructure, traffic regulations, driver habits, etc.? (c) How to adopt autonomous vehicles to match with the mindset of pedestrians and drivers in different geographical aspects? (d) Who is liable in case of an accident of fully autonomous and non-autonomous vehicles? Answers to such questions are not clear yet and to be discussed or to be considered before framing any legal roadmap and deployment of an autonomous vehicle on the road.

The development and deployment of autonomous vehicles are going to change the nature of the insurance service sector. Decision making in extreme and unavoidable cases that end with a fatal accident is the key question of the time. While human beings are judgmental and condemnable subjects, the decision on a pre-programmed algorithm does not work all the time. Cases like this where insurance plays a vital role and in which the algorithm developer will predetermine the collateral damage in case of an accident and this will generate a different insurance coverage.

**Ethical Issues:** Transition to fully automated driving will require regulations that will restrict some personal freedom and it is not clear if that is balanced by the benefits. There are many parameters to be considered and taken into account for this to be acceptable to every user, especially in complex situations involving the ethical factor as a prime [14]. Yet moral choice solutions not made available, for example, in case of an emergency situation (a) Whether a vehicle ended up on a wall or to the person on the road? (b) Would the death of children be more important than an elder? (c) Should a pregnant woman count as two lives? Lastly, in the case of an accident which causes only injuries, but no fatalities, whether the pre-programmed algorithms are enough to define the priority of the decisions by severity, types of injuries as well as life affected by it?

## 3.11   Cyber-Physical Systems (CPS) Concerns

We all know that driving is a complex task and to make it easy or smoother will need plenty of programming capability in case of the autonomous vehicle. By doing this, the system has the issue of vulnerability. The efficiency and reliability of autonomous vehicles totally depended on the computing power, competency and network effectiveness, which can fail or even hack by the hacker. In the context of malware and ransomware putting into the system during the upgradation of software, how to protect the vehicle? Intelligent vehicles have several electronic control units (ECUs), which are connected with an internal network of the fulfillment of various tasks. Attacking these ECUs and breaching the data line will cause numerous unknown complications which never happened before. On the way of deployment of such vehicles issues related to the infringement of data is not resolved yet. Broadly, the open questions related to data privacy include, (a) Who will keep the data? (b) What is the size of data storage (e.g.

Daily, weekly, etc.)? (c) Who provides security to store data? (d) If data is stolen, by which law one can be punished?

### 3.12    Impact on Employment, and Costing of Vehicles

Driving is a socioeconomic entity, and hence, by the implementation of an autonomous vehicle on the road will create serious employment issues in many countries. If so, it will push out some sort of criminal activity and increase the poverty level in society. In particular, developing nations will face drastic changes in their political domain as a number of people are going to unemployed suddenly. Deployment of an autonomous vehicle for the developing nations is not feasible due to infrastructure facilities, and especially they have already fought with a higher unemployment rate. In light of these, the governments have to find some suitable way of employment before adapting an autonomous vehicle.

Although, there is a tremendous development during the recent time for the autonomous vehicle technology, still, the costing of a single unit is not predicted well enough. There are lots of factors affecting the costing, include what kind of the infotainment system provided, what level of security provided, where the unit is manufactured, and what is another extra package demanded by the customer.

### 3.13    Climate Change, Global Warming, Electric-Vehicles

Autonomous vehicle technology came up with the revolutionary change in the day to day life. Of course, it comes up with a profound effect on the environment, but whether it is good or bad will depends on the regulatory authorities that how they will manage and/or define the rules and regulations. In the midst of various driver-assist and autonomous vehicle technology development, one of the greatest challenge comes across is global warming. This is because yet not clear whether the greenhouse gas (GHG) and emission reduction guaranteed by adopting autonomous vehicles. It depends on how many AVs are on the road, nature of congestion on road, and fuel efficiency per mile traveled by the AVs are among the other prime factors. One of the solutions is to prepare the future road to electrical autonomous vehicles (EAVs). EAVs should be integrated with the vehicle sharing and public transport system to ensure the reduction in the level of emission.

## 4    Limitations of the Survey

As the survey was conducted via different web-based platforms, hence, there are no specific participatory restrictions imposed on participants. That's why it has seen that we recorded a high number of responses from one part of the world, while it is not true for the rest, for example, the total number of respondents counted from Brazil was 728 and at the other end only single respondents from counties like Ecuador, Paraguay, Haiti, etc. which may affect the results of whole Latin America. Furthermore, it was assumed that adequate information provided with the survey page was enough for the participants to understand the concept of automated driving and autonomous vehicles. Although, we were available online for any kind of help throughout the time of the survey period. It may be observed that findings from the survey conducted are largely based on descriptive and qualitative. Hence, future research is needed to comprehend and investigate diverse analyses based on the near real-time or simulator-based study to ensure the facts presented.

## 5 Conclusions

The way in which it portrays the usefulness of automated driving and the importance of autonomous vehicles for the society as a next-generation intelligent transportation system, there is no doubt that it will work largely for the benefit of a common man. But, in a journey of driver-assistance to driver replacement, we should not forget the key player "human". By considering these implications, it will help to the policymakers and regulatory authorities to put autonomous vehicles in more acceptable and meaningful ways.

**Acknowledgments.** This work has been supported by the Portuguese Foundation for Science and Technology (FCT – Fundação para a Ciência e Tecnologia) within the R&D Units Project Scope: UIDB/00319/2020. The authors would like to thankful all the anonymous participants for their valuable contribution to the online survey.

## References

1. Healey, J., Picard, R.W.: Detecting stress during real-world driving tasks using physiological sensors. IEEE Trans. Intell. Transp. Syst. **6**(2), 156–166 (2005). https://doi.org/10.1109/TITS.2005.848368
2. Rigas, G., Goletsis, Y., Fotiadis, D.I.: Real-time driver's stress event detection. IEEE Trans. Intell. Transp. Syst. **13**(1), 221–234 (2012). https://doi.org/10.1109/TITS.2011.2168215
3. Stanton, N.A., Young, M.S.: Driver behaviour with adaptive cruise control. Ergonomics **48**(10), 1294–1313 (2005). https://doi.org/10.1080/00140130500252990
4. Groeger, J.A.: Understanding Driving: Applying Cognitive Psychology to a Complex Everyday Task. 1st edn. Psychology Press (2000)
5. Chung, W., Chong, T., Lee, B.: Methods to detect and reduce driver stress: a review. Int. J. Autom. Technol. **20**, 1051–1063 (2019). https://doi.org/10.1007/s12239-019-0099-3
6. The Society of Automotive Engineers (SAE): Taxonomy and definitions for terms related to on-road motor vehicle automated driving systems - J3016 (2014). https://www.sae.org/standards/content/j3016_201401/
7. The Society of Automotive Engineers (SAE): Taxonomy and definitions for terms related to on-road motor vehicle - J3016 (2016). https://www.sae.org/standards/content/j3016_201609/
8. The Society of Automotive Engineers (SAE): Taxonomy and definitions for terms related to driving automation systems for on-road motor vehicles - J3016 (2018). https://www.sae.org/standards/content/j3016_201806/

9. Montemerlo, M., Jan, B., et al.: Junior: the stanford entry in the urban challenge. J. Field Robot. **25**(9), 569–597 (2008). https://doi.org/10.1002/rob.20258

10. Anna, C., Xavier, D., Jacqueline, E., Stefan, R. : Road infrastructure support levels of automated driving. In: Proceedings of 25th ITS World Congress, Copenhagen, Denmark, pp. 1–10 (2018). https://www.inframix.eu/wp-content/uploads/ITSWC2018-ASF-AAE-Final-paper_v4.pdf

11. Wattles, J.: Tesla on autopilot crashed when the driver's hands were not detected on the wheel (2019). https://edition.cnn.com/2019/05/16/cars/tesla-autopilot-crash/index.html

12. Lubben, A.: Self-driving uber killed a pedestrian as human safety driver watched (2018). https://news.vice.com/en_us/article/kzxq3y/self-driving-uber-killed-a-pedestrian-as-human-safety-driver-watched

13. Robert, L.P.: Are automated vehicles safer than manually driven cars? AI Soc. **34**(3), 687–688 (2019). https://doi.org/10.1007/s00146-019-00894-y

14. Bonnefon, J.F., Shariff, A., Iyad, R.: The social dilemma of autonomous vehicles. Science **352**(6293), 1573–1576 (2016). https://doi.org/10.1126/science.aaf2654

# Perception and Processing in Automated Driving – A Dual Process Application

Vanessa Sauer[1](✉), Alexander Mertens[1], Madeleine Reiche[2],
Christoph Mai[2], Jens Heitland[3], and Verena Nitsch[1]

[1] Institute of Industrial Engineering and Ergonomics, RWTH Aachen
University, 52056 Aachen, Germany
v.sauer@iaw.rwth-aachen.de
[2] School of Business, Economics and Society, Friedrich-Alexander-Universität
Erlangen-Nürnberg, 90403 Nuremberg, Germany
[3] AUDI AG, 85045 Ingolstadt, Germany

**Abstract.** This work investigates the applicability of the elaboration likelihood model and its dual process mechanism to explain how features of the automated driving experience are perceived and, in turn, are processed by passengers to evaluate the driving experience in terms of passenger well-being. For this purpose, a user study with real-world experience of automated driving using a Wizard of Oz prototype was conducted. Eighty-four participants were assigned randomly to four different groups of elaboration likelihood by manipulating their motivation and ability to perceive and process features of the automated driving experience. Results indicate that the elaboration likelihood model and its two routes of processing apply to automated driving. Participants with higher levels of elaboration likelihood perceived more features of the driving experience, spent more cognitive effort on processing them, and consulted a larger variety of passenger needs to determine the effect of features on passenger well-being. Understanding the underlying mechanism of how passengers perceive and process features of automated vehicles may assist in design decisions of such vehicles to create a pleasant experience, high levels of passenger well-being, and ultimately boost the acceptance and willingness to use automated vehicles.

**Keywords:** Automated driving · Perception · Elaboration likelihood model

## 1 Introduction

The role of health and well-being is gaining importance in the design of passenger cars [1]. Both research and industry are investigating concepts to increase physical and mental well-being while driving, such as active seating concepts [2, 3] to reduce biomechanical stress in prolonged seated positions, or affective computing applications using data from physiological sensors to control sound, lighting, air conditioning, and seat massage functions among other interior features [4].

Increasing vehicle automation may provide new design strategies beyond concepts possible in manually driven cars to enable and foster passenger well-being. New design opportunities may arise from the enablement of non-driving related tasks (NDRTs)

© Springer Nature Switzerland AG 2020
C. Stephanidis et al. (Eds.): HCII 2020, LNCS 12429, pp. 193–206, 2020.
https://doi.org/10.1007/978-3-030-59987-4_14

facilitated by the transfer of control and responsibility from the driver to the automated vehicle. The transfer of control is particularly important for the driver, who may now also assume the role of a passenger for limited time periods (SAE level 3 automated driving [5]) or extended time periods (SAE level 4 and 5).

The transfer of control in higher levels of automation provides the foundation for new and more variable vehicle and interior layouts. Novel layout and interior designs have been proposed in numerous concept vehicles for different automation levels. They include features such as increased leg space, collapsible steering wheels, new seat concepts including larger backrest angles or seat rotation, and make new service ideas related to NDRTs possible (e.g., Audi Aicon [6], Mercedes-Benz F 015 [7] or Volvo 360c [8]).

A prerequisite to creating high levels of passenger well-being in automated vehicles is the understanding of how features of the vehicle affect passenger well-being. This includes insights on which vehicle features passengers perceive while traveling in the car. Further, knowledge on how passengers process the perceived features and to what extent the features ultimately affect passengers' level of well-being in an automated vehicle is required.

Research in psychology and marketing offers different models that attempt to explain underlying mechanisms of processing information and resulting beliefs and behaviors. One of these models is the elaboration likelihood model (ELM, [9]), which is a commonly applied model with applications in driving contexts. For example, the model has been used to explain the formation of trust [10] and acceptance [11], or how different personality traits lead to different HMI evaluations [12]. However, to the authors' knowledge, ELM has not yet been investigated in regards to its applicability to explain the processing mechanism used by passengers to determine their level of passenger well-being in an automated vehicle or other subjective evaluations of the driving experience. Therefore, the applicability of ELM in automated driving contexts to explain the perception and processing of vehicle features and the resulting level of passenger well-being is investigated in this work with a user study.

## 2  Related Work

The passenger's subjective evaluation of the travel experience in different transport modes has long been considered by measuring comfort [13]. Lately, research on passenger well-being has grown. Across different transport modes, definitions of passenger well-being draw from definitions of subjective well-being (e.g. [14–16]). In automated driving contexts, passenger well-being can be defined as "a positive self-evaluation of one's current affective state triggered by the travel experience" [17, p. 240].

One approach to understanding how the travel experience in an automated vehicle leads to passenger well-being is investigating the applicability of ELM. ELM is one of the major models in research on persuasive communication [18] and provides a framework to understand when and how information is processed and how attitude changes may result. As a dual process model, ELM suggests two routes of processing [9]. The route for processing information depends on the likelihood of elaboration, i.e., "the extent to which a person thinks about the issue-relevant arguments contained in a message" [9, p. 128]. If elaboration likelihood is high, information tends to be processed extensively and cognitively via the central route. In case of low elaboration likelihood, information is processed more superficially and affectively via the peripheral route. Elaboration likelihood does not have to be strictly high or low, but it can vary between different levels. Therefore, processing of information does not have to be exclusively via one of the routes but can also be a combination of both routes [9].

The level of elaboration likelihood depends on situational and personal circumstances, which determine a person's ability and motivation to deal with and process information. Ability and motivation are driven by different factors such as distraction, need for cognition, and personal involvement, among other variables [9].

Applying the concept of ELM to this context, it is argued that tangible and intangible features of the automated driving experience pose as a source of information to the passenger. The likelihood of the passenger to elaborate on these features depends on their motivation and ability. In automated driving contexts, passengers experiencing automated driving for the first time may be especially motivated for different reasons such as curiousity or concerns. Another source of motivation may be passengers' involvement and high interest in cars [19]. Recurring positive experiences with automated driving may reduce passengers' need for information [20], and thus, motivation to deal with the driving experience may decrease.

Passengers' ability to deal with the experience may be determined by distraction [9]. In the case of automated driving, NDRTs may be a particular source of distraction for passengers. Especially with higher levels of automation, passengers, including the driver, can engage in lengthy, visually, and mentally demanding tasks taking away the passengers' attention from the vehicle [21].

Depending on the motivation and ability of the passenger to deal with the vehicle and the resulting level of elaboration likelihood, the extent to which features of the automated driving experience are perceived may vary. High elaboration likelihood leads to more information being processed compared to low elaboration likelihood [22]. Thus, it is hypothesized:

*H1: Passengers with high levels of elaboration likelihood perceive more vehicle features than passengers with lower levels of elaboration likelihood.*

In line with ELM, low elaboration likelihood increases the likelihood of processing features via the peripheral route. In contrast, high elaboration likelihood increases the likelihood of processing features via the central route. Central route processing entails a more detailed, cognitive evaluation of features [23]. Consequently, it is expected that higher elaboration likelihood corresponds to a higher cognitive analysis of the perceived features.

*H2: Passengers with high levels of elaboration likelihood analyze the perceived features more cognitively than passengers with lower levels of elaboration likelihood.*

*H3: Passengers with low levels of elaboration likelihood process more features via the peripheral route than passengers with higher levels of elaboration likelihood.*

Everyday experiences show that passengers who process information from the automated driving experience cognitively (i.e., central route processing) are frequently able to pinpoint exactly why a feature has a certain effect on their level of passenger well-being. For example, an ergonomically-designed car seat may lead to higher levels of well-being due to higher levels of comfort. Or intransparent driving behavior of the vehicle may have detrimental effects due to lack of trust. This experience from daily life indicates that central route processing may include a cognitive assessment of need fulfillment by the driving experience. Prior research has identified different needs relevant in transportation. These range from trust, perceived safety, physical well-being to aesthetics, and symbolic value, among other needs [17, 24].

*H4: Passengers with high levels of elaboration likelihood consider more passenger needs in central processing than passengers with lower levels of elaboration likelihood.*

## 3 Method

To determine the applicability of ELM for perception and processing in automated vehicles, the four hypotheses developed above were investigated with a user study. The user study allowed a real-world experience of automated driving with the help of the Wizard of Oz method [25] letting participants experience automated driving. For this purpose, a right-hand-drive production car was fitted with a mock-up driver's workplace (pedals, steering wheel, interfaces) on the left passenger side (c.f. Fig. 1). This gave participants the impression to be sitting in the driver's seat in right-hand traffic. The wizard driver controlled the car from the right side and was separated from the participant with a screen. To increase the realism of the automated driving experience, the wizard driver was instructed to mimic the driving behavior of an automated vehicle by adhering to traffic regulations and following guidelines by Festner et al. [26].

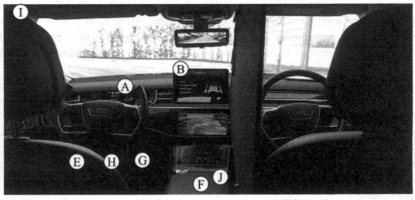

| A: Status indicator | E: Seat | I: Privacy glass |
| B: Driving style adjustment | F: Arm rest | J: Storage |
| C: Driving dynamics | G: Leg space | K: Fragrancing |
| D: Driving noise | H: Materials | |

**Fig. 1.** Wizard of Oz Setup with highlighted features queried in the user study.

## 3.1    Experimental Setup

A study design with two between-subject factors (motivation (low/high) and ability (low/high)) was used to create different levels of elaboration likelihood. From this design, four different groups of participants with varying levels of elaboration likelihood resulted (c.f. Table 1). The participants were randomly assigned to one of the four experimental groups while ensuring comparable groups regarding age and gender.

**Table 1.** Experimental groups with different levels of elaboration likelihood based on different levels of ability and motivation.

| Group | 1 | 2 | 3 | 4 |
|---|---|---|---|---|
| Elaboration likelihood | High | Medium | Medium | Low |
| Motivation | High | High | Low | Low |
| Ability | High | Low | High | Low |

The level of elaboration likelihood was considered as an independent variable in this study, while the number of perceived features from the automated driving experience, the level of cognitive analysis, the processing route, and the type of passengers were collected as dependent variables.

## 3.2    Experimental Procedure

To avoid biasing the participants, the focus of the study on investigating perception and processing in automated vehicles was not communicated to prospective participants. Instead, they were informed that the study focused on the acceptance of automated vehicles. Participants agreeing to be part of the study were welcomed at the study site, and informed consent was obtained. Participants proceeded to complete a demographic questionnaire. In the next step, the Wizard of Oz method was briefly explained to avoid confusion, and the participants were instructed on how to behave during the following automated driving experience according to their group (c.f. Table 2). Participants were asked to imagine that they were traveling in an automated vehicle. The automated drive lasted, on average, ten minutes with a maximum speed of 30 km/h, oncoming traffic, and other road users. After returning from the automated driving experience, participants were interviewed regarding their perception and processing of the driving experience. The interview had the following questions to collect the relevant measures:

1. Which features of the driving experience did you perceive while experiencing automated driving?
2. Did you perceive any of the 11 features detailed in Fig. 1 (if not already mentioned in the answer to question 1)?
3. For each feature that you perceived, how much effort did you spend to think about the feature (on a scale of 1: very low, 5: very high)?

**Table 2.** Information used to prime participants to induce high and low levels of ability and motivation.

|  | High | Low |
|---|---|---|
| Ability | You do not have to do any specific task. However, please refrain from using your phone or other personal devices | Please complete the reading comprehension tasks on the tablet in the center console |
| Motivation | Please imagine that you plan on purchasing an automated vehicle. You have already driven the car manually. Now you want to try out the "autopilot" function. Behave like you would if this were a real test drive, and you would actually decide on buying | In this study, we want to investigate how suitable regular vehicle sensors integrated into the interior are to measure passenger well-being. You do not have to do anything specific while in the car |

4. For each feature that you perceived, did the feature affect your level of passenger well-being? If yes, how did the feature have an effect (effect cannot be determined/general impression or via one or multiple passenger needs)?

After the interview, participants were debriefed and received information on the actual study purpose. On average, participants spent 45 min to complete the study.

### 3.3  Measures

To ensure comparability and control for interpersonal differences, participants were not only asked what features they perceived through an open-ended question (see Sect. 3.2). In addition, participants were asked which features they had perceived from a list of eleven features (see Fig. 1). The list of features was derived from related work to include physical and intangible features with relevance to passenger well-being that could be displayed in the Wizard of Oz vehicle.

The intensity of cognitive analysis for each perceived feature was measured on a 5-point scale (1: very low, 5: very high). To determine the route via which a feature was processed, participants could indicate that the feature had a general effect on well-being and they could not give a specific reason for the effect (peripheral processing). To indicate central processing, participants could select one or more passenger needs from a list of nine needs as a reason why a feature had an effect on their passenger well-being. The passenger needs suggested by [17] were used as a predefined list and divided into hedonic and utilitarian needs:

- Utilitarian needs: safety, trust, control, physical well-being, usability
- Hedonic needs: comfort, aesthetics, spatial feeling, symbolism

For additional insights on the sample, the interest in cars in general, and prior experience with advanced driving assistance systems was measured on a 5-point scale (1: very low, 5: very high).

## 3.4  Participants

Eighty-four participants (48 male, 36 female) participated in the study. The participants were aged between 18 and 58 years (M = 33.51 years, SD = 9.37 years). They had, on average, a high interest in cars in general (M = 4.26, SD = .81) and a moderate to high level of prior experience with advanced driving assistance systems (M = 3.99, SD = .84). Of the 84 participants, 61 had a technical background while the remaining 23 had a non-technical background.

## 3.5  Data Analysis

The hypotheses are analyzed with one-factor ANOVAs using different elaboration levels (c.f. Table 1) as a between-subject factor. For H1, the number of perceived features per participant is used as dependent variable. H2 is investigated using the median level of cognitive analysis across all perceived features per participant as dependent variable. H3 is analyzed by considering the proportion of features processed peripherally as dependent variable. Finally, the variety of passenger needs considered across all centrally processed features is used as dependent variable to analyze H4.

H1-H4 hypothesize not only group differences depending on elaboration likelihood but also a trend. H1, H2, and H4 suggest an increasing trend for the dependent variable with increasing elaboration likelihood, while H3 suggests a decreasing trend. To investigate the suggested trends, a Jonckheere-Terpstra test is performed for each hypothesis.

# 4  Results

In the following, the results of the one-way ANOVAs and the Jonckheere-Terpstra tests for each hypothesis are summarized.

## 4.1  Number of Perceived Features

ANOVA shows a significant difference between the four elaboration likelihood groups for the number of perceived features ($F(3, 80) = 15.68$, $p < .001$) with a large effect size ($\eta_G^2 = .37$). Post-hoc tests with Bonferroni correction show that participants in the low elaboration likelihood group perceived significantly fewer features (M = 7.91, SD = 2.23) than any of the other groups. There are no differences between the medium and high elaboration likelihood groups (c.f. Fig. 2).

The overall trend that with increasing elaboration likelihood the number of perceived features increases is supported ($J = 1733$, $p < .001$). Thus, H1 is supported.

## 4.2  Level of Cognitive Analysis

In terms of cognitive analysis, a significant difference between the four elaboration likelihood groups is evident as well ($F(3, 80) = 6.14$, $p = .001$) with a medium effect ($\eta_G^2 = .19$). Interestingly, participants in the medium elaboration likelihood groups spent the most cognitive effort on analyzing the perceived features (M = 3.17, SD = .76

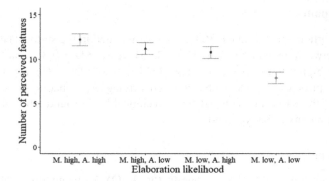

**Fig. 2.** Plotted average mean of perceived features (H1), error bars: Fisher's least significant difference, M: motivation, A: ability.

and M = 3.36, SD = .60, c.f. Fig. 3). Post-hoc tests indicate that the low elaboration likelihood group had significantly lower levels of cognitive analysis than the other groups. Further, the Jonckheere-Terpstra test does not yield support for the hypothesized trend (J = 1284, p = .063).

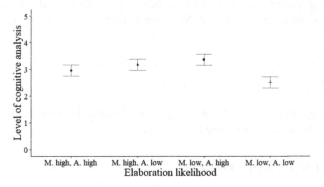

**Fig. 3.** Plotted average mean of cognitive analysis (H2), error bars: Fisher's least significant difference, M: motivation, A: ability.

## 4.3    Elaboration Likelihood and Processing Routes

There is no statistical evidence that lower elaboration likelihood leads to features being processed stronger via the peripheral route (H3) as ANOVA finds no significant group differences (F(3, 80) = .64, p = .59, $\eta_G^2$ = .02). Further, no decreasing trend of peripheral processing with increasing elaboration likelihood is visible (J = 1119.5, p = .557, c.f. Fig. 4).

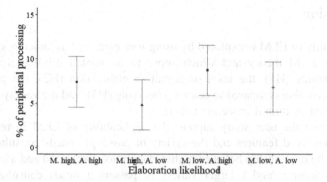

**Fig. 4.** Plotted average mean of the proportion of peripheral processing (H3), error bars: Fisher's least significant difference, M: motivation, A: ability.

### 4.4 Elaboration Likelihood and the Variety of Passenger Needs Considered

ANOVA investigating H4 suggests significant differences between elaboration likelihood groups regarding the variety of needs considered in central processing ($F$ (3, 80) = 8.18, p < .001, $\eta_G^2$ = .23). The average variety of needs considered in each elaboration likelihood group follows the hypothesized trend. In the high elaboration likelihood group 8.0 needs are considered on average (SD = 1.54), while the medium elaboration likelihood groups consider both on average 7.67 needs (SD = 1.85 and .97). The low elaboration likelihood group considered the smallest variety (M = 5.67, SD = 2.22, c.f. Fig. 5). Further, post-hoc tests show that the low elaboration likelihood group has considered a significantly smaller variety of needs than the other three groups (p < .01). The Jonckheere-Terpstra test supports the trend visible in Fig. 5 (J = 1576, p < .001).

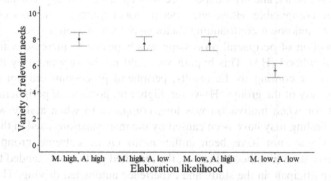

**Fig. 5.** Plotted average mean of the variety of passenger needs considered (H4), error bars: Fisher's least significant difference, M: motivation, A: ability.

## 5  Discussion

The applicability of ELM is explored by using four measures as indicators, which were derived from ELM theory and which apply to automated driving: the number of perceived features (H1), the level of cognitive elaboration (H2), the proportion of peripheral processing compared to central processing (H3), and the variety of passenger needs consulted in central processing (H4).

Results from the user study support the applicability of ELM in regards to the number of perceived features and the variety of passenger needs consulted in central processing. The relationship between higher elaboration likelihood and a larger number of perceived features and a larger variety of passenger needs consulted in central processing respectively is clearly visible (c.f. Figs. 2 and 5). Consequently, passengers willing and motivated to deal with the automated driving experience are likely to engage more with the vehicle and be more attentive to different features. As discussed above, especially novel users may fall into this category and have higher levels of elaboration likelihood. Thus, car manufacturers and service designers should design the features of automated vehicles and corresponding mobility services with this in mind. The features should be carefully designed to fulfill a large variety of passenger needs and, in turn, contribute to passenger well-being.

In regards to H2 and H3, empirical evidence is not as straight forward. The level of cognitive analysis is expected to increase with elaboration likelihood. However, the highest level of cognitive analysis is observed for the low motivation/high ability group, followed by the other medium elaboration likelihood group (c.f. Fig. 3). Only the medium elaboration likelihood groups are significantly different from the low elaboration likelihood group. The high elaboration likelihood group does not differ significantly from any of the other groups. This counter-intuitive finding may be explained by the fact that motivation and ability are not the only determinants of elaboration likelihood. Rather, ELM suggests additional factors such as personal differences can play a role [9]. Of the collected demographics (age, gender, background, general interest in cars, and prior experience with advanced driving assistance systems), the groups are comparable. However, other personal characteristics not considered in the study or an unknown confounding factor may have played a role.

The proportion of peripheral processing was expected to increase with decreasing elaboration likelihood (H3). This hypothesis could not be supported by the results of the user study. According to the results, peripheral processing did not significantly differ between any of the groups. However, higher proportions of peripheral processing were evident for when motivation was low, compared to when ability was low (c.f. Fig. 4). This finding may have been caused by the manipulations used in the study. The manipulations may not have been sufficient to create extreme group differences regarding elaboration likelihood. Further, the recruited participants tended to be excited to be able to participate in the study and experience automated driving. This may have counteracted the manipulations causing mixed processing routes to be used in the majority of cases [18].

Overall, the measures used to test ELM applicability do not give a clear indication of whether elaboration likelihood in automated driving is stronger driven by ability or by motivation. Group differences between the two medium elaboration likelihood groups and between the medium and high elaboration likelihood groups are not significant for any of the measures used in this study. Merely the low elaboration likelihood group differs significantly from some of the other groups (H1, H2, H4). This may suggest that an increase in either motivation or ability is sufficient to raise elaboration likelihood and cause passengers of automated vehicles to engage stronger with the automated driving experience.

Given these results of the study, the perception and processing mechanism in automated driving with regards to determining the level of passenger well-being can be explained as depicted in Fig. 6. Elaboration likelihood of a passenger is determined by motivation and ability to engage in the automated driving experience. Depending on elaboration likelihood, a passenger perceives a number of features of the automated driving experience. The number of perceived features increases with elaboration likelihood. These perceived features are either processed via the central route with the help of utilitarian and hedonic passenger needs to determine the resulting level of passenger well-being. Or processing of the perceived features can be less cognitive and more affective via the peripheral route. Depending on the level of elaboration likelihood features are processed dominantly via the central (high elaboration likelihood) or the peripheral routes (low elaboration likelihood) or a combination of both.

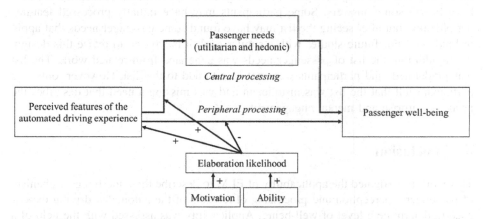

**Fig. 6.** Perception and processing mechanism for automated driving contexts with regard to passenger well-being.

## 5.1 Limitations

The results and implications from this study have to be viewed under consideration of the limitations of the study design and method. The Wizard of Oz method was used to allow participants to experience automated driving as realistically as possible. However, due to the vehicle set up and to avoid confusion, participants were informed that the vehicle is driven by a wizard driver, and they should imagine traveling in an automated vehicle. The majority of participants mentioned that they were able to do so after returning from the drive. In addition, given the technology currently available, a

Wizard of Oz setup is an efficient way to allow for real-world automated driving experiences.

The results of this study also depend on the used vehicle and its specific features. In this study, a production vehicle was modified to allow the Wizard of Oz setup. Yet, the original interior design was kept as much as possible. Therefore, the results of this study may be generalizable to other passenger cars as well.

Further, the route used in the study corresponded to city traffic (max. speed 30 km/h), and the overall drive lasted, on average, 10 min. Effects may have been different for longer exposure to automated driving and for different routes. Driving on highways or in cities with higher speeds (e.g., 50 km/h) may have changed the perception of the driving experience, for example, in regards to motion sickness.

In terms of study design suggestions for improvements for future studies can be provided. The manipulations of ability and motivation appeared to be insufficient to create distinct groups of high, medium, and low elaboration likelihood. An additional influencing factor may have been the recruited participants who were mostly excited to participate and may have dominated low elaboration likelihood manipulations. Results may differ if recruiting participants with low interest in cars in general or more experienced participants for whom automated driving is not a novelty.

The study design included a query of applicable passenger needs in case of central processing with the help of a predefined list. This design with the predefined list may have biased some answers. Some participants may have initially processed features peripherally, but after seeing the list may have found some passenger needs that apply in hindsight. For future studies with a similar goal, it is advised to revise this design.

In addition, the list of passenger needs was generated from related work. The list was predefined, and participants were not able to add to this list. However, only one participant felt that the list was insufficient and was missing a need that describes the need for surprise and mental engagement.

# 6   Conclusion

This work investigated the applicability of ELM to describe the underlying mechanism of passengers' perception and processing of features of the automated driving experience to determine a level of well-being. Applicability was assessed with the help of a user study utilizing a real-world automated driving experience. Participants' motivation and ability to deal with the automated vehicle and the resulting driving experience was deliberately manipulated to create groups with different levels of elaboration likelihood. In the study, four measures describing the key assumptions of ELM in the context of automated driving were collected. Three of the four measures and their corresponding hypotheses find empirical support. Thus, providing support that ELM can, in fact, be used to describe the underlying mechanism of perception and processing in automated driving (c.f. Fig. 6).

Implications for research and industry can be drawn from this work. Insights into how passengers perceive and process features can help the understanding of how passenger well-being is created and may fuel the growing research field of passenger well-being in automated driving. Further, the understanding of the underlying processing mechanism can shed light on what features of the automated driving experience are relevant to create passenger well-being for different user groups. This may be helpful to tailor future automated vehicles and mobility services to different target groups that differ in ability and motivation to deal with the automated vehicle. For example, mobility services targeting passengers who want to work while traveling, and thus, have a lower ability to engage with the vehicle can design their service accordingly.

**Acknowledgments.**   The authors would like to thank AUDI AG, Germany, for their contribution to this research. The contents of this paper are solely the responsibility of the authors and do not necessarily represent the views of AUDI AG, Germany.

# References

1. Addam, M., Knye, M., Matusiewicz, D.: Automotive Health in Deutschland. Wenn die Gesundheitsbranche auf die Automobilindustrie trifft. Springer, Wiesbaden (2018). https://doi.org/10.1007/978-3-658-20876-9
2. JLR: Jaguar Land Rover's New Shape-Shifting Seat of the Future Makes You Think You're Walking (2020). https://www.jaguarlandrover.com/news/2020/01/jaguar-land-rovers-new-shape-shifting-seat-future-makes-you-think-youre-walking. Accessed 16 Jan 2020
3. Hiemstra-van Mastrigt, S., Kamp, I., van Veen, S.A.T., Vink, P., Bosch, T.: The influence of active seating on car passengers' perceived comfort and activity levels. Appl. Ergon. **47**, 211–219 (2015). https://doi.org/10.1016/j.apergo.2014.10.004
4. Mercedes-Benz: Ganzheitliches Konzept für mehr Wohlbefinden und Fitness: Mercedes-Benz "Fit & Healthy": Komfort wird noch intelligenter (2017). http://media.daimler.com/marsMediaSite/de/instance/ko/Ganzheitliches-Konzept-fuer-mehr-Wohlbefinden-und-Fitness-Mercedes-Benz-Fit–Healthy-Komfort-wird-noch-intelligenter.xhtml?oid=15181280. Accessed 11 May 2018
5. SAE: Taxonomy and Definitions for Terms Related to On-road Motor Vehicle Automated Driving Systems, 2016th edn. SAE (SAE J3016) (2016)
6. AUDI AG: Audi Aicon (2017). https://www.audi-mediacenter.com/en/audi-aicon-2017-9299
7. Daimler: Mercedes-Benz F 015 Luxury in Motion (2015). https://media.daimler.com/marsMediaSite/ko/de/9906573. Accessed 7 Jan 2020
8. Volvo Car Group: Volvo Cars' New 360c Autonomous Concept: Reimagining the Work-life Balance and the Future of Cities (2018). https://www.media.volvocars.com/global/en-gb/media/pressreleases/237020/volvo-cars-new-360c-autonomous-concept-reimagining-the-work-life-balance-and-the-future-of-cities. Accessed 16 Apr 2020
9. Petty, R.E., Cacioppo, J.T.: The elaboration likelihood model of persuasion. Adv. Exp. Soc. Psychol. **19**, 123–205 (1986). https://doi.org/10.1007/978-1-4612-4964-1_1
10. Kraus, J.M., Forster, Y., Hergeth, S., Baumann, M.: Two routes to trust calibration: effects of reliability and brand information on trust in automation. Int. J. Mob. Hum. Comput. Interact. **11**(3), 1–17 (2019). https://doi.org/10.4018/IJMHCI.2019070101
11. Liu, P., Xu, Z., Zhao, X.: Road tests of self-driving vehicles. Affective and cognitive pathways in acceptance formation. Transp. Res. Part A: Policy Pract. **124**, 354–369 (2019). https://doi.org/10.1016/j.tra.2019.04.004

12. Forster, Y., Hergeth, S., Naujoks, F., Krems, J.F.: How usability can save the day - methodological considerations for making automated driving a success story. In: Proceedings of the 10th International Conference on Automotive User Interfaces and Interactive Vehicular Applications - AutomotiveUI 2018, Toronto, ON, Canada, 23–25 September 2018, pp. 278–290. ACM Press, New York (2018). https://doi.org/10.1145/3239060.3239076

13. Oborne, D.J.: Passenger comfort - an overview. Appl. Ergon. 9(3), 131–136 (1978). https://doi.org/10.1016/0003-6870(78)90002-9

14. Ahn, Y.-J., Kim, I., Hyun, S.S.: Critical in-flight and ground-service factors influencing brand prestige and relationships between brand prestige, well-being perceptions, and brand loyalty: first class passengers. J. Travel Tour. Mark. 32(sup1), S114–S138 (2015). https://doi.org/10.1080/10548408.2015.1008666

15. Senn, T., Falter, M., Ruster, P., Hadwich, K.: Automated driving - creating gain or reducing pain? An empirical study of direct and mediated effects on wellbeing. In: GMFC 2018, pp. 1580–1583 (2018). https://doi.org/10.15444/GMC2018.13.08.01

16. Ma, L., Zhang, X., Ding, X., Wang, G.: Bike sharing and users' subjective well-being. An empirical study in China. Transp. Res. Part A: Policy Pract. 118, 14–24 (2018). https://doi.org/10.1016/j.tra.2018.08.040

17. Sauer, V., Mertens, A., Heitland, J., Nitsch, V.: Exploring the concept of passenger well-being in the context of automated driving. Int. J. Hum. Factors Ergon. 6(3), 227–248 (2019). https://doi.org/10.1504/IJHFE.2019.104594

18. Klimmt, C.: Das Elaboration-Likelihood-Modell, 1st edn. Nomos, Baden-Baden (2011)

19. Brunner, C.B., Ullrich, S., Jungen, P., Esch, F.-R.: Impact of symbolic design on brand evaluations. J. Prod. Brand Manag. 25(3), 307–320 (2016)

20. Reilhac, P., Moizard, J., Kaiser, F., Hottelart, K.: Cockpitkonzept für das teilautomatisierte Fahren. ATZ 118(3), 44–49 (2016)

21. Kim, J., Kim, H.-S., Kim, W., Yoon, D.: Take-over performance analysis depending on the drivers' non-driving secondary tasks in automated vehicles. In: ICT convergence powered by smart intelligence. ICTC 2018: the 9th International Conference on ICT Convergence, Maison Glad Jeju, Jeju Island, Korea, 17–19 October 2018, pp. 1364–1366 (2018)

22. Radford, S.K., Bloch, P.H.: Linking innovation to design: consumer responses to visual product newness. J. Prod. Innov. Manag. 28(S1), 208–220 (2011). https://doi.org/10.1111/j.1540-5885.2011.00871.x

23. Homburg, C., Schwemmle, M., Kuehnl, C.: New product design: concept, measurement, and consequences. J. Mark. 79(3), 41–56 (2015). https://doi.org/10.1509/jm.14.0199

24. Ahmadpour, N., Lindgaard, G., Robert, J.-M., Pownall, B.: The thematic structure of passenger comfort experience and its relationship to the context features in the aircraft cabin. Ergonomics 57(6), 801–815 (2014). https://doi.org/10.1080/00140139.2014.899632

25. Dahlbäck, N., Jönsson, A., Ahrenberg, L.: Wizard of Oz studies - why and how. In: Gray, W.D. (ed.) Proceedings of the 1st International Conference on Intelligent User Interfaces. 1st international conference on Intelligent user interfaces, Orlando, Florida, USA, 04–07 January 1993, pp. 193–200. ACM, New York (1993). https://doi.org/10.1145/169891.169968

26. Festner, M., Eicher, A., Schramm, D.: Beeinflussung der Komfort- und Sicherheitswahrnehmung beim hochautomatisierten Fahren durch fahrfremde Tätigkeit und Spurwechseldynamik. In: Uni-Das, E.V. (ed.) 11. Workshop Fahrerassistenzsysteme und automatisiertes Fahren, Walting im Altmühltal, Germany, 29–31 March 2017, pp. 63–73 (2017)

# A Practical View of the Similarity and Differences Among the Impaired Driver States in Legal Driving

Dan Shen[ID], Taryn Spisak[ID], Yaobin Chen[ID], and Renran Tian[✉][ID]

IUPUI, Indianapolis, IN 46202, USA
{danshen,tspisak,ychen,rtian}@iupui.edu,
https://tasi.iupui.edu

**Abstract.** Detection and intervention of various impaired driver states have been intensively studied with corresponding technologies widely implemented in modern vehicles. Different algorithms are proposed to detect certain states or conditions, with intervention means like driver alerts or vehicle active safety features being developed and optimized accordingly. However, there lacks a unified view of all of these different driver states. In order to support the development of vehicle systems, this study tries to compare the commonly-seen impaired driver states in terms of their detection features as well as the effects on degraded driving performance. A meta-analysis is conducted to identify the overlapping and disjoint spaces among them from the angle of the vehicle design. The research finds some answers about the driver behavior and environment features that the vehicle system shall pay attention to and the degraded driving performance that the vehicle shall prepare for, when impaired driving happens in different ways in the reality.

**Keywords:** Impaired driver states · Driver state sensing · Feature detection · Degraded driving performance

## 1 Introduction

Impaired driving is a commonly used term of abnormal driving states in recent years with the rapidly development of automated vehicles, which means operating a vehicle while under the influence of sleepiness, distraction, or mind wandering and so on. Since impaired driving states can significantly reduce drivers' visual scanning capability and cognitive process of concentrating on the driving tasks, they are main causes of vehicle crashes. When happening, drivers will not be able to grip the steering wheel or step on the brake pedal in time during some emergency situations. Thus, the impaired driver states will affect the driving safety with degraded driving performance on the road. Considering the complexity in this area, impaired driver states in this paper are limited to those happening during legal driving like mind wandering, angry, fatigue, distraction

© Springer Nature Switzerland AG 2020
C. Stephanidis et al. (Eds.): HCII 2020, LNCS 12429, pp. 207–220, 2020.
https://doi.org/10.1007/978-3-030-59987-4_15

and drowsiness, which can link the occurrence of many potential road accidents with higher risks.

The research on driver distraction began in early 1990s, when inattention caused by cell phones were proved to have huge impact on drivers' capability of responding to the critical driving conditions. The 100-Car Naturalistic Driving Study found that almost 80% of all crashes and 65% of all near-crashes involved driver distraction [1]. Based on police reports, the US National Highway Traffic Safety Administration (NHTSA) conservatively estimated that a total of 100,000 vehicle crashes each year are the direct result of driver drowsiness [2]. These crashes resulted in approximately 1,550 deaths, 71,000 injuries and $12.5 billion in monetary losses [3]. Reference [4] reported that lane departure was dramatically greater while driver has mind wandering as well as a narrow visual attention. For angry driving state, drivers tend to be more aggressive with faster speed and less headway distance while following the lead vehicle [5]. Meanwhile, driver fatigue is one of the major implications in transportation safety and accounted for up to 40% of road accidents [6]. Therefore, the above five impaired driver states can interfere with driving tasks affecting divers' concentration, reaction time, and capability to maintain adequately direct attention to the critical scenarios in legal driving.

Since drivers may intentionally or unintentionally make mistakes while driving on the roadway due to different types of impaired driving states, in-vehicle driver state sensing (DSS) systems are currently equipped and utilized in some level 2 or higher level automated vehicles to monitor human driving status and provide the corresponding information to the automated driving system. Through the DSS systems, drivers' driving behaviors can be detected based on visual features, which mainly involve eye tracking, head movement, and facial expressions. By analyzing these features, the system can accurately estimate driver status and determine whether the driver is capable to control the vehicle. If drivers are in any types of above-mentioned impaired driving status, the control authority will be transferred from human to the machine. Thus, the DSS is critical to future autonomous vehicles due to its importance of transition process from auto-control to manual-control.

Different methods are proposed to detect certain impaired driver states in the literature for driver alerts or other vehicle active safety features accordingly. However, there lacks a unified view of all these different driver states. The isolated studies of these driver states and the theoretical comparisons among them, provide limited guidance in developing vehicle systems to efficiently intervene impaired driver states in practical situations involving dynamic and complex states. This paper will mainly focus on the commonly-seen impaired driver states happening in legal driving, and generate a practical view of the similarity and differences among them in terms of the detection features and negative effects on driving performance. A meta-analysis will be conducted to identify general abnormal driver states, and then compare their detection features as well as the reported effects in degrading driving performances. The main outcomes of the paper are the most important features the driver state sensing system should pay more attentions and what are the potential degraded driving performances the automated system needs to be prepared when impaired driving occurs on the road.

## 2 Common Impaired Driver States

To control the research scope, this paper excludes the impaired driver states for illegal driving conditions like drug or alcohol. Medical concerns are also not included. After excluding these conditions, this section summarizes impaired driver states that are widely investigated in the literature. For each state, commonly used definitions and ground-truth measurements are discussed.

### 2.1 Fatigue

Fatigue is an impaired driving states happened in normal driving because of feeling overtired, with low energy and a strong desire to sleep, which interferes with safe driving activities. Fatigue generally happens with the following three potential root causes: lifestyle factor, physical health conditions, and mental health issues. For driving purpose, fatigue generally means that the driver possesses the deficient functions of physiology and mentality after a long driving time. During the driving process with fatigue, the skills and response time will decline with higher risk levels comparing with the normal driving status. The current installed in-vehicle driver state monitoring system can detect fatigue by capturing the grip strength of steering wheel, eyelid movements, Electrocardiogram (ECG) or driver visual features, such as yawning [6–9].

### 2.2 Drowsiness

Drowsiness is commonly known as people feeling abnormally sleepy or tired during the daily life. It can lead to some related symptoms, such as fatigue, forgetfulness or falling asleep at inappropriate times. Similar to fatigue, multiple reasons may cause drowsiness, which can range from mental health and other lifestyle factors to some serious medical situations. Although "Fatigue" and "drowsiness" are usually confused and interchangeably, they are significantly different. Fatigue generally refers to the feeling of tiredness or exhaustion, drowsiness specifically means the precise state right before sleep. Therefore, fatigue can result into drowsiness, or we can say drowsiness is the relevant aspect of fatigue during driving. Since we have no control during this time period, the vehicle may have higher risk levels than fatigue from a driving safety perspective. The DSS also has the ability to detect drowsiness by capturing drivers' eye blink, facial features, and questionnaires and so on [10–15].

## 2.3  Distraction

Driver distraction (DD) is defined as an activity performed by a driver that diverts the attention away from the primary activity (vehicle longitudinal and lateral control) potentially leading to safe driving degradation. It appears due to some event, activity, object, or person within or outside the vehicle, which compels or induces the driver's attention away from the primary task [16]. Thus, it is a significant cause of fatal accidents. Distraction has also been extended by Regan et al. [17], adding the similar concept of driver inattention, which means insufficient or no attention to critical activities for safe driving toward a competing activity. Driver distraction is commonly classified into 3 categories, namely manual distraction, visual distraction and cognitive distraction. The detection methods for driver distraction have been widely studied, using eye and head movement, vehicle dynamics and assessment questionnaires and so on [18–23].

## 2.4  Angry

Angry is another risk factor for driving in recent years due to high-intensity and high-paced life. According to [5], drivers tend to be more aggressive with faster speed, less headway distance while following the front car in an angry state. Greater deviations in lateral position and acceptable shorter turning radius were also observed when driver is angry. Thus, it is also a significant factor can lead to fatal traffic collisions. From research point of view, angry driving is different from "road rage". Road rage is one of the extreme type of aggressive driving, which intends to commit a criminal behaviors, such as intentionally colliding pedestrian and using weapons to harm other drivers. The angry driving state discussed in this paper includes speeding, changing lanes without signaling and so on. All illegal driving states and behaviors will not be considered. Nowadays, eye movement data and braking pressure are generally used to detect angry drivers since they scan a narrower area and brake harder to compensate for the delay of initial braking when in an angry state [24–26].

## 2.5  Mind Wandering

Mind wandering is also called task unrelated thought, which is the experience of attention and thoughts not maintaining on the original single task for a relative long time period, and it is specifically dangerous when people are engaged in task requiring concentration and attention, such as driving. Texting, reading or talking to other people are all possible causes for driver mind wandering. Drivers will not be able to take an appropriate actions when facing with critical conditions since the brain cannot process both task-relevant and task-irrelevant sensing information in detailed way. Lane deviation and speeding were possibly two significant degrade driving performance from mind wandering [26]. Variables of vehicle speed, lateral position deviation and hazard response time are some commonly applied features for detecting driver mind wandering [27,28].

# 3   Methodology

By using the key words of each impaired driver sates, a number of research papers were found, which contain papers and reports following the PRISMA meta-analysis guidelines including: title, abstract, methods, results and discussion and so on [10]. All the papers being included consist of conference papers, journals, book chapters, and some other works that can satisfy all the following rules:

- The paper had to be published within 2010 and 2020.
- It had to be revolved around the impaired driving states; mind-wandering, fatigue, drowsiness, anger, and distraction.
- With-in the study it needs to mention degraded driving performances that the impaired state may cause and discuss the measurable features that were used to conduct the study.

Figure 1 demonstrates the selection process of papers for consideration in this meta-analysis. A total of 197 papers were collected initially according to the search results using the keywords of all the impaired driver states. For studying the detection features of these impaired driver states, 135 papers that contain the measurable features were kept, with 26, 54, 10, 33, 12 papers were used for impaired driver state of distraction, drowsiness, angry, fatigue, and mind wandering, respectively. For studying the degraded driving performance, similar criteria was applied which excludes illegal driving states and requires degraded driving performance measurements in the studies, and 32, 19, 15, 23, 16 papers were utilized in the meta-analysis for different impaired driver states as previous.

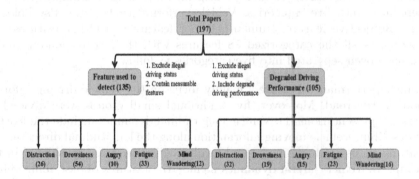

**Fig. 1.** Selection of publications included in the meta-analysis.

## 3.1   Detection Features

Although there are many publications about impaired driving states and their detection methods, there is not a uniform and commonly agreed set of features to be collected and used. Several features very often overlapped and mixed with other driver states, such as drowsiness and distraction. The methodology of how we explore this issue will be introduced in the following sections.

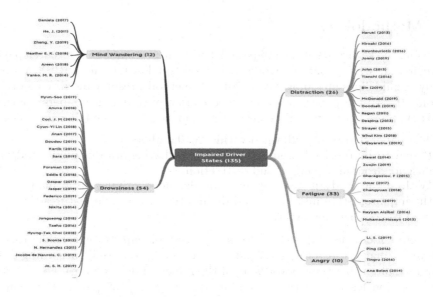

**Fig. 2.** Data collection methods used in the feature selection for detecting impaired driver states.

**Data Extraction.** Depicted in Fig. 2, 135 reference papers were selected for meta-analysis of feature detection, with 78 common features extracted from the literature over decades of research. Specifically, all the measurable features can be separated into five categories: Vehicle-performance Feature, Psychological feature, Subjective feature, Human-behavior feature and Other features. The Fig. 3 depicts all the categorized 78 features with their corresponding index, which have been separated into five categories as follow.

1. Vehicle-performance Feature - mainly focus on the vehicle driving information on the road. Moreover, five additional small groups were divided for better representations. 1). Vehicle longitudinal dynamics include the features of describing vehicle moving information along the longitudinal direction, and features as use of brake pedal and headway distance were considered in this group; 2). Vehicle lateral dynamics include the features of describing vehicle moving information along the lateral direction, and features as vehicle lateral position and lane deviation were discussed; 3). Steering wheel includes the variables of describing human steering maneuvers while driving, and features of steering wheel acceleration and steering wheel movement were taken into considerations; 4). The road properties containing vehicle driving environment were also utilized for detection such as lane width and road curvature and so on; 5). Vehicle lane change frequency and total number of cars the ego vehicle passes are features in the group of other related features.

2. Psychological feature - a feature of the mental life of a living organism, which is critical for detecting drivers with impaired driving states. This kind of feature will reflect the cognition and reaction time of drivers in some emergency situations. Blood pressure and electrocardiogram were two commonly used features to recognize the impaired driver states.

3. Subjective feature - a feature of subjective report or designed questionnaires. For example, a common used questionnaires for detecting driver drowsiness is Karolinska Sleepiness Scale (KSS) [29], which is listed in Fig. 3;

4. Human-behavior feature - this type of feature is influenced by a number of factors from human behavior, and these factors also belong to several categories. In this meta-analysis, six following categories were taken into account. 1). Eye features are used in many research papers, which include eye tracking, eyelid movement and blink frequency and so on. 2). Face features were also applied by using computer vision algorithms with face orientation and facial morphological. 3). Driver mouth status is also a critical and effective way to detect abnormal driving status. The most commonly used two features are mouth opening and yawning. 4). As the largest organ of the body, human skin has many information reflecting driver mental states and healthy conditions, such as nervous with sweating and drowsiness with fever. Thus, the skin conductance level can be used to detect these two types of impaired driver states. 5). Body skeleton features include all of the bones, cartilages, and ligaments of the body, and can generate driver movement through muscles. 6). The last category is time information of driver, such as continuous driving time and braking reaction time. These variables are also a supplemental features to help estimate the impaired driver states.

5. Other features - excluding from all above categories, there are still some features we need to collect for the evaluation of driver status. Several driving activities were labeled in some learning methods for better predicting the distracted driving behavior, such as texting and talking. Some researchers also did capture the lightning conditions to describe the driving environment and detect the abnormal driver states.

**Data Analysis.** In order to better understand current trends of feature selection for detecting impaired driver states, the frequency of 78 extracted features being used in the studies were calculated and compared. Since each category has different numbers of papers, the usage frequency of detection was computed by dividing the frequency number over the total paper number of each impaired driver state.

Furthermore, some features were individually utilized to detect one specific abnormal driver state, but some features were shared to use for detecting at least two of the impaired driver states. All shared features will be collected and connected to the five impaired driver states with usage frequency.

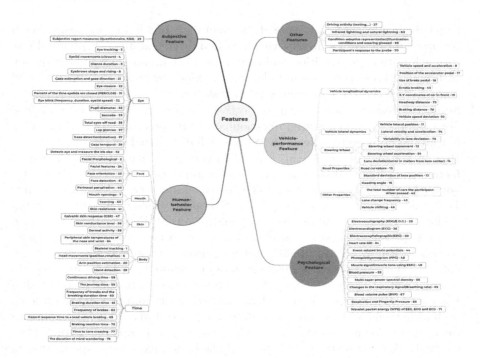

**Fig. 3.** Feature collection used for detecting impaired diving states.

## 3.2   Degraded Driving Performance

When conducting the study there are various impaired driving states that can occur. From this we evaluated five impaired driving estates categorized as distraction, drowsiness, mind wandering, anger and fatigue and the correlation to degraded driving performances. Presented in Fig. 4, 105 references were selected for a meta-analysis.

**Data Extraction.** Throughout the literature, there were common outcomes for the impaired driving states. The outcomes can be broken down into four main categories: speed, lane position, headway and reaction time. Figure 5 illustrates the results of the impaired driver state degraded driving performance and the number of findings in the research papers. Based on the research papers the four subsequent categories are defined, as follows.

1. Speed - Evaluating the study baseline speed and then the speed the driver was going when they recorded the impairment driving state, determines if there was an increase or decrease speed.
2. Headway - Increase and decrease in headway relates to the distance between the driver's car and the car in front of it. If there is less distance between the driver's car and the car in front, it is considered a decrease in headway. If there is more distance between the driver's car and the car in front, then it would be considered an increase.

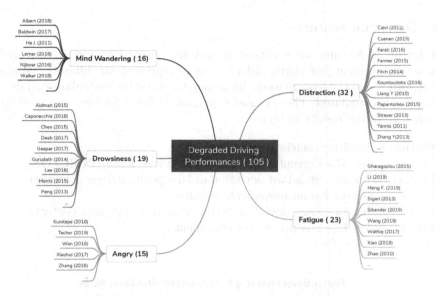

**Fig. 4.** Data collection methods used in the degraded driving performance for detecting the impaired driver state.

3. Reaction time - Relates to the amount of time a driver responds to the situation. The increase in reaction time indicates the additional amount of time to react.
4. Lane position - Increase and decrease in lane position refers to how often drivers will change lanes. When lane position increases, the driver will demonstrate changing lanes more frequently.

**Data Analysis.** 105 papers were analyzed in investigating the common occurrences of the impaired driving state in relation to degraded driving performance. The study revealed four different degraded driving performances: reaction time, headway, speed and lane position.

## 4   Results

This section consists of two parts, one is the analysis results for detection features and the second one is effects on driving performance. For detection features, the usage frequency of each feature was calculated, and the shared features with the corresponding weights was also generated. For effects on driving performance, the impaired driver states mapping with the degraded driving performance was demonstrated.

## 4.1    Detection Features

A total of 78 features were extracted and summarized in Fig. 5. As can be seen in the segment bar chart, different colors represent for different impaired driver states, and the feature usage frequency for detecting each abnormal driver states was accumulated. The six most commonly utilized features can be clearly obtained from the results as below:

1. Feature Index 10 - Vehicle speed deviation
2. Feature Index 31 - Percent of the time eyelids are closed (PERCLOS)
3. Feature Index 13 - Standard deviation of lane position/lane detection
4. Feature Index 4 - Eyelid movements (closure)
5. Feature Index 14 - Lane deviation (error in meters from lane center)
6. Feature Index 12 - Steering wheel movement

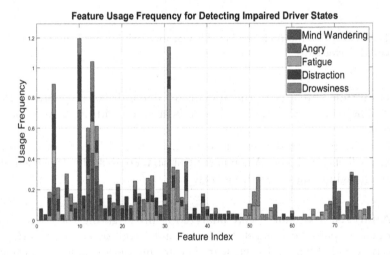

**Fig. 5.** Feature Usage Frequency for detecting the impaired driver state.

Shared features were also collected and shown in Fig. 6. In this paper, shared features are defined for features that can detect at least three abnormal driver states. Thus, a total of 23 features were shared to detect impaired driver states among all 78 extracted features. In the figure, the common features were connected to the related impaired driver states with the usage frequency; The number of shared features for detecting each impaired driver state are 10 for angry, 23 for drowsiness, 23 for distraction, 20 for fatigue, and 8 for mind wandering. Different colors of connection lines show different groups of shared detection features with usage frequency. The detailed descriptions of each shared features are listed in Fig. 3.

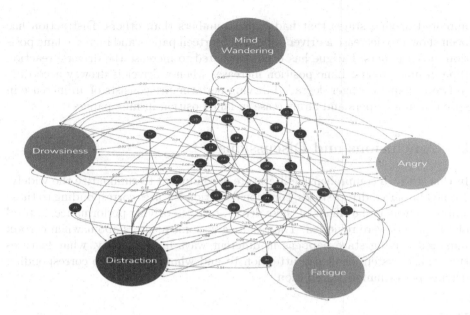

**Fig. 6.** Feature Usage Frequency for detecting the impaired driver state.

## 4.2 Effects on Driving Performance

Figure 7 illustrates the connections among impaired driver states and degraded driving performances. There were certain degraded driving performances and

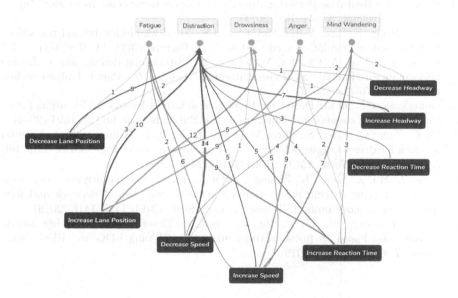

**Fig. 7.** Results of the impaired driver state with the degraded driving performances

impaired driving states that had higher numbers than others. Distraction has been shown to decrease a driver's speed in fourteen papers and increase lane position in ten papers. Fatigue has been associated to increase the drivers' reaction time in nine papers. Lane position increases when a driver is drowsy according to twelve papers. Anger degraded driving performance consists of an increase in speed in nine papers and an increase in lane position in nine papers.

## 5    Conclusions and Discussions

In this study, a comprehensive literature is conducted to summarize the widely-studied impaired driver states, common detection features corresponding to these states, as well as the effects of these driver states on driving performance. A total of 197 papers were reviewed. The results give some answers about when certain impaired driving state happens in different ways in the reality, what features the vehicle system shall pay attention to and what may be the corresponding driving performance degradation.

## References

1. Botta, M., Cancelliere, R., Ghignone, L., Tango, F., Gallinari, P., Luison, C.: Real-time detection of driver distraction: random projections for pseudo-inversion-based neural training. Knowl. Inf. Syst. **60**(3), 1549–1564 (2019). https://doi.org/10.1007/s10115-019-01339-0
2. Sayeed, A., Sadi, S.A.: Driver drowsiness detection using face monitoring and pressure measurement. Res. Rev. J. Embed. Syst. Appl. **5**(3), 12–18 (2018)
3. Kumari, K.: Real time detecting driver's drowsiness using computer vision. Int. J. Res. Eng. Technol. **3**, 147–151 (2014)
4. He, J., Becic, E., Lee, Y.-C., McCarley, J.S.: Mind wandering behind the wheel: performance and oculomotor correlates. Hum. Factors **53**(1), 13–21 (2011)
5. Zhang, T., Chan, A.H.S., Ba, Y., Zhang, W.: Situational driving anger, driving performance and allocation of visual attention. Transp. Res. Part F Traffic Psychol. Behav. **42**, 376–388 (2016)
6. Gharagozlou, F., et al.: Detecting driver mental fatigue based on EEG alpha power changes during simulated driving. Iranian J. Public Health **44**(12), 1693 (2015)
7. Li, Z., Yang, Q., Chen, S., Zhou, W., Chen, L., Song, L.: A fuzzy recurrent neural network for driver fatigue detection based on steering-wheel angle sensor data. Int. J. Distrib. Sens. Netw. **15**(9), 1550147719872452 (2019)
8. Xiao, Z., Hu, Z., Geng, L., Zhang, F., Wu, J., Li, Y.: Fatigue driving recognition network: fatigue driving recognition via convolutional neural network and long short-term memory units. IET Intel. Transp. Syst. **13**(9), 1410–1416 (2019)
9. Wang, H., Cong, W., Li, T., He, Y., Chen, P., Bezerianos, A.: Driving fatigue classification based on fusion entropy analysis combining EOG and EEG. IEEE Access **7**, 61975–61986 (2019)

10. Aidman, E., Chadunow, C., Johnson, K., Reece, J.: Real-time driver drowsiness feedback improves driver alertness and self-reported driving performance. Accid. Anal. Prev. **81**, 8–13 (2015)
11. Arefnezhad, S., Samiee, S., Eichberger, A., Nahvi, A.: Driver drowsiness detection based on steering wheel data applying adaptive neuro-fuzzy feature selection. Sensors **19**(4), 943 (2019)
12. Baccour, M.H., Driewer, F., Kasneci, E., Rosenstiel, W.: Camera-based eye blink detection algorithm for assessing driver drowsiness. In: 2019 IEEE Intelligent Vehicles Symposium (IV), pp. 987–993. IEEE (2019)
13. Murukesh, C., Padmanabhan, P.: Drowsiness detection for drivers using computer vision. WSEAS Trans. Inf. Sci. Appl. **12**, 43–50 (2015)
14. Guede-Fernández, F., Fernández-Chimeno, M., Ramos-Castro, J., García-González, M.A.: Driver drowsiness detection based on respiratory signal analysis. IEEE Access **7**, 81826–81838 (2019)
15. Gurudath, N., Bryan Riley, H.: Drowsy driving detection by EEG analysis using wavelet transform and K-means clustering. Procedia Comput. Sci. **34**, 400–409 (2014)
16. Westin, M., Dougherty, R., Depcik, C., Hausmann, A., Sprouse III, C.: Development of an adaptive human-machine-interface to minimize driver distraction and workload,. In: Proceedings of International Mechanical Engineering Congress and Exposition, San Diego, CA, USA, pp. 1–13 (2013)
17. Regan, M.A., Hallet, C., Gordon, C.P.: Driver Distraction and Driver Inattention: definition, relationship and taxonomy. Accid. Anal. Prev. J. **43**, 1771–1781 (2011)
18. Alberto, F., Usamentiaga, R., Carús, J.L., Casado, R.: Driver distraction using visual-based sensors and algorithms. Sensors **16**(11), 1805 (2016)
19. Graichen, L., Graichen, M., Krems, J.F.: Evaluation of gesture-based in-vehicle interaction: user experience and the potential to reduce driver distraction. Hum. Factors **61**(5), 774–792 (2019)
20. Jin, L., Niu, Q., Hou, H., Xian, H., Wang, Y., Shi, D.: Driver cognitive distraction detection using driving performance measures. Discrete Dyn. Nat. Soc. **2012** (2012)
21. Kawanaka, H., Miyaji, M., Bhuiyan, M. and Oguri, K.: Identification of cognitive distraction using physiological features for adaptive driving safety supporting system. Int. J. Veh. Technol. **2013** (2013)
22. Koma, H., Harada, T., Yoshizawa, A., Iwasaki, H.: Considering eye movement type when applying random forest to detect cognitive distraction. In: 2016 IEEE 15th International Conference on Cognitive Informatics & Cognitive Computing (ICCI* CC), pp. 377–382. IEEE (2016)
23. Strayer, D.L., Turrill, J., Cooper, J.M., Coleman, J.R., Medeiros-Ward, N., Biondi, F.: Assessing cognitive distraction in the automobile. Hum. Factors **57**(8), 1300–1324 (2015)
24. Wan, P., Wu, C., Lin, Y., Ma, X.: Optimal threshold determination for discriminating driving anger intensity based on EEG wavelet features and ROC curve analysis. Information **7**(3), 52 (2016)
25. Kumtepe, O., Akar, G.B., Yuncu, E.: Driver aggressiveness detection via multisensory data fusion. EURASIP J. Image Video Process. **2016**(1), 1–16 (2016). https://doi.org/10.1186/s13640-016-0106-9
26. Barragan, D., Roberts, D.M., Chong, S.S., Baldwin, C.L.: Comparing methods of detecting mind wandering while driving (2017)
27. Zheng, Y., Wang, D., Zhang, Y., Weiliang, X.: Detecting mind wandering: an objective method via simultaneous control of respiration and fingertip pressure. Front. Psychol. **10**, 216 (2019)

28. Alsaid, A., Lee, J.D., Roberts, D.M., Barrigan, S., Baldwin, C.L.: Looking at mind wandering during driving through the windows of PCA and t-SNE. In: Proceedings of the Human Factors and Ergonomics Society Annual Meeting, Los Angeles, CA: vol. 62, no. 1, pp. 1863–1867. SAGE Publications (2018)
29. Shahid, A., Wilkinson, K., Marcu, S., Shapiro, C.M.: Karolinska Sleepiness Scale (KSS). In: Shahid, A., Wilkinson, K., Marcu, S., Shapiro, C. (eds.) STOP, THAT and One Hundred Other Sleep Scales. Springer, New York (2011). https://doi.org/10.1007/978-1-4419-9893-4_47

# Expert Cyclist Route Planning: Hazards, Preferences, and Information Sources

Mary L. Still[⊠]

Old Dominion University, Norfolk, VA 23529, USA
mstill@odu.edu

**Abstract.** Cycling in the United States has continued to increase, but relatively few empirical studies examine cycling behavior outside of commuting. A focus on commuting is potentially problematic as recreational cycling is the most common form of cycling in the US. In this study, cyclists who ride extensively on the roads primarily for recreation were surveyed. The results indicate that expert cyclists share many safety concerns with commuters (heavy traffic loads, high-speed traffic, and other hazardous conditions) but differ in other factors they consider during route planning. The data also suggest that computer applications do not meet expert cyclists' route planning needs as they report a preference for getting route information from fellow cyclists or local bike shops and clubs. Therefore they seek advice from sources that are not always easily accessible. The development of successful technology to support bicycle route planning is an ongoing challenge. Bicycle route generation requires the incorporation of nuanced and dynamic information (e.g., traffic load by time of day). This study highlights a disconnect between the resources recreation cyclists use to plan new cycling routes and the resources available.

**Keywords:** Bicycling · Route planning · Safety

## 1 Introduction

Cycling has been purported as a way to address public health, environmental, and transportation concerns. While the activity has continued to increase in popularity in the United States [1], a variety of challenges may limit continued growth. For cyclists, one challenge is knowing where to ride. The purpose of this study is to examine the factors expert cyclists consider when planning a route and the resources they use when planning routes. A relatively unique aspect of this study is the focus on cyclists who are best categorized as recreational cyclists who ride long distances on the road each year. The majority of existing route planning research focuses on utilitarian route planning and commuting. Obvious differences exist between these groups, but it is currently unclear whether those differences meaningfully impact route planning. Another unique element of this study is an examination of the resources expert cyclists use to plan routes (e.g., other cyclists and computer applications such as Strava, Map My Ride, and Google Maps). Even though the scientific literature has limited data on route planning for recreational cycling, it is possible that other entities, particularly those that already serve recreational cyclists, would offer route planning resources. Therefore, an indirect

© Springer Nature Switzerland AG 2020
C. Stephanidis et al. (Eds.): HCII 2020, LNCS 12429, pp. 221–235, 2020.
https://doi.org/10.1007/978-3-030-59987-4_16

measure of cyclist preferences could be inferred from the specific resources they value when planning a route. Because of this, the data from this study have the potential to fill a gap in the literature regarding recreational cyclist preferences and have the potential to inform the development of more effective route planning applications.

## 1.1   Factors Considered During Route Planning

Safety is hypothesized to play a major role in planning a route. In Winters, Davidson, Kao, and Teschke's (2011) stated preference study, nine of the top ten deterrents to cycling were related to safety with primary concerns associated with vehicle interactions and hazardous surfaces. Similarly, Xing, Handy, and Mokhtarian (2010) found a positive correlation between the distance cyclists ride and the perceived safety of the ride; that is, greater distances are associated with higher levels of perceived safety, and shorter distances are associated with lower levels of perceived safety. Some hazards could be mitigated through route planning. The existing route planning literature covers a variety of factors ranging from infrastructure [4] to health [5] and safety to societal norms [e.g., 3] to individual cyclist characteristics [e.g., 6]. The most comprehensive collection of work examines bicycle infrastructure and route planning.

In general, studies collecting stated preference and revealed preference (e.g., GPS tracking) data have shown that cyclists prefer physical separation from motor vehicles. When riding on shared roadways, they prefer streets with less and slower-moving traffic as well as those with no on-street parking [for a review see 7]. This type of research has been used as evidence that improved bicycle infrastructure may lead to increases in bicycle commuting. One tacit assumption of this research is that, if available, cyclists will incorporate bicycle infrastructure into their routes.

Even with substantial evidence that cyclists prefer to ride where there is cycling infrastructure [7: 1], there are challenges in translating those preferences into predictions about how an individual cyclist will plan a route. One challenge in the United States is the relative lack of continuous cycling infrastructure. That is, it is common for a single route to include segments with no infrastructure along with some shared infrastructure (designated bike routes or sharrows), or some dedicated infrastructure (e.g., painted bike lanes, multiuse paths). Along these lines, Buehler and Dill's (2016) review of the literature indicates that even though cyclists in the US and Canada prefer separate cycling facilities, the majority (50–90%) of the distance covered in their rides takes place on roads with no dedicated bicycle facilities.

A second challenge in applying existing research to route planning for US cyclists is that most of the data are related to commuter behavior. Recreational cycling is far more prevalent than commuting in the United States [3] and this trend is unlikely to change [c.f., 8]. This is problematic as evidence is mixed as to whether or not these two types of cycling are influenced by the same factors [3]. There are notable differences between cycling for recreation or fitness and cycling for utilitarian purposes like commuting. One major difference is that utilitarian rides have specific destinations. Individuals commuting from home to work have a fixed point of origin and a fixed destination; the only variation would be in how they travel between those points. Recreational routes are comparatively unconstrained from that perspective. This flexibility presents its own challenges. For instance, Priedhorsky, Pitchford, Sen, and

Terveen (2012) tested algorithms that were designed to create personalized bicycle routes. While they report that initial tests of the algorithms were successful and they were feasible to implement, challenges remain in understanding and modeling the subjective experience of recreational cyclists (e.g., what makes a "good" route). They specifically note the repeated request for routes that are loops instead of out-and-back routes.

Beyond the possibility that priorities for utilitarian and recreational routes differ, there are subtleties within the utilitarian literature suggesting that individual differences and even slight differences in task demands impact route planning. Aultman-Hall, Hall, and Baetz (1996), for instance, found two distinct types of cyclists – those who take more direct routes on busier roads and those who actively avoid busier roads. In a similar vein, Broach, Dill, and Gliebe's (2012) revealed preference study identified different preferences between routes used for commuting and those used for utilitarian purposes like shopping (i.e., rides that were not a commute and not for exercise). Distance traveled was a greater concern when commuting than when riding for other utilitarian purposes; commuters also were reported to be "somewhat more sensitive to riding in high volumes of mixed traffic" (p. 1737). These subtilties within the utilitarian category lend credence to the idea that activities with much different goals (commute vs. exercise, for instance) would be associated with different demands.

## 1.2   Route Planning Resources

Commuters and recreational cyclists alike must engage in route planning. While route planning resources have the most apparent benefits for cyclists who are new to the activity or new to an area, expert cyclists can also benefit from these resources. Regular cyclists may want to ride while on vacation or after moving residences. Recreational cyclists may need to find a route to work as they transition to commuting by bicycle [see 6 and 12 for evidence that some commuters begin as recreational cyclists]. Even experienced recreational cyclists may need to plan a new route if they want to ride to a new location or simply want to incorporate a new route into their exercise routine. A benefit of considering route planning in expert cyclists is that, on balance, they should have been exposed to a wider variety of routes than those who travel less distance on the roadways or those who primarily travel fixed routes.

A variety of resources are available to help cyclists plan new routes. The route planning features available within each resource are heavily influenced by the stake-holders involved and by the original intended use of the resource. For example, some route planning resources are related to public policy and infrastructure design. Because of this, they may highlight the availability of specific bicycle infrastructure, safety data, and typical traffic volume. Some route planning resources are specialized for specific areas (e.g., bicycle tourism for a city), so they might include unique points of interest and entertainment or recreational areas. Resources facilitating long-distance bicycle travel (e.g., biking across the country) and bikepacking include options for locating food and drink and lodging. Resources supporting bicycle fitness may prioritize data associated with the speed or effort associated with the ride.

Because the present study was designed to examine the preferences of cyclists who ride extensively for recreation or exercise and because some applications are not well known [e.g., Biketastic, 13] only those resources that are relevant and more well-known were examined in this study. Considerable overlap exists between the applications, so these sources are examined according to relevant features they provide (Table 1).

**Table 1.** Major route planning features and applications that provide them

| | Google Maps | Strava | Garmin | Map My Ride | Ride with GPS | Bikemap | Komoot |
|---|---|---|---|---|---|---|---|
| Full cycling routes with subjective data | | | | | X | X | X |
| Full cycling routes others have ridden | X | X | X | X | X | X | X |
| Specific sections ofroads or routes | X | X | X | | | | |
| Road maps | X | X | X | X | X | X | X |
| Road maps with street view | X | | | | X | X | X |
| Road maps with bicycle frequency data | | X | | | | X | |
| Road maps indicating bicycle facilities | X | | | X | X | X | X |
| Maps indicating surface types | X | X | X | | | X | X |
| Points of interest | X | | | X | X | X | X |
| Leader boards | | X | | | | | |
| Social groups | | X | X | X | | | X |

The applications examined can be sorted into three categories. First, Google Maps [14] is a general road map and navigational tool that has been expanded to include bicycle infrastructure overlays and specific considerations for bicycle navigation. Second are applications best categorized as fitness trackers: Strava [15], Garmin Connect [16], and Map My Ride [17]. The primary utility of these apps involves accurate tracking of location, speed, and other performance metrics; they have been expanded to differing degrees to generate routes and facilitate social networking. Third, are applications best categorized as user-developed content with routes built on OpenStreetMap's OpenCycleMap resource. The Ride with GPS [18], Bikemap [19], and Komoot [20] applications provide platforms that facilitate more lengthy descriptions of routes along with the integration of photos and points of interest on the routes.

Despite the existence of a variety of route-planning resources, it is unclear whether they address cyclists' needs. Previous research suggests that cyclists are primarily concerned with safety in relation to vehicle traffic, but only Google Maps provides live indicators of traffic volume. Similarly, it does not appear as if any of the applications integrate accident data. From the perspective of recreational cyclists, only Garmin and Strava generate bicycle route loops from a set location; the absence of this feature could be problematic for cyclists who don't want to specify destinations in order to create a route. Anecdotally, it seems even popular applications that cater to recreational cyclists have failed in providing adequate route planning. In evaluating a new routing feature in Strava, popular blogger, DC Rainmaker reports, "I'm actually impressed. I had relatively low expectations for such a feature, mostly because it feels like every time we see companies try and do automated route generation, it either ends up being too stiff or too focused on data driven by commuters – which aren't really ideal for workouts (where sustained speed and non-stops are of higher importance)" [21]. His comments highlight what may be a long-standing trend of disparity between the factors considered in route planning applications and cyclist needs.

### 1.3    Present Study

The purpose of this study is to examine the resources expert cyclists rely on when planning a route as well as conditions they consider when planning a route. This extends previous research by surveying cyclists who primarily ride for recreation, by examining the influence of additional road hazards on route planning, and by asking cyclists to rate various sources, they would consider when planning a cycling route.

## 2    Method

### 2.1    Participants

Cyclists for this study were recruited using a snowball technique through social media. An invitation to participate was posted on a Facebook page representing an 1800 member, Virginia-based, cycling group. The invitation was then shared to a few individual cyclist's pages and to at least two additional cycling groups. Only individuals who reported living in the state of Virginia and had taken the Virginia drivers' license exam were considered for the study. Of the 145 respondents who met those requirements and indicated they were cyclists, 37 did not complete the survey, and an additional 18 respondents did not meet the minimum yearly distance requirement (2000 miles) to be considered expert cyclists.

Ninety cyclists remained in the dataset after excluding those who did not complete the survey or meet the mileage criteria. All cyclists reported riding at least once a week, all exceeded the 2000 miles/year criterion, and all of them reported riding a bicycle on the road. This sample of cyclists had extensive experience with an average of 20.85 years of experience riding a bicycle and riding an average of 4394 miles each year (varied from 2000 to 12000 miles). Also, 58% reported having specific expertise related to bicycling, which included amateur and professional racing, providing bicycle tours, promoting cycling events, leading group rides, racing, and riding various disciplines (road, gravel, cyclocross, track, and mountain biking), and coaching. Participant demographics were typical for expert cyclists in the region; older males with higher socioeconomic status (69% male, average age 52 years old, 88% Bachelors' degree or higher).

## 2.2  Materials and Procedure

The data for this study were gathered using a more extensive stated preference online survey that included: demographics, bicycle-related law, perceived hazards, and route planning. The data related to knowledge of bicycle-related law and perceived hazards were examined in a separate study [22].

Participants were asked to identify and rate factors they consider when planning a bicycle ride. Broadly, those factors included potentially hazardous road conditions, interactions with motorists, navigation ease and efficiency, presence of bicycle infrastructure, route familiarity, and local attractions, services, or scenery. To facilitate a more comprehensive analysis, participants were asked to consider a few perspectives. First, they were asked to select from a list of 21 factors *all* of those they would consider when planning a bicycle ride. The factors overlap with those examined in previous route planning studies [e.g., 2]. To encourage liberal responding, cyclists were asked to "select all that apply". Second, participants rank-ordered nine general factors by indicating which were most to least influential when planning a typical ride (e.g., traffic concerns, weather conditions, road quality, time constraints, landmarks/sights/events, number of stops). Finally, participants were asked to rate how often specific conditions influenced their route selection. The specific conditions associated with this item overlapped with some factors that were assessed by the "select all" item, but this item also included additional hazards that had been examined in Still and Still (2020). The conditions were rated on a scale of 1 to 5 for how often they influence route selection (*never, sometimes, about half the time, most of the time, always*). Because some of the "hazardous" conditions being examined in this study are not common in the route planning literature (e.g., speed bumps, drains), data related to participant perception of these hazards was included as well. Perceived hazards were measured by asking cyclists to rate how hazardous (1 – *not at all hazardous*, 5 – *very hazardous*) they believe specific conditions or situations would be to them if they were riding their bike.

Participants were also asked to identify and rate the resources they use when planning a new route. This portion of the study was intended to provide an indirect measure of the utility of current route planning resources and applications. For example, if cyclists prefer routes generated using fitness tracking applications over Google Maps, it might reveal underlying preferences for the factors considered in those applications. The list of resources examined is not exhaustive; it was developed from an informal survey of expert cyclists, online bicycling forums, and bicycling publications (e.g., *Bicycling* magazine). To measure the variety of resources participants use, they were asked to indicate which of nine resources they would consider when planning a new route in an area they are familiar with (new destination where they live). To see if their preferences depend on familiarity with the location, they were also asked to indicate what resources they would use in an area they are unfamiliar with (city they have never visited before). To further explore the usefulness of existing resources, they were asked to rate how safe, enjoyable, and fast or efficient they would expect a local route to be if recommended by, or developed using, those resources. The rating scale ranged from 1 (*not at all likely*) to 5 (*very likely*) and included a sixth option, *do not know*.

# 3    Results

Only data from the 90 expert cyclists, as defined in the Method section, were included in these analyses. When hypothesis testing was employed, a probability of .05 was used as the criterion for determining statistical significance. No outliers were identified, excluded, or replaced.

## 3.1    Factors Considered During Route Planning

Participants were first asked to identify from a list of 21 factors which ones they consider when planning *any* bicycle ride. Of the 21 factors (listed in Table 2), the mean number of factors identified by an individual participant was 10.79, suggesting that expert cyclists consider several factors when planning a route.

When examining these individual factors (see Table 2), the majority of expert cyclists consider safety issues related to interactions with motor vehicles and road conditions when planning a route. Bicycle infrastructure and "bike friendly" features are considered by many cyclists, but not to the same extent as other safety issues. Factors commonly associated with other forms of recreation (e.g., tourism) are only regularly considered by a minority of expert cyclists. These data suggest that few expert cyclists use cycling in combination with other forms of recreation.

While multiple factors are considered in route planning, it is unlikely those factors have equal importance. Therefore, participants were asked to rank nine general factors in order from most to least influential in making their route decision. *Traffic concerns* were ranked as having the greatest influence on route selection, followed by *weather conditions* and *time constraints*. *People they expect to ride with* (e.g., group rides) and *average speed for the route* were ranked nearly the same (4th and 5th) in the middle of the list. *Road surface quality* and *familiarity with the route* were ranked slightly lower and *landmarks, sights, or events*; and *number of stops/slowdowns* were ranked as having considerably less influence on route selection.

When asked to rate potential hazards on the roadway, consistent with previous findings, expert cyclists were most concerned with the risk associated with motor vehicles, potholes or broken road surfaces, and glass or sharp objects in the road (see *Hazard Rating* in Table 3). Across all potential hazards, participants' hazard ratings

**Table 2.** Conditions expert cyclists consider when planning any bicycle ride.

| Cyclist consideration | Potential route conditions | Proportion of cyclists |
|---|---|---|
| Most consider (70–90%) | Amount of automobile traffic | .89 |
| | Time of day or night | .81 |
| | Automobile speed | .78 |
| | Road surface quality | .74 |
| | Presence of snow or ice on the road | .72 |
| Majority consider (50–69%) | Personal experience with close calls or accidents on the route | .63 |
| | Wind direction or strength | .62 |
| | Presence of water on the road | .61 |
| | Presence of shoulders on the road | .59 |
| | Availability of bike lanes | .51 |
| Some consider (30–49%) | Availability of separate bike paths | .49 |
| | Road width | .49 |
| | Number of stops (stop signs or lights) | .48 |
| | Ease of navigation (number of turns or road changes) | .46 |
| | Picturesque sights during the ride | .44 |
| | Availability of marked bike routes | .42 |
| | Availability of food and drink (e.g., coffee house, brewery, restaurants) | .30 |
| Few consider (0–30%) | Availability of nutrition (e.g., gas stations, vending machines) | .27 |
| | Availability of aid (e.g., other cyclists or emergency services) | .21 |
| | Amount of pedestrian traffic | .21 |
| | Proximity to attractions (tourist stops, activities, events) | .11 |

were positively correlated with route influence rating; that is, more hazardous conditions were associated with greater influence over route planning.

When asked to rate how often these potential hazards and other conditions influence route selection, only risk of vehicles passing too closely and risk of being hit by a distracted driver were considered more than half of the time. Five additional conditions and hazards were rated as being considered about half of the time when planning a route: potholes/broken road surfaces, broken glass/sharp objects, standing water, gravel/sand, and speed they can ride on the route (*Route Influence Rating* in Table 3).

**Table 3.** Ratings (mean and standard deviation) of how much influence specific conditions or situations have on route selection and how hazardous those same conditions are rated. Spearman's rho correlations between measures are reported. * $p < .05$, ** $p < .01$, *** $p < .001$

| Condition or Situation | Route influence rating | Hazard rating | Correlation |
|---|---|---|---|
| Risk of motor vehicles passing too closely | 3.68 (1.18) | 4.73 (0.54) | .39 *** |
| Risk of being hit by a distracted driver | 3.69 (1.30) | 4.32 (1.04) | .30 ** |
| Risk of colliding with an open car door | 2.82 (1.34) | 4.33 (0.87) | .23 * |
| Risk of crash with a pedestrian | 2.17 (1.35) | 3.79 (1.14) | .25 * |
| Risk of crash with another bicycle | 2.01 (1.23) | 3.17 (1.13) | .46 *** |
| Risk of unexpected pedestrian crossing | 2.04 (1.16) | 3.54 (1.16) | .29 ** |
| Risk of unexpected animal crossing | 2.09 (1.15) | 3.66 (1.08) | .45 *** |
| Potholes or broken road surfaces | 3.06 (1.21) | 3.89 (1.00) | .51 *** |
| Broken glass or other sharp objects in the road | 3.07 (1.41) | 3.98 (0.96) | .36 *** |
| Sticks, rocks, or other small debris in the road | 2.61 (1.26) | 3.44 (0.91) | .48 *** |
| Boxes, furniture, other large debris in the road | 2.54 (1.51) | 3.74 (1.18) | .51 *** |
| Speed bumps or other uneven road surfaces | 2.48 (1.15) | 3.21 (1.00) | .42 *** |
| Metal grates, manhole covers, storm drains | 2.46 (1.21) | 3.51 (1.00) | .39 *** |
| Standing water on the roadway | 3.06 (1.31) | 3.44 (0.97) | .49 *** |
| Gravel or sand on the roadway | 2.94 (1.31) | 3.59 (0.97) | .50 *** |
| Number of stoplights/stop signs on the route | 2.33 (1.05) | 2.63 (1.02) | .42 *** |
| Hills and road gradients | 2.30 (1.26) | n/a | n/a |
| How fast you will be able to go on the route | 3.04 (1.13) | n/a | n/a |
| Likelihood of ticketing for traffic violations | 1.20 (0.62) | n/a | n/a |

## 3.2    Resources Used for Route Planning

**Local vs. Unfamiliar Locations.** To index the general types of resources cyclists use when planning a new route, participants were provided with ten resource options and asked to select all resources they would typically consider. This was done for both familiar (e.g., town they live in) and unfamiliar (e.g., a city never visited before) locations. The majority of expert cyclists reported they would consider routes recommended by a local cycling club or bike shop and routes recommended by acquaintances familiar with the area. They also report using approximately four sources of information when planning a new route (i.e., 3.9 resources when planning a local ride and 4.6 resources when planning a ride in an unfamiliar location).

As indicated in Table 4, the data suggest that while expert cyclists use similar resources when planning routes in familiar and unfamiliar locations, there are some differences. For instance, routes obtained from local clubs and stores are valued the most in both situations, but acquaintances who are familiar with the area are valued more when the cyclist is riding in an unfamiliar location than in a familiar location. There is also more reported reliance on public and private maps of routes, cyclist frequency data (e.g., heatmaps), and identified segments in an unfamiliar location compared to a familiar location. While this finding is not surprising, it does show that when planning for an unfamiliar location, expert cyclists use more resources and they are more likely to use technological resources like applications.

**Table 4.** Sources of information cyclists report typically using when planning a new route. Values represent the proportion of total cyclists who reported using each source.

| Information source | Familiar location | Unfamiliar location |
|---|---|---|
| Routes recommended by a local cycling club or bike store | .80 | .88 |
| Routes recommended by acquaintances familiar with the area | .66 | .81 |
| Google Maps | .54 | .52 |
| Public maps identifying full routes others have ridden (e.g., Map My Ride) | .47 | .61 |
| Public maps showing frequency of logged rides on specific roads (e.g., Strava heat maps) | .40 | .57 |
| Public maps identifying specific section of roads or routes (Strava Segments) | .47 | .48 |
| Private maps of routes acquaintances have ridden (e.g., Garmin friends' activity) | .43 | .52 |
| Other map programs with no street view | .10 | .10 |
| Accident data | n/a | .07 |
| No outside resource, only use own knowledge of the area | .10 | .01 |

**Expected Quality of Route Planning Resources.** To further explore specific applications and the expectations cyclists have when using specific resources, participants rated how safe, enjoyable, and fast and efficient, they expect a route to be when using those resources. These ratings were completed in the context of finding a new local bicycle route. This framing was intended to establish an evaluative context in which cyclists might use their knowledge and experience to consider the quality of routes informed by various resources.

A few results are noteworthy. First, participants had the option to indicate that they "do not know" how safe, enjoyable, or fast and efficient a route would be. The percentages listed in Fig. 1 indicate those who *did not* select "do not know". From those data, it is clear that expert cyclists were less familiar with, or confident about, the

Komoot and Bikemap applications. They were more willing to rate Ride with GPS and Map My Ride and even more so Garmin, Strava, and Google Maps. This higher willingness to provide ratings suggests they have more familiarity or experience with those applications.

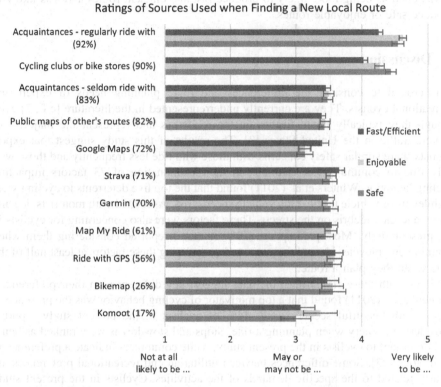

**Fig. 1.** Mean ratings (standard error) for how fast and efficient, enjoyable, and safe participants think a route would be based on the information source. Sources are listed in descending order based on the percentage of participants who rated the source (e.g., 17% rated Komoot; 83% reported not using Komoot).

A second trend in the data reveals higher ratings for routes informed by acquaintances the cyclist regularly rides with and cycling clubs or bike stores than the other resources (see Fig. 1). To test this trend, a composite rating was calculated for each resource by finding the average rating across the three dimensions (fast/efficient, enjoyable, safe). A significant effect of resource type was obtained, $F(10, 140) = 18.07$, $p < .001$, using this metric. Post hoc tests using the Bonferroni correction revealed that the composite rating for acquaintances they regularly ride with and for cycling clubs or bike stores are significantly higher than the composite ratings for all other resources. The only other significant difference between sources was a higher composite rating for acquaintances they seldom ride with compared to Google Maps and Komoot.

Finally, while the three ratings tend to vary together, there were some exceptions. For instance, while cyclists expected that acquaintances they regularly ride with and cycling clubs and stores were more than likely to provide safe and enjoyable routes, they ranked those sources as being slightly less likely to produce fast and efficient routes. The opposite pattern was found for Google Maps where, relative to one another, it was rated as being more likely to produce fast and efficient routes and less likely to produce safe or enjoyable routes.

# 4  Discussion

It is crucial to consider the preferences and route planning needs of expert and recreational cyclists. They are currently underrepresented in the literature [c.f., 7] even though they typically travel further on the roadways and represent the majority of bicycle traffic in the United States [3]. The results of this study suggest that expert cyclists share similar safety concerns with those who ride less frequently and those who only ride to commute. For example, in their examination of 73 factors impacting cycling behavior, Winters et al. (2011) found that the top five deterrents to cycling were high levels of vehicle traffic, high vehicle speeds, risk associated with motorists, ice and snow, and glass/debris on the streets. These factors were also concerning for cyclists in the present study. Most participants (70% or more) reported considering them when planning any bicycle ride and they reported considering these factors at least half of the time when they plan a route.

Even with these similarities, the data suggest key differences in their preferences. Winters et al. (2011) found that a top motivator of cycling behavior was the presence of routes with beautiful scenery; only 44% of cyclists in the present study reported considering scenery when planning a ride. Stops and slowdowns were ranked as being less important to cyclists in the present study, while commuters indicate a preference to limit stops [23]. Some differences between utilitarian and recreational preferences are clearly related to the specific demands of the activities. Cyclists in the present study considered wind direction in route planning. Commuters with fixed origins and destinations would have little flexibility to change their route to accommodate wind direction. Similarly, commuter behavior may be impacted by the facilities at their destination, such as showers and secure bike storage; these factors would not be expected to be relevant for recreational cycling.

The results of this study also highlight a potential disconnect between the resources expert cyclists use to plan a new cycling route and the resources available to create or discover those routes. Cyclists rely on other cyclists to recommend routes over applications that may be used for route planning. They also rate those human sources as being more likely to provide routes that are safe, enjoyable, and fast and efficient. This result is somewhat surprising given applications like Strava, Garmin, and Map My Ride allow users to view routes their "connections" have created and/or rode themselves. In other words, it seems cyclists could find the same routes from their acquaintances simply by looking at the activities in their acquaintances' digital profiles. While there are some potential barriers to doing this (e.g., some users make their activities private and some cyclists do not use these applications) it makes the ratings disparity initially seem unusual.

There are a couple of reasons why cyclists might not value routes they find using applications to the same extent as routes they could obtain from someone they regularly ride with or from a local bike shop. One challenge with bicycle routes that use roads with vehicular traffic is that they are subject to dynamic conditions. Route conditions associated with traffic volume, dangerous drivers, presence of ice/water/sand, broken glass, and potentially even potholes may change throughout the day. While fellow cyclists or those associated with bike stores or clubs may not know the current conditions, they can convey what the conditions are typically like. For instance, there may be roadways that typically have low levels of traffic in the morning but have substantially more traffic in the afternoon and evening. A cyclist might recommend the route only during the low traffic times. Similarly, there may be areas where an individual regularly encounters a portion of a route with broken glass or other debris; they could easily convey that information to a fellow cyclist. These dynamic changes are not well represented in current applications.

Another challenge involves the decision making process cyclists utilize when determining preferred routes over less-preferred routes. Complex situations can arise where a cyclist might use a cut-through [c.f., 11] that saves time or avoids a perceived hazard when an application would not. Similarly, while more applications are being developed to accommodate cyclist preferences to avoid multilane roads, high-speed roads, or hills, it is not clear that they produce what would be considered a preferred route. It is possible that cyclists might accept a short distance with non-preferred conditions if the rest of the route were subjectively better than an alternative that completely avoids those undesirable features. The results of several studies suggest bicycle route planning does involve these types of tradeoffs [10, 11]. Accordingly, researchers have begun examining those tradeoffs. For example, specific route features (bicycle infrastructure, on-street parking, number of stops) can be assigned positive and negative values to help quantify how they tradeoff in route selection [23, see also 24]. At this point, it is not clear route planning applications have been implemented to account for those tradeoffs in a way that would be like that of an expert cyclist. Ultimately, though, because utilitarian and recreational cyclists share similar safety concerns, and those are identified as primary concerns, there may be technological solutions for route planning that appeal to both groups as long as the applications can account for more dynamic and complex situations.

If developers intend to improve cycling route planning applications they will need to overtly accomodate different types of cycling activites. Even a cyclist who primarily rides for fitness may occasionally commute. Having the option to select a ride type - such as commuting, running errands, exercising, sight-seeing - could allow attributes that are most important for that activity to be considered during route generation. The same functionality could help accommodate different user types (e.g., someone who only commutes or only rides for exercise). Another consideration for developers will be how to obtain and incorporate more dyamic information into initial route planning. One way to do this would be to highlight areas on the route where hazardous conditions are anticipated. The hazard information could be based on historic traffic volumes, accident data, or subjective ratings provided by cyclists who have previously ridden through that area. To provide better estimates of the hazards, the application could prompt users to input the time at which they intend to begin their ride. The start time, along with expected rate of travel, could be used to estimate traffic volume when they reach critical portions of the route. This type of information could also be pushed in real time to cyclists' fitness trackers, warning them of increasing traffic volume at their current location or on an upcoming portion of the route. Weather alerts, segment information (e.g., Strava), and even missed calls and messages can already be pushed to many fitness trackers when enabled by the user. Capturing some of the nuanced aspects of route planning that cyclists expect from other experienced cyclists, could improve the usefulness of applications and expert cyclist reliance on applications.

# References

1. Le, H.T.K., Buehler, R., Hankey, S.: Have walking and bicycling increased in the US? A 13-year longitudinal analysis of traffic counts from 13 metropolitan areas. Transp. Res. Part D **69**, 329–345 (2019)
2. Winters, M., Davidson, G., Kao, D., Teschke, K.: Motivators and deterrents of bicycling: comparing influences on decisions to ride. Transportation **38**, 153–168 (2011)
3. Xing, Y., Handy, S.L., Mokhtarian, P.L.: Factors associated with proportions and miles of bicycling for transportation and recreation in six small US cities. Transp. Res. Part D **15**, 73–81 (2010)
4. Dill, J.: Bicycling for transportation and health: the role of infrastructure. J. Public Health Policy **30**, S95–S110 (2009)
5. Rasmussen, M.G., Grontved, A., Blond, K., Overvad, K., Tjonneland, A., Jensen, M.K., Ostergaard, L.: Associations between recreational and commuter cycling, changes in cycling, and Type 2 Diabetes risk: a cohort study of Danish men and women. PLoS Med **13**(7), e1002076 (2016)
6. Park, H., Lee, Y.J., Shin, H.C., Sohn, K.: Analyzing the time frame for the transition from leisure-cyclist to commuter-cyclist. Transportation **38**(2), 305–319 (2011)
7. Buehler, R., Dill, J.: Bikeway networks: a review of effects on cycling. Transp. Rev. **36**, 9–27 (2016)
8. Pucher, J., Buehler, R.: Why Canadians cycle more than Americans: a comparative analysis of bicycling trends and policies. Transp. Policy **13**, 265–279 (2006)
9. Priedhorsky, R., Pitchford, D., Sen, S., Terveen, L.: Recommending routes in the context of bicycling: Algorithms, evaluation, and the value of personalization. In: Proceedings of the ACM 2012 conference on Computer Supported Cooperative Work, New York, New York, US, pp. 979–988. Association for Computing Machinery (2012)
10. Aultman-Hall, L., Hall, F.L., Baetz, B.B.: Analysis of bicycle commuter routes using geographic information systems: implication for bicycle planning. Transp. Res. Rec. **1578**, 102–110 (1996)
11. Broach, J., Dill, J., Gliebe, J.: Where do cyclists ride? A route choice model developed with revealed preference GPS data. Transp. Res. Part A **46**, 1730–1740 (2012)
12. Sener, I.N., Eluru, N., Bhat, C.R.: Who are bicyclists? Why and how much are they bicycling? Transp. Res. Rec. **2134**, 63–72 (2009)
13. Reddy, S., Shilton, K., Denisov, G., Cenizal, C., Estrin, D., Srivastava, M.: Biketastic: sensing and mapping for better biking. In: Proceedings of the 28th International Conference on Human Factors in Computing Systems, pp. 1817–1820. Association for Computing Machinery, New York (2010)
14. Google Maps. https://www.google.com/maps. Accessed 16 June 2020
15. Strava. https://www.strava.com. Accessed 16 June 2020

16. Garmin Connect. https://www.connect.garmin.com, last accessed 2020/6/16
17. Map My Ride. https://www.mapmyride.com. Accessed 16 June 2020
18. Ride with GPS. https://www.ridewithgps.com. Accessed 16 June 2020
19. Bikemap. https://www.bikemap.net. Accessed 16 June 2020
20. Komoot. https://www.komoot.com. Accessed 16 June 2020
21. Rainmaker, D.C.: Strava rolls out significant new routes feature (2020). https://www.dcrainmaker.com/2020/03/strava-rolls-out-significant-new-routes-feature.html. Accessed 16 June 2020
22. Still, M.L., Still, J.D.: Sharing the road: experienced cyclist and motorist knowledge and perceptions. In: Stanton, N. (ed.) AHFE 2019. AISC, vol. 964, pp. 291–300. Springer, Cham (2020). https://doi.org/10.1007/978-3-030-20503-4_27
23. Sener, I.N., Eluru, N., Bhat, C.R.: An analysis of bicycle route choice preference in Texas. US. Transp. 36, 511–539 (2009)
24. Dey, B.K., Anowar, S., Eluru, N., Hatzopoulou, M.: Accommodating exogenous variable and decision rule heterogeneity in discrete choice models: application to bicyclist route choice. PLoS ONE 12(11), e020830 (2018)

# The Situation Awareness and Usability Research of Different HUD HMI Design in Driving While Using Adaptive Cruise Control

Jianmin Wang[1], Wenjuan Wang[1], Preben Hansen[2], Yang Li[1],
and Fang You[3(✉)]

[1] Car Interaction Design Lab, Tongji University, Shanghai 201804, China
{wangjianmin, wenjuanwang, 1633000}@tongji.edu.cn
[2] Stockholm University, 164 55 Kista, Stockholm, Sweden
preben@dsv.su.se
[3] Shenzhen Research Institute of Sun Yat-Sen University, Shenzhen, China
youfang@mail.sysu.edu.cn

**Abstract.** Head-Up display (HUD) is increasingly applied to automobiles. However, HUD might have also shortcomings causing new driving problems. This paper investigates the effects of different Human Machine Interfaces (HMI) of HUD under ACC function on situation awareness (SA) and system usability for cut-in driving scenarios. The laboratory-based controlled experiment conducted used a driving simulator with a total of 8 participants. Each participant performed three different tasks, using three different HMIs including two HUD HMI and one baseline HMI (dashboard HMI). The results indicate that HUD display can influence the participants' SA and system usability, and that different HUD design can have different effects. The HUD design with dynamic directivity of augmented reality brings about better SA and system usability. The research suggest that it is possible to improve the SA and system usability through improved HUD-HMI design.

**Keywords:** Situation awareness · Usability · HUD-HMI design · ACC · Driving simulator

## 1 Introduction

### 1.1 Adaptive Cruise Control

During the last years an increasing number of Advanced Driver Assistance Systems (ADAS) has been developed to improve the driving safety and comfort. ACC is one of the most important semi-automated functions which is a longitudinal support system that can adjust the speed and maintain a time-based separation from the vehicle in front. In order to achieve the speed and headway, the ACC system has authority over the throttle and brakes.

ACC systems can have positive and negative effects on driving safety. ACC provides a potential safety benefit in helping drivers maintain a constant speed and

© Springer Nature Switzerland AG 2020
C. Stephanidis et al. (Eds.): HCII 2020, LNCS 12429, pp. 236–248, 2020.
https://doi.org/10.1007/978-3-030-59987-4_17

headway [1]. Therefore, the driver has more resources available to attend to other tasks, such as looking at route signs and traffic signals. Also, when ACC is provided, drivers pay more attention to lateral control than when ACC is not provided [2]. However, drivers may glance "off-road" more frequently and longer when using ACC [3], which decreases safety. As drivers rely on the ACC system, they do not monitor the surrounding as carefully and might thus lose some of their situation awareness [4]. Overall, human drivers and vehicles need to drive together when using ACC, which requires an exchange of information between the person and the car. Therefore, for the designer, it is necessary to consider the general mental model of the driver when using ACC, so as to design the better HMIs of ACC function.

## 1.2 Head-up Display (HUD, Including Windshield HUD (W-HUD) and Augmented Reality HUD (AR-HUD))

HUD technology in aviation has been known about since the 1940s. It keeps the pilot's attention focused outside of the cockpit and supports aircraft control by information visualization within the pilot's main sight line on a transparent combiner [5]. In the automobile industry, General Motors employed color W-HUD first time in 1988 [6]. Today, there is a growing interest in HUD form vehicle manufacturers following considerable advances and maturity in the technology [7]. W-HUD uses the windshield of a car as display device directly. The position of the W-HUD picture is floating above the bonnet, in front of the street. This picture can cover critical traffic environments outside of the windshield. In recent years, with the development of AR technology, more and more car manufacturers have begun to work on the development of AR-HUD. AR-HUD picture can be shown not only in drivers' line of sight, but also matching the real traffic environment and providing a true augmented experience.

It is found that HUD allows improving "eyes on the road" time by reducing the number of glances to the in-vehicle [8, 9]. HUD allows more time to scan the traffic scene [10] and enhances understanding of the vehicle's surrounding space particular under low visibility conditions [11]. This benefit in terms of increasing situation awareness can impact the probability a driver will success in detecting a time-critical event [12]. However, Stanton and Young find that provision of a head-up display (HUD) reduces reported situation awareness [25]. Perhaps one of the reasons for this finding is that with the instrument cluster display, drivers can have discretion over when they want to sample the information, whereas with the HUD the data is displayed all the time. Therefore, the HUD might have made the driving task more visually complex and reduced overall situation awareness.

In some studies, researcher also give some design suggestion of automotive HUD. According to Wang et al. [32], the information elements of HUD-HMI are mainly presented in two forms: text and graphic symbols. It is also found that prompt and warning information should be in the state of low brightness or no brightness in general, and the driver's attention should be aroused by increasing brightness, flashing or making prompt sound when necessary [33]. For some large automotive industries (e.g. BMW, Audi, Benz and Volvo), we find that all of the HUD constant information is displayed in white. We also find that the HUD information elements basically contain speed, navigation and warning by comparing the HUDs of different cars. One of the main differences is that if the vehicle is equipped with driving assistance system, the design elements of driver assistance features will be supplemented in HUD, such as Lane Departure Warning (LDW). And another main difference is that HUD design of different cars may have different color combinations, for example, BMW uses white, green and orange, while Benz uses white, blue and red.

### 1.3 Situation Awareness

When driving, situation awareness can be defined as the driver's mental model of the current state of the vehicle and mission environment [13]. This indicates that the driver's situational awareness of the ACC system and the road environment is very important for driving performance during the use of ACC. A formal definition of SA is "The perception of the elements in the environment within a volume of time and space, the comprehension of their meaning, and the projection of their status in the near future" [14]. The SA model encompasses three levels of SA. Level 1 includes the perception of elements in the current situation (e.g. reading the set speed and time gap), level 2 is the comprehension of the current situation (e.g. knowing whether the vehicle is following a leading vehicle), and level 3 is the projection of future status (e.g. anticipating status changes of vehicle, and avoiding conflict) [13]. Driving can be thought of as a dynamic control system in which system input variables change over task time. In theory, the construct of SA in dynamic systems fits very well to this domain [15]. Though advanced automation technologies have been expected to improve system and operator safety, efficiency and comfort, such technologies may also generate negative effects on driver behavior [16]. Then some researchers put forward the view that increasing the driver's situation awareness is a key to successful automation [17].

There are four classes of approaches to evaluate situation awareness—process measures, direct measures, behavioral and performance measures [18]. Process measures include eye tracking, information acquisition, and analysis of communications [19]. Direct measures of SA attempt to directly assess a person's SA through subjective measures and objective measures. Subjective measures ask the users to rate their SA on a scale. Objective measures collect data from users on their perceptions of the situation and compare them to what is actually happening to score the accuracy of their SA [19]. Behavior measures infer the operators' level of SA based on their behavior. Performance measures infer SA based on how well an operator performs a given task as compared to a predetermined standard, or how good the outcomes of a scenario are (e.g., number of successful missions) [18].

In this experiment, performance measure and objective measure are adopted. We measure the driving performance by the driver's lateral control of the vehicle. And we measure objective SA by Situation Awareness Global Assessment Technique (SAGAT). The SAGAT assesses level 1 (perception), level 2 (comprehension) and level 3 (projection) SA by asking the driver questions related to the relevant features of the car and external environment necessary for safe driving [20]. In the experiment of this paper, because the program pause will affect the execution of task, participants complete the SAGAT immediately after each task. Endsley's study has shown that SA data are readily obtainable through SAGAT for a considerable period after a stop in the simulation (up to 5–6 min) [20]. In this experiment, the execution time of each task is about 1 min, so SAGAT can be used after each task without affecting the SA inquiry effect as much as possible.

### 1.4   Usability Test

For the development and design of ADAS, system usability should be improved while ensuring safety. The definition of usability that can be found in the ISO DIS 9241-11 [21] is "The effectiveness, efficiency and satisfaction with which specified users can achieve specific goals in particular environments." [22]. The system with high usability can perform functions effectively, by which users can complete tasks efficiently and have a high degree of satisfaction with the interaction process. In the usability study, the System Usability Scale (SUS) is a classic scale [23] and consists of 10 topics including a positive statement of odd items and a negative statement of even items, requiring participants to score 5 points for each topic after using the system or product. Several empirical studies have shown that SUS works well [17, 24]. There are also large sample studies indicate that the reliability coefficient of SUS is 0.91 [17]. Our usability test will use the SUS framework.

Endsley [25] argues that interface design should ideally provide an overview of the situation and support projection of future events, as well as providing cues of current mode awareness. Thus, in our case, it is important to know the exact influences of the HUD design on SA when using ACC.

## 2   Research Question

In this study, we evaluate the HUD design under the ACC function, and mainly propose the following two hypotheses:

1. HUD designs can increase drivers' situation awareness and system usability when using ACC.
2. Compared to static HUD design, HUD design with dynamic guidance can increase situation awareness and system usability better.

Based on the outcome of the research question above, we will make suggestions for HUD design under ACC function.

## 3   Experimental Method

### 3.1   Participants

8 participants including students, teachers and other school staff from the Tongji University, China were recruited. One male and seven females. They were aged between 20 and 50 (M = 26.13, SD = 7.27). All participants had valid driving licenses, 5 of them (62%) had a driving license for 1–5 years, and 3 of them (38%) had a driving

license for 6–10 years. 1 people (12%) knew nothing about ACC, 5 people (63%) knew something about ACC but never use it, and 2 people (25%) had ever used ACC.

In this study, we explained everything about ACC and the simulator operations to all participants before experiment. And the traffic conditions in the experimental tasks are relatively simple, so the participants could handle them with common real-life driving experience. In order to minimize the impact of driving experience on the experimental results, the subjects did undergo a complete training session to be fully familiar with the driving simulator before starting the experimental tasks.

### 3.2    Technical Equipment

The experiments with the driving simulator was conducted in a laboratory at the Tongji University, Shanghai, China. There are two driving simulators. One serves as the main test vehicle and the other as the auxiliary test vehicle. Main test vehicle consisted of longitudinally adjustable seat, Logitech G27 force-feedback steering wheel and pedals. During the experiment, three LED screens were designed and used to display the driving scene. Auxiliary test vehicle consisted of Logitech G27 force-feedback steering wheel, pedals and three LED screens. The programs in both driving simulators, are developed based on Unity software. They all have basic driving functions, and the two test vehicles run in the same traffic scene and can see each other. In addition to the basic driving functions, the main test vehicle has the function of ACC (including adjusting the set speed, adjusting the time gap, normal follow-up, etc.) with dashboard display and HUD display. When the auxiliary test vehicle is running, the experimenter can see the value of relative distance and THW which are used for the experimental conditions.

In the experiment setting (Fig. 1), the participants carried out the test task by driving the main test vehicle, and the experimenter completed the cut in working condition with the main test vehicle by driving the auxiliary test vehicle. The Supervisory Control and Data Acquisition system (SCADA) was also used in the experiment to record and save the driving data such as speed and steering wheel angle to the csv file in real time, so that the data can be statistically analyzed after the experiment.

**Fig. 1.** Experimental Equipment (a is the main test vehicle, c is the auxiliary test vehicle, and b is SCADA).

### 3.3 Experimental Design

A dual-task within-subject approach was applied. The experimental dependent variables are drivers' situation awareness and system usability. The experimental independent variables are three different HMI design schemes, dashboard HMI design, dashboard and HUD1 HMI design, dashboard and HUD2 HMI design (referred to as dashboard-HMI, HUD-HMI1 and HUD-HMI2).

1. Dashboard-HMI (Fig. 2): The HMI of ACC is only displayed on the dashboard. Design elements of ACC have been adapted and displayed with reference to vehicles equipped with ACC on the market. These design elements include speed, ACC logo, setting speed, identifier of leading vehicle and time gap.

**Fig. 2.** Dashboard-HMI (baseline HMI that design elements are displayed only on the dashboard).

2. HUD-HMI1 (Fig. 3): Compared to dashboard-HMI, the display mode of HUD (including W-HUD and AR-HUD) is added. And we use the same design elements for the dashboard and the HUD.

**Fig. 3.** HUD-HMI1 (the AR time-gap bar is relatively stationary with the main test vehicle).

3. HUD-HMI2 (Fig. 4): Compared to HUD-HMI2, the design form of AR time-gap bar is different. The time-gap bars in the two design schemes display the time gap information of the ACC. The difference is that the AR time-gap bar in the HUD-HMI1 is relatively stationary with the main test vehicle, and the AR time-bar in the HUD-HMI2 dynamically points to the leading vehicle.

**Fig. 4.** HUD-HMI2 (the AR time-bar dynamically points to the leading vehicle).

### 3.4 Experimental Tasks

The cut-in event is a typical scenario of ACC [26, 27] and it's fairly common in day-to-day driving. In this experiment, each participant performs three tasks corresponding to three different HMI design schemes, all of which are in the cut in scenario involving the ACC function enabled. When the auxiliary test vehicle is cutting in, the speed of both vehicles is 30 km/h and the distance is about 20 meters (THW ≈ 2.4 m/s). In order to avoid a learning effect, these three HMI designs are presented to each participant in random.

### 3.5 Experimental Process

The experimental procedure was as follows:

1. First, demographic information was collected from the participants, including name, age, time of possession of driver's license, frequency of driving, and understanding of ACC.
2. The researcher introduced the purpose of the experiment and the general experimental procedure to the participants.
3. After the introduction, the participants were allowed to sit in the driver seat of the simulator for 10 to 15 min in order to familiarize themselves with the basic driving controls and the operation of the ACC (turning on/off, adjusting the set speed, adjusting the time gap). The researcher then introduced the HMI display of the ACC on the instrument panel. To avoid possible learning effects, the traffic scene during the practice session is different from the traffic scene of formal test session.
4. Each participant was asked to keep the simulated vehicle straight in the lane under ACC while braking if any unexpected events should emerge. Each participant completed the experimental tasks after they familiarized themselves with ACC function.
5. Between each task, the participant was asked to rate the situation awareness, system usability via commonly recommended SAGAT and SUS.
6. The process of performing the task on the screen was computer captured and the whole user-simulator interaction process videotaped to facilitate the search and verification after the experiment.

# 4 Results and Preliminary Findings

To investigate the effects of different HMI designs on situation awareness and system usability, we collected user feedback scores of SAGAT and SUS for three different HMI conditions. We also recorded the lateral control data—steering angle of steering wheel through SCADA. Only descriptive statistics were reported, given that there was not enough data to justify confirmatory analyses. The following is the statistical analysis results.

## 4.1 Situation Awareness

**SAGAT.** Average SAGAT scores was broken down by design schemes (Fig. 5). As Fig. 5 shows, the SA scores of HUD (HUD-HMI1 and HUD-HMI2) are both higher than dashboard-HMI, indicating that the subject is aware of fewer of the environment and car under HUD conditions, which is consistent with the Hypothesis 1. Compared to HUD-HMI1, the SA score of HUD-HMI2 is higher, indicating that dynamic HUD design can increase situation awareness, which is also consistent with the Hypothesis 2. Moreover, the SAGAT is designed to evaluate SA from the three dimensions: level 1 (perception), level 2 (comprehension) and level 3 (projection). The driver's scores in different dimensions are shown in Fig. 6. In contrast to best perception (Level 1 SA), participants have worst projection (Level 3 SA) under Dashboard-HMI condition. Participants have the same understanding (Level 2 SA) in the three different design schemes. Generally speaking, HUD-HMI2 reports higher overall situation awareness.

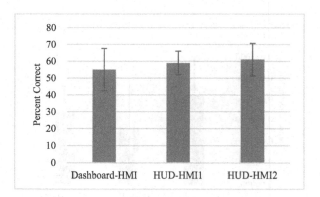

**Fig. 5.** Average overall SAGAT percent correct score. Error bars represent 95% confidence intervals.

**Driving Performance.** During the execution of the experimental task, ACC longitudinally controls the vehicle, liberating the driver's feet, and the driver only needs to operate the steering wheel to laterally control the vehicle. Therefore, we analyze driving performance by the driver's lateral control of the vehicle. In this experiment, we calculate the overall standard deviation (SD) of steering wheel angle from the time

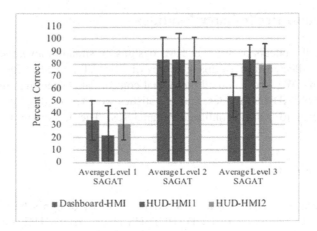

**Fig. 6.** SAGAT score of three levels of situation awareness. Error bars represent 95% confidence intervals.

the auxiliary vehicle starts to cut in to that the main test vehicle follows the leading vehicle steadily, which is used to characterize the driver's lateral control. The greater the value of the SD, the more unstable drivers' lateral control of the vehicle. As Fig. 7 shows, the standard deviation of steering wheel angle of dashboard-HMI is the highest, then HUD-HMI2, and HUD-HMI1 is the lowest. We found that HUD conditions report more stable lateral control than dashboard condition. And HUD-HMI1 condition reports the best driving performance.

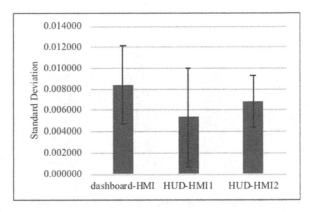

**Fig. 7.** Standard deviation of steering wheel angle. Error bars represent 95% confidence intervals.

## 4.2    Usability

As shown in Fig. 8, the HUD-HMI2 score is higher than both dashboard-HMI and HUD-HMI1, and the scores of dashboard-HMI and HUD-HMI1 are the same.

This result is consistent with the Hypothesis 2. For level of usability, both dashboard-HMI and HUD-HMI1 are level D. However, HUD-HMI2 is level C, indicating that different HMI design of HUD may result in different results, improving or reducing usability. Taken together, usability of ACC system is better under HUD-HMI2 in this study.

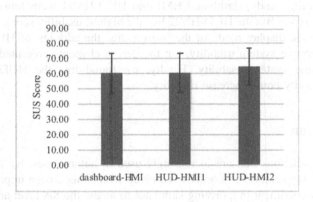

**Fig. 8.** SUS score of three HMIs. Error bars represent 95% confidence intervals.

## 5 Discussion

The result indicates that the participants demonstrated lower overall SA with the dashboard-HMI than HUD-HMI1 and HUD-HMI2. Previous studies [25] found that since the HUD data were displayed all the time, the HUD may have caused the driving task more visually complex and reduced overall situation awareness. Our experimental results show another conclusion. Similar to what Rutley [28] found, the HUD speedometer could increase the awareness of speed. From the analysis of the three different levels of SA, participants had lower perception of relevant elements in the driving environment with HUD, but at the same time they had higher projection. It is possible that HUD may capture too much attention from the drivers, a phenomenon known as cognitive capture [29]. This may lead to that the drivers may focus more on the elements of the HUD, than on the elements in the real world. However, since HUD highlights more driving information related to ACC status [30], drivers begin to process the information contained in the ACC status earlier and more often allowing them to be better prepared for upcoming traffic scenarios. This may lead to a higher level of SA. In our study, we also found that the SA of HUD-HMI2 was higher than HUD-HMI1. This suggests that dynamically changing elements that followed the real traffic scenario could further increase the drivers' SA.

Accidents are caused by drivers who fail to perceive important elements in the driving environment, and do not understand how these elements interact with each other, and/or are unable predict what will happen in the near future [31]. In other words, a lack of situation awareness leads to unsafe driving. In the same way, low SA leads to unstable lateral control when using ACC. In our study, participants have more stable lateral control with HUD than only dashboard, which is consistent with the self-reported SA result. However, the driving performance and SAGAT score are inconsistent under HUD-HMI1 and HUD-HMI2 conditions. One reason for this could be that the small sample size of the data may cause inaccurate statistical results. Moreover, slight numerical changes may not represent the difference in actual driving performance.

In the usability study, dashboard-HMI and HUD-HMI1 were found to have the same usability score. But the HUD-HMI2 had the highest usability score. This indicates that, based on the display mode of the instruments, the addition of HUD would not necessarily improve system usability, but the design elements presented on the HUD would determine system usability. Finally, we found that the HUD design with dynamic directivity could increase usability.

## 6 Conclusion

For the ACC functions that are increasingly used in automobiles, we have designed three HMI display solutions. In order to come up with better design improvements, we conducted an experiment in a driving simulator to assess the SA level and usability of different HMI design in cut-in scenarios of ACC. Our results show that HUD display affects the situation awareness of the participants and system usability. Our study also shows that different HUD design have different effects on situation awareness of drivers and system usability. Based on the research results, HUD design suggestions are proposed.

In this experiment, we used two HUD designs that were compared to a baseline dashboard design. Compared to the dashboard-HMI, the HUD design which is static relative to the main vehicle (HUD-HMI1) increases drivers' SA and reports the same system usability, the HUD design with dynamic guidance effect (HUD-HMI2) increases both SA and system usability.

In summary, the design of the HUD has an important impact on driving, and an important contribution of this study is to propose that the HUD design with dynamic directivity of augmented reality should be recommended as a way of increasing drivers' SA and usability.

## 7 Limitations

The most obvious limitation was the number of participants. A larger population subjects may give more clearer results. In addition, this experiment requires the cooperation of the experimenter. Although the experimenter has rich experience, manual control may cause the instability of the experimental task.

Moreover, this experiment evaluates the HUD design only in the cut in scenario of the ACC function and without the traffic lights and complex traffic conditions under non-motorized vehicles.

# 8  Future Work

The study of HUD design is of great significance to the driving safety. Further research topic continues to focus on HUD design research. In future research, larger cohorts of participants with multiple ages and multiple driving experiences will be used for statistical analysis. Furthermore, we will develop the driving simulator to achieve more traffic scenarios and allow subjects to complete tasks independently without the cooperation of experimenter. In addition to situation awareness and usability, more psychological factors such as workload, trust and so on are studied to evaluate the HUD design from the perspective of cognition and design.

**Acknowledgement.** This work is partially supported by Shenzhen Collaborative Innovation and Technology Program - International Science and Technology Cooperation Project; National Social Science Fund(19FYSB040); Tongji University's Excellence Experimental Teaching Project; Shanghai Automotive Industry Development Fund (1717); Graduate Education Research Project, Tongji University(2020JC35).

# References

1. Davis, L.C.: Effect of adaptive cruise control on traffic flow. Phys. Rev. E **69**(6), 1–8 (2004)
2. Ohno, H.: Analysis and modeling of human driving behaviors using adaptive cruise control. Appl. Soft Comput. **1**(3), 237–243 (2001)
3. Thompson, L.K., Tönnis, M., Lange, C., Bubb, H., Klinker, G.: Effect of active cruise control design on glance behaviour and driving performance. Paper presented at the 16th World Congress on Ergonomics, Maastricht the Netherlands, 10–14 July 2006
4. MarkVollrath, S.S., Gelau, C.: The influence of cruise control and adaptive cruise control on driving behaviour – a driving simulator study. Accid. Anal. Prev. **43**(3), 1134–1139 (2011)
5. Tuzar, G.-D., Van Laack, A.: White paper. Augmented reality head-up display HMI impacts of different field-of-views on user experience (2016). http://docplayer.net/33909881-White-paper-augmented-reality-head-up-displays-hmi-impacts-of-different-field-of-views-on-user-experience.html
6. Weihrauch, M., Melocny, G.G., Goesch, T.C.: The first head-up display introduced by General Motors (SAE Technical Paper No. 890228). Society of Automotive Engineers, New York (1989)
7. Pauzie, A.: Head up display in automotive: a new reality for the driver. In: Marcus, A. (ed.) DUXU 2015. LNCS, vol. 9188, pp. 505–516. Springer, Cham (2015). https://doi.org/10.1007/978-3-319-20889-3_47
8. Horrey, W.J., Wickens, C.D., Alexander, A.L.: The effects of head-up display clutter and in-vehicle display separation on concurrent driving performance. In: Proceedings of the Human Factors and Ergonomics Society Annual Meeting, p. 1880 (2003)
9. Kiefer, R.J.: Effects of a head-up versus head-down digital speedometer on visual sampling behavior and speed control performance during daytime automobile driving (SAE Tech. Paper 910111). Society of Automotive Engineers, Warrendale (1991)
10. Liu, Y.C.: Effect of using head-up display in automobile context on attention demand and driving performance. Displays **24**, 157–165 (2003)
11. Charissis, V., Papanastasiou, S.: Human–machine collaboration through vehicle head up display interface. Cogn. Technol. Work **12**, 41–50 (2010)

12. Gish, K.W., Staplin, L.: Human factors aspects of using head up displays in automobiles: a review of the literature. DOT HS **808**, 320 (1995)
13. Hicks, J.S., Durbin, D.B., Morris, A.W., Davis, B.M.: A Summary of Crew Workload and Situational Awareness Ratings for U.S. Army Aviation Aircraft. ARL-TR-6955 (2014)
14. Endsley, M.R.: Design and evaluation for situation awareness enhancement. In: Proceedings of the Hunan Factors Society 32nd Annual Meeting, vol. 32, no. 2, pp. 97–101 (1988)
15. Ma, R., Kaber, D.B.: Situation awareness and workload in driving while using adaptive cruise control and a cell phone. Int. J. Ind. Ergon. **35**(10), 939–953 (2005)
16. Ward, N.J.: Automation of task processed: an example of intelligent transportation systems. Hum. Factors Ergon. Manuf. Service Ind. **10**(4), 395–408 (2000)
17. Bangor, A., Kortum, P., Miller, J.: Determining what individual SUS scores mean: adding an adjective rating scale. J. Usab. Stud. **4**(3), 114–123 (2009)
18. Endsley, M.R., Jones, D.G.: Design for Situation Awareness-An Approach to User-Centered Design, 2nd edn., pp. 259–266. CRC Press of Taylor and Francis Group, London (2004)
19. Endsley, M.R., Jones, D.G.: Design for Situation Awareness-An Approach to User-Centered Design, 2nd edn., p. 58. CRC Press of Taylor and Francis Group, London (2004)
20. Endsley, M.R.: Measurement of situation awareness in dynamic systems. Hum. Factors J. Hum. Factors Ergon. Soc. **37**(1), 65–84 (1995)
21. ISO: Ergonomics of human-system interaction -Part 11: Usability: Definitions and concepts (ISO 9241-11) (2008). https://www.iso.org/obp/ui/#iso:std:iso:9241:-11:ed-2:v1:en
22. Jordan, P.W.: An Introduction to Usability, pp. 5–7. CRC Press, London (1998)
23. Brooke, J.: SUS-A quick and dirty usability scale. In: Jordan, P.W., Thomas, B., Weerdmeester, B.A., McClelland, A.L. (eds.) Usability Evaluation in Industry, pp. 189–194. Taylor and Francis, London (1996)
24. Tullis, T.S., Stetson, J.N.: A comparison of questionnaires for assessing website usability. In: Proceedings of Usability Professionals Association (UPA) 2004 Conference (2004)
25. Stanton, N.A., Young, M.S.: Driver Behaviour with ACC. Ergonomics **48**(10), 1294–1313 (2005)
26. Feng, Z., Ma, X., et al.: Analysis of driver initial brake time under risk cut-in scenarios. In: The 14th International Forum of Automotive Traffic Safety (2018)
27. Gu, R., Zhu, X.: Summarization of typical scenarios of adaptive cruise control based on natural drive condition. In: Proceedings of the 11th International Forum of Automotive Traffic Safety, pp. 387–393 (2014)
28. Rutley, K.: Control of drivers' speed by means other than enforcement. Ergonomics **18**, 89–100 (1975)
29. Tufano, D.R.: Automotive HUDs: The overlooked safety issues. Hum. Factors J. Hum. Factors Ergon. Soc. **39**(2), 303–311 (1997)
30. Gabbard, J.L., Fitch, G.M., Kim, H.: Behind the glass: driver challenges and opportunities for ar automotive applications. Proc. IEEE **102**(2), 124–136 (2014)
31. Endsley, M.R.: Toward a theory of situation awareness in dynamic systems. Hum. Factors J. Hum. Factors Ergon. Soc. **37**(1), 32–64 (1995)
32. Wang, J., Luo, W., et al.: Design of the human-machine interface for automobile HUD. Process Autom. Instrum. **36**(7), 85–87 (2015)
33. Sun, Y.: Symbol design of interface information based on user cognitive psychology. Art Technol. **4**, 303 (2014)

**Interaction in Intelligent Environments**

# Simplicity and Interaction in "Buddhist-Style" Chinese Ink Animation Short Films

Aihua Cao(✉)

College of Media and Art, Nanjing University of Information Science and
Technology, Nanjing, China
3527491414@qq.com

**Abstract.** Originating from the simple and tasteful minimalist aesthetics of the design community and the Buddhist-style attitude towards life, combined by explorers of animation creation, simple Chinese ink animation short films have rapidly caught the attention of "Buddhist-style" animators and animation enthusiasts, with the gratitude towards the resonance of the temperament expressed in Chinese ink painting and the casual attitude of Buddhist style. The simple short films of ink animation that places a great emphasis on cutting simple frames to express the poetic and artistic conception and forge vivid and vital conditions of characters in pursuit of creative aesthetics, are permeated with the so-called "Buddhist-style" nature not only in the production team and the choice of creative themes, but also in the pursuit of creative effects. They advocate the simplicity of the frame and the abstractness of the image in a formal language.

**Keywords:** Buddhist-style · Temperament · Ink animation films · Simplicity

## 1 Introduction

With the fast pace of work and life, some Internet terms have suddenly become popular in recent years, among which "simple" and "Buddhist-style" appear particularly frequent among young people in the workplace. The original meaning of the so-called "Buddhist-style" refers to the ordinary and forthright temperament of inactivity. On the current network, it is often used to describe the attitudes of those who are leisurely, attached to nothing in particular, and have few desires for life. The social stage we are in now is an era of high efficiency and speed. There are competitions everywhere, from city to countryside and coastal areas to inland. People get increasingly faster working pace and feel more life pressure, so that many workers often have an indescribable sense of high pressure from the inner psychology and the work environment. For this reason, many people in the workplace need to take advantage of this so-called "Buddhist-style" attitude to reduce mental stress and the burden of work by adopting a life attitude that shirks complexity and serious matters. In this way, the mixture of the simple and tasteful minimalist aesthetics that originates from the design community and the "Buddhist-style" attitude of life produced by the young people in the workplace from the perspective of life immediately becomes "chicken soup" for the souls of exhausted and stressed workers that need spiritual comfort in the society. Accordingly,

© Springer Nature Switzerland AG 2020
C. Stephanidis et al. (Eds.): HCII 2020, LNCS 12429, pp. 251–260, 2020.
https://doi.org/10.1007/978-3-030-59987-4_18

in the field of animation, the creation of Chinese ink animation short films under digitization has become one of the creative directions for "Buddhist-style" animation designers and the focus of animation fans with "Buddhist-style" temperament. For example, the reason why Erhu and other such short animated films that express the spiritual connotation of Chinese national art with the help of traditional Chinese ink painting can quickly become popular on the Internet is because of their artistic context of simplicity and delicate elegancy which agree with the so-called "Buddhist-style" pursued in a certain level. As such, the majority of animation enthusiasts and professional appreciate this type of animation style.

Why are animation designers and enthusiasts projecting their eyes on the Chinese ink painting form under the simple fashion? To explain this relationship, we must first explore the aesthetic connotation and expression of traditional Chinese ink painting.

The famous landscape painter Chuanxi Chen pointed out in his book History of Chinese Landscape Painting that the aesthetic source of Chinese ink painting was metaphysics that flourished in the Wei and Jin Dynasties of China, and metaphysics originated from traditional Chinese Taoist thought, which were of the same origin with Buddhist doctrines from India on the spiritual level. They both emphasize "emptiness", "inaction", "empty fantasy", etc. And such thoughts collided with each other during this particular historical period of the Northern and Southern Dynasties of China, forming the Zen thought that ancient scholars of China had a special liking for. Through the history of Chinese cultural thought, what people can perceive is that Chinese Buddhism is actually restrained by Taoist doctrines, which has resulted in a high degree of coherence between Buddhist and Taoist in the profound artistic philosophy. Therefore, the artistic function of traditional Chinese ink painting based on the Buddhism and Taoism is the "naturalness" and "inaction" of the Taoist pleasure and self-content, and its artistic expression must also connote the Buddhist peace and quietness, as well as simplicity and ethereality.

There is no doubt that the simple and ethereal painting style of traditional Chinese ink painting based on Zen thought is highly consistent with the aesthetic pursuit of "Buddhist style" of current animation designers. With the increasing number of the so-called "Buddhist-style" people, and with the development of ink painting styles of animation films labelled as "Buddhist-style" driven by strong social customs and demands for aesthetic taste, the number of China's simple short films of ink animation has rapidly increased. Many young animation designers with a certain complex for traditional ink painting do not want to be bound by popular animation styles and have free spirits. They have become more and more obsessed with the production of the so-called "Buddhist-style" ink style animation short films. In this way, the ink "Buddhist-style" animation films are immediately favored by workers with "Buddhist-style" temperament, forming such an appealing loop. Although these ink-and-wash animations are titled as "Buddhist-style", they do not indicate that these so-called "Buddhist-style" ink paintings are casually created or simply produced. This kind of short films is actually similar to the freehand brush work of Chinese ink painting. It expresses concise shapes and strokes, and simple black and white supported by playful artistic techniques that are plain, simple, and disinterested with an inactive life attitude and aesthetic pursuit. It refers to the means of animation production to reflect the art form of Chinese ink animation style, which strengthens the artistic characteristics of Chinese ink painting for animation production and manifests itself in the pursuit of simplicity and clearness in characters, and deepness and ethereality in the artistic conception.

## 2 The Resonance of the Temperament Expressed in Chinese Ink Painting and the Casual Attitude of "Buddhist Style"

Traditional Chinese culture has always respected "imagery". The Book of Changes has been revered by Confucianists as the head of the Six Classics. Its "creating images to deliver meaning", and the cultural concepts originated from the "dense and subtle images" have a profound effect on Chinese calligraphy and painting. Since then, the traditional Chinese aesthetics and the arts of all Chinese dynasties have adopted the esthetical principle of "heeding more connotation than form", and all have created art around the core of "imagery", which has become the most important aesthetic standpoint of traditional Chinese art theory. "Imagery", accompanying the development of Chinese culture throughout, is the foundation of forming the unique landscape of Chinese culture and art. The freehand and spirit-focusing intentions of Chinese ink paintings are, on the basis of the subjective aesthetic observation of artistic creator, portrait and expression of the mental "images" of natural objects. This "imagery" in traditional Chinese aesthetics is the literary and artistic transformation of natural objects with a strong subjective mood of the creative subject. The meaning in "image" is the spiritual pursuit of Chinese ink painting works. Specifically, the creation of Chinese ink painting is based on the simple and general calligraphy strokes and ink to express the spiritual state of mind and inner charm of natural objects. That is, the image contains the subjective feelings of the creator beyond the form. Obviously, the visual image with the strong subjective feelings of the subject in the creation of Chinese ink painting is a unity of subjectivity and objectivity, which is both subjective and objective, both concrete and abstract as well.

This subjective and objective, concrete and abstract Chinese ink image emphasizes the "constant logic" of the expressed object, rather than its "constant form" only. The art master of the Northern Song Dynasty, Shi Su, said, "Mountains, rocks, and trees; clouds, water, and mist, although they do not have constant forms, they have a constant logic. The failure of delivering the constant form is known to everyone; while the failure of delivering the constant logic is unknown to even those who understand paintings well." It precisely shows that images expressed in Chinese ink paintings are both non-objective and not completely true. However, it is also objective and real, which is the realness of subjective and objective fusion, that is, the "constant logic" of artistic images. From this point of view, the "constant logic" of artistic images is actually the subjective and objective image of the "unity of object and self" generated by Chinese painters in the process of artistic creation by means of imagery modeling, which is a type of image between "likeness and unlikeness" compared to the actual image of natural objects. The "likeness" is because the "constant logic" is not lost. The "unlikeness" is a new art image and artistic style that merges with the creator's subjective feelings and true temperament.

This kind of creative mentality and mental state, which is rooted in the subject's creative mood, has, from a shallower level, resonated with the "Buddhist-style" mentality that is self-pleasing and not bound by external objects. "Buddhist style", as a social and cultural phenomenon that is popular among young people in the workplace, highlights that these young people are unwilling to be restrained and persecuted by the modern rhythm. Their casualness in pursuing "Buddhist style" reflects their life attitude of seeking their true selves: this truly is a deliberate reaction of the casual and self-involved youngsters against the pursuit of utilitarianism and materialism. They choose a simple and tranquil lifestyle they love according to their inner needs in a detached attitude. When reflected in the artistic forms represented by the creation of animation short films, their life attitude and aesthetic pursuit of the "Buddhist style" naturally spurt artistical sparks in the interaction with the "Buddhist-style" ink animation films. Whether it is the creation of short ink animation films or the favor of a "Buddhist-style" people, their artistic direction is invariably creating a visual image that fully reflects the strong subjective feelings of the creative subject. This visual image must be both subjective and objective, concrete and abstract, and must be full of subjective and objective harmony, natural and simple artistic style.

## 3 The Status and Characteristics of the "Buddhist Style" in the Creation of Short Ink Animation Films

Currently many animation designers are quietly changing the attempt of achieving the educational function of "learning in fun" or the pursuit of pure commercial value of past animation creation. They are more and more concerned about the release of their inner emotions by the type and style of animation. They use the art style of traditional Chinese ink painting to express their "Buddhism-style" mentality in the form of simple ink painting, which makes the display of animation films more diversified and more personalized. As a result, it is bound to make this kind of ink animation short films similar to the sketch of Chinese painting to be accepted by audiences feeling increasing pressure at all levels, especially the young white-collar workers in the workplace.

At the moment, the ink animation short films that are simple, creative and "Buddhism-style" created by young animation designers as mentioned before exemplifies a strong influence of Chinese ink painting style on the image style and character modeling. The simple painting style, non-thematic content and self-expression of the individual's temperament have touched the hearts of young workers in many ways and gained wide recognition from the younger generation. The status quo and characteristics of the creation of this kind of simple ink animation short film are as follows:

### 3.1    The "Buddhist-Style" Creation Team

At present, most of the groups that explore the creation of ink animation films in China are individual animation creators and small teams. Such creative teams are generally not large. They are not interested in ink animation blockbusters with grand scenes, many characters, and complex plot structures, but are passionate about simple ink animation films conducive to the improvisation of the mind and straightforward expression. These creators do not follow the traditional rules, nor strive for fame, so they are spiritually detached, and their minds are free and reposeful. It seems that they are the same as the young people today, but their spiritual pursuits and lifestyles are different from those who are struggling in the workplace: they are very concerned about their true inner preferences. Following the selves and paying attention to the truth is always the first tenet of their lives. They break away from the constraints of rules, the pressure of the workplace, and the temptations of the material. The have the spirit of a hermit which is carefree and indifferent, creating in any way and rhythm they want.

### 3.2 The "Buddhist-Style" Creative Themes

The simple and short "Buddhist-style" Chinese ink animation films completely origi-nate from the expression of the creator's personal mood, which reveals a non-commercial creative tendency that has been thematically weakened. These non-commercial and thematically weakened short films apply the stroke and ink techniques of Chinese ink painting and the ethereal and peaceful oriental artistic style to the creation of animation short films. The simple ink animation short films they create generally have the characteristics of perfectly expressing the traditional poetic mood of traditional Chinese ink painting and pursuing the distant spiritual realm. This creative mode and style fit their "Buddhist-style" spiritual pursuit of releasing the pressure of the soul, which is the main purpose of creating a new spiritual utopia.

### 3.3 The "Buddhist-Style" Creative Effects

In these ink animation short films that pursue the "Buddhist style", modern video production methods are incorporated into the Chinese ink painting form, and the minimalist approach is used to picturesquely depict the creator's free and boundless imagination. Digital technology combined with plane modeling is the main creative form of these Buddhist-style ink animation films. That is, while drawing on the graphic CG technical performance, it also draws on the simple and clean composition of the traditional Chinese ink painting, revealing the inner calm and the pursuit of a peaceful mind, which is in line with the aesthetic taste of modern "Buddhist-style" audiences that favors simplicity.

## 4   3 the Beauty of the "Buddhist Style" in Simple Ink Animation Short Films

### 4.1 The Pervading Poetic Quality

The artistic conception in this kind of "Buddhist-style" simple ink animation short films is just like the sketch of Chinese ink painting, which fully reflects the poetic pursuit and artistic conception of freehand ink painting. With the help of the fresh brushwork and elegant style of Chinese ink painting, the "Buddhist-style" ink animation short films create an eternal poetic realm and atmosphere that is quiet, ethereal and full of vitality. The short films are suffused with romantic and quiet poetry which slowly diffuses into the viewer's heart as the plot unfolds. In the "Buddhist-style" ink animation short films, the themes, objects, and scenes in the frame are small, leaving a large blank space to show the fresh, delicate and elegant air of smoke and water. They may be as simple and solemn as Zongyuan Liu's "an old man in straw cape on a lonely boat, is fishing alone against snow in the river cold" in Fishing in the Cold River Alone; or as quiet and flexible as Wei Wang's "the bright moon glows in pine branches; while clean water bubbles upon stones" in Autumn Dusk in the Mountain. In this way, poetic conception and ink painting are so ingeniously blended in animated short films. This poetic and artistic beauty is a kind that has achieved harmony and unity. It is a beauty that turns complexity into simplicity, a beauty featured conciseness and pureness, and a mature beauty that returns to be plain after flourishing, which resembles the flowing paintings of the Song Dynasty. "Most of the pictures are blank or distant horizontal fields, with only a little painting on one corner, which seems vast and makes people feel relaxed." [1].

In the animated short film, The Cowherd's Flute, which is fully "Buddhist-style", the creator uses simple and concise ink to shape the rural landscape. On the winding country path, "the cowherd is playing a flute on the buffalo; the music resounds melodiously in the field". The music also seems to penetrate time and space, sending the fragrance of willow leaves in the early spring, taking people into a fairyland, giving rise to endless reverie and bringing spiritual comfort. Just as the great master of aesthetics Zehou Li said, "in a limited set of scenes, objects, themes, and layouts, a specific and strong poetic and artistic meaning is conveyed" [2]. The frame is simple and harmonious which can arouse the feelings of people and is pleasing to the body and mind. People seem to be able to enter a wonderful new world (Fig. 1).

**Fig. 1.** Stills of animated film "The Cowherd's Flute"

### 4.2    Vigorous Atmosphere and Deep Artistic Conception

"Spirit" in the traditional Chinese aesthetics refers to the spirit of the expressed object in the artistic work, and the external image of the expressed object is called form. The form and spirit of the depicted object in a successful art works are interdependent and mutually enhanced. The so-called vigorous atmosphere means that the form and spirit, which is the external forms and internal contents of the objects, in the artwork are highly integrated and fully displayed in an extremely concise stroke and ink language, thereby highlighting the vividness of the depicted objects and subjective feelings of the creator. The simple and short "Buddhist-style" animation films inherit the artistic expression form of Chinese ink painting in a good way and strive for the combination of form and spirit in artistic images with minimalist brushwork. In this way, the more non-themed traditional ink animation short films are, the more "Buddhist-style" and concise the ink painting is, the more they pursue the vigor and vitality of the works, the more they pay attention to the artistic mood of artistic works that transcend the worldly affairs.

Artistic conception is the highest artistic realm advocated by traditional Chinese art (including poetry and painting). It is a blend of subjective feelings and objective sceneries and is a deep spiritual connotation of Chinese poetry and painting. It is also the pursuit of the implication of poetry and painting and artistic beauty of expressing infinite meaning in a limited dimension. This beauty is the feeling of being touched from the depths of the heart, which realizes the freedom of the heart and the paintbrush and is a spiritual conversion. To put it simply, the reason why the simple ink animation style of the "Buddhist style" attracts so many sincere people is that, in addition to the extrinsic beauty of its elegant ink painting form, it contains the true temperament deep from the creator's own heart.

# 5    The Conciseness and Abstraction of the Form Language of Ink Animation Films

## 5.1    The Abstraction of Film and Television Language

Ink animation short films with the implication of "Buddhist style", from the perspective of "Buddhist style", tentatively re-combine the artistic features of the traditional Chinese ink painting, especially the minimalist form of simple ink painting, with digital film and TV animation forms in digital production. Therefore, they not only have the characteristics of narrative methods and story structure of film and television frames such as lenses, scenes, and picture composition in traditional film and television production, but also incorporate the language of Chinese ink painting and the poetic quality of Chinese painting, acquiring a unique artistic connotation. These ink animation short films often have simple narrative structures due to their improvisational and non-thematic quality, and expression of inner peace (there are no tortuous plots like large-scale, thematic animation films). The character settings are extremely general and refined, and the rhythm of sub-lens is also gentle. Most of the short films determine the big panorama based on the needs of expressing emotions and meanings.

In the digital video category of the 2012 International Digital Art Biennial, the gold winner in animated short films Erhu is such one with strong "Buddhist style". It properly integrates traditional Chinese ink art form with modern animation production technology. With the help of real-life images, its shape is illusory and ink-washed, and then it is narrated in a dynamic form. In this film, the ink painting technique is used to blur the background and the image of the characters. It seems to fade the color of time and narrate the childhood memories with the dream-like illusionary ink painting. Driven by the storyline, the scenes of childhood memories flash brightly or darkly in front of the viewer's eyes; the soothing and beautiful tunes in the background seem to be the loving voice of grandmother telling fairy tales in the cool summer nights under the stars. The short film Erhu seems to have a prose-like narrative structure with no ups and downs or dramatic conflicts. The whole film is very relaxed and soothing, and slightly dreamy. In short, the creator uses extremely simple and highly concise black-and-white language to display slowly on the screen. Not eager or impatient, it shows the Chinese charm, full of elegancy and profoundness of ink painting, in a proper pace, but it also gives people a mood of "Buddhist style" that is casual and carefree, and heartfelt sorrow that emanate from it.

In most simple animated short films pursuing "Buddhist style", there are generally no large changes in the positions of the characters and the scenery. The portrayals of the characters are often based on the dynamic movements of real people or the characteristic outline of characters with the ink lines of Chinese painting. Generally, they have no fine depiction on the five sense organs, and only blur the details of the character's face. On the basis of the generalization of the character image, the background music rhythm is used to drive the scene change. In the description of the scene, the illusion of ink is used to express specific emotions and moods, or to create the melody and rhythm (Fig. 2).

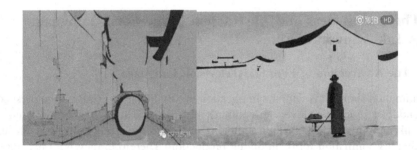

**Fig. 2.** Stills of animated film "Erhu"

## 5.2    Ink-Washed Form Language

From the perspective of form language, all the short animation films striving to be simple and "Buddhist-style" inherit the characteristics of Chinese ink painting, showing the aesthetic form and style of traditional Chinese ink painting. It is also due to the concise style of traditional Chinese ink painting that the ink animation is grafted on, it must present the expression form of Chinese ink animation with oriental artistic connotation. Similar to Chinese ink cartoons sixty years ago, this type of ink animation short films still continues the image characteristics of traditional Chinese ink painting by drawing lines with calligraphy strokes to depict characters. The short films emphasize more on the blending of lines and ink colors and the resemblance of the character image. What is most outstanding that, compared with short Chinese ink animation films 60 years ago, today's ones pursuing the "Buddhist style" are mainly designed to combine the unique Chinese ink charm with the animation of fun, and with the help of simple forms of Chinese ink painting such as "landscape depicted in the corner or along the edge" and sketches of figure paintings, to not only convey the "freehand" effect of the distant and artistic mood of ink painting in pursuit of simplicity, but also express the indifferent and leisurely life attitude and artistic feelings of the "Buddhist-style" creative subject.

"Buddhist-style" short animation films with ink-washed form language generally have the following characteristics:

First, the traditional method of "leaving blank space" in traditional Chinese ink painting is still the most important method for the frame design of simple and short ink animation films. Short ink animation films can effectively form empty and psychedelic virtual scenes by using blank space, creating an ethereal and elegant spiritual style. This kind of short films, holding the charm in the depicted scenes while containing endless affections in the blank space with extremely simple stroke and ink, has created the oriental ethereal and artistic mood and the pursuit of inaction in life, with a strong aesthetic style of Chinese painting.

Second, they represent a colorful ink-and-wash virtual space and subjective world. The space layout in traditional Chinese ink painting is often based on a simple perceptual proportion. As it is said in the Landscape Theory written by Wei Wang, a poet and painter of the Tang Dynasty, the space of Chinese painting is set according to the rule: "one zhang (3.3 m) of mountain is proportionate to one chi (0.33 m) of tree; one cun (0.033 m) of horse is proportionate to one fen (0.0033 m) of the person. Far-off people have no eyes, remote trees have no branches, and distant mountains in the shape of eyebrows have no stones; water far away has no ripples and could reach as high as the clouds." In addition to the simple perceptual proportion, the most important thing is the shade gradation of traditional ink painting – "five colors of ink". They can express the near and distant space in the artistic work and also create the atmosphere of the virtual world through the wet and dry shades of ink. (The ancient Chinese believed that "ink is color", and the "five colors of ink" meant dense, thick, heavy, light, clear, or thick, light, dry, wet, and black. It meant that ink color in ink painting had a rich level, like the hue changes of many colors such as cyan, yellow, purple, and green.)

The current ink animation short films pursuing the "Buddhist style" are also based on the artistic characteristics of the "five colors of ink" in traditional Chinese ink painting. With the help of the form language of "using ink" in ink painting and the change of intensity of ink colors in the animation film, they can express spatial rhythms and at the same time shape the situational atmosphere of the virtual world.

Once the ink animation short film Qiu Shi created by the ink animation creation team led by Professor Lijun Sun of Beijing Film Academy came out, it won the favor of the creators who are committed to ink animation. The short film inherits the freehand tradition of Chinese ink painting and integrates the artistic ideas that promote the innovation of ink animation into modern animation production. Specifically, the short animated film Qiu Shi not only inherits the style of freehand brushwork of Chinese freehand flower and bird paintings, pays attention to the refinement of stroke and ink, emphasizes the simplicity of the picture, but also ingeniously integrates with the most cutting-edge digital technology elements in the contemporary era. The flatness of Chinese painting and the spatiality of the film are integrated into one, conveying a strong oriental art charm. The style of the short film is very simple and fresh, the painting environment is fresh and elegant, and the atmosphere is casual and indifferent, which is very consistent with the aesthetic taste of "Buddhist-style" people (Fig. 3).

**Fig. 3.** Still of animated film "Qiu Shi"

In general, the prevalence of short ink animation films is brought about by both the fashion and the charm of the traditional Chinese ink painting art. The so-called "Buddhist style" is precisely the attitude and mental state of life that in some ways coincide with the aesthetic pursuit of Chinese ink painting with the traditional paintings of men of letters as the core. It also reflects the return of people's sentiment towards the slow life period and the retrospection of the life situation in the farming era in artistic fields represented by animation production in the current fast-paced digital era.

## References

1. Li, Z.: The Course of Beauty, p. 179, SDX Joint Publishing Company (2014)
2. Abad, S., Bonnet, N., Bouvry, D., et al.: La corticothérapie, une cause de rhabdomyolyse chez les asthmatiques en réanimation **40**(4), 180 (2019)

# Design of Real-Time Individualized Comfort Monitor System Used in Healthcare Facilities

Yanxiao Feng, Nan Wang, and Julian Wang$^{(\boxtimes)}$

Department of Architectural Engineering, University Park,
Pennsylvania 16802, USA
julian.wang@psu.edu

**Abstract.** There is an increasing need to address the issue of achieving and maintaining a healthy and comfortable indoor environment in healthcare facilities, such as hospitals, nursing homes, etc. The occupants can identify the environmental variables that contribute to the indoor quality; however, different people would have their individual needs, health conditions, preferences, and expectations of the environment. An individualized comfort model is a new approach to enhance the occupants' comfort in a monitored micro-environmental condition. The proposed individualized comfort model in this work integrates three primary types of input parameters: micro-environmental data, individual physiological signals, and individual-specific data. This paper intends to form the framework of the individualized indoor comfort model by leveraging wearable sensors and data-driven methods that address the real-time data collection and monitor. This comfort model is more about the thermal and visual comfort level at this stage. The measurement methods of the input, output, and third factors (e.g., confounding and mediating variables) will be discussed. The hardware (Arduino platform, wristband, camera module) and the software (smartphone application, webserver) are proposed in this real-time individualized comfort monitor system. Also, the modeling workflow to develop such personalized comfort models will be explained. This developed personal comfort model with long-term input data is expected to have a more accurate prediction accuracy.

**Keywords:** Responsive control · Real-time monitor · Event alert

## 1 Introduction

There is an increasing need to address the issue of achieving and maintaining a healthy and comfortable indoor environment for the patients and the staff with the increasing demand for healthcare facilities in recent years due to the aging population worldwide and the growth of the people diagnosed with chronic diseases [1]. The health and comfort of the physical environment of the hospitals have been studied in various projects and been perceived as having significant influence that does not only contribute to the healing process of the patients but also the workers' satisfaction [2]. The associated indoor environmental comfort aspects include thermal comfort, indoor air quality (IAQ), visual comfort, and acoustic comfort, among which indoor thermal comfort and air quality are typically deemed as the factors that are most likely to affect

© Springer Nature Switzerland AG 2020
C. Stephanidis et al. (Eds.): HCII 2020, LNCS 12429, pp. 261–270, 2020.
https://doi.org/10.1007/978-3-030-59987-4_19

the occupants' overall indoor comfort [3]. Secondarily, the effect of indoor lighting environment on occupants' visual comfort has been highlighted in a few studies of indoor environment quality since the visual quality can impact occupants' comfort, health, and productivity. Furthermore, some studies have explored the multisensory effects among these indoor comfort aspects, for example, the influence of daylight on occupants' thermal responses and overall comfort [4].

The occupants can identify the environmental variables that contribute to the indoor quality [5]; however, different people, especially the patients with various physical and mental conditions, would have their individual needs, preferences, and expectation of the environment. The indoor comfort could be assessed by subjective ratings, instrument measurements of indoor environmental quality (IEQ), and occupant-related indicators [6]. For instance, currently, the thermal comfort models suggested by the ISO 7730 standard, which are predicted mean vote (PMV) and predicted percentage dissatisfied (PPD), are widely used for the evaluation of mean indoor thermal comfort level. The PMV model considers two types of variables including environmental conditions: air temperature, relative humidity, air velocity and mean radiant temperature, and human factors: metabolic rate and clothing insulation. Nevertheless, as mentioned above, there have few considerations that are given to the personal differences and psychophysics that may influence individual comfort preference and assessment [7]. In most actual building control situations, indoor quality adjustment still relies on the space- or even building-based sensors, regardless of the individual characteristics. For instance, in our previous studies, we demonstrated that a thermostat's position in a conventional office setting might cause significant thermal variations and discomfort due to a lack of local environmental sensing and control and the different window properties [8, 9].

An individualized comfort model is a new approach to enhance the occupants' comfort in a monitored micro-environmental condition. Recently developed personalized thermal comfort models, inheriting from the PMV model, adopted the machine learning algorithms by measuring the associated variables using wearable sensors and wireless technique. Clothing insulation, indicated by ISO 7730 standard as an essential personal variable, can primarily affect the occupants' comfort level [10]. However, it is typically simplified or assumed because of the difficulty of automatic measurement and impacts the prediction accuracy [11]. Another concerned problem of comfort monitor in the hospital setting is to integrate the real-time tracking data of patients' monitor system to the individualized comfort model and to predict the comfort level of the patients who may or may not be able to describe their desired requirements. The wearable sensors and devices used to measure the input variables have rarely been developed to stream the real-time data, synchronize the data uploading and mark the events when the variation of the signal over threshold values.

This work intends to propose and design a real-time personal comfort monitor system that allows real-time data streaming from the wearable sensors and predicts the individualized thermal and visual comfort levels. The hardware of this real-time personalized visual comfort monitor system is designed based on the Arduino platform with wearable sensors. Accessing and manipulating the collected real-time database enable labeling the event of signals variation over the threshold value which may indicate the change of occupants' comfort sensation. Eventually, a framework is developed to compute and predict the individualized comfort level using machine learning techniques based on the sensor data. The developed personal comfort models with long-term input data are expected to have a more accurate prediction accuracy.

# 2 Related Work

Some studies have been done to develop the personal environmental control (PEC) systems that focus on the thermal or visual comfort with the technology of distributed sensing, context-awareness, machine learning, and the internet of things (IoT) proliferating. In this section, we will have a brief review of the recent researches on the approaches developed or implemented in the personalized thermal comfort models and visual comfort models, as well as the research limitations. Also, the critical parameters related to the environment condition and individuals fed to the personal comfort model will be discussed and selected for the machine learning algorithms.

## 2.1 Occupant-Responsive Thermal Comfort System

Aiming to implement individual control of the indoor climate, mainly the room temperature, connected sensors, and wireless technology are utilized to integrate personal comfort models into the building HVAC control system. The participation and response of the occupants on the ambient conditions are used to assess their comfort sensation and preference, feed to the machine learning algorithms, predict the personal thermal sensation and even adjust the HVAC systems based on the decision framework.

Some of the earlier studies that involving humans' thermal votes for comfort sense inherited from the PMV models and mainly focused on the occupant's participatory feedback as the signals to adjust the thermostats instead of predicting the comfort level. Authors of [12] developed a real-time thermal correction of the temperature setpoint by using a customized cell phone application and web-connected HVAC system. The thermostat correction value was the difference between the calculated PMV value and the thermal sensation value which is provided by the occupants based on the 7-point ordered scale suggested by standards: hot, warm, slightly warm, neutral, slightly cool, cool. This design implemented the participation of the occupants; however, it used the fixed value for most of the parameters in the PMV model, estimated some parameters and overlooked personal variations. Researchers in [13] designed a smart PMV-based personalized office thermal control system that introduced the personal model to correct the existing PMV model by showing the sensation difference of the current user from an average person. It used multiple sensors to measure the environmental variables but estimated the users' clothing level and activity level. Similarly, to capture the occupant's desired temperature setpoint, [14] designed a participatory-sensing system using the smartphone voting to shape the occupants' A/C setting habit. Most of these PMV-based model studies focused mainly on capturing the preferred temperature setting point through users' votes and required the frequent involvement of the occupants which was laborious. However, these studies ignored the other thermal model parameters and have limitations in accurately shaping the thermal preference.

At the same time, some researchers [15–19] aimed to model or predict the occupants' thermal sensation by measuring the environmental or personal parameters to facilitate the integration of more individual-related parameters, at the same time, control the HVAC system by utilizing wireless sensors and adaptive learning systems. Moreover, different thermal sensation scales were modified and tried to improve their modeling accuracy. For example, a thermal comfort adaptive system to predict the user's satisfaction was designed [15] by aggregating the measured environmental conditions (temperature and relative humidity), and predefined user information (clothing insulation and user activity) into its adaptive fuzzy system. In this proposed system, the wireless sensor networks (WSN) technology was used to control the distributed thermostats through system learning from the user's actions on the thermostat according to the external environmental condition variations. [16] designed a smartphone application to gather the feedback of users' thermal preference to improve data acquisition by proposing a 3-level thermal preference scale (from cooler to warmer). In this study, the ambient conditions variables were measured to assess their influence on the thermal preference prediction, and it was concluded that the 3-level preference scale outperformed the ASHRAE 5-point scale. A similar satisfaction-based control system was proposed in [18] using the one-class classifier model based on the hot/cold complaints input with environment conditions collected. Given that there are diverse comfort-related factors from human physiology, there is an upward trend in integrating the environmental factors and human data into the prediction model to improve the overall thermal comfort. An individualized HVAC control framework was developed by [19] and this study integrated the environmental and personal factors in the decision loop to improve prediction accuracy. It produced a smartphone application, used the cloud database to store data, and adopted the classification algorithms to predict thermal preference. The supporting hardware and software in this human-focused control system made progress in dynamically controlling the environment. Some of the limitations in the current studies could be addressed in the system control process through data collection, streaming, and management with the technological advancements in sensing, computing and data management.

## 2.2 Visual Comfort Measuring and Monitor

More and more researchers have adopted the approach that combines the methods of subjective surveys and questionnaires with simulation analysis to study the visual comfort to reduce the interference with the occupants' daily activity. Researchers [20–22] conducted experimental studies to assess visual comfort using lighting indicators such as illuminance, glare and brightness, and developed functions or models to predict visual comfort. Most of these studies required professional instruments such as expensive cameras and illuminance meters and cannot transfer the image data to analysis software conveniently. A personalized visual comfort control system was proposed by authors in [23] using a smart mobile APP, illuminance sensor, and wireless light sensor node to control task light based on user's light preference from historically collected data. This study was implemented in an office with multiple occupants. For a personal small workstation or a patient's private area, portable lighting measurement devices without disturbing the users' daily life could be explored.

# 3  Methodology

This paper intends to present an individualized comfort monitor system that provides a real-time thermal and visual comfort data collection by using wearable sensors, smartphone APP, and window servers and enables documenting and predicting patients' individual thermal and visual comfort ratings. The main goals of this study are to form a framework that can: (1) autonomously monitor the data of environmental and human factors collected by the environment sensor and wristband via the cloud; (2) process measuring data and automatically detect "events" referring to the potential ambient environment changes; (3) collect users' comfort voting when there is an "event alert" automatically detected; and (4) enable comfort prediction modeling using machine learning algorithms and its application in the control loop.

This individualized comfort monitor system includes the hardware components to measure the thermal and visual comfort-related factors and software components to storage, transfer, and process data. The details of the comfort monitor system are shown in Fig. 1. It can be categorized into four major technological components: (1) data measurement and collection; (2) data storage and event alert process via web server; (3) Alert-based voting through smartphone APP; (4) Model selection and output.

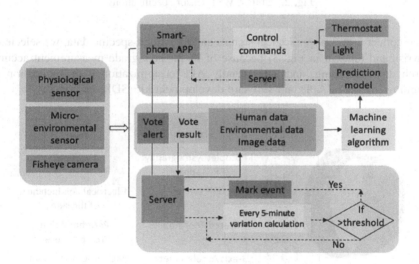

**Fig. 1.** Framework of the individualized thermal and visual comfort system.

## 3.1  Data Collection

Both environmental and human factors will be collected to develop this real-time monitor system. A portable environmental sensor is selected to measure the data of the ambient environment in the users' body proximity, and this enables the users to live a daily life without location limitations. It needs to be pointed out that the collected environment data and image data would be paired with the time-stamped personal physiological data and fed into the machine learning model, so there is no need to confine the data collection location to a specific room. The industrial-grade UbiBot WS1 is selected to measure the environment data (shown in Fig. 2) that includes temperature, humidity, light, and vibration. This smart environmental sensor could be connected to the internet via WIFI and enables data auto synchronization to its IoT platform. The friendly feature about UbiBot is its function of data forwarding and HTTP interaction which allows the data transfer to the personal web server that will be customized to set event alert that will be discussed in 3.2 section.

| Sensor | Range | Precision |
|---|---|---|
| Temperature sensor | -4°F to 140°F | ±0.3°C |
| Humidity sensor | 10% to 90% | ±3%RH |
| Ambient light sensor | 0.01 to 83K lux | ±2% |
| Vibration index sensor | - 16 to 16g | 4mg |

**Fig. 2.** UbiBot WS1 sensor specifications.

To collect users' physiological signals and individual-specific data, we selected the E4 wristband (shown in Fig. 3) because of its medical-grade measurement accuracy, smooth data streaming, and user-friendly APP customization with application programming interface (API) and software development kit (SDK) provided.

| Sensor | Signal |
|---|---|
| Photoplethysmography (PPG) sensor | Heart rate |
| GSR Sensor | Electrical conductance of the skin |
| Infrared Thermopile | Peripheral skin temperature |
| 3-axis Accelerometer | Motion-based activity |

**Fig. 3.** E4 wristband sensors

The camera module with the Arduino platform is mainly used to capture the lighting condition for discomfort factor assessment (Fig. 4a). The camera has a mini fisheye lens that could simulate the human field of vision and capture the full-resolution RAW image (Fig. 4b) which makes it compatible with IoT application. The Serial Peripheral Interface (SPI) interface supports camera commands and enables data stream. Discomfort

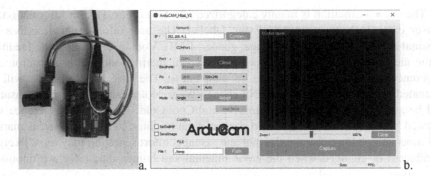

**Fig. 4.** Arducam module: a. Camera with Arduino connection; b. Desktop App.

factors of illuminance and glare are included in this design because they can lead to discomfort quickly and could be solved from the control point of view [24].

### 3.2 Data Streaming and Event Alert

Patients will be asked simply to behave as they usually do, but also to wear these personal sensor modules. The data streaming among the sensors, smartphone APP and web server could be described in Fig. 5a for thermal comfort monitor and Fig. 5b for visual comfort. The web server is used in this study to store and process the real-time data uploaded from UbiBot, E4, and Arduino-based Arducam camera. This database integrated the time-stamped environmental, image, and personal data together into one variation calculation command which is programmed to calculate the variation of the mean value for each parameter in a 5-minute period. This ongoing program is used to mark an event and send out an alert to the user's smartphone APP to request a thermal sensation vote when the variation values exceed the threshold set for each parameter. The threshold value for each setting depends on its scale and the approximate range of variation. The vote results are collected via the APP interface and transferred to the database server.

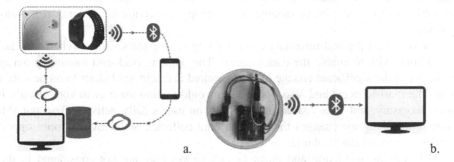

**Fig. 5.** Real-time data streaming: a. thermal comfort monitor; b. visual comfort data monitor

The data information is mainly categorized into four types: 1) User information; 2) Sensor data; 3) Vote results; 4) Event labeled. The user information describes the personal-specific factors (user ID, age, gender, BMI). Vote results collect the feedback at the alert time, and the questions will be about thermal and visual sensation and preference based on the principles of simpleness. The thermal preference will be evaluated by using "Want warmer/No change/Want cooler" and the thermal sensation will be assessed by using "Hot/Warm/Neutral/Cool/Cold." The visual preference will be rated by using "Want dimmer/No change/Want brighter." The event alert is marked and time-stamped because the thermal and visual comfort sensation may most likely to be affected or changed when the environmental and human data have a pronounced fluctuation.

### 3.3    Model Selection and Commands Control

The users' responses to their thermal and visual sensation and preference, as the dependent variable or output, are the categorical data type. The machine learning techniques via R software, including linear methods, non-linear methods, trees, and rules, can be conducted to get the predicted response of the model based on the collected real-time data from amounts of participants. The model selection should take into account the prediction accuracy, prediction consistency and convergence which are mentioned in [25] and have been discussed in detail in [26]. The Wi-Fi smart thermostat and lighting control are recommended in this study to make it easier to control the HVAC and lighting system which should be designed to communicate with this control technology.

## 4    Discussion and Conclusions

The proposed real-time monitor system integrates four primary types parameters exploited as the input or independent variables: 1) environmental data, 2) image data, 3) human physiological signals, and 4) human-specific data. Also, human subjective votes data will be served as dependent variables. The individualized indoor comfort model can be established by various modeling techniques and these above-mentioned datasets. This study discussed some of the opportunities and limitations of using wearable sensors and camera modules to develop an individualized comfort monitor system.

We proposed the real-time data synchronizing among the sensors, web server, and smartphone APP to enable the data monitor. The ongoing back-end monitor program could detect the significant change of the measured data and send alerts to request for a vote. The marked event and alert notification would remind the user to vote when it is most necessary and thus reduce interventions on user's daily activity. The portable environmental sensor changes the way the data collected and provides more opportunities to expand data volume.

The clothing insulation and mean radiant temperature are not considered in this individualized model. The clothing insulation could be measured using a heat flux sensor, but it cannot be uploaded in real-time with other factors. The mean radiant temperature and air velocity of the environmental variables are also not considered in this proposal because, in most indoor environmental situations, they could be easily pre-determined. This framework is intended to stream the measured real-time data and change the way of data collection and processing, so it relies on the smart sensor and technology at the sacrifice of a few factors that cannot be measured in real-time.

**Acknowledgments.** We acknowledge the financial support provided by Environmental Protection Agency P3 SU836940.

# References

1. Barker, R.: 2030 The Future of Medicine, Avoiding a Medical Meltdown. Oxford University Press Inc., New York (2011)
2. Zborowsky, T., Kreitzer, M.J.: Creating optimal healing environment in a healthy setting. Minn. Med. **91**, 35–38 (2008)
3. Hwang, R.-L., Chien, J.-H., Lin, T.-P., Cheng, M.-J.: Patient thermal comfort requirement for hospital environments in Taiwan. Build. Environ. **42**(8), 2980–2987 (2007)
4. Chinazzo, G., Wienold, J., Andersen, M.: Combined effects of daylight transmitted through coloured glazing and indoor temperature on thermal responses and overall comfort. Build. Environ. **144**, 583–597 (2018)
5. Andrade, C., Lima, M.L., Fornara, F., Bonaiuto, M.: Users' views of hospital environmental quality: Validation of the perceived hospital environment quality indicators (PHEQIs). J. Environ. Psychol. **32**(2), 97–111 (2012)
6. Bluyssen, P.M.: Towards new methods and ways to create healthy and comfortable buildings. Build. Environ. **45**(4), 808–818 (2010)
7. Havenith, G., Holmér, I., Parsons, K.: Personal factors in thermal comfort assessment: clothing properties and metabolic heat production. Energy Build. **34**, 581–591 (2002)
8. Duan, Q., Wang, J.: Thermal conditions controlled by thermostats: an occupational comfort and well-being perspective. Civ. Eng. Architect. **5**, 173–179 (2017). https://doi.org/10.13189/cea.2017.050502
9. Duan, Q., Wang, J.: A parametric study of the combined effects of window property and air vent placement. Indoor Built Environ. **28**(3), 345–361 (2019)
10. Ergonomics of thermal environment-Analytical determination and interpretation of thermal comfort using calculation of the PMV and PPD indices and local thermal comfort criteria. ISO/FDIS 7730 (2005)
11. Alfano d'Ambrosio, F.R., Palella, B.I., Riccio, G.: The role of measurement accuracy on the thermal environment assessment by means of PMV index. Build. Environ. **46**, 1361–1369 (2011)
12. Erickson, V.L., Cerpa, A.E.: Thermovote: participatory sensing for efficient building HVAC conditioning. In: Proceedings of the Fourth ACM Workshop on Embedded Sensing Systems for Energy-Efficiency in Buildings, pp. 9–16. ACM (2012)
13. Gao, P.X., Keshav, S.: SPOT: a smart personalized office thermal control system. In: Proceedings of the Fourth International Conference on Future Energy Systems, pp. 237–246 (2013)
14. Hang-yat, L.A., Wang D.: Carrying my environment with me: a participatory-sensing approach to enhance thermal comfort. In: Proceedings of the 5th ACM Workshop on Embedded Systems for Energy-efficient Buildings, pp. pp. 1–8. ACM (2013)

270     Y. Feng et al.

15. Bermejo, P., Redondo, L., de la Ossa, L., Rodríguez, D., Flores, J., Urea, C., et al.: Design and simulation of a thermal comfort adaptive system based on fuzzy logic and on-line learning. Energy Build. **49**, 367–379 (2012)
16. Jazizadeh, F., Marin, F.M., Becerik-Gerber, B.: A thermal preference scale for personalized comfort profile identification via participatory sensing. Build. Environ. **68**, 140–149 (2013)
17. Zhao, Q., Zhao, Y., Wang, F., Jiang, Y., Zhang, F.: Preliminary study of learning individual thermal complaint behavior using one-class classifier for indoor environment control. Build. Environ. **72**, 201–211 (2014)
18. Wang, F., et al.: Experimental comparison between set-point based and satisfaction based indoor thermal environment control. Energy Build. **128**, 686–696 (2016)
19. Li, D., Menassa, C.C., Kamat, V.R.: Personalized human comfort in indoor building environments under diverse conditioning modes. Build. Environ. **126**, 304–317 (2017)
20. Bian, Y., Ma, Y.: Subjective survey & simulation analysis of time-based visual comfort in daylit spaces. Build. Environ. **131**, 63–73 (2018)
21. Borisuit, A., Linhart, F., Scartezzini, J.-L., Münch, M.: Effects of realistic office daylighting and electric lighting conditions on visual comfort, alertness and mood. Light. Res. Technol. **47**(2), 192–209 (2015)
22. Buratti, C., Belloni, E., Merli, F., Ricciardi, P.: A new index combining thermal, acoustic, and visual comfort of moderate environments in temperate climates. Build. Environ. **139**, 27–37 (2018)
23. Shareef, P.K.A., Kumar, A., Harn, K.T., Kalluri, B., Panda, S.K.: ReViCEE: a recommendation based approach for personalized control visual comfort & energy efficiency in buildings. Build. Environ. **152**, 135–144 (2019)
24. Anthierrens, C., Leclercq, M., Bideaux, E., Flambard, L.: A smart sensor to evaluate visual comfort of daylight into building. Int. J. Optomechatron. **2**, 413–434 (2008)
25. Kim, J., Schiavon, S., Brager, G.: Personal comfort models – a new paradigm in thermal comfort for occupant-centric environmental control. Build. Environ. **132**, 114–124 (2018)
26. Liu, S.C., Schiavon, S., Das, H.P., Jin, M., Spanos, C.J.: Personal thermal comfort models with wearable sensors. Build. Environ. **162**, 106281 (2019)

# Interfacing the City

## Media Theory Approach to Cognitive Mapping of the Smart City Through Urban Interfaces

Jakub Ferenc[✉] iD

Department of Philosophy, University of West Bohemia,
Pilsen, The Czech Republic
jferenc@kfi.zcu.cz

**Abstract.** The aim of the paper is to analyse the interface as a cognitive map of the smart city from a media-theoretic perspective. The issue of cognitive mapping in the context of urbanism was articulated in Lynch's *The Image of the City* where the notion of "image ability" or constructing a mental map of the spatial and environmental features of the city played the major role in how humans experience the city. Media theory sees the city as an information-processing medium that consists of both physical and digital layers, making the (smart) city a hybrid product made of "atoms and bits". Following Manovich, the paper argues that there is no necessary link between the digital data and their form, as digital material is a material without qualities which requires a certain form, that is an interface, to be perceived. The paper argues that the interface is 1) a relation between the visible surface layer and the deeper, invisible layer of a medium and 2) Norman's cognitive artefact which helps humans with information complexity and overload. Applying Haken and Portugali (2003), the paper asserts the information-centric view of the smart city. Lynch claimed that the future form of the city should allow experiencing the city as a whole by constructing a synthetic image. The paper suggests that the only solution to Lynch's requirement in the age of the smart city is designing an urban interface. Finally, the paper defines the urban interface and offers a brief selection of historical and contemporary examples of urban interfaces.

**Keywords:** Cognitive mapping · Image ability · Kevin lynch · Media theory · Smart city · Urban interface

## 1 Introduction

At the beginning of the 20th century, the Swiss modernist architect Le Corbusier regarded the city and individual buildings as both "living machine" and "the machine for living". Influenced by the avant-garde Bauhaus school, Le Corbusier [1] envisioned in his book *Towards a new architecture* the future that would not be governed by old historical architectonic styles and superfluous ornaments but new forms inspired by rational aesthetics of cars, planes, and mass-production that were better-suited for the revolutionary aspects of modern age. In 1970 s the co-founder of M.I.T. Media Lab, Nicholas Negroponte [2] belonged to early proponents of responsive architecture where

© Springer Nature Switzerland AG 2020
C. Stephanidis et al. (Eds.): HCII 2020, LNCS 12429, pp. 271–285, 2020.
https://doi.org/10.1007/978-3-030-59987-4_20

sensors and latest technology would be embedded into urban structures, making buildings and cities smart, interactive, and responsive to human needs and the contextual changes in the environment. This idea embodied the broader concept of smart city and was further explored at Xerox PARC, the birthplace of graphical user interface and important research in human-computer interaction and user experience design. Mark Weiser [3], who worked at PARC as the chief scientist, proposed the concept of *ubiquitous computing*, the vision in which computational capabilities and data processing are fully integrated into the fabric of environment and everyday objects, enabling computers to become invisible, their transparent mediation, and natural user interfaces [4]. As more urban services and processes shifts from the physical space to the information space, managing the city starts to be a design problem about managing the information flows and media channels.

In Kevin Lynch's concept of "image ability", a good mental model of the city's form and affordances improve cooperation among people, satisfaction, orientation and enhance experiences of being a citizen [5]. As this paper argues, however, it is unlikely for citizens of smart cities to make a clear mental image of the city due to the general shift of its services, processes, and affordances from the physical to digital space. What is needed is the stance that a city is an information-processing medium, or simply *a computer*, and to achieve positive user experiences can be satisfied increasingly only by affording proper tools for cognitive mapping, namely designing urban interfaces which synthesize a holistic picture mediating a relationship between the city and its citizens.

The paper will offer a media-theoretic analysis of the interface as a tool for cognitive mapping of the smart city and as a potential solution for increasing complexity of contemporary urban life.

## 2   The City as a Medium

Many media theorists argue that technology has merged with the existing urban infrastructure to such extent that the city itself generates a large amount of data and computational power. Far from being a passive set of objects and buildings, the city has become an active agent shaping our lives, the stack of multiple interrelated physical and digital layers, infrastructural space, or a sociotechnical medium enabling interaction among human and non-human actors.

The interest of media theorist in the city can be traced to the revolution in media theory in the middle of 20th century. Several Canadian media theorists affiliated with the University of Toronto argued for the active role of technological media in our society and their impact on human thinking and perception. Marshall McLuhan became the most visible proponent of the novel approach in media studies. His famous phrase "the medium is the message" invites various interpretations and is often misinterpreted. The interpretation advocated here is that what matters to a media theorist is not a particular YouTube video, story in a book or what contents a train carries but the technological form and infrastructure that enable the medium to exist in the first place: the internet, printing press, railroads and steam engine respectively. For that reason, McLuhan equated media with technology and explored the connection between the form of technology and the cognitive and perceptual changes which its introduction exerts on the society and individual minds. McLuhan commented on the city as a medium in the context of his general theory in which media are extensions and modifiers of our senses, bodily, mental, and social processes. For McLuhan, housing and the city were technological extensions of skin and heat control of the body which inherently transform how citizens see the world: urban plan and early technologies, such as outdoor electrical lights prolonging a day, shape and rearrange the ways whereby we perceive the world and how we associate with each other and build social communities [6, pp. 125-130].

Friedrich Kittler treated the subject in his *The City is a Medium* essay where, following Lewis Mumford, the city is a medium for communication which "translate[s] its products into forms that could be stored and reproduced [...] By means of its storage facilities (buildings, vaults, archives, monuments, tablets, books), the city became capable of transmitting a complex culture from generation to generation [7]. Even before digitalisation, there were postal services, telegraphs, telephones, car traffic and railway stations as a part of network of nodes that communicated with each other. The network of nodes that comprises the city can work only because the city has information-processing capabilities and, according to Kittler, that is why the city is a computer, or medium. However, data would be semiotically meaningless unless they can be accessed and formatted. Kittler notices that "[m]edia are only as good and fast as their distributors": ancient scrolls could have the same content as the modern book format, but the ability to give each page number and show readers an "interface" like a table of contents made the data easier to find and read.

The Dutch media theorist Mark Deuze synthesized a large corpus of data and theories about the role of media in our lives. Deuze in his book *Media Life* [8] argues that media are ubiquitous and structure our everyday experiences, but also create experiences that would not be available without the mediating "third" or "in-between" element. Deuze analyses how living in the mediated life looks like and what values and ethical concerns stem from it. The city and urban space are natural places where to investigate such question as the increasing number of world population migrate to urban areas and the city becomes a laboratory of mediated life.

Using the theories behind the concepts of "Mediapolis" and "Media city", Deuze argues that we live in a hybrid or extended reality where we are simultaneously at two or more places at once due to intermixing of the physical and digital layers of our lives. De Jong and Schuilenburg from the urban platform Studio Popcorn, cited by Deuze, claim that "we have to consider the geographical space of the city an open area or a media infrastructure that can continually update themselves" [9, pp. 21]. For Deuze and other media theorists, the city has become a *hybrid material* which designers and urban planners can exploit to create new conceptualization of public space in which the spatial domain is becoming less important than affordances, services, and functions that the city offers for its citizens.

Martin de Waal in his *The City as Interface* [10] introduces the concept of *urban media*, a collective term for media technologies that can influence the experience of a city's physical space. Urban media can be either "experience markers" or "territory devices". Experience markers are media that can record and store data about the urban space, with Instagram, Foursquare and other social media being the prime examples of repositories of urban everyday life. On the other hand, territory devices do not focus on *the representation of what is present but presentation of the absent*: urban media have power to add new layers of meaning and affordances to the current physical location which we occupy; for example we can be connected at instant with our family and friends, or we can look up information and Instagram photos of the place where we stand. Urban media used as territory devices can dramatically influence our relationship with the place, since its meaning and our emotional attachment to it are not fixed, but are co-constructed and negotiated anew during each interaction, because the relevant contextual aspects of each interaction differ each time [9, 10].

For William Mitchell and Malcolm McCullough [9], the hybridisation and merging of the physical and digital worlds should incentivize new design strategies. For example, McCullough suggests that goals of architecture and new media studies now converge in a new "public ambient space" [8, pp. 25] where interactive design should enrich the set of established architectural methods. These ideas reflect radical ideas of responsive architecture developed already by Negroponte and also point to the fact that interaction design and user experience design should claim public urban space as their own next frontier where bits and atoms are design materials for creating new user-citizen experiences.

There is an important corollary to describing digital bits as a design material. Materials in general influence what potential forms and functions are accessible: while physical materials restrict forms that they can take, the digital material has little physical limitations, except for the computational power to run the code. Following Löwgren and Stolterman [11], the digital material is better understood as "a material without qualities", because what UX, interaction, or digital designers use for their work depends on the ongoing developments in computer science, information technology, urbanism, architecture, but also social sciences, humanities, and other fields. I believe that the ontological qualities of the digital material that are conditioned on the sociotechnical context is in itself a quality. Therefore, the general malleability or fluidity of the digital material could be used as its essential feature.

Another possible fundamental quality of the digital material, discussed in Lev Manovich's foundational text in new media studies, is that there is no necessary link between the digital data and the form of their representation. It is the task of a designer to find a suitable auditory, tactile, visual, or other sensual [1] form for the data. For example, contrary to Renaissance painters who used the visual strategy of mimesis, designers cannot copy the existing form of data, because there is none. Instead they have to design an interface that would *construct an appropriate relationship* between the digital data and their invented (visual) form, so that a human can *make sense of the data* whose raw binary ontological and epistemological complexity lie beyond the mental abilities of humans. For any thoughtful digital designer, it is essential to understand that their work does not involve only in making of tangible products. In the information and post-industrial societies, it increasingly involves *knowledge construction* [11, pp. 2] and

---

[1] I am deliberately using the semantic ambiguity of the word "sensual". I refer both to the ability of a form-interface to seduce our senses, following Don Norman's approach to design elaborated his Emotional design [18] and the general goal of User Experience Design to create attractive and meaningful user experiences. But also, I refer to a form-interface that can be presented to and affect our senses.

*managing of the information-cognitive complexity.* In fact, historical analysis of digital revolution of the 20th century reveals that all the pioneers of the era – Vannevar Bush [12], J. R. Lickider [13], and Douglas Engelbart [14] – explicitly stated that their ideas of interfaces and human-machine symbiosis originated from thinking about the issue how to tackle the increasing knowledge and information complexity of the modern world. For them, the interface is a much needed cognitive artefact [15] which navigates humans through the information overload by "augmenting our intellect" and extending our natural cognitive abilities by being a mediator that reduces the complexity of the world and information systems down to a form that is easily digested by humans. As this paper argues, it is also the only way to understand the smart city, because with the interface, designers can synthesize both the physical and digital, data-based layers of the city and design a synthetic "image" or "map" of the city and means to affect it back via the interactive feedback loop (which other non-digital, non-interactive interfaces such as paper maps, graphs, or photographs cannot do).

For further elucidation of the interface as an image of the city, I will turn to Kevin Lynch's concept of "imageability" of the city and my own analysis of the "interface".

## 3    The Image, Cognitive Map and Imageability of the (Smart) City

Even before the onset of massive digitalization of the city, Lynch argued that the increasing complexity of the urban space requires from architects and urban planners to design a good "imageability" or legibility of the city, which is "a crucial condition for the enjoyment and use of the city" [5, pp. 18]. In other words, for deeper and positive user-citizen experiences, people should be able to construct in their heads a clear mental image or cognitive map of the city and all its affordances [5, pp. 5][2].

In the pre-digital era, Lynch considered in his seminal book *The image of the city* (1960) only the physical layer of the city. His empirical research revealed that people make sense of the spatial and environmental conditions in the city with the help of five visual elements related to the city: paths, edges, nodes, districts, and landmarks that contributed most to high imageability or legibility of the city.

In Lynch's view, people form cognitive maps of the city as a result of "two-way process between the observer and his environment" [5, pp. 7] or the combination of an *external image* of the environment that "suggests distinctions and relations" and the *internal processing* of a human mind that "selects, organizes, and endows with meaning" what a person sees. The image created in such way, however, is not static,

---

[2] This paper acknowledges the difference between the mental image and cognitive map. While the cognitive map introduced by [43] and used regularly in cognitive science and psychology refers to the internal mental model that a person keeps in the head, the mental mapping as practiced in Lynch (1960) and subsequently urban geography in general refers to an externalised cognitive model, usually in the form of a drawing when research based on Lynch's work gives humans a task to create a drawing of the urban area. For the discussion on the origins of the cognitive map see [44]. This paper uses the terms interchangeably.

but updates continually against the "filtered perceptual input in a constant *interacting process*" [5, pp. 6, emphasis added].

When Lynch argues that the environment "suggests distinctions and relations", his notion strongly resembles the concept of "affordance" that has been imported from Gibson's ecological psychology [20] to human-computer interaction literature by Norman [19]. Contrary to Gibson's controversial claim that environmental affordances can be directly "picked up" in a perceptual (optic) flow by an observer without any cognitive processing, Lynch would agree with Norman's view that affordances must be interpreted by an observer and thus are emergent and partly subjective result of the human agent's cognition interpreting and interacting with the physical environment. The mental image of the city is never its perfect *representation,* but a necessary *abstraction* (a medium or interface) due to limitations of human memory and cognition, but also the subjective input such as personal knowledge, memories, moods through which our perception of the city is filtered. If the faithful mental image of the city inside our heads is impossible even in theory, what is its purpose and how do we evaluate what type of urban planning and architectural structures lead to mental images better than others?

According to Jiang [21], contemporary theorist such as Haken and Portugali [22] build on Lynch and developed "an information view, which argued that it is information, in particular semantic information that cities or city art[e]facts have, that makes the cities or city art[e]facts imageable or distinguishable". [21]. The information view suggests that to achieve a good image and positive experiences, the semantic information must have an appropriate scale, fidelity, and level of abstraction. The information view of cognitive mapping and development of the mental image of the city fits well with the analysis of the contemporary smart city as an information-processing medium which consists of physical and digital layers. If we take the information view seriously, it is the digital layer that functions as the primary resource of data with which a user interfaces to get the information. The building, street or statues carry limited amount of information about themselves within its physical layers, however by using any average smartphone connected to the internet, websites like Wikipedia and location-sensitive mobile apps like Google Maps open "a window" to the information-rich digital layer where anybody can search for expert-level information. The GPS-powered apps like Instagram, Flickr or Google Earth enable citizens to experience any urban space at several different scales: from an interior of a local café to the urban layout of the whole city. Jiang adds that "the increasing amounts of social media data (e.g., Flickr and Twitter) can be used for cartographic and cognitive mapping" of geometric, topological and semantic attributes of the city [21].

The continual broadening of the concept of cognitive mapping can be seen in the work of postmodern theoretician Fredric Jameson who notices that even though Lynch was predominantly interested in the phenomenological aspects of immediate perception of the city, there is also the need to understand the abstracted totality of the city that shapes and is shaped by the perceptual local data of a perceiving subject-citizen-user. A Marxian theorist, Jameson thinks that the geographical and experiential alienation that people feel when they are unable to construct a cognitive map of the city can be applied to the same problem that a person faces in terms of his or her relation towards political ideology and capitalist economic systems: "the incapacity to map socially is as crippling to political experience as the analogous incapacity to map spatially is for urban experience. It follows that an aesthetic of cognitive mapping in this sense is an integral part of any socialist political project" [23]. We do not need to subscribe to Jameson's socialist politics to recognize that a good experience of the local and particular requires having a good cognitive map of the totality of the social experience. Interestingly, both Jameson and user experience design agree that the totality, or the system view has to be taken into account to understand and design for positive user experiences.

Jameson's expansion of the concept of cognitive mapping moves beyond the urban geography and includes any complex physical or even an immaterial system such as political ideology. This paper assimilates both Lynch and Jameson so that the smart city, consisting of physical and digital layers, should be also included within the scope of cognitive mapping.

Lynch introduced the concept of imageability decades before the digital revolution, but wrote a prediction, resonating with the concept of smart city, that the future synthesis of city form will be required to experience the city as a whole and that a "large city environment *can* have sensuous form" but "to design such form is rarely attempted today" [5, pp. 118, emphasis added]. Moreover, Lynch wrote that such synthetic form for experiencing the city in a holistic manner will be:

> "a complicated pattern, continuous and *whole*, yet intricate and *mobile*. It must be *plastic* to the perceptual habits of thousands of citizens, *open-ended* to change of function and meaning, receptive to the formation of new imagery. It must invite its viewers to explore the world" [5, pp. 119, emphasis added].

The plasticity and mobility of the "sensuous form" that would let humans experience the city holistically seems an impossible task for the "old-fashioned" material made from atoms: even the most innovative contemporary designs in responsive architecture are far from being able to design physical structures mobile and responsive enough so that they can process thousands of individual citizens simultaneously. For more than forty years, however, we have had a ready-made solution to the problem how to visualise complexity of any kind and for last ten years it has become truly mobile, responsive, open-ended and customisable for the individual needs of each user. We have been interfacing with digital data through computers and smart devices, specifically through various modality paradigms of the interface.

# 4  Interface

In the context of computing, the straightforward definition of the interface would be following: the interface is a piece of technology which came to being by an intentional design activity that enables humans to interact with functions of a given technology by hiding or compressing its internal complexity into a perceivable and actionable modality of representation. A standard definition within the field of HCI says that the interface is "the means of communication between a human user and a computer system, referring in particular to the use of input/output devices with supporting software" [35].

Paul Dourish [36] in his historical analysis of interaction reminds us that the interface underwent a gradual evolution: from a specialized symbolic and text-based interfaces – where the knowledge of command-line control commands had to be memorised – to current ubiquitous graphical user interfaces that employ the desktop metaphor for its visual design language. Dourish introduced to the human-computer interaction community and discourse terminology and ideas from cognitive science and phenomenological philosophy when he coined the new paradigm called "embodied interaction" – the form of interface that exploits the natural human abilities used for social communication and physical interaction with the world. For example, we intuitively understand turn-taking and empathise with chatbots which simulate a real-life social conversation with a human being; or we exploit our understanding of folk physics of how the world works when we interact with touch-based or movement-based interaction. In this regard, the embodied interaction appears to be a theoretical exploration of the natural user interfaces (NUI) [4] and tangible user interfaces (TUI) developed at MIT Media Lab which consciously go beyond the traditional desktop metaphor of graphical user interfaces (GUI) and focus on augmented and virtual reality devices like Microsoft Kinect, Microsoft HoloLens, Oculus Rift, Google Glass, Apple's VR software kit for Apple devices and so on.

In 1997, Steven Johnson wrote in his book [32] one of the first treatments of the role of interfaces on our society from the humanities-centric perspective. He defined the interface as "software that shapes the interaction between user and computer. The interface serves as a kind of translator, mediating between the two parties, making one sensible to the other. In other words, the relationship governed by the interface is a *semantic* one" [31, pp. 14, emphasis added].

McLuhan used the term "interface" as a passing note already in 1962 by borrowing it from the field of physics where the term means a general event of "the meeting and metamorphosis of two structures" [33, pp. 149]. In his poetic style, McLuhan commented that when two structures meet or "touch", they do not destruct each other, but their meeting inherently changes them. This "transformation without destruction" quality which he called "interfaciality" became a major point in McLuhan's medium theory whose most mature version is explored in the Laws of Media [34]. Here McLuhan articulates his influential thesis that there are always two sides of the medium: the *figure* and *ground*. The *surface*, perceivable layer that he called "figure" can be equated with the visible content with which humans (users) directly interact with technological media – for example a text opened in a PDF file, menu bars on a web page or buttons and displays of virtual reality headsets. The *deeper*, hidden layer which he called "ground" refers to the totality of infrastructural, technological, physic, or social structures. The interface is "where the action is" [34, pp. 102], meaning where all these structures can interact with each other. In fact, McLuhan stated that the figure and ground layers of the medium can interact only through an interface, because there is no direct connection between them [34, pp. 109].

McLuhan's media-theoretic approach to the interface resembles Norman's analysis of artefacts as cognitive artefacts that amplify our natural cognitive abilities by the virtue of providing better representations of a given cognitive problem. Norman himself made a distinction between the "surface representations" and "internal representations". Mirroring McLuhan's categorization, Norman agrees that there is a surface layer of technologies that consists of visible representations employing semiotic tools such as symbols, indexes or icons to form a consistent visual metaphor through which we interact with the other, to users invisible layer of internal representations.

It seems clear that for McLuhan and Norman an interface is not merely a visual part of a software application. Instead, the interface is a fundamental *relation* between the surface and depth layers of a technological medium (e.g. the city).

While the surface layer of the medium is most of the time framed with a computer screen that designates the dimensions of the surface layer, answering where the deeper ground layer starts and ends is more difficult. We can ask: Where does the smartphone start and end? Similarly, what are the physical and digital boundaries of the smart city? It cannot be the object itself, as any current digital infrastructure is interconnected worldwide and thus extends beyond the observable physical boundaries of "objects" such as the smartphone or smart city. The digital layer of objects is, as it were, spread out in the world which renders impossible to locate the object at specific geographic coordinates.

The smart city is massively distributed in time and space, therefore it is not an object directly accessible to our everyday phenomenological perception, which is a trait of any hybrid – both physical and digital – complex system as Nick Srnicek argues in his analysis of another non-object, neoliberal capitalistic economic system [29]. Drawing on Keller Easterling [30, pp. 13], I also understand the city and its physical and digital spaces as informational infrastructure space. However, for information to be an in-formation, it must be available to human senses in a perceptible and meaningful form, i.e. via an interface whose form gives the information meaning and affordances to influence back the dataflow within the infrastructure space.

Working on another model of the city as informational infrastructure, Bratton developed a formal model of technologically mediated society called The Stack. It is a model of "planetary-scale computation (e.g., smart grids, cloud computing, mobile and urban-scale software, universal addressing systems, ubiquitous computing, and robotics, and so on) not as isolated, unrelated types of computation but as forming a larger, coherent whole" [31, pp. 15]. Bratton borrows the metaphor of a stack from information technology where the Open Systems Interconnection (OSI) and TCP/IP models of the internet abstract individual layers, codifying for network engineers, system programmers and application developers a shared common language that has enabled the development of the internet and its services like email or world-wide web as we know them today. Like the OSI and TCP/IP models, Bratton's Stack comprises six interdependent layers: *Earth, Cloud, City, Address, Interface, User.* As we can see, the (smart) city is represented as one of several layers in a larger whole, which, as I believe, gives us a better picture of where the smart city starts and ends: it is one of many layers of the Stack. The top layer of the Stack represents user-citizens who can interact with the lower layers only in a mediated manner through the Interface layer, which is consistent with the analysis in this paper. Although the full reflection of Easterling's infrastructure space or Bratton's Stack is beyond the scope of this paper, it is worth noting what Bratton has to say about the role of the interface within the model that is compatible with the city-as-medium.

Bratton asserts the view of this paper that the interfaciality of the interface resides in its ability to translate and mediate "from a set of possibilities into a visual instrument", which is "necessary for our comprehension of any network we might encounter [31, pp. 212]. For Bratton, the interface is a synthetic image, map or instrument which synthesises cognition into a syntax of a (graphical user) interface whereby the interface gives a user synthetic, yet total image of the geography of all the lower layers, including the City layer. Because the interface as discussed here is based on the digital technology, it is not only a static visual representation, but also an interactive image-map-instrument and can affect the lower layers back via the interactive feedback loop. Lastly, Bratton agrees that "some visual interfaces also work as regularized *cognitive maps* of the urban interfacial territories in which they are situated, and as such, their semantic content can function as a binding collective representation of The Stack's geography" [31, pp. 152, emphasis added]. It is this property of interfaces to function as cognitive maps which helps to make sense of the smart city and amplify the internal cognitive abilities with the aid of external representations what is still needed to analyse.

### 4.1    Interface as a Cognitive Map/Artefact

From the perspective of contemporary cognitive science, the human mind would not be able to function to the fullest potential without the aid of external devices. The artefacts whose one of the primary functions is to aid human memory and problem-solving capabilities are called *cognitive artefacts*. [15]

This special class of artefacts does not refer primarily to hypermodern technologies of the 21st century, but consists of mundane objects such as paper, pencil, notebooks, post-it notes or even a well-organized filing cabinet without which, according to Norman, modern business in the 20th century would not have been possible [16, pp. 161]. In Norman's view, notebooks or post-it notes do not change our internal biological capacity for memory, instead their power as cognitive artefacts lies in their ability to change *the nature and structure of the task* so that instead of demanding cognitive computation we use our excellent perceptual and patter-recognition skills to *see* and *interpret* visual or other forms of spatial re-presentations of a given task. By *off-loading* the computational demands from brain to an interface of an artefact, cognitive artefacts amplify and extend cognition and human performance.

The design problem of creating cognitive artefacts shifts to finding mapping rules that transform cognitively demanding tasks to an appropriate representation. Norman comments that the notion of "appropriateness" is connected to subjective feeling and experience of "naturalness". Norman defines the naturalness of cognitive artefacts based on how the artefact, or interface, reduces the complexity of a relation between the surface or figure and the depth of ground or, in other words, between the representation and what is being represented [15].

Another contemporary interpretation of the naturalness of interfaces of artefacts is found in Dourish's definition of embodied interaction which claims that natural user interfaces are those which exploit most the natural human abilities of social intelligence, direct manipulation of objects, and pattern matching and recognition. Moreover, Dourish shows that the evolution of interaction and interfaces follow this rule consistently. Compared to symbolic assembly languages and text-based command-line interfaces, graphical user interfaces are powerful cognitive artefacts that afford cognitive mapping, because they translate the complex tasks of management of information into the management of two-dimensional bitmap space of a computer screen [36].

It is worth noting that Norman's cognitive artefacts represent a conservative approach to studying how artefacts, media, and technological objects shape the human cognition. Norman and scholars like Andy Clark [24], Edwin Hutchins [25], Mark Rowlands [26], Lambros Malafouris [27], Donna Haraway [28], Peter-Paul Verbeek [10] and others in contemporary schools of thought in cognitive science working under the umbrella of *4E cognition, cognitive anthropology, post-phenomenology*, and *philosophy of mind* consider external objects to be not only external guides to our internal cognitive processes, but also argue that external objects at specific occasions participate in co-constituting cognitive processes themselves so that cognition is distributed over biological and non-biological parts.

## 5  Urban Interfaces

The (smart) city is an information medium, infrastructure space, non-object and a part of the larger Stack. To go beyond a situated, phenomenological position of our local time and geographical location, we need an interface that would help us form a more complete image of the city. Without the interface used as a cognitive map, the imageability of the city as a whole is impossible, which is especially true for the smart city that comprise of both physical and digital layers producing a large amount of data that need a specific kind of interface that translates them for a human. This specific interface has been called the *urban dashboard* or *urban interface* [38, 39].

The urban interface is any interface that extends natural-born human abilities so that a user-citizen experiences the city as much in its physical-digital hybrid totality as possible. After more than five decades when in 1962 Douglas Engelbart gave his "Mother of all demos" presentation and almost forty years after the introduction of the first Macintosh in 1984 featuring then revolutionary graphical user interface, I agree with Shannon Mattern that despite advancements in NUI and TUI paradigms and various advancements in displays "embedded in buildings, kiosks and furnishings", there exists "the common equation of 'interface' with 'screen'" [38], especially rectangular screens of computer and smart phone displays. Mattern provides a comprehensive overview of current projects at the intersection of art, design, and technology building functional prototypes and experiments in apps, urban dashboards and publicly accessible online portals that enable citizens to interface with various data about the city such as locations of farmer's markets or air quality. One of the projects that Mattern cites, Urbanscale, offers a critique of using merely screens for representing data:

"[w]e don't believe that any particularly noteworthy progress will be made by dumping data on a screen and calling it a day, let alone transposing an utterly inappropriate "app" model from smartphones to large, situated displays […] municipal, commercial or citizen-generated, data only becomes understandable and usefully actionable when it's been *designed*: when it's been couched in carefully-considered cartography, iconography, typography and language" [38].

To stimulate the imagination for creating new urban interfaces that would revolutionize the relationship between humans and the city, the approaches in media archaeology and humanities in general explore historical precedents. Throughout the recent media history, various media were used to capture the city from novel perspectives that did not rely merely on a digital screen but still challenged our understanding of the city and its dynamics.

For example, John Snow's map of cholera outbreaks in 19th century London may be regarded as one of the first examples of urban interface. Snow used the map of London's urban layout and drew dots at the place where there was recorded an incident of cholera. With the help of this analogue data visualisation, he could spot the correlation between the number of incidents and the geographic locations of specific water pumps. Snow inferred that these pumps must be contaminated, which proved to be correct.

William Playfair's graphical representation of how quantitative economics data change throughout the time introduced into the vocabulary of data visualisation the element of timeline. Charles Marville's mapping of Paris in 1850 s, followed by Nadar's famous aerial photographs were the first attempts at capturing the totality of the city by freezing the city in time with photographic representation. On the other hand, the development of film medium enabled creative filmmakers like Walter Ruttmann and Dziga Vertov to probe the nature and dynamics of city life by their "city-symphony" films.

One of the most ambitious political projects to automate the economic system of a country was the Cybersyn project in Allende's socialist Chile in 1970 s. According to historian of technology Eden Medina, Cybersyn was designed as a cybernetically-enhanced and decentralized system that was supposed to gather real-time economic data from the whole country in order to automate the process of economic decision-making and allocation of materials and capital [37]. Factories and other economically relevant places produced data that were sent in real-time to the futuristic-looking operational centre. Here, the data were processed and shown on computer interfaces for human operators who were supposed to make data-informed decisions and corrections to otherwise automated system.

A contemporary, 21st century example of novel approaches to mapping and interfacing the urban data is the Selfiecity project [42] led by Lev Manovich and his team affiliated with Software Studies Initiative. The project uses the theoretical lens of digital humanities and new media studies[3] to "understand how people construct meanings from their interactions, and how their social and cultural experiences are mediated by software" [41]. Manovich and his team downloaded from Instagram, an image-sharing social medium, 140 000 photos that were further analysed to select 640 self-portraits photographs or "selfies" from five global cities: Bangkok, Berlin, Moscow, New York, and Sao Paulo. The photographs were analysed by custom-made software and visualised with the software for big data visualisation. The final data

---

[3] The arguments for the new media and software studies and analytical tools for studying new media technologies were for the first time analysed in a systematic fashion in Manovich's seminal work The Language of New Media [40]

visualisation featured variables such as demographics, pose, facial expression or mood. How does the project relate to urban interfaces? Using a large data set generated by Instagram users voluntarily, the project had a unique opportunity to uncover the patterns in how users experience the city and how their subjectivities are mediated by technology. Up until the recent past, such data and technology to process them were not available. The project is a thus a prime example of how we can interface with urban data of interpersonal communication and technologically mediated human behavior and use the information for further design and sociological research to design better user experiences and management of information-cognitive complexity of living in and experiencing the (smart) city.

## 6 Conclusion

The aim of this paper was to analyse the interface as a cognitive map of the smart city from a media-theoretic perspective. The issue of cognitive mapping in the context of urbanism was for the first time articulated in Lynch's *The Image of the City* where the notion of "imageability" or constructing a mental map of the spatial and environmental features of the city played the major role in how user-citizens experience the city. Lynch wrote on the topic before the digital revolution; therefore, he only considered the physical layer of the city as relevant to the construction of the image of the city.

Using theories of media theoreticians like Kittler, Mumford, McLuhan, Deuze, de Waal, Mitchell or McCullough, I showed that media theory has dealt extensively with the topic of the city. Moreover, media theory sees the city as an information-processing medium that consists of both physical and digital layers, thus making the (smart) city a hybrid made of "atoms and bits" material. Following Manovich, the paper argues that there is no necessary link between the digital data and their form, as digital material is essentially a material without qualities which requires a certain form, that is an interface, to be perceived. The interface thus should not be viewed as an artefact, but rather as a relation between the visible surface layer and the deeper, invisible layer of a medium. Moreover, because the interface gives the data a form that makes them perceivable, the interface functions as a knowledge construction tool, or Norman's cognitive artefact which helps humans to deal with information complexity and overload, which was the preoccupation even of early pioneers of digital revolution.

Next, the paper focused on a closer analysis of Lynch's imageability. Whereas Lynch did not go beyond the physical layout of the city, Jameson applied cognitive mapping in the context of political ideology, which paved the way for applying cognitive mapping unproblematically to the smart city, especially its digital layer. Applying Haken and Portugali (2003), the paper asserted the information-centric view of the smart city. Lynch claimed that the future form of the city should allow experiencing the city as a whole by constructing a synthetic image which would be a complicated pattern, whole, mobile, plastic to perceptual habits of citizens, open-ended to change, receptive to the formation of new imagery.

The paper claimed that the only solution to Lynch's requirement in the age of smart city is designing an appropriate interface. The interface was then analysed through the lens of media theory and Norman's conceptualization of cognitive artefacts. The paper argues for seeing the interface as a cognitive artefact.

Finally, the paper defined the urban interface and offered a brief selection of historical and contemporary examples of urban interfaces.

# References

1. Corbusier, L., Etchells, F.: Towards a New Architecture. Dover Publications Inc., New York (1927)
2. Negroponte, N.: The Architecture Machine. MIT Press, Cambridge, Massachusetts (1970)
3. Weiser, M.: the computer for the 21st century. Sci. Am. **265**(30), 94–104 (1991)
4. Wigdor, D., Wixon, D.: Brave NUI World. pp. 137–144, Morgan Kaufmann (2011)
5. Lynch, K.: The Image of the City. MIT Press, Cambridge, Massachusetts (1960)
6. McLuhan, M.: Understanding media. MIT Press, Cambridge, Massachusetts (1994)
7. Kittler, F.A., Griffin, M.: The City is a Medium. New Literary History **27**(4), 717–729 (1996)
8. Deuze, M., Izdná, P., Šlerka, J.: Media life. Univerzita Karlova v Praze, nakladatelství Karolinum, Praha (2015)
9. De Waal, M.: City as Interface. NAi010 Publisher (2014)
10. Verbeek, P.-P.: Beyond interaction. Interactions **22**(3), 26–31 (2015)
11. Löwgren, J., Stolterman, E.: Thoughtful Interaction Design. MIT Press, Cambridge, Massachusetts (2007)
12. Bush, V.: As we may think. The Atlantic Monthly **176**(1), 101–108 (1945)
13. Licklider, J.C.R.: Man-computer symbiosis. IRE Trans. Human Factors Electron. **HFE-1**, 4–11 (1960)
14. Engelbart, D.C.: Augmenting Human Intellect: A Conceptual Framework, Summary Report AFOSR-3233. Stanford Research Institute (1962)
15. Norman, D.A.: Cognitive artifacts. In: Carroll, John M. (ed.) Designing interaction. Cambridge University Press, Cambridge (1991)
16. Norman, D.A.: Things That Make Us Smart: Defending Human Attributes in the Age of the Machine. Basic Books, New York (1994)
17. Norman, D.A.: The Invisible Computer. MIT Press, Cambridge, Massachusetts (1999)
18. Norman, D.A.: Emotional Design: Why We Love (or Hate) Everyday Things. Basic Books, New York (2005)
19. Norman, D.A.: The Design of Everyday Things: Revised and, Expanded edn. Basic Books: Revised edition, New York (2013)
20. Gibson, J.J.: The Ecological Approach to Visual Perception. Houghton Mifflin, Boston (1979)
21. Jiang, B.: Computing the image of the city. arXiv:1212.0940 (2012)
22. Haken, H., Portugali, J.: The face of the city is its information. J. Envir. Psychol. **23**(4), 385–408 (2003)
23. Jameson, F.: Cognitive mapping. In: Nelson, C., Grossberg, L. (ed) Marxism and the Interpretation of Culture, University of Illinois Press, pp. 347–60 (1990)
24. Clark, A.: Natural-Born cyborgs: minds, technologies, and the future of human intelligence. Canadian J. Sociol. **29**(3), 471 (2004)
25. Hutchins, E.: Cognition in the Wild. A Bradford Book (1996)
26. Rowlands, M.J.: The New Science of the Mind: From Extended Mind to Embodied Phenomenology. MIT Press, Cambridge, Massachusetts (2010)

27. Malafouris, L.: How Things Shape the Mind. MIT Press, Cambridge, Massachusetts (2013)
28. Haraway, D.J.: Simians, Cyborgs and Women: The Reinvention of Nature. Free Assn Books, London (1996)
29. Srnicek, N.: Navigating Neoliberalism: Political aesthetics in an age of crisis. After us Issue 1 (2015)
30. Easterling, K.: Extrastatecraft: The Power of Infrastructure Space. Verso, London (2016)
31. Bratton, B.H.: The Stack on Software and Sovereignty. MIT Press, Cambridge, Massachusetts (2016)
32. Johnson, S.A.: Interface Culture: How New Technology Transforms the Way We Create & Communicate. Basic Books, New York (1997)
33. McLuhan, M.: The Gutenberg Galaxy: the making of typographic man. University of Toronto Press, Toronto (1962)
34. McLuhan, M., McLuhan, E.: Laws of Media: The New Science. University of Toronto Press, Toronto (1988)
35. Hookway, B.: Interface. MIT Press, Cambridge, Massachusetts (2014)
36. Dourish, P.: Where the Action is the Foundations of Embodied Interaction. MIT Press, Cambridge, Massachusetts (2001)
37. Medina, E.: Cybernetic Revolutionaries: Technology and Politics in Allende's Chile. MIT Press, Cambridge, Massachusetts (2014)
38. Mattern, S.: Interfacing Urban Intelligence. Places Journal, 49–60 (2015)
39. Mattern, S.: Mission Control: A History of the Urban Dashboard. Places Journal (2015)
40. Manovich, L.: The Language of New Media. MIT Press, Cambridge, Massachusetts (2001)
41. Manovich, L.: The Algorithms of Our Lives. The Chronicle of Higher Education. http://chronicle.com/article/The-Algorithms-of-Our-Lives/143557/. Accessed 1 June 2020
42. Tifentale, A.: The Selfie: Making sense of the "Masturbation of Self-Image" and the "Virtual Mini-Me". www.selfiecity.net. Accessed 01 June 2020
43. Tolman, E.C.: Cognitive Maps in Rats and Men. Psychol. Rev. 55(4), 189–208 (1948)
44. Kitchin, R.M.: Cognitive Maps: what are they and why study them? J. Envir.l Psychol. 14(1), 1–19 (1994)

# Ubiquitous Display: Research on Interaction Design Based on Flexible Display

Xinwei Guo[✉]

School of Mechanical Engineering, University of Science and Technology,
Beijing, China
guoxinwei@ustb.edu.cn

**Abstract.** From a cathode ray tube (CRT) based graphical user interface
(GUI) to a flat panel liquid crystal display (LCD) based natural user interface
(NUI), From e-ink based e-readers to organic light-emitting diode (OLED)
based consumer electronics products, and virtual space display based on VR/AR
technology, etc. The development of display technology promotes the development of information carriers towards more diverse characteristics. We will
find that the carrier displayed on the interface changes from fixed to movable,
from real to virtual. Imagine that the carrier of future information will eventually
surpass our traditional screen, and develop from ubiquitous computing to
ubiquitous display. This article describes the product morphological characteristics and interaction design challenges in flexible user interfaces. Based on
literature research and design case analysis, the key points in the design of
flexible display interfaces are introduced in three aspects: the dimensions of the
information architecture, the form of information display, and the definition of
interaction behavior. Finally, the article explores future ubiquitous display
application scenarios, and proposes design possibilities such as the integration of
information space and physical space, the extension of design objects, and more
ecologically intelligent feedback.

**Keywords:** User interface design · Interaction design · Ubiquitous display ·
Flexible display

## 1 Display Technology Promotes the Diversification of Information Carriers

Karim Rashid mentioned in his book "I Want to Change the World" that the world we
design should be full of "blobjects" [1]. It describes the shape of a product, which is
characterized by smooth curves and no sharp edges. The word is considered a compound word, an abbreviation of "blob" and "object" referring to a surface-filled form.
This property is not available in LCD displays because it does not have the property of
changing its planar state or screen shape.

With the maturity of Organic Light-Emitting Diode (OLED) display technology,
Nokia Corporation conceptualized the application of flexible OLED displays on mobile
phones for the first time in February 2008, and released Morph's concept design

C. Stephanidis et al. (Eds.): HCII 2020, LNCS 12429, pp. 286–297, 2020.
https://doi.org/10.1007/978-3-030-59987-4_21

(see Fig. 1) [2]. It created the concept of using flexible display screens in consumer electronics devices.

**Fig. 1.** Morph concept design [2]

The development and popularization of electronic inks, OLED displays, organic compounds, electronic textiles, sensors, and computer-controlled materials have enriched a variety of information display carriers and platforms. Interfaces based on flexible display technology provide richer scenarios and contexts for the development of user interfaces and user experiences.

At the same time, it will also bring new challenges and requirements in the design process. The design forms, information interaction methods and future application scenarios in the flexible display interface will be the focus of this article.

## 2 Classification of Morphological Features of Flexible Interfaces

### 2.1 Flexible Display Interface

The flexible display interface mainly refers to a deformable display screen, such as folding, bending, curling, etc. In addition, the process of screen deformation is also one of the ways for users to input information.

In January 2019, Xiaomi Inc. released an engineering prototype of a dual-folding phone. In February of the same year, Huawei Inc. released the industry's first 5G folding phone. In recent years, more and more consumer electronics products have applied flexible display technology to mobile phones, wearable devices, and more abundant smart products.

### 2.2 Shape Display Interface

The shape display interface [3] is also called non-planar display, and the shape can be a curved surface, a sphere, a cylinder, or the like.

Visionox Inc. (see Fig. 2) has done many years of research and exploration in the field of OLED display, as shown in the Fig. 2, smart home jewelry boxes, smart water cups, e-books, etc. As well as design applications in the automotive field, the curved display of the steering wheel in the cockpit of the car and the full-screen center console are typical scenarios based on OLED display technology in the shape display interface.

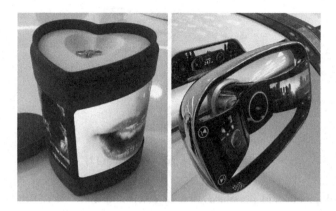

**Fig. 2.** Shape display interface

## 2.3 Dynamic Display Interface

The dynamic display interface can change different shapes or states. By actively sensing the environment or being controlled by a computer, a multi-scenario application can be defined.

LG Inc. has developed a flexible TV [4] for the first time at CES 2018 (see Fig. 3). The TV display has three states, the full screen state provides a "Full View" experience, and the curled state provides a "Line View" experience. Collapse all is a "Zero View" experience, when the user can use the audio system.

**Fig. 3.** LG flexible TV [4]

# 3  Challenges for Interaction Design in Flexible Display Scenarios

## 3.1  Changes in User Interface Display Status and Area

We can see consumer electronics products ranging from keyboard phones to full-screen phones to various flexible screens (see Fig. 4). The difference between the display area in the interface and the well-known graphical user interface is more obvious. We need to reconsider the display area range of the flexible interface in different states and the user's operating scene. Major technology companies such as Apple have applied for patents on the interface design of flexible display screens in different sizes.

**Fig. 4.** Changes in the screen display area

Different operating systems have their own layout specifications for the graphical user interface corresponding to different sizes of display screens. In the foreseeable future, flexible display-based forms will no longer be static. On the one hand, we can fold, bend, and fold the flexible interface like paper or plastic sheets. On the other hand, as mentioned in the previous chapter, the shape of the interface can be deformed by computer algorithms or perceived changes in the environment to actively adapt to the user's physical environment, the form of data, or the user's needs.

From flat and relatively static interfaces to deformable and driving interfaces. The layout presented in the interface, such as the display area, operation area, and classification of functional areas are changed. These changes need to be redefined, according to different states and the user's operating scene, different product application scenarios, target user characteristics, product design goals, and so on.

## 3.2  Changes in Interaction Behavior and Methods

Interaction logic covers two aspects, one is the design of interaction behavior, and the other is the judgment of interaction efficiency.

From the initial mouse and keyboard-based input, to the touch input of the multimedia interface, and the multi-modal input in the multi-channel user interface. From the setting of single-touch gestures in the early Android system to the setting of operation gestures for the multi-touch screen in the iOS system. The design of interactive methods has always been one of our research focuses. In the interactive design of flexible display, how we will interact with various shaped display interfaces, how we will enter information, and how the system will give feedback to users, these will directly affect the efficiency of the system and the user experience.

As mentioned at the beginning, the development of display technology has promoted the development of user interface and human-computer interaction. When the development of flexible display technology will produce a curved, flexible, or any other form of carrier as a display medium, we need to consider the user's handholding posture while considering user input methods, so as to consider the reasonable interactive area more accurately.

### 3.3 Re-establishment of Interactive Efficiency Standards

The second direction we need to think about the way of interaction is to judge the efficiency of interaction, and it is also an important factor affecting the user experience. User experience evaluation often uses experimental methods to obtain data, such as usability tests, user facial expression recognition, eye tracking, and so on. Combining these data with task settings can allow people to more intuitively and accurately analyze the effectiveness of the design. In the graphical user interface, Microsoft Corporation defines the interface layout of different locations for different devices in the Windows system based on interaction efficiency and availability.

In the traditional mouse click-based graphical user interface (GUI) and the natural user interface (NUI) through touch and gesture interaction, Fitts'Law is widely used in the evaluation of human-computer interaction efficiency. Queens University Media Lab has tested and studied the operating efficiency of flexible display screens according to Fitts'Law, and the results show that the bending input is highly related to Fitts's law in both position and speed control [5]. It can be seen that in non-planar user interfaces, for some input methods, we can still continue the basic rules of Fitts'Law to evaluate interaction efficiency.

However, due to the changes in curvature in the flexible display, the diversity of display content, and the characteristics of interaction behavior, how to establish a comprehensive evaluation of interaction efficiency requires further testing and research.

## 4    Elements of Interaction Design in Flexible Display Scenarios

In the process of user interface design, the important link between design prototype and mass production practice is the establishment of standards and specifications. From the technical specifications of hardware products to the development specifications of algorithm programs and design specifications for visual presentation, user interfaces under different systems and service software under different hardware standards need to run on the basis of platform design principles or themes. The author compared the design specifications of the three major mobile operating platforms today, which can basically be summarized into three major branches: information architecture, display form, and interaction logic.

## 4.1    Multi-dimensional Presentation of Information Architecture

Information architecture is the organization of data. The research content is data, which organizes, classifies, and reorganizes data into information groups, and integrates information in series according to different logics to form different types of information architectures. In the non-planar display flexible interface, it has more dimensional paths and multi-state display than the traditional flat interface. The process of user information acquisition and the state of the interface display have a corresponding relationship with the physical space.

As shown in Fig. 5, normal information is a traditional tree-like hierarchical information architecture. When the flexible interface is in dynamic or deformed, the information will adapt to the change of the interface shape and change. When the flexible interface is in a deformed state, the information is presented in a folded state.

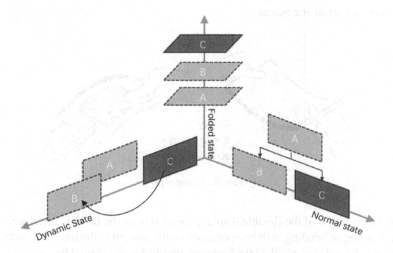

**Fig. 5.** Multi-dimensional information architecture

When we consider the organizational structure of the information and the navigation logic of the system, we can more vividly associate the logical relationship of the data with the flexible spatial relationship. The main purpose of the design of the Material system is also that the interaction methods tend to be natural, and the visual presentation returns to life. The design theme of the Material operating system is that the interaction and visual style tend to converge with nature and life. Among them, in the definition of Navigation, the three-dimensional spatial relationships of X, Y, and Z in the information hierarchy are mentioned. It maps the actions of paper stacking and extraction to the logic of the system's information architecture, achieving the effect of a natural interaction experience.

Information architecture is the medium through which users communicate with information. Representation of abstract information is the task of information architecture in interface design. The naturalization of design language and the non-perception of interaction behavior are one of the commonly used expressions in interaction design.

## 4.2    Space-Adaptive Interface Layout

When migrating the content from a relatively static screen to a flexible screen with variable form and curvature, we need to define design specifications based on flexible display while considering the hardware structure.

The Android system has redesigned and standardized the layout of some folding mobile phones, and standardized the layout changes of the interface content when the mobile phone is in the folded state and the expanded state. Dave Burke, vice president of Android engineering, described this feature: "As you expand, the system's applications will be seamlessly transferred to a larger screen without missing any details."

Gummi (see Fig. 6) is a prototype design of a flexible credit card [6]. The application scenario is an interactive subway map. When there is no external force, the rigidity of the flexible base can restore it to a flat state. When the screen is bent by external forces, the subway map will zoom in or out, and the touch screen on the back allows users to scroll the screen.

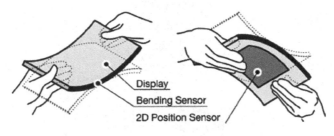

**Fig. 6.** Gummi [6]

In the interaction of the flexible display, operations on the flexible interface, such as folding, flipping or bending, will be operations on the content of the interface itself. When the display area and range of the interface are variable due to external forces, this requires us to achieve consistent physical operations and display of interface element controls when defining the layout of the interface. For example, the inward folding operation interface elements are squeezed inward, and the outer folding operation is the expansion of interface elements outward. In the interaction of the curl screen, the interface content is enlarged or reduced in the same direction as its corresponding curl strength.

## 4.3    The Combination of Software and Hardware: What You Do Is What You Get

The definition of input and output behavior is an important part of the interface design process, and it has a significant weight in the user experience of the product. In the graphical user interface, the input device and the output device are different and separable. The user inputs instructions through the mouse and keyboard, and the display outputs information. This separated interaction is usually indirect for interaction with physical objects [7]. Input and output are indistinguishable in the flexible display interface. The user can complete part of the input by operating the product hardware.

With the change of the screen state, the content of the interface is changed to adapt to the new form. The output and input are presented as a true mapping, and the behavior is consistent with the information conveyed by the interface.

Paper Phone (see Fig. 7) is one of the first interface designs to introduce bending gestures on a real flexible screen. For actions with strong directional cues, the bending gestures have strong consistency with the interface information. They are simpler in concept, less physically demanding, and more natural for users to interact with [8]. As mentioned in the article, the variability and diversity of interface states enrich the user's input experience. Design an intuitive interactive experience based on using a natural interaction language and respecting the user's mental model. Realize the natural matching of the interface display information with the user's input gesture, so as to achieve the resonance of the input and output in the flexible display, and achieve what you do is what you get.

**Fig. 7.** Paper Phone [8]

# 5  Ubiquitous Display: Future User Interface Scenarios

## 5.1  Information Depth Embedded in Physical Space

One of the researches on user interface that we usually talk about is the collation, refinement and arrangement of information. The data scattered in the space is presented in a certain logical structure, and displayed in a visual and interactive state in a two-dimensional plane space based on the X\Y axis. With the increasing variety of information interaction methods, the learning cost for users to obtain information is gradually reduced. The popularity of gesture operations, somatosensory interactions, facial recognition, and voice interactions allows users to obtain information in multiple paths and channels. At the same time, with the characteristics of the flexible interface, it provides more possibilities for the display of information. Information can make the two-dimensional space from the X\Y axis gradually develop to the three-dimensional space from the X\Y\Z axis.

The design of the "transparent" A-pillar in the smart cockpit is an application of flexible display in smart car scenarios (Fig. 8). Utilizing the characteristics of flexible AMOLED, the screen is wrapped around the A-pillar, and the image blocked by the A-pillar is relied on the camera on the outside mirror of the car to transfer it to the on-board computer. It is then placed on a flexible display inside the A-pillar to simulate the effect of a "transparent" A-pillar, solving the problem of visual blind spots and greatly improving driving safety.

**Fig. 8.** "Transparent" A-pillars in cars [9]

Take advantage of the flexible, deformable, and bendable material characteristics of flexible screens, based on the information logic foundation of traditional flat user interfaces. Fusion of abstract information architecture with concrete physical space will be one of the development directions of organic user interfaces in the future.

At the same time, combining IoT technology and artificial intelligence algorithms to fuse information with space will open up wider user scenarios and application values for ubiquitous displays.

## 5.2   Design Objects Expand from Behavior-Oriented Research to Definition of the Environment

In 2001, Richard Buchanan proposed a "fourth orders of design" model [10]. From symbolic graphic design, to the definition of things in industrial design, to the study of behavior in interaction design, the fourth dimension is the concern for the environment (see Table 1). This also corresponds to the three dimensions of design mentioned by Donald Norman in emotional design: instinct, behavior, and reflection. No matter what kind of display carrier is based on, our research on user interface will eventually go beyond our definition of traditional screens. Our design objects are ultimately concerned with the integration of technology and environment to build the relationship between man and nature, and man and the environment.

**Table 1.** Fourth order of design [10]

| Symbols | Things | Action | Thought |
|---|---|---|---|
| Graphic design | | | |
| | Industrial design | | |
| | | Interaction design | |
| | | | Environmental design |

There is always a mutually beneficial symbiotic relationship between technological exploration and design innovation. The vision of the Internet of Things (IoT) and the Display of Things (DoT) is imminent. As our design objects and contexts expand from interfaces to lifestyles and living environments. Data information and product services in traditional user interface research have also migrated. From two-dimensional flat display to infinite multi-dimensional extension. The intelligence and diversity of organic forms, the integration of input and output, the diversification of interaction methods, and intelligent feedback in the ecosystem will all bring new design challenges and broad opportunities for exploration and innovation.

When the flexible display screen is integrated with smart life, ubiquitous computing and display can make the general public experience the intelligent life scene of active perception more naturally.

## 5.3 More Ecologically Intelligent Feedback

Traditional user interfaces usually wake up the system with inputs and trigger outputs. For example, unlock it with a swipe gesture, wake up the smart speaker with your voice, or swing a ball in a somatosensory game. The system calculates and completes tasks preset by the system through user actions. With the increase of new driving devices and intelligent materials, future flexible scenarios will be able to actively sense the user's ecological environment, data form and interface functions, and actively change their interface content and screen shape to give intelligent feedback.

In 1954, architect Frank Lloyd Wright advocated that human settlements live in harmony with the natural world. He emphasized the interconnectedness of all things, the symbiotic order system of nature [11]. The Al Bahr tower (see Fig. 9) is a classic case of combining smart materials and drives with buildings and the environment. Its appearance is a protective layer composed of 2,000 umbrella-shaped glass elements, which can be automatically opened and closed according to the intensity of sunlight. This adjustable sun visor can reduce the heat generated by sunlight in the room by about 50%.

As scholars continue to explore smart display materials in the future, any medium may present a realistic carrier. From ubiquitous computing to ubiquitous display, our definition of the interface display carrier will also go beyond the traditional screen. It will turn the natural world into an interface and the interface into a natural world. The redefinition of any life scene is worthy of the designer giving it organic and flexible life. The scenario of flexible user interface design empowers the reconstruction of ecology and environment, while saving energy consumption, making the ecology or environment grow and adapt to human survival [13].

**Fig. 9.** Al Bahr tower [12]

# 6   Conclusion

Under the development trend of Display of Things (DoT), breakthroughs in display technology can bring about disruption in human-computer interaction and application scenarios. The application based on flexible display has promoted the data information and product services in the traditional graphical user interface from a limited flat display to an infinite multidimensional extension. The diversity of flexible forms, the integration of input and output, and the diversification of interaction modes, whether for hardware manufacturers or content service providers, will bring new challenges and broad opportunities for exploration and innovation.

There are also some problems with the design and application of flexible interfaces. For example, most of the current designs are flexible display products with folding mobile phones as the core form. The production cost is high, and whether there are more suitable application scenarios is worthy of our further exploration.

At the same time, there is still a lot of space for exploration of smart materials. When we closely combine the biological characteristics and driving characteristics of materials with our living environment. And take full advantage of the possibilities of various design scenarios provided by these emerging technologies. Human beings will ultimately benefit from the green and sustainable development of natural ecology.

**Acknowledgments.**   The work described in this paper was generously supported by the Fundamental Research Funds for the Central Universities, Beijing, China. (FRF-BR-18-007A)

# References

1. Rashid, K.: I Want to Change the World. Universe Publishing, Bloomington, Indiana (2001)
2. Nokia Research Center (February 2008). "The Morph Concept". Nokia. 12 Feb. (2013)
3. Vertegaal, R., Poupyrev, I.: Organic user interfaces. Commun. ACM **51**(6), 26–30 (2008)
4. LG flexible TV. https://www.lg.com/global/lg-signature/oled-tv-r9
5. Burstyn, J., Carrascal, J.P., Vertegaal, R.: Fitts' law and the effects of input mapping and stiffness on flexible display interactions. In: Chi Conference. ACM (2016)
6. Schwesig, C., Ivan, P., Eijiro, M.: Gummi: a bendable computer. In: Proceedings of the SIGCHI Conference on Human Factors in Computing Systems (2004)
7. Holman, D., Vertegaal, R.: Organic user interfaces: designing computers in any way, shape, or form. Commun. ACM **51**(6), 26–30 (2008)
8. Lahey, B., Girouard, A., Burleson, W., Vertegaal, R.: Paperphone: understanding the use of bend gestures in mobile devices with flexible electronic paper displays. In: Proceedings of the SIGCHI Conference on Human Factors in Computing Systems, pp. 1303–1312. ACM (2011)
9. "Transparent" A-pillars in cars, http://www.visionox.com/news/show-1292.html
10. Buchanan, R.: Design research and the new learning. Des. Issues **17**(4), 3–23 (2001)
11. Sokolina, A.P.: Biology in architecture: the goetheanum case study. The Routledge Companion to Biology in Art and Architecture. pp. 80–98. Routledge (2016)
12. AI tower. https://unbindarch.wordpress.com/category/architectural-style/#jp-carousel-1736
13. Nabil, S., Thomas, P., David, S.K.: Interactive architecture: Exploring and unwrapping the potentials of organic user interfaces. In: Proceedings of the Eleventh International Conference on Tangible, Embedded, and Embodied Interaction (2017)

# Exploring the Design of Interactive Smart Textiles for Emotion Regulation

Mengqi Jiang[1], Martijn ten Bhömer[2], and Hai-Ning Liang[1(✉)]

[1] Xi'an Jiaotong-Liverpool University, Ren'ai Road. 111,
Suzhou 215000, China
{Mengqi.Jiang,HaiNing.Liang}@xjtlu.edu.cn
[2] University of Nottingham Ningbo China, Taikang East Road. 199,
Ningbo 315100, China
martijn.ten.bhomer@nottingham.edu.cn

**Abstract.** The present study aims to investigate the design of interactive textiles for emotion regulation. In this work we proposed a design which allows users to visualize their physiological data and help regulate their emotions. We used the Research through Design method to explore how physiological data could be represented in four different interactive textiles and how movement-based interaction could be designed to support users' understanding and regulation of their emotional state. After an initial user interview evaluation with several textile prototypes, light and vibration were selected as modalities within the biofeedback-based interaction. A smart interactive shawl that reacts to changes in emotional arousal was designed to help the users know their emotion and adjust it, if necessary, with the support of electrodermal activity sensor and pressure-based sensors. The results of the second study showed that the smart shawl could help the user to visualize their emotions and reduce their stress level by interacting with it.

**Keywords:** Design · Smart textiles · Emotion regulation · Interactive textiles · Research through Design

## 1 Introduction

Emotional fluctuations, caused by work stress, academic examinations, challenging relationships, physiological diseases, happen regularly in many people's lives and affect our behaviour and decision-making to a considerable extent. Despite emotions, such as depression, fear, anxiety, and nervousness being an essential part of the life experiences, it may not be ideal for people to be regularly trapped in an overwhelming emotional state for a long time without realizing it. We are encouraged to self-regulate our emotions, and it has been reported that emotion self-regulation plays a significant role in effectively restoring physical and mental health [28].

The prevalent strategies of emotion self-regulation include psychological counselling, self-reflection, physical exercise, yoga, meditation, and catharsis. Conventionally, people rely on their subjective will to regulate their emotions through different approaches; however, in extreme cases, maintaining a rational and calm mindset may

© Springer Nature Switzerland AG 2020
C. Stephanidis et al. (Eds.): HCII 2020, LNCS 12429, pp. 298–315, 2020.
https://doi.org/10.1007/978-3-030-59987-4_22

not be possible, given that many people may occasionally be overwhelmed by strong emotions. Therefore, researchers have explored ways to support the process of emotion regulation with digital technology. Biofeedback, as a body-mind technique that involves using visual, auditory or haptic feedback to control involuntary body functions, can help the user better control body's reactions and behaviours and understand their internal emotional states more explicitly [33]. The classical biofeedback design is a kind of one-way augmented feedback; that is, users can reflect on their physiological state through augmented feedback. However, as Yu [32] mentioned, biofeedback can also be functional and allow bidirectional, dynamic, adaptive feedback base on user's states and interaction [31]. We hope that users have more autonomy in emotional regulation. In this research, we aim to help people self-regulate their emotions by not only providing biofeedback but also allowing the wearer to actively interact with the 'visualized' biofeedback on clothing that they typically wear. However, what remains unclear is how to design bidirectional adaptive biofeedback-based interaction to regulate emotion.

Although many HCI researches are paying attention to emotion engaged interaction design [9, 10, 30], very few studies have explored how interactive design could be used to regulate emotion, especially with interactive textiles. Interactive textiles can sense the stimuli or signals from the user and the environment, then react and properly adapt to them [4]. Besides, interactive textiles have the advantage of traditional textiles, while also being able to integrate technology and can be unobtrusively worn close to the source of physiological signals—i.e., the user. As such, they are well suited for supporting users with needs of short- and long-term emotion self-regulation. The goal of this research is to explore how interactive textiles can be designed to let users better engage in interacting with their own emotions. Our research also aims to explore whether an interactive system built around smart textiles could be used for emotion regulation.

## 2   Related Work

Emotion regulation and interactive textiles are two distinct domains, which both involve communication through the user's body and feelings. Advances in the development of smart textiles and emotion engaged interaction design have also helped drive the integration of these two domains.

### 2.1   Emotion Engaged Interaction

As we know, emotion not only has an impact on how we think and behave, but also plays a pivotal role in self-expression, social communication, and physical health. Norman [19] introduced the concept of emotional design, highlighted the importance of emotion in design, and took pleasant emotional experience as a standard to evaluate the success of a design product. In Picard's Affective Computing [23], she describes computing that relates to, arises from, or influences emotions. She tried to empower computer with the ability to recognize, understand, and even to have and express emotions, especially with wearable computers. With the advances in interaction design, affective design is no longer limited to the emotional data coding and presentation but turns to emotion engagement, affective loop interaction and experience centred soma design [11, 20], which emphasises the role of physical participation in the emotional interaction, including physiological signals participation and body movements participation.

In these studies, emotion-related bio signals such as electromyogram (EMG), blood volume pulse (BVP), electrodermal activity (EDA) and electroencephalogram (EEG) were extracted for biofeedback and embodied interaction. For example, Picard et al. [22] designed a pair of skin conductivity gloves to measure the wearer's skin conductivity levels as indicators of physiological arousal. This glove-like device used light to map the degree of arousal in the human body. The visual presentation can clearly show people's emotional arousal levels in different activities. The Brightbeat App [13] was designed for stress relief with users being able to observe their heart-beats; it slowed their breathing and improved self-reported calmness and focus. These design practices help users to understand their physiological state better, based on their subjective understanding and self-reflection.

Except for the emotion-related bio signal-based interaction, body motion was also explored within affective interaction research. These types of experiences were applied in Höök's SenToy Doll project [10], in which the user could express their physical and emotional state by using various kinds of emotional gestures to interact with a doll. In her another project, an instant messaging application could transform the user's gestures into emotional expressions—for example, when angry gestures were visualized into a strong aggressive colourful background [27], the receiver would then sense the emotion of the sender by interacting with the system.

Mood Swings is an interactive artwork designed by Bialoskorski et al. [2], which recognises affective movement characteristics expressed by a person and displays a colour that matches the expressed emotion. These design cases combine body biodata or movement with a feedback mechanism to achieve an affective experience and showed the potential of supporting emotional well-being. Users often experienced more autonomy in this process. On the other hand, the potential of smart textiles in this field has not been much developed, although they are more advantageous in supporting body and experience centred affective design.

## 2.2 Affective Smart Textiles

In affective smart textiles design, Stead [26] put forward her thinking about the relationship between fashion, emotion, and technology through practice-based research, and preliminarily investigated how clothing can both represent and stimulate emotional response through technology. Uğur [30] reported her study on the theory and design practice of wearing embodied emotions and designed several kinds of smart wearable products which expressed wearers' emotional state. She explored the definition of new body boundaries and the possibilities of expressing emotions in wearable design with technology and stated that emotional embodiment through wearable technology can help people to regulate their emotions. Ashford [1] more specifically researched the relationship between EEG signals and emotional states. In her projects, she attempted to integrate EEG signals into visualized embodied designs and found that potential users are very interested in the personalized aesthetics design of wearables and applied the design to inspire confidence with quantified self. In 2013, the SENSOREE company also designed a GER Mood Sweater collar to allow visualizing the user's emotional status with LED lights and brought it to the market [24]. The main function of these designs and research is to embody emotions on smart textiles and to arouse users' self-reflection and attention to them. Although these cases are textile-based augmented biofeedback and took advantage of e-textiles, they have not involved functional bidirectional biofeedback interaction between users and the textiles.

Another design case is the Affective sleeve [21], which produces rhythmic tactile movements with warm and slight arm pressure to promote calmness and reduce anxiety. The researcher found that the speed of the sleeve's tactile movements affects the participants' breathing rate and perception of calmness. It affects the user's emotional state with detailed vibrotactile feedback. According to the results, the feedback mechanism is also a potential factor to consider about in emotion regulation.

# 3  Methodology

The research followed a combination of the Research through Design (RtD) approach [14, 29] and mixed research method. Explorations during two design cycles served as stimuli to define the research direction and gather further feedback. In the first cycle, four types of modalities were integrated into textiles to represent biofeedback. These four modalities were evaluated during a qualitative user study, which resulted in the selection of visual, tactile feedback and hand gesture interaction as the starting point for the second design cycle. A shawl providing tangible emotional feedback was then designed. Touch motion was used for the user to interact with their embodied emotions. To verify the prototype's effectiveness and obtain further user feedback, a second mixed research evaluation was conducted with the prototype.

## 3.1  First Design Cycle: Visualized Biofeedback on Textiles

Emotion expression and recognition is the premise of emotion regulation. So, at the beginning of the first design cycle, it was our goal to explore the design space of textile-based biofeedback visualizations. Following the RtD approach, we first designed several textile-based biofeedback visualizations and observed how the user would interact with these smart textile prototypes to drive the design and further research inquiries.

Four kinds of textile prototypes were designed that could represent the user's emotional arousal level based on different feedback modalities: light, vibration, colour change (based on thermochromic ink), and shape change. Table 1 shows an overview of the four textile prototypes. An EDA sensor placed on the finger measured the user's emotional arousal level. The data was then used as input for the visualization in the textiles.

During the evaluation, six participants were invited to interact with these textiles and place these textiles in their comfortable position, whether attached or spread around parts of their body. Most participants preferred to place the fabric on their upper body

**Table 1.** Four feedback modalities for the smart textiles in our designs and their user feedback.

| Textile prototypes | Textile | Feedback modality | Description | User feedback |
|---|---|---|---|---|
| | Smocked scuba knitting fabric with LED lights | Visual feedback (colour and brightness) | The LED light embedded in 3D fabric structure. The brightness and colour change according to the emotional arousal level. | The LED light mode is more intuitive and effective. It has more diversified forms of expression. |
| | Quilted scuba knitting fabric with vibration motors | Tactile feedback (Vibration frequency) | The vibration intensity of the motors inside the textile changes according to the emotional arousal level. | Vibration mode is more private, the hand is more sensitive for vibration than the body. |
| | Overlapped non-woven thermochromic stripes with EeonTex heater fabric | Thermal-Visual feedback (red, blue, black colour saturation) | Fabric is made of stripes, dyed with different thermochromic pigments. The temperature changes with the emotional arousal level, which leads to colour change. | It has delayed emotional bio-feedback, but easy to wear. |
| | Laser-cut non-woven fabric with motor | Shape-changing feedback (Rotation angle) | The fabric texture surface moves driven by motors underneath with thread pulling the texture. | It feels cool, has a better visual effect, suits the younger user, but soft material is not easy to manipulate. |

(near their arms and chest) where they can touch it, while their emotional arousal level was displayed using the feedback modality.

After the participants finished interacting with the prototypes, they were interviewed about their subjective experiences. Two participants stated that they would not mind if other people see their emotional states, while four participants were very concerned about their privacy. Most participants mentioned that the visualization of emotions could be more useful for overly stressed people, while healthy (less stressed) people do not necessarily need to visualize their emotions all the time. It could be important for people under chronic, continuous stress to have ways to vent (or let out) their negative emotions to prevent them from bottling up these feelings.

Some key reactions from participants about the different types of feedback modalities are summarized in the last row of Table 1. Overall, visual and tactile feedback modalities are more widely accepted, because they can be easily perceived and placed around users' body and have more diversified forms of expression. They were concerned about the thermochromic feedback, because the temperature change was too slow to feedback the EDA level. Some participants showed interest in the fabric shape changing caused by the mechanical motor—for example, they said it feels interesting to have the fabric move on their body. Also, they thought young people may be more likely to accept the shape changing fabric, but the fabric structure of the sample is relatively soft and unstable. When considering the possibility of daily use, they agreed that visual feedback and vibration feedback were more realistic. Besides, participants said that they did not want to wear them every day as the form of clothes, but they would like to wear them as accessories like a scarf or wristband which are more flexible.

In the interaction between participants and smart fabrics, we observed that they showed more interest in some fabrics with special texture and would like to keep touching them. The initial fabric texture design was to better integrate textiles and electronic components, such as the smoked sewing texture in visual feedback and the quilted sewing structure in vibration feedback. During the study, participants used their hands and fingers to poke the bubble-like fabric textures. When asked about this behaviour, participants mentioned that it reminded them of the action of popping bubble in certain plastic wraps. This action could help them to release their stress because the action of pressing the material combined with the sound of the popping bubbles made them feel more relaxed. However, they did not take many actions on the thermochromic and motion feedback textiles. Except for the reflection caused by being able to visualize their emotions, this insight could help frame the design of interactions that deal with motions [16, 17], and led us to ask whether we can regulate the user's emotion through motion-based interaction and how-to bring motion-based interaction into the smart fabric system.

## 3.2    Second Design Cycle: Designing the Interactive Smart Shawl

According to the first experimental results and user feedback, a new prototype was then designed which could be used to further explore the role of interaction for self-regulation. The final prototype is a shawl, designed for people who want to regulate their emotions in real, actual environments during their daily activities, such as going for outdoor activities, communicating with people, etc. This design is expected to help users balance their emotions and reduce the negative impact of aggressive emotions on their health and social life (see Fig. 1).

Emotions are complicated and complex, there is no single bio-signal that can accurately capture all the emotional states. Some studies have shown that a combination of multiple biological signals can be used to determine users' emotion [12, 15]. Because the focus of this research is on the exploration of how movement-based

**Fig. 1.** User scenarios: The smart shawl aims to help people to self-regulate emotions in their daily lives, like social activities or outdoor activities.

interaction plays a role in the self-regulation of emotion, we have not focused on emotion recognition technology. Therefore, we selected a Grove EDA sensor to measure the general emotional arousal level.

Based on the reactions from the participants during the exploratory study, the light feedback and vibration feedback were more preferred for visualizing and sensing the dynamic data from the EDA sensor. Moreover, an interactive action was added to the visualization that could be utilized when users feel stressed or emotionally aroused. Inspired by the action of popping bubble wrap, users can relieve their stress by poking each fabric bubble to change the emotion arousal triggered from the light or vibration feedback, thus allowing them to calm their emotion down (see Fig. 2). When the user feels nervous, the location of the shoulder and chest is more natural to provide comfort; therefore, the product is designed as a shawl, which users can wear on their shoulders.

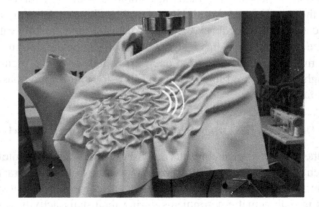

**Fig. 2.** User scenarios: The smart shawl aims to help people to self-regulate emotions in their daily lives, like social activities or outdoor activities.

**Smart Shawl Prototype Composition.** The functional part of the shawl consists of 14 separate fabric bubbles, each of which integrates a pressure sensor made by Velostat foil (pressure-sensitive material based on piezo-resistive effects), a LED light, and a vibration motor. When the wearer's arousal level changes, each fabric bubble module will react by changes in intensity (see Fig. 3).

**Fig. 3.** The electronic components integrated with the pressure sensor, LED and vibration module, as an independent interaction unit.

**Interaction Modes and Interaction Flow.** The smart shawl has two modes for users to choose in different scenarios, the light and vibration modes. The light mode is a public mode, in which the people around the wearer can perceive the wearer's emotional state through the colour and brightness of the light. In the weak emotion arousal state, it will light up slightly with tint colour. In a stronger emotion arousal state, the light will be brighter and show stronger colour changes. The vibration mode is considered as the privacy mode because its feedback can only be sensed by the wearers themselves. Vibration intensity also changes depending on the emotional arousal level as measured by the EDA sensor.

The interaction flow is displayed in Fig. 4. The shawl first visualizes the wearer's emotional state through light or vibration, which allows the wearer to be aware of and reflect on their emotional state; based on this visualization they can further interact with the smart shawl. In the light mode, when the wearer feels stressed or nervous, the EDA sensor measures the state after which, the light would turn on, and the wearer could poke each fabric bubble with his/her finger for a brief period to make the corresponding light to turn off. The vibration mode works this way as well. The module stops working as feedback to the user's behaviour. The wearer can repeat this interaction with the smart shawl constantly to relieve their stress or let out their negative emotions until they are somewhat calmer. Based on the prototype the shawl was tested to verify whether it could help wearers to self-regulate their emotion.

**The Emotion Regulation Loop.** In this study, emotion regulation was implemented based on the following three steps. In the first step, the emotion data was acquired by the EDA sensor and processed to identify the emotion variation level based on the wearer's emotional arousal. In the second step, the emotional state was visualized, which would transform the arousal data into lights or vibration within the smart textiles. In the third step, the user could interact with the smart textiles to self-regulate their emotions. The shawl would show the state of the user's emotional arousal and allow

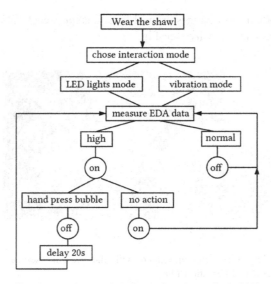

**Fig. 4.** The interaction flow of each textile bubble.

the user to interact with the visualized emotions. Moreover, because of the interplay between the emotions and the user's actions, their emotions could change continuously. As such, this process could form a dynamic loop to guide the user back to the ideal emotional level. Besides, interaction can be both conscious and unconscious. If it is a conscious interaction, there could be a reflection step before interaction and the user's reflection may also affect his or her emotion (see Fig. 5).

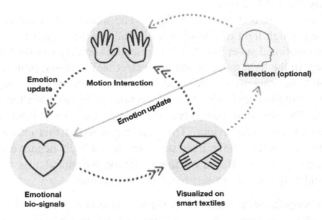

**Fig. 5.** Emotion regulation loop process with visualized biodata in the smart shawl prototype.

## 4   Smart Shawl Prototype Experiment

We recruited 15 unpaid volunteers from a local University to participate in the experiment. There were 9 females and 6 males (aged between 18 and 26; Mean = 21.2, SD = 2.072). They came from different backgrounds, including industrial design, architecture, computer science, media art, and were all recruited from a social media platform. The participants were selected based on their interest to participate in this study. The experiment was carried out in a design studio. To explore the attitude of the users, an emotion induction interview and a semi-structured interview were conducted. During the interviews, we recorded participants' EDA data for quantitative analysis and their reactions to the prototype for qualitative analysis. The test had the following three goals:

- To further understand the participants' attitude towards emotion regulation and how they handle it;
- To induce the emotional response of the participants, then test the effect of the prototype for emotion regulation;
- To elicit participants' experience and feedback on the prototype.

### 4.1   Procedure and Apparatus

According to the objective of the study, a preliminary semi-structured interview outline was compiled, and four students were pre-interviewed based on the outline. Two emotion induction methods were compared: video emotion induction and recall emotion induction [25]. Based on the results and feedback from the participants, the recall emotion induction method was selected since it resulted in a stronger emotional response from the participants (measured by the EDA sensor), while the video induction method resulted in too much variance between the participants based on their personal preference for video content—that is, for the same video content, some people are more excited, some people are more insensitive. The outline of the interview was finally formed after the modifications.

Before the interview began, the general interview process was introduced, including duration, purpose, and the prototype itself. The participants signed informed consent to voluntarily participate in the study (see Fig. 6). Then participants were interviewed with the following pre-set questions.

**Fig. 6.** Steps of the experiment process.

- Are you bothered by emotion problems in your daily lives?
- What kind of emotion are you dealing with? And which scenario?
- How do you deal with this kind of emotional fluctuation in their daily life?
- What's your explanation of your coping behaviour?

After the interview, several questions were asked for emotion induction.

- When did your last emotional fluctuation happened?
- Could you recall what happened?

Then participants filled in the first Self-Assessment Manikin (SAM) form [3]. After the emotion induction, the participant was encouraged to experience the prototype. Finally, the participants were asked to self-evaluate their emotions again with the second SAM form and express their feelings and opinions about the prototype.

## 4.2 Results

The data collected during the interview included data from the EDA sensor, video recordings and written text on the forms. This data was used as input for the analysis to evaluate the prototype. Within the data presented in this section, F and M represent the gender of the participants, and the numbers after the letters represent the order of the participants.

**Coping Behaviours of Emotional Fluctuation.** As part of the unstructured interview, we asked the participants to recall their behaviour after they experienced stress or strong emotions in their daily lives and to give their interpretation for these behaviours. Their coping behaviours vary, including tearing paper, doing exercises, hugging people, etc. Based on their responses, we were able to categorize them into five types of interpretation: positive intervention, venting negative emotion actions, increasing sense of control, attention diversion and unconscious behaviours they could not explain clearly. The full list of behaviours and our interpretations grouped in categories are summarized in Table 2.

**Table 2.** The participants' behaviours and their interpretation when dealing with stress or emotion variations.

| Interpretation of their actions | Behaviours when participants were experiencing stress/emotion variation |
|---|---|
| Positive intervention | Hugging other people or plush toys |
| Venting actions | Paper tearing, tearing other things apart, rubbing hands, doing exercise, running, poking bubbles, throwing the pillow |
| Increase control | Pressing a pen |
| Attention diversion | Pulling hair, playing phones |
| Unconsciousness behaviour | Walking up and down, scratching head, swinging hands, swinging feet, more gestures |

**Emotion Induction and EDA Data.** The emotion induction method evoked fluctuation in participants' emotions. Figure 7 shows each participants' average EDA data before and after emotion induction. A paired t-test on the data showed there was significant difference (t = 10.512, P < 0.05). Specific comparisons showed that the average EDA value after emotion induction (218.33 ± 54.86) was significantly higher than the average EDA value before induction (71.67 ± 21.85).

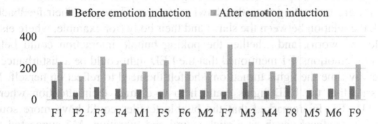

**Fig. 7.** The participant's EDA data comparison before and after emotion induction.

**SAM Tests Before and After Experiencing the Shawl.** Based on the assumption that participants' emotional reflection is significant, the SAM test was conducted to evaluate the participants' subjective emotional variations. We invited the participants before and after interacting with the prototype to complete the SAM questionnaire, which measures emotional variations on a scale from 0–9 for three aspects: emotional valence, arousal, and dominance. Figure 8 shows the graphs of the values for the three SAM aspects. The values of valence1, arousal1, and dominance1 are the data after the emotion induction interview, but before they interacted with the prototype. Emotional valence2, arousal2, and dominance2 are the data after they interacted with the prototype.

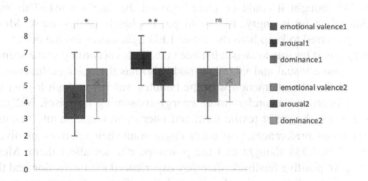

**Fig. 8.** The participants' SAM box plot (*P < 0.05, ** P < 0.01, ***P < 0.001).

We did 3 paired t-tests on the data. The results are as follows: (1) The emotional valence value increased from 4.40 ± 1.35 to 5.20 ± 1.08, after the completion of the test, and it was found that the difference between the two groups was significant, t = − 2.567, P = 0.022 < 0.05, indicating that the interactions with the prototype improved the general positive emotion of the participants. (2) After the experiment, the results of emotion arousal level showed that the difference between the two conditions was significant, $t = 5.870$, $P < 0.01$. It shows that the prototype is conducive to the recovery of users' emotion arousal level. (3) Although the emotion dominance score increased from $4.80 \pm 1.15$ to $5.27 \pm 0.88$, there was no significant difference between the two conditions after the experiment.

**User Feedback.** Participants were encouraged to express their feeling and opinions when they were interacting with the shawl prototype. They gave their feedback about the shawl, the relation between the shawl and their body (for example, where else could the textiles be worn), and whether the poking bubble interaction could help them regulate their emotions. F1 mentioned that the LED light could be a disturbance for her because every time the lights turned on, she felt the need to reflect on herself. M1 and F3 discussed that the LED lights could help to distract their attention when being stressed. M1, F5, F6 remarked that the bubble textiles could have more sources of multi-sensory feedback, such as a click sound and vibration. M5 suggested that the LED lights could light up one by one, while simultaneously creating rhythmical musical feedback.

Regarding the form of poking bubble in the textile, some participants liked the shawl and would like the functional part to be placed around the shoulder as they thought it could be more comfortable. F5 suggested that the smart shawl could also integrate a hug function and heating function to give comfort to the user. F8 preferred it to be placed on the arm or hand, so it could be easier to wear, and its reaction could be seen more clearly. The participants also had some concerns, because the shawl might not be tight enough to be in contact with the skin, and the user had to look down at the fabric to see the lights when it was in LED light mode. F4 mentioned that the interactive textile could also be used in handbags for women, for example by measuring the EDA data when they were holding the bag. F7 suggested it should be integrated into a wristband. M5 thought it could be placed around the user's waist. This participant recalled that when he is angry, he would put his hands on his waist. Most of the participants preferred to keep both the public LED light mode and the private vibration mode so they could be able to switch between the modes according to the scenario. The light mode is more visual and vibration mode also has the massage function.

F7 thought that the interaction with the bubbles was not enough for her to let her emotions out because she prefers more energy-consuming exercises. M2 mentioned that for real users, the smart textile form and interaction mode should be customized based on personal preferences, and users might want their relatives involved in the interaction. F1 and M4 thought that the prototype did not affect them. Most of the participants gave positive feedback after they experienced the interaction and thought it could help people with emotional self-regulation. Some of them mentioned their expectations for smart textile products with improved performance.

# 5 Discussion

## 5.1 Two Design Cycles

Following the RtD approach, four smart textiles and one smart shawl were designed to help us explore the interactive smart textile design for emotion regulation and verify its feasibility with the hybrid research method.

In the first design cycle, we tested four smart textiles and interview and got the user's feedback on emotional visualization and feedback mode based on different types of smart textiles, then chose visual and vibrotactile as the feedback modes. Another discovery is the gesture interaction triggered by fabric samples in the RtD process. We realized that both body motion and interaction have an impact on emotional state. Therefore, the second study attempts to combine movement and feedback mechanism with interaction to amplify the effect on emotion.

The results of the second design cycle indicated that the movement-based interactive emotion self-regulation design of the smart shawl could help the stressed user to reflect and manipulate their emotional states.

From the participants' feedback, it seems that each person's emotions might be aroused by different triggers, but the negative emotional experiences are similar, such as depression, impatience, nervous, etc. In Table 2, we tried to categorize participants' instinctive responses to emotions into four types. The participants' interpretations of these behaviours are not necessarily the only ones, since there are many complex factors behind emotion and response behaviours. However, the participants' explanations may help us to design effective interactions strategies for emotion regulation.

After the interview emotion induction, the SAM questionnaire results show that, in general, the prototype had a greater impact on the participants' emotional valence and arousal after they interacted with the prototype. From the qualitative interviews, we found that most participants showed a positive attitude towards the design of the prototype and put forward their suggestions for further improvements. Male participants preferred to position the smart textiles on the arm or hand, while female participants wanted to place it around the chest. The participants' response is consistent with Uğur's survey [30] on the somatic sensation of emotions, which indicates that the chest and shoulders have more feelings when participants are emotionally aroused. Some participants also expressed the expectation that the interactive textile prototype could be combined with gloves, wristbands, and handbags, to further integrate it into their daily life. Many participants expressed their expectations for richer interactive feedback. For example, when visualizing emotion with lights or vibration, there could be additional sound feedback or interaction guidance to achieve a better interactive experience and emotional relief.

## 5.2 Reflection

Several aspects may affect the emotional status of participants in the experiment, such as the speed of emotional recovery of the participants, the novelty of a new prototype, personal preferences of materials, etc. Above all things, movement-based interaction and feedback mechanism are the most important factors.

In previous studies, it has been suggested that there is a bi-directional relationship between emotion and body motor behaviour [5, 6]. Body movements can be used not only to express emotions but also to influence how we feel due to the mirror neurons. Body movement exercises, such as TaiChi, yoga [8], have long been used in emotion regulation and this concept has been applied in dance/movement therapy. However, what remains unclear is how to design motion-based interaction to affect emotion. Hand Interactions such as popping sealed air capsules have been shown to be effective for nervous or stressed individuals since it can help to release muscle inhibition [7]. These types of interactions have also been applied in digital user interfaces. For example, the NetEase music application recently introduced a stress release mode in which users can poke virtual bubbles or break the virtual glass on the screen to relieve stress [18] and received positive feedback from users.

Emotion self-regulation methods through body motion can be determined by different types of emotions. Besides poking fabric bubbles, we may consider different types of interactive hand actions, and a wider range of body actions for interaction. Compared with the physiological state, we can better control our body movement, muscle movement and respiratory rhythm to a certain extent. This advantage should be more integrated into the interaction design for emotion regulation, rather than just receiving the information conveyed by biofeedback.

In the smart shawl, the feedback mechanism plays multiple roles: (1) Visualizing the emotion-related physiological information; (2) Causing users to reflect on their emotional state; and (3) Motivating users to interact with their emotion visualizations with actions. Different feedback modes also affect users' emotional state. In our design, we let users choose their own preferred feedback modalities to interact with the smart shawl. Although the results of SAM test show that the overall both modalities results seem to be effective on emotional regulation, the difference of impact between two feedback mechanisms remains unknown, which is the part we will follow up in the future research.

Future developments of smart textile products do not only concern technological breakthroughs but also about designing interaction styles that fit these close-to-the-body products to improve the user's experience. There is an intimate relationship between the human body and the products we carry around, such as our clothing. Smart textile products, in particular, will be more dynamic and flexible and can be tailored according to the user's physical and psychological states. Embodied interaction design can further expand the functions of smart textiles while improving users' emotional experience. This can help them to further communicate with themselves and others, based on their emotions in a dynamic and real-time basis.

### 5.3   Further Development

To test the effect of the movement-based interaction in smart textiles, the prototype design is based on a simple interaction model. In the future, we plan to design richer interactions in the system to improve the user experience. Also, we will explore further usage scenarios and user acceptance and feedback in real-life contexts.

Further, when designing interactions based on emotions it is necessary to consider the appropriate interaction location on the body, fabric selection, emotion visualization modes, and other kinds of physiological signals which can be used to measure emotion states. How to personalize the emotional self-regulation products according to the different scenarios to achieve the best user experience will be a topic for further research.

# 6 Conclusion

The affective interaction of the prototype is self-supportive, a closed-loop, avoids privacy issues, gives users autonomy and, at the same time, helps users to understand and interact with their embodied emotions. Because many factors affect human emotions, it is difficult to design interactions which react to a specific aspect of our emotions. However, the emotional experience can be designed. In this case, user's emotional experience was affected through embodied interaction. Our prototype helps people to regulate emotion by letting them see and 'interact' with them. The emotion regulation smart textile system may also benefit the family members or friends since they are also closely related to users' emotional states. The research application can be extended to the design of emotion regulation for social relationships. According to users' cultural backgrounds and preferences, products can be designed for self-supportive users and also for users to communicate with their families or friends.

The approach of this research is based on Research through Design. The process of combining making and testing in iterative cycles helped identify the research direction and reflect on the research question. With the development of interactive textiles, designers will face the situation of solving multi-disciplinary involved design problems. The proposed smart textile design methods and experiences will help them explore functional and aesthetic possibilities in their projects.

**Acknowledgement.** The authors would like to thank all the participants for the time and the reviewers for their comments. This research was supported in part by Xi'an Jiaotong-Liverpool University (XJTLU) Key Program Special Fund (KSF-A-03), and XJTLU Research Development Fund (RDF-17-01-54).

# References

1. Ashford, R.: Responsive and Emotive Wearable Technology: physiological data, devices and communication, Doctoral dissertation, Goldsmiths, University of London (2018)
2. Bialoskorski, L.S., Westerink, J.H., Van den Broek, E.L.: Experiencing affective interactive art. Int. J. Arts Technol. 3(4), 341–356 (2010)
3. Bradley, M.M., Lang, P.J.: Measuring emotion: the self-assessment manikin and the semantic differential. J. Behav. Therapy Exp. Psychiatry 25(1), 49–59 (1994)
4. Cherenack, K., van Pieterson, L.: Smart textiles: challenges and opportunities. J. Appl. Phys. 112(9), 091301 (2012)
5. Damasio, A.R.: The feeling of what happens: body and emotion in the making of consciousness. Houghton Mifflin Harcourt (1999)

6.  de Rooij, A.: Toward emotion regulation via physical interaction. In: Proceedings of the Companion Publication of the 19th International Conference on Intelligent User Interfaces, pp. 57–60 (2014)
7.  Dillon, K.M.: Popping sealed air-capsules to reduce stress. Psychol. Rep. **71**(1), 243–246 (1992)
8.  Francis, A.L., Beemer, R.C.: How does yoga reduce stress? Embodied cognition and emotion highlight the influence of the musculoskeletal system. Complementary therapies in medicine (2019)
9.  Fritsch, J.: Understanding affective engagement as a resource in interaction design. Nordes 3 (2009)
10. Höök, K., Laaksolahti, J.: Empowerment: a strategy to dealing with human values in affective interactive systems (2008)
11. Höök, K.: Affective loop experiences – what are they? In: Oinas-Kukkonen, H., Hasle, P., Harjumaa, M., Segerståhl, K., Øhrstrøm, P. (eds.) PERSUASIVE 2008. LNCS, vol. 5033, pp. 1–12. Springer, Heidelberg (2008). https://doi.org/10.1007/978-3-540-68504-3_1
12. Jeon, M.: Emotions and affect in human factors and human–computer interaction: Taxonomy, theories, approaches, and methods. In Emotions and Affect in Human Factors and Human-Computer Interaction, pp. 3–26. Academic Press (2017)
13. Khut, G.: Designing biofeedback artworks for relaxation. In: Proceedings of the 2016 CHI Conference Extended Abstracts on Human Factors in Computing Systems, pp. 3859–3862 (2016)
14. Koskinen, I., Zimmerman, J., Binder, T., Redstrom, J., Wensveen, S.: Design research through practice: from the lab, field, and showroom. Elsevier (2011)
15. Lisetti, C.L., Nasoz, F.: Using noninvasive wearable computers to recognize human emotions from physiological signals. EURASIP J. Adv. Signal Process. **2004**(11), 929414 (2004)
16. Nanjappan, V., Shi, R., Liang, H.N., Lau, K.K.T., Yue, Y., Atkinson, K.: Towards a taxonomy for in-vehicle interactions using wearable smart textiles: insights from a user-elicitation study. Multimodal Technol. Inter. **3**(2), 33 (2019)
17. Nanjappan, V., Shi, R., Liang, H.N., Xiao, H., Lau, K.K.T., Hasan, K.: Design of interactions for handheld augmented reality devices using wearable smart textiles: findings from a user elicitation study. Appl. Sci. **9**(15), 3177 (2019)
18. Netease Cloud Sati Space Introduction. https://baijiahao.baidu.com/s?id=1620172495110902700&wfr=spider&for=pc. Accessed 10 June 2020
19. Norman, D.A.: Emotional design: why we love (or hate) everyday things. Basic Civitas Books (2004)
20. Nunez-Pacheco, C., Loke, L.: Crafting the body-tool: a body-centred perspective on wearable technology. In: Proceedings of the 2014 Conference on Designing Interactive Systems, pp. 553–566 (2014)
21. Papadopoulou, A., Berry, J., Knight, T., Picard, R.: Affective sleeve: wearable materials with haptic action for promoting calmness. In: Streitz, N., Konomi, S. (eds.) HCII 2019. LNCS, vol. 11587, pp. 304–319. Springer, Cham (2019). https://doi.org/10.1007/978-3-030-21935-2_23
22. Picard, R.W., Scheirer, J.: The galvactivator: a glove that senses and communicates skin conductivity. In: Proceedings 9th International Conference on HCI (2001)
23. Picard, R.W.: Affective Computing. MIT Press, Cambridge (2000)
24. Sensoree. Mood Sweater collar to visualize the user's emotion. http://sensoree.com/. Accessed 10 June 2020
25. Siedlecka, E., Denson, T.F.: Experimental methods for inducing basic emotions: a qualitative review. Emot. Rev. **11**(1), 87–97 (2019)

26. Stead, L.J.: 'The emotional wardrobe': a fashion perspective on the integration of technology and clothing, Doctoral dissertation, University of the Arts London (2005)

27. Sundström, P., Ståhl, A., Höök, K.: eMoto: affectively involving both body and mind. In: CHI 2005 Extended Abstracts on Human Factors in Computing Systems, pp. 2005–2008 (2005)

28. Terry, M.L., Leary, M.R.: Self-compassion, self-regulation, and health. Self Identity 10(3), 352–362 (2011)

29. Toeters, M., ten Bhömer, M., Bottenberg, E., Tomico, O., Brinks, G.: Research through design: a way to drive innovative solutions in the field of smart textiles. In: Advances in Science and Technology, vol. 80, pp. 112–117. Trans Tech Publications Ltd. (2013)

30. Uğur, S.: Wearing Embodied Emotions: A Practice Based Design Research on Wearable Technology. Springer, Milan, Italy (2013). https://doi.org/10.1007/978-88-470-5247-5

31. Wensveen, S.A., Djajadiningrat, J.P., Overbeeke, C.J.: Interaction frogger: a design framework to couple action and function through feedback and feedforward. In: Proceedings of the 5th Conference on Designing Interactive Systems: Processes, Practices, Methods, and Techniques, pp. 177–184 (2004)

32. Yu, B.: Designing biofeedback for managing stress (2018)

33. Yucha, C., Montgomery, D.: Evidence-based practice in biofeedback and neurofeedback. AAPB, Wheat Ridge, CO (2008)

# FlowGlove: A Liquid-Based Wearable Device for Haptic Interaction in Virtual Reality

Lijuan Liu[1,2], Cheng Yao[1(✉)], Yizhou Liu[1], Pinhao Wang[1],
Yang Chen[1], and Fangtian Ying[3]

[1] College of Computer Science and Technology, Zhejiang University,
Hangzhou, China
{liulijuan,Yaoch}@zju.edu.cn
[2] Ocean College, Zhejiang University, Hangzhou, China
[3] School of Industrial Design, Hubei University of Technology, Wuhan, China
yingft@gmail.com

**Abstract.** Current hand-worn haptic devices can render a variety of tactile sensations. However, few studies focus on providing a real liquid tactile experience with those devices in virtual reality scenes. To address this gap, we extend the potential of liquid sensation with the FlowGlove, an innovative wearable device with the tactile sensation of pressure, vibration, and temperature enabling virtual reality haptic interactions. FlowGlove system includes five sections: a liquid bladder, cooling system, pneumatic actuation, vibration section, and command operation. FlowGlove in active mode delivers sensations through water flowing in the liquid bladder and can provide cold feeling under the action of the water cycle cooling system. It can also render haptic feelings of touch, fondle, and grip, which generates sensation in different parts of hands. Studies evaluated the material properties and pneumatic effect of FlowGlove. We also explored several applications leveraging this liquid-based haptic approach. In different scenarios, FlowGlove provides users dynamic haptic sensation experience that enhances interaction in water-related virtual reality scenes.

**Keywords:** Wearable device · Liquid sensation · VR scene · Water interaction

## 1 Introduction

Currently, VR technology is maturing quickly and has been widely applied to different fields, such as entertainment, education, and social activities [1]. Consumer VR devices such as the Oculus Rift and HTC Vive are capable of rendering visual and audio content, and handheld controllers further improve the interaction and the sense of presence. Liquid-related VR scenes usually appear in VR games or VR water sports. Most of them provide visual feedback or relay on external devices to spray liquid directly into the human body, which would cause trouble in some specific scenarios. Very limited efforts have considered offering liquid perceptions in the virtual reality scenes. Inspired by that, we present a new wearable device that can be used in the VR scenes to provide a variety of liquid feelings and interactions.

© Springer Nature Switzerland AG 2020
C. Stephanidis et al. (Eds.): HCII 2020, LNCS 12429, pp. 316–331, 2020.
https://doi.org/10.1007/978-3-030-59987-4_23

Haptic perception and other body experiences have a significant impact on immersion and presence. Many of the haptic technologies were designed to improve feedback of the hand and fingertip [2]. However, most of these haptic devices primarily serve applications with virtual objects and impede the user's natural cutaneous sensations and dexterity for the benefits offered by the immersive haptic rendering [3]. Users are unable to touch and feel virtual objects the same way they interact with real ones [4]. Especially in the VR scene, users perform operations through HMD or handheld controller, and they can only visually observe the water environment and cannot perceive more tactile experience.

To provide better liquid sensation experiences, a wearable haptic interface Flow-Glove is introduced, which has the water surrounding tactile for the hand (Fig. 1a). It includes a liquid bladder, a pneumatic system, vibration actuators, and a cooling system (Fig. 1b). We control the system by computer and Arduino UNO. The liquid bladder was designed to wrap the hand to provide a sense of being surrounded by water, and the cooling system can reduce liquid temperature to provide cold feeling. The pneumatic system includes 8 airbags which can be inflated and deflated independently to provide targeted water force perception. We also set up 4 vibration actuators to provide vibrotactile. When users move their hands, they can perceive the water flow, which can enhance the water stimulation experience. We also presented several example applications that highlight the functionality of our device. Our contributions of this work include:

**Fig. 1.** FlowGlove: a. appearance of FlowGlove; b. internal structure of FlowGlove; c. application in VR game.

1) Presenting a new wearable device that can provide liquid sensation in VR scenes.
2) Combining pneumatic with liquid to simulate water pressure and water flow.
3) Exploring the interaction ways (input and output) with water.
4) Examining the usability of FlowGlove through a comparative experiment with the standard VR controller.

## 2  Related Work

Our work relates to liquid sensation in the water-related virtual reality scenes aiming to create an immersive underwater experience. There are extensive researches on the field of VR experience design, and we limit our review of related work to liquid-based VR experience and device for liquid sensation.

### 2.1  Liquid-Based Experience

The experience design of the VR liquid environment means that in the constructed virtual scenes, users can interact with the contents, and the system can give perceptual feedback. According to the content of the virtual scene, users receive various physical stimuli from the visual, tactile, auditory, olfactory, and motion perception. Liquid sensations can strengthen the immersion of liquid environments in VR scenes. At present, the experience design of liquid-based VR is mainly used for entertainment such as games, aquariums, and marine amusement parks. These liquid-based VR experiences are presented in two ways: experiences in real water environments and experiences on land.

**Experiences in Real Water Environments.** Such experiences occur in a real water environment, and body perception is produced by real water. For example, AquaCAVE was designed for enhancing swimming experience, using a combination of CAVE-like projection-based virtual reality with a swimming pool, swimmers can be immersed in synthetic scenes [5]. Wenlong Zhang [6] presented an underwater VR device prototype, a simple HMD, that can be used underwater, but in this structure, the air enters the device, which greatly increases the buoyancy, making swimming uncomfortable. Another project developed this approach comes from Hiroyuki Osone [7]. He designed an optimal HMD for swimming. Because there was no air layer in the HMD, it was expected that buoyancy would not be an issue, and the HMD could easily be worn while swimming. All these devices need to be used underwater, and they focus on giving users the virtual visual experience in the real underwater environment. They are not portable, and require users to enter the real water environment to get liquid feeling, and cannot be experienced in a regular VR environment.

**Experiences on Land.** This type of experience occurs on land, where devices provide liquid sensation in the body. The devices' sensors, actuators, and unique materials simulate the liquid sensation. Amphibian was a virtual reality system providing an immersive SCUBA diving experience through an available terrestrial simulator [8]. This system incorporated sensations of sight, hearing, kinesthetic sense, temperature, and balance, but had not focused much on tactile sensation. Yi-Ya Liao focused on the perception of the face and presented a liquid mask that can simultaneously produce thermal changes and vibration responses by filling liquid into the mask [9]. There are also researchers using special materials to simulate water feedback. Keishiro Uragaki [10] proposed the visual liquidness impression with fluidized sand and the augmented reality technique. While these approaches provide the water-related experience in VR scenes, they did not focus on the haptic perception produced by various forms of underwater interaction, such as the difference between the haptic perception produced by the floating up and diving down. This paper aims to create the underwater perception experience for liquid-related VR scene and to explore haptic effects that can be better created with liquid, vibration, and pneumatic actuation.

## 2.2    Device for Liquid Sensation

There are several object properties associated with haptics in general-such as pressure, temperature, size, or weight [11]. Researchers have explored rendering tactile [11, 12], force [13, 14], ship [15], vibration [1] with wearable devices. Liquid has been explored in designing haptic and tangible interfaces. There are three main ways for the generation of liquid sensation: simulate the liquid sensation with electronic components, use smart liquid material, and use real water materials.

**Simulated Sensation with Electronic Components.** Researchers have used electronic components to stimulate liquid sensations, such as vibration and pneumatics [3, 16]. Vibration is one of the most promising approaches for haptic perception because of the small size of vibration actuators, such as HapCube [14], WAVES [17]. Konishi et al. presented a Synesthesia Suit, which utilizes 26 vibration tactile actuators on a full-body suit for enhancing VR gaming experiences [18]. Ali Israr and Ivan Poupyrev showed arrays of vibration actuators that can provide the perception of smooth motion on the back [19]. Pneumatic actuation technology has also been a popular choice for enabling soft, shape-changing interfaces for tangible and haptic interactions. Liang He [20] created a novel wearable haptic interface by gently pressing on the skin using compliant shape-changing nodes. Another project called Pneumatibles [21], with a single pneumatically driven actuator that simulated a button. Frozen Suit is a full-body haptic interface by using jamming patches at joints position to create an experience of a frozen body in VR games [22]. Additionally, body pneumatic feedback systems are utilized to reproduce various experiences, such as being hugged [23, 24]. The process of constructing and controlling of pneumatic actuation enabled people to explore the effect of various structural and control-related parameters on the actuator's tactile performance [21].

**Smart Liquid Material.** Smart liquid material has been well studied in recent years, such as magnetorheological (MR) fluid, electrorheological (ER) fluid, and ferro fluid [25–27]. These materials provide unique touch feedback because of their non-rigid surfaces and been shown to be effective in providing liquid stimuli. Martin Schmitz proposed Liquido [28] to embed liquids into 3D printed objects while printing to sense various tilting and motion interactions via capacitive sensing. Follmer et al. [29] explored how jamming of granular particles can be used in designing malleable, flexible and shape-changing interfaces. Qiuyu Lu et al. [30] presented LIME, Liquid Metal interfaces for non-rigid interaction. Haptic Canvas [31] was a haptic entertainment system presented by dilatant fluid with the controlling grove, and users can have the experience of distinct multimodal haptic sensations. Designers and researchers have brought special liquid material into digital interaction experiences, and liquid material has been explored in applications of deformable and tangible UIs.

**Real Water Material.** The real water is involved in the haptic system and is used to provide the liquid sensation. Compared with the other two ways, real water can provide a more direct and realistic sensation. Teng Han et al. [3] proposed HydroRing and provided the tactile sensations of pressure, vibration, and temperature on the fingertip via liquid flow. Chih-Hao Cheng proposed GravityCup, a liquid-based haptic feedback device that simulated realistic object weights and inertia when moving virtual handheld objects [32]. Liquid Jets [33] was a fluid user interface as a logic-computing input/output device based on touching small jets of water. Then the fuzzy logic could be demonstrated by smooth variations in fluid flow control. The above works demonstrated the haptic applications of liquid or fluid in the HCI field, but had different design goals from ours. With FlowGlove, we leverage flowing water to produce sensations on the hand. By combining the liquid with pneumatics and vibrations, FlowGlove is able to provide liquid sensation in VR scenes.

## 3 System Description

The FlowGlove system consists of five sections: the liquid bladder, cooling system, pneumatic actuation, vibration section, and command operation (Fig. 2a). The liquid bladder can wrap the entire hand and provides a sense of underwater immersion. The cooling system includes a water pump and a cooling unit. It can help lower the temperature of the water and keep it at a certain temperature range. The vibration section has 4 mini vibration actuators controlled by Arduino. It is designed to provide an underwater vibration feeling. Pneumatic actuation can support underwater force, including 8 airbags, mini pumps, and 2-way solenoid valves. The user can also give commands via the membrane switch, and the Inertial Measurement Unit can identify the user's hand position. The overall system intends to present a different liquid sensation experience through a prototype of multi haptic feedback. The layout of the internal devices is shown in Fig. 2b, which includes the membrane switch, liquid bladder, vibration actuators, and airbags from the inside to the outside.

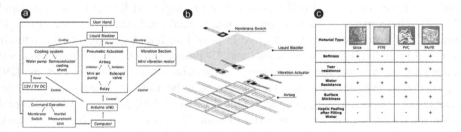

**Fig. 2.** a. Overview of the FlowGlove system. b. The layout of internal elements of FlowGlove. c. Comparison of the properties of the four materials-Silica, PTFE, PVC, and PA/PE.

## 3.1  Wearable Design

Diving gloves are an indispensable protective tool in deep diving. It plays a protective role when encountering sharp marine creatures in the deep sea. Moreover, it can also help keep warm because of the lower temperature in the underwater environment. This haptic wearable is designed as a diving glove in water-related VR scenes, which has an adjustable strap on the side to comfortably fit the user's hand type with various sizes. The material we used is a diving fabric, a composite of Styrene-Butadiene Rubber (SBR) and polyester fabric. This material has the properties of elastic, shockproof, heat resistance, and tears resistance. The device is fixed by velcro, and the user can wrap it according to the personal situation to ensure a firm fit. Some triangular decorations are designed and attached to the surface of FlowGlove, which are printed with a 3D printer (Fig. 1a).

## 3.2  Liquid Bladder

We customized a liquid bladder that can wrap the user's hand to create an underwater immersion experience. The liquid bladder was divided into two separate bags from the middle. Each area has a liquid inlet and a liquid outlet, and the two bags are symmetrically distributed. We set the size of the liquid bladder by referring to the size of the adult's hand. The entire format is $290 \times 230$ mm in the unfolded state and $145 \times 230$ mm in the folded state.

The material of the liquid bladder would affect the skin haptic, and different materials will present different tactile experiences. We choose material according to the elements of softness, tear resistance, water resistance, surface stickiness, and skin haptic feeling after filling water. We compared four materials: Silica, Polytetrafluoroethylene (PTFE), Polyvinyl chloride (PVC), the composite material of Polyamide and Polyethylene (PA/PE) (Fig. 2c).

By comparing the properties of the material, we chose the composite material made of PE and PA with 50 microns thick, which has a pleasant softness and can wrap the hand comfortably. It also has strong tear resistance to allow the user to grip at will. Viscous material will stick to the skin and affect the skin haptic. This composite material has a lower viscosity to provide a smoother experience. As for the type of liquid, we tested freshwater and seawater. The results showed that the fluidity of the two liquids was similar, and the skin sensation was not much different, so we chose freshwater as the experimental liquid because it is easy to obtain. After testing, the hand felt better when the water volume is 400 ml in each space of liquid bladder so that the liquid can flow and wrap the hand without uneven distribution in various hand postures.

## 3.3  Cooling System

Seawater temperature represents the thermal condition of the ocean. The annual average water temperature of oceans is about 17.4 °C [34]. To create a realistic liquid sensation experience, we designed a cooling system to lower the liquid temperature with a semiconductor cooling sheet through cold water circulation. Two valves were placed in each liquid bladder. A tube with an inner diameter of 2.5 mm was placed in the valve, and a water pump can be connected to ensure the liquid is cooling. The pump can draw water from a reservoir. A semiconductor cooling sheet can be used for cooling liquid, and the system is able to deliver liquid in the range from 17–25 °C to ensure users' comfort (so as not to expose the user to temperatures that are too cold). 25 °C is what we consider the typical indoor temperature. The cooling system takes about 25 s to cool 400 ml of liquid by 5°. Users can set an initial temperature value in the temperature range. Arduino UNO can control the cooling sheet, and a basic control algorithm was programmed. When the probe detects that the liquid in the reservoir is 0.5° above the target temperature, the repeater activates the semiconductor cooling sheet to achieve cooling. When it is 0.5° below the target temperature, the cooling will stop.

### 3.4    Pneumatic Actuation

Eight airbags were installed on the device, and this density was sufficient to implement the sense of water force across the hand. Figure 3a highlights the allocation of airbags: there are 4 airbags at the back of the hand and others on the palm. Each airbag has a valve for inflation and deflation and can be controlled separately. The size of each airbag is $110 \times 70$ mm. Two PVC tubes with an inner diameter of 2.0 mm were placed in the valve, the shorter tube was set in the valve, and an external mini-pump (ZT030-01-12120, airflow 0.3L/m) was connected, which can pump air into the airbag. The longer tube ran through the valve and was connected to the mini 2-way solenoid valve (DC 3 V) for deflation. The eight sets of mini air pump and solenoid valve were connected to 8 relays, which can be controlled by Arduino UNO. UNO was connected to the computer through USB. The hardware and the VR game were coordinated through serial communication.

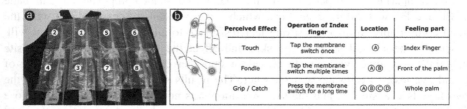

**Fig. 3.**  a. The layout of airbags. b. Positions of vibration actuators and the interaction ways.

### 3.5    Vibration Haptic

Four fixed high-frequency mini vibration actuators were placed between the liquid bladder and the airbags. Commands from the VR game can be transmitted to the Arduino UNO via USB to control the vibration actuators. The positions of vibration actuators are shown in Fig. 3b. These positions correspond to the four airbags below the palm. The entire vibration actuators can be adjusted to single vibration and combined vibrations according to users' interaction ways. When the index finger taps once on the membrane switch, the A vibration actuator works, which can render the feeling of touch. When the index finger taps multiple times on the membrane switch, the A and B vibration actuators work, the front of the palm can sense the vibration to simulate the interactive situation of fondling. When the index finger presses the membrane switch for a long time, all vibration actuators will work together, and the whole palm can feel the water vibration to simulate the haptic of catching (Fig. 3b).

### 3.6 Command Operation

Users can send commands via FlowGlove, which can synchronize with the VR picture content and the hardware. FlowGlove includes an Inertial Measurement Unit (IMU) to detect the three-dimensional position of the hand. The detected data is transmitted to the computer through the SerialPort class of Unity 3D to control VR screen content. A single-button membrane switch was installed on the FlowGlove liquid bladder, which corresponded to the user's index finger operating position. When users press the membrane switch, the button status is transferred to the computer VR program via Unity 3D's SerialPort class, which is converted into instructions by the program and sent to the Arduino. Arduino can control the vibration motors according to the command category to give feedback when the button is pressed.

## 4  Experiment and Evaluation

To improve and evaluate the performance of FlowGlove and to understand how users would use our system, we conducted two user studies with 16 participants (8 male and 8 female), ages 18–34 (M = 24.88, SD = 4.03). All participants experienced VR before, and three of them have the experience of water-related VR scene experience. Participants were recruited from our university with 10 dollars each as compensation.

### 4.1  Study 1: Pneumatic Actuation Effect

The purpose of this experiment is to test the pneumatic actuation of FlowGlove. We compared the force effect of a single airbag and the same airbag covered with the liquid bladder. We also examined the pressure that they put on the palm and back of the hand. In this study, users were asked to participate in 3 tests. The whole study was carried out on the desk. Users put down the palm in the natural state, and the force should not be added deliberately.

Test 1-Single Airbag. The hand was placed on the airbag (the same size as the airbag used on FlowGlove), and the Force Sensing Resistor (FSR 402 P/N: 30-81794) [35] was placed between hand and airbag to detect pressure data. The airbag was inflated and deflated by an air pump and a solenoid valve. FSR measured pressure and recorded data every 0.3 s. We marked the positions of airbag and FSR to ensure that the pressure was added and tested in the same area each time.

Test 2-Airbag Covered with the Liquid Bladder. Users were required to wear FlowGlove and maintained the same gesture. The FSR was placed between the palm and the liquid bladder. This position was the same as the FSR position of Test 1. The airbag was adjusted to the same area, and then was inflated and deflated to detect pressure values on the hand palm.

Test 3-Airbag Covered with the Liquid Bladder. Users were required to wear FlowGlove and maintained the same gesture and adjusted the position of airbag above the hand. One FSR was placed between the liquid bladder and the back of the hand to detect the pressure value.

**Result.** The experiment results showed that the pneumatic actuation acted on the liquid bladder can simulate water force on the hand. As shown in Fig. 4b, the maximum force of the FlowGlove single airbag is about 7.74 N, and the maximum pressure generated by the single airbag without liquid bladder is about 1.02 N (Fig. 4a). Longer inflation time is required to achieve maximum force after wearing FlowGlove, and the results of Test 2 indicated that the time of deflation is shorter than the inflation, which means that the hand can feel the pressure disappear when the air is deflated. By comparing the pressure on the palm and the back of the hand, we found that the force added at the back of the hand was slightly larger than the palm, and the maximum pressure detected at the back of the hand was about 9.21 N (Fig. 4c). This is because there is also the weight from the liquid bag on the back of the hand. Our findings from Study 1 indicated that the combination of pneumatic and liquid could produce water pressure on the hand and increase the pressure effect. The pressure on the back of the hand is greater than that on the palm. The liquid bag will affect the inflatable effect of the airbag, and the airbag covered with the liquid bag will inflate for a longer time.

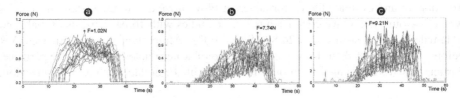

**Fig. 4.** a. Test 1, the hand is placed on the airbag and the FSR is placed between the hand and airbag. b. Test 2, FSR was placed between the palm and the liquid bladder. c. Test 3, FSR was placed between the liquid bladder and the back of the hand.

### 4.2 Study 2: Haptic Simulation in Different Hand Gestures

In this section, we compared the haptic simulation effects in three hand gestures: palm down, palm forward, and palm to side. The interactive scenario we used is that a whale is gradually approaching the player, and the player can perceive the pressure of the water flow caused by the whale swimming. We measured the force values at four positions on the palm under different gestures. Participants were required to wear the FlowGlove device to experience the haptic effect of the whale approaching in three gestures, and four FSRs were placed between the palm and the liquid bladder to detect pressure. The four positions were the same as the positions of 4 vibration actuators (Fig. 3b). In the test, every participant maintained the hand posture and did not move.

**Result.** In the same VR scenario, FlowGlove supported different haptic feeling in different gestures. When the palm was down, the airbags 1, 2, 5, and 6 (Fig. 5a) were simultaneously inflated, and squeezing the liquid bladder to generate water force; then the airbags 3, 4, 7, and 8 (Fig. 5b) were inflated. During this process, the finger part felt the pressure first, as shown in Fig. 6a, the force values of A and B are larger than C and D. After that, the rest of the hand can sense the pressure, the force values of C and D are larger than A and B. This haptic effect can be used to simulate the experience that the whale is getting closer to the user.

**Fig. 5.** When the whale is approaching, (a) (b) palm down, the airbags 1, 2, 5, 6 are inflated, then airbags 3, 4, 7, 8 are inflated; (c) palm forward, the airbags 5, 6, 7, 8 are inflated.

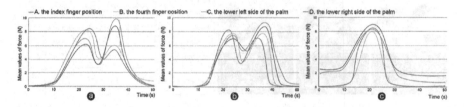

**Fig. 6.** Mean force values of 4 positions. The positions of A, B, C, and D are same as the positions of 4 vibration actuators. a. palm down; b. palm forward. c. palm to side.

When the palm was forward, the 5, 6, 7, and 8 airbags (Fig. 5c) were inflated and the palm was under pressure. Figure 6b shows that data of C and D is larger than A and B. This is because when the palm is straight forward, the water in the liquid bladder flows to the bottom to press the palm with the effects of gravity.

When the palm faced to the side, seem like palm down (Fig. 5a, b), the airbags 1, 2, 5, and 6 were first inflated, and then the airbags 3, 4, 7, and 8 were inflated. When 1, 2, 5, and 6 were inflated, these 4 FSR values all increase (Fig. 6c). When 3, 4, 7, and 8 were inflated, the pressure felt by the hand was strong, while the force of the A, B positions can also feel pressure under the water flow.

## 5  Application

To explore applications for FlowGlove, we built several scenes according to the Ocean Rift [36] VR game and Poly webpage [37]. The VR scenes were set to explore the seabed. Players can swim freely in the sea and interact with the ocean creatures.

FlowGlove will provide corresponding haptic feedback. Players need to wear the VR device (HTC VIVE) and our FlowGlove prototype in the game. We invited 12 users to experience our prototype to elicit qualitative feedback on our device and their haptic experience.

## 5.1  Underwater Moving

This application highlights the ability of FlowGlove to render the underwater moving haptic. In this scene, the player wore FlowGlove in his left hand and took the standard controller in his right hand. Pull the trigger to turn on the moving mode to explore the underwater environment freely (Fig. 7a). Both the standard controller and the Flow-Glove can control the direction of the scene, and the player's position was reflected by the virtual hand in the picture. FlowGlove provided haptic feedback based on the player's gesture and motion (Fig. 7d). For example, when the user performed a dive down interaction with the palm down gesture, the 5, 6, 7, and 8 airbags were inflated, squeezing the liquid bladder and the palm. The system would stop inflating while releasing the trigger so that the player can stop diving.

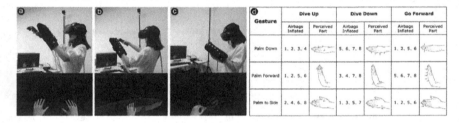

**Fig. 7.** Application scenes of the FlowGlove based on an ocean VR game: a. underwater moving; b. interact with the whale; c. catch one fish. d. The force perceived parts of hand in different gestures when moving underwater.

## 5.2  Interaction with the Creature

This application is to reflect the liquid sensation with vibration. In this VR scene, a whale swam near the player, and the player could interact with it through FlowGlove by moving hand closer and petting the whale (Fig. 7b). The corresponding hand operation was that the index finger repeatedly pressed the membrane switch to trigger the vibration actuators A and B (Fig. 3b) to work on the liquid bladder, and the finger can sense the vibration of the water flow to simulate the feeling of petting the whale. When the player stopped pressing the membrane switch, the vibration actuators would stop working.

Players can also capture fish through FlowGlove: move the hand close to the fish, then long-press the membrane switch to catch the fish (Fig. 7c). Then the four vibration actuators can work together, and the whole palm can feel the vibration to simulate the experience of catching one fish. If the player releases the membrane switch, the fish will escape from the palm. If the player holds the membrane switch and throws the fish to the whale, the fish will be eaten.

## 5.3  User Feedback

To better understand the performance of our device, we invited an additional 12 users (8 male, 4 female) from our university who had not tried the device before to provide feedback on its use. All 12 participants had the VR experience, and 5 of 12 had the water-related VR experience. We wanted to understand how our FlowGlove device compared to the standard HTC VIVE controller (off-shelf). During the study, participants tried two of our example applications: the underwater moving scene and the interaction with the whale scene. Before the study, users would get an introduction to the device and the head-mounted display.

They were allowed to get used to our equipment in a simple tutorial scenario. Over the next thirty minutes, participants tried the two scenes using both our device and the standard HTC VIVE controller. Participants explored the scenarios and then provided feedback on their experiences through semi-structured interviews. Our questions focused on the haptic experience, and we also conducted a test to evaluate the device's usability. Participants were asked, "How well did the FlowGlove match your haptic impression of the liquid scene," and rated the usability of the device on a 5-point Likert scale. 6 participants experienced each scene with HTC VIVE firstly and then worn the FlowGlove and the VIVE controller. Another 6 participants experienced each scene with FlowGlove firstly and then worn the VIVE controller and FlowGlove.

Participants were very interested in our design and were pleasantly surprised by the whole experience. 8 users said that when they used FlowGlove, they felt the flow of water and the cool sense, which provided a more realistic haptic. In the Underwater Moving scene, P6 commented that "FlowGlove made me feel the pressure of water when I was moving under the sea"; P2 pointed out that the haptic perception matched his movement, which made him feel that the operation was functional. In the scene of interaction with the whale, 1 participant said that the petting of the whale was unreal because the vibration feeling was strong, but the experience of catching fish was enjoyable. 3 of 12 users said that FlowGlove was heavy, and they felt tired when worn for a long time, and 1 user said that he was not used to wearing our device with his left hand and operating the controller with the right hand, which would decrease the experience.

The haptic feeling of our device is better than the standard controller. As shown in Fig. 8, FlowGlove could provide better water immersion sense ($M = 4.50$) with the liquid bladder wrapped the hand. The sense of water force ($M = 4.00$) and cold feeling ($M = 4.40$) are also better than the standard controller. However, the operation experience of FlowGlove ($M = 3.30$) is worse than the standard one ($M = 4.30$). Responses of Wilcoxon signed-rank tests showed that these differences were significant for the Operation Experience ($Z = 2.76$, $p = 0.006$), Water Force Feeling ($Z = 3.13$, $p = 0.002$), Water Vibration Feeling ($Z = 2.83$, $p = 0.005$), Water Immersion Sense ($Z = 3.15$, $p = 0.002$), and Cold Feeling ($Z = 3.11$, $p = 0.002$).

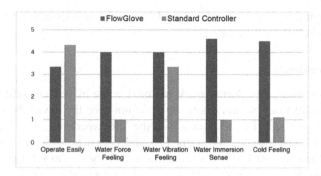

**Fig. 8.** Comparison of FlowGlove and the standard controller on the liquid sensation experience. The results showed that the haptic experience of FlowGlove is better than the standard controller but weaker at operation.

## 6   Discussion, Limitation and Future Work

FlowGlove is an attempt of the liquid sensation in the VR scene. It transcends the visual experience and explores a variety of haptic sensations that can be added to the VR experience. The system mainly consists of the liquid bladder, pneumatic actuation, and vibration module, which make the entire device somewhat bulky and can be fatigued for long-term wear. We use cold water circulation to keep the lower temperature of the water in the liquid bladder. This also provides new applications for game design. For example, it can change the liquid temperature according to the interaction scenarios. In the future, we will improve the cooling system and optimize the pneumatic actuation to allow for a free experience and rich haptic perception.

It is unsurprised that the FlowGlove system does not afford the full functions of the standard controller. But in this paper, our device focuses on the liquid sensation, and the device can achieve more functions using the standard controller. However, when users use the FlowGlove device only, it can also afford the basic functions.

The system will send instructions when the user presses the switch, and the membrane switch and finger would also be squeezed simultaneously when the airbag is inflated, possibly erroneously triggering the membrane switch. It is just a potential problem now. We have not seen this phenomenon in the current experimental tests. In the future, we will make targeted experiments to improve this problem.

The system's eight airbags can be operated independently and synchronously, and each airbag is sized to $110 \times 70$ mm due to the limitation of the valve. This size can be reduced in the future so that a greater number of airbags can be distributed for more accurate target position pressure sensing. Moreover, each airbag can achieve multiple effects of different inflation speeds, which will require complex design implementations.

We will continue to delve into improving the experience, operability, and usability of the current prototype to create a better immersive liquid sensation. We will also study the specific range of pressure values for each haptic effect to provide a more realistic haptic experience. In the future, FlowGlove is expected to offer more haptic experiences, such as feelings of plants and shells. We will also make virtual liquid sensation research on other parts of the body, such as the head and neck. In the future, we will further explore the new applications of FlowGlove in education to help people have a better understanding of the water environment.

## 7   Conclusion

This paper introduces FlowGlove, a liquid-based wearable haptic interface that provides underwater pressure and vibration haptic sensations using pneumatic airbags, vibration motors, and liquid bladder. Compared to traditional technologies, this system offers underwater immersion, water flow, and lower temperature sensation on the hand haptic. To verify the efficiency of this approach, we have conducted a series of user studies and evaluated the haptic perception. FlowGlove can provide the liquid sensation in water-related VR scenes, which will be used in education and entertainment to help people have a rich experience and a good understanding of the water environment.

**Acknowledgment.** We thank all the volunteers, and all publications support and staff, who wrote and provided helpful comments on previous versions of this document. This research was supported by the National Natural Science Foundation of China (No. 51675476).

## References

1. Zhao, Y., et al.: Enabling people with visual impairments to navigate virtual reality with a haptic and auditory cane simulation. In: Proceedings of the 2018 CHI Conference on Human Factors in Computing Systems, Montreal QC, Canada, pp. 1–14. ACM (2018)
2. Delazio, A., Nakagaki, K., Klatzky, R.L., Hudson, S.E., Lehman, J.F., Sample, A.P.: Force jacket: pneumatically-actuated jacket for embodied haptic experiences. In: Proceedings of the 2018 CHI Conference on Human Factors in Computing Systems, Montreal QC, Canada, pp. 1–12. ACM (2018)
3. Han, T., Anderson, F., Irani, P., Grossman, T.: HydroRing: supporting mixed reality haptics using liquid flow. In: Proceedings of the 31st Annual ACM Symposium on User Interface Software and Technology, Berlin, Germany, pp. 913–925. ACM (2018)
4. Abtahi, P., Follmer, S.: Visuo-haptic illusions for improving the perceived performance of shape displays. In: Proceedings of the 2018 CHI Conference on Human Factors in Computing Systems, Montreal QC, Canada, pp. 1–12. ACM (2018)
5. Yamashita, S., Zhang, X., Rekimoto, J.: AquaCAVE: augmented swimming environment with immersive surround-screen virtual reality. In: Proceedings of the 29th Annual Symposium on User Interface Software and Technology, Tokyo, Japan, pp. 183–184. ACM (2016)
6. Zhang, W., Tan, C.T., Chen, T.: A safe low-cost HMD for underwater VR experiences. In: Proceedings of the SIGGRAPH ASIA 2016 Mobile Graphics and Interactive Applications, Macau, China, pp. 1–2. ACM (2016)
7. Osone, H., Yoshida, T., Ochiai, Y.: Optimized HMD system for underwater vr experience. In: Cheok, A.D., Inami, M., Romão, T. (eds.) ACE 2017. LNCS, vol. 10714, pp. 451–461. Springer, Cham (2018). https://doi.org/10.1007/978-3-319-76270-8_31

8. Jain, D., et al.: Immersive terrestrial scuba diving using virtual reality. In: Proceedings of the 2016 CHI Conference Extended Abstracts on Human Factors in Computing Systems, San Jose, USA, pp. 1563–1569. ACM (2016)
9. Liao, Y.Y., Hong, Y.F., Han, P.H., Ko, J.C.: LiquidMask: utilizing liquid-based haptic for multiple tactile sensation in immersive virtual reality. In: Proceedings of the ACM SIGGRAPH 2019 Virtual, Augmented, and Mixed Reality, Los Angeles, USA, p. 1. ACM (2019)
10. Uragaki, K., Matoba, Y., Toyohara, S., Koike, H.: Sand to water: manipulation of liquidness perception with fluidized sand and spatial augmented reality. In: Proceedings of the 2018 ACM International Conference on Interactive Surfaces and Spaces, Tokyo, Japan, pp. 243–252. ACM (2018)
11. Rietzler, M., Geiselhart, F., Frommel, J., Rukzio, E.: Conveying the perception of kinesthetic feedback in virtual reality using state-of-the-art hardware. In: Proceedings of the 2018 CHI Conference on Human Factors in Computing Systems, Montreal QC, Canada, pp. 1–13. ACM (2018)
12. Schorr, S.B., Okamura, A.M.: Fingertip Tactile devices for virtual object manipulation and exploration. In: Proceedings of the 2017 CHI Conference on Human Factors in Computing Systems, Denver, USA, pp. 3115–3119. ACM (2017)
13. Chinello, F., Malvezzi, M., Pacchierotti, C., Prattichizzo, D: Design and development of a 3RRS wearable fingertip cutaneous device. In: Proceedings of the 2015 IEEE International Conference on Advanced Intelligent Mechatronics (AIM), Busan, pp. 293–298. IEEE (2015)
14. Kim, H., Yi, H., Lee, H., Lee, W.: HapCube: a wearable tactile device to provide tangential and normal pseudo-force feedback on a fingertip. In: Proceedings of the 2018 CHI Conference on Human Factors in Computing Systems, Montreal, QC, Canada, pp. 1–13. ACM (2018)
15. Benko, H., Holz, C., Sinclair, M., Ofek, E.: NormalTouch and TextureTouch: high-fidelity 3D haptic shape rendering on handheld virtual reality controllers. In: Proceedings of the 29th Annual Symposium on User Interface Software and Technology, Tokyo, Japan, pp. 717–728. ACM (2016)
16. Bermejo, C., Hui, P.: A survey on haptic technologies for mobile augmented reality (2017)
17. Culbertson, H., Walker, J.M., Raitor, M., Okamura, A.M.: WAVES: a wearable asymmetric vibration excitation system for presenting three-dimensional translation and rotation cues. In: Proceedings of the 2017 CHI Conference on Human Factors in Computing Systems, Denver, USA, pp. 4972–4982. ACM (2017)
18. Konishi, Y., Hanamitsu, N., Outram, B., Minamizawa, K., Mizuguchi, T., Sato, A.: Synesthesia suit: the full body immersive experience. In: Proceedings of the ACM SIGGRAPH 2016 VR Village, Anaheim, California, p. 1. ACM (2016)
19. Israr, A., Poupyrev, I.: Tactile brush: drawing on skin with a tactile grid display. In: Proceedings of the SIGCHI Conference on Human Factors in Computing Systems, Vancouver, BC, Canada, pp. 2019–2028. ACM (2011)
20. He, L., Xu, C., Xu, D., Brill, R.: PneuHaptic: delivering haptic cues with a pneumatic armband. In: Proceedings of the 2015 ACM International Symposium on Wearable Computers, Osaka, Japan, pp. 47–48. ACM (2015)
21. Gohlke, K., Hornecker, E., Sattler, W.: Pneumatibles: exploring soft robotic actuators for the design of user interfaces with pneumotactile feedback. In: Proceedings of the TEI 2016: Tenth International Conference on Tangible, Embedded, and Embodied Interaction, Eindhoven, Netherlands, pp. 308–315. ACM (2016)
22. Al Maimani, A., Roudaut, A.: Frozen suit: designing a changeable stiffness suit and its application to haptic games. In: Proceedings of the 2017 CHI Conference on Human Factors in Computing Systems, Denver, USA, pp. 2440–2448. ACM (2017)

23. Takahashi, N., et al.: Sense-roid: emotional haptic communication with yourself. In: Virtual Reality International Conference (VRIC 2011), pp. 6–8 (2011)
24. Teh, J.K.S., Cheok, A.D., Peiris, R.L., Choi, Y., Thuong, V., Lai, S.: Huggy Pajama: a mobile parent and child hugging communication system. In: Proceedings of the 7th International Conference on Interaction Design and Children, Chicago, USA, pp. 250–257. ACM (2008)
25. Jansen, Y., Karrer, T., Borchers, J.: MudPad: localized tactile feedback on touch surfaces. In: Proceedings of the Adjunct Proceedings of the 23nd Annual ACM Symposium on User Interface Software and Technology, New York, USA, pp. 385–386. ACM (2010)
26. Liu, Y., Davidson, R., Taylor, P.: Touch sensitive electrorheological fluid based tactile display. Smart Mater. Struct. 14(6), 1563–1568 (2005)
27. Davidson, R., Liu, Y., Taylor, P.: Investigation of the touch sensitivity of ER fluid based tactile display. Smart Struct Mater. 1, 92–99 (2005)
28. Schmitz, M., Leister, A., Dezfuli, N., Riemann, J., Müller, F., Mühlhäuser, M.: Embedding liquids into 3d printed objects to sense tilting and motion. In: Proceedings of the 2016 CHI Conference Extended Abstracts on Human Factors in Computing Systems, San Jose, USA, pp. 2688–2696. ACM (2016)
29. Follmer, S., Leithinger, D., Olwal, A., Cheng, N., Ishii, H.: Jamming user interfaces: programmable particle stiffness and sensing for malleable and shape-changing devices. In: Proceedings of the 25th Annual ACM Symposium on User Interface Software and Technology, Cambridge, USA, pp. 519–528. ACM (2012)
30. Lu, Q., Mao, C., Wang, L., Mi, H.: LIME: liquid metal interfaces for non-rigid interaction. In: Proceedings of the 29th Annual Symposium on User Interface Software and Technology, Tokyo, Japan, pp. 449–452. ACM (2016)
31. Yoshimoto, S., et al.: Haptic canvas: dilatant fluid based haptic interaction. In: Proceedings of the ACM SIGGRAPH 2010 Emerging Technologies, Los Angeles, USA, pp. 1–1. ACM (2010)
32. Cheng, C.H., et al.: GravityCup: a liquid-based haptics for simulating dynamic weight in virtual reality. In: P Proceedings of the 24th ACM Symposium on Virtual Reality Software and Technology, Tokyo, Japan, pp. 1–2. ACM (2018)
33. Hu, A.Z., Janzen, R., Lu, M.H., Mann, S.: Liquid jets as logic-computing fluid-user-interfaces. In: Proceedings of the on Thematic Workshops of ACM Multimedia 2017, California, USA, pp. 469–476. ACM (2017)
34. Sea Water Temperaturel, https://baike.baidu.com/item/%E6%B5%B7%E6%B0%B4%E6%B8%A9%E5%BA%A6/4756271?fr=aladdin. Accessed 13 Dec 2019
35. Force Sensing Resistor, https://www.interlinkelectronics.com/. Accessed 18 Apr 2019
36. Ocean Rift, https://store.steampowered.com/app/422760/Ocean_Rift/. Accessed 13 Dec 2019
37. Whale, https://poly.google.com/view/5p9B6IebY-A. Accessed 11 Dec 2019

# Tableware: Social Coordination Through Computationally Augmented Everyday Objects Using Auditory Feedback

Yanjun Lyu[1,2]([✉]), Brandon Mechtley[1,2]([✉]), Lauren Hayes[1]([✉]),
and Xin Wei Sha[1,2]([✉])

[1] School of Arts, Media + Engineering,
Arizona State University, Tempe, AZ, USA
{ylyul6,bmechtley,lauren.s.hayes,xinwei.sha}@asu.edu
[2] Synthesis Center, Arizona State University, Tempe, AZ, USA

**Abstract.** This research develops a novel way of rethinking cultural and social behavior using computationally augmented artifacts. These 'instruments' provide various types of auditory feedback when manipulated by certain actions within social contexts, such as a bar or dining space. They foster affective social engagement through the habitual and explorative actions that they afford in everyday contexts, and their resulting auditory feedback. The goal is not only to observe how social interactions are affected by the manipulation of augmented artifacts, but also to observe how the sounds and manipulations affect psycho-sociological [1] changes towards more collaborative social relations during the processes of participatory sense-making [2]. In this paper, we present: a) a study of dynamic social interaction and how we instrumented tangible artifacts to reflect and induce engagement, b) a literature review that provides background for our design methodology, c) 'vocal prototyping'–a responsive media technique for developing action-sonic mappings, d) our experimental prototype based on this design methodology.

**Keywords:** Tangible user interaction · Computationally augmented interface · Participatory sense-making · Ensemble interaction · Social interaction · Dynamic of coordination · Engagement · Social cognition · Action-sonic coupling · Affective computing · Responsive media · Embodied interaction

## 1 Introduction

The main thrust of our research is an exploration of the effects that augmenting and mediating human auditory perception may have on ad hoc social interaction by enabling people – who may start out as complete strangers – to cultivate meaningful relationships and friendships using familiar everyday objects that have been altered and enhanced for that purpose. The interdependent acoustic feedback resulting from the interaction of real computationally augmented artifacts in such a setting can contribute to a dynamic social engagement. *Tableware* consists of a set of ordinary objects–such as plates, glasses, chairs–that are equipped with electronics in order to sense how they are manipulated in space and time and to drive real-time media, including digital audio

© Springer Nature Switzerland AG 2020
C. Stephanidis et al. (Eds.): HCII 2020, LNCS 12429, pp. 332–349, 2020.
https://doi.org/10.1007/978-3-030-59987-4_24

synthesis, in response to the activity. For our project, we built a specific set of table-ware objects, namely, wine glasses that can double as musical instruments. These are intended to affect and inspire participants to interactively explore the dynamics of coordination [2, 3] while simultaneously allowing participants to progress in their understanding of others and thus help them to sustain interactions, form relations, and, ultimately, to interact more collaboratively and efficiently. Using these computational everyday objects, we seek to explore spontaneous social coordination, asking the following questions:

- How can social experiences be extended through explorative, improvisatory, sonic-action couplings?
- How do sounds influence users' feelings while they are performing tasks with an enhanced device instead of just passively listening?
- How do people relate to each other differently when their activities jointly affect and influence a resultant sonic texture?
- How is the dynamic transition from individual exploration to a social interaction successfully influenced by the coupling of sound and the manipulation?

Progress in learning and discovery is facilitated by coupling actions to sonic feedback in expected and intuitive ways as well as through designing unusual and novel relationships. This embodied, enactive interplay of participants and augmented objects elicits better social dynamics and helps raise people's awareness of conversational resonance, sympathy [1, 21, 22]. This is a socially engaging, non-verbal communication in which the interpersonal relations are articulated via sound and actions. The regulated coupling of sound and action as an extension of body language can help people build trust and empathy though ensemble fusion. In her work on enactive music cognition, author Hayes has developed bespoke techniques for interdisciplinary improvisation using both sound and movement to foster such collaborative behaviours and group dynamics (see [4]). While this work specifically concerns performance practice, the scaffolding of such collaborative interactions through technological means is crucial to fostering and developing such relationships.

It is necessary to clarify the following questions in order to illustrate why we choose the specific way of measuring the responsive sounds and physical objects as significant in the domain of social coordination:

- Why are everyday objects chosen instead of explicitly designed manufactured ones?
- Why is a certain object used–glasses in particular—as measuring instruments rather than forks/chairs/tables?
- Why is the data being collected from the interactions with the object, rather than directly from participants themselves through, for example, physiological data such as heartbeat, breath, brain activity, and so on, especially given that we are interested in gauging emotional factors of social interaction?

As Coccia [5] has observed, everyday objects absorb social, cultural, personal memories precisely because they have endured as commonplace, familiar things, and thus charge the spaces in which they are situated, with meaning and affect. That is, they participate in the production of the social meaning of the spaces in which they are used. He suggests that we never have a relationship with our homes as bare geometric spaces, because those geometries are abstractions, but instead we develop our lived experience in relation to the objects that furnish our everyday lives. Objects lend the otherwise imaginary and abstract space a sense of concrete reality–a room is merely a room until a bed *makes it a bedroom*. It is the dining table that makes a space the room for communal meals. The cup makes the surface it sits on a site of potential refreshment. The number of glasses on top of a table determines whether it is an individual, dyadic, or an ensemble social setting. Because it can be used in a more symbolic way such as libation or toasting—functions that are above the mere taking of food or drink–the glass is a more charged social symbol, especially when compared with other kinds of tableware, which are more pedestrian in their function. It is for this reason that we opt for glasses as the primary measuring instrument. We think of affective social engagement in terms of animating "boundary objects" [6, 34], that intertwine and co-articulate intentions of and interpretations by multiple parties emerging through use[1]. Moreover, we choose to augment objects so that they not only intermediate every day or canonicalized social activity in relation to ordinary use, but also to offer potentially extraordinary affordance [32] within a social scenario. For example, in our case, the ordinary glass and the wine within provides the affordance to drink or grab (habitual actions), while simultaneously affording the sonic responses caused by actions performed with the glass, actions that immediately transform it into an extra-ordinary object. Also, an empty glass may offer more possibilities for playful engagement than one containing liquid, where the sound feedback is caused by explorative actions. Boundary objects automatically register the relations between and among people in a social space. The objects we called *instruments* that regulate the relationship between the people and the sounds that are correlated to specific activities. By contrast, the way in which directly facilitating the participants' role in the process may not be not as explicit as our observations suggest–this data can be misleading–especially from an affective/emotional perspective.

We can also regard these boundary objects as "cultural probes" [29] that make tangible the enactment of social relations among a group of people. Cultural probes such as what we have built have been employed in design research since the 1990's [30]. In our work, by augmenting ordinary tableware with motion sensors and gesturally modulated, computationally synthesized sound, we can precisely calibrate the extraordinariness of the 'voicing' of their movement and vary the mapping from movement or people's relational activity to sound as extra-linguistic sonic field correlated to their activity. Most importantly, computational control allows experimentalists and the participants to repeat the effect in a reproducible way to gain experiential knowledge. This approach is informed by Satinder Gill's work on *tacit engagement* and collective, relational engagement via embodied skilled practices [11].

---

[1] In Leigh Star and Griesemer's formulation: "Boundary objects are objects which are both plastics enough to adapt to local needs and constraints of the several parties employing them, yet robust enough to maintain a common identity across sites. They are weakly structured in common use and become strongly structured in individual-site use. They have different meanings in different social worlds, but their structure is common enough to more than one world to make them recognizable, a means of translation. The creation and management of boundary objects is key in developing and maintaining coherence across intersecting social worlds." [34, p 393].

Based on our research, our prototyping extends from single dyadic interaction forms–which was discussed in [7]–to larger scale ensemble social models. By 'ensemble' we mean that the experience involves more than two subjects that cannot be reduced to individual or dyadic interaction. A simple example would be something like an "All for one! And one for all!" salute. A more subtle one could be seen in the continuous field of tensions, relaxations and propensities at play during a performance of a musical ensemble (see [33]). The key is the mapping of habitual and explorative actions and the evolution of their impact as they fluctuate from isolated atomic experience to ensemble experience. From an enactive point of view, by dyad (two autonomous agents) and ensemble interaction we mean the process of actively exploring and influencing actions toward some social environment based on embodied skills and generating new or meaningful interactions [8]. For example, in our case, by perceiving the other's actions and acquiring resultant sounds to react to, similar meaningful performative reactions will be generated and incorporated synchronously. In forwarding this view, Fuchs and De Jaegher proposed the idea of "enactive inter-subjectivity," [8, p341] a variation of interaction theory where social understanding is thought to be created through coordination between two or more embedded agents, which they described as "mutual incorporation." [8, p341]

We are interested in designing everyday spaces to more adequately enable situations of conviviality[2] and interaction involving groups of people who may or may not know each other, who may or may not share a common social or cultural background. To that end, we study everyday settings where people are already gathered socially, such as when taking refreshment–food and drink–together in a shared, perhaps public space such as a dining room, cafe, or restaurant. We are interested in how feelings of caring and empathy, and conviviality may be mediated even when people do not share enough of a common epistemic context to speak the same language. Knowing that sonic nuance–such as 'tone of voice'–and ambient sound can greatly affect the felt or perceived meaning of an action [9–11] and the sense-making of a lived experience, we ask: how can the extra-linguistic sonic modalities of mediation in the course of social dining or drinking enable (or hinder) the emergence of sense[3], more pointedly, the sense of care or conviviality of the social event?

In Sect. 2, we discuss related works which present different methods to facilitating human-human engagement in socially rich contexts and which also influence our research method. Section 3 presents more specific research methodology for discussing social interaction from the perspective of both individual experience and collective experience, where we incorporate augmentation logic to accommodate various social forms. Section 4 describes a sampling of experimental outcomes and a general mapping primitives and more future considerations and suggestions will be presented in the conclusion.

---

[2] We thank and acknowledge Shomit Barua for this formulation in terms of conviviality [28].

[3] Where we use "sense" as a verb, we explicitly take it to mean the way a human (or a living organism) takes stock of its relation to its ambient. We take a Deleuzian interpretation of the noun sense as the bundle of "processes of [differentiation], transformation, resistance or appropriation inflicted on a thing." [24, p. 10]

## 2   Related Works

Auditory displays are increasingly found in everyday products, due to advances in microfabrication and embedded computation. Sound quality studies provide, indirectly, some insights into the relationship between acoustical features of sounds and emotions in relation to different spaces. Such conceptual innovations can serve psycho functional purposes, such as making an electric car emit sound to affect emotional appeal, for example. Electric vehicles are completely silent, and by adding an appropriate 'roar', the user's perceived power of the engine is enhanced. Auditory displays therefore can similarly play an important role in stimulating emotional responses before, during, and after user interaction. Rafaeli and Vilnai-Yavetz [14] present a model to demonstrate factors that induce emotion through the use of artifacts, describing "how the artifact fits an ascribed function or how usable it is, aesthetic qualities, such as visual color, sonic timbre, symbolism, which relates to how the artifact is interpreted in a certain cultural context." [1, p1] Discussing the computationally-augmented glass, entitled *The Flops* [1], Lemaitre states how such augmented artifacts can elicit emotion based on the quality of sound and the difficulties of the manipulation that will produce the sounds. Their user study monitors twenty-five participants' feelings from three arousal, valence, and dominant scales by producing various sounds from the single action of pouring the glass. They concluded that a pleasant sound paired with simple action will encourage more engagement in the activity. The interplay of action and sound determines the level of engagement that transpires. This study is useful to us as a good theoretical and empirical example of research that supports the appeal and utility of this relationship between sound and action.

Van Reekum, Johnston and colleagues [15, 16] also focus on how to elicit emotional responses through the use of computational artifacts. In their report, they used a computer game to create affective engagement in adolescents. Successfully completing a level of the game (goal-conducive event) or alternately, losing a ship (goal obstructive event) were operationalized. Pleasant and unpleasant sounds associated with these events were used to measure the agreeableness of the game experience. Their results confirmed that the addition and manipulation of goal conduciveness and pleasant feedback affect psychological changes positively during the process. This concept of creating goal consistency can also be used as a method in a social setting, where sound and manipulation in some way persuade participants to cooperate in order to achieve the goal consistency associated with the rewards or losses [17–19]. Our work differs from Van Reekum et al. in that our participants do not have to have a specific task-oriented goal.

*The Flops*: Negotiating Between Habitual and Expressive Gestures [20] is a study that details another example of sonic manipulation using an interactive artifact. It enumerates eight habitual actions associated and their corresponding effects of sounds. These actions involve both habitual and non-habitual actions. They provide a way to interact with the designed glasses–3D printed–through habitual gestures, resulting in different types of sounds. For example, a non-habitual gesture will produce an unexpected sound, such as the sound of wind or of birds. When the movement is synchronous, the same light and sound patterns are displayed. For example, the connective sound might become stronger as the users perform exploratory actions. A game-based sonic interaction can be used as a method to induce strangers' engagement with each other in public scenarios. For example, the intensity and pitch of a sound or a light will vary accordingly–'rewarding' or 'punishing'–in response to the same action, failure to act, or error.

*GameLunch*: Forging a Dining Experience Through Sound [21] is a sonically augmented dining table. The project investigates the closed loop between interaction, sound, and emotion by exploiting the power and flexibility of physically based interactive sound models. Compared to *Flops*, *GameLunch* uses a more paradoxical approach by making the user encounter unexpected and often contradicting sonic feedback while performing ordinary dining actions such as cutting, slicing, pouring, and so on. The authors note the importance of environmental sound in everyday acts. They introduce a "per absurdum" [21, p2] aspect. For example, the action of pouring a liquid into a decanter will produce a continuous friction/braking sonic feedback unrelated to the sound we usually associate with fluids. A contradictory perception of the flow of the liquid alters the user's reaction and helps her challenge her preconceptions. *GameLunch* defined an innovative method for thinking about contradictory sonic feedback produced by habitual actions, challenging human preconceptions and material perception in order to attract their attention and curiosity, which stimulates emotional impact and makes for more engaged social settings.

In antecedent work by Fantauzza et al. [27] created instrumented 'hacky-sacks' and clothing that sonified *ad hoc* gestures, and could be used to augment non-verbal, embodied interaction between people[4]. This 'softwear' was part of a stream of work in expressive wearables that first and foremost could be felt and treated as jewelry or clothing, rather than as electronic devices. We used these *softwear* to study human-human engagement in socially rich contexts. In addition to the performative applications, *softwear* and actors were used as social/cultural probes to study the dynamics of engagement and disengagement.

In another antecedent work, Krzyzaniak et al. [35] synthesized music varying as a function of degree of correlation between time-series of orientations reported by inertial sensors worn by dancers. We conjectured that (1) orientation of some parts of the body could better signal intention than simply position or velocity which could reflect many non-intentional factors, and (2) correlation of time-series of orientations from corresponding body parts could perhaps index joint intention, as an alternative measure of synchrony. Correlation measures, by design, can detect, temporally shifted patterns that nonetheless have some parallel form; thus, they could serve to detect a synchronizing *passage* of intention from one person to another, even if the bodies may exhibit non-isomorphic forms and non-parallel velocities in any given instant.

---

[4] https://vimeo.com/tml/ubicompdemo (3:57- 5:40), https://vimeo.com/tml/ubicomp

# 3   Research Methodology

## 3.1   *In Situ* Experiential Research

The deep problem of intersubjectivity is to extend accounts of individual experience to accounts of collective experience and qualities of experience that are functions of relations or even of ambient situations *that cannot be reduced to unidimensional relations between two subjects* (such as distance, age, or some abstract social index like "is-parent-of"). Therefore, we design our augmentation logics to accommodate ensemble as well as dyadic and individual activities, and to accommodate concurrent as well as responsive action.

We underline that our research methodology is predicated on understanding social, experiential, affective engagement mediated by ordinary objects augmented by computational media, used in thick, *in situ*, ordinary social settings. Author Sha has established an antecedent Topological Media Lab[5] to study how ordinary gestures and environments, through various means of socio/technological/artistic augmentation, may constitute sense and meaning or affective relation in the course of ad hoc ordinary as well as marked [26] or rehearsed activity [12, 13]. Specifically, we ask: "How can ordinary actions in everyday environments acquire symbolic charge? What makes some environments enlivening and others deadening?" [12, p63] This *in situ* experiential approach aligns with a scientific methodology of observing how people and technical objects (see Simondon [25]) enact social-aesthetic experiences in everyday, ordinary settings. Instead of having people manipulate stimulus-action-response cycles in abstract laboratory conditions, we insert our everyday objects-cum-instruments into the thick context of ordinary social situations. By thick, we refer to the "rich magma of social, imaginative, and erotic fields within which people play even in ordinary situations, situations in which we perform without first analyzing and cutting up our experiences into analytic layers." [36, p38] We also are "mindful of Clifford Geertz's sociological and anthropological approach to describing culture in all of its rich social patterns and dynamics without orthogonalizing it a priori into categories and schemata that we would bring to bear on that culture. The dynamical potential field of experience should be designed in a pre-orthogonalized way by the composers and enjoyed by the participants without requiring that they make any cognitive model of their world in order to perform in it." [13, p72] By algorithmically controlling the computationally augmented behavior of those objects, we can precisely and reproducibly vary their behavior in concert with how people manipulate them in *ad hoc* and unconstrained yet conditioned activity. This embedded approach informs our research methodology, as described in the section on prototyping process.

## 3.2   Social Interaction

De Jaegher and Di Paolo [3] state that social interaction plays an important role in facilitating social cognition and motivates novel experimental designs from embodied

---

[5] Topological Media Lab, 2001- present, http://topologicalmedialab.net

and enactivist perspectives. De Jaegher, in *Participatory Sense-making* [2], states that the interactive process itself often has an affective dimension in the sense that it allows us to feel varying degrees of connectedness with others. It is also a crucial factor in deciding whether to sustain the social interaction itself when forming social relationships. Social cognition [3], a general term used to describe cognition involving the understanding of others' emotion, intention, and action in forming relations, sustains these interactions. But, importantly, social cognition is more than just understanding *of* others; rather, it is understanding *with* others. Fuchs and De Jaegher [8] proposed the idea of "enactive intersubjectivity," [8, p341] a variation of interaction theory in which social understanding is thought to be created through coordinated interactions between two embodied agents. From a phenomenological perspective, they called this "mutual incorporation." Mutual incorporation [8] is the reciprocal interaction of agents where each agent reaches out to embody the other in some tangible way. In other words, action from oneself and reaction from others under a certain social setting are reciprocal. The effect of an action directly prompts a reaction in response to its effect on the other. It is possible to say that the other person's action becomes incorporated into a participant's body schema in the sense that their perception and action are closely coordinated with the presence of it. These agents, of course, are not mutually incorporated from the start. Through the oscillation between matches, mismatches, in-phase and phase-delayed states, two bodies coordinate with each other, then start to present in a synchronized or choreographed manner. To accommodate non-isolatable, non-dyadic qualities of shared experience, our designs enable ensemble activity among any number of participants.

### 3.3 Dynamics of Coordination

The importance of being familiar with interactive processes has been highlighted in studies of dynamic coordination in dynamical system theory by Richardson and Shockley [22, 23]. Their respective work allows us to view interactions as processes extended in time with a rich structure that is only apparent at the relational level of the collective dynamic. Synchronization is an essential type of coordination, but it is not the *only* kind of coordination possible; many cases of appropriately patterned behaviour, such as mirroring, anticipation, imitation, and so on, are more general forms of coordination [2]. Another important distinction is that between concurrent coordination versus *call and response*, or more generally *responsive* coordination. Concurrent coordination requires a perfect synchronization. An example of this is when participants raise or set down their wine glasses together at the same time; that is, when they are performing the same actions. Responsive coordination, by contrast, has a much wider range of possibilities, as there are no such transitions from one strictly coherent state to another. Systems in responsive coordination do not entrain perfectly. Instead, they show phase attraction [2], which means that they tend to approach perfect synchrony, but in an inadvertent way. An example of this is when the host stands, raises a glass, and says "Auguri!" at which point everyone else raises their own glass and

Table 1. Design criteria in different social modes

| Dynamic Social Modes | Actions | Interaction Modes |
|---|---|---|
| Individual | **Habitual:** Drink, Slide, Tilt<br><br>**Explorative:** Tilting (four directions), Velocity (four directions), Horizontal / vertical movement, Circular swirling, Shaking | An explorative process allows participants to acquire knowledge through the individual sense-making process through the use of the augmented objects. |
| Dyad | Same as above | Imitation/ Mirroring: Two participants may mirror or imitate each other's action. |
| Dynamic of Coordination | Same as above | Call and Response:<br><br><br><br>Black dot represents the initiator of the action, and blue dots represent respondents. From left to right: Two people respond to two hosts' calls, one host actively calls an action to the other three, and three participants actively call an action to a person.<br><br>Concurrent:<br><br><br><br>Four participants do the same action at the same time, such as any of the habitual or explorative actions listed. |

responds with "Auguri!" in unison[6]. We borrowed the concept of dynamic forms of coordination from concurrent and responsive perspectives to use in our criteria to develop the design of our prototype below (see Table 1).

Our design makes use of three social modes: single, dyadic, and extended social coordination. We assume people rely on habitual action to interact with the object initially, but this is not prerequisite. These three modes do not necessarily have a prescribed sequence to follow during interaction and can occur out of order. The process is flexible. In order to give participants a sense of the interaction between themselves and the object through common actions, we introduce an individual interaction mode, which helps participants individually be mindful of the interaction with the computational object in question. Because we aim to facilitate understanding on a person-to-person level, the dyadic and social coordination modes feature and rely on sensorimotor coordination between people. Through their experience and relation with the object, participants acquire a sense of playfulness. They begin to discover the multiple forms of interaction that are possible, such as actions that correspond with each other, actions that mirror other actions, actions that change the timbral parameters of a sound, etc. The coordination of intentional activity in interaction affects individual sense-making and a new domain of social sense-making can take place, that is participatory sense-making [2]. By following the study of dynamic coordination, relative coordination can be interpreted through *call and response* (as a special case of phase attraction [2]). For example, in our four-person social setting, a) call and response coordination takes place when all participants do not act entirely synchronously, but a phase attraction exists such that their actions are patterned in such a way as to form a coherent social form; or b) *concurrent* coordination takes place when similar actions take place at the same time. For example, call and response coordination could take place when four participants move or tilt in the same direction and another two move or tilt in contrary directions. Each pair's action is concurrent, but the two pairs are acting in call and response.

The following section, prototyping process, will detail how we incorporate technology to generate the vocal prototyping of the generating sound to movement and movement to sound mappings.

## 4   Prototyping Process

Based on the research study of social dynamic interaction structure and incorporated technology, we propose the following questions to consider: What ideas or fragments are worth pursuing? How could we implement them with the technology? Without any contextual or previous instruction, how would participants start a conversation using the 'instrument' within the social setting? How might a particular vocalized sound be reinterpreted or generated during the process of participatory sense-making?

---

[6] Concurrent or responsive coordination, and synchronization are first approximations to the richer phenomena of coordination via rhythm as generalized, multidimensional or aperiodic, temporal form, in work by Garrett Johnson and the last author [31], and with Adrian Freed, Todd Ingalls, Julian Stein, Gabrielle Isaacs at Synthesis.

## 4.1 Technology and Mapping Overview

We want to recognize and respond to people's social need for engaging in collectively meaningful actions in the heat of social engagement, so it is important that our instruments can create appealing sound during freely improvised movement. To achieve this, we map sensor values from embedded sensors to real-time digital audio instruments. A wireless 3-axis fusion sensor (accelerometer, gyroscope, and orientation) is connected to a Feather M0[7] microcontroller and embedded into each glass. The microcontroller is programmed to simultaneously convert raw data into an Open Sound Control (OSC) data stream and send it via WIFI to a computer running Max/MSP, which maps sensor data to several digital synthesizers. The sound is played back through mini speakers which are embedded in the bar/table somewhere near the glass. All sensing features (floating point values, scaled 0–1) are transformed from raw data using low-level mathematical operations to map actions to sonic feedback. All these input values will directly control the parameters of the synthesizers. Each feature is directly mapped to one or more parameters of an instrument. This allows participants to freely explore new joint-actions. For example, freely moving in a horizontal/vertical way will additively combine two separate instances of sonic feedback produced by each independent action.

## 4.2 General Mapping Primitives

This section describes the transformations applied to the raw data in order to produce useful audio control signals and also describes the application of these control signals to specific sound generation strategies. Where possible, to allow for freely improvised movement, we develop mappings between raw sensor features and the audio instruments by defining a continuously valued feature vector with values normalized between 0 and 1. Using continuous mappings, and avoiding mutually exclusive mappings, affords more expressive, nuanced gestures that can deviate from any predefined schema, as might be memorized by a machine learning algorithm. Additionally, since the feature mappings ensure a wider coverage of the space of potential manipulations of the cups, participants are more able to freely improvise with the instrument using continuously nuanced movement rather than selecting among a finite set of sounds pre-designed by the experimentalist.

**IMU Sensors.** The BNO055 sensor[8] is programmed to send a UDP packet containing 9 feature values at a programmable frame rate to a configurable IP address and wireless network. We have found a frame rate of approximately 50 Hz to be most reliable with the least amount of latency or packet loss.

Specifically, we denote linear acceleration at timestep $t$, $a_t = a_{t,x}, a_{t,y}, a_{t,z}$, angular velocity about each axis, $\omega_t = \omega_{t,x}, \omega_{t,y}, \omega_{t,z}$, and absolute orientation, $R_t = R_{t,x}, R_{t,y}, R_{t,z}$.

---

[7] Adafruit Feather M0. https://www.adafruit.com/product/2772

[8] Adafruit BNO055 Absolute Orientation Sensor. https://learn.adafruit.com/adafruit-bno055-absolute-orientation-sensor

The acceleration and orientation of the cup is first calibrated to remove constant acceleration due to gravity and so that orientation can be defined with respect to the seated guest, facing forward, independent of which direction the sensor is facing. At the beginning of each session, the cups are placed on the table and average acceleration and orientation are computed over a short duration, to be subtracted from subsequent readings.

$$a'_t \equiv a_t - \frac{\sum_{i=1}^{C} a_i}{C} \tag{1}$$

$$R'_t \equiv R_t - \frac{\sum_{i=1}^{C} R_i}{C} \tag{2}$$

Derived quantities then include:

*Acceleration Magnitude.* Total acceleration magnitude is defined as the Euclidean norm of the linear acceleration vector:

$$AccelMagnitude \equiv \sqrt{a'_x2 + a'_y2 + a'_z2} \tag{3}$$

*Directional Acceleration.* We then define horizontal and vertical acceleration along each axis and acceleration in each direction in three-dimensional space:

$$AccelHorizontal \equiv a'_x, \tag{4}$$

$$AccelVertical \equiv a'_y, \tag{5}$$

$$AccelLeft \equiv \max(-a'_x, 0), \tag{6}$$

$$AccelRight \equiv \max(a'_x, 0), \tag{7}$$

$$AccelForward \equiv \max(a'_y, 0), \text{ and} \tag{8}$$

$$AccelBack \equiv \max(-a'_y, 0). \tag{9}$$

*Spin.* We define the orientation about the Z axis (orthogonal to the table) as the "Spin," scaled 0-1:

$$Spin \equiv \frac{R'_z}{360}. \tag{10}$$

*Tilt.* We also compute the angle of tilt away from an upright orientation as a continuous value between 0 and 1:

$$Tilt \equiv \frac{\max\left(R'_x, R'_y\right)}{90}. \tag{11}$$

*Tilt left, right, forward, and back.* We detect which direction the cup is tilted in by measuring un-calibrated acceleration along each axis to determine which axis is aligned with gravity:

$$TiltLeft \equiv Tilt \times \frac{\max(-a_x, 0)}{9.8}, \tag{12}$$

$$TiltRight \equiv Tilt \times \frac{\max(a_x, 0)}{9.8}, \tag{13}$$

$$TiltBack \equiv Tilt \times \frac{\max(-a_y, 0)}{9.8}, \tag{14}$$

$$TiltBack \equiv Tilt \times \frac{\max(a_y, 0)}{9.8}, \tag{15}$$

$$TiltHorizontal \equiv \max(TiltLeft, TiltRight), \text{ and} \tag{16}$$

$$TiltVertical \equiv \max(TiltForward, TiltBack). \tag{17}$$

*Circular Motion Detection.* We define circular motion as moving the cup in a circular pattern parallel to the plane of the table. This should result in no change in data from the gyroscope, as the orientation of the cup remains constant. We detect a continuously valued circular motion vector by training a continuously valued neural network that takes in a vector of the most recent N acceleration and angular velocity values with two continuously valued scalar outputs, *CircleClockwise* and *CircleCounterclockwise:*

$$Input_t \equiv a_{t-N,x}, a_{t-N,y}, a_{t-N,z}, \ldots, a_{t,x}, a_{t,y}, a_{t,z}. \tag{18}$$

For real-time gesture following using deep neural networks, we use the Wekinator [36] application, which allows training and real-time output over OSC. For training, we have used a variety of sizes and speeds of circular gestures over the course of five minutes of training.

(a) Scaled value should pass the threshold to the instrument

(b) Scaled feature value directly controls the instrument.

**Fig. 1.** Signal Flow-Direct Mapping

## 4.3 Manipulation to Sound to Manipulation

**Direct Mapping.** Each linear/non-linear movement is directly mapped to various synthesizers (see Fig. 1).

*Directional Acceleration to FM Synthesizer Coupling.* We map the magnitude of acceleration in each direction to a separate FM synthesizer, which has a unique, pre-determined carrier frequency. The acceleration values are then mapped directly (see Fig. 1(b)) to the harmonicity ratio and amplitude of the synthesizer. By modifying the harmonicity ratio as well as determining the amplitude by acceleration, we allow the participant to expressively control the timbral characteristics of the sound with the quality of their movement. This results in linear acceleration giving rise to four different sounds, depending on the direction of movement. For example, if a participant rapidly moves the cup back and forth horizontally or vertically, a continual sequence of two frequencies will be heard.

*Spin to Resonant Frequency Sweep.* The orientation of cup orthogonal to its base is mapped directly to two resonant bandpass filters filtering white noise input. The orientation is also mapped to amplitude, but it is mapped such that there is zero amplitude when the cup is facing forward (0°) and maximum amplitude when it is facing backward (180°). Since we map spin to amplitude using absolute orientation rather than change in orientation, this allows the participant to use the cup as a "dial," using more precise movement to tune the bandpass filter center frequency and amplitude of the instrument.

*Drinking (tilting back).* It will result in amplitude modulation producing a tremolo effect. We used the mapping of tilting back to start a drinking action sequence. In our direct mapping, we give a specific curve to amplitude. Two sounds are modulated by separate nonlinear curves which determine their amplitude as a function of tilt angle. In the first sound, the tilt, from starting to drink (slight tilt) until finishing drinking (>90°), controls the modulation rate and amplitude of a low frequency oscillator modulating the amplitude of a sinusoid with a pre-tuned frequency. A greater tilt angle will result in a louder, effervescent ('fizzier') sound. The second sound's maximum amplitude is reached at a specific angle which indicates that the drinking sequence is completed.

This sound's later presence in the drinking sequence causes a "surprise" at the end. Since this sound is only present during drinking, while there is liquid in the cup, this may impose scarcity on the instrument's use during play.

*Circular movement to granular synthesis modulation.* The detection value for circular movement from *Wekinator* is mapped to the amplitude, and the linear acceleration magnitude is mapped to the playback rate of a time-stretching granular synthesizer. A sliding window, of a predetermined width, advances throughout a sound at a given playback rate. The granular synthesizer stochastically samples from this region uniformly. Circularly sliding the cup more slowly or quickly will decrease or increase the playback rate, causing the instrument to play the sound back more slowly or quickly without decreasing or increasing its pitch.

**Concurrent Coordination.** We have created mappings for concurrent coordination between participants through simple expressions of the sensor features of multiple cups. As table one shows, we map two types of coordination: call-response and concurrent coordination. Simple concurrent coordination mappings can be achieved through expressions of multiple feature vectors between participants. For example, denoting the current tilt of the $n$-th cup as $Tilt_n$, a continuous value between 0 and 1 that indexes the concurrent tilting (or drinking) of cups between guests, could be expressed as $Tilt_1 \times Tilt_2 \times Tilt_3 \times Tilt_4$ (see Fig. 2), whereas a feature that maps asymmetric tilting between two groups of guests could be expressed as $Tilt_1 \times Tilt_2 \times (1 - Tilt_3) \times (1 - Tilt_4)$. These combined feature vectors can then be mapped to the amplitude of instruments that should play during synchronous action.

In future experiments, we have also considered detecting of synchronous and call-and-response action (see Table 1) between participants by using estimates of autocorrelation of the raw sensor values and derived features between cups, allowing us to detect phase differences between participants for call-and-response action and to map synchronous activity at different time scales. This method can also allow for more variability in how the movements are expressed between participants (such as moving left and right in synchrony, but with lower or greater force).

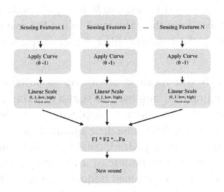

**Fig. 2.** Signal Flow - Combined Features Mapping

# 5  Conclusion and Further Work

The goal of our design criteria is to encourage participants to collectively explore, through a process of trial and error, an improvised orchestrated movement, creating unexpected, new sounds through the use of concurrent actions. In each of the experimental outcomes outlined above, we strove to maintain intuitive mappings between physical movement and sound. The mappings implemented were therefore intentionally simple. More complex mappings, which require careful, more nuanced consideration and thorough in situ playtesting should be explored in the future. The development of such mapping will be foundational for further investigation in the field, including measures of concurrent and responsive activity between participants.

Once a relationship between sound and ensemble movement is perceived, we ask if the activity articulates a social relation between the participants. And how can we then engage the participants in future social activity. A user-testing plan should anticipate these questions, especially from a perspective of sonic affect, as the agreeableness and playfulness of an activity will persuade participants to actively engage in more similar activities. From a technical perspective, the sensor electronics employed are small and relatively unobtrusive in order to minimize the amount by which the sensor board distracts from freely improvised movement or social activity. Finally, as we understand the potential space of social protocols of conviviality [28], we will enrich the suite of augmented tableware and related props or furniture together with possibly other ambient media modalities, such as variable haptic feedback or responsive lighting, in order to provide a more flexible environment for embodied social coordination.

**Acknowledgments.** For critical and technical support, we thank our research colleagues at the Synthesis Center and in the School of Arts, Media and Engineering at ASU: Shomit Barua, Assegid Kidane, Seth Thorn, Tejaswi Gowda, Connor Rawls, Todd Ingalls, and Peter Weisman.

# References

1. Lemaitre, G., et al.: Feelings elicited by auditory feedback from a computationally augmented artifact: the flops. IEEE Trans. Affect. Comput. 3(3), 335–348 (2012). https://doi.org/10.1109/t-affc

2. De Jaegher, H., Di Paolo, E.: Participatory Sense-Making. Phenomenol. Cogn. Sci. 6(4), 485–507 (2007). https://doi.org/10.1007/s11097-007-9076-9

3. De Jaegher, H., Di Paolo, E., Gallagher, S.: Can social interaction constitute social cognition? Trends Cogn. Sci. 14(10): 441–447 (2010). https://doi.org/10.1016/j.tocs

4. Hayes, L.: Beyond Skill Acquisition: Improvisation, Interdisciplinarity, and Enactive Music Cognition. Contemporary Music Review. Taylor & Francis, London (2019)

5. Coccia, E.: Reversing the New Global Monasticism. Fall Semester, 21, Apr. https://fallsemester.org/2020-1/2020/4/17/emanuele-coccia-escaping-the-global-monasticism (2020)

6. Fox, N.J.: Boundary Objects: Social Meanings and the Success of New Technologies. Sociology 45(1), 70–85 (2011)

7. Lyu, Y., Hayes, L.: Exploring social coordination through computationally augmented artifacts using auditory feedback. In: 26th International Symposium on Electronic, Montreal, Canada (accepted, 2020)
8. Tanaka, S.: Intercorporeality and Aida: developing an interaction theory of social cognition. Theory Psychol. **27**(3), 337–353 (2017)
9. Gendlin, E.T.: Experiencing and the Creation of Meaning: a philosophical and psychological approach to the subjective. Free Press of Glencoe, New York (1962)
10. Gendlin, E.T.: Thinking beyond patterns: Body, language and situations. Focusing Institute, Spring Valley (1991)
11. Gill, S.P.: Tacit engagement: beyond interaction. AI & Soc. **34**(1), 163 (2016). https://doi.org/10.1007/s00146-016-0681-4
12. Sha, X. W.: The Atelier-Lab as a Transversal Machine. Revue rancaise d'etudes americaines, pp. 62–78 (2011)
13. Sha, X.W., Freed, A., Navab, N.: Sound design as human matter interaction. Extended Abstracts on Human Factors in Computing Systems, April 2013, pp. 2009–2018. https://doi.org/10.1145/2468356.2468718
14. Rafaeli, A., Vilnai-Yavetz, I.: Instrumentality, aesthetics and symbolism of physical artifacts as triggers of emotion. Theoret. Issues Ergon. Sci. **5**(1), 91–112 (2004). https://doi.org/10.1080/1463922031000086735
15. Johnston, T., Van Reekum, C., Hird, K., Kirsner, K., Scherer, K.R.: Affective speech elicited with a computer game. Emotion **5**(4), 513–518 (2005)
16. Van Reekum, C., Johnston, T., Banse, R., Etter, A., Wehrle, T., Scherer, K.: Psychophysiological responses to appraisal dimensions in a computer game. Cogn. Emot. **18**(5), 663–668 (2004)
17. Kaiser, S., Edwards, T.: Multimodal emotions measurement in an interactive computer game: a pilot-study. In: Proceedings of the VIIIth Conference of the International Society for Research on Emotions, vol. 13, no. 1, pp. 19–124 (1999)
18. Ravaja, N., Timo, S., Jani, L., Kari, K, Mikko.: The psychophysiology of video gaming: phase emotional response to game events. In Proceedings of the Digital Game Research Association (DiGra)conference: changing views -World in play (2005)
19. Ravaja, N., Turpeinen, M., Saari, T., Puttonen, S., Jarvinen, L.: The psychophysiology of games bond: phasic emotional response to violent video games. Emotion **8**(1), 114–120 (2008)
20. Franinovic, K.: The Flops: Negotiating Between Habitual and Explorative Gestures. New Interfaces for Musical Expression (2011)
21. Polotti, P., Monache, S.D., Papetti, S., Rocchesso, D.: Gamelunch: forging a dining experience through sound. In: Proceeding of the Twenty- Sixth Annual CHI Conference Extended Abstracts on Human Factors in Computing Systems- CHI (2008). https://doi.org/10.1145/1358628.1358670
22. Shockley, K., Richardson, D.C., Dale, R.: Conversation and coordinative structures. Topics Cogn. Sci. **1**(2), 305–319 (2009)
23. Richardson, M.J., et al.: Rocking together: dynamics of intentional and unintentional interpersonal coordination. Hum. Movement Sci. **26**(6), 867–891 (2007)
24. Voss, D.: Deleuze's Rethinking of the Notion of Sense. Deleuze Stud. **7**(1), 1–25 (2003)
25. Gilbert, S.: On the Mode of Existence of Technical Objects. Translated by Cecile Malaspina and John Rogove, Minnesota (2015)
26. Kean, M.L.: Markedness. In International encyclopedia of linguistics, v. 2. Edited by W. Bright, pp. 390–391. Oxford University Press, Oxford (1992)
27. Fantauzza, J., Berzowska, J., Dow, S., Iachello, G., Sha, X.W.: Greeting Dynamics Using Expressive Softwear. Ubicomp (2003)

28. Barua, S., Lyu, Y.: Conviviality Cafe. Connectivity_Café (2020). http://synthesiscenter.net/projects/connectivity-cafe/(2019-2020)
29. Gaver, B., Dunne, T., Pacenti, E.: Cultural Probes. Interactions, Jan-Feb 21–29 (1999)
30. Graham, C., Rouncefield, M.: Probes and participation. In: Proceedings of the Tenth Anniversary Conference on Participatory Design, pp. 194–197(2008)
31. Sha, X.W., Johnson, G.L.: Rhythm and textural temporality: experience without subject and duration as effect. In: Crespi, P., Manghani, S. (eds.) Rhythm and Critique: Technics, Modalities, Practices,. Edinburgh (2020)
32. Rietveld, E., Kiverstein, J.: A rich landscape of affordances. Ecol. Psychol. **26**(4), 325–352 (2014)
33. Hayes, L.: Enacting Musical Worlds: Common Approaches to using NIMEs within both Performance and Person-Centred Arts Practices. In: Proceedings of the International Conference on New Interfaces for Musical Expression, pp. 299–302. Baton Rouge, USA (2015)
34. Leigh Star, S.: The structure of Ill-structured solutions: boundary objects and heterogeneous distributed problem solving. In: Hubs, M., Gasser, L. (eds.) Readings in Distributed Artificial Intelligence 3. Morgan Kaufmann, Menlo Park (1989)
35. Krzyzaniak, M., Anirudh, R., Venkataraman, V., Turaga, P., Sha, X.W.: Towards realtime measurement of connectedness in human movement. Movement and Computing (2015)
36. Sha, X.W.: Poiesis and Enchantment in Topological Matter. MIT Press, Hoboken (2013)

# Research on Interaction Models of Interactive Digital Art and Its Application in Designing User Control

Suyuan Pan(✉)

School of Media Arts and Communication,
Nanjing University of the Arts, Nanjing, China
pan_music@163.com

**Abstract.** In recent years, digital art forms such as digital image, electronic music, and virtual reality have resorted to various interactive technologies to enhance the control and presentation of artworks. Based on human's interactive behavior, this paper discusses the structural features and control behavior design of the common regional fixed-point interactive model, portable interactive model and wearable interactive model in digital art, and determines the basic model structure for the interactive control in different interactive models, so as to fix positions and make use of multiple forms of interaction, enhance the artistic expression of digital artworks under the premise of effective control.

**Keywords:** Digital art · Image art · Interactive control · Behavior design · Artistic expression

## 1 Introduction

Digital art is a form of art developed together with computer technology. Interactive experience is an important means for digital art to connect artworks with the audience. Interaction has been a hot topic in the field of digital art since past few years. Hypertext, together with virtual immersion and interaction, forms the aesthetic structure of digital art. The development of human-computer interactive technology has enriched the control methods of digital artworks on parameters. In recent years, digital art forms such as digital image, electronic music, digital devices, and virtual reality have resorted to various interactive technologies to enhance the control and presentation of the content of artworks. The development of the digital image, electronic music and digital devices has been closely related to the interactive mechanism. The innovation of human-computer interactive mechanism breaks the limit of human's control of computer and other digital systems, from the traditional contraposition switch control to remote control to the control of somatosensory and even brainwave [1].

Based on the relationship between music and interaction, the scholar Todd Winkler summarized the interactive mode of electronic music as three different modes of "quasi symphonic conducting", "quasi chamber music quartet" and "quasi jazz improvisation" [2], which respectively represent three different relations between human and the computer. One is the quasi symphonic conducting mode, in which man as the subject directly controls every operation flow of the computer, and the computer as the object is responsible for receiving and executing the commands from the subject controller, which is mostly close to the traditional subject control mode. The other is the quasi chamber music quartet mode, in which man as the creative subject can control settings while leaving some room for change. The changing space can be modulated appropriately according to the on-site conditions during the performance, and the affected conditions include cooperation with other actors, feedback from the audience, etc. In this mode, the man and computer are cooperative. The third is the quasi jazz improvisation mode, in which man as the guide preset the limitations, development trends and other information, and keep the multiple possibilities for change while determining the main direction. In musical composition and performance, more work will be carried out by the computer. If the simulation results turn to a negative direction (such as the music melody does not conform to the conventional aesthetics), real-time correction by humans will lead the computer operation into a more reasonable direction, which can be called as human interference guided mode.

Todd Winkler's summary of the above interactive modes of electronic music is also applicable to the interpretation of the control relationship between humans and computers in digital visual art or digital installation art with interactive functions. From the perspective of computer operation mode, interactive control is actually to digitize various human behaviors, decompose and transform them into quantitative digital information and correspond to the controlled parameters in the internal computer program [3]. There are different standards for the classification of interactive technologies in different fields. Based on the interactive control behavior, this paper classifies the commonly used interactive models in digital art into three basic models: regional fixed-point interaction, portable use interaction and wearable motion interaction. On this basis, this paper analyzes and discusses the structural characteristics of different human-computer interactive models and the control behavior design so as to carry out positioning and make use of multiple forms of interaction, enhance the artistic expression of digital artworks under the premise of effective control.

## 2 Structural Features and Control Behavior Design of Regional Fixed-Point Interactive Model

### 2.1 Structural Features of Regional Fixed-Point Interactive Model

The interactive components in the regional fixed-point interactive model are all fixed in a specific position in the sensing space, and the behavior in the sensing space is monitored. If we compare the regional fixed-point interactive model to an instrument, the most similar one should be the organ. They are all set in a fixed space before being used. To play the organ, the organist has to sit in front of the organ keyboard; to trigger interaction of the regional fixed-point interactive model, the interactive object must be in the sensing range, and the user cannot move these devices or carry them to other places at any time. The regional fixed-point interactive model needs to be installed, modulated and set parameters according to the space environment every time it is displayed. The sensors used include infrared sensor, sound detector, graphic detector and other sensors that can scan and collect area information. The advantage of this kind of model lies in that the interactive object does not need to carry or wear any other equipment, so it is often applied to the interactive devices in public space.

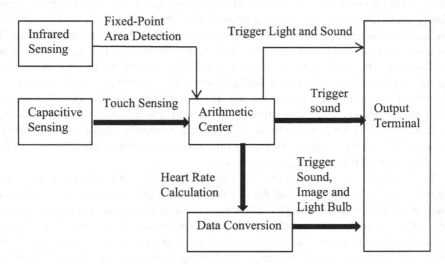

**Fig. 1.** Operation flow chart of the biometric table

Joseph Butch Rovan, a composer and new media artist of the Multimedia and Electronic Music Experimental Center (MEME), Brown University, USA, has been engaged in electronic music composition and electronic instrument device design for many years. In 2009, he created "The Biometric Table", a multimedia audition device combining electronic technology with traditional art concepts, which applied the regional fixed-point interactive model design [4]. The interaction of the whole set of device is divided into three interactive structures: the first part detects whether someone is approaching through the infrared sensor, and when someone enters the sensing range, the pre-designed lighting effect, background sound and acoustic information will be triggered; in the second part, when the participant put his hands on the capacitive touch sensor on the desktop, the computer will calculate his heart rate based on the capacitive information and trigger another acoustic information; in the third part, the system will generate corresponding video and acoustic information based on the heart rate calculation data, and the bulb on the desktop will be lit to complete the whole interaction process and artistic presentation (see Fig. 1).

Combined with the flow chart and on-the-site snapshots (see Fig. 2), it can be found that this system is highly participatory, with no dedicated operator, and can be triggered at any time by anyone entering the sensing range. Moreover, only those who enter the sensing area can interact with the system and trigger the artistic content.

**Fig. 2.** On-the-site snapshots of the biometric table

The regional fixed-point interactive model can give full play to its interactive performance, as long as there is a certain space for placement, whether it is on a fixed stage or in a public space, which can be used as a device that allows everyone to participate in, or as a professional musical instrument.

## 2.2  Analysis of Information Control Mode and Interactive Behavior Design of Regional Fixed-Point Interactive Model

Interactive behavior control allows users to "communicate" with computers in a more diverse way, through different ways of information communication. However, the ultimate goal of interaction alongside rich behavioral varieties is to control the computer. Therefore, the interaction should be designed according to the detection features of different interactive media. According to the interactive media in the regional fixed-point interactive model construction, special attention should be paid to the following three conditions during the operation.

### Spatial Validity of Detection Behavior

As mentioned above, the regional fixed-point interactive model enables anyone in all relevant areas to start interactive control by placing interactive devices in a specific space, in other words, the spatial limitations greatly affect the interactive behavior of such models. Once the area involved in the interactive behavior is too large and beyond the detection range, it will cause the interactive object loss. For devices like Kinect that needs to fix position before detection, the object loss can have serious impacts on performance and control. The effective behavior in the detection area includes two effective conditions: the behavior effectively exists in the detection area and the behavior effectively reaches the detection minimum unit value.

That the behavior effectively exists in the detection area means that all controlled interactions only occur in the detection range where stable and continuous output signals can be obtained. Spatial limit conditions are the primary essential factors when using small-scale detection external devices such as Wacom and digital cameras. Taking Leap Motion as an example, the limit detection range of its external device can reach about 40 cm in height, 60 cm in width and 50 cm in depth, but the effective detection range in practical use does not include the outer space, with 30 cm in height, 40 cm in width and 40 cm in depth as the basic reference threshold. When the hands move too close to the edge area, the external device may lose object and get out of control at any time due to detection misjudgment.

The most important thing when using large-scale detection external devices is that the behavior should effectively reaches the minimum unit of detection. Microsoft Kinect's standard detection range can cover up to 4 m wide and 2 m high, and Christie Air-Scan's multi-point infrared detector can even cover up to 10 m wide. This kind of large-scale detectors usually uses approximate fuzzy algorithm to reduce the extra operations caused by small motions, so the behavioral dynamic value generated can only be effective if it is higher than the maximum value of the fuzzy algorithm. For example, when using Microsoft Kinect, significant numerical changes can be obtained by swinging the arm, but the data obtained by rotating the arm cannot be effectively controlled, because the dynamics generated by rotating the arm are too small to be used for control.

### The Control Timeliness of Performative Behavior

In addition to controlling the computer, interactive control behaviors are often presented as a way of visual performance, while performative behaviors such as instrumental performance and dancing are also used as interactive control behaviors. And the time attribute of music also determines that the control information generated by performative behaviors must be time-efficient.

From the technical point of view, timeliness is mainly reflected in the relationship between the speed of performance behavior and the capture refresh rate. When performing motions generate too much information in a short time, the detection equipment and software system will lose some intermediate data due to the insufficient refresh rate, and the retrieved data will skip, which is similar to the "frame loss" of digital video. A quick motion of the detected object in front of the camera or a high-speed wave within the range of the Leap Motion can cause the control information to lose its stability and make the linear variation jump. Therefore, if the performance behavior is used to control the linear parameters, the stable relationship between motion speed and detection refresh rate is very important.

In addition to speed control, control timeliness is also related to the detection similarity of performance behaviors. The detection mode of the sensor device can cause the information detected to be different from the information seen by humans. Using different fingers on Wacom does not change the coordinate parameters obtained from the sketchpad, nor does facing or backing Kinect change the positioning of the skeleton in space. Therefore, some seemingly different motions will generate data with high similarities. If the generated data are very similar, some corresponding data will become invalid parameters, resulting in the loss of timeliness of the control behavior.

**Behavior Design and Difference Between Switch Parameter and Linear Parameter**

Control information for a computer includes switch control and linear control. When designing interactive behaviors, motions with different features are required for different control information. The behavior used to control the switch needs to be sufficiently dynamic to enable the detector to detect significant data changes in the region. For example, when using Leap Motion to detect the grasping-motion, it is necessary to bend all fingers to ensure that the finger length is lower than the limit value of the detector. Clenching a fist can be quickly and effectively recognized to trigger the switch, while slowly bending the fingers will lead to detection misjudgment, making the switch unable to trigger in time.

On the contrary, linear parameter control requires more stable, uniform and slow behavior design. Just as when using Microsoft Kinect or Leap Motion, the displacement value generated by constant speed movement is relatively smoother when the movement change is lower than the detected refresh rate, and the acceleration data generated by uniform acceleration are easier to control, while the instantaneous variable speed movement beyond the detected refresh rate will reduce the stability of linear parameters and the control ability of behaviors.

## 3 Structural Features and Control Behavior Design of the Portable Interactive Model

### 3.1 Structural Features of the Portable Interactive Model

The interactive components in the portable interactive model are characterized by small size, which can be carried by the controller and used for interaction when necessary. Just as the regional fixed-point interactive model can be compared to the musical instrument organ, the portable interactive model is more like the orchestra instrument, which can be played in a fixed position, or can be played while walking and moving, as long as the instrument is held in hand. The most common portable interactive models are those wireless access controllers, such as wireless mouse, keyboard, Bluetooth game handle, etc. Now most smartphones can be portable interactive controllers by installing remote control applications. A typical portable interactive model generally includes toggle, infrared sensor, triaxial accelerometer, gyroscope, and magnetometer. These models are all based on a core controller, which is the origin for spatial judgments and through which all interactive data are sent.

Wii Remote is the main game controller for Nintendo's Wii host, just like the "Nunchaku" which is made up of a master hand controller and an auxiliary hand controller. In addition to the switch buttons of the conventional handle, the controller also has an infrared positioning sensor and a motion sensing module composed of a gyroscope and a triaxial accelerometer. Because its signal is stable and can be directly connected to the computer through OSC signal, it is favored by lots of interactive artists, so it is often used as a typical portable interactive controller in various works. In 2009, composer Alexander Schubert and violinist Barbara Lüneburg combined violin playing with the interactive technology of Wii Remote to create Weapon of Choice [5], a multimedia interactive electronic music piece. During the performance, the violinist also had to control the Wii Remote through some motions to change the violin sound after digital sampling (see Fig. 3). In subsequent versions, to make the violin perform better, the musician disassembled the Wii Remote auxiliary hand controller and only installed the motion sensing module at the end of the bow, but the interaction technology used remained unchanged.

In Weapon of Choice, the composer transformed Wii Remote and the violin bow into an integrated design, which is also a common way for many designers who use the portable interactive model. Combining the controller with other objects held in the hand will not interfere with the performance, and the controller can be used as a performance prop while implementing interactive control. As long as the control model is within the range of receiving and sending signals, it can be controlled interactively wherever it moves, thus getting rid of the limitation of performance area, but it also has another limitation, that is, it must carry interactive controls.

**Fig. 3.** On-the-spot snapshot of weapon of choice and sample drawing of original Wii remote controller

### 3.2 Analysis of Information Control Mode and Interactive Behavior Design of Portable Interactive Model

The interactive control generated by the portable interactive model can control parameters with more free behavior motions. Many artists are searching for a behavior mode that combines control and performance. Interactive electronic music based on portable interactive devices is often combined with instrumental performance, dance, physical performance and other forms. However, no matter what form of performance is combined, in order to achieve effective behavior control and accuracy, the following three aspects are inevitable in the design of control behavior.

**Control Behavior Design and Detection Data Validity**
The interactive system based on the portable interactive model can interact with the computer in a more natural manner through carrying and motion control. After getting rid of the limitation of space area, people can make more motions and behaviors, but the more varied and complex motions can be, the more likely for "invalid control" to occur.

Most human's motions are performed by multiple muscles of the body at the same time. Even behaviors with strong purpose will produce additional motions due to years of exercise habits and physical conditions. In the performance of musical instruments, these behaviors also become a part of the performer's performance characteristics. However, aiming at parameter control, such additional stylized behavior motions will show an obvious inclination of causing control interference or even control signal error. For example, when testing the behavior control of Nintendo's Wii handle, the sample testers' holding habits led to the complete deviation of the data. Eight of the ten sample testers held the Wii controller with the button facing up and parallel to the ground, and the x-axis data acceleration and displacement parameters were stable when moving horizontally, while the other two accidentally flipped their wrists due to their habit as they moved, causing the sensor perpendicular to the ground. Although it is only a small motion deviation, this motion directly causes the quadrant of the gyroscope sensor on the sensing component to flip, and the corresponding data directly cause serious errors.

Therefore, it is necessary to pay great attention to the influence of body habits in the design of related control motions. When designing control behaviors, we should try to avoid not too complicated motion structures or difficult motion flows. Moreover, the threshold value and other attributes of control parameters need to be modified through multiple tests.

**Mapping Relationship between Complex Control Behavior and Control Parameters**

Complex control behavior refers to the combination of motions that simultaneously generate multiple changes in sensing information, such as rotating the body while the arm moves in a vertical circle, or flipping the wrist while pushing the arm forward. The complex skeletal and muscular structure of the human body makes it easy for people to make similar combined motions, but such combined motion information can generate a large amount of combination data after the decomposition of sensing components.

Even the simplest wrist-turning motion can be detected by the triaxle gyroscope and then decomposed into three data groups, and the three messages are related to each other in human motion behavior. By mapping the related data to the parameter set which has the relation type, the synchronization control of multiple information can be realized quickly to achieve more effective control effect, such as the output ratio of multiple oscillators, the relationship between the frequency and loudness of sound, or coordinate information of the image. On the contrary, if the correlation data is mapped to parameters that have no correlation or even need independent control, the control force will decline or even fail.

Another case is data superposition or cancellation caused by complex motions. The most representative superposition is that the hand holding the device and the body rotate in the same direction at the same time. Due to the rotation of the body, an angle difference $\alpha$ is generated, while the rotation of the hand produces another angle difference $\beta$. At this point, the angle value obtained by the sensor is $\gamma\alpha + \beta$. Similarly, when the hand and body rotate in the same direction, the value detected by the sensor is the difference between the two angles. Reasonable application of data superposition and cancellation can enhance the performance of the motion under the premise of stable control, but the improper use will also cause the increase in error.

In the interactive behavior design, what is more important is to design simple control behaviors first, and then combine relevant parameters with behaviors and motions to obtain spacing control ability and visual effect, rather than to blindly pursue the beauty of motions at the expense of control force. In addition, it also needs a lot of practice to use complex motions to control multiple groups of related information synchronously, and more stable parameter control can be achieved by the reinforcement of the control of limbs to form a habit.

**Control Signal Interference and Resolution of Invalid Behavior**
During the performance, a large number of unexpected behaviors will be generated for the purpose of visual aesthetics or motion coherence. Some of the data generated by these behaviors have no impact on parameter control, while others will interfere with the control. These types of behaviors that are not applicable for parameter control but are unavoidable are collectively called invalid behaviors.

On the one hand, invalid behavior can be reduced by reasonable motion design; on the other hand, it can also be reduced by using the mapping methods of segment control and condition triggering control when mapping data. Segmented control is to turn on the mapping relationship between sensor data and corresponding parameters in corresponding chapters or time according to the development of music, and cut off the mapping relationship before and after. In this way, it can effectively reduce the interference of invalid behavior to other sections of the music by combining motion design at corresponding time points. Conditional trigger control is to use additional conditions to restrict the data mapping generated by behaviors. For example, if the switch button on the handle is taken as the limiting condition, the behavior data will form a mapping relationship with the corresponding parameters only when it is turned on, and if multiple switch controls are used, the cross mapping between the sensing data and the parameters can be realized.

# 4   Structural Features and Control Behavior Design of Wearable Motion Interactive Model

## 4.1   Structural Features of Wearable Motion Interactive Model

The interactive components in the wearable motion interactive model are directly worn on the controller in different forms, and the interactive behavior is realized through the motions generated by the controller.

In national arts around the world, bells or metal pieces are often tied to the body or clothes. When dancing, they make sounds along with motions and form music together with accompanying instruments, which is also the original wearable instrument. The ultimate goal of human-computer interaction is to realize "unconscious interaction", that is, to associate human consciousness directly with computer without any bridging tools. The current technology cannot directly realize this concept, but all kinds of sensors for human body have already been able to directly collect human motion information to achieve natural behavior interaction. Wearable interactive models have been widely used in today's movie special effects production, human motion research and other fields. With the development of science and technology, continuous break-throughs have been made—smaller size, lower cost, and improved sensing accuracy, which also makes wearable devices more applicable to daily life. Now there are various wearable interactive devices developed for a variety of human body information in the market, such as MindWave for brain wave detection, MYO for arm motion detection, Gest for hand motion detection, etc. In addition to being compatible with most detectors in the portable interactive model, the wearable interactive model may also use many of the common modules in medical and ergonomic applications, such as Elec-troencephalogram (a.k.a. EEG), Electromyography (a.k.a. EMG), Flex sensors, etc. The interaction is realized through the detection of human bioelectricity as well as that of behaviors and motions.

In 2015, Thalmic Lab launched MYO wristband, a wearable interactive device consisting of a triaxle accelerator, gyroscope, magnetometer and eight EMG sensors that can recognize arm motions and some hand motions. In the same year, the artist Ensemble Topographic combined MYO wristband with electronic music, digital video and dance art to lead the multimedia art project Llac [6]. In this work, the dancer wearing MYO wristband performs an impromptu dance with music, and data are collected through the wristband to correlate music information with the dancer's motions (see Fig. 4). Because the interactive device is worn directly on the body, the dancer will not be limited by the space at all, and the audience can also focus on the performance itself.

The wearable interactive model gives the interactive object the maximum degree of freedom, and the area limitations, bright conditions and handheld devices do not interfere with the image interactive behavior design. However, the wearable interactive model also has its own problems, such as the selection of highly sensitive sensing data and control information, device stability, motion design, data information mapping and so on, which are the technical difficulties to be further solved for wearable devices.

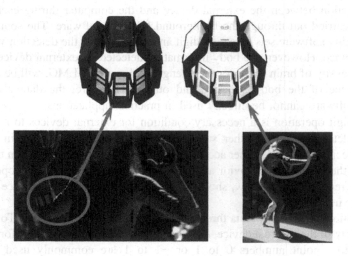

**Fig. 4.** On-the-spot snapshots of llac and sample drawing of original MYO controller

## 4.2   Analysis of Information Control Mode and Interactive Behavior Design of Wearable Motion Interactive Model

Some techniques used in wearable interactive model are the same as those used in portable interactive model, such as triaxle gyroscopes and accelerometers. Therefore, the interactive behavior design of the wearable interactive model also needs to refer to the rules of the portable use interactive model in some cases. In addition, the interactive behavior design of the wearable interactive model has the following elements.

**Accurate Detection and Standardized Wearing**
The external devices used in the wearable interactive model must be fixed in the corresponding position of the human body during the interaction to ensure the normal data detection. Equipment falling off, shaking, or shifting during movement can cause misdetection. External devices such as MYO wristbands or interactive gloves, which are used to detect the interactive behavior of limbs, are very easy to shift when doing strenuous actions. Therefore, most designers will design relatively gentle motions as control behaviors, and some artists will also use other methods for auxiliary fixation, such as taping or wrapping to increase the adhesion between components and the skin.

All wearable interactive devices must abide by the principle of standardized wearing, which means that the initial angle, position, direction and other information detected by the sensor should be consistent with the initial value set by the software when wearing the external device. For example, wearing the external device of MYO wristband requires the initial position of its core controller to be parallel to the ground light and close to the wrist end, while wearing the Mind-Wave requires the relatively fixed position of the brainwave damper on the forehead. Although different objective environments may have a certain impact on the wearing of external devices, standardized wearing can effectively reduce the difference. Compared with adjusting parameters by software, standardized wearing is always a more effective way.

**Conversion of Individual Behavioral Characteristics and Detection Data**
The connection between the external device and the computer during each wearable motion is carried out through the background bridging software. The source code of these bridging software sets a general digit and threshold for the detection value of the external device. However, the body information detected by external devices, whether it is the intensity of brain waves or the strength and speed of EMG, will be affected by the difference of the body structure and others. Therefore, the data generated by bridging software cannot be directly used in practical applications.

High-digit operation is a necessary condition for external devices to realize high-precision detection, and whether such high-digit operation is needed in interactive design is decided by the designer according to specific requirements. When the changes caused by the interaction behavior are of low precision, using low-digit operation can effectively reduce the data flow, shorten data transmission time and reduce data delay from receiving to mapping.

In addition to operands, data threshold conversion is also necessary. To ensure the commonality of the external device, developers tend not to set thresholds for open data, while floating point numbers 0 to 1 or $-1$ to 1 are commonly used for closed parameters. The universal threshold for MIDI signal (0,127) or the threshold of color level parameters (0,255) is far different from that of the sensor (0., 1.). Therefore, the most important process of data mapping is to convert data threshold. Similarly, the values of acceleration, electromyography and so on are also affected by individual muscle strength, motor ability and other factors. Suppose that the acceleration value generated by a trained adult male waving his arm can reach (−0.8, 0.8), while that of an untrained female may only be (−0.6, 0.6). At this point, it is necessary to perform threshold positioning according to the wearer's personal characteristics and then convert it into the relative threshold of the control parameters.

The wearable motion interactive model has no space limitation of regional fixed-point interactive model, nor does it need to deliberately operate external devices to interact like the portable model. The interactive system based on this model directly converts the natural information generated by human body into control information through the comprehensive use of various detection technologies, making the unconscious natural interaction possible. But every coin has two sides. Although non-operation interaction is the advantage of wearable motion interactive model, it is more difficult to accurately control the data generated by the interactive information due to the lack of deliberate control behavior. Therefore, more practice and running-in work are needed to control the interactive behavior with wearable devices.

## 5   Conclusion

With the development of digital technology, more kinds of interactive devices are used in digital art. Compared with the traditional control behavior, the behavioral motions in the interactive process are more agreeable in vision, more natural in operation and more varied in motion. Even so, today's human-computer interaction still cannot be separated from three basic interactive models: regional fixed-point interaction, portable use interaction and wearable motion interaction. Some small-scale artworks mostly make use of one interactive model in the design according to the control requirements and performance features, while some large-scale integrated digital media art will use a variety of interactive models according to the creation objectives, venues, performance mechanisms and other conditions to derive a multi-dimensional composite interactive model. As the most important medium to achieve the goal control, the interactive behavior design, on the one hand, should ensure the applicability, feasibility and accuracy of its behavior to the parameter control; on the other hand, it should consider the user's personal characteristics, performance and aesthetics. How to find and grasp the balance point of the control and expression of interactive control behaviors is the major issue of human-computer interaction in digital art, and the focus topic for every digital artist and researcher.

# References

1. Li, S.: An Introduction to Digital Media Arts (3rd Edn.). Tsinghua University Press, Beijing (2015)
2. Winkler, T.: Composing Interactive Music: Techniques and Ideas Using Max [M]. The MIT Press, London (2001)
3. Kutz, M.: Eshbach's Handbook of Engineering Fundamentals Eshbach 5th Edition. John-Wiley, New Jersey (2009)
4. Joseph Butch Rovan's works "The Biometric Table". http://www.soundidea.org/rovan/research_biometric_table.html, last accessed 2019/2/14
5. Alexander Schubert and Barbara Lüneburg's works "Weapon of Choice". http://www.alexanderschubert.net/works/weapon.php. Accessed 20 February 2019
6. Ensemble Topogràfic's works "Llac". http://www.ensembletopografic.com/discography. Accessed 26 February 2019

# Interactive Visualization of the Thoughts in Traditional Chinese Culture

Jin Sheng[✉]

School of Media Arts and Communication of Nanjing University of the Arts,
Nanjing, China
nysmsj@163.com

**Abstract.** *The Book of Changes*, Taoism, Confucianism and Buddhism, which are important parts of the traditional culture of China with a profound history of more than 5000 years, represent the diverse traditional Chinese philosophical ideology. In order to better protect and inherit the historic, extensive and profound cultural spirit with unique national characteristics, the visual expression of interactive thoughts between human, nature and society is used, which can facilitate the spread and promotion of the traditional culture of China. Therefore, this paper focuses on how to transform written texts in the traditional culture of China to images and videos, and tries to interpret the extensive and profound connotation of the traditional culture of China via visual expression enabled by multimedia technology.

**Keywords:** Traditional culture · Interactivity · Visualization

## 1 Introduction

The Chinese nation's over 5000 years of history has given birth to a wealth of culture and ideas. Starting from the Book of Changes, a mainstream cultural ideology integrating multiple schools of thought, including the Tao Te Ching of Laozi, Confucianism, and the thoughts of Zhuangzi and Mozi and Buddhism, gradually came into being. Our ancestors comprehended the essence of nature and grasped the origin of the universe from the cosmic laws of nature, which later evolved into Taoism that advocates learning from nature, inaction and coexisting with nature, Confucianism that emphasizes an ideal society featuring the doctrine of the mean, harmony, virtue and justice, and Buddhism that believes everything is illusion and ultimate liberation can be achieved by transcending life and death and eliminating afflictions. All these ideas form the spirit and social ideology that are unique to China (Fig. 1).

C. Stephanidis et al. (Eds.): HCII 2020, LNCS 12429, pp. 363–380, 2020.
https://doi.org/10.1007/978-3-030-59987-4_26

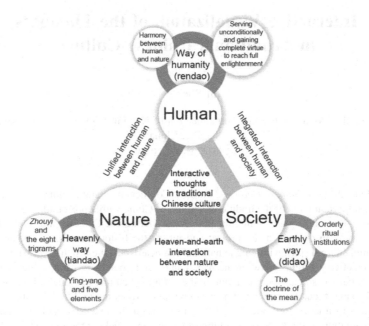

**Fig. 1.** Thoughts in the traditional culture of China

## 2 The Heaven-and-Earth Interaction Between Nature and Society

### 2.1 The Eight Trigrams (Bagua) in *the Book of Changes*—the Cyclical Interaction Within the Universe

*The Book of Changes*, an ancient and rich classic, is the root of Chinese culture. It describes the change, non-change, and simplicity of things with symbols and writing systems, and represents Chinese people's understanding of the universe and the world in ancient times. Its inner philosophical ideas and unique logical system constitute the framework of Chinese philosophy and Chinese culture. The eight trigrams (Bagua) have two arrangements, namely the Primordial and the Manifested. The Primordial Bagua is also known as Fu Hsi Bagua, named after Fu Hsi, the first ancestor of the Chinese nation in ancient mythology. The Bagua invented by Fu Hsi consists of Qian, Kun, Zhen, Xun, Kan, Li, Gen and Dui, representing Heaven, Earth, Thunder, Wind, Water, Fire, Mountain and Lake respectively. Ancient people comprehended the hardness and softness of each hexagram through the changes of heaven and earth, and discovered the law of life of all things in the universe. They fully observed the nature of things, thoroughly understood the heavenly principles and gained insight into the earthly issues, gradually comprehending the way to cultivate their minds through developing their moral characters and cultivating their temperament, and govern the state through improving people's living standards and strengthening governance abilities. The sequence of the hexagrams in the Primordial Bagua is Qian as 1, Dui as 2,

Li as 3, Zhen as 4, Xun as 5, Kan as 6, Gen as 7 and Kun as 8, among which the former four are Yang hexagrams arranged anticlockwise, and the latter four are Yin hexagrams arranged clockwise. Each hexagram represents one natural phenomenon, with Qian representing Heaven, Kun representing Earth, Zhen representing Thunder, Xun representing Wind, Kan representing Water, Li representing Fire, Gen representing Mountain and Dui representing Lake. Each hexagram forms a pair with the one opposite the other, leading to the mutual transformation and balance between Heaven and Earth, Wind and Thunder, Water and Fire, Mountain and Lake. Interactions in nature are the reasons for the bloom and fading of lives, which present themselves in a three-dimensional form in the natural environment (Fig. 2).

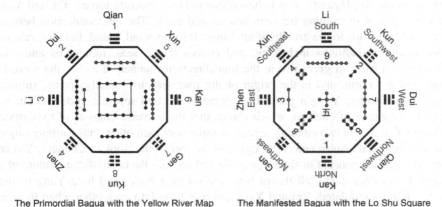

The Primordial Bagua with the Yellow River Map     The Manifested Bagua with the Lo Shu Square

**Fig. 2.** The primordial bagua and the manifested bagua

The Manifested Bagua is also known as King Wen Bagua. King Wen of Zhou, with surname being Ji and first name being Chang, was the leader of the feudal lords in Western China during the late Shang Dynasty. It is said that after careful study, King Wen of Zhou standardized the Primordial Bagua and made it more organized, creating sixty-four trigrams and three hundred and eighty-four Yao (broken or unbroken lines), as well as hexagram statements and Yaoci (line texts). This is later known as Zhouyi. It elaborates on the complicated social phenomena through simple images and numbers as well as the changes of Yin and Yang. The sequence of each hexagram in the Manifested Bagua is Kan as 1, Kun as 2, Zhen as 3, Xun as 4, Qian as 6, Dui as 7, Gen as 8, Li as 9, which is arranged in accordance with the Lo Shu Square (Luoshu). Each hexagram represents one direction, with Kan being the north, Kun being the southwest, Zhen being the east, Xun being the southeast, Qian being the northwest, Dui being the west, Gen being the northeast and Li being the south. Each hexagram forms a pair with the one opposite the other, leading to the mutual correspondence and balance between the south and the north, the east and the west, the southeast and the northwest, the southwest and the northeast. Geographical interactions promote the integration and changes of ethnic groups, which present themselves in a two-dimensional form in the natural environment.

The organic combination of the Primordial Bagua and the Manifested Bagua forms the cyclical interaction within the universe. This type of corresponding combinations of interaction lays the foundation for social development.

## 2.2 Ying-Yang and Five Elements—the Generating and Overcoming Interactions Between Things

The Book of Changes · XiCi (Commentary on the Appended Phrases) Part One states, "the reciprocal process of Yin and Yang is called the Dao. That which allows the Dao to continue to operate is human goodness, and that which allows it to bring things to completion is human nature." The concept of Yin and Yang came into existence as early as in the Xia Dynasty. It is believed that the two opposite forces, Yin and Yang, are the origin of everything between heaven and earth. The interconnection between Yin and Yang leads to the growth of all things. It forms wind, cloud, thunder, rain and other weather conditions in heaven, and creates rivers, seas, mountains and other landforms on earth. It gives rise to the four directions, namely the east, the west, the south and the north, and is the origin of the four seasons, namely spring, summer, autumn and winter. Yin-yang and five elements are two separate systems. Yin and Yang is a concept of dualism, which claims that the universe consists of two aspects (Yin and Yang). The two contrary aspects complement each other, thus forming objects and lives between heaven and earth. Lying in the core of the Book of Changes, Yin and Yang is a general concept to signify, explain and identify the contradictory nature of all things. Laozi once said, "all things bear Yin on their backs and hold Yang to their front." Being interrelated, Yin and Yang can transform into each other when there are external changes. Its characteristics go through cyclical changes during the continuous process of contradiction and integration.

The theory of the five elements was put forward by Jizi, a nobleman in the late Shang Dynasty. According to Shangshu (the Book of Documents) · Hongfan (the Great Plan), Jizi introduced the five elements, namely metal, wood, water, fire and earth, to King Wu of Zhou, and deemed them as the fundamental elements to form all things in the world. The theory of the five elements emphasizes the concept of system in the physical world, and describes the internal structural relations and forms of movement of all things. Unlike Yin and Yang which is an ancient theory of contradiction and unity, the theory of the five elements is a primitive study of systems and a theory of the composition of substances in ancient China. There are both generating and overcoming interactions between the five elements. For generating interactions, wood fuels fire. Fire forms earth with ashes left after the burning. Earth generates metal, as most metals are buried under the earth. Metal generates water, as metal would melt into liquids at high temperatures. Water feeds wood, as plants need to be watered to grow. As for overcoming interactions, wood separates earth, as plant seeds, initially buried underneath, will break through the soil when they grow, or farming tools, most of which are made from wood, can loosen the soil. Metal penetrates the wood, as sharp metal tools can chop wood. Fire overcomes metal, as despite the hardness of the metal, fire can melt it into liquids at high temperatures. Water destroys fire by putting it out. Earth overcomes water, as piles of earth can dam water. The generating and overcoming interactions between the five elements

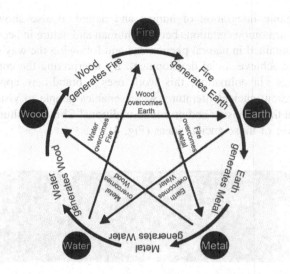

**Fig. 3.** Diagram of the generating and overcoming interactions between the five elements

form the interconnection between things, which also demonstrate the internal structural relations of all things as well as a holistic ideology (Fig. 3).

If we interpret the interrelations of things from the perspective of the generating and overcoming interactions between the five elements, we will discover that nothing in nature is isolated and static. Instead, things maintain balance through continuous generating and overcoming interactions. The concept of Yin-yang and the five elements together form a combined theory. It is a systems theory of contradiction and unity which believes that all things achieve mutual improvement and development through contradiction and interactions.

## 2.3    Interactive Visual Expression Between Nature and Society

In his book the Book of Changes Studies and Astronomy, Professor Yang Lu from Nanjing University studies the celestial events and calendars described in the Book of Changes and Yizhuan (a collection of commentaries to the Book of Changes), and points out that "ancient people did not intend to explore the nature of celestial bodies or the universe, nor did they plan to figure out the mechanism of celestial bodies, and therefore the purpose of their astronomical observation does not have modern astronomical meaning. However, by looking up into the universe, they acquired the knowledge and wisdom needed to survive on earth".

Changes, a video with animated effects created by Jin Sheng, reflects the cyclical interaction within the universe. The work starts by focusing on the universe and astronomical and geographical phenomena, demonstrating the transformation process from Fu Hsi's Primordial Bagua to King Wen of Zhou's Manifested Bagua. The video presents the natural phenomena in the Bagua in a dynamic way, thus revealing the interactions between all things in nature in a more direct manner. The combination of mathematical principles in the ancient Lo Shu Square and phenomena in nature signifies the organic integration of human and nature. It also shows that only by interpreting the harmonious relations between human and nature in accordance with the law of change contained in natural phenomena and following the way (Dao) of heaven and earth can we achieve social development. By interpreting the core culture of the Book of Changes via animation, this work uses a brand-new approach of visual expression to present ancient literature, which enables people to visually and cognitively understand the extensive and profound traditional Chinese culture, and learn and master the essence of those ancient ideas (Fig. 4).

**Fig. 4.** Changes, an animated video by Jin Sheng, video length: 5′10″

The basic formation of Origin, a video installation work by Jin Sheng, is a system of different parts inspired by the Yin and Yang dualism, which states that the Supreme Ultimate (Taiji) generates the two modes (the Yin and Yang), and the two basic modes generate the four basic images, which then generate the eight trigrams. Cool and warm colors are used to represent Yin and Yang respectively, and the texture of the mixed media reflects the changes in this big, wonderful world. This work also projects the language symbols and the graphical images of the 28 Mansions onto the installation to show the law of nature that the universe is ever-changing, so as to reflect on the insignificance and uncertainty of human beings, and remind people that only by respecting nature and following the laws of nature can we achieve the coordination of Yin and Yang and a harmonious society (Fig. 5).

**Fig. 5.** Origin, a video installation work by Jin Sheng, dimensions: 610 × 110 cm

The above two works both make use of modern visualization to express ideas in the traditional culture, a more direct way of expression by transforming written texts to artistic visual languages. The principles of interactions between nature and society derived from the changes of the laws of nature, with their ever-developing dialectical ideas and inclusive attitude, have been integrated into the values of the Chinese nation, becoming an integral part of Chinese culture.

## 3  The Unified Interaction Between Human and Nature

### 3.1  The Harmony of Human and Nature–the Harmonious Coexistence of Human and Ecological Environment

There is a saying in Dao Te Ching of Laozi, "Human models himself after the earth, the earth models itself after heaven, the heaven models itself after Dao and Dao models itself after nature". [1] This saying means the harmony of humans and nature. Even the "heaven" should run in accordance with the "Dao". The "nature" does not mean the natural world but the natural state. Laozi believed that only in a natural state can a man be completely happy and free. In Laozi's point of view, the culture is not the result of the improvement of natural state, but the degeneration of civilization, because the so-called benevolence and reason are produced by the loss of "Dao". The existence of benevolence and propriety is only necessary when the "Dao" is deserted, the country is in chaos and the family is not at peace. Therefore, only by abolishing the benevolence and propriety can we truly be filled with morality, benevolence and righteousness, and we can allow them to be natural state, which is the "inaction" advocated by Laozi. In accordance with the "inaction", a man may assist in the course of nature and not presume to interfere, which means letting all things grow based on their nature without any interference [2].

In the process of transforming nature, human beings start by destroying it. By taking a look at the impacts of various disasters caused by an ecological imbalance on human and society in today's world, we can know that the harmonious coexistence of human and nature is the foundation of social development. We should respect nature, pursue the harmony between heaven, earth and human, worship the heaven and earth, help to nurture life, protect people and nourish things.

In the natural world, heaven, earth, and human are connected with each other. Chuang-tzu· Dasheng says, "The heaven and the earth are parents of all things." The Dao of three powers is stressed in the Book of Changes. The importance of human position is illustrated by the juxtaposition of heaven, earth and human and the centrality of human. The Dao of heaven is to "start from all things"; the Dao of the earth is to "produce all things". The Dao of human is to "make all things". Concretely speaking, the Dao of heaven means Yin and Yang, the Dao of the earth means softness and hardness and the Dao of human means benevolence and righteousness. The heaven, earth and human have their own ways, but they correspond to each other.

The foundation for the harmonious coexistence of human and ecological environment is to respect the heaven and fear the earth so that green mountains and clear water are developed. To respect the heaven is to respect the natural law of the universe, and to fear the earth is to follow the ecological principle. Only in this way can we get the proper response from the nature, and human beings can then rest and procreate.

## 3.2  Perfect Virtue—Human's Transcendence and Ascension of the Material World

Indian Buddhism was introduced into China in the early years of the Eastern Han Dynasty. After a long period of spreading and continuous development, eight sects were founded in the Sui and Tang Dynasties, developing into Chinese Buddhism with Chinese national characteristics.

"Buddha nature" has become one of the central issues in the discussion of Buddhism in China since its introduction into China. Daosheng Zhu strongly advocated the idea that everyone has a Buddha-nature and that everyone can become a Buddha, which was generally welcomed by Chinese society, and eventually became the main theme of Chinese Buddhist philosophy. Zen Buddhism fully affirms the possibility of liberation for everyone in ordinary life by highlighting the role of every individual. The spiritual and humanistic tendency of Chinese Buddhism has been implemented into the heart and current life of every ordinary person. The Buddha-nature theory, namely "the heart is the Buddha", "the human is like Buddha" and "all saints are equal", has become one of the important characteristics of Chinese Buddhism, which is consistent with traditional Chinese thoughts. [3]

Under the Buddhist concept – "all beings are equal", everyone can escape from misery and become a Buddha by his own efforts. Influenced by "ignorance" and "covetousness", all living beings inevitably have various good and evil behaviors, which will lead to their souls' reincarnation from the heaven, the earth, the beast, the hungry ghost, the hell to the Asura after death, and they are unable to get relief from the agony of living and dying. To eliminate suffering and to enter nirvana, we shall follow the eight righteous ways of positive view, positive thinking, positive language, positive occupation, positive life, positive growth, positive mindfulness, and positive fineness. Only when all troubles are completely eliminated can the practice of Buddhism be completed and the reincarnation of living and dying be forever removed, which is the ultimate ideal state of Buddhism.

In the process of realizing the ideal, human should put aside all vain pursuits and comprehend the dialectical relationship between human and the natural ecological environment from the thought of "in absolute accordance with what is right". This thought reflects Buddhism's pursuit of the harmonious relationship between human and the objective environment, and has become Buddhism's basic position in dealing with the relationship between the subjective and objective, human and nature. This also has important reference significance for the construction of modern ecological theory [4].

## 3.3  Interactive Visual Expression Between Human and the Material World

In Chapter 21 of Dao Te Ching written by Laozi, "the thing that is called Dao is elusive, evasive. Elusive, evasive, yet latent in it are forms. Elusive, evasive, yet latent in it are objects." This saying indicates that the "Dao" has no fixed form. There is the form in the latent and there is the object in the latent. In Dao The, an interactive video installation work by Jin Sheng, with the full text of Laozi's Dao Te Ching as the background and the vessel "bowl" as the carrier, the dynamic transformation of material objects is realized by fragmentary words to reflect the infinite state of Laozi's "Dao", which is "the shape is without shape and the form is without form". At the same time, it also reflects the transformation of heaven, earth and human from intangible to tangible and it is the benevolence that makes "Dao" become true (Fig. 6).

**Fig. 6.** *Dao The*, an interactive video installation work by Jin Sheng, dimensions: 50 × 50 × 9 cm

In Book 6 of Surangama Sutra, "there are no other ways to return to the origin, but there are many ways to cultivate yourself. There are many ways to be divine regardless of good times or bad times. The speed may be different in the initial method of entering Samadhi." The meaning of the saying is: if we enter into our own nature and see ourselves as what we are, we shall find that we are the same. There are many ways and means to enter into our own nature, all of which are convenient methods with no difference. Our own nature is ultimate without external, tiny without internal. It is encompassing and inclusive so we can get into nature with any method. However, the initial method of entering Samadhi must be determined according to the basis of each individual. Some may enter Samadhi faster or some may enter slower.

In Return, a video installation work by Jin Sheng, three matrixes of 108 Buddhas are arranged and combined into many methods to reflect the diversity of learning approaches. The 32 sutras from Diamond Sutra overlap the images by means of moving images, enhancing the interaction between the gradual concave movement of the Buddha and the Buddha, the sutras and the audience, aiming at changing the impetuous mentality of the masses. We should achieve compassion, because compassion is a reflection of a person's wisdom and it can eliminate impetuous mentality.

We should keep our minds pure and unstained so that we can get the joy of silence (Fig. 7, Fig. 8).

**Fig. 7.** Return, a video installation work by Jin Sheng, dimensions: 250 cm × 250 cm × 3

## 4   The Integrated Interaction Between Human and Society

A review of the development of Confucianism over the past two thousand years, from Confucius' principle of "benevolence" and "rite" to Mencius' principle of "benevolence against tyranny", shows that the relationship between human and society is the prerequisite for the normal development of society. On the one hand, "The Three Cardinal Guides and The Five Constant Virtues" with "benevolence" as the core is the basis and norm of the social order. On the other hand, the Doctrine of the Mean, as the highest thinking concept and the code of conduct of the Chinese people, embodies the responsibility and obligation of individuals in society. The integration of the two sides is more conducive to the healthy development of the country.

### 4.1   Ritual System—the Responsibility and Obligation of Human in Society

The ritual system reflecting the supremacy of royal power, patriarchal blood relationship, ancestor worship and other elements of traditional Chinese culture is one of the important features of ancient Chinese civilization. Rites have a strong social function of "governing the state, stabilizing the country, arranging the people in order and benefiting the heirs" (The Commentary of Zuo·The Eleventh Year of Yingong). Since Duke Zhou made the rite, the influence of rite on the political, economic and moral life of traditional Chinese society has lasted for thousands of years. The rulers use the ritual system to guide political decisions and regulate the behavior of all social members, so as to achieve the harmony and stability of the country. Chinese traditional ritual culture regulates the relationship between individuals and others, individuals and clans, and individuals and groups through a set of symbolic behaviors and procedural structures, clarifying the identity boundaries among people from the perspective of

**Fig. 8.** Return, a video installation work by Jin Sheng, dimensions: 250 cm × 250 cm × 3

ethics, so as to stabilize the moral order within the community of various groups. And it also facilitates the construction of the social operation mode of patriarchal clan hierarchy, and fundamentally solves the order problem of the operation of traditional Chinese social and political life, making the communication relations in social and political life show the characteristics of etiquette and ethics [5].

Confucianism believes that family etiquette education is the premise of etiquette life, and it is the basis for developing people's behavior. Only by cultivating and learning the basic etiquette in the unique patriarchal blood relationship of the family, can we deal with the relationship of family and ethics beyond utility, so that parents can love their children and children are filial to their parents. The filial piety that Confucius attached great importance to is the natural embodiment of this sincere feeling, and also the code of conduct and moral basis for people to enter the society. Therefore, as long as we continue to educate the masses morally, we will surely enable people to improve their moral self-control and abide by social norms from the bottom of their hearts, so as to maintain the social stability and order.

### 4.2    The Doctrine of the Mean – Human Should Guarantee the Appropriate "Degree" in the Society

In the doctrine of the mean ("中庸" in Chinese characters) of Confucianism, "中" means suitable, and "庸" means doing things in an appropriate way. It is spreading goodness that you can do it for a long time if you do it in the right way. As the traditional culture, the spirit of doctrine of the mean is the moderation, which urges us to do things in a moderate way, and strives to keep within a reasonable range.

Yuechuan Wang, professor of the Peking University, pointed out in The Position of the Doctrine of the Mean in the Chinese History of Thought that in essence, the doctrine of the mean is not ordinary but the theorizing and philosophizing of the rite, because it is transformed from the "rite". This rite is not a system of rules and regulations, but the basic requirements of people's ideology and value system from the psychological structure. This means that the doctrine of the mean is not mediocrity and indulgence, neither the daily loosening or inappropriateness. However, it means that we need a higher requirement of "rite" to restrain ourselves so that people would not pursue too much external material accessories, would not be too greedy, and would not excessively want reputation, status and wealth. Otherwise, people will suffer heavy pain, annoyance and anxiety. In real life, we should guarantee the appropriate "degree" and can get the true "degree" if we learn to get something out of life. We should do things in an impartial way, not do some "strange and disorderly" things, and follow the normal and ordinary rules of life. The doctrine of the mean enlightens people to abstain from greed, impetuosity, lust and fullness. After abstinence, people would not be real people, and will become a gentleman of integrity [6].

The Doctrine of the Mean is an important moral code of Confucianism and the highest standard of conduct pursued by Confucianism. In the process of pursuing and practicing the highest level of the Doctrine of the Mean, Confucius thought that he did not reach the ideal level, which showed that man's self-awakening has great limitations. If you want to be a gentleman of integrity, you should start from small things. "We can see a person's character from the subtlest words and deeds." As Bei Liu from The Three Kingdoms said, "Do not do it because it's a small bad thing, and do not care because it's a small good thing." "Climbing must start from a low place, and a long journey must start from a near place". People should start with small things and start with themselves first, so that they can do big things and could go far. Only in this way can the doctrine of the mean be implemented.

### 4.3   Interactive Visual Expression of Human and Society

Health Preservation, an interactive design work by Jin Sheng, is based on the health preservation secret script in the inscription of Laojun, in Bozhou, Henan Province. It combines the principle of Yin-yang, eight trigrams and five elements in the Book of Changes to restore the combination meaning of the combined characters from the perspective of Daoist health preservation. With the visual presentation of words and animation, it also interprets the secrets of Laozi's health preservation and shows the philosophy and art of the combined characters in ancient China in an interactive way (Fig. 9).

Circulation, a video installation work by Jin Sheng, uses the installation form to combine the four gods of Qinglong, Baihu, Zhuque, Xuanwu and the plate from Han Dynasty to imply heaven and earth. It uses the terrestrial branch on the plate, the hexagrams and solar terms in the video, to make the astronomical and geographical atmosphere of ancient Chinese philosophy. The experimental head images of all living beings in the middle overlap show the natural law of the world's Yin-yang transformation, the alternation of life and death, and the harmony between human and nature. In this way, people are inspired to overcome their laziness, and strive to break the evil and cultivate the good, so as to reach the other side which is ideal, good and beautiful (Fig. 10).

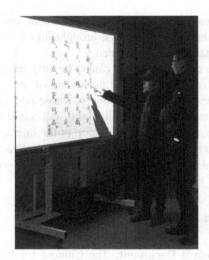

**Fig. 9.** Health preservation, interactive design work by Jin Sheng

**Fig. 10.** Circulation, a video installation work by Jin Sheng, dimensions: 210 × 210 cm

## 5   The Future Value of the Interactive Visual Expression

The traditional Chinese culture is broad and profound. Its core ideas cannot be dispensable from the school of Changes and have been continued and developed with the cultural nourishment from Confucianism, Buddhism and Taoism theoretically. As for the interaction among human, nature and society, the contents and principles from these schools of thoughts are interlinked, in spite of their different names, since they all build the ecological environment with respect and protection towards the nature as their main goal. Only with the creation of a harmonious natural and social environment, can the role and efficacy of the socialization of the humanistic spirit be brought into full play and a perfectly harmonious society for human beings be created.

As exceptional as the traditional Chinese culture can be, it cannot be only stayed at the expression level of words. For the further inheritance and promotion of the traditional cultural thoughts, the application of the new media technology, whose purpose is to actualize the visual transformation of the traditional cultural thoughts, is granted with social value and realistic significance for the study and dissemination of the interactive thoughts in the Chinese traditional culture. In terms of the future value of the interactive visual expression, the historical, aesthetic and dissemination values in the field of social value have been mainly developed.

## 5.1    The Historical Value of Theory and Practice

**The Theoretical Refinement of the Historical Document.** The Chinese traditional culture and thoughts have been retained in the form of documents after thousands of years of inheritance. As a consequence, the core part of the Chinese traditional culture and thoughts must be refined and extracted if the visual expression is applied to the interactive thoughts of the traditional Chinese culture. In the process of clarifying the Chinese traditional culture and thoughts, it has been found that the elaboration of the classical theories cannot do without the balance among human, nature and society.

All theories and thoughts are used to educate and guide people to be optimistic and kind, so as to maintain the functionality of the society. Ideologies that have been appreciated by the ancient sages from the laws of nature are of universal enlightenment. For example, the on-going interactive movement of the universe has been included in the eight diagrams (eight combinations of three whole or broken lines formerly used in divination) of the Book of Changes; meanwhile the material attributes of Ying-yang and five elements in nature are all the balanced interaction of mutual reinforcement and neutralization, which constitute the living environment for the society and are also the material basis for the survival of human beings and the productive forces to promote social development. The harmony between human and nature will inevitably reach the ideal state of "oneness", which is called "perfect virtues and merits" in Buddhism. The basic principle of being human beings have been positioned by the set of etiquette and doctrine of mean in Confucianism. Thus, to reasonably measure the extent is an important factor for the enhancement of personality. The harmony and unity among human, nature and society can be achieved only by the transcending of people themselves. Therefore, the analysis and refinement of the Chinese traditional culture and thoughts from the perspective of history not only enriches the theoretical system for the visual transformation of the Chinese traditional culture, but also offers vital theoretical basis for the interactive visual expression between nature and society.

**Practical Transformation of Historical Context.** In the process of visual transformation of interactive thoughts in the Chinese traditional culture, we need to respect the historical context of the classical culture and interpret them from the perspective of the ancients. The visualization of document is not just the simple schema, but also the reflection of the ancient social and historical spirit.

"Historical Contextualism" proposed by Quentin Skinner (1940-), a renowned contemporary English thinker, has changed the research method of traditional history of thought and it has opened up a new perspective for the study on the history of political thought. He insists that it is an indispensable link for the study on the history of thought through the restoration of the specific context generated by the text to examine the author's intentions [7].

The research method of historical context is equipped with extensive guiding hints for the visualizing reappearance of classical documents. In the process of interactive visual expression, we need to understand the behaviors and intentions of the thinkers by entering the specific ideological context of history. The content of the original work must be first of all satisfied in the form, while the artistic techniques in the practice can be flexible and changeable, based on which the forming of the interactive video work can be both in line with the ideological connotation of the original author and equipped with artistic tastes, allowing the modern audience to feel the subtleties of the Chinese traditional culture among the interactive experience of work.

## 5.2   The Artistic Value of Aesthetics and Experience

**The Aesthetic Enhancement of Artistic Expression.** The visual presentation of the Chinese traditional culture and thoughts is not just the respect to and the inheritance of the traditional culture, but an artistic activity, which in the form of art is the combined expression of the new media and traditional art. High-quality visual expression can only be reached with the support of the digital technology through the multi-angle and comprehensive presentation of the new media, because the Chinese traditional culture and thoughts cannot be fully presented by the expression of the traditional art.

The creation of the art works with the digital extension can not only achieve the artistic effects of the real works through the modelling, color and material of the art entity, but also build a virtual art world. Our aesthetic vision is expanded by such kind of artwork with the combination of virtuality and reality. Even the single display of the specific artwork can also be presented through multiple angles. Digital art techniques allow the interaction between works and audience, with the virtual scenes and sound effects "narrating" the process of art creation. Besides, the virtual reality artistic technique enables the omnidirectional deconstruction of the art works, displaying the thinking process of the whole art creation from thought to the technological realization. A new-brand visual feast is given to us by the visual and real presentation of these art works. [8]

**Experiential Richness of Interactive Art.** Multimedia interactive art is used to create art works through the multimedia interactive technology, with art works mainly presented in the form of interactive devices, hereby achieving the interaction with works through human-machine interaction in the process of creating art works. In the visual presentation of the Chinese traditional culture and thoughts, this bidirectional communication can stimulate the initiative of viewers' active participation to the maximum extent and meet the personalized appreciation needs of the people in the pure appreciation mode, allowing viewers have face-to-face intelligent interaction with the art works in accordance with their interests and hobbies.

As the innovations of the times, new and fresh appreciation feelings have been added by the interactive function of the multiple digitalization. Virtual space, 3D remote sensing system and face-to-face touch system has been adopted by the virtual interaction system. The viewers can enter into a virtual space with the art works in the designated area by wearing special glass and high-tech helmet, allowing them to touch the art works that suit their tastes and access all information about the Chinese traditional culture and thoughts displayed by the art works. This new kind of high-tech artistic expression enhances both the personalized value of the art works and the emotional interaction experience between viewers and the artwork.

### 5.3    The Communication Value of Timeliness and Expansion

**The Strengthened Timeliness of Text Dissemination.** There are 48 modes of dissemination expressed in the *Communication Models*, written by Denis McQuail, a well-known English expert in the field of communications. In this book, three of the modes are most important, namely, one-way linear communication mode, two-way circular communication mode and multi-directional interactive communication mode. With the rapid development of the science and technology, the multi-directional interactive communication of new media, such as network and smart phone is the most effective way of communication for the mass media in the current society.

The interactive video work formed after the visual reconstruction of the texts in the Chinese traditional culture and thoughts is more prone to the information dissemination in the network era, especially the multi-directional interactive communication mode. In the Chinese traditional cultural environment, the culture change is a different type of cultural mode that takes place, including the material culture featured by the transformation of the basic material for human survival, the health culture of behavioral characteristics with the enhancement of the living quality for mankind as the tenet, the social political culture featured by the recognition and respect toward the common social order and organization as well as the aesthetic culture characterized by the pursuit of beauty in the leisure life [9]. These cultural phenomena are spreading globally with the fastest speed. Thus, works of the Chinese traditional culture and thoughts after the expression of the interactive video are more granted with the timeliness of communication, which is not just the effective inheritance of classic documents but the reemergence of the second life for history and culture.

**The Regional Expansion of the Cultural Communication.** Cultural communication is a kind of subjective cognition activity for mankind to encode and decode, which is manifested in the perception and understanding of human beings. Such cognitive activity is subjected to the constraint or disturbance of a series of subjective factors, whether at the stage of perception or understanding. In the long process of development, the dissemination of the Chinese traditional culture and thoughts are relatively refined in a certain geographical region. From the global perspective, cultural exchanges should not just remain in the level of text document but break through the historical constraints and regional barriers.

Today, our world is undergoing the unprecedented cultural revolution. Especially, with the arrival of the 5G era, the sense of distance in the world is diminishing gradually, the trend of the integration of all ethnic groups is becoming more obvious and the multi-cultural exchanges are more frequent. The Chinese traditional culture and thoughts are not just the wealth for the Chinese people, but the precious heritage for the people around the world. From this level, the inheritance and dissemination are of vital importance. Therefore, the mutual understanding and appreciation among different groups and cultures in the modern society is crucial to the happiness and peace of family, community, the whole society and even the world. As a consequence, inter-active visual expression of the Chinese traditional culture is obviously equipped with special significance and value for the regional expansion of cultural communication.

# 6 Conclusion

The interactive visual expression of the Chinese traditional culture is the visualized art creation built on the interpretation of the Chinese traditional culture, which is not just a schematic reemergence of the classic documents, but a secondary creation of the core thoughts in the ancient Chinese philosophy. Starting from Origin, the case work of the interactive visual expression elaborates that the natural instinct of adapting to the nature asks for the match of Yin and Yang; then enhances the "initiative realm" from the perspective of Morality and changes the impetuous mentality of the masses from Healthcare and Return for which the former asks for the nourishment of heart and the latter asks for the return of the heart. At last, based on the above-mentioned infor-mation, we obtain the knowledge and wisdom needed for survival from Changes and jump out the repetition of Cycle, reaching the ideal world of beauty and goodness.

The creation of the above-mentioned video works not only involves the combi-nation of traditional culture and digital technology, but the experimental thinking after the interpretation of the classical texts. In order to reach the visualized image trans-formation of the ancient texts, they attempt to make an organic combination of tradi-tional and modern, content and form, and technology and art with the innovative image device language. From the angle of the multi-dimensional modality of the works, this thinking process of art creation is the dynamic expression of psychology and behavior, the virtual and real combination of objects and images. The ancient philosophical flavor given out of the works from inside to the outside permeates and fills the psychological space of the audience, triggers the feelings of the audience and arouses their sensibility, hereby generating resonance and sublimation. The interactive thought of the Chinese traditional culture is achieved through diverse ways such as static image, dynamic image, physical devices and composite materials. This is a relatively grand topic that requires further adherence and exploration for the protection and inheritance of the traditional culture and thoughts. Only in this way, can the faith and wisdom of the ancient sages convert into the driving force for social development.

Everything in the universe has its own nature!

# References

1. Chapter 25 of *Lao-tzu*
2. Zhao, X.R.: A Study on the thought of "harmony between nature and man" in the Chinese traditional culture and its development. Sichuan Academy of Social Sciences, Sichuan (2017). (in Chinese)
3. Hong, X.P.: Elaboration on the main characteristics and humanistic spirit of Chinese buddhist thought. J. Nanjing Univ. (Philos. Hum. Soc. Sci.) **38**(3), 66 (2001). (in Chinese)
4. Li, L.: A Study on the ecological aesthetic wisdom of Chinese Buddhism. Doctorate Degree Dissertation of Shandong University (2009). (in Chinese)
5. Sun, C.C.: Pre-QIn confucian etiquette, ethics and its modern value. Res. Ethics **5**, 41–42 (2015). (in Chinese)
6. Wang, Y.C.: The position of *the Doctrine of the Mean* in the Chinese history of thought. J. Southwest Minzu Univ. **12**, 60 (2007). (in Chinese)
7. Yin, J., Wang, Q.: Context analysis method and historical explanation. Acad. J. Jinyang **2**, 88 (2015). (in Chinese)
8. Sheng, J.: Study on the digital extension of chinese static works of art. J. Nanjing Arts Inst. (Fine Arts Des.) **6**, 18 (2019). (in Chinese)
9. Sheng, J.: Study on the System Design of Digital Art Application in the Exhibition of Museum. Jiangsu People's Publishing Ltd., Jiangsu (2019). (in Chinese)

# Simulation Model for Mapping the Causes and Effects of Human Error in Product Development

Sven Tackenberg[✉] and Sönke Duckwitz

Laboratory for Industrial Engineering, OWL University of Applied, Sciences and Arts, Campusallee 12, 32657 Lemgo, Germany
`sven.tackenberg@th-owl.de`

**Abstract.** The applications of new information technologies in the field of product development lead to a significant change in work processes. Due to new assistance systems, companies further reduce the available time for the product developers. Based on this observation, a research hypothesis regarding the effects of the variable "amount of available time" on the quota of flawless product development is formulated. This hypothesis was empirically analyzed by conducting a laboratory experiment. The results lead to the development of a Bayesian network. The network describes the probability that a human can process a task without an error at required times. According to the structure of the Bayesian network, the paper introduces an actor-oriented model that can be used for person-centered simulation of the occurrence and effects of errors. Finally, the paper provides insight into the use of a formal model in the case of a simulation study.

**Keywords:** Actor-oriented simulation · Human reliability · Product design

## 1 Introduction

With the developments and applications of new information technologies, including Internet of Things (IoT), mobile internet and artificial intelligence, etc., the work processes in companies have changed. While the shop-floor of a company is in the focus of discussion about benefits and implementation strategies of IoT, indirect departments of a company are subordinated. In particular, the consequences for product development departments are not the focus of the current discussion. This is quite astonishing because digital solutions, such as Product Lifecycle Management-Systems and Computer-Aided Design, are already implemented in companies. Individuals use the interactive design software to iteratively draft, develop and construct products, providing a competitive advantage for the fulfillment of product requirements and the level of work efficiency [1]. However, so far, the use of these tools is a rarely analyzed area of human-machine systems [2].

Through human-computer interaction, individuals should be empowered to meet the product and process requirements. Thereby, the high complexity between components and functions has to be considered. Furthermore, the component and functions

© Springer Nature Switzerland AG 2020
C. Stephanidis et al. (Eds.): HCII 2020, LNCS 12429, pp. 381–396, 2020.
https://doi.org/10.1007/978-3-030-59987-4_27

are often very dynamic during the product development process. The fulfillment of these requirements can still not be done automatically by software tools. Therefore, a high level of human input is still essential [1]. However, due to new software functions and individual support by assistance systems, it can be observed that companies further reduce the available developing time. As a result, the time pressure experienced by individuals increases, and the probability of human reliability decreases. However, due to the interplay of different influencing factors of the person, product, and process during product development, it has so far been challenging to predict the occurrence of an error and its effect.

In this paper, first of all, the static taxonomy for description and analysis of human reliability in the product design of Djaloeis et al. is introduced [2]. The taxonomy is mainly based on the semiotic model of human-machine interaction of Luczak et al. [3] and the multi-aspect taxonomy of human malfunction by Rasmussen [4]. Based on the introduced theoretical fundament, the paper presents a Bayesian network and an actor-oriented simulation model to describe the likelihood of an error as well as the cause and effects. Furthermore, an empirical study was conducted under laboratory conditions. The focus of these experiments was the gaining of knowledge about the emergence and effects of errors in order to parameterize the developed simulation model.

## 2   Literature Review

Rasmussen defines human reliability as the human ability to fulfill the required functions at required times [5]. Based on this definition, Rasmussen develops a taxonomy, in which several aspects of human reliability interact and influence the probability and scope of requirement fulfillment (see Fig. 1) [4]:

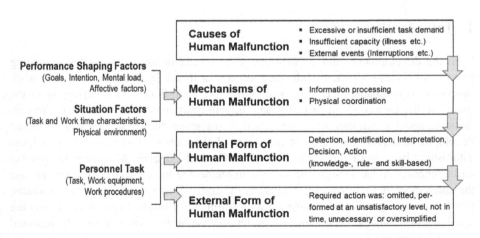

**Fig. 1.** Static taxonomy for description and analysis human reliability (based on [2])

- The issue *Personnel Task* describes the task to be performed by an individual,
- Internal reasons for inappropriate human action, such as inappropriate human information processing, or human inference (*Mechanisms of Human Malfunction*),
- External reasons for inappropriate human action, such as external interruption, excessive task demand, or the health of the individual (*Causes of Human Malfunction*).
- The issue of *Situation Factors* describes the amount of available time, the task characteristics, or the physical environment which not directly cause malfunctions.
- The issue *of Performance Shaping Factors* includes situations factors that are not directly observable.

Rasmussen's generic taxonomy of human malfunction can be adapted to define human reliability in computer-aided product design. The taxonomy in Fig. 1 summarizes the situational fulfillment of product- process-, environment-related product design. However, due to the static description, the taxonomy does not consider the iterative, time-dependent nature of product design. Therefore, Djaloeis et al. present a product development model with three phases which are executed iteratively [2]:

- Start of a task of the product design process ($t \leq 0$) – time-persistent factors are of interest.
- During the processing of a task ($0 \leq t < T$) – the time-persistent and situation-dependent factors of product design are relevant.
- End of task processing ($t \geq T$) – related to individual and product.

Therefore, a simulation model has to be developed, which reflects the internal and external reasons for inappropriate human action and sufficiently reflects the dynamics of product development.

## 3  Laboratory Experiment

For human reliability in the context of processing weakly structured work processes, only a few empirical data are available. In order to ensure a well-founded development and verification of the actor-oriented simulation model, the taxonomy of human reliability of Djaloeis et al. [2] is used and compared with the decision variables of a previous version of our simulation model [6]. Therefore, the focus lies only on the factor "amount of available time". The following research hypothesis was formulated:

- H1: "The more time is available for a task, the higher the quota of fulfilled product requirements."

This hypothesis has been previously examined for more basic, non-creative tasks, and creative-informative tasks related to product design. However, there is a lack of empirical research, when an error occurs and when it is identified during the process. Based on the above mentioned research hypothesis, an experimental design with a basic, multi-part product design process was developed and conducted. Each task requires creative-informative input and corresponds to one level of systematic engineering design, focusing on the functional, working, and constructional levels. The available processing times for the tasks are the independent variable. The results achieved and the number of errors are the dependent variables. Besides, there was a verbal, qualitative self-confrontation with the solutions developed. In this setting, the participants of the study have to design a bicycle crank, using the following tasks:

- $T_{1a}$: Handwritten sketch of the component structure based on an explosive drawing.
- $T_{1b}$: Handwritten sketch of the functional structure of the product as well as the links between component and functional structure,
- $T_2$: Preparation of a handwritten schematic sketch to illustrate options for an improvement of the existing product for the respective applications,
- $T_{3a}$: Designing the bicycle crank with a CAD software tool,
- $T_{3b}$: Assembly of the developed crank, using a CAD software tool.

The experiment was carried out under laboratory conditions in the Institute of Industrial Engineering and Ergonomics at RWTH Aachen University. A between-subjects design was chosen, and each individual participated precisely once in this experiment. Each person worked with a standard Windows desktop computer and a 21-inch TFT monitor. The sample consisted of 112 junior engineers, all of them students in higher semester engineering classes at RWTH Aachen University, which had a comparable level of knowledge about design methodology and the software tools used. The participants were divided into four groups (Table 1), which were categorized by the amount of available time.

**Table 1.** Processing times per group for the product development tasks

| Subtask | Group 1 | Group 2 | Group 3 | Group 4 |
| --- | --- | --- | --- | --- |
| 1a, 1b | 5 min | 8 min | 10 min | 12 min |
| 2 | 10 min | 12 min | 16 min | 20 min |
| 3a | 5 min | 8 min | 10 min | 13 min |
| 3b | 10 min | 12 min | 16 min | 20 min |
| Total | 30 min | 40 min | 52 min | 60 min |

The results of the preliminary study have proved that within the sample, there is no correlation between previous experience or rather spatial imagination and the quality of the achieved work results. For the evaluation of the results, the proportion of realized product requirements is evaluated. Four categories are used to differentiate the solutions:

- Category 1: The solutions fulfill the product requirements completely.
- Category 2: The solution meets most of the product requirements and has no serious errors regarding design and function.
- Category 3: The solution proportionally meets the product requirements and has several errors regarding design and function.
- Category 4: The solution does not meet the requirements to a large extent.

A design expert from the Chair and Institute of Engineering Design at RWTH Aachen University evaluated the work results of the participants. The Kruskal-Wallis test applied to the data set shows at a significance level of 0.01 that there is not an even distribution of the quota of fulfilled product requirements and available time for all subtasks. A further analysis of the rank correlation with Spearman Roh confirms the presumed highly significant correlation between the quality of the results of the five tasks and the available time with a bilateral significance level of 0.01. The graphical description employing error bar charts as well as the pairwise comparison of the groups using the post hoc Mann-Whitney test show that the corresponding null hypothesis $H_{01}$ can be rejected (see Fig. 2). The statistical evaluation implies for the simulation model the development of a probability-based relationship between the simulated time taken to process a task and a faulty execution result.

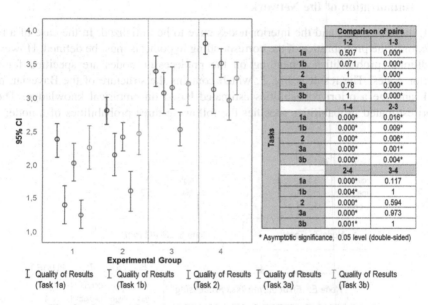

**Fig. 2.** Quality of results concerning the four-time groups and tasks

# 4   Bayesian Network for Inappropriate Human Action

A formalism for processing uncertain knowledge is Bayesian networks, also known as belief networks [7]. Bayesian networks are directed acyclic graphs. Such a graph consists of a large number of nodes connected by directed edges. Each node contains information about the probability of a priori defined events. A hypothesis describes the occurrence of a specific event and is assigned to a node. The resulting relations between nodes describe the dynamic dependencies between the probabilities of hypotheses. The following Bayesian network is based on the considerations in Jameson [8] and Kipper et al. [9].

An individual has to process a task. In this context, it would be interesting to examine whether an error occurs. According to the results of Djaloeis et al. [2], at least the knowledge of an individual, the difficulty of the task as well as the required processing time must be taken into account. The higher the knowledge of an individual or the easier the task is, the higher the likelihood that the individual will not make an error during task processing. On the other hand, there is a correlation between a present error and the observed processing time. Four nodes will be introduced which represent the following hypotheses:

- The individual has a high or low skill level to process the task (Node $S$).
- The task has a low, medium, or high complexity (Node $T$).
- During the processing of the task, an error or no error occurs (Node $E$).
- The required processing time is low or high (Node $D$).

### 4.1    Initialization of the Network

First, the root nodes and the interior nodes have to be initialized. In the case of a root node, only the probabilities of the corresponding hypothesis must be defined. However, conditional probabilities depending on the predecessor nodes are specified for the interior nodes. The result is Fig. 3, which contains the structure of the Bayesian network and the a priori probabilities estimated based on empirical knowledge. The a priori estimated probabilities specifies the following three probabilities of a node:

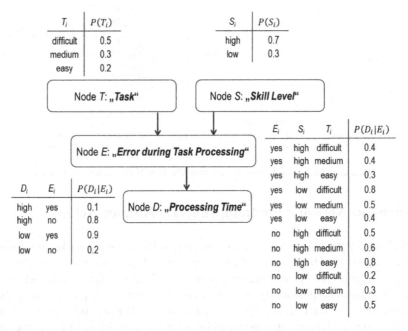

**Fig. 3.** A-priori probabilities of the Bayesian network for the Use Case

- π-Value: Current strength to support the hypothesis of the node through the predecessor nodes.
- λ-Value: Degree of support of the hypothesis of the node through its successor nodes.
- BEL-value: Overall confidence that the hypothesis is true.

The BEL-value of a hypothesis $H_i$ of node $N_i$ is calculated from the π-value and the λ-value of the same node according to formula (1):

$$BEL(H_i) = \alpha \cdot \lambda(N_i) \cdot \pi(N_i) \text{ with } \sum_{i=1}^{n} BEL(H_i) = 1 \qquad (1)$$

During the initialization phase, the probability values of the successor nodes of the root notes have not been defined. Therefore, the λ-values are therefore initially assumed to be "1":

$$BEL(T) = \alpha \cdot \lambda(T) \cdot \pi(T) = \alpha \begin{pmatrix} 1 \\ 1 \\ 1 \end{pmatrix} \times \begin{pmatrix} 0.5 \\ 0.3 \\ 0.2 \end{pmatrix} = \begin{pmatrix} 0.5 \\ 0.3 \\ 0.2 \end{pmatrix} \qquad (2)$$

The value BEL(S) is determined analogously. All values of the network are shown once again in Fig. 4. The interior nodes are calculated from the π-vectors of their predecessor nodes. Thereby, the λ-vectors for the successor nodes are also initially assumed to have the value 1. The basis for determining the values for the interior nodes

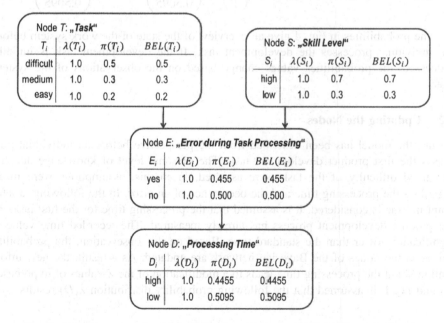

**Fig. 4.** Bayesian network after initialization of the probability values of all nodes

is the *"formula of the total probability"* [14]. This results in the $\pi$-proportion of the probability of an error (Skill levels $j$: 2| Complexity levels $k$ of the task: 3):

$$\pi(E_1) = \sum_{j=1}^{2} \sum_{k=1}^{3} P(E_1|S_j, T_k) \cdot \pi(S_j) \cdot \pi(S_k) \tag{3}$$

$$\pi(E_1) = 0.14 + 0.084 + 0.042 + 0.12 + 0.045 + 0.024 = 0.455 \tag{4}$$

$$\pi(E_2) = \sum_{j=1}^{2} \sum_{k=1}^{3} P(E_2|S_j, T_k) \cdot \pi(S_j) \cdot \pi(S_k) = 0.5 \tag{5}$$

The probability of a high or low execution time is carried out analogous to:

$$\pi(D_1) = \sum_{j=1}^{2} (D_1|E_j) \cdot \pi(E_j) = 0.1 \cdot 0,455 + 0.8 \cdot 0.5 = 0.4455 \tag{6}$$

$$\pi(D_2) = \sum_{j=1}^{2} (D_2|E_j) \cdot \pi(E_j) = 0.9 \cdot 0,455 + 0.2 \cdot 0.5 = 0.5095 \tag{7}$$

On the basis of the $\pi$-values, the following *BEL*-vectors for the nodes $E$ and $D$ are calculated:

$$BEL(E) = \alpha \cdot \lambda(E) \times \pi(E) = \alpha \cdot \begin{pmatrix} 1 \\ 1 \end{pmatrix} \times \begin{pmatrix} 0.455 \\ 0.500 \end{pmatrix} \underset{with\alpha=1}{=} \begin{pmatrix} 0.455 \\ 0.500 \end{pmatrix} \tag{8}$$

$$BEL(D) = \alpha \cdot \lambda(D) \times \pi(D) = \alpha \cdot \begin{pmatrix} 1 \\ 1 \end{pmatrix} \times \begin{pmatrix} 0.4455 \\ 0.5095 \end{pmatrix} \underset{with\alpha=1}{=} \begin{pmatrix} 0.4455 \\ 0.5095 \end{pmatrix} \tag{9}$$

The probabilities in Fig. 4 give an overview of the state of the work system before the individual processes the development task. If the development task is initially processed, the probabilities values change based on the observations of the system state.

## 4.2    Updating the Nodes

So far, the model has been described from the perspective before an individual processes the first product development task. The personal level of knowledge and the perceived difficulty of the task were assessed. From this, assumptions were made regarding the processing time and the occurrence of an error. In the following, a later point in time is considered. It is assumed that the processing time for the first tasks of the product development process has already measured. The recorded time value is significantly lower than the standard time. Based on this observation, the probability values in the nodes of the Bayesian network are updated. As a result, the new information about the processing time leads to a modification of the $\lambda$-values of hypotheses $D_1$ and $D_2$. It is assumed that the following probability distribution $\lambda(D)$ results:

$$\lambda(D) = \begin{pmatrix} 0.2 \\ 0.8 \end{pmatrix} = \begin{matrix} observedtime \geq standardtime \\ observedtime < standardtime \end{matrix} \quad (10)$$

The modification of $\lambda(D)$ results in new values for the *BEL*-vector of node $D$:

$$Bel(D) = \alpha \cdot \lambda(D) \times \pi(D) = \begin{pmatrix} 0.2 \\ 0.8 \end{pmatrix} \times \begin{pmatrix} 0.4455 \\ 0.5095 \end{pmatrix} = \begin{pmatrix} 0.0891 \\ 0.4076 \end{pmatrix}$$

$$= \alpha \cdot \begin{pmatrix} 0.0891 \\ 0.4076 \end{pmatrix} \underset{with\alpha=2.0129}{=} \begin{pmatrix} 0.1794 \\ 0.8206 \end{pmatrix} \quad (11)$$

Once a significantly shorter processing time has been observed, it is no longer plausible to assume an equal probability values for the occurrence of an error or no error. Consequently, the new information should affect the *BEL*-vector of node $D$ in such a way that the probability for hypothesis $E_1$ (occurrence of an error) increases, while it decreases for hypothesis $E_2$ (no occurrence of an error). For this purpose, a $\lambda$-message is sent from the node $D$ to the predecessor node $E$ with $e_i$ elements (see Fig. 5).

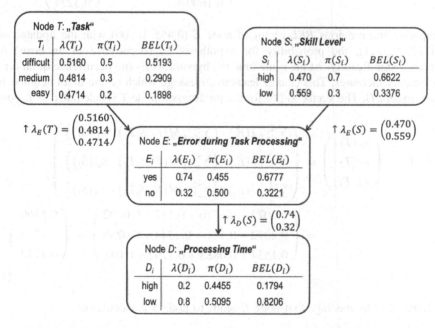

**Fig. 5.** Based on the observed processing time, modified probabilities of the Bayesian network

Once significantly shorter processing time is observed, it is no longer plausible to assume an equal probability value for the occurrence of an error or no error. Consequently, the new information should affect the $BEL$-vector of node $D$ in such a way that the probability for hypothesis $E_1$ (occurrence of an error) increases. At the same time, the hypothesis $E_2$ (no occurrence of an error) decreases. For this purpose, a message is sent from the node $D$ to the predecessor node $E$ with $e_i$ elements:

$$
\lambda_D(E) = \begin{pmatrix} \lambda_D(E_1) \\ \lambda_D(E_2) \end{pmatrix} = \begin{pmatrix} \lambda(D_1) \cdot P(D_1|E_1) + \lambda(D_2) \cdot P(D_2|E_1) \\ \lambda(D_1) \cdot P(D_1|E_2) + \lambda(D_2) \cdot P(D_2|E_2) \end{pmatrix} \tag{12}
$$

$$
= \begin{pmatrix} 0.2 \cdot 0.1 + 0.8 \cdot 0.9 \\ 0.2 \cdot 0.8 + 0.8 \cdot 0.2 \end{pmatrix} = \begin{pmatrix} 0.74 \\ 0.32 \end{pmatrix}
$$

After receiving the $\lambda_D$-message, the probability values within the node $M$ are recalculated:

$$
BEL(E) = \alpha \cdot \lambda(E) \times \pi(E) = \begin{pmatrix} 0.74 \\ 0.32 \end{pmatrix} \times \begin{pmatrix} 0.455 \\ 0.500 \end{pmatrix} = \begin{pmatrix} 0.3367 \\ 0.1600 \end{pmatrix}
$$

$$
= \alpha \cdot \begin{pmatrix} 0.3367 \\ 0.1600 \end{pmatrix} =^{with \alpha=2.0129} \begin{pmatrix} 0.6777 \\ 0.3221 \end{pmatrix} \tag{13}
$$

Comparing the previous $BEL$-vector of node $E$ (0.455, 0.500) with the updated one (0.6777, 0.3221), the probability for hypothesis $E_1$ (occurrence of an error) has decreased significantly. At the same time the hypothesis $E_2$ (no occurrence of an error) significantly increases. This change leads to a message which is sent to all neighboring nodes, except $D$. The vector $\lambda_E(T)$ for the predecessor node $T$ is calculated as follows:

$$
\lambda_E(T) = \begin{pmatrix} \lambda_E(T_1) \\ \lambda_E(T_2) \\ \lambda_E(T_3) \end{pmatrix} = \begin{pmatrix} \sum_{i=1}^2 \lambda(E_i) \cdot \left( \sum_{i=1}^2 M(E_1|S_jT_1) \cdot \pi_E(S_j) \right) \\ \sum_{i=1}^2 \lambda(E_i) \cdot \left( \sum_{i=1}^2 M(E_1|S_jT_2) \cdot \pi_E(S_j) \right) \\ \sum_{i=1}^2 \lambda(E_i) \cdot \left( \sum_{i=1}^2 M(E_1|S_jT_3) \cdot \pi_E(S_j) \right) \end{pmatrix}
$$

$$
= \begin{pmatrix} 0.2072 + 0.1776 + 0.112 + 0.0192 \\ 0.2072 + 0.111 + 0.1344 + 0.0288 \\ 0.1554 + 0.0888 + 0.1792 + 0.048 \end{pmatrix} = \begin{pmatrix} 0.5160 \\ 0.4814 \\ 0.4714 \end{pmatrix} \tag{14}
$$

Similarly, the message that node $E$ sends to node $S$ is calculated:

$$
\lambda_E(S) = \begin{pmatrix} \lambda_E(S_1) \\ \lambda_E(S_2) \end{pmatrix} = \begin{pmatrix} 0.470 \\ 0.559 \end{pmatrix} \tag{15}
$$

Following the λ-messages sent from node $E$ to the predecessor nodes $T$ and $S$, the probabilities are updated:

$$BEL(T) = \alpha \cdot \lambda(T) \times \pi(T) = \alpha \cdot \begin{pmatrix} 0.5160 \\ 0.4814 \\ 0.4714 \end{pmatrix} \times \begin{pmatrix} 0.5 \\ 0.3 \\ 0.2 \end{pmatrix}$$

$$= \alpha \cdot \begin{pmatrix} 0.2580 \\ 0.1445 \\ 0.0943 \end{pmatrix} \underset{with\,\alpha=2.0129}{=} \begin{pmatrix} 0.5193 \\ 0.2909 \\ 0.1898 \end{pmatrix}$$

(16)

$$BEL(S) = \alpha \cdot \lambda(S) \times \pi(S) = \alpha \cdot \begin{pmatrix} 0.470 \\ 0.559 \end{pmatrix} \times \begin{pmatrix} 0.7 \\ 0.3 \end{pmatrix}$$

$$= \alpha \cdot \begin{pmatrix} 0.3290 \\ 0.1677 \end{pmatrix} \underset{with\,\alpha=2.0129}{=} \begin{pmatrix} 0.6622 \\ 0.3376 \end{pmatrix}$$

(17)

The comparison of the previous $BEL$-vector with the modified one shows that the two $BEL$-vectors are only slightly changed by the recalculation.

The Bayesian network covers the three central factors of human reliability, described by Rasmussen: Personnel Task, Mechanism, and Causes of Malfunction. Based on a current observation of the processing time, the complexity of a task and the individual skill level, the probability of the occurrence of an error is modified. These calculation rules can be used in the simulation model to illustrate the possibility of an error.

## 5   Simulation Model

The product development process consists of several related and independent tasks that have to be processed. Due to the resulting degrees of freedom, an individual can process these tasks using different tasks sequences and processing modes. To analyze the relations, setting up a simulation model is a suitable approach. Simulation provides a way of experimenting with a model of a work process to understand its dynamics under various settings of decision variables and constraints. A simulation study usually consists of independent, iteratively processed simulation runs to generate data for statistical analysis. A taxonomy for classifying organizational models and the corresponding simulation approaches is subject to the German standard VDI 3633, Part 6. According to this standard, the pivotal point is the simulated level of individual activities within an organization. In activity-oriented models, the simulated dynamic is determined by the modeled activities, whereas in actor-oriented models, the simulated behavior of persons causes the dynamic of the model. Both approaches are further differentiated according to the level of human behavior represented in the simulation model: task-centered, personnel-integrated, and person-centered. This paper presents an actor-oriented, person-centered model. The simulated work person can make autonomous decisions based on a behavioral model, and the task is individually processed.

### 5.1 Actor-Oriented Simulation Approach

Precedence relations of tasks describe the functional and/or chronological relationship. To each task $j \in J$ a set of precedence relations $Pred(j)$ is assigned, with the exception of the initial task $j = 0$, $Pred(j) = \emptyset$. All tasks in $Pred(j)$ must be sufficiently processed before task $j$ can be initially started. Pre-emption of tasks is allowed, therefore the degree of processing $\delta_i$ of tasks in $Pred(j)$ has to be considered instead of start times and durations of $Pred(j)$. In the absence of a clearly defined sequence of task processing, an individual decides independently and according to their judgment which task is processed next. Empirical studies indicate that humans are prone to seeing short-term tasks as more important than long-term ones. In the case of product development, a task is often preferably selected if the desired result can be reached with low workload, the task is perceived as an interesting challenge or the time frame until the required completion date greatly decreases. In the literature, this behavior is referred to as bounded rational behavior [10]. Steel and König [11] include the time factor in a prioritization rule to describe the forms of decisions and actions taken, referred to as Temporal Motivational Theory. Organizing the executable tasks by a human is based on evaluating the positive and negative aspects of processing task $j$ at time $t$. Supporting aspects of selecting a specific task $j$ are the importance $I_j$ and the urgency of $j$. The criterion of urgency is expressed by the period between the desired deadline $t_{j\_dead}$ of $j$, the present time $t$ as well as the attained degree of processing $\delta_j$, in relation to the planned time exposure $a_{j,m}$. Negative aspects are described by the familiarization of the individual with the task $\delta_{STpj}$ and the preparation time $a_{STj}$ if a task is initially processed or being resumed after an interruption. The influence of the individual character on decision making is taken into consideration by the factors $F_w$ and $F_{STw}$ and $\Gamma^+$. The priority of a task is expressed as [13]:

$$Priority_j(t) = \frac{I_j \cdot F_w}{1 + \Gamma^+ \left( \frac{t_{jdead} - t}{a_{j,m}(1 - \delta_j)} \right)} - \left( (1 - \delta_{STj}) a_{STj} \cdot F_{STw} \right) \tag{18}$$

The implemented algorithm runs through the same sequence of events and states during a simulation run (see Fig. 6). The simulated behavior of the individual leads to a prioritization of all work tasks in the task pool. Afterward, the individual selects the task with the highest priority and checks the availability of the required work equipment and work objects (status "*Organize*"). If both are available, the state changes from "*Organize*" to "*Processing*". If the task with the highest priority cannot be processed, the individual selects the task with the second-highest priority, and so on. In the case that no task can be treated, the new state is "*Unemployed*". Such a status can occur due to insufficient processing of previous tasks by other individuals. During task processing, the processing stage of the task increases. Furthermore, the individual continuously checks whether the task has been completed or whether a specified period has expired. In both cases, the individual switches to the status "*Organize*", prioritizes the task pool, and selects a new or the same task for processing. If the task is fully processed, the corresponding work object is created. This object represents the necessary input for the initial processing of the subsequent tasks. Such a work object can be a real or virtual object, a document, or information.

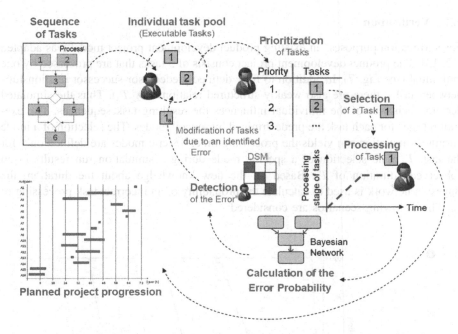

**Fig. 6.** Actor-oriented simulation model to analyze the consequences of errors

Based on the empirical study, the correlation between the required processing time of a task, and human reliability has been included in the model. The algorithm captures the completion time of a task and determines the required processing time. The structure of the Bayesian network is used to calculate the current probability of an error based on the processing time. Additional factors influencing the probability are the complexity of the task and the competence level of the individual. If the probability determines the existence of an error during the processing of a specific task, the corresponding work object is assigned the attributes *"Error Time"* {*Task ID*}, *"Error type"* {*Error ID*}, *"Error known"* {*yes, no*}. The processing of the subsequent tasks is carried out up to the point where the individual identifies the error. The probability of identifying an error depends on the subsequent tasks, and a corresponding value is assigned to each task. If an error is detected, the individual has to process already completed tasks and/or additional work on future tasks is necessary. The required information required is mapped in a Design Structure Matrix for a specific error:

- Probability of identifying the error during processing a specific task,
- Tasks that have to be iteratively processed due to the error,
- Time required for an iterative processing of already completed tasks,
- Extra time for tasks which have not yet started.

Based on the point in time when the error is identified, the algorithm determines the number of tasks to be processed iteratively as well as the time required to rectify the error. The processing of the modified tasks is based on the simulated individual decision behavior and selection of tasks.

## 5.2    Verification

For verification purposes, an existing product development project model was adapted [12, 13]. The product development project consists of 5 tasks that are processed by one individual (see Fig. 7). In addition to fully defined predecessor-successor relationships between tasks, there are also weakly structured relations ($T_2$, $T_3$). Thus the simulated decision behavior of the individual influences the resulting task sequences. The execution times for each task are predetermined by several modes. The selection of a mode during a simulation run yields the processing time. Several modes are defined only for the task $T_4$. The selection of a specific mode during a simulation run results in an "observed" duration of $T_4$. Based on the new knowledge about the duration, the Bayesian network is used to calculate the probability of an incorrect task processing of $T_4$. The following scenarios are considered:

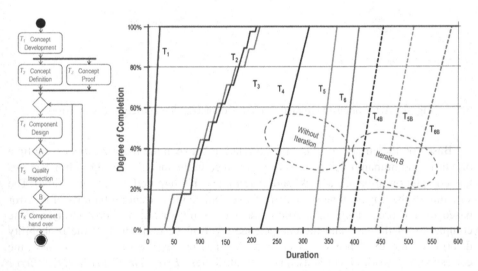

**Fig. 7.** Simulation results (Scenario 1: without an error | Scenario 2: detection of an error at point B)

- Scenario 1: The standard times of all tasks are sufficiently assessed.
- Scenario 2: The standard time of task $T_4$ is reduced significantly.

A further variable during a simulation run was the time of identifying the error. Based on whether an error occurs, the task at which an error occurs and the task at which the error is identified, the simulated project processes different.

The probability for the detection of an error when finalizing task $T_4$ is assumed to be 50%. If the error is detected, 50% of the initial work of $T_4$ has to be repeated to fix the error. The corresponding DSM of the error contains both values. When the error is not detected at point $A$, the probability rises to 80% after finalizing task $T_5$. If the simulated individual detects the error at point $B$, an iteration loop occurs, and 50% of the initial work of task $T_4$ and $T_5$ has to be repeated.

The axis of abscissas shows the duration of the development project (see Fig. 7). The ordinate shows the cumulated amount of work spend to finish the project. The heterogeneity of the simulated duration results from the additional amount of work resulting from the time of the error occurrence and identification. Flawless processing of the tasks results in a duration of 387 time units (TU). If the simulated individual detects the error after $T_4$, an iteration of $T_4$ is necessary, and the total duration increases to 535 TU. Figure 7 illustrates the effect of late error detection. Due to an iteration loop covering two tasks, the duration increases to 584 TU.

## 6 Conclusion and Outlook

In this paper, we simulate the occurrence and the impact of different errors on the progress of a product development project. We used an actor-oriented, person-centered simulation model to illustrate individual decision making during product development. The results of the laboratory experiment lead to an enhancement of the existing actor-oriented work process simulation models [6] by considering bounded human reliability and its influence on development projects. The introduced Bayesian network describes the probability that an error occurs. Thereby, the observed system states regarding the activity durations lead to a dynamic adjustment of error probabilities. Therefore, the simulation model enables managers to identify the origin and impact of an error during a future product development process. Thus function allows the user to optimally solve the trade-off between the standard time of a task and the error occurrence. The results contribute to a better understanding of product design processes and a more detailed analysis of human reliability in this field of work. For further development of the simulation model, a follow-up experiment could include collaborative work on tasks and interruptions with a higher disruptive force (e.g., simulated telephone calls).

## References

1. Pahl, G., Beitz, W., Feldhusen, J., Grote, K.-H.: Engineering Design. Springer, London (2007). https://doi.org/10.1007/978-1-84628-319-2
2. Djaloeis, R., Duckwitz, S., Hinsch, M., Feldhusen, J., Schlick, C.M.: Analysis of human reliability in computer-aided design. In: SMC 2012: Conference Proceedings of 2012 IEEE International Conference on Systems, Man, and Cybernetics (IEEE SMC 2012), Seoul, October 2012, pp. 868–873. IEEE, Piscataway (2012)
3. Luczak, H., Springer, J., Schmidt, L.: Ergonomics of CAD systems. In: Karwowski, W. (ed.) International Encyclopedia of Ergonomics and Human Factors, vol. 1, 2nd edn. Taylor & Francis, London, New York (2006)

4. Rasmussen, J.: Human errors. A taxonomy for describing human malfunction in industrial installations. Journal of Occupational Accidents **4**, 311–333 (1982)
5. Rasmussen, J.: Notes on Human Error Analysis and Prediction. Risø National Laboratory, Risø (1978)
6. Tackenberg, S., Duckwitz, S., Schlick, C.: Activity- and actor-oriented simulation approach for the management of development projects. Int. J. Comput. Aided Eng. Technol. **2**(4), 414–435 (2010)
7. Abramson, B.: On knowledge representation in belief networks. In: Bouchon-Meunier, B., Yager, Ronald R., Zadeh, Lotfi A. (eds.) IPMU 1990. LNCS, vol. 521, pp. 86–96. Springer, Heidelberg (1991). https://doi.org/10.1007/BFb0028092
8. Jameson, A.: Knowing what others know. studies in intuitive psychometrics. PhD-Thesis, University of Amsterdam, Amsterdam (1990)
9. Kipper, B., Brants, T., Plach, M., Schäfer, R.: Bayessche Netze: Ein einführendes Beispiel. Technical Report 4, Graduiertenkolleg Kognitionswissenschaft, Saarbrücken, Universität des Saarlandes (1995)
10. Kahneman, D.: Maps of bounded rationality: a perspective on intuitive judgment and choice. In: Frängsmyr, T. (ed.) Prize Lecture, Les Prix Nobel, The Nobel Prizes 2002. Nobel Foundation, Stockholm (2003)
11. Steel, P., König, C.J.: Integrating theories of motivation. Acad. Manag. Rev. **31**(4), 889–913 (2006)
12. Duckwitz, S., Tackenberg, S., Kobelt, D.: Simulationsmodell zur Abbildung der Ursachen und Auswirkungen von menschlichen Fehlern in der Produktentwicklung. In: GfA (eds.): Frühjahrskongress 2019, Dresden Arbeit interdisziplinär analysieren – bewerten – gestalten. Dresden (2019)
13. Duckwitz, S., Tackenberg, S., Schlick, C.M.: Simulation of human behavior in knowledge-intensive services. In: Ganz, W. (ed.) Productivity of Services Next Gen - Beyond Output/Input: RESER 2011, p. 208. Fraunhofer Verlag, Stuttgart (2011)
14. Dallmann, H., Ester, K.-H.: Einführung in die höhere Mathematik, vol. III. Gustav Fischer Verlag, Jena (1992)

# Aspects of Form, Interface, and Interaction in the Design of Wearable Devices

Ziqiao Wang[✉]

School of Media Arts and Communication of Nanjing University of the Arts,
Nanjing, China
549950413@qq.com

**Abstract.** Wearable device is a collective wearable device that compromises big data and intelligent sensor technology. It has become the focus of the public under the circumstance social economy is developing rapidly, the internet is widely spreading, and intelligent sensor technology is developing overall. Nowadays, society has given space to express one's distinguishing feature for everyone to the most extent. Personalized pursue of sentiment has become the characteristic of the epoch. However, the acceleration of social pace has already made social pressure spread among individuals and groups in an unprecedented speed. How to meet personal needs, relieve stress, make happiness, and create value, has become the question in need of an urgent solution when designing wearable devices. This paper discusses the design of wearable devices from three aspects: form and appearance, which includes the shape, scale, material and color, classifications, graphic elements and typography of the visual interface, and the man-machine interactions such as operational procedure, input means, and feedback experience.

**Keywords:** Wearable devices · Design of form and appearance · Design of visual interface · Design of man-machine interaction

## 1 Introduction

Wearable device is a collective wearable device which compromises big data and intelligent sensor technology. Its notion and definition have different versions. Generally speaking, wearable device refers to a kind of portable device which could be worn on the body or integrated to the clothes or the accessories. Meanwhile, as an intelligent device, it is also called "intelligent wearable device," and "intelligent wearables means using wearable technology to do intelligent design on daily wears, thus, to develop wearable devices, such as eyeglasses, gloves, clothes, and shoes, etc." [1].

Wearable devices could be divided into two types: product and platform. Wearable devices for product type are mainly for a particular function, the aim of its research and development is to strengthen some kind of lateralization function, take Jawbone and Fitbit for example, they are the kind of wearable devices which are used to measure exclusive statistics of the body. They have some singlet functions such as measuring heart rate, calorie consumption, daily walking step number, etc. Product wearable

© Springer Nature Switzerland AG 2020
C. Stephanidis et al. (Eds.): HCII 2020, LNCS 12429, pp. 397–410, 2020.
https://doi.org/10.1007/978-3-030-59987-4_28

devices have relatively low requirements for learning cost, which means they are easy to use, and consumers could learn with high efficiency. Different from product wearable devices, platform types focus more on the complexity of the functions and establishing a shareable platform. They also gather various kinds of functions together. Their complexity forces the consumers to spend more time in familiarizing their operations. At the same time, compounding devices are generally inserted hardware compositions individually, whose allocations could support the software system of third parties, such as Apple Watch, Galaxy Gear 2, Google Glass, etc. The design of both the product type and the platform type should be focused on the three aspects: form and appearance, visual interface, man-machine interaction.

## 2 Design of Form and Appearance for Wearable Devices

The form is the most direct language for the product to express itself, it is the dominant method to tell the characteristic of the product and show the information of the product. Generally, the excellent design of form can produce proper physiology and psychological experience and trigger a series of ongoing sentimental activities, such as relaxation, joyous, fascination, and expectation. "Form" refers to the shape of the product and outline appearance after proportions and harmonization, "appearance" mainly refers to the gestures and expressions of the product, which mainly contains color, select material, quality, etc. As a compound word, the form contains not only the implication of form but also the stimulation of sense organ. Therefore, exquisite and diverse shapes, scale after adaptation to a specific condition, inappropriate material measure, and color with brightness and shade are indispensable elements of form.

### 2.1   Exquisite and Diverse Shape

With the increase of aesthetic standards, people have already been tired of the monotonous shape, and personalized shape thus becomes a compelling way to attract people's attention. The conceptual modular smartphone called Project Ara, published by Google in 2015, was a representative of personalized-designed of a portable electronic device. Although this type of mobile phone does not belong to wearable devices, it contains the necessary potentials and characteristics for wearable devices in the future. As Fig. 1 shows, the block model machine uses standard hardware interface (general electromagnet adsorption interface), every model could connect by exchange interface and steel structures of a frame in order to give a unique shape to every model. Users can make the models alternate between arrangement and composition at all time, thus, to create a unique layout. With 3D printing technology continually mature and perfect, users in the future can create their model shape by themselves, which means that realizing the thought into reality.

The shape of design which is direct to the heart would make an impression on us, and to stimulate the appetite to buy. The nature of people's desire for beautiful things impels people to select more beautiful things constantly, which requires the products to be more diverse in design and give consumers abundant imagination. Different and graceful design shapes of wearable devices expressed increase consumers' viscosity

**Fig. 1.** Modular general-used frame and assembling method (Source: https://www.toodaylab. com/69585)

effectively and trigger the infinite dream of the products. What is more, the design shape with active, positive emotion is also a necessity. Usually, emotion is expressed in the form of sentiments. As everyone has different emotions and sentiment, detecting individual sentiments for everybody appropriately is a humanistic core for the design of wearable devices. The function of expressing sentiments could also be expressed in the shape of wearable devices. Therefore, designers could use hyperbolic art shapes to express these particular sentiments.

Generally speaking, in shape of the design, designers should start from the aspect of ergonomics, after doing some analysis on the target audience and corresponding settings to individual consumer's physical quality, such as physique, weight, and height, and then acquire the underlying model structure which is reliable and dependable. After knowing the sophisticated basic model structure, users still have the setting right to increase, reduce and change modular part by themselves, thus to make the users to play their full imagination, create a new modular part according to their own characteristics, design on the basic modular structure initially, and generate marks suitable for their personality.

## 2.2 Scale After Adaptation to Specific Condition

For the users, if diverse shape design is a prior admission ticket, proper function in an appropriate scale is a permanent license. Wearable devices focus on the word "wear," the essential element is function. Whether the device is comfortably worn, decides whether it is accepted by the body, and wearing comfortably requires the scale of wearing devices to be suitable for the body structure. Therefore, in the process of designing wearable devices should take a broad view of different body parts and adapt suitable scale setting.

At the same time, design for the scale should be divided into two aspects: products and users. As far as the angle of products, for one thing, the design of wearable devices should pay attention to the scale between using area and supporting area, solve the relationship between the whole and the part. Increase the area of the visible part to the full on the basis of not affecting use in order to provide the consumers with a good user experience. For another, the scale of the product itself should be set strictly according to the size of the users, for example, wearable devices in the form of wristband should be adapted according to the scale of the users' limbs, and trunk, the ones in head-mounted form should be designed according to the users' pupillary distance.

As far as the angle of users, the design of wearable devices should fully abbey the scale of users' five senses: auditory sense, touch sense, visual sense, olfactory sense, and taste sense, not limited to the minimal requirements to the users, but to express the depth of five senses more directly, that is to say, it should be designed to the scale of the depth of senses which matches the sensing ability of different users. For example, the design of wristband devices aims to fit the touch sense, and the design of head-mounted devices to fit the visual sense.

### 2.3   The Material in Appropriate Measure

Material is not only the bone of the product but also the outer garment. Appropriate material could make the structure of the product briefer and the appearance more charming. In the design of wearable devices, the constitution of multi-material could increase the comparison among the components of the device, thus, to make the users distinguish the components more conveniently. Meanwhile, the selection for the material also meets for people's nature of loving beautiful things. For example, in ancient China, the buildings with wooden structures were decorated by Cornices Brackets, Brocade satin was decorated by floral border, glazed tiles were decorated with grains. These different materials illustrate that decoration to the objects is an advanced method for the people to express beauty. The selection of materials for wearable devices should take decoration into consideration and is the same as the overlying of multi-material. As a kind of decoration, the material could improve the aesthetic degree of the wearable products, which means increasing products' fascination from the level of aesthetic.

Material is also a way of abstraction perception in daily life. When people are touching the surface of the object, they are sensing its material at the same time and arouse their user experience. Therefore, the process of using touch sense to stimulate memory is also a process of skeuomorphism, which also means the experience of playing games. The function of skeuomorphism of the material arouses the users' memory at the exact moment of touching, and utilizing this kind of biological property compounds unique wearable functions with a tactile sense of relevant material, which plays a leading role in the function performing.

### 2.4   Color with Brightness and Shade

After the products facilitated with shape, scale, and material, the color becomes the catalyst to distillate the overall effect. As human beings have long lived in the multifarious colorful world, after years and years' sense and experience of the stimulation from the outside world, human beings have acquired a large amount of sense experience. When contacting with some kind of concrete color, the consciousness in the heart would be triggered to help the main body remember the object which color represent. A famous British psychologist Gregory said: "the sense of color is meaningful to human beings—it is the core of visual sense and impresses our emotional state deeply" [2]. Color is the first impression of abstraction of natural objects, this kind of feeling can be broadly adopted in the design of wearable devices and arouse users' affective association. Based on this point, using color appropriately could serve people to express complicated feelings and emotions. The appliance of color should pay attention to national characteristics and regionalism. Same color would express different sentimental connotation in different countries and regions, for example, in ancient China, the empires were more likely to use yellow to represent noble and red for joyous, however, in western countries, yellow is usually used to express the emotion of jealous, timid and overcautious, red is used to express violence. The design of color should be selected according to the cultural regulations in different countries, which is the principle for wearable devices design to follow.

Besides applying the fixed collocation formed by national, ethnic, and regional culture, color collocation also depends on color's harmonization and comparison to maneuver users' active sentiment effectively. Harmonization and comparison have the relationship of the unity of opposites, just like one coin has two sides. Single comparison would trigger fierce stimulated feelings to cause people uncomfortable, and complete harmonization would cause visual sense to lose weight and finally lead to a feeling of debility of the color. Thus it is needed to mix under an appropriate scale, which is more evident in wearable devices. The function of colors on wearable devices could be divided into two parts: requirements of function and fashion aesthetic. From the part of function requirement, the color of wearable devices should give more focus on the functional characteristics of the devices, which means that users could imagine the function of the devices from the color alone, at the same time, some essential parts should be highlighted and form a differentiated color relationship. From the part of fashion aesthetic, the color focus of wearable devices should achieve the aim of the unity of the general character and individuality. On the one hand, it is needed to correspond to the group psychology of users. On the other, it should magnify users' aesthetic character, including pursuing differences and eccentricity to make people of different ages, genders, professions, cultures, and faith acquire the color they are fond of.

## 3  Design of Visual Interface for Wearable Devices

From biological angle, the visual sense is a process of sensing, receiving, and analyzing information. This process is also the process of anastomosing and transferring information from outside and individual thoughts of the receiver himself. Among the five senses, visual sense plays the role of receiving the most information, that is to say, visual sense plays a crucial role in handling the information from outside and make right judgment, which means that wearable devices must carefully consider how to design their visual interface in order to lead and regulate users' behavior correctly.

The nature of wearable visual interface games refers to the plan and regulation of the interface visual procedure and visual effects. Generally, the visual procedure is constituted of viewpoint paths that are passed by body vision when perceiving information from out space. These optical paths are divided into three perceptual procedures, including the chief first impression after perception with physiological photoreceptor cell as the leading supporter purely, part of detail impression concerned by explicit consciousness (second impression), and supplementary judgment formed by psychological reflection after people's awareness (reflective impression). Because of the limitation of the body's vision, when observing a visual interface, users usually would move optical line of sight based on instinct, gaze at every element on the visual interface. If we lead this kind of optical line of sight incorrectly and greatly harm the user experience. Visual effects usually contain some essential elements in graphic design, including icon elements and typography. Therefore, the result of the visual effect usually decides the users' intention to use. Visual effects and visual procedures should consider the limitation of its design space, which means visual interface types, advantages, and disadvantages of wearable devices should be listed and analyze the design principles of visual procedures and the visual effects correspondingly.

### 3.1 Classification of Visual Interface

In case of nowadays technology, wearable devices' visual interface are divided into two types: the first is traditional visual interface based on fixed screen, such as TV screen, mobile phone screen, and computer screen, etc., the second is virtual holographical visual interface based on projection, such as virtual reality, augmented reality and mixed reality.

The visual interface of fixed screen mainly appears on wearable devices such as wristband and watch. As virtual technology is immature nowadays, size-fixed screen still has some advantages. Firstly, a size-fixed screen gives regulation to the scale of vision in order to regulate the point position and the proportion the visual images appear. Secondly, size-fixed screen gives a medium for people to operate, which makes the feedback more reliable. Meanwhile, there still exists a significant defect in the visual interface. First of all, as such kinds of devices are smaller than mobile phones, they need to do scaling correspondingly when designing an interface. Besides, the appearance of a visual interface is limited to the fixed screen, so if the users want to acquire information, they need to make the screen appear in the visual threshold, like taking mobile phone out of pocket to check the incoming telegram or the message. The process of moving screens is the process of transferring the center of sight point in nature. Although nowadays people have already formed a habit of moving screen repeatedly, no matter how rapid to move the screen, the moving screen will still consume some time and produce some trouble. We can also say that the process of moving impedes the efficiency of users to percept and accept information promptly.

Vision interface under Virtual reality projection and Augmented reality projection mainly appear in wearable devices. In the aspect of solving visual information, everyone will make different decisions on the same object according to their understanding. Differentiated understanding may lead to errors in prejudgment and fault on operating. On the above problem of accepting and solving information, the appearance of virtual reality, which is used to augment reality, undoubtedly provides the right solution. Wearable devices with projecting virtual images function could combine the environment of the field of view and vision of the device to display the interface, thus, to display the corresponding transfer of virtual data to people's standard field of vision. This measure has put the screen before people's eyes directly in nature, which broadens people's field of view virtually. When users are using wearable devices with augmented reality function, they can acquire the information of the picture in their field of view promptly, which significantly increase the efficiency of information-accepting and avoid the trouble of moving screen repeatedly. Virtual image also has other advantages. Besides the primary function of displaying information, it also has the function of augmenting reality, such as prettifying spectacles in the field of view, adding decorations, creating platforms for users to express personalities. Vision interface with the function of augmenting reality could even make the users select the pictures, words, language, and marks which can express their personality and emotion to mark the scene they like, and make the strange Infotips more sincere, which is both the way of personality expression and charming of emotional interest.

## 3.2  Regulation of Graphic Elements

Generally speaking, graphic is the symbol with a clear, direct connection, and plays a vital role in visual language in the design of visual interface. The quality of visual language is essential to the efficiency and significant effect of information feedback on wearable devices. Graphic element should avoid using materialized icons which occupy sizeable internal storage but to do streamline design based on flattening principle. Flattening principle usually means a design method that is not focused on reappearing the object's shape, color, and material in reality. Its most apparent characteristic is sublating some decoration effects, such as shallow and sense of reality, but using concise abstract shape, outline, and a color lump to sketch the form of the object. Based on the designing thought of flattening, when designing the icons for such kind of wearable devices, we should first give these icons high identifiability. Nevertheless, the increase of identifiability should depend on building productive relationships among the concrete objects between icons and real life, which means that we should find out the mapping relationship between icons and objects in nature, or we call it "metaphor." "Metaphor" is generally divided into three forms: conceptual, enactive, and symbolic, each form has its appliance scale and expression technique. The conceptual metaphor focuses on highlighting the nature and classification of the objects. For example, the icons for musical Apps usually choose musical note, and enactive metaphor focuses on expressing the using method and action principle. For example, icons for basketball App will choose the moment of dunking picture, and symbolic metaphor is a process of abstraction, it usually simplified extracts the shape of the object and finally acquire the simplified and concise image, for example, the icons for camera usually mix-use abstract graphic shape, such as rectangular and circle, as the identified symbol.

Besides identifiability, the design of the icons for wearable devices should also consider its operability. "In order to take the scene and environment as a part of the interface, we should try to take the icon interface as supplement of the scene but not the copier" [3], as wearable devices are usually used in the process of exercising, the users would touch the devices and cause error on touch position, such kind of error would make the devices miss accepting the order and giving response. As a result, the whole device would not work correctly, and the users would get a misconception of inefficiency. Therefore, the size and position showed on the screen of every icon would be different from the size and position in real operation, thus need to adjust according to the conditions of the users.

### 3.3  Typography

Texts are not only the visual symbolic expression of language but also the most critical measure to spread information except graphic elements. The advantages of texts lie on that they can express complete information that images could not in order to make perfection to the visual function of edition. Typography is a crucial part of format design. As the fruit of human being's language symbol, typography can not only express correctly to the information but also transfer diversified emotion in the visual interface design of wearable devices. Accurate and orderly typography could not only improve the stability in users' accepting information, but also touch the users' heart deeply, and interact with other furthermore.

Typography aims at establishing a process reflecting the primary and secondary sequence in reading, which is mainly decided by the three elements in texts, they are fonts, font size, and kerning. The font is an abstract expression of the art style of texts, different forms and compositions make up different fonts, which show their characteristics individually. These characteristics would generate a unique aesthetic feeling naturally when reading. In the process of perceiving the beauty of the fonts, people can also improve their reading efficiency and accuracy. However, for the number of fonts that been used in one visual interface, more is not better. In the limited space of the screen in wearable devices, the use of a unified font could increase the integrity of the edition to the most substantial extent and reduce complexity.

Font size is a static expression form of the characteristic of fonts. The amount of font size could show out whether a passage is essential or not directly. Large-size fonts usually get people's attention because they are highly active. The prior level of being detected is high as a consequence. On the contrary, the smaller the font size is, the lower their prior level is on. However, large-size fonts could get the stability of small-size fonts. Therefore, in wearable device's interface design, the designer should use large-size fonts to mark the contents people use, weaken the functions less frequently used, use small-size fonts to make up crumby structure information annotation, thus, to increase the integration of the interface.

Kerning is the space between letters, and also, the part needs to pay the most attention to in language association. From the practical-use angle, whether the kerning is appropriate, decides whether the texts could be read in sequence, and at the same time, decide the level of the readers' reading ability. The harmony between size and style of fonts is usually achieved by controlling kerning. In wearable devices' visual interface format design, the comparison between kerning can largely protrude the scene the designer wants to build, for example, utilizing larger kerning to express a kind of alienation, and tense kerning to express the sense of compression.

## 4  Design of Man-Machine Interaction for Wearable Devices

Interactive design is also called Interaction Design and activity of regulating the behavior and creating communicating language between human beings and computers.

With mature sensing technology and constant improvement of motion identification means, identifying brain waves and carrying out bone sensing signal is not far-fetched area. Wearable devices have already transferred into the new medium expressed by interactive design and become a new method to express personality.

## 4.1 Concise Operational Procedure

In the real process of wearing wearable devices, users need to try their best to recurrent designers' procedure fixed in the process of designing a product, which means operation control. The focus of operation procedure lies in making the settings of devices and instincts of users generate direct relationships, thus to make users master the vital operational points when facing the devices for the first time, establish confidence, and acquire a sense of fulfillment. Excellent procedures can also impel the operation of the device lean close to the instinct of the users, which significantly reduces learning cost. Based on the procedures, the users can not only recurrent the designers' settings quickly, but also make their self-expression according to their personality. At the same time, for one thing, the interaction of wearable devices should simplify the procedures of identifying signals and accepting information, reduce the difficulty of logical identification of interactive design, for another, wearable devices should respect individual's differences, try hard to design according to users' unique format, quantize users' behavior. Under the conditions of inferring users' behavior correctly, increase the identification appropriately, increase the sense of experience, focus on recreation and relaxation, and avoid intricate operational procedures.

On the operational structure part, the interactive design of wearable devices requires to increase the using proportion of linear processes, reduce the element of the compound procedure. At the same time of one order getting carried out and triggering relative function, it should also be provided selections based on the users' characteristics. Meanwhile, keeping the basic structure of wearable device system constant and creating diversified visual transferring effects can ensure normal exemplify of the function of wearable devices effectively, thus, to increase the users' sense of belonging and identity. Such as Fig. 2 says, Samsung's Galaxy Gear 2 smartwatch adopts the procedural structure of linear and hierarchical form, break up some essential functional model, creating some unique menu icons for necessary models, and set some multi-list selections under elementary for the users to choose. The users can also modify the icons and position under the elementary menu according to personal interests at any time in any place. The operational procedure should take both personality and sequence into consideration.

## 4.2 Multidimensional Input Means

Besides its operative feature, interaction is still a process of input and output. Furthermore, because wearable devices touch closely with the body, the devices could detect body movement and psychological movement more accurately, which makes wearable devices different from traditional portable electronic devices. As far as wearable devices' technology, there are three mature input methods: motion input, speech input, and visual input. The most frequently used input way is no more than motion input, which concentrates on the upper limbs, such as finger touch, gesture transformation, wrist turnover, etc. With the daily changing of technology, the medium

**Fig. 2.** Customized menu of Samsung watch's setting (Source: https://g.pconline.com.cn/x/462/ 4627638.html)

to identify the interactive activities of wearable devices and motion is also changing rapidly. Nowadays, there are four kinds of general-used mediums, touch screen, camera, infrared ray, and millimeter-wave. The first three kinds are mainly used to perceive two-dimension static state and trends or other gestures between two-dimension and three-dimension. Millimeter-wave could detect body gestures Omni bearing, which makes the users separate themselves from the limitations of the fixed screen, use three-dimension gestures for order inputting more, which effectively solve the problem of inconvenient operation caused by the small-size of touching area in some wearable devices, such as wristband and watch, and enlarge the potential of gesture input, broaden the diversity of gestures. In addition, wearable devices supporting gesture-input can also make the users' hands be in the state of freedom always. Meanwhile, such devices enable the users to come back to main tasks on hand immediately, these considerations have exemplified free and the characteristics of freedom of interaction deeply.

At the same time of paying attention to enlarge gesture's diversity and free hands, the relationship between body movements also needs to be attached importance to by the designers. There is a specific sequence between body movements. Every moment of action change could also be understood as the prelude before the next movement. This kind of prelude can be transferred into the signals representing the switch-on of particular functions in wearable devices. According to this kind of sequence, the design of wearable devices should provide function defined by the user himself to the users, which means that users are capable of setting personal action semantics for some function and regulate specific behavior to use the function. For example, the Samsung Company has taken a series of overall designs on the body's coherent induction technology, as Fig. 3 says Samsung's Galaxy Gear 2 has a "wrist lift" function, G-Sensor chipset inside can perceive the movement of flicking of the wrist, end black at a proper time, and display its sensitization time. The start mode, which is suitable for body movement and nerve accepting habit, is also a form of play behavior that reflects personality and emotion. Figure 4 and Fig. 5 are wearable devices in glass forms developed by Microsoft Company, named Hololens. Users can use the association of gesture to create illusory objects in visional field of view, and then enter into reality and

**Fig. 3.** Samsung watch's "wrist lift" function (Source: https://tech.sina.cn/mobile/pc/2013-09-05/detail-iavxeafs2830944.d.html?vt=4&sid=56938)

unique area which surpass reality. This kind of creative behavior, which reflects personality, generates an immersive operation feeling to improve the design effect of gestures.

Besides motion input, speech input and visual input also become mature and mature. Speech input is the closest method to the body's instinct. Users can just use utterance to do input control according to their own will, which reduces the steps of input and increases the accuracy and speed of acquiring information. Just as Fig. 6 says, Google Project Glass developed by Google Company has taken this technology to free human being's hands thoroughly, and the information interaction between users and devices all take speech interaction directly. As Fig. 7 says visual input is a kind of input way generated from dynamic change of users' eyes viewpoint. When the users' viewpoint changes, the devices will adjust accordingly. Vision input can dodge many problems triggered by users' particularity. For example, when searching for information, because of differences in personality, everyone may use different keywords to describe the same object. As a result, differences in inputting keywords may lead to significant divergences when giving feedbacks, which adds obstacles for users to acquire accurate information. Vision input overcomes this drawback and projects the generated virtual interface into the retina to mix with live-action. By such a kind of visual interface, users can acquire the accurate information of all the objects in vision directly and avoid the occurrence of the inaccuracy of the input information resource, which effectively reduces the possibility of information consuming when transferring. Google Project Glass has applied this principle and shows the characteristic of "first-grade" amplification in vision, which presents all the scenes added with all kinds of illusions to the public. This technology makes vision directly input into diversion curb, which means seeing is information input resource. According to users' habit accumulated day by day, the system can not only list all the frequently used selections automatically when users are taking actions but also make prejudgment on the behavior which most likely to happen in order to help the users to make a valid selection.

Fig. 4. Hololens (Source: https://gpc.pconline.com.cn/611/6111956_1.html)

Fig. 5. The interface of creating personalized object and virtual reality in reality (Source: http://tech.163.com/15/0123/10/AGKT0RO800094P0U.html)

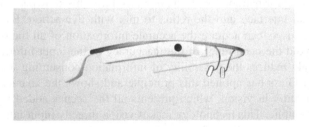

Fig. 6. Google glasses (Source: http://gc.zbj.com/20150910/n16731.shtml)

## 4.3 Steric Feedback Experience

Wearable devices' changes in interaction contain not only operation procedures and input methods but also man-machine feedback. Appropriate ways of feedback could make the operators get an overall understanding on whether the wearable devices

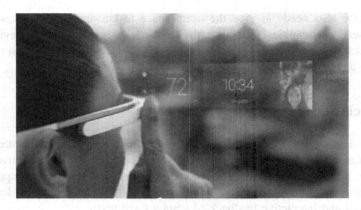

**Fig. 7.** The technology of augmented reality (Source: https://m.zol.com.cn/article/4148110.html)

accept the order made by himself rapidly. Appropriate ways can also enable the users to be clear on the state of wearable devices. With newly born reality-based interaction sophisticated day by day. The contents of man-machine feedback of the existing wearable devices have been different from previous interactive feedback under graphical user interface, which is composed of visual sense and audio sense. The visual sense is the fundamental feedback method and accord with the acceptance ability of biological vision. However, because of its limitations, which means that vision would easily be shaded and could meet the requirement of timing, therefore, vision sense is mainly suitable for the devices with large-size screens and separated from the human body. As a kind of penetrated medium, the sound has compared an advantage on the dimension of space. However, it is easy to affect other people and bad for constituting privacy. Therefore, to wearable devices that focus on information timeliness and personal privacy, besides retaining the feedback from visual sense and audio sense, it still needs to increase body sense feedback, which is an essential virtual reality element.

Body sense feedback can also be called force feedback, mainly refers to the activities that measuring wearable devices' operators by computers and imitating force sense close to the real-world and respond to the ones exerting force. This kind of force feedback is the most suitable feedback for the body's instinct and consciousness experience, is also a feedback model that has minimum learning cost and is easy for the operators to master, and what is more, it is an exciting form of feedback. Therefore, when designing force feedback in wearable devices, on the one hand, the designers should simulate nature and respect body's habitual feedback formed in natural world, then make one-to-one design for the direction of the force and strength, such as the object's weight, elasticity, texture of material and tactile impression, on the other hand, an effective interface is not just the imitation to present world, but also needs to do irreal and artificial order setting. Therefore, body sense design can also be made in a diametrically opposite way, which means making symbolic design, exaggerating, or reversing the concept of force in common sense. Body sense design should allow the learners to study and adjust to the setting of human-made feedback sense and shape feedback from different from reality. At the same time, designing force feedback symbolically also needs to give the users space to customize and re-design, fully respect users' personalities. Of course, the feedback design of wearable devices is not the feedback of a single sense organ but multi-sense organ feedback, which mix visual feedback, audio feedback, and body sense feedback.

## 5 Conclusion

Wearable devices make the product mixed with natural and unnatural, perceptual and rational elements in design through the way of presenting reasonably and diversified in the shape, proportion, material, and color of the form and appearance, appliance of multi-measure and multi-dimension on the aspect of visual interface, including orderly arrangement and interactive feedback of graphics and texts.

## References

1. Chen, G.: Intelligent Wear could Change the World: Next Business Boom. Electronic Industry Publisher, Beijing (2014). (in Chinese)
2. Richard, G.: Visual Sense Psychology. Beijing Normal University Publisher, Beijing (1986). (in Chinese)
3. Sun, X., Feng, Z.: Research on wearable devices' interaction design. Decoration 2, 28–33 (2014). (in Chinese)

# Interactive Relationships in Animation Art Ecology

Yue Zhou[✉]

College of Media and Art, Nanjing University of Information Science
and Technology, Nanjing, China
824497078@qq.com

**Abstract.** Animation art ecology refers to the state of existence between animation and related art, animation and people, and animation and environment, and the interlocking artistic relationship between them. The study of the ecological relationship of animation art should include some relevant contents and discussion discourses related to natural ecology, social ecology, cultural ecology and even intelligent ecology. The interactive ecological law of animation art is formed by the interaction and restriction between animation art behavior and environment, which reflects the nature of interaction among individuals, groups and the whole of art ecology. By clarifying the various interactive ecological relationships inside and outside animation art, we can better understand and grasp the relationship between animation and human, give ecological respect and protection to animation art, and establish a long-term relationship of interdependent and sustainable development with it.

**Keywords:** Animation art · Interactive ecology · Ecological relationship

## 1 Animation Art Ecology

The origin of ecology begins with the study of individual organisms. Nowadays, ecology has penetrated into various fields, and people of different cultural backgrounds have different definitions of "ecology".

### 1.1 Animation Art

Animation art is a comprehensive artistic expression means that integrates many related art forms such as literature, painting, dance, music, etc. As a cultural carrier, its communication phenomenon is also a collection of symbolic meanings. Cultural elements are given to it through specific design and artistic expression, conveying the unique spiritual value and cultural connotation of animation films.

Animation has broken away from the past professional boundaries and established the concept of "pan-animation", which means that the study of animation opens up a whole new path [1].

© Springer Nature Switzerland AG 2020
C. Stephanidis et al. (Eds.): HCII 2020, LNCS 12429, pp. 411–424, 2020.
https://doi.org/10.1007/978-3-030-59987-4_29

## 1.2   Art Ecology

Art ecology refers to the state of existence between art and art, art and human, and art and environment, and the interlocking artistic relationships between them. The study of the art ecological relationship should include some related contents and discussion discourses related to natural ecology, social ecology, cultural ecology and even intelligent ecology. The observation and intervention of the art ecology is to better maintain the benign interactive ecological relationship of art.

## 1.3   Ecological Characteristics of Animation Art

**Ecological Nature of Animation Art.** The scope of the animation art ecosystem can be large or small and intertwined. The interaction effects between ecological elements differ from being explicit and implicit, strong and weak. But in essence, around the interaction between works and people, the material and spiritual energy flow and circulation in the animation art ecosystem are always continuous.

**Ecological Characteristics of Animation Art.** *1. Ecological Objectivity.* Regardless of whether people are concerned about ecological implementation, ecology and ecological relations always exist. They affect human beings and human life in a realistic and objective way. Like all forms of art, once the animation is created, there will be a corresponding animation art ecology, and the ecological interaction relationships among them are the problems and questions that must be faced and considered by animation creation, communication, and groups of appreciation. Moreover, the objectivity of ecology requires people to establish a thorough ecological consciousness providing a prerequisite for the harmonious continuation of the artistic ecology.

*2. Ecological Balance.* The ecological relationship of animation art displays as the action and reaction between animation art and people and artistic environment factors. And as a complete, dynamic and relatively stable ecosystem, the interaction and restriction between internal and external factors and links tend to be balanced.

*3. Ecological Interactivity.* The constituent elements within the ecosystem are intertwined, and changes in one of them will lead to chain interactions in other links, and even the linkage and reaction of the entire ecosystem.

# 2   Interactive Ecological Law of Animation Art

## 2.1   Establishing Interactive Awareness of Animation Ecology

The ecological interactive consciousness of animation refers to the awareness and attention of creators, social media and audiences to the existence of animation art.

The existence state of animation art includes the interaction between animation art and its internal links and elements such as external environmental condition. If interaction refers to the mutual response and two-way influence behavior between people and people, things and the environment in a certain behavioral process, then the interactive ecology of animation art tends to study the restrictions and dependencies on the surface and deep layers formed by this response and influence behavior.

There is a crisscross interactive relationship in the ecological area of animation art. The establishment of the ecological awareness of animation art, on the one hand, is based on the initiative of artistic (creative behavior) consciousness; on the other hand, it should pay due respect to the laws of artistic ecology. To establish interactive ecological consciousness of animation art, in the actual animation art activities, organically unifying the production process of art with its artistic goals is vital to the development of animation art.

## 2.2  Understanding the Logical Relationship of the Animation Ecology

The logical influence relationship of animation ecology refers to the explicit and implicit restriction and influence in the animation art ecology. The explicit relationship is manifested as: around the value of animated artwork, there is an interactive and restrictive relationship between the author's creative intention, the audience's interpretation ability and the media's discourse power. They are the core direct influence relationship in the animation ecology. The implicit influence relationship is more complicated. It contains the constraint and promotion of external context factors such as political climate, moral trends, artistic thought, and technological level. They are indirect influence factors in the middle and outer parts of the animation ecology.

## 2.3  Grasping the Interactive Laws of the Art Ecology

The interaction law of animation art ecology mainly includes three aspects. First, the research object of animation ecology is the unified whole of animation and environment. The action and reaction of animation art and environment in the whole is the primary interaction law of animation ecology. Second, with the development of animation art, the animation ecosystem is always in a dynamic state of development from equilibrium to imbalance and back to equilibrium. Artistic creation, interpretation, evaluation, and the environment affect each other and restrict each other. They are in a relatively stable dynamic equilibrium state for a certain period of time, and will also change the ecological interaction relationship due to the strength of all parties in the development. Third, regional action and reaction of artists, artworks, audiences, and the environment are the laws of energy flow and material circulation in the art ecosystem, and their essence is interactive.

In addition, the impact of the external social environment on the creation of animation art sometimes appears in an implicit way, and sometimes exhibits explicit characteristics. For example, the rise of an artistic trend of thought will affect the artistic creation and interpretation of the environment. There are various levels and regions of the animation art ecosystem. The type, form, style, and related art exploration of animation art itself are the research contents of animation art ecology.

# 3 Interactive Ecological Relationship of Animation Art

## 3.1 Human-Nature Interaction

The birth of animation is relatively late compared to painting, sculpture and architecture, but the sprout of animation can be traced back to prehistoric cave paintings, in which we can vaguely identify the causes of the origin of human civilization and art.

**Revealing Awe in Piety from Imitating Nature.** Animation art was born in the mid-nineteenth century, but the bud of animation art can be traced back to the Paleolithic Age. This can be seen from the ancient cave rock paintings. Humans' paintings started from a simple record of life, and soon evolved into a description of activities and things in life. The contents of the paintings are mostly things that can provide survival energy in nature. The Paleolithic hunters and painters thought they can possess what they paint and control what they portrayed. It is not so much to say that they used painting to show their expected results as to pray, so animals in cave paintings often appear to be stabbed and shot. It looks rather like witchcraft than an aesthetic taste (Fig. 1).

**Fig. 1.** Stone age cave painting (Source: https://www.donsmaps.com/lascaux.html)

Later, with the development of planting and animal husbandry, mankind entered a new cultural stage. People were aware of the restrictive effects of weather, such as wind, rain, lightning, hail, plague and drought, and they realized there was a mysterious force controlling them. People believed in animism. Perseverance and bewilderment of food, and instinct feelings and emphasis on reproduction all showed the human awe for nature. Artistic creation was more instinctively around the core of survival. The original art developed gradually in the imitation of nature by human beings in respect and with fear. It is also the beginning of human understanding of nature. In this stage of art interactive ecology, human beings are passive because of their weakness.

**Gaining the Satisfaction of Mastering the World in the Process of Depicting Nature.** The course of all arts depends on the development of human society and the maturity of material civilization. Various art forms transit from early naturalism to the material world, and the development of painting, sculpture, and architecture, whether being secular or religious art, are still material in essence. At the same time, based on the basic material guarantee, spiritual needs were born. Art developed beyond simple depiction and further to symbolism. People no longer simply imitated nature, but tried to create a corresponding, opposite, and independent existence. The aesthetic needs of art have gradually matured. In this stage of art interactive ecology, human initiative has obviously risen to a dominant position.

Once animation was produced, it directly entered the new cultural era. The development of related arts such as literature, painting, music, and movies provided a rich soil for animation. The development of animation was also driven by desire. People were constantly seeking to enhance the ability to present the dynamic and static condition of everything in the world. The presentation not only pointed to the attention to the material world, but also reflected the human desire to control the world.

**Pursuing the Expression of Spiritual Consciousness in Creation Beyond Nature.** If the origin of art activities is based on the attention and imitation of the material world, and the Neolithic art undergoes beautification and idealization, then in later art practices, the relationship between human and nature changes from passive imitation to mastery and to active presenting. In the series of changes, the pursuit of the spirit of art is gradually revealed and dominates. Under the domination of theology and religious art, art, with the alternation of the secular art and the religious art, experienced the symbiosis of classicism and naturalism, and the artistic harmony pursued in the middle of the Renaissance is indeed a utopian world.

The focus on self-spiritual needs begins with opposition to impersonal constraints. Arts have always been more focused on the expression of emotions. They rely on the material to express illocutionary meaning, and pursue self-consciousness and the freedom of spiritual expression in artistic creation.

**Yearning for the Harmony Between Man and Nature in the Gradual Realization of Returning to Nature.** For thousands of years, culture, art, nature and society have been in a state of change. Although culture and art draw nutrients from nature, they have always sought consistency with society. On the one hand, the creative group has experienced difficulties in the contradiction between self-expression demands and social acceptance consciousness and has tried to strike a balance. On the other hand, due to the rapid development of science and technology, art has been held hostage by the sudden emergence of technology, and is obsessed with achieving sensual assaults and flaunting techniques, increasingly deviating from nature. The behavior that neglects the fundamental will inevitably lead to artistic creations that are gorgeous and stunning, but spiritually shallow and weak. The artistic activities are in an unprecedented loss, and caught in blindness and impetuousness of the relationship between self and nature.

## 3.2    Human-Social Interaction

**Echoing the Mainstream Consciousness of Society.** Political consciousness includes national policy, power guidance of intermediary and media discourse, and social mainstream values. National policy and national spirit are the core elements of cultural dissemination. To a certain extent, media, venues and other art intermediary agencies represent the will of the country to conduct reviews and judge, encourage excellent artworks that can positively shape the national spirit and promote national culture.

Animation and digital media are core components of the creative and pioneering nature of the cultural industry. Animation, as an efficient cultural communication medium and art symbol, has the significance of appearance and interpretation of national culture. At the same time, animation art is the main art form in the new period undertaking the culture inheritance, art dissemination, and spirit promotion. Its coordinated development will effectively promote the construction of material and spiritual civilization.

**Matching the Audience's Aesthetic Taste.** First, animation creation needs multiple dimensions of design for its content, structure, and form of the work to make them serve the same theme of the film. Second, the creator uses the organization of audiovisual elements and rhythmic style to grasp the expressive power of film production art and enhance the contagiousness of the work, in order to arouse the audience's conscious identity, emotional resonance, and aesthetic pleasure. In addition, animation, as a medium carrying ideological culture and moral concepts, is also a bridge between the author and the audience. The creator conveys an aesthetic experience from an artistic perspective and outputs a value judgment. As a form of communication art full of wisdom and imagination, animation seeks a high degree of unity of story, aesthetics and education (Fig. 2).

**Fig. 2.** Hayao Miyazaki's *Castle in the Sky* (Source: http://i.mtime.com/ly5434/blog/4857699/)

**Coordination with the Social Industrial Economy.** The industrial and economic chain of animation revolves around market, marketing, planning, distribution, and promotion of multiple business models. Box office and derivatives development have become the commercial focus of animation art behavior.

The dual attributes of animation art are artistry and commerciality. Animation is an art form deeply loved by the public. Therefore, we have no doubt about the artistry of animation, and the commerciality of animation is also gifted. Good animation will always be culturally rooted, entertaining, and commercial, so that it touches and appeals to the people, and drives consumption. The triumph of a successful animation does not stop at the box office, but it can succeed in expanding a derivative space. The expansion of the living space of animation largely depends on whether it can expand the audience and drive the development of industrial economy (Fig. 3).

**Fig. 3.** Despicable *Me* 2010 (Source: https://pic.newyx.net/gallery/8018.htm)

### 3.3  Human-Cultural Interaction

The coverage of culture is huge. It contains all the aspects of human life including clothing, food, shelter, and transportation, which is a material and spiritual whole of all groups. It is the existence of all social phenomena from the past to the future and the inherent human spirit and the sum of inheritance, creation, and development.

Human culture is divided into material culture and spiritual culture. Artistic creation nourishes from culture, expresses and spreads in the form of culture, and forms new cultural concepts and cultural phenomena in the process of cultural interpretation and cultural criticism. The development ecology of culture always presents the interaction of the three main forces of the creator, the media and the audience around the meaning and value of the work. The origin of the interaction is the creator, the feedback is from the audience, and social media is the bridge and bond of artistic interaction. Art speaks through works and seeks resonance from audiences through the media.

This kind of artistic interaction not only gives the audience a beautiful experience and spiritual guidance, but also spreads the national, regional, historical, realistic, material, spiritual cultural characteristics and concepts, forms the flow and accumulation of culture, and will be written into the cultural history of art as the cultural reality of art together with artistic works.

**Drawing Nourishment from Historical Culture and Forming Personal Cultural Ideas.** Culture is a collective consciousness that reflects people's habitual lifestyle and spiritual value orientation. All artistic creations are built on this basic consciousness. Animated works are cultural carriers, and their contents, forms and purposes have cultural characteristics. Art creators, through the extraction and processing of artistic languages and information symbols, assign their own observation perspectives, conceptual intentions, and value judgments to projects which are spread to the mass audience through the art medium. Interpretation of the audience and social evaluation are cultural dissolution processes. Artworks' receiving resonance or rejection is a cultural phenomenon. They will eventually precipitate into a symbol of consciousness, a spiritual and cultural power, and return to the cyclical development of society and culture.

Chinese culture has a long history and rich heritage. Chinese animation should absorb more of the essence of the traditional Chinese culture, such as paper cutting, ink painting, and Peking opera. It is well known to us that only the national characteristic is welcome to the world [2]. Animation designers should put animation creation in the soil of his/her own nation, based on his/her own experience and real life, absorb elements from national culture, and draw lessons from classical literature, historical stories, traditional customs and modern life, and apply his/her own linguistic methods and narrative logic to reorganize materials, share his/her perspectives and reflections in novel and unique ways, form personal values and aesthetic judgments, and create animation work with his/her own language style. Only by searching for materials in culture and creating for the future can the content of the work be enriched, and the author's concept is conveyed.

**Getting Inspiration from Real-life Events and Defining Artistic Motivation.** During the evolution of human civilization, in each specific period, culture has synchronic characteristic. Various thoughts, schools, and forms are horizontally intertwined and influential. It involves astronomy and geography, and worldly wisdom, shows traditional customs, life habits, laws and regulations, contains religious beliefs, ways of thinking, values, and aesthetic tastes, and condenses literature and art, spiritual totems, and so on. Art creation requires art creators to have sufficient accumulation and certain opinions. What is more important for them is to discover perspectives, find suitable opportunities to express the concept of the theme, find the "points" that move the audience, and then determine in what ways to organize and construct logical clues, advance the plot, and reproduce the real life plots and emotions in the animation space and time, so that the audience resonates, so as to reflect our living reality and pass our thoughts, beliefs and opinions.

**Enriching Narrative Means of Animation by Referring to Related Art.** Animation is the most special and comprehensive art form that's most related to others among the many art forms, especially the traditional two-dimensional animation. Its pictures are painted, its script is literary, its lens language is photography, its logic is cinematic. Thus the art of animation is inherently subjected to the nourishment of literature, painting, music, drama, and movie. It incorporates the genes of those precedent related arts, absorbs and mixes the essence of national culture in various regions, and has experienced the baptism of various cultural trends of thought. With the exploration and integration of traditional and digital technologies, it has grown rapidly and has been constantly superimposed into human spiritual and material cultural nutrients, gestating the future of world culture (Fig. 4).

**Fig. 4.** *Up* (Source: https://luoedu.com/movies/1787.html)

As the animation art matures, its creative concept has become more and more independent, but its formal language has become more and more inclusive. It relies on multiple designs of visual and auditory sensations to enrich the narrative means, explore more transmission methods in the olfactory and somatosensory changes, and let the audience experience a kind of physiological, psychological and spiritual guidance of "creating something out of nothing".

### 3.4  Human-Machine Interaction

In the development of animation art, there has always been an interactive and changing ecological relationship between technology and art. Two-dimensional animation has more inherited the expression language of painting, while stop-motion animation has a manual formal texture, and three-dimensional animation relies on digital advantages, which has incomparable advantages in realistic reproduction of reality. No matter what type of animation, it will always depend on technology to be created.

Looking objectively at the differentiation of animation today, we can see two trends. The strength of technical force naturally divides the technical trend of animation. The strong one is supported by technology, and continuously strives to upgrade visual shock, sensory experience, interaction and control, etc. The weak one takes stylization as the way out, and seeks to realize artistic value in terms of narrative style, aesthetic expression, value and judgment.

Today's virtual reality technology has gradually come into people's notice and art. When virtual reality images meet with animation, the traditional animation expressions and ways of viewing have undergone profound changes. The thinking logic of audiovisual languages, time and space clues and ways of expression are further open. If we say that the interaction we talked about before is the interaction of various factors in the entire ecosystem of animation art, it is a broad concept. Then, the interaction in the virtual reality animation is narrow. It refers to the autonomous choice, the reading of the content and the course of the audience through people's interaction with machines. Virtual reality animation, as a form of future animation, is close at hand.

Although the main and accompanying positions alternate on the surface, in fact, animation is inseparable from the support of artistic concepts and technology. Art and technology are the dual attributes of animation art that cannot be sidelined. Corresponding to the needs of today's industrialized society, the ecological status of animation itself depends on the coordination and balance between its technology and artistic power.

The most perfect state is the free integration of art and technology. It refers to the return of the two to their attributes. The shock of technology to the senses must be controlled, and the communication of art to the spirit must be based on matter.

**Advancements of Hardware and Software.** The technical starting point of animation can be traced back to 1895. The Lumiere brothers first publicly showed films, such as the famous *The Arrival of a Train* and *Shower in the Sea*, which brought the film into a new era. The spread of animation always depends on a certain carrier and a media platform. If the spread of animation has been limited for a hundred years in the early stage of animation, with the development of modern media technology, it has been barrier-free. Today all media terminals can carry dynamic expressions. The traditional way of static expression has been greatly impacted, and animation is in its element because of its inherent dynamic nature. Various terminal media such as outdoor advertising, TV screens, computers, and mobile phones are all seeking ways to win in the market competition.

The upgrade of the software makes the collection and output of the animation upside down the traditional thinking, making the hardware performance more optimized and the quality of the work better. Through the application of various software, some images and special effects can be produced. The production speed and quality of movie special effects have been greatly improved. Producers can complete more delicate, real and shocking picture effects on the computer. For example, Maya software can be used to create effects such as storms, lightning, landslides, ghosts, aliens, house collapses, volcanic eruptions, tsunamis and other effects that cannot be completed with actual shooting or props. You can also use Maya software to make simulated characters such as The mice in *Stuart Little*, the squirrels in *Ice Age*, the master Yoda in *Star Wars* and so on. The rapid animation production technology integrates body motion capture, expression capture, finger capture, virtual shooting, etc., which can realize real-time synchronous data recording of full body motion capture and automatic refinement of plug-in data at a later stage. This not only greatly improves work efficiency, but also enhances the quality of animation.

**Machine Intelligence.** With the development of science and technology, the intelligent life enjoyed by humans has undergone a process from quantitative change to qualitative change, and has become unable to extricate themselves from machines. The reaction of people has changed from the sigh of surprise and joy at the beginning to artificial intelligence products, to the perplexed and alarmed feeling of future artificial intelligence.

Human's sense of superiority and security has always come from his ability and confidence to control the world. The worry about artificial intelligence is not what it can do now or in the future, but that it may be independent of human instructions. When humans are still anticipating what to do, they may already be beyond the scope of human's "sight".

The collision between intelligence and art may not just produce sparks, but an unstoppable trend. Art creation will not be a human patent. For example, the inheritance of styles in cartoons is not a problem at all, and any classics that have existed in history can be infinitely derived and immortal. Imagine that if a painting can be transformed into "Picasso style" and "Van Gogh style", then a film can certainly be of a "Picasso" style language or of a "Van Gogh" logic. With the unlimited growth space of hardware and software, all this is waiting for us not far away, and history and the future are facing a "reunion".

On the other hand, today's art evaluation is still relying on experts, the media, and the audience. Maybe tomorrow, the experts, the media, and the audience will be replaced by big data collection. Machine after learning can completely generate more rational and stable professional opinion. The authority and history of art criticism will also be subverted and rewritten.

Undoubtedly, artificial intelligence's involvement in art has become a reality, and it will definitely continue to expand from shallow to deep, and thus expand territory. So, human beings have to think about several issues: does our artistic creation still have human emotions when we rely more on science and technology or artificial intelligence? Is human's art enjoyment becoming richer or more monotonous? Can we always control the machine to do what we think, and can it replace the happiness that original sketching brings?

In the interaction with artificial intelligence, human beings need to prudently and effectively exercise guidance, limit and control power to ensure that the situation is always under human's control.

# 4   Interactive Ecological Strategy of Animation Art

## 4.1   Taking Interactive Ecological Consciousness as the Premise of Artistic Creation

In the interactive relationship between art and society, there is no doubt that good works of art have a positive guiding effect on the basic conscience and value judgment of the broad audience.

If art can't give the audience spiritual cultivation, improve the social aesthetic ability, and output value and judgment, then the existence of art will lose its fundamental meaning, or even go to the opposite. If artistic communication deviates from truth, goodness, and beauty, so that the false, evil, and ugly things can circulate, over time, people will be assimilated by the environment until the customs are destroyed, which will bring serious evil consequences to society. It will be as the saying goes, "living with unhealthy people is like staying in a shop of salted fish, you will not smell the stink over time, but become accustomed to it" [3].

The creation and dissemination of animation art should pay attention to the changing cultural and spiritual needs of the audience, take interactive ecological consciousness as the premise of artistic creation, and give ecological respect to the existing rules and industrial phenomena of animation art.

## 4.2   Taking Historical and Cultural Inheritance as the Basis of Artistic Creation

In a certain sense, culture is gradually formed by the development of history. History is a "cultural collection" of many social developments and national experiences with vertical causality and correlation. The interpretation of culture should be based on the historical context. Skinner insists that examining the author's intention through the restoration of the specific context produced by the text is an indispensable link in our study of the history of thought [4]. Culture is obviously horizontal and synchronic. It is based on the sum of society, folklore, morality, fashion, aesthetics, creativity and values on the basis of social development. Compared with culture, history has the characteristics of verticality and extension. It is a diachronic spiritual characteristic and cultural line of material and spiritual continuation. It also reflects the influence of the early culture on future cultures and shows the understanding and inheritance of the ancestors' thoughts and achievements by later generations.

Culture and history are intertwined and support each other. The study of the culture of any nation is inseparable from the study of its history. To study any period of history, we must start with cultural phenomena. Therefore, the connotation of art itself includes a comprehensive understanding and expression of history and culture. Artistic creation bears the heavy responsibility of describing human experiences, expressing human emotions, embodying human spirit, and inquiring about human nature. Artistic creation should highly unify material representation and spirit of history and culture, creating features in the inheritance and integration of history and culture.

### 4.3    Communicating with Artistic Spirit to Meet the Aesthetic Needs of the Audience

The meaning of artistic existence is "beauty and aesthetics". Artists provide beautiful images, artistic conception, beautiful emotional mobilization and emotional experience, so that the audience can obtain different sensory experience. In this way, the creators and audiences have an exchange of ideas, emotional resonance and aesthetic interaction.

On the basis of the established aesthetic cognition, in addition to providing beautiful images and feelings, artistic creation must also provide aesthetic value judgments and aesthetic cognition orientation. Similarly, the artistic aesthetic value of an animation film is also multi-dimensional, including the theme and content, form and method, image and emotion, culture and spirit. The aesthetics of animation art is embodied in narrative strategies, image shaping, cultural integration, etc. There should be first aesthetic ideas and aesthetic tastes that meet the requirements of the times, and second, the pursuit of perfect unity of content and form. In addition, attention should be paid to moving the audience with artistic spirit and emotional appeal. The aesthetic appeal of animation art not only aims at the audience's current aesthetic taste, but also expands the audience's cognitive horizon, creates a beautiful context space, and guides and enhances the audience's aesthetic and value orientation.

### 4.4    Driving Industrial Economic Cycle with Aesthetic Cultural Consumption

Animation has been inextricably linked to the economy since its birth. The contradiction of art as a commodity is reflected in the conflict between the pursuit of artistic value and the pursuit of commercial value. This contradiction is gradually resolved with the unity of understanding of all parties. Commercial investment is the foundation to ensure the quality of creative art, and the quality of creative art is the fundamental to ensure the realization of commercial goals.

In the commercialized context of today's society, animators should change their thinking and bring the audience's aesthetic guidance and cultural consumption guidance into the team's artistic creation goals. The connotation of animation art must not only be rooted in history and culture, but also refer to the times and fashions, so that the aesthetic impact and emotional impulses in the animation film, from the content to the form, are continued and extended to a touchable temperature in the derivative products, and move from the animation film into people's lives, driving the consumption of aesthetic culture. "Animation" is not only an artistic phenomenon, but also a way that can affect our daily lives. Let art, technology, culture and creativity form the aesthetic driving force of animation art and gradually build an industrial ecological relationship that aesthetically drives consumption.

# 5   Conclusion

Studying the real state and ecological relationship of animation should be based on an understanding of the vertical growth of animation development and evolution, and it is more necessary to summarize the horizontal influence factors of its artistic creation.

In the process of animation art practice, the artistic expression of the creative group is constantly innovating, new demands for technical realization are constantly generated, and a new art ecology is constantly formed. Under the collision of contemporary multiculturalism and the penetration of modern art, people's aesthetic horizons have been widened and their aesthetic experience has been enriched. Even the aesthetic concepts, aesthetic psychology, and aesthetic value orientations have presented a pluralistic trend. Therefore, when creating animation, creators should use their own experience as a basis, take real life as a model, absorb elements from national culture, reorganize materials with their own language and narrative logic, and use a novel and unique way to share their perspectives and thoughts, form personal values, aesthetic judgments, and create animation works with their own language style. They should reproduce the real life plots and emotions in the animation space and time, and make the audience resonate, so as to reflect the reality of our lives and to convey our thoughts, beliefs, and opinions.

On the one hand, animation exists as an art, and its ecological relationship is mainly reflected in the interaction and coordination of the author, the media, and the audience. The creator's intention, the evaluation of the intermediary, and the audience's interpretation jointly determine the meaning of the work. The bias of either party will lead to the deviation of animation art from its creative purpose and social responsibility.

On the other hand, under the background of the era of market economy, the survival of animation should be market-oriented, mass-oriented and industrialized.

In the commercialized context of today's society, animators should change their thinking and bring the audience's aesthetic guidance and cultural consumption guidance into the team's artistic creation goals. In short, only by understanding the interactive ecological relationship between the inside and outside of the animation art, can we better understand the relationship between people and art, apply ecological respect and protection to the animation art, and build a long-term relationship of interdependent and sustainable development.

# References

1. Zhu, M.J.: Introduction to Animation. Hubei Fine Arts Publishing House, Wuhan (2008). (in Chinese)
2. Jia, F., Lu, S.Z.: An Introduction to Animation. Communication University of China Press, Beijing (2005). (in Chinese)
3. Wang, G., Wang, X.: Kongzi Jiayu. Zhong Hua Book Company, Beijing (2014). (in Chinese)
4. Yin, J., Wang, Q.: Context analysis method and historical explanation. Acad. J. Jinyang **2**, 88 (2015). (in Chinese)

# A Novel Context for the Expression of Art Through Interactive Multimedia Electronic Music Installation—Taking the Work of Rainbow Cliff and Dusk as an Example

Xiaoni Zhuang[✉]

School of Media Arts and Communication,
Nanjing University of the Arts, Nanjing 210013, China
85839863@qq.com

**Abstract.** Under the background of the era of science and technology, the pursuit of technological innovation has become a trend. The distinction of the identity between engineers and musicians is no longer clear, and the artists' pursuit of sound and its expression form know no boundaries. The present paper mainly focuses on computer composition and programming thinking. Nowadays, the multimedia installations of audio-visual integration span music, art design, computer, and other domains, making contemporary artists more and more equipped with the professional ability of compound talents. The audio-visual integrated installation with real-time interaction provides the audience with a new immersive and interactive aesthetic experience, transforming them gradually from the audience to participants and passive creators. Therefore, it has gradually become a research direction for practitioners to study the installations with real-time interaction characteristics, the mode of combination of specific specialties behind them, the professional technologies in the works, and the specific knowledge structure of cross-disciplines implemented in the curriculum. Taking a specific work as an example, the author briefly discussed the technology and art involved in interactive multimedia electronic music installation from the perspective of music science and technology.

**Keywords:** Interactive music controller · Multimedia installation · Electronic music

## 1 Real-Time Interactive Multimedia Electronic Music Installation (Controller)

An ordinary box, like a music box in our memory, sits quietly in the center of the stage. The performer removes its lid and slowly twitches the bobbin pole twined by the strings in the box, awakening the sound of bells and the change of the light and shadow of the stage. The nursery rhyme is sung by the performer and the bell sound adds radiance and beauty to each other as if reminiscing about the footsteps of past life, with some steps of expectation and some of the confusion, some of the hesitation and some of the determination. All the experiences of hopes and disappointments look like this

C. Stephanidis et al. (Eds.): HCII 2020, LNCS 12429, pp. 425–440, 2020.
https://doi.org/10.1007/978-3-030-59987-4_30

flowing string, surrounding the artist layer upon layer around the ring of the bell, and the light and shadow, which can no longer return into the box. The reproduction of the memory constructs the definition of "who I am". Every circle seems to have formed but no intentions, just like the clue of the past and the track of the year. Does not it look like our life? Every crooked string finally built into a circle. This is the premiere of the Rainbow Cliff and Dusk at the concert hall of Brown University in 2013, which was created, designed, produced and performed by artist Akiko Hatakeyama[1]. Figure 1 below is a screenshot of the performance.

**Fig. 1.** The scene of the performance of *Rainbow Cliff and Dusk* (Akiko, H. (2013). *Rainbow Cliff and Dusk* [photograph] form *BLIND | The world where I can't be but you live in - SECTION 3-4*.concert hall, Brown University. Retrieved from http://akikohatakeyama.com/v_michi_higure.html) by artist Akiko Hatakeyama

What this work embodies behind the stage performance is the integration of multidisciplinary technology. It is a multimedia work of interactive electronic music that uses Hall Sensor to trigger signals and simultaneously controls sound and light through computer mapping. By using the computer mapping algorithm and the audiovisual integration, the artist plays several roles in this work to bring novel forms of expression to the stage. This is the new situation of artworks exhibition under the combination of technology and art.

The author visited the Centre for Future Music of the University of Oregon for academic purposes in 2018. Under the tutorship of Professor Hatakeyama, I have personally experienced the interactivity and practicability of the digital-driven interactive multimedia controller (installation) in the United States and experienced its cutting-edge creativity and cross-disciplinarily through participating in the design and performance. Therefore, I would like to take the professor's work Rainbow Cliff and Dusk as the starting point to discuss my understanding of art and technology in this type of works.

---

[1] Akiko Hatakeyama, Assistant Professor, Center for Future Music, School of Music and Dance, University of Oregon. Her research interests include improvisation, real-time computer interaction and visual media.

As a new art form, the interactive multimedia electronic music installation combines the connotations of multiple disciplines. In the process of design and creation, it is very important to have an understanding of each art form and concept, which can provide correct control at the macro level for the direction of creation and the final result. Next, the author will briefly analyze the concept of real-time interactive multimedia electronic music installation and the relationship among multimedia art, installation and interactive electronic music through the work *Rainbow Cliff and Dusk*.

## 1.1 The Disciplinary Concept of the Work

Real-time interactive electronic music belongs to the category explored by avant-garde artists in the development of electronic music. Electronic music is a new discipline derived from the development of multimedia art, with its research purpose being not only to use electronic means to spread music, but also to use electronic machinery to make and synthesize new sounds.

Real time is defined as the actual natural time in which something happens, and interaction is defined as the interplay between two or more objects. Therefore, the concept of real-time interactive electronic music can be simply understood as the artistic performance that makes use of the technology of real-time data collection by computer to influence the music during music composition and improvisation.

Interactive music installation (controller) involves multiple disciplines, including programming, human-computer interface, musicology, psychology, stage performances, etc. Through the circulation and combination of the identity of the creator in the category of art, science, and technology, sensibility and rationality, it reflects progressive development of subjects in the context of the integration of science, technology, and art.

Since the beginning of the 21st century, composers have gradually begun to carry out technical transformation. They are no longer limited to the traditional means of music creation and performance, and are more inclined to explore the integration of multidisciplinary technical languages. As for the principle of realizing interaction, that is, the way of transmission and processing between data, different technologies including audio sampling, video acquisition, signals received by different sensors and computer algorithm programming, etc. also came into being. The interaction principle of *Rainbow Cliff and Dusk* is derived from magnetoelectric sensors among many sensor technologies.

To better study this kind of multimedia art and realize its application, domestic and foreign countries gradually set up corresponding courses. Take the Center for Future Music of the University of Oregon as an example, the Sensor Musik course offered by the department mainly focuses on multimedia art of audiovisual combination, and teaches related technologies and art forms generated by sensors. Students mainly study the design and production of interactive electronic music works and complete their works in classes under the guidance of the instructor. And finally, they should finish the course in the form of a concert or performance. During the author's visit, the course was taught by Professor Hatakeyama.

This course covers music performance, composition, and improvisation, as well as the fundamentals of the interface design for microprocessors and sensors. Students should learn to use microprocessors and external installation for the Arduino hardware/software platform, different types of sensors, electronic circuits design, digital numbering systems, logic operators, and basic knowledge of C programming language and integrated development environment (IDE).

How to create art in the transition between the data-mediated performance of gestures and sound (music) is the most creative and valuable part of this course. The technical principles of the work presented in this paper are included in the course. Various installations with interactive performance functions developed through the course can be called interactive installations, which work by using real-time data to drive a controller that synchronously interacts with lights or video signals and electronic music.

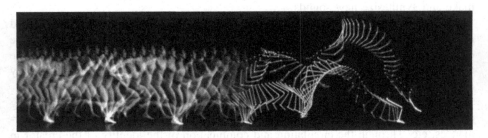

**Fig. 2.** The Dynamic screenshot of the work *Let us imagine a straight line* (2009)

For example, in another work *Let us imagine a straight line*[2] (see Fig. 3), it can be observed that in the table there are two brass handrails for placing the palms of your hands, and this is the tactile feedback system of data gloves designed and produced by Butch Rovan[3], a professor at Brown University (Professor Hatakeyama's supervisor at Brown University). The trigger is the brass handrail-like installation, which is actually a biometrics meter that works like a cardio meter. When the audience places their hands on the brass sensor, the installation will calculate their heart rates. After the completion of the calculation, the table will light up and send the measurement data, triggering sound events (six sound installations) and video movements on the screen so that the audience can see and hear their own heartbeats (Fig. 2).

[2] Butch, R. (2011) *Let us imagine a straight line*. [photograph]. WRO, Wroclaw, Poland, the 14th Biennial Exhibition of Media Art; ISEA2011, Istanbul (online gallery), International Electronic Art Symposium; June 2010, Stony Brook, State of New York, International Computer Music Conference; Sydney, Australia, the Architecture International Movie Night; October - November 2009, the Cougut Center for the Humanities of Brown University.
Retrieved from http://www.soundidea.org/rovan/portfolio_imagine_photogallery.html.

[3] Butch Rovan (USA), professor of music at Brown University, multimedia artist, composer, performance artist, computer music multimedia programmer. His research interests include custom-designed interactive systems for music performance and visual media.

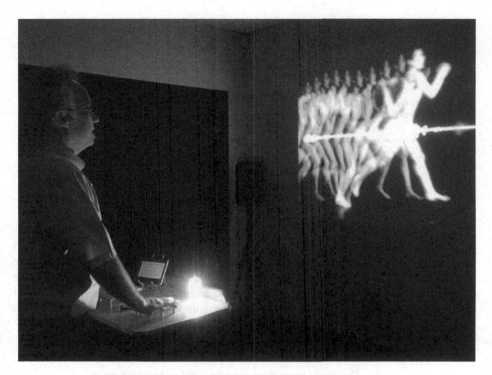

**Fig. 3.** One of the audiences is experiencing the installation and interacting with the work *Let us imagine a straight line* in the exhibition

Professor Rovan says on his website that he has been working on systems of enhanced acoustic installations, as well as new photography and video technologies so as to provide more tools for capturing and analyzing subtle gestures.

This work is also a typical real-time interactive multimedia electronic music installation. On the basis of the traditional installation art of exhibition type, the interactive multimedia installation increases the interactivity, which brings a sense of experience to the audience and increases possibilities for the stage performance of the artists. As a consequence, how to make the gesture of control more artistic and how to make the way of control more mysterious and magical has gradually become the design focus of the artists (Fig. 4).

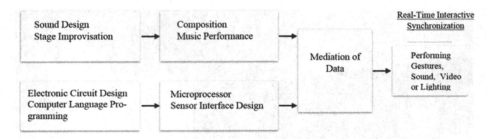

**Fig. 4.** Workflow chart of sensor music course

## 1.2   The Interaction and Control of Multimedia Installation Art

Multimedia art was born in the 20th century. It is based on digital technology, compatible with computer, film, photography, video recording, video, sound, installation interaction and other comprehensive means for creation. It is a kind of pure art that is the embodiment of the innovation and technology of the artists' ideas in the process of the evolution of the times and the continuous attempts and expansions of the combination of spatial and temporal dimensions. Figure 5 lists the important contexts of the development of multimedia since its birth and the main contents studied in different periods.

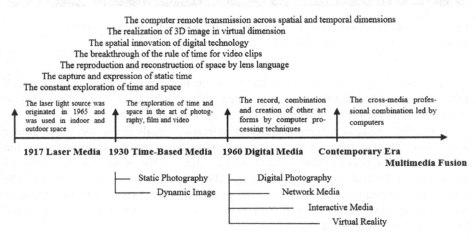

**Fig. 5.** The development of multimedia art

It is not difficult to see from Fig. 5 that technology leads to the pace of multimedia development, which is predominantly characterized by the integration of multiple disciplines. Multimedia installation can be used for public art exhibitions, for example, parks, squares, plazas, museums, and schools can all become its stage. Different from traditional art, interactivity not only brings a sense of experience but also makes the audience a part of the work. For example, in Fig. 6, the work *Forest of Resonating*

*Lamps*[4], light and music shine up as people get closer, and the pace of each mover in the immersive experience is woven into the clues of the light. In Fig. 7, the work *The Sculpture of Time Distortion in a Mirror*[5], the movement of the light completely follows the pace of the music, casting different light and shadow spaces constantly. All of these works use interaction to express their creativity and infinite imagination, but behind the interaction is the strict and meticulous control of the computer. To learn the control behind the work, we need to go back to the content of the previous section on the sensor music course.

**Fig. 6.** Forest of resonating lamps - one stroke, metropolis

**Fig. 7.** The sculpture of time distortion in a mirror

In summary, the interactive multimedia electronic music installation is a comprehensive display of "venue + materials + emotions". The interpretation with both sound and light on the stage constitutes a multimedia form, and various interactive devices which were designed and made for the performance "venue" (or stage) are "materials", and the language for conveying "emotions" is the audiovisual electronic music and lighting system. In the following section, the author will interpret Professor Hatakeyama's approach of using the interactive electronic music context to tell the audience about emotions step by step.

---

[4] Team Lab. (2018). *Forest of Resonating Lamps - One Stroke, Metropolis.* [photograph]. teamLab borderless, Shanghai, China. Retrieved from https://borderless.team-lab.cn/shanghai/ew/Forest_of_resonating_lamps_icecave_shanghai/
Interactive Installation, Murano Glass, LED, Endless, Sound: Hideaki Takahashi.

[5] Team Lab. (2019). *The Sculpture of Time Distortion in a Mirror.* [photograph]. teamLab borderless, Shanghai, China. Retrieved from https://borderless.team-lab.cn/shanghai/ew/sea_of_clouds_shanghai/
Light Sculpture - Line, Sound: Hideaki Takahashi.

## 2 Technical Analysis of the Work

### 2.1 The Music Part of Rainbow Cliff and Dusk

The music part is the "emotional" part of the interactive multimedia electronic music installation. It is also the link for artists to convey emotions through the language of music. Empathizing first and then subliming is the most effective way to gain an audience's recognition within the effective time. If the language of music (melody, rhythm, mode, tone, harmony, polyphony, texture, etc.) is too complex and exceeds the average understanding level of the audience, it will enhance the audience's thinking ability while they are accepting the work. Due to the relatively new performance materials (or installation) in performing forms and gesture controls, there is no lack of works with "complex materials (installation) + complex emotions (music)". Therefore, some contemporary installation of interactive electronic music requires the audience to have a certain artistic quality. But Professor Hatakeyama's work is more about conveying the feeling of empathy, and people of any class can be touched by it.

The work consists of three parts: vocal singing, self-made installation (controller) of glockenspiel (the artist calls it "Hako", which means music in Japanese) and a lighting modulation system. The total length of the work is 10 min and 15 s. The first 4 min are performed by a female vocalist, and then the glockenspiel performance of the self-made device (controller). The polyphonic ensemble between the human voice and the glockenspiel instrument starts at 6 min and 13 s.

The music part of the work belongs to the emotional category, which is invisible and untouchable during the performance. The emotion and rhythm presented on the stage are completely dominated by the artist, so it is relatively subjective and changeable in spaces (variability).

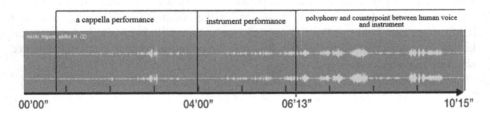

**Fig. 8.** Audio time node of *Rainbow Cliff and Dusk*

The prologue of the work is almost silent. The artist walks up to the stage in the dim light slowly. The vocal Accapella starts at 00:40 s. It can be observed from the waveform and Fig. 8 that the singing voice gradually increases. Subsequently, the artist holds the installation to complete the Accapella, which is the musical theme of the whole work. The movement of the body and the vocal singing of humans during the performance are integral parts of the entire work. In the eyes of the artist, what she has accomplished is an artistic ritual act, not a pure performance.

Before 04:00, music in this work is still a purely auditory expression. After 04:00, with the real-time mapping from the computer to the Hall sensor, lighting systems and the parameters of installation (musical instrument controllers), the music is converted into the visual lighting effect in real-time when it is heard.

This song has a ABA'B'C structure. The pure fifth between the small *a* and one-line octave *e* is the core motivation in the parallel phrase in passage A. The dense melody of passage B contrasts with the relatively soothing melody of passage A. The climax of the work is in the reproduction part of passage B', where the enhancement of volume and speed has pushed the entire work to its highest point. The subsequent passage C slowly introduced new material with a second and slowly ended. The artist's self-made controller (instrument box Hako) works much like a music box. The speed of the cylinder produced by the Hall Effect is controlled by the Max software in the computer, which simultaneously controls the rhythm of the music and the brightness of the light. The music box reminded the artist of her childhood, so she chose the bell tone to match it in terms of color. Polyphonic echoes between human voices and musical instruments are the ways to convey the core concepts of the work (Figs. 9, 10, 11, and 12).

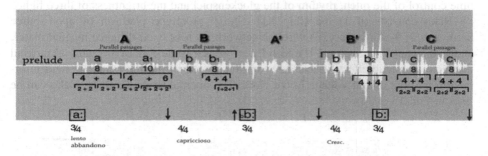

**Fig. 9.** Structure analysis of *Rainbow Cliff and Dusk*

**Fig. 10.** Stave of passage A

**Fig. 11.** Stave of passage B        **Fig. 12.** Stave of passage C

## 2.2   The Music Installation (Controller) System of "Hako"

The part of the installation is relatively objective hardware. The steps from design to implementation are very specific, with no tolerance of fault being allowed. It is also the most challenging part of the artist's creation.

In the performance of this work, the Hako music box (hereinafter referred to as Hako) was designed by the artist as a music box with strings drawn outward unidirectionally. Through changing the speed of the rotation of strings, the artist can take real-time control of the pitch, rhythm of the glockenspiel and the brightness of three lights.

Hako consists of 1) the Chip KIT Uno32 prototype platform of open-source hardware, 2) 9-volt battery, 3) wireless network, 4) four fixed-distance magnet plates, and 5) the Hall Effect sensor. The Hall Effect[6] sensor is the core of this work. As a kind of electromagnetic effect, it acts as a transducer, converting the magnetic field information into the output voltage in the work. The internal structure of the Hako can be seen in Fig. 13.

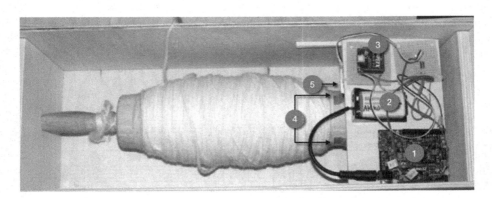

**Fig. 13.** Five main units of the internal structure of Hako

---

[6] This phenomenon was discovered by the American physicist E. H. Hall (1855–1938) in 1879 when he was studying the conductive mechanism of metals.

[1] When the current passes through the conductor perpendicular to the external magnetic field and the carrier deflects, an additional electric field is generated perpendicular to the direction of the current and magnetic field, resulting in a potential difference between the two ends of the conductor. When the magnet is placed close to the potential difference carrier, the Electro Rheological Effect will be motivated to produce electromagnetic signals.

The Hall sensor first sends the electromagnetic pulses to Chip KIT Uno32, which converts the pulse into MIDI and then transmits the MIDI signal to the Max software on the computer via the wireless network Xbee WBee. The 9-V battery is used to power the Uno32 so as to solve the problem of an external power cord, thus making the music box not limited by range, and facilitating the visual performance (stage movement) of the performers (Figs. 14 and 15).

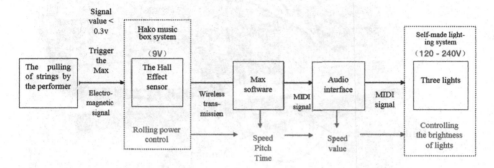

**Fig. 14.** The schematic diagram of system operation

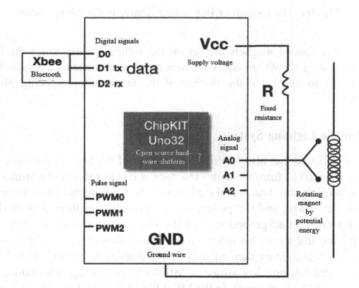

**Fig. 15.** The circuit diagram of Hako system

When the rolling sheathing is rotated, the magnet attached to it will continuously pass through the Hall Effect sensor, thus generating a magnetic field effect. When the magnet approaches the Hall Effect sensor, the patch in Max (the software used for mapping data interactively in the computer) will get a value close to 0 (0.004) (see Fig. 16 below), thus triggering the switch. On standby, when there are no magnets around the sensor, the value of the patch is 0.7 or so. A timing trigger is set in the Max system to receive values below 0.3.

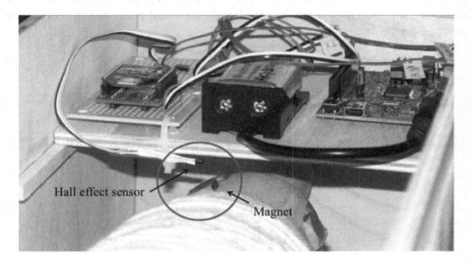

**Fig. 16.** The position of Hall Sensor relative to the rolling sheath

Four equally spaced magnets are set on the rolling sheath. Since the four mean values of the rolling sheath are equal for each rotation, the mean values can be set as a fixed parameter to determine the rhythm of the music samples being played by a glockenspiel.

### 2.3    Self-made Lighting System

The Hako installation can also control the intensity of the light at the same time. The speed value transferred from the audio interface is connected to the self-made lighting system to control the brightness and darkness of the three lights. These three lights are placed under the stage, and the performers are projected as three sets of **silhouettes from behind** on the background wall of the stage in an upward manner, creating a confined, private and somewhat lonely space. The shadows magnify the movements of the performers, highlighting their identity and increasing instability (Fig. 17).

Professor Hatakeyama has edited a MIDI file containing information of pitch, velocity-time and MIDI channels. In the MIDI file, channel 1 is set to receive pitch and speed information from the music. The patch software of Max is mainly used to map fundamental tones and speed information and send this information to the Sub-patch that manages sound samples. Within this sub-patch, each sound sample is mapped to a separate MIDI number. For example, in the play of the sound, the number 48 sent by the MIDI file corresponds to the pitch of C3 in the audio file of the object.

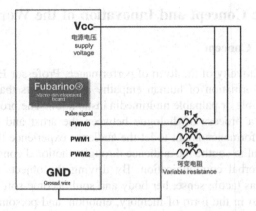

**Fig. 17.** The circuit diagram of lighting system of Hako installation

The LED lighting installation was a self-made system designed by Butch Rovan (Professor Hatakeyama's supervisor during her study for a master's degree at Brown University). In this system, the PWM is adopted instead of DMX for dimming control, which increases the convenience and flexibility of the lighting system. The system can also be adapted to different international standards of voltages (120–240 V). In this regard, the author believes that Professor Hatakeyama's design is worth learning. Voltage conversion is a common problem encountered in international exhibitions, which directly affects the performance of the work. As a part of the work, it can be designed in the early stage of creation, which can effectively avoid many inconveniences in the later period (Fig. 18).

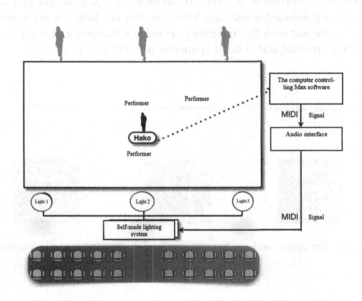

**Fig. 18.** The visual effect drawing of the stage

# 3   The Artistic Concept and Innovation of the Work

## 3.1   The Artistic Concept

Different from the novelty of the form of performance, Professor Hatakeyama's works focus on the transformation of human empathy and thoughts that are not visible or audible into an audible or palpable multimedia installation. The process of work design and production is a process of dialogue between the artist and her inner self. The purpose of live performance is not to let the audience experience the artwork or know the artist, but a ritual to soothe the audience through emotional consensus and settle the soul through nonverbal communication. By driving the objects of sound and light perception as well as tactile sense, her body and soul become soft and her exploration of time is embodied in the form of memory, emotion, and personal experience.

The part of the song is the artist's recollection of her childhood. Professor Hata-keyama chose to sing in Japanese in the American public performance in the hope that the audience could understand the melody in their way and not be guided by language directionality. The act of pulling strings from a box is a metaphor for recalling a hidden memory. *"I usually cannot guess what triggers the memory. The connection to trigger memory is sometimes random and sometimes clear. It may take a long time to retrieve the memory, but once I recall it, a lot of the past flows out. Sometimes I hesitate to release certain memories whose change is in parallel with the rhythm of the music and the pulling of the body movement. The clues (the efforts and traces of recollection) lie on the floor forming a net, as if old memories were hopelessly trying to capture new ones without letting them slip away, which is also a ritual of protecting what was lost in the past."* (Excerpt from master's degree thesis of Akiko Hatakeyama).

Ultimately, Professor Hatakeyama sets the goal of the installation as the music box that each of us has owned at one time or another (the material and cultural entities consumed or not consumed in our daily lives). At the same time, the combination of the language of music and with lighting effect can make it perform a new artistic act of the mass' recalling spiritual and cultural connotation of the past (Fig. 19).

**Fig. 19.** The correspondence between conceptual ideas and concrete techniques

## 3.2    The Artistic Innovation

In the performance of this work, there are multiple transforming processes: 1) the traditional instruments used for playing are transformed into devices made by the composer; 2) the emotion itself has completed the concretized transformation and experienced the progressive process of memory-consciousness-unconsciousness; 3) the transmission channel has completed the transformation of information abstraction, and the computer has translated language symbols into sound symbols for transmission; 4) the creator has completed the transformation from a conductor to a performer; 5) the whole work itself is a transformation process of using technology to express art.

The technological revolution of the combination of self-made installation + new performance mode + traditional language of music provides more possibilities for forms of music expression. The diversified development of artists' knowledge structure-music sound system-noise system-computer language programming also reflects the current development trend of multimedia artistic expression means.

Finally, it should be pointed out that the difference between highly skilled people and artists lies in the expression of emotion and the source of artistic inspiration. In the process of technological development, there will appear many branches in blind pursuit of technological innovation, which is of necessity from an objective point of view. However, from the perspective of artistic expression, the display technology and the use of advanced technology to effectively express emotion are completely different. The following speech given by Professor Jeffrey Stolet[7] in the 2012 Kyma Annual Conference can express this difference.

*"The sound made by my pet cat on the piano is just the objective feedback of movement and behavior. However, the sound played by the pianist Glenn Gould is music. Why? Because my cat does not understand how the instrument works, and knows nothing about the mapping involved in it and what keys are associated with what sound. But the pianist Glenn Gould knows that when he plays a note called central C, there is a certain pitch, which means that he can play the music consciously. However, my cat, without the knowledge in this regard, gets no opportunity to compose for her intentions of performance.*

*Therefore, the structures generated throughout the past, present and future of music are designed, and the playing of instruments is a purpose-driven performance to convey emotions and cultures."*

Some artistic concepts such as language problems, the traveling to distant places, the death of relatives, etc. are universal. People of different ages and genders have different experiences of these emotions, but they have all experienced them before. When most avant-garde artists are in their prime, they will develop in two different directions: the pursuit of continuous technological innovation and the extreme expression of individualism. Without an understanding of the artist's life background, the main source of inspiration for the works and the main innovative technology, the audience can hardly understand the works.

---

[7] Jeffrey Stolet (USA), Director of the Center for Future Music, College of Music and Dance, University of Oregon.

Multimedia art is an art form that evokes many associations. It establishes an environment and attitude that is humanely close to art and technology, implying that we can take artists as mediators and explorers of the Internet. Although the technology of transmission is constantly innovating and the audio-visual experience is constantly upgrading, the concepts transmitted are often the eternal empathy and emotion of human beings.

**Acknowledgements.** This article is one of the research products of Jiangsu Provincial Philosophy and Social Science Research Program for Colleges and Universities titled "Research on the Application of Interactive Music Controller in the field of Electronic Music Installation" (No. 2018SJA0361).

I sincerely thank Professor Jeffrey Stolet and Professor Akiko Hatakeyama for the meticulous guidance I received during my academic visit at the University of Oregon. At the same time, I also thank them for providing valuable information in the process of writing the paper! Finally, I would like to express my sincere thanks to assistant teacher Iris Wang for her careful guidance and explanation of the electronic circuit in the paper.

# References

1. Hatakeyama, A.: Blind | The world where I can't be but you live in Written in May 2013 Revised in November for Xiaoni Zhuang (2017)
2. Stolet, J.: Twenty-three and a half things about musical interfaces. In: 2012 Kyma International Sound Symposium (2012)
3. Arnheim, R.: Visual Thinking. Chinese Translation by Teng Shouyao. Guangming Daily Press, Beijing (1986)
4. Zettl, H.: Sight, Sound, Motion: Applied Media Aesthetics (2003). Chinese Translation by Miaomiao. Z Communication University of China Press, Beijing. https://doi.org/10.1007/978-1-4615-1119-9_2

# Digital Human Modelling
and Ergonomics

# Leveraging Muscular Fitness Surrogates to Classify Cardiorespiratory Fitness Status in Youth: A Supervised Machine Learning Approach

Toyin Ajisafe[(⊠)]

Texas A&M University – Corpus Christi, Corpus Christi, TX, USA
toyin.ajisafe@tamucc.edu

**Abstract.** Cardiorespiratory fitness (CRF) is linked with anxiety, depression, and cardiovascular disease risk. Assessing CRF is time consuming, space-prohibitive, and may require specialized equipment. Therefore, it is not routinely assessed in schools or clinical settings. This study aimed to leverage muscular fitness surrogates, anthropometrics and demographics to build optimal CRF classifiers that can be easily deployed across multiple settings. $VO_{2PEAK}$ was estimated using a prediction equation that integrated the 20-m Progressive Aerobic Cardiovascular Endurance Run dataset from 210 youth (116 males) ($9.7 \pm 1.08$ years; $138.6 \pm 9.4$ cm; $42.3 \pm 14.4$ kg). Muscular fitness (i.e., 90° push-up, curl-up, etc.) was assessed. Several models (e.g., Support Vector Machine (SVM), Naïve Bayes, and Logistic Regression) were trained using both the originally imbalanced dataset and a balanced dataset resulting from synthetically oversampling the minority class. Metrics, including Area Under Curve (AUC) and True and False Positive Rates (TPR and FPR) were used to compare performance between models. The most salient model was a Logistic Regression model with nine features (i.e., sex, age, sit-and-reach, body mass, trunk lift, BMI, curl-up, 90° push-up, and height) (accuracy = 89.5%; AUC = 0.96; TPR = 0.86, FPRs = 0.08). This model correctly classified 100% and 100% of positive and negative class observations, respectively. A Logistic Regression model (accuracy = 85.7%; AUC = 0.92; TPR = 0.84, FPRs = 0.14) with four features (i.e., sex, age, sit-and-reach, and body mass) correctly predicted 100% and 91% of positive and negative class observations, respectively. Results demonstrate the feasibility of leveraging muscular fitness, anthropometrics, and basic demographics to develop accurate, streamlined models that can be easily deployed across multiple settings in order to facilitate routine CRF assessment in youth.

**Keywords:** Machine learning · Cardiorespiratory fitness classification · Weight status · Hispanic/latino youth · School fitness surveillance

## 1 Introduction

Cardiorespiratory fitness (CRF) is the capacity to perform whole-body movements (e.g., walking briskly, running, and negotiating stairs) at a moderate to vigorous intensity without quick onset, debilitating fatigue [1]. CRF has been linked with

© Springer Nature Switzerland AG 2020
C. Stephanidis et al. (Eds.): HCII 2020, LNCS 12429, pp. 443–454, 2020.
https://doi.org/10.1007/978-3-030-59987-4_31

anxiety, mood, depression, and cardiovascular disease risk [2]. CRF can be directly measured as $VO_{2PEAK}$ during max and sub-max treadmill and ergometer protocols. Further, it can be estimated using field tests. However, regardless of the method, assessing CRF is time consuming, space-prohibitive, and may require specialized equipment. These barriers likely underlie its continued lack of adoption in clinical settings [3] and preclude its recurrent assessment in schools. Muscular fitness (i.e., the capacity to exert sustained muscular force against some resistance) and CRF fitness are inextricably linked. The cardiorespiratory system transports oxygen to active skeletal muscles, where it is metabolized (via an aerobic metabolic pathway) to generate energy. Upper body strength and endurance (measured using grip strength) is associated with cardiometabolic risk [4]. There is a predictive relationship between muscular strength and endurance (assessed using push-up and curl-up tests) and clustered cardiometabolic risk [5]. Relatedly, muscular fitness associates with CRF [6, 7]. Therefore, it is important to leverage tractable surrogates that can deployed by clinicians, physical education teachers, public health practitioners, and possibly parents to recurrently surveil CRF in youth.

A number of studies have reported cut-points for CRF in children and youth in the US and Europe using clustering of a range of cardiometabolic markers, including systolic blood pressure and triglycerides [8, 9]. F Lobelo, RR Pate, M Dowda, AD Liese and JR Ruiz [9] reported $VO_{2PEAK}$ cut-points of 36.0 and 35.5 mL.kg$^{-1}$.min$^{-1}$ for 12–15- and 16–19-year-old girls and cut-points of 44.1 and 40.3 mL.kg$^{-1}$.min$^{-1}$ for 12–15- and 16–19-year-old boys, respectively, during a submaximal treadmill protocol [9]. Using similar markers and a maximal ergometer bike test, AR Adegboye, SA Anderssen, K Froberg, LB Sardinha, BL Heitmann, J Steene-Johannessen, E Kolle and LB Andersen [8] reported $VO_{2PEAK}$ cut-points of 37.4 and 33.0 mL.kg$^{-1}$.min$^{-1}$ for 8–11- and 14–17-year-old girls and cut-points of 43.6 and 46.0 mL.kg$^{-1}$.min$^{-1}$ for 8–11- and 14–17-year-old boys, respectively [8]. JR Ruiz, FB Ortega, NS Rizzo, I Villa, A Hurtig-Wennlof, L Oja and M Sjostrom [10] reported $VO_{2PEAK}$ cut points of 37.0 and 42.1 mL.kg$^{-1}$.min$^{-1}$ for 9–10-year-old girls and boys, respectively. Despite the associations between muscular fitness and CRF, no studies have leveraged established CRF cut-points to develop optimal classifiers that make its recurrent assessment (at multiple time points across the school year) feasible and practical.

The Progressive Aerobic Cardiovascular Endurance Run (PACER) is commonly used to assess CRF in the field [11]. However, although the PACER increases the feasibility of assessing CRF in settings such as school gyms, it requires ample space and is impractical in clinical settings. Machine learning approaches have been commonly applied to classification problems involving predicting disease risk owing to their capacity to leverage several different methods and identify multivariate interactions and patterns that are optimally predictive of specified endpoints [12]. Supervised learning has been used to classify fundamental locomotor skills (e.g., hopping, running, etc.) [13], activity type (e.g., walking, standing stationary, etc.), predicting physical activity patterns in older adults [14], and classifying obesity among youth [15]. Machine learning techniques are increasingly applied to classification problems in health (Fig. 1). Although studies have approached prediction problems around using predetermined classification methods, inherent peculiarities related to shared contexts (ecological and sociocultural) suggest that it is important to explore multiple models and identify the best performing ones for the specific problem and dataset. Consistent with this framework, FS Abdullah, NS Abd Manan, A Ahmad, SW Wafa, MR Shahril, N Zulaily, RM Amin and A Ahmed [15] found that decision tree performed the best at classifying childhood obesity using features that included push-up test, partial curl-up, step-up, and sit-and-reach test in 12-year-old Malaysian children. It is best to implement multiple approaches (e.g., Random Forest, and SVM) as methods tend to be differentially suited to various classification problems. For example, while Logistic Model Tree algorithms showed the highest classification accuracy (79–92%) for activity classification, SVM models performed best at classifying obesity among youth [15].

The capacity to surveil and predict disease risk is central to public health efforts aimed at reducing the burden of disease [12]. While the evidence supporting the causal effect of low CRF on obesity is less salient, the inverse association between them is well established. Further, CRF associates (independent of muscular fitness) with anxiety, mood, depression, and cardiovascular disease risk. Therefore, the purpose of this study was to identify and leverage muscular fitness surrogates to build optimal classifiers that can be easily deployed to identify CRF status across a variety of settings.

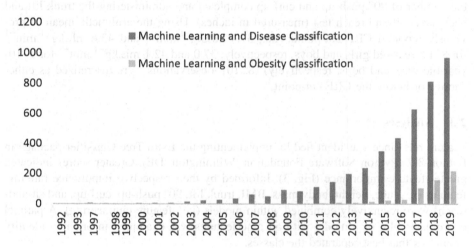

**Fig. 1.** Peer-reviewed machine learning publications trend by year from Web of Science

## 2 Methods

### 2.1 Sample

Data were collected from school children (n = 218; 116 males) (9.7 ± 1.08 years; 138.6 ± 9.4 cm; 42.3 ± 14.4 kg) (84% Hispanic/Latino) in Corpus Christi, Texas, between September-November 2016. Directly measured $VO_{2PEAK}$ values were not available; therefore, $VO_{2PEAK}$ was estimated using the FITNESSGRAM prediction equation (i.e., $VO_{2PEAK} = 0.353(Laps) - 1.121(Age) + 45.619$) involving the number of laps successfully ran on the 20-m PACER [16]. Muscular fitness was assessed using trunk lift, 90° push-up, curl-up, and sit-and-reach per FITNESSGRAM® protocols.

BMI (quotient of weight (kg) and the square of height (m)) z-score percentiles for age and sex were used to delineate weight status [17]. Texas A&M University-Corpus Christi Institutional Review Board approved this study (IRB # 122-17).

## 2.2 Variables

Height and body mass were measured to the nearest 0.1 m and 0.1 kg, respectively. BMI was calculated as the quotient of weight (kg) and the square of height (m). Resulting scores were standardized as z-scores and used to determine respective percentiles for age and sex according to the Centers for Disease Control and Prevention (CDC) growth charts [17]. Underweight, healthy weight, overweight, and obesity were defined as BMI < 5th percentile, 5th $\leq$ BMI < 85th percentile, 85th $\leq$ BMI < 95th percentiles, and BMI $\geq$ 95th percentile, respectively [17, 18]. Given the unequal distances between the percentile-based classifications, the weight classes were discretized as follows: underweight was "0," healthy weight was "1," overweight was "2," and obesity was "3."

Muscular fitness (i.e., strength, endurance, and flexibility) was assessed by counting the number of 90° push-up and curl-up completed and administering the trunk lift and back saver sit-and-reach test (measured in inches). Using the arithmetic mean of previously reported CRF cut-points (i.e., 37.4 mL.kg$^{-1}$.min$^{-1}$ and 43.6 mL.kg$^{-1}$.min$^{-1}$ for 8–11-year-old girls and boys, respectively; 37.0 and 42.1 mL.kg$^{-1}$.min$^{-1}$ for 9–10-year-old girls and boys, respectively) [8, 10], observations were discretized as either "above or below the CRF cut-point."

## 2.3 Analyses

Feature relevance was identified by implementing the Extra Tree Classifier package in Python 3.7 (Python Software Foundation, Wilmington, DE). Greater scores indicated greater feature importance (Fig. 3). Informed by their respective importance ranking, features (sex, age, height, body mass, BMI, trunk lift, 90° push-up, curl-up, and sit-and-reach) were recursively combined within models (i.e., feature engineering). A parallel coordinates plot of a model with all nine features was examined in order to identify predictors that best separated the classes.

Classifiers were built using MATLAB R2019b (Mathworks, Natick, MA). After imputing missing data points using the median of observations in each class, 90% of the dataset was used to train several models (e.g., Decision Tree, Support Vector Machine (SVM), Naïve Bayes, and Ensemble), while 20% was retained for validation. A 5-fold cross validation was employed to prevent overfitting. Features namely age, sex, height, body mass, BMI, trunk lift, 90° push-up, curl-up, and sit-and-reach were recursively combined within models (i.e., feature engineering). Models were evaluated using Receiver Operating Characteristics curve analyses. The associated Area Under Curve (AUC) (where AUC $\geq$ 8 is good discrimination), True Positive Rate (TPR) (i.e., Sensitivity), and False Positive Rate (FPR) (i.e., 1 - Specificity) indicated model quality and performance. Given its importance to the problem at hand (i.e., classifying CRF status relative to recommended cut-points), False Negative Rate (FNR) was also calculated. Precision (i.e., the capacity to identify only the relevant cases) and recall (i.e., the capacity to identify all cases of interest within a dataset) were also calculated. Maximal precision decreases the incidence of false positives, while maximal recall reduces the instances for false negatives. F-Measure (harmonic mean of precision and recall) was also adopted, because it penalizes extreme values of precision and recall.

## 3 Developing Classifiers from Imbalanced Datasets

Broadly, a dataset is described as imbalanced, if the discrete categories or class to be classified are not roughly equally represented in the dataset. In the context of disease classification (where "0" represents the negative class and "1" represents the positive class), an imbalance would be indicated, if the number of observations in the positive class were disproportionally fewer than the observations in the negative class or vice versa. Considering CRF (as examined and delineated in the current study), any considerable discrepancy between the number of observations that are above and below the specified cut-point would constitute an imbalance. In this study, 66% of the total observations were below the age- and sex-indicated CRF cut-points and therefore categorized as the positive class. The remaining 34% of total observations were above the age- and sex-indicated CRF cut-points and categorized as the negative class. As such, "0" represented the negative class (i.e., not at risk for chronic disease) and "1" represented the positive class (i.e., at risk for chronic disease). This imbalance in distribution of the target classes could potentially bias the performance of classifiers in the direction of majority class [19]. Although the cost of misclassifying the positive class far exceeds that of the reverse error, it is often important to leverage methods that help mitigate any effects of class imbalance in order to optimize model performance by minimizing both Type and I and II errors. One such method is Synthetic Minority Over-Sampling Technique (SMOTE) [12, 19]. SMOTE simply generates new data points between a data point and its nearest neighbor in space. These new data points are generated along the same line as the original (i.e., non-synthetic) data points. In the current study, the minority class (within the training dataset) was oversampled by approximately 210%, thereby resulting in 133 observations. Therefore, the balanced and imbalanced datasets consisted of 266 and 196 observations, respectively. Owing to the relative small size of the dataset, 10% of the training set was withheld for further validation (in addition to 5-fold cross validation implemented during training). Figure 2 shows the workflow associated with the development of classifiers.

**Fig. 2.** Data processing workflow

# 4 Discussion

## 4.1 Feature Relevance

In the current study, 34% of the total initial observations scored above the cut-point for CRF and were classified as "0" (i.e., not at risk for chronic disease). Further, 39% of the training dataset belonged to the minority class prior to oversampling. Additionally, 41%, 18%, and 41% of the total observations had healthy weight, overweight, and obesity, respectively. Results of The Extra Tree Classifier show that age and sex are key contributory features to classifying CRF even with dataset imbalance (Fig. 3).

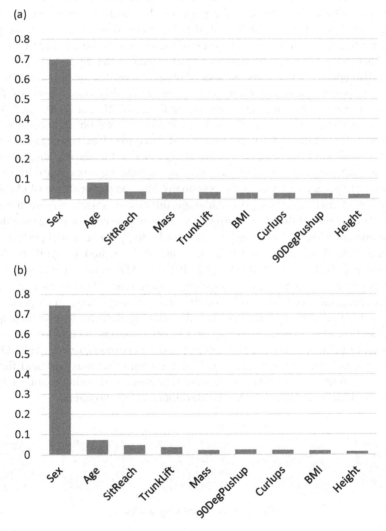

**Fig. 3.** Bar chart showing feature relevance/importance scores from (a) the imbalanced dataset and (b) the balanced dataset using Random Forest and Extra Tree Classifier. The features are sex, age, height, body mass, BMI, trunk lift, 90° push-up, curl-up, and sit-and-reach scores

**CRF Classifiers Trained Using an Imbalanced Dataset.** The most salient models trained using the imbalanced dataset are presented first. All model quality and performance metrics are presented in Table 1. A Logistic Regression model (accuracy = 86.1%; AUC = 0.92; TPR = 0.89, FPRs = 0.17) with all nine features (i.e., sex, age, sit-and-reach, body mass, trunk lift, BMI, curl-up, 90° push-up, and height) emerged salient (Table 1). When deployed using the test data, this model correctly predicted 100% and 91% of observations below (i.e., positive class) and above (i.e., negative class) the referenced cut points for CRF (using estimated $VO_{2PEAK}$), respectively. Comparatively, a Logistic Regression model (accuracy = 87.2%; AUC = 0.92; TPR = 0.88, FPRs = 0.14) with six features (i.e., sex, age, sit-and-reach, body mass, trunk lift, BMI) correctly predicted 100% and 91% of observations the positive and negative classes, respectively. Similarly, a Medium Gaussian SVM model (accuracy = 87.2%; AUC = 0.90; TPR = 0.89, FPRs = 0.16) with five features (i.e., sex, age, sit-and-reach, body mass, and trunk lift) correctly predicted 100% and 91% of observations the positive and negative classes, respectively. A Logistic Regression model (accuracy = 85.7%; AUC = 0.92; TPR = 0.84, FPRs = 0.14) with four features (i.e., sex, age, sit-and-reach, and body mass) (Table 1) correctly predicted 100% and 91% of positive and negative class observations, respectively. In contrast, a Naïve Bayes model (accuracy = 87.2%; AUC = 0.90; TPR = 0.86, FPRs = 0.10) with 8 features (i.e., sex, age, body mass, BMI, trunk lift, 90° push-up, curl-up, and sit-and-reach) correctly predicted 91% and 91% of previously withheld positive and negative class observations, respectively. A Cosine K-Nearest Neighbor model (accuracy = 87.2%; AUC = 0.89; TPR = 0.87, FPRs = 0.24) with seven features (i.e., sex, age, sit-and-reach, body mass, trunk lift, BMI, curl-up) correctly predicted 91% and 91% of positive and negative class observations, respectively. A Medium Gaussian SVM model (accuracy = 88.8%; AUC = 0.91; TPR = 0.89, FPRs = 0.13) with three features (i.e., sex, age, and sit-and-reach) (Table 1) correctly predicted 100% and 82% of positive and negative class observations, respectively. A Weighted KNN model (accuracy = 89.3%; AUC = 0.92; TPR = 0.89, FPRs = 0.11) with two features (i.e., sex and age) correctly predicted 82% and 91% of positive and negative class observations, respectively. Lastly, as a reference, a Fine Gaussian SVM model (accuracy = 68.9%; AUC = 0.57; TPR = 0.10, FPRs = 0.97) with one feature, namely sex, correctly classified 27% and 0% of the positive and negative classes, respectively. Notably, there were several other high performing models (not reported), including a Logistic Regression model (accuracy = 87.2%; AUC = 0.93; TPR = 0.86, FPRs = 0.12) with three features (i.e., sex, age, and mass) that correctly predicted 100% and 91% of positive and negative class observations, respectively. Additional model performance metrics, (e.g., recall, precision, and F-Measure) are presented in Table 1.

**Table 1.** Additional CRF classification models with greater than 85% accuracy and associated Receiver Operating Characteristic (ROC) curve analysis metrics

| Model | Accuracy (%) | AUC | TPR | FPR | FNR | Recall | Precision | F-Measure |
|---|---|---|---|---|---|---|---|---|
| *Imbalanced dataset* | | | | | | | | |
| Logistic Regression[9] | 86.1 | 0.92 | 0.89 | 0.17 | 0.11 | 0.84 | 0.89 | 0.86 |
| Naïve Bayes[8] | 87.2 | 0.90 | 0.86 | 0.10 | 0.14 | 0.90 | 0.86 | 0.88 |
| Cosine KNN[7] | 87.2 | 0.91 | 0.86 | 0.11 | 0.14 | 0.89 | 0.86 | 0.87 |
| Logistic Regression[6] | 87.2 | 0.92 | 0.88 | 0.14 | 0.12 | 0.86 | 0.88 | 0.87 |
| Medium Gaussian SVM[5] | 87.2 | 0.90 | 0.89 | 0.16 | 0.11 | 0.85 | 0.89 | 0.87 |
| Logistic Regression[4] | 85.7 | 0.92 | 0.84 | 0.14 | 0.16 | 0.84 | 0.86 | 0.85 |
| Support Vector Machine[3] | 88.8 | 0.90 | 0.84 | 0.13 | 0.11 | 0.89 | 0.87 | 0.88 |
| Weighted KNN[2] | 89.3 | 0.92 | 0.89 | 0.11 | 0.11 | 0.89 | 0.89 | 0.89 |
| Fine Gaussian SVM[1] | 68.9 | 0.57 | 1.00 | 0.97 | 0 | 0.51 | 0.51 | 0.67 |
| *Balanced dataset* | | | | | | | | |
| Logistic Regression[9] | 89.5 | 0.96 | 0.86 | 0.08 | 0.14 | 0.92 | 0.86 | 0.89 |
| Logistic Regression[8] | 89.8 | 0.95 | 0.85 | 0.05 | 0.15 | 0.94 | 0.85 | 0.90 |
| Logistic Regression[7] | 89.8 | 0.95 | 0.85 | 0.05 | 0.15 | 0.94 | 0.85 | 0.90 |
| Logistic Regression[6] | 89.5 | 0.95 | 0.84 | 0.05 | 0.16 | 0.94 | 0.84 | 0.89 |
| Logistic Regression[5] | 90.2 | 0.95 | 0.85 | 0.05 | 0.15 | 0.94 | 0.85 | 0.90 |
| Bagged Tree Ensemble[4] | 90.2 | 0.94 | 0.89 | 0.08 | 0.11 | 0.92 | 0.89 | 0.90 |
| Logistic Regression[3] | 89.5 | 0.94 | 0.83 | 0.05 | 0.17 | 0.94 | 0.83 | 0.88 |
| Logistic Regression[2] | 88.3 | 0.93 | 0.81 | 0.05 | 0.19 | 0.94 | 0.81 | 0.87 |
| Cubic SVM[1] | 67.7 | 0.68 | 0.62 | 0.27 | 0.38 | 0.69 | 0.62 | 0.66 |

Abbreviations: Receiver Operating Characteristics, ROC; Area Under Curve, AUC; True Positive Rate, TPR; False Positive Rate, FPR; False Negative Rate, FNR; K-Nearest Neighbor, KNN; Support Vector Machine, SVM. Subscripts indicate the number of features included in the model in order of importance/relevance.

**CRF Classifiers Trained Using a Balanced Dataset.** The most salient model trained using balanced dataset was a Logistic Regression model (accuracy = 89.5%; AUC = 0.96; TPR = 0.86, FPRs = 0.08) with all nine features (i.e., sex, age, sit-and-reach, body mass, trunk lift, BMI, curl-up, 90° push-up, and height) (Figs. 4 and 5) (Table 1). When deployed using the test data, this model correctly predicted 100% and 100% of the positive and negative class observations, respectively.

Additionally, a Logistic Regression model (accuracy = 89.8%; AUC = 0.95; TPR = 0.85, FPRs = 0.05) with 8 features (i.e., sex, age, body mass, BMI, trunk lift, 90° push-up, curl-up, and sit-and-reach) correctly predicted 100% and 91% of observations in the positive and negative classes, respectively. A Logistic Regression model (accuracy = 89.8%; AUC = 0.95; TPR = 0.85, FPRs = 0.05) with seven features (i.e., sex, age, sit-and-reach, body mass, trunk lift, BMI, curl-up) correctly predicted 100% and 91% of positive and negative class observations, respectively.

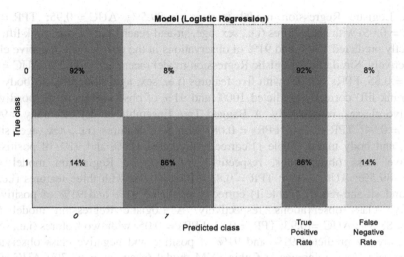

**Fig. 4.** Confusion matrix of a Logistic Regression model for cardiorespiratory (CRF) status classification. Shown in the figure are the percentages of observations that were correctly and erroneously classified as above or below the specified cut-point based on all nine features, namely sex, age, height, body mass, BMI, trunk lift, 90° push-up, curl-up, and sit-and-reach scores.

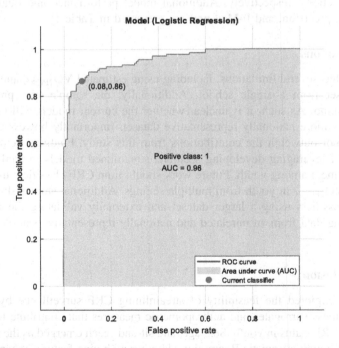

**Fig. 5.** Receiver Operating Characteristic (ROC) curve of a Logistic Regression model for cardiorespiratory (CRF) status classification. Shown in the figure are the Area Under Curve and True and False Positive Rates relevant to the performance of the classifier.

A Logistic Regression model (accuracy = 89.5%; AUC = 0.95; TPR = 0.84, FPRs = 0.05) with six features (i.e., sex, age, sit-and-reach, body mass, trunk lift, BMI) correctly predicted 100% and 91% of observations in the positive and negative classes, respectively. Similarly, a Logistic Regression model (accuracy = 90.2%; AUC = 0.95; TPR = 0.85, FPRs = 0.05) with five features (i.e., sex, age, sit-and-reach, body mass, and trunk lift) correctly predicted 100% and 91% of observations in the positive and negative classes, respectively. A Bagged Tree Ensemble model (accuracy = 90.2%; AUC = 0.94; TPR = 0.89, FPRs = 0.08) with four features (i.e., sex, age, sit-and-reach, and body mass) (Table 1) correctly predicted 100% and 91% of positive and negative class observations, respectively. A Logistic Regression model (accuracy = 89.5%; AUC = 0.94; TPR = 0.83, FPRs = 0.05) with three features (i.e., sex, age, and sit-and-reach) (Table 1) correctly predicted 91% and 91% of positive and negative class observations, respectively. A Logistic Regression model (accuracy = 88.3%; AUC = 0.93; TPR = 0.81, FPRs = 0.05) with two features (i.e., sex and age) correctly predicted 91% and 91% of positive and negative class observations, respectively. As a reference, a Cubic SVM model (accuracy = 67.7%; AUC = 0.68; TPR = 0.62, FPRs = 0.27) with one feature, namely sex, correctly classified 18% and 0% of the positive and negative classes, respectively. There were several other high performing models (not reported), including a Logistic Regression model (accuracy = 88.7%; AUC = 0.94; TPR = 0.83, FPRs = 0.06) with three features (i.e., sex, age, and mass) (Table 1) correctly predicted 100% and 91% of positive and negative class observations, respectively. Additional model performance and quality metrics, (e.g., recall, precision, and F-Measure) are presented in Table 1.

## 4.2    Limitations

This study has several limitations, including using estimated $VO_{2PEAK}$ and a relatively small dataset from a single school. Additionally, the sample was predominantly Hispanic/Latino. As such, it is unclear whether the current models will perform similarly with a more nationally representative dataset. Importantly however, these limitations do not outweigh the contributions from this study. Findings demonstrate the feasibility of leveraging developing accurate, streamlined models to facilitate routine CRF assessment among youth. Future work should train CRF classifiers using directly measured $VO_{2PEAK}$ in youth from multiple settings. Additional studies should explore building classifiers using a larger dataset and externally validating the most salient models using data from an unrelated and nationally representative sample of children and youth.

## 4.3    Conclusion

This paper explored the feasibility of streamlining CRF surveillance by leveraging muscular fitness surrogates and anthropometric measures that contribute to accurately classifying CRF status in youth. Sex, age, and sit-and-reach emerged as the most salient features. Although a Logistic Regression classifier with nine features recorded the best performance (i.e., identified 100% of positive cases) at classifying the training dataset, a number of other classifiers correctly classified 91% of the positive and negative classes. These results suggest several machine learning algorithms can be leveraged to develop accurate, streamlined models that can be deployed to assess CRF in children in a variety of settings, including schools, doctors' offices, and public health intervention sites. For example, a simplistic model with only sex, age, and sit-and-reach accurately classified 91% of positive cases CRF and could dramatically decrease the temporal, spatial, and equipment burden associated with testing, thereby encouraging practitioners such as physical education teachers to recurrently surveil CRF (similar to academic progress reports) and inform physical activity programming, accordingly. While using a balanced training dataset yielded the most salient model, several other models trained on imbalanced dataset performed relatively accurately when deployed to classify the test data. Surprisingly, 90° push-up did not rank as one of the most relevant muscular fitness surrogate features in the current research.

# References

1. Saltin, B.: In Limiting Factors of Physical Performance (Oxygen Transport by the Circulatory System During Exercise in Man): Stuttgart. Thieme Publishers, Germany (1973)
2. Ortega, F.B., Ruiz, J.R., Castillo, M.J., Sjostrom, M.: Physical fitness in childhood and adolescence: a powerful marker of health. Int. J. Obes. (Lond.) 32(1), 1–11 (2008)
3. Yang, J., et al.: Association between push-up exercise capacity and future cardiovascular events among active adult men. JAMA Netw. Open 2(2) (2019)
4. Peterson, M.D., Saltarelli, W.A., Visich, P.S., Gordon, P.M.: Strength capacity and cardiometabolic risk clustering in adolescents. Pediatrics 133(4), e896–903 (2014)
5. Burns, R.D., Brusseau, T.A.: Muscular strength and endurance and cardio-metabolic health in disadvantaged Hispanic children from the U.S. Prev. Med. Rep. 5, 21–26 (2017)
6. Sacheck, J.M., Amin, S.A.: Cardiorespiratory fitness in children and youth: a call for surveillance, but now how do we do it? Exerc. Sport Sci. Rev. 46(2), 65 (2018)
7. Ajisafe, T.: Association between 90(o) push-up and cardiorespiratory fitness: cross-sectional evidence of push-up as a tractable tool for physical fitness surveillance in youth. BMC Pediatr. 19(1), 458 (2019)
8. Adegboye, A.R., et al.: Recommended aerobic fitness level for metabolic health in children and adolescents: a study of diagnostic accuracy. Br. J. Sports Med. 45(9), 722–728 (2011)
9. Lobelo, F., Pate, R.R., Dowda, M., Liese, A.D., Ruiz, J.R.: Validity of cardiorespiratory fitness criterion-referenced standards for adolescents. Med. Sci. Sports Exerc. 41(6), 1222–1229 (2009)
10. Ruiz, J.R., et al.: High cardiovascular fitness is associated with low metabolic risk score in children: the European Youth Heart Study. Pediatr. Res. 61(3), 350–355 (2007)
11. Meredith, M.D., Welk, G.: Fitnessgram/Activitygram: Test Administration Manual, 3rd edn. Human Kinetics, Champaign (2004)
12. Selya, A.S., Anshutz, D.: Machine learning for the classification of obesity from dietary and physical activity patterns. In: Giabbanelli, P.J., Mago, V.K., Papageorgiou, E.I. (eds.) Advanced Data Analytics in Health. SIST, vol. 93, pp. 77–97. Springer, Cham (2018). https://doi.org/10.1007/978-3-319-77911-9_5
13. Ajisafe, T., Um, D.: Exploring the feasibility of classifying fundamental locomotor skills using an instrumented insole and machine learning techniques. In: Duffy, V.G. (ed.) HCII 2019. LNCS, vol. 11581, pp. 113–127. Springer, Cham (2019). https://doi.org/10.1007/978-3-030-22216-1_9

14. Zheng, Y., Xie, J., Vo, T.V.T., Lee, B.C., Ajisafe, T.: Predicting daily physical activity level for older adults using wearable activity trackers. In: Zhou, J., Salvendy, G. (eds.) HCII 2019. LNCS, vol. 11593, pp. 602–614. Springer, Cham (2019). https://doi.org/10.1007/978-3-030-22015-0_47

15. Abdullah, F.S., et al.: Data mining techniques for classification of childhood obesity among year 6 school children. Adv. Intell. Syst. **549**, 465–474 (2017)

16. Burns, R.D., et al.: Cross-validation of aerobic capacity prediction models in adolescents. Pediatr. Exerc. Sci. **27**(3), 404–411 (2015)

17. Kuczmarski, R.J., et al.: 2000 CDC growth charts for the United States: methods and development. Vital Health Stat. **11**(246), 1–190 (2002)

18. Racette, S.B., Yu, L., DuPont, N.C., Clark, B.R.: BMI-for-age graphs with severe obesity percentile curves: tools for plotting cross-sectional and longitudinal youth BMI data. BMC Pediatr. **17**(1), 130 (2017)

19. Chawla, N.V., Bowyer, K.W., Hall, L.O., Kegelmeyer, W.P.: SMOTE: synthetic minority over-sampling technique. J. Artif. Intell. Res. **2002**(16), 321–357 (2002)

# Evaluating the Effect of Crutch-Using on Trunk Muscle Loads

Jing Chang[1], Wenrui Wang[2], Damien Chablat[3]($\boxtimes$), and Fouad Bennis[4]

[1] Tsinghua University, Beijing 100084, China
les_astres@tsinghua.edu.cn
[2] Ecole Centrale de Nantes, 44300 Nantes, France
wwr.1122@163.com
[3] Laboratoire des Sciences du Numérique de Nantes, UMR CNRS 6004, 44300 Nantes, France
damien.chablat@cnrs.fr
[4] École Centrale de Nantes, LS2N, UMR CNRS 6004, 44300 Nantes, France
fouad.bennis@ec-nantes.fr

**Abstract.** Crutch is the most common tool for temporary or permanent ambulation assistance. Crutch-using transforms human kinematic chain, and therefore is hypothesized to have dynamical influence on the trunk. In this paper, two different crutch gaits were analyzed with regard to their associated risks of scoliosis. A numerical human-crutch model was constructed on the OpenSim software, then both unilateral crutch gait (denoted as single crutch walking) and bilateral crutch gait (denoted as double crutch walking) were simulated to represent the situation where ones' right foot gets injured and bears 10% of body weight at most. The kinematics of one single moment in the weight-transferring phase were constructed through joint space. The inverse dynamics calculation and the static optimization algorithm were conducted to compute joints load and muscles activation level at this moment. Attentions were paid to eight muscle groups that are closely associated with the occurrence of scoliosis. As the results, the average muscle activation level of the eight muscle groups were 31% in the case of single crutch walking and 9% for the double crutch walking, as compared with 1% in a normal gait. Muscle activation asymmetry was more severe for single crutch gait than that of a double crutch gait. It is suggested that the unilateral crutch walking brings higher risk of scoliosis than the bilateral crutch walking in the partial weight bearing gaits.

**Keywords:** Crutch · Trunk muscle · Scoliosis · Muscle load · OpenSim

## 1 Introduction

Dating back to ancient Egypt, the crutch was used to overcome gait disorders for thousands of years [2]. Being one of the most traditional and widely used exoskeletons, the crutch is today mainly used for rehabilitation and assistance

© Springer Nature Switzerland AG 2020
C. Stephanidis et al. (Eds.): HCII 2020, LNCS 12429, pp. 455–466, 2020.
https://doi.org/10.1007/978-3-030-59987-4_32

to the elderly, to help the handicapped, patients and the elderly in necessary activities such as walking and climbing stairs.

It has been reported that approximately 600,000 Americans use crutches each year [9], including people with spinal cord injuries (SCI). It is estimated that IBS affects the quality of life of more than 250,000 Americans and that this number is increasing by 11,000 each year [6]. Despite the remarkable development of the lower limb exoskeletons, the crutch remains the first choice of SCI patients for mobility assistance. The use of crutches is becoming even more widespread as society ages. People over 65 years of age represent 17.5% of the EU population in 2011 [3] and this number is estimated to rise to 29.5% in 2060. The crutch transfers the ground reaction force from the lower limbs to the upper limbs, which largely changes the kinematic chain of the human body. This transformation of the kinematic chain induces a redistribution of loads between the muscles. It is possible that inappropriate use of crutches could lead to excessive or unbalanced loading on the muscles, which would cause secondary health problems. Therefore, it is necessary to evaluate the effect of crutch use on muscle loads.

Most previous studies on the use of crutches have focused on the upper limbs. Fischer et al. [4] investigated the pressure on the forearm caused by the use of crutch on 20 healthy adults. The results showed that the maximum pressure on ulnar reached 41 kPa in three different motions, suggesting a high risk of hematoma and pain. Slavens et al. [12] presented an inverse dynamics model that estimated the loads on all upper limb joints when the crutch is applied to the elbow. Experiments on handicapped children showed that the greatest joint reaction force was in the posterior direction of the wrist, and the greatest joint reaction moment was the flexion moments of the shoulder.

Studies have also clearly shown how the crutch affects the upper extremities and highlighted its potential risks. In particular, the work of Vankoski et al. [13] has demonstrated that the loads on lower limb muscle decrease when a crutch is used. However, the effect of the use of crutches on the trunk muscles remains unstudied for no reason. Indeed, the work of Chang et al. [1] revealed a significant relationship between loads on the arm muscles and loads on the back muscles. In addition, as Requejo et al. [8] reported, for users with unbalanced lower limb force generation, arm loads were greater on the opposite side than on the weaker side of the lower limb. In this case, it is very likely that the loads on the trunk muscles are also unbalanced, leading to a high risk of scoliosis.

The objective of this study is to evaluate the effect of the use of crutches on trunk muscle loads. A numerical model of a human musculoskeletal crutch was built in the OpenSim software to simulate the case of a foot injury. An inverse dynamic analysis was performed on three walking cases, then the activation levels of the trunk muscles were calculated and compared. Particular attention was paid to the bilateral balance of the trunk muscles.

## 2    Methods

### 2.1    Walking Gaits with Crutches

There are many reasons in real life for people to use crutches, congenital or acquired. If one person has an injury to a foot and the injured foot can still support some of its weight, he may choose to use either a single crutch or a pair of crutches. The corresponding walking patterns are different.

When walking with only one crutch, the crutch must be located on the non-injured side. In the first phase of a gait cycle, the crutch and the injured foot are stretched, during which the weight of the body is supported by the healthy foot. The second phase starts when the crutch and the injured foot are on the ground and then the centre of gravity begins to move forward. In this phase, the body weight is distributed between the crutch and both feet. In the finial phase, the centre of gravity is between the crutch and the injured foot. At this time, the latter foot leaves the ground and moves forward. A whole walking cycle ends when the injured foot reaches the ground, as shown in Fig. 1.

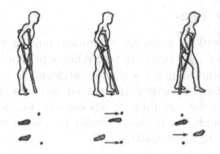

**Fig. 1.** A gait cycle of single-crutch walking [5]

Double crutch walking begins when the crutch on the healthy side is extended, followed by the injured foot. At the same time, the centre of gravity shifts forward to reach the extended crutch and foot. Then the crutch behind moves forward, followed by the last foot, as shown in Fig. 2.

### 2.2    Crutch Model and Musculoskeletal Modeling with OpenSim Software

OpenSim is an open source software for biomechanical modeling, simulation and analysis [10]. Users are enabled to build their own model. In this study, a human-crutch model is built based on the full-chain model developed by the LS2N [1]. The basic model has 46 bodies, 424 muscles and 37 degrees of freedom, while the double-crutch model has two more bodies and four other degrees of freedom. The constructed model covers the muscles of the kinetic chain of the whole body. With OpenSim software, the inverse kinematics as well as the inverse dynamics

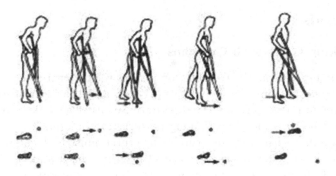

**Fig. 2.** A gait cycle of double-crutch walking [5]

can be easily evaluated. The calculated joint moments can be distributed between each muscle by an optimization algorithm according to their properties (MVC: maximum voluntary contraction).

### 2.3   Simulation Settings

In this study, three walking cases are examined: normal walking, walking with one crutch and walking with two crutches. When a person is injured on one foot, but it still provides some support, a single crutch can be used to assist walking. However, when this foot is particularly injured and cannot provide this part of support, or when both feet are injured, but can also provide partial support, at this time a single crutch can no longer assist people to walk, choose a double crutch It is necessary to assist walking [11].

### 2.4   Single Crutch Walking

Suppose that the experimenter's right foot is injured and can only bear 10% of the body weight [7]. The left hand uses a single crutch to perform a three-point gait. At this time, the gravity is mainly borne by the left foot and the crutch as shown in Fig. 4.

### 2.5   Double Crutches Walking

Suppose the experimenter's right foot is injured and can only support 10% of the body weight [7]. Double crutches are used for four-point walking. At this time, the right foot and the double crutches have moved forward, and the center of gravity has moved forward, so that the gravity is mainly supported by the right foot and double crutches. The next procedure is to lift the left foot and move close as shown in Fig. 5.

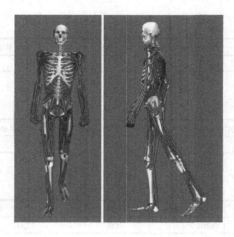

**Fig. 3.** Normal walking

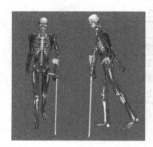

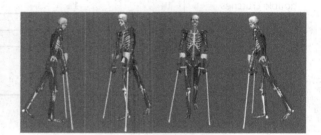

**Fig. 4.** Walking with a single crutch

**Fig. 5.** Walking with double crutches

## 3   Results of the Simulations

We calculated the degree of activation of different muscles through experiments. These muscles are as follows:

- Rectus abdominis muscles (2 muscles);
- Iliacus muscles (22 muscles);
- Abdominal external oblique muscles (12 muscles);
- Abdominal internal oblique muscles (12 muscles);
- Quadratus lumborum muscles (36 muscles);
- Iliocostalis muscles (24 muscles);
- latissimus dorsi muscles (28 muscles);
- Longissimus muscles (10 muscles).

During normal walking, walking with a single crutch and walking with a double crutches, the average degrees of muscle activation obtained were: 1%, 31%, 9%, respectively. From these results, we can see that using crutches to assist walking

**Table 1.** Trunk muscle activation

| | Rectus abdominis muscle | | Iliacus muscle | |
|---|---|---|---|---|
| | right | left | right | left |
| health | 6% | 1% | 1% | 1% |
| single crutch | 100% | 100% | 1% | 68% |
| double crutches | 100% | 100% | 2% | 2% |

| | Abdominal external oblique muscle | | Abdominal internal oblique muscle | |
|---|---|---|---|---|
| | right | left | right | left |
| health | 2% | 1% | 4% | 1% |
| single crutch | 34% | 83% | 50% | 100% |
| double crutches | 31% | 27% | 77% | 81% |

| | Quadratus lumborum | | Iliocostalis | |
|---|---|---|---|---|
| | right | left | right | left |
| health | 1% | 1% | 1% | 1% |
| single crutch | 1% | 78% | 1% | 92% |
| double crutches | 1% | 1% | 1% | 1% |

| | latissimus dorsi | | Longissimus | |
|---|---|---|---|---|
| | right | left | right | left |
| health | 1% | 1% | 1% | 1% |
| single crutch | 1% | 15% | 1% | 80% |
| double crutches | 1% | 1% | 1% | 1% |

weighs more than normal walking, and we can also find that the muscles that use single crutch bears more load than those that use double crutches.

The rectus abdominis is a long flat muscle that connects the sternum with the pubic junction, shown in Fig. 6. It is an important posture muscle, responsible for flexion of the lumbar spine. The activation levels of the left and right abdominal muscles are 6% and 1%, respectively, for the normal walking. When walking with one or two crutches, the level of activation of the two right abdominal muscles is 100%. This suggests a high load on the right abdominal muscle when using crutches.

The iliacus is a flat, triangular muscle. It forms the lateral part of the iliopsoas, providing flexion of the thigh and lower limb at the hip joint, shown in Fig. 7. It is important for lifting (flexing) the femur forward. From Table 1, we can see that the activation levels of the left and right iliacus muscles are 1% when a person walks normally. But when people walk with only one crutch, the activation levels of the left and right iliacus muscles are 68% and 1%. Although there is no additional load on the right muscles, they are overloaded by the left muscles. We can see that when people walk with only one crutch, the left iliacus muscles cause a lot of load.

This results in asymmetrical muscle activation. Prolonged asymmetry leads a risk of scoliosis. When people walk with double crutches, the activation levels of the left and right iliacus muscles are both 2%. The muscles symmetry of the

**Fig. 6.** Rectus abdominis muscle

double crutches are perfect, and the muscles load is minimal, which is similar to normal walking. As the right foot is injured, the left leg has to support more force than usual when walking with a single crutch. However, because the right foot is injured, the right leg does not play an important role in the gait process. The muscles do not support any additional load. Long-term muscle asymmetry can also lead to a deformation of the spine connected to these muscles, causing scoliosis.

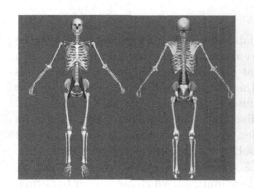

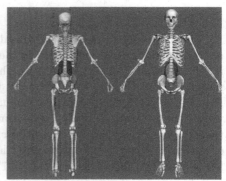

**Fig. 7.** Iliacus muscle activation          **Fig. 8.** Quadratus lumborum Muscles

The quadratus lumborum muscle is a paired muscle of the left and right posterior abdominal wall. It is the deepest abdominal muscle and commonly referred to as a back muscle, shown in Fig. 8. It can first perform a lateral flexion of the spine and an ipsilateral contraction. Second, it can extend the lumbar spine and contract bilaterally. Thirdly, it can perform vertical stabilization of the pelvis, lumbar spine and lumbosacral junction, preventing scoliosis. Fourthly, it can tilt the pelvis forward, it is the contralateral lateral pelvic rotation.

From Table 1, we can see that the activation levels of the left and right quadratus lumborum muscles are both 1% when a person walks normally. But when people walk with only one crutch, the activation levels of the left and right quadratus lumborum muscles are 78% and 1%. This situation causes the asymmetric activation of the muscles. Prolonged asymmetry carries the risk of scoliosis. When people walk with a double crutches, the activation levels of the left and right quadratus lumborum are both 1%. The muscles symmetry of the double crutches are perfect, and the muscles load is minimal, which are similar to normal walking.

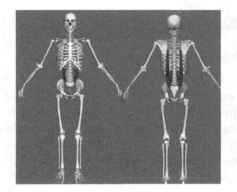    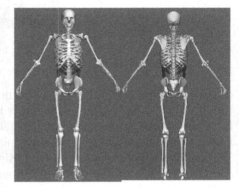

**Fig. 9.** The iliocostalis muscles          **Fig. 10.** The external oblique muscles.

The iliocostalis is the muscle immediately lateral to the longissimus that is the nearest to the furrow that separates the epaxial muscles from the hypaxial, shown in Fig. 9. From Table 1, we can see that the actication levels of the iliocostalis muscles are 92% and 1%. Although there is no additional load on the right muscles, it is overloaded by the left muscles. It can be seen that when people walk with one crutch, the left iliocostalis muscles are more activated. This leads the asymmetric activation of the muscles. Prolonged asymmetry carries the risk of scoliosis. When people walk with double crutches, the activation level of the left and right iliocostalis muscles is 1%. The muscles symmetry of the double crutches is perfect, and the muscles load are minimal, which are similar to normal walking.

The abdominal external oblique muscle is the largest and outermost of the three flat abdominal muscles of the lateral anterior abdomen. The external oblique is situated on the lateral and anterior parts of the abdomen. It is broad, thin, and irregularly quadrilateral, its muscular portion occupying the side, its aponeurosis the anterior wall of the abdomen. It also performs ipsilateral side-bending and contralateral rotation. So the right external oblique would side bend to the right and rotate to the left. The internal oblique muscle functions similarly except it rotates ipsilaterally, shown in Fig. 10. From Table 1, we can see that the activation levels of the left and right abdominal external oblique muscles are 1%

when a person is walking normally. But when people walk with a single crutch, the activation levels of the left and right abdominal external oblique muscles are 83% and 34%. It can be seen that when people walk with a single crutch, the left abdominal external oblique muscles cause a lot of loads. This situation cause the asymmetric activation of the muscles. And the load on the left and right muscles is much higher than normal walking. When people walk with a double crutches, the activation levels of the left and right abdominal external oblique muscles are 27% and 31%. Although the muscles load are higher than during normal walking. They are more symmetrical than when people walk with a single crutch. This muscles are responsible for torso rotation. From this, we can see that when the human body rotates left to right under normal conditions, the force used is the same, and it is easy. When the right foot is injured, the rotation of the human body becomes much more difficult, especially in the case of a single crutch. Due to the injury of the right foot, the human body's torso is not flexible to rotate to the right, so this part of the muscles need to provide a lot of energy to help the torso rotate.

The abdominal internal oblique muscle is an abdominal muscle in the abdominal wall that lies below the external oblique muscle and just above the transverse abdominal muscle, shown in Fig. 11. Its fibers run perpendicular to the external oblique muscle, and the lateral half of the inguinal ligament. Its contraction causes ipsilateral rotation and side-bending. It acts with the external oblique muscle of the opposite side to achieve this torsional movement of the trunk. From Table 1, we can see that the activation level of the left and right abdominal internal oblique muscles is 1% when a person is walking normally. But when people walk with a single crutch, the activation levels of the left and right abdominal internal oblique muscles are 100% and 50%, respectively. It can be seen that when people walk with a single crutch, the left abdominal internal oblique muscles cause a lot of loads. This situation cause the asymmetric activation of the muscles. And the load on the left and right muscles is much higher than normal walking. When people walk with double crutches, the activation levels of the left and right abdominal internal oblique muscles are 81% and 77%, respectively. Although the muscles load is higher than when walking normally, it is more symmetrical than when people walk with a single crutch. The main roles of these muscles are to maintain the stability of the trunk and to assist the external oblique muscles to help with the trunk rotation. The mechanism is similar to that of the external oblique muscles, but from the results, we can see that maintaining this stability consumes a lot of energy.

Abdominal external oblique muscles and abdominal internal oblique muscles are directly connected to the bones. When the muscles on both sides are in an asymmetric state for a long time, it is easy to cause the muscles on one side to be overdeveloped, causing the spine bend to the side of the muscles and cause scoliosis.

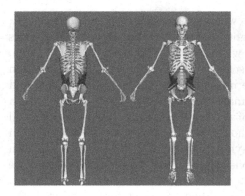

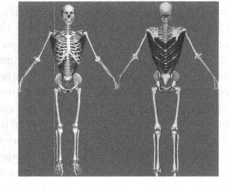

**Fig. 11.** Internal oblique muscles         **Fig. 12.** Latissimus dorsi muscle group

The latissimus dorsi is a large, flat muscle on the back that stretches to the sides, behind the arm, and is partly covered by the trapezius on the back near the midline, shown in Fig. 12. The latissimus dorsi is responsible for extension, adduction, transverse extension also known as horizontal abduction, flexion from an extended position, and (medial) internal rotation of the shoulder joint. It also has a synergistic role in extension and lateral flexion of the lumbar spine. From Table 1, we can see that the left and right latissimus dorsi muscles activation levels are both 1% when a person is walking normally. But when people walk with a single crutch, the left and right latissimus dorsi muscles activation levels are 15% and 1%. Although there is no additional burden on the right muscles, they are overloaded by the left muscles. It can be seen that when people walk with a single crutch, the left latissimus dorsi muscles cause a lot of burdens. This situation causes the asymmetric activation of the muscles. When people walk with a double crutches, the left and right latissimus dorsi muscles activation levels are both 1%. The muscles symmetry of the double crutches is perfect, and the muscles load is minimal, which is similar to normal walking.

Here we can see that when people walk with a crutch, the arm provides a part of the force, and latissimus dorsi muscles transfer this part of the force to the torso. Because the right foot is injured and the left hand uses a crutch. In this case the force on the left will increase. The right hand is not exerted extra load, so the activation of the right muscles is the same as normal walking. As this part of the muscles is directly connected to the spine, an asymmetrical state of the back muscles over a long period of time can bend the spine and thus create scoliosis.

The longissimus dorsi is lateral to the semispinalis, shown in Fig. 13. It is the longest subdivision of the erector muscles of the spine and extends forward into the transverse processes of the posterior cervical vertebrae. From Table 1, we can see that the activation levels of the muscles of the left and right longissimus are both 1% when a person walks normally. But when people walk with a single crutch, the activation levels of the left and right longissimus muscles are 80% and 1%. Although there is no additional load on the right muscles, they are

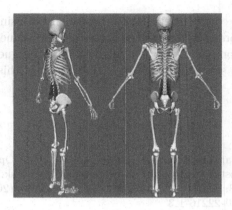

**Fig. 13.** The longissimus dorsi (lumbar part) muscle group.

overloaded by the left muscles. It can be seen that when people walk with a single crutch, the left longissimus muscles cause a lot of burdens. This situation causes the asymmetric of the muscle activation. When people walk with double crutches, the activation of the left and right longissimus muscles is 1%. The muscles symmetry of the double crutches are perfect, and the muscles load are minimal, which are similar to normal walking.

## 4  Discussions

We simulated the process of walking with crutches, and obtained the levels of activation of the human trunk muscles during normal walking, using a single crutch and double crutches. By comparing the activation levels of these muscles, we can see that the use of crutches, especially a single crutch, can lead to a large difference in the activation level of the back muscles on the left and on the right sides. This long-term difference can lead to muscle degeneration and scoliosis. Compared to normal walking, the double crutches used in this experiment increased stress, but they are still acceptable. The symmetry of activation of the muscles on the left and right sides is better than using a single crutch for walking.

## 5  Conclusions

In this article, we found that people using double crutches for walking use less force than when they use single crutches and the activation of their muscles is more symmetrical. However, although we have currently evaluated the use of single and double crutches, we only studied a small sequence for our analysis. Although the sequence we have chosen is very representative, more precise evaluations still require dynamic analysis. In addition, our results come only from numerical simulations. In order to verify the accuracy of the simulations, real experiments will be conducted to verify these analyses using ART motion capture systems and force platforms. The information obtained will then be used in OpenSim to be compared with our simulations. A fatigue model will be used to identify the most stressed muscles and the impact of this fatigue in postural changes.

# References

1. Chang, J., Chablat, D., Bennis, F., Ma, L.: A full-chain OpenSim model and its application on posture analysis of an overhead drilling task. In: Duffy, V.G. (ed.) HCII 2019. LNCS, vol. 11581, pp. 33–44. Springer, Cham (2019). https://doi.org/10.1007/978-3-030-22216-1_3
2. Epstein, S.: Art, history and the crutch. Clin. Orthopaed. Related Res.® **89**, 4–9 (1972)
3. Eurostat, E.: Population Structure and Ageing. Luxembourg, European Commission (2014)
4. Fischer, J., Nüesch, C., Göpfert, B., Mündermann, A., Valderrabano, V., Hügle, T.: Forearm pressure distribution during ambulation with elbow crutches: a cross-sectional study. J. Neuroeng. Rehabilit. **11**(1), 61 (2014)
5. Healthy, D.: Necrosis of the femoral head: 4 ways to walk using a cane correctly! close it! https://kknews.cc/zh-my/health/j88z9bq.html. Accessed 16 Feb 2017
6. Jackson, A.B., Dijkers, M., DeVivo, M.J., Poczatek, R.B.: A demographic profile of new traumatic spinal cord injuries: change and stability over 30 years. Arch. Phys. Med. Rehabilit. **85**(11), 1740–1748 (2004)
7. Li, S., Armstrong, C.W., Cipriani, D.: Three-point gait crutch walking: variability in ground reaction force during weight bearing. Arch. Phys. Med. Rehabilit. **82**(1), 86–92 (2001)
8. Requejo, P.S., et al.: Upper extremity kinetics during lofstrand crutch-assisted gait. Med. Eng. Phys. **27**(1), 19–29 (2005)
9. Russell, J.N., Hendershot, G.E., LeClere, F., Howie, L.J., Adler, M.: Trends and differential use of assistive technology devices: United States, 1994. US Department of Health and Human Services, Centers for Disease Control and ... (1997)
10. Seth, A., et al.: Opensim: simulating musculoskeletal dynamics and neuromuscular control to study human and animal movement. PLoS Comput. Biol. **14**(7) (2018)
11. Shoup, T., Fletcher, L., Merrill, B.: Biomechanics of crutch locomotion. J. Biomech. **7**(1), 11–19 (1974)
12. Slavens, B.A., Bhagchandani, N., Wang, M., Smith, P.A., Harris, G.F.: An upper extremity inverse dynamics model for pediatric lofstrand crutch-assisted gait. J. Biomech. **44**(11), 2162–2167 (2011)
13. Vankoski, S., Moore, C., Statler, K.D., Sarwark, J.P., Dias, L.: The influence of forearm crutches on pelvic and hip kinematics in children with myelomeningocele: don't throw away the crutches. Dev. Med. Child Neurol. **39**(9), 614–619 (1997)

# Determining Endurance Limit Under Intermittent Physical Operations Based on a Combined Fatigue-Recovery Model

Jiawei Fu and Liang Ma[✉]

Department of Industrial Engineering, Tsinghua University, Beijing, China
liangma@tsinghua.edu.cn

**Abstract.** Intermittent physical tasks are prevalent in physical manual operations, and engineers must be provided with effective guidelines for intermittent job design to reduce work-related musculoskeletal disorders (WMSDs) resulting from repetitive intermittent operations. In this paper, we combine a local muscle fatigue and a recovery model to determine the endurance limit under intermittent operations. We preliminarily validated the endurance limit model by comparing the predicted endurance limits and the endurance limits measured in a 50% MVC intermittent task. The endurance limit under intermittent isometric operations could be determined using a muscle fatigue-recovery model and individual fatigue attributes. Estimation of the WMSD risk associated with spectrum loadings in a series of intermittent tasks using the proposed endurance limit model is a promising approach.

**Keywords:** Muscle fatigue · Intermittent task · Endurance limit model

## Nomenclature

| | |
|---|---|
| $F(t)$ (%MVC) | current executable maximum force, current muscle strength as a percentage of the MVC |
| $F_{load}$ (%MVC) | external workload on muscle as a percentage of the MVC |
| $k$ (min$^{-1}$) | local muscle fatigue rate |
| $R$ (min$^{-1}$) | local muscle recovery rate |
| $T_{cycle}$ (min) | cycle time of an intermittent operation |
| $D_{cycle}$ | duty ratio of a cycle |
| $E$ (min) | loading period, which is equal to $T_{cycle} \times D_{cycle}$ |
| $P$ (min) | rest period, $P = T_{cycle} - E$ |
| $F_i^s$ (%MVC) | executable maximum force at the start of the loading period in the $i^{th}$ cycle |
| $F_i^e$ (%MVC) | executable maximum force at the end of the loading period in the $i^{th}$ cycle |
| $\alpha$ | threshold coefficient; the external intermittent operation cannot be sustained when the muscle strength $F(t)$ falls below the threshold load $\alpha \times F_{load}$ |
| $N$ | maximum sustainable number under an intermittent task |
| $c$ | fatigue risk index resulting from cumulative intermittent tasks |
| $N_i$ | maximum sustainable number for the $i^{th}$ intermittent loading condition |
| $n_i$ | number of exposure cycles for the $i^{th}$ intermittent loading condition |

Supported by the National Natural Science Foundation of China [grant number 71471095 and 71942005].

# 1    Introduction

Although technological advancements have reduced the number of heavy manual operations for workers, work-related musculoskeletal disorders (WMSDs) remain a widespread issue leading to increased financial and societal costs [1,12]. Several risk factors are known to be associated with WMSDs. Among the most commonly accepted physical risk factors are exposure to tasks involving high force demands, tasks involving high rates of repetition, tasks involving awkward postures, and tasks of long duration [2,11,25]. A number of researchers have attempted to determine the acceptable limit of workload, repetition and duration to provide occupational guidelines that could effectively lower the risk of WMSDs [6,7,13,14,23,24].

The acceptable limit associated with prolonged static tasks has been studied extensively to aid physical task design; the most well-known and developed approach is the maximum endurance time (MET) and its corresponding model [9,16,19]. The MET has been used to determine the acceptable duration of maintaining a static muscular contraction and to provide reference for physical task design in international standards [15,16,19]. Despite research on the MET over several decades, a large proportion of occupational tasks are more flexible than prolonged static tasks, such as intermittent tasks.

Similar to the MET for static tasks, the maximum endurance duration for intermittent tasks is also critical for guiding operation design. Experimental studies and corresponding modelling have been performed in the literature to quantify the acceptable endurance duration limit and its influencing factors [3, 16,21]. Based on experimental data, several empirical models predicting the endurance duration have been developed to support repetitive isometric tasks design and its assessment [10,13,14,26]. However, the strong task dependency of the models limits the generalization of those models to other intermittent task designs [13] because task parameters and individual fatigue attributes are not considered as variables in those empirical models.

Different from empirical models, physiology-based muscle fatigue modelling has been found to be a promising approach to account for task parameters and individual fatigue attributes in intermittent operations and to provide generalized mathematical forms to describe muscle fatigue progression. Some muscle physiological models have been developed to predict force decline during repeated contractions [4,28,30]. Those models are often used to determine the maximum acceptable effort and then to limit workload in physical operations. However, the true situation is that the workload is fixed and cannot be changed easily, and the acceptable duration is more essential for task design. Moreover, none of these models have been associated with physical operation design to determine the endurance limit under intermittent operations.

Therefore, the aim of this study was to determine endurance limit for intermittent tasks. In Sect. 2, a typical intermittent operation is described, and the endurance limit is defined. The endurance limit is determined based on a combined fatigue-recovery model. In Sect. 3, we carried out an preliminary validation experiment to which compared the predicted endurance limits and the measured one. In Sect. 6, the potential applications of the endurance are discussed.

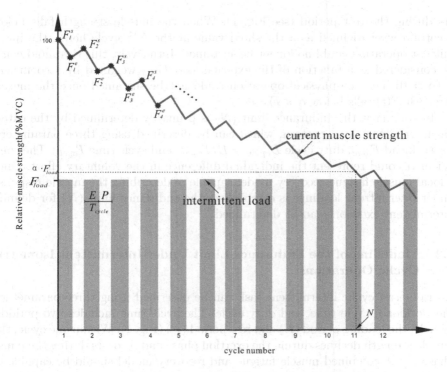

**Fig. 1.** Muscle physical response under external intermittent load (Parameters are explained in Nomenclature.)

# 2 Endurance Limit Under Intermittent Operations

## 2.1 Endurance Limit Under Intermittent Operations

For a given subject, the endurance duration limit under intermittent physical operations is primarily determined by muscle fatigue and individual voluntary effort in maintaining the physical task. Here, we used muscle physiological behaviour featuring repetitive isometric contractions, or intermittent contractions at the same force level to illustrate the endurance limit under intermittent operations (see Fig. 1). Under intermittent tasks consisting of repetitive isometric contractions, the actual profiles of the external load and internal muscle force are approximately cyclic. The load profile in an intermittent task can be assumed to comprise work-rest cycles. Each cycle with a duration of $T_{cycle}$ comprises a loading period ($E$) and rest period ($P$). The external load ($F_{load}$) is assumed to be constant under isometric contractions.

Similar to the MET, the endurance limit($N$) is the maximum sustainable number of a cyclic physical operation under given intermittent conditions. According to muscle physiology, the muscle strength declines while outputting power against external loads in a physical operation [29]. Under intermittent circumstances, the force decreases during the loading period and partially recovers during the rest period (see Fig. 1). When the muscle strength falls below a certain level (defined as a threshold value at the $N^{th}$ cycle here), the intermittent operation could no longer be sustained. Intuitively, this threshold could be considered as a function of the external load $F_{load}$ weighted by a coefficient $\alpha$ ($\alpha > 0$), i.e., the physical operation could not be sustained once the muscle strength $F(t)$ falls below $\alpha \times F_{load}$.

In summary, the endurance limit $(N)$ is primarily determined by the external intermittent load pattern, which can be described using three parameters: its workload $F_{load}$, duty cycle $D_{cycle} = E/T_{cycle}$, and cycle time $T_{cycle}$. The coefficient $\alpha$ could represent the individual difference in the voluntary effort. Once a local muscle fatigue-recovery model capable of describing the muscle response under intermittent loadings is established, the endurance limit $(N)$ for definite intermittent exertions can be determined.

## 2.2  Modelling of the Endurance Limit Under Intermittent Isometric Cyclic Operations

An isometric cyclic intermittent task can be described using three parameters: the workload, cycle time, and duty cycle. The cycle time includes two periods, namely, the loading period $(E)$ and rest period $(P)$ (Fig. 1). Within one cycle, the muscle strength declines during the exertion phase and recovers during the pause phase [8]. A combined muscle fatigue and recovery model should be capable of describing the changing strength within the work cycle.

Ma et al. [17,18] proposed and validated a general muscle fatigue model (Eq. 1) and a recovery model (Eq. 2), respectively. The fatigue and recovery models include external task parameters and a time course that are suitable for calculating the endurance limit under intermittent operations. The fatigue and recovery models have been applied in some industrial practical projects to estimate fatigue risk [5,27]. Other models, such as those proposed by [30] and [4] can also predict force decline during repeated contractions; however, these models contain some parameters regarding muscle fibre and neuro activity (activation) that are difficult to identify in practice. Models with fewer parameters may be suitable for industrial applications.

$$\frac{\mathrm{d}F}{\mathrm{d}t} = -kF_{load}\frac{F}{MVC} \tag{1}$$

$$\frac{\mathrm{d}F}{\mathrm{d}t} = R(MVC - F) \tag{2}$$

The fatigue-recovery model is based on the assumption that muscle physical behaviour during one cycle can be divided into two different periods: one fatigue period and one recovery period. Each period was described using its specific model. Then we could combine the fatigue and recovery models to describe the force profile in an intermittent cycle (Eq. 3). Detailed explanations on the parameters are given in the Nomenclature.

$$
F(t) = \begin{cases} MVCe^{\int_0^t -k\dfrac{F_{load}(u)}{MVC}\,du} & nT_{cycle} < t \leq nT_{cycle} + E \\ F_{ini} + (MVC - F_{ini})(1 - e^{-Rt}) & nT_{cycle} + E < t \leq (n+1)T_{cycle} \end{cases}
$$

$$(3)$$

Here, $F_{ini} = F(nT_{cycle} + E)$, where $n = 0, 1, 2 \ldots$, represents the muscle strength at the end of the loading period.

## 2.3   Numerical Computation of Endurance Limit

To determine the endurance limit $N$, we must first determine the cycle at which the muscle strength fails against the load. If the initial muscle strength in each cycle is known, then the cycle for which failure may occur can be determined. In the $n^{th}$ cycle, we only considered the muscle capacity at two critical points: the strength at the beginning of the loading period denoted as $F_n^s$, and the strength at the end of each loading period denoted as $F_n^e$ (see Fig. 1).

Using the fatigue-recovery model, given in Sect. 2.2, we derived the recurrence relation with two initial muscle strengths of neighbouring cycles (see Eq. 4) as follows:

$$
F_n^s = F_{n-1}^s e^{\dfrac{A}{F_{n-1}^s}} B + F_{n-1}^s (1 - B)
$$

$$
F_n^e = F_n^s e^{\dfrac{A}{F_n^s}}
$$

$$(4)$$

where $A = -k \int_0^E F_{load}(u)du$, $B = e^{-R \times P}$, $F_1^s = MVC$, and $n = 1, 2, 3\ldots$.

To maximize the flexibility of this model, we used a relatively unit-less measure of muscle force as a percentage of the maximum voluntary contraction ($\%MVC$). Therefore, $F_n^s$ and $F_n^e$ are equivalent to the task-specific muscle force in $\%MVC$.

An analytical expression of $N$ cannot realistically be derived, as we could not obtain general term forms of $F_n^s$ and $F_n^e$ with a transcendental function in the recurrence relation ($e^{\frac{A}{F_{n-1}^s}}$). Therefore, with this recurrence relation, we applied a numerical method to solve $N$. The corresponding programming pseudo code is given as follows. Because $F_n^e$ is lower than $F_n^s$, we compared $F_n^e$ with $F_{load}$ to simplify the judgement regarding whether the muscle can still sustain the external load.

**Data:** $F_{load}$, $T_{cycle}$, $D_{cycle}$

**Result:** Determine Endurance Limit by using Numerical Algorithm

Initialisation $F_1^s = MVC$, $F_1^e = F_1^s e^{\frac{A}{F_1^s}}$, n=1, A, B;

**while** $F_i^e > \alpha F_{load}$ **do**

$\quad n = n + 1$

$\quad F_n^s = F_{n-1}^s e^{\frac{A}{F_{n-1}^s}} B + F_{n-1}^s (1 - B)$

$\quad F_n^e = F_n^s e^{\frac{A}{F_n^s}}$

**end**

**Algorithm 1:** Numerical algorithm to determine Endurance Limit

## 3    Preliminary Validation of the Endurance Limit Model

**Experimental Set-up.** We validated the numerical solution directly by comparing the predicted endurance limits with the measured ones. The endurance limit was predicted by optimizing $k$ and $R$ of a given subject in an intermittent isometric operation ($\alpha = 1$), and the true endurance limit was measured for the same subject under the same intermittent isometric operation until exhaustion.

Ethical approval for this study was obtained in advance, and a total of 12 subjects participated in the study (all male, age $26.5 \pm 1.6$ yrs, all right-handed). Each participant was told to be seated with their upper arms and back tight against the chair back. Body movement was mechanically restrained by straps that immobilized the trunk and shoulder to the chair. The testing arm was bared, and the participants were asked to keep their right forearm perpendicular to the upper arm. The biceps brachii, triceps brachii, and brachioradialis muscles generated the force against the lever. All the strengths in the experiment for holding the lever against external load were measured using the BTE PrimusRS®(BTE Technologies, Baltimore, MD, United States). During the entire experiment, we closely observed participants to ensure that they maintained a posture as still as possible (see Fig. 2(a)).

Each subject completed three sessions: a session for measuring MVC, a session for measuring the individual fatigue attributes under intermittent isometric operation, and a session for measuring endurance limit under intermittent isometric operation. A 24-h break was enforced between each session, and the subjects were not allowed to conduct heavy physical operations during the break.

In the MVC session, the MVC was determined as the greatest exerted force upon the posture described in Fig. 2(a). At least three MVC trials (each lasting 3 s) were performed, with a 5-min rest interval in-between. The mean of the three measurements was recorded as the participant's MVC (denoted as the subject's initial maximum strength $F_1^s$).

In the fatigue attribute measurement session, subjects performed the arm holding intermittent operation ($F_{load} = 50\%$MVC, $T_{cycle} = 20$ s, $D_{cycle} = 0.5$) for 5 successive cycles. In each cycle, brief MVC measurements (sub-MVC) were conducted immediately after the loading period and rest period for 2 s (see Fig. 2(b)). For the $n^{th}$ cycle, the sub-MVCs measured after the loading period were denoted as $F_n^e$, and the sub-MVCs measured after the rest period were denoted as $F_{n+1}^s$. Each sub-MVC measurement was paired with a 2-s rest break [28] to diminish the effect of the MVC measurement. The fatigue and recovery rate ($k$ and $R$) were then determined by minimizing the differences between the experimental sub-MVCs ($F_n^e$ and $F_n^s$) and theoretical curves as functions of $k$ and $R$ (Eq. 5). Once $k$ and $R$ for a given subject are known, the endurance limit ($N$) could be predicted using Algorithm 1.

$$G(k, R) = \min \sum_i [F_{pred}(t_i, k, R) - F_{obs}(t_i)]^2 \tag{5}$$

In the endurance limit session, each subject performed the same operation as that in the fatigue attribute measurement session until the subject self-reported failure. They received non-threatening verbal encouragement throughout the exercise duration. The cycle number at failure was recorded as $N$.

**Results.** The predicted and measured endurance limits are listed in Table 1 and shown in Fig. 3. The mean values of the predicted and measured endurance limit are both 14.8, implying that our endurance limit model performs well at the group level (paired t-test, p = 0.947; ICC = 0.58, p = 0.08).

Furthermore, for each subject, individual errors were more substantial between the predicted endurance limit and measured endurance limit. We calculated the goodness of fit ($R^2$) and used the measured endurance limit to calculate $\alpha$ for each subject. The former $R^2$ indicates how well the force decline is predicted by using the fatigue and recovery model, and the latter $\alpha$ indicates the individual threshold in maintaining the intermittent operation. A few subjects (e.g., subject 8) stopped the intermittent operation according to their voluntary willingness, and with the threshold is far away from $F_{load}$; moreover, the fatigue attributes ($k$, $R$) of a few subjects may not have been accurately obtained from the experiment (e.g., subject 10).

## 4  Effects of the Task Parameters on the Endurance Limit

Earlier experimental results provide important details regarding the influences of three task parameters (workload, cycle time, and duty ratio) on the endurance duration or muscle fatigue [6,7,13,14,23,24]. Using the proposed model of the endurance limit, we obtained the general derivatives with $T_{cycle}$, $D_{cycle}$ and workload, and verified the effects of the two parameters ($T_{cycle}$ and $D_{cycle}$) on the load-number diagrams (or stress-number (S-N) diagram). Figure 4a shows the relationship between the $N$ with loading for different cycle times, and Fig. 4b shows the relationship between $N$ with loading for different duty cycles.

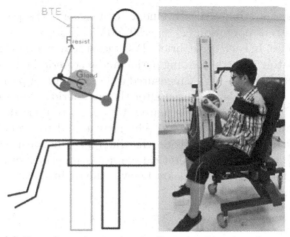

(a) Seated static posture in the experiment and materials used in the experiment.

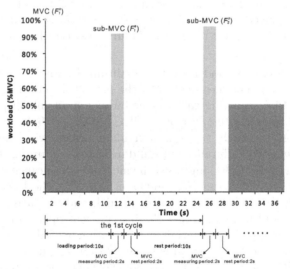

(b) All experimental conditions consisted of an effort of submaximal intensity being held for 10 seconds, followed by a brief MVC and rest. Each MVC was paired with a rest break of matching duration (in this example, 2 seconds followed by 2 seconds).

**Fig. 2.** A: Seated static posture in the experiment and materials used in the experiment. B: The experimental condition consisted of an effort of 50% MVC intensity being held for 10 s and a rest period for 10 s. Every period was followed by a brief sub-MVC measurement and rest. Each sub-MVC measurement was paired with a rest break of matching duration (in this example, 2 s followed by 2 s).

**Table 1.** Comparison of the predicted and measured endurance limits

| Subject item | Measured values | Predicted values | $R^2$ | $k$ | $R$ | $\alpha$ |
|---|---|---|---|---|---|---|
| 1 | 10 | 10 | 0.71 | 1.01 | 2.58 | 1.00 |
| 2 | 23 | 19 | 0.74 | 0.88 | 6.39 | 0.92 |
| 3 | 18 | 16 | 0.65 | 0.46 | 1.06 | 0.96 |
| 4 | 14 | 14 | 0.79 | 0.95 | 4.57 | 1.00 |
| 5 | 16 | 14 | 0.97 | 2.51 | 11.79 | 0.95 |
| 6 | 15 | 17 | 0.86 | 0.86 | 5.41 | 1.05 |
| 7 | 15 | 12 | 0.50 | 1.27 | 5.66 | 0.90 |
| 8 | 18 | 11 | 0.92 | 1.28 | 5.18 | 0.78 |
| 9 | 11 | 9 | 0.75 | 1.49 | 4.87 | 0.93 |
| 10 | 13 | 21 | 0.43 | 1.14 | 8.76 | 1.20 |
| 11 | 10 | 13 | 0.90 | 1.00 | 4.52 | 1.10 |
| 12 | 15 | 21 | 0.83 | 0.82 | 6.57 | 1.15 |
| Mean | 14.8 | 14.8 | 0.75 | 1.14 | 5.61 | 0.995 |
| SD | 3.6 | 3.9 | 0.16 | 0.48 | 2.62 | 0.11 |

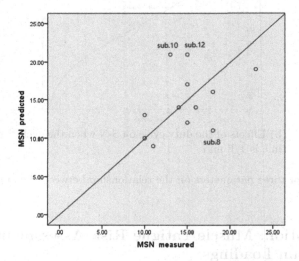

**Fig. 3.** Comparison of the predicted and measured endurance limits

The results show that $T_{cycle}$, $D_{cycle}$ and the workload have negative effects on the endurance limit. A higher relative load or duty ratio (longer duty cycle) results in fewer tasks being sustained. This finding is consistent with previous experimental results [13] and [6].

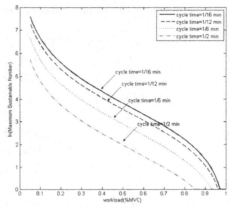

(a) Effects of the cycle time on S-N when the duty cycle is 1/2

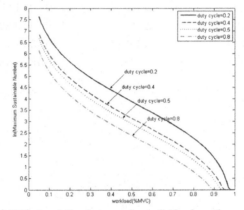

(b) Effects of the duty cycle on S-N when the cycle time is 1/6 min

**Fig. 4.** Effects of three parameters on the relationship between the applied load $F_{load}$ and $N$

## 5    Implication: Muscle Fatigue Risk Assessment for Spectrum Loadings

In daily manual operation, a physical task might include several different intermittent tasks, which can be considered as equivalent to spectrum loadings in material science.

The most common method of assessing or predicting damage resulting from spectrum loadings is the linear cumulative damage rule for fatigue life. This rule was proposed by Palmgren and Miner [20,22] and is shown in Eq. 6 (the parameters are explained in the Nomenclature). For muscle-fatigue risk assessment, Gallagher et al. [10] introduced the Palmgren-Miner rule for ergonomics applications on the basis of material science, and concluded that approach could satisfactorily assess the risk of cumulative damage to muscle.

$$c = \sum_{i=1}^{k} \frac{n_i}{N_i} = \frac{n_1}{N_1} + \frac{n_2}{N_2} + \ldots + \frac{n_k}{N_k} \qquad (6)$$

The Palmgren-Miner rule often provides a useful approximation of the accumulation of fatigue damage in a material; however, it is just an approximation. The results of this study would help in simplifying the job design for spectrum loadings, and the overall fatigue risk could be determined by adding the risks of each intermittent task. Moreover, the effectiveness of rotation between different tasks in reducing muscular fatigue or exposure can be assessed. This finding may refine recommendations of organizational strategies to mitigate musculoskeletal injury risk associated with intermittent work.

# 6 Discussion

## 6.1 Endurance Limit Under Intermittent Operations

In this paper, a model to determine the endurance limit for a given intermittent task was developed. Based on the muscle fatigue-recovery model, we could predict the $N$ with satisfying results considering the task parameters and muscle fatigue attributes. With the endurance limit model, engineers can obtain a quantitative measure, that indicates when workers should stop working to avoid WMSD risks. The endurance limit model provides insight into the relationship between the workload ($F_{load}$), cycle time ($T_{cycle}$), duty ratio ($D_{cycle}$) and endurance limit. The objective of the model is to support work design, e.g. selecting an appropriate schedule among different intermittent schedules or selecting the most effective improvement strategy such as increasing the rest time and decreasing the work time. In determining the endurance limit, several assumptions were made to simplify the problem. However, a detailed analysis of the intermittent operation cycle based on a muscle fatigue and recovery model could be an effective approach to obtain a new perspective on intermittent task design and WMSD prevention.

## 6.2 Limitations

This paper was primarily based on studies featuring repetitive isometric contractions, or intermittent contractions at the same force level. The fatigue-recovery model and the numerical algorithm could consider more dynamic tasks, but we could only derive a simple formula of endurance limit ($N$) for an external load with simple form, such as repetitive isometric contractions. Thus, we used a muscle physiological behaviour featuring intermittent isometric contractions to illustrate the endurance limit under intermittent operations.

However, these types of simple contraction patterns are not generally reflective of industrial work; as a result, these ergonomic tools may not provide accurate predictions of risk for use in ergonomics. Additional research should aim to improve the model to allow for accurate fatigue predictions during sustained isometric, dynamic and complex contraction patterns.

The fatigue-recovery model is based on the assumption that muscle physical behaviour during one cycle can be divided into two different periods: one fatigue period and one recovery period. Each period was described using its specific model. This assumption helps to simplify the motor unit activity and to derive simple strength decline formula under intermittent isometric operations. However, this assumption may require some adjustment and improvement when generalized to more complex or dynamic tasks.

# 7    Conclusion

In this study, we proposed a model to determine the endurance limit for an intermittent task. This model could be solved by either numerical solution or by an approximation method with acceptable accuracy. Optimizing the $k$ and $R$ coefficients for the fatigue-recovery model resulted in good predictions of muscle strength during intermittent submaximal force patterns. Along with the Palmgren-Miner rule, this endurance limit model could be applied to evaluate muscle fatigue risk for spectrum loadings.

# References

1. AAOS: The burden of musculoskeletal diseases in the United States: prevalence, societal and economic cost. Rosemont, IL (2008)
2. Bernard, B.P., Putz-Anderson, V.: Musculoskeletal disorders and workplace factors; a critical review of epidemiologic evidence for work-related musculoskeletal disorders of the neck, upper extremity, and low back (1997)
3. Björkstn, M., Jonsson, B.: Endurance limit of force in long-term intermittent static contractions. Scand. J. Work Environ. Health **3**(1), 23–27 (1977)
4. Callahan, D.M., Umberger, B.R., Kent, J.A.: Mechanisms of in vivo muscle fatigue in humans: investigating age-related fatigue resistance with a computational model. J. Physiol. **594**(12), 3407–3421 (2016)
5. De Sapio, V., Howard, M., Korchev, D., Green, R., Gardner, R., Bruchal, L.: Demographic specific musculoskeletal models of factory worker performance, fatigue, and injury. In: 2016 IEEE Aerospace Conference, pp. 1–13. IEEE (2016)
6. Sood, D., Nussbaum, M.A., Hager, K., Nogueira, H.C.: Predicted endurance times during overhead work: influences of duty cycle and tool mass estimated using perceived discomfort. Ergonomics (2017). http://dx.doi.org/10.1080/00140139.2017.1293850
7. Dickerson, C.R., Meszaros, K.A., Cudlip, A.C., Chopp-Hurley, J.N., Langenderfer, J.E.: The influence of cycle time on shoulder fatigue responses for a fixed total overhead workload. J. Biomech. **48**(11), 2911–2918 (2015)
8. van Dieen, J., Toussaint, H., Thissen, C., Van de Ven, A.: Spectral analysis of erector spinae EMG during intermittent isometric fatiguing exercise. Ergonomics **36**(4), 407–414 (1993)
9. Imbeau, D., Farbos, B., et al.: Percentile values for determining maximum endurance times for static muscular work. Int. J. Ind. Ergon. **36**(2), 99–108 (2006)

10. Gallagher, S., Schall Jr., M.C.: Musculoskeletal disorders as a fatigue failure process: evidence, implications and research needs. Ergonomics 60(2), 255–269 (2017)
11. Hoogendoorn, W.E., van Poppel, M.N., Bongers, P.M., Koes, B.W., Bouter, L.M.: Physical load during work and leisure time as risk factors for back pain. Scand. J. Work Environ. Health 25, 387–403 (1999)
12. Horton, R.: GBD 2010: understanding disease, injury, and risk. The Lancet 380(9859), 2053–2054 (2013)
13. Iridiastadi, H., Nussbaum, M.A.: Muscle fatigue and endurance during repetitive intermittent static efforts: development of prediction models. Ergonomics 49(4), 344–360 (2006)
14. Iridiastadi, H., Nussbaum, M.A.: Muscular fatigue and endurance during intermittent static efforts: effects of contraction level, duty cycle, and cycle time. Hum. Factors 48(4), 710–720 (2006)
15. ISO: Ergonomics-Evaluation of static working postures-ISO11226, Geneva (2000)
16. Kahn, J., Monod, H.: Fatigue induced by static work. Ergonomics 32(7), 839–846 (1989)
17. Ma, L., Chablat, D., Bennis, F., Zhang, W.: A new simple dynamic muscle fatigue model and its validation. Int. J. Ind. Ergon. 39(1), 211–220 (2009)
18. Ma, L., Zhang, W., Wu, S., Zhang, Z.: A new simple local muscle recovery model and its theoretical and experimental validation. Int. J. Occup. Saf. Ergon. 21(1), 86–93 (2015)
19. Miedema, M.C., Douwes, M., Dul, J.: Recommended maximum holding times for prevention of discomfort of static standing postures. Int. J. Ind. Ergon. 19(1), 9–18 (1997)
20. Miner, M.A.: Cumulative fatigue damage. J. Appl. Mech. 12(3), A159–A164 (1945)
21. Nussbaum, M.A.: Static and dynamic myoelectric measures of shoulder muscle fatigue during intermittent dynamic exertions of low to moderate intensity. Eur. J. Appl. Physiol. 85(3–4), 299–309 (2001)
22. Palmgren, A.G.: Die lebensdauer von kugellagern. Zeitschrift des Vereins Deutscher Ingenieure 68(14), 339–341 (1924)
23. Potvin, J.R., Calder, I.C., Cort, J.A., Agnew, M.J., Stephens, A.: Maximal acceptable forces for manual insertions using a pulp pinch, oblique grasp and finger press. Int. J. Ind. Ergon. 36(9), 779–787 (2006)
24. Potvin, J.R.: Predicting maximum acceptable efforts for repetitive tasks: an equation based on duty cycle. Hum. Factors 54(2), 175–188 (2012)
25. Punnett, L., et al.: Estimating the global burden of low back pain attributable to combined occupational exposures. Am. J. Ind. Med. 48(6), 459–469 (2005)
26. Rose, L.M., Beauchemin, C.A., Neumann, W.P.: Modelling endurance and resumption times for repetitive one-hand pushing. Ergonomics 61, 1–39 (2018)
27. Seo, J., Lee, S., Seo, J.: Simulation-based assessment of workers muscle fatigue and its impact on construction operations. J. Constr. Eng. Manag. 142(11), 04016063 (2016)
28. Sonne, M.W., Potvin, J.R.: A modified version of the three-compartment model to predict fatigue during submaximal tasks with complex force-time histories. Ergonomics 59(1), 85–98 (2016)
29. Vøllestad, N.K.: Measurement of human muscle fatigue. J. Neurosci. Methods 74(2), 219–227 (1997)
30. Xia, T., Frey Law, L.A.: A theoretical approach for modeling peripheral muscle fatigue and recovery. J. Biomech. 41(14), 3046–3052 (2008)

# Evaluation of Occupant Comfort and Health in Indoor Home-Based Work and Study Environment

Xingzhou Guo[1] and Yunfeng Chen[2(✉)]

[1] Construction Animation, Robotics, and Ergonomics (CARE) Lab,
School of Construction Management Technology (SCMT),
Purdue University, West Lafayette, IN 47907, USA
guo529@purdue.edu
[2] CARE Lab, SCMT, Purdue University, West Lafayette, IN 47907, USA
chen428@purdue.edu

**Abstract.** Most companies in the United States (U.S.) have asked their employees to work from home (WFH) since the COVID-19 pandemic. Therefore, work environment changed from office to home. However, home environment is designed for living purpose instead of working purpose. People may experience different levels of comfort visually, thermally, etc. when WFH. Because occupants can be affected differently by indoor environmental quality factors in office (e.g., difficult temperature adjustment based on personal preference) and at home (e.g., easy temperature adjustment), which could increase the experience of sick building syndrome (SBS). Evaluation of occupant comfort and health in office environment was widely explored before. Less research was conducted to explore occupant comfort and health when WFH. Therefore, this study compiled a comprehensive list of key factors and indicators of occupant comfort and health from previous literature. Then, a survey was designed and distributed in the U.S. to evaluate occupants' satisfaction of home-based work or study environment and experience of SBS. The demographic analysis shows that diverse types of occupants were covered. Then, occupants' satisfaction and experience of SBS when WFH were compared with regular work or study. The findings show that occupants' satisfaction slightly increased while experience of SBS slightly decreased when WFH. More importantly, ocular symptoms were the top concern in regular work or study and WFH. This study shows the differences of satisfaction and experience of SBS between regular work or study and WFH, which also indicates a direction for future technologies to improve home environment, well-being, and health.

**Keywords:** Indoor work environment · Home-based work · Sick building syndrome · Health · Comfort · COVID-19

## 1 Introduction

Since March 2020, an increasing number of the United States (U.S.) based companies has asked their employees to work from home (WFH) to practice social distancing in response to the highly contagious disease, COVID-19 [1]. Shortly after that, some

© Springer Nature Switzerland AG 2020
C. Stephanidis et al. (Eds.): HCII 2020, LNCS 12429, pp. 480–494, 2020.
https://doi.org/10.1007/978-3-030-59987-4_34

companies announced that the option is offered to employees to remain working from home even after the COVID-19 pandemic becomes under control. Home becomes the new work environment for people to not only live, but also work, study, etc. However, home is originally designed for living purpose while office is the one designed for working purpose. Due to this sudden change of work environment from office to home, there is not sufficient time to evaluate whether home-based work environment is appropriate for working activities, studying activities, etc.

Poor indoor environmental quality (IEQ) factors can increase the presence of sick building syndrome (SBS), which refers to occupants' experience of discomforts in terms of ocular symptoms, oropharyngeal symptoms, cutaneous symptoms, lethargy and cognitive symptoms, respiratory and nasal symptoms, and general symptoms when they work or study in an indoor environment [2–8]. Word Health Organization reported that 30% of buildings, especially sealed indoor environment, can cause SBS because occupants are dissatisfied with the IEQ factors and experience discomfort, such as visual discomfort, thermal comfort, etc. [9–12]. There are no shortage of studies on occupant comfort and health when working in office. However, less studies are conducted on exploring occupant comfort and health when working at home.

This study first identified factors and indicators measuring comfort and health by reviewing literature related to satisfaction of IEQ factors, occupant comfort, occupant well-being, work-life balance, and SBS symptoms, and by compiling key items across literature and removing redundant items. With identified measurement factors and indicators, a survey was designed and distributed to professionals and students in the U. S. Collected data was then analyzed to explore professionals and students' comfort and health in the new work environment. This study aims to disclose the differences of satisfaction of indoor environment and experience of sick building syndrome between regular work (RW) or study and work or study from home, which can also provide insights in designing indoor environment control systems or technologies to improve occupant comfort and health for future long-term working from home and potential new crisis.

# 2  Literature Review

WFH has inevitably became a new way to work for organizations and individuals. However, current research has mainly focused on exploring the relationship between IEQ factors and occupant comfort and health in regular office environment. For example, advanced heat, air ventilation, and cooling systems have been developed to adjust office environment by analyzing office workers' real time-feedback [13–15]. While the research focusing on home-based work environment is much less. The influencing factors can impact occupants differently between office and home. For example, office workers can be affected by co-workers' conversion, while home-based workers can be interrupted by family members.

IEQ can affect occupant comfort, through visual comfort, thermal comfort, acoustic comfort, indoor air quality, layout and work-related factors and psychological factors [9, 10. 12, 16], which is used in this study to evaluate occupant satisfaction of home-based work environment. In addition, SBS is used to reflect occupant health conditions [9].

Common SBS includes ocular symptoms, oropharyngeal symptoms, cutaneous symptoms, lethargy and cognitive symptoms, respiratory and nasal symptoms, and general symptoms [6]. The goal of this paper is to explore the differences of occupant comfort and health when working in regular office and from home.

## 3 Methodology

A survey was designed to solicit professionals and students' home-based work or study experience, such as satisfaction of IEQ and experience of SBS, through a five-point Likert Scale. The survey includes five parts. The first part collected demographic information. The second part gathered information about participants' work performance and productivity. The third part focused on the effect of influencing factors of indoor environment on occupant comfort and health. The fourth part surveyed participants about the impacts of home-based working or studying and COVID-19. Lastly, chances were provided to leave comments and suggestions. In this paper, the demographic analysis was conducted to summarize the background information of participants. Then mean and standard deviation (SD) were used to compare the change of participants' satisfaction of IEQ and SBS experience before and during WFH A five-point Likert scale was employed in this research to reflect participants' evaluation for (1) satisfaction of IEQ during RW and WFH with one for very dissatisfied and five for very satisfied, and (2) SBS experience during RW and WFH with one for very rare and five for very often.

This survey was distributed to more than 13,000 professionals and students in the U.S. via email, LinkedIn, other social media, and 15 professional associations. Up to May 25th, 2020, 774 responses were received (response rate: 6%). 204 complete responses received for the third part of the effect of influencing factors of indoor environment on occupant comfort and health.

### 3.1 Participants

Employees from both academia and industry as well as students are the focus of this survey. A detailed occupation description for all participated occupations can be found in Table 1. In addition, this survey has reached different states in the U.S. including Indiana, Michigan, Florida, etc.

**Table 1.** Summary of participants' occupation

| Categories | Occupation description |
|---|---|
| Academia | Education staff whose work is administration |
| | Teachers or instructors whose work is teaching |
| | Researchers whose work is research |
| | Professors whose work includes both teaching and research |
| Student | Students without assistantship who does not need to do research, teaching, or other tasks to get paid |
| | Students with assistantship who needs to do research, teaching, or other tasks to get paid |
| Industry | On-site workers who usually work outdoor |
| | Project management workers who usually work indoor on project |
| | Industry staff whose work includes company administration and support |

## 3.2 Measurement Factors and Indicators

In order to evaluate occupant comfort and health, a two-step procedure was conducted to capture the key measurement items of occupant comfort and health. First, the literature related to satisfaction of IEQ factors, occupant comfort, occupant well-being, work-life balance, and SBS symptoms was reviewed. Second, a complete and precise list of factors and indicators in measuring comfort and health was developed by compiling key items across literature and removing redundant items. For example, artificial lighting was found to be one of the physical factors which can influence visual comfort, therefore corresponding indicators related to artificial lighting (e.g., your ability to turn on/off artificial lighting, etc.) were also found and adopted. In addition, family related indicators were also adopted because family members may create extra influencing factors at home. The key seven factors and 52 indicators were extracted for measuring impact of influencing factors, satisfaction and comfort of work environment. And six factors and 29 indicators were extracted for measuring occupant health, as shown in Table 2 and Table 3 with their corresponding sources. Then, professionals' and students' comfort and health were evaluated through a five-point Likert scale.

**Table 2.** Measurement factors and indicators of satisfaction

| Measurement factors of satisfaction | Indicators and corresponding sources |
|---|---|
| Visual factor | Artificial lighting [17] |
| | Your ability to turn on/off artificial lighting [3] |
| | Your ability to adjust brightness [18, 19] |
| | Natural lighting [20] |
| | Your ability to control natural lighting [21] |
| | Glare level [22] |
| | Window area [23] |
| | Distance to window [21] |
| | Curtain type [24] |
| | A view of outside [21] |

(*continued*)

**Table 2.** (*continued*)

| Measurement factors of satisfaction | Indicators and corresponding sources |
|---|---|
| Thermal factor | Temperature [25] |
| | Your ability to control temperature [26] |
| Acoustic factor | Noise [16] |
| | Your ability to control noise [6] |
| Layout factor | Space area [5, 20, 27] |
| | Space layout [5, 20, 27] |
| | Color of room [27] |
| | Color of furniture [28] |
| | Cleanliness [29] |
| | Maintenance [29] |
| Air quality factor | Natural ventilation [30] |
| | Your ability to control natural ventilation [30] |
| | Mechanical ventilation [30] |
| | Your ability to control mechanical ventilation [30] |
| | Air pollution emission [9] |
| | Your ability to control air pollution emission [9] |
| | Humidity [11] |
| | Your ability to control humidity [31] |
| | Air freshness [32] |
| | Your ability to control air freshness [32] |
| Work-related factor | Type of work [27] |
| | Workload [32] |
| | Work schedule [33] |
| | Company/institution policy [34] |
| | In-person communication [35] |
| | Online communication [36] |
| | Electronic facility [37] |
| | Online platform [38] |
| | Team working atmosphere [39] |
| | Peer pressure [40] |
| | Interest in work [41] |
| | Privacy [42] |
| | Interruptions by other people [43] |
| | Relationship with partners [44] |
| | Cozy clothes [45] |
| Psychological factor | Mental health [39] |
| | Work stress [46] |
| | Emotional health [47] |
| | Self-regulation [48] |
| | Self-efficacy [48] |
| | Relationship with friends/family members/etc. [44] |
| | Work-life balance [49] |

**Table 3.** Measurement factors and indicators of SBS

| Measurement factors of SBS | Indicators and corresponding sources |
|---|---|
| Ocular symptoms | Eye irritation [6] |
| | Tired eyes [50] |
| | Itchy or watery eyes [17] |
| Oropharyngeal symptoms | Dry throat [6, 7] |
| Cutaneous symptoms | Dry, itchy or irritated skin [7] |
| Lethargy and cognitive symptoms | Fatigue [6, 7] |
| | Difficulties in concentrating [6, 7] |
| | Difficulty in remembering things [15] |
| | Feeling heavy headed [2] |
| | Headache [7, 9] |
| Respiratory and nasal symptoms | Chest tightness [51] |
| | Asthma [7] |
| | Shortness of breath [7] |
| | Sneeze [7] |
| | Wheezing [7] |
| | Cough [7] |
| | Blocked or stuffy nose [7] |
| | Runny nose [7, 10] |
| General symptoms | Dizziness [9] |
| | Pain in neck, shoulders or back [9, 52] |
| | Nausea or upset stomach [46] |
| | Heart stroke [7] |
| | Increasing blood pressure [7] |
| | Fainting [7] |
| | Hearing issues [7] |
| | Vomit [52] |
| | Itching ears [6] |
| | Nervous feeling [52] |
| | Depression [7] |

# 4 Data Analysis

## 4.1 Demographic

Participants' age range is from 19 to 79. The majority of participants' age is from 31 to 50 (42%), 30 or under (35%), over 50 (23%), and one participant preferring not to disclose the age. The age distribution indicates the collected data covered different ages of employees and students. The majority of participants was male (74%) as shown in Fig. 1. In addition, 24% of participants were female, and other 2% of participants preferred not to disclose, or selected non-binary or not listed.

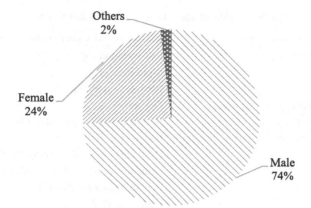

**Fig. 1.** Participant's gender distribution

Figure 2 shows the distribution of different occupations of participants. The majority of participants' occupation is professor, which accounted for 23% (47 responses). The occupation of project management worker also accounted for a large portion of all responses with 17% (35 responses). Then students with assistantship and students without assistantship contributed 16% (32 responses) and 13% (26 responses) respectively. Education staff and researchers shared the same portion 6% (13 responses for each occupation). Industry staff and teacher follows with 6% (12 responses) and 5% (11 responses). To summarize, there are 86 responses received from academia, 58 responses received from students, and 60 responses received from industry. The data gathered can be utilized to evaluate different occupations' opinion about satisfaction of IEQ and experience of SBS.

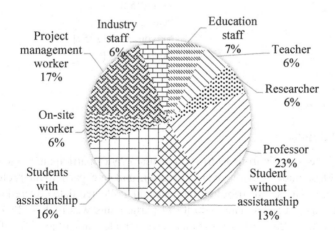

**Fig. 2.** Participant's occupation distribution

## 4.2    Satisfaction of Indoor Environmental Quality Factors

Satisfaction can reflect whether occupants are satisfied with work environment. This study considered key factors including visual, thermal, acoustic, layout, air quality, work-related, and psychological factors as shown in Table 4. The mean of scores of each indicator was calculated and used as the score of the corresponding factors.

For RW, professionals and students were less satisfied with thermal conditions (3.59), acoustic conditions (3.63), and air quality factors (3.82), compared with visual factors (3.92), layout factors (4.07), psychological factors (4.08), and work-related factors (4.15). While, for WFH, professionals and students were less satisfied with psychological factors (3.97), acoustic factors (3.99), and work-related factors (4.11), compared with layout factors (4.19), air quality factors (4.30), thermal factors (4.32), and visual factors (4.33). In addition, based on the difference result, occupants became less satisfied with work-related factors and psychological factors when changing from RW condition to WFM condition. This situation can be explained by characters of different work environments (i.e., office and home). Office is usually a multi-occupancy space where people need to share the same thermal condition, air quality condition, etc. [25, 53]. Therefore, thermal conditions and air quality conditions cannot always meet occupants' need. In addition, acoustic conditions can become worse due to the lack of enclosed private space and daily office activities [42]. Therefore, part of occupants can easily experience discomfort caused by unfavorable thermal condition, acoustic condition, and air quality condition. However, when they work or study at home, it is usually a single-occupancy space where occupants can adjust the temperature, control air freshness, etc. based on their preference. Therefore, occupant satisfaction at home became better. As for the less satisfied work-related factors and psychological factors when WFH, it is a result of that professionals and students lack the opportunity and convenience when they need to communicate with others in person and when need team working atmosphere [39]. Instead, they have to utilize online platform such as WebEx, OneDrive, Zoom, etc. to virtually communicate with others. In addition, professionals and students can also be affected by noise from family members, which explains the low satisfaction of acoustic condition.

Table 4.    Satisfaction of RW and WFH by measurement factors

| Measurement factors | RW | | WFH | | Difference (RW - WFH) |
|---|---|---|---|---|---|
| | Mean | SD | Mean | SD | Mean |
| Visual factors | 3.92 | 1.48 | 4.33 | 1.07 | −0.41 |
| Thermal factors | 3.59 | 1.49 | 4.32 | 1.01 | −0.73 |
| Acoustic factors | 3.63 | 1.41 | 3.99 | 1.21 | −0.35 |
| Layout factors | 4.07 | 1.17 | 4.19 | 1.08 | −0.12 |
| Air quality factors | 3.82 | 1.45 | 4.30 | 1.09 | −0.48 |
| Work-related factors | 4.15 | 1.15 | 4.11 | 1.21 | 0.04 |
| Psychological factors | 4.08 | 1.12 | 3.97 | 1.21 | 0.11 |

The change of satisfaction for RW and WFH among different occupations is shown in Table 5. Education staff, teachers, researchers, professors, students with assistantship, project management workers, and industry staff who usually need to work indoor reported an increase of satisfaction when changing from RW to WFH. This is a result of that home-based work can provide them with a more customized environment such as having fully control over room temperature, lighting, etc. without the need to consider other occupants in a shared room (e.g., co-workers who share the space with you) [25, 54], and organizing the room layout based on personal preference to create comfort [20].

On the other hand, students without assistantship who do not need to stay in lab to conduct research and on-site workers who usually work outdoor claimed that they are less satisfied with home-based work or study environment. The working activities that on-site workers normally perform require on-site workers to visit the site in person. Therefore, it creates inconvenience when they have to work from home, thus less satisfied with the home-based work environment. Similarly, students without assistantship may also feel home-based studying is overall less satisfied because they used to study at places where they found comfortable like library, study rooms, etc. Now, they have no other options but study at home.

**Table 5.** Satisfaction of RW and WFH by occupations

| Categories | Occupations | RW | | WFH | | Difference (RW - WFH) |
|---|---|---|---|---|---|---|
| | | Mean | SD | Mean | SD | Mean |
| Academia | Education staff | 3.60 | 1.20 | 4.42 | 0.89 | −0.81 |
| | Teacher | 3.93 | 1.31 | 4.12 | 0.90 | −0.19 |
| | Researcher | 3.88 | 1.51 | 3.98 | 1.40 | −0.10 |
| | Professor | 3.87 | 1.17 | 4.15 | 1.06 | −0.28 |
| Student | Student without assistantship | 3.82 | 1.33 | 3.75 | 1.28 | 0.07 |
| | Students with assistantship | 4.12 | 1.36 | 4.27 | 1.23 | −0.15 |
| Industry | On-site worker | 4.71 | 1.29 | 4.52 | 1.03 | 0.18 |
| | Project management worker | 3.94 | 1.20 | 4.17 | 1.01 | −0.23 |
| | Industry staff | 4.33 | 1.25 | 4.66 | 1.08 | −0.32 |

### 4.3 Frequency of Sick Building Syndrome

Frequency of SBS reflects how frequent occupants experience different SBS, which indicates their health condition. This study considered commonly experienced symptoms including ocular symptoms, oropharyngeal symptoms, cutaneous symptoms, lethargy and cognitive symptoms, respiratory and nasal symptoms, and general symptoms as shown in Table 6. The mean of scores of each indicator was calculated and used as the score of the corresponding factors.

For RW, professionals and students had experienced the symptoms in the following order: ocular symptoms (3.07), lethargy and cognitive symptoms (2.90), general symptoms (e.g., dizziness, etc.) (2.85), cutaneous symptoms (2.80), oropharyngeal symptoms (2.78), and respiratory and nasal symptoms (2.67). While, for WFH, professionals and students experienced the symptoms in the following order: ocular symptoms (2.97), general symptoms (e.g., dizziness, etc.) (2.71), lethargy and cognitive symptoms (2.68), cutaneous symptoms (2.60), respiratory and nasal symptoms (2.51), and oropharyngeal symptoms (2.50). In addition, the difference result indicated that professionals and students experienced less symptoms when working or studying at home. More importantly, it should be noticed that ocular symptoms were the most frequently experienced symptoms under both RW and WFH. Because nowadays, most working activities and studying tasks rely on the computer use which increases the frequency of ocular symptoms [50]. In addition, people tend to wear contact lens when working in office, which leads to an increase of chances of having ocular symptoms [55]. Conversely, the chances of ocular symptoms decreased when people do not need any visual support or tend to wear regular glasses at home. Also, previous studies showed that there is a significant positive correlation between the frequency of symptoms and hours spent on working or studying on computer. Therefore, people have more flexible schedule when WFH, which can lead to a positive difference result (RW – WFH > 0: less symptoms experienced by professionals and students when working or studying from home) [50, 56].

**Table 6.** SBS experience of RW and WFH by measurement factors

| Measurement factors | RW | | WFH | | Difference (RW - WFH) |
|---|---|---|---|---|---|
| | Mean | SD | Mean | SD | Mean |
| Ocular symptoms | 3.07 | 1.74 | 2.97 | 1.69 | 0.11 |
| Oropharyngeal symptoms | 2.78 | 1.77 | 2.50 | 1.67 | 0.28 |
| Cutaneous symptoms | 2.80 | 1.82 | 2.60 | 1.73 | 0.20 |
| Lethargy and cognitive symptoms | 2.90 | 1.62 | 2.68 | 1.58 | 0.22 |
| Respiratory and nasal symptoms | 2.67 | 2.02 | 2.51 | 1.98 | 0.16 |
| General symptoms | 2.85 | 2.11 | 2.71 | 2.08 | 0.14 |

The change of SBS experience for RW and WFH among different occupations is shown in Table 7. Education staff, teachers, professors, on-site workers, and project management workers reported decreased frequency of SBS experience from RW to WFH. For teachers and professors, a common approach to teaching after the stay-at-home order is recording videos for students to watch through online teaching platforms, which eases teachers' preparation work for classes and explains for decreased frequency of SBS experience when working from home. The tasks that on-site workers need to do may also be delayed due to the requirement of practicing social distance. Therefore, they can also have less SBS experience. On the other hand, researchers, students with assistantship, students without assistantship, and industry staff claimed that they had experienced more SBS in home-based work or study environment. Students can choose their preferred places to study relatively free compared with professionals who usually have to stay at offices. Therefore, when students are asked to stay at home, they may experience more SBS, which is consistent with the previous finding in this paper (i.e., students without assistantship are less satisfied with WFH). However, a further study by considering working hours and habits will be conducted to study the frequency of different occupations' SBS for RW and WFH, because working hours and habits have significant impact on SBS [50, 57].

**Table 7.** SBS experience of RW and WFH by occupations

| Categories | Occupations | RW | | WFH | | Difference (RW - WFH) |
|---|---|---|---|---|---|---|
| | | Mean | SD | Mean | SD | Mean |
| Academia | Education staff | 2.44 | 1.63 | 2.27 | 1.64 | 0.17 |
| | Teacher | 2.27 | 1.81 | 1.83 | 1.43 | 0.44 |
| | Researcher | 2.70 | 2.08 | 2.74 | 2.12 | −0.04 |
| | Professor | 2.78 | 1.87 | 2.70 | 1.86 | 0.09 |
| Student | Student without assistantship | 2.83 | 1.87 | 2.86 | 1.88 | −0.04 |
| | Students with assistantship | 3.07 | 2.06 | 3.08 | 2.08 | −0.01 |
| Industry | On-site worker | 3.92 | 2.16 | 2.61 | 1.95 | 1.31 |
| | Project management worker | 2.88 | 1.94 | 2.66 | 1.83 | 0.22 |
| | Industry staff | 2.20 | 1.73 | 2.27 | 1.94 | −0.07 |

# 5   Discussion

The data analysis part has shown the difference between different occupant satisfaction of work environment in regular office and at home, and the difference between the frequency of occupants' SBS experience. Three main findings are discussed here. First, home was designed for living purpose not working purpose. Therefore, it is needed to explore how home-based work environment affects occupants. The result shows that, the overall satisfaction score of home-based work environment is slightly higher than the overall satisfaction score of office work environment, mainly because occupants can better control temperature, lighting, etc. based on their personal preference and occupants can have flexible schedule. This explains the second finding that the frequency of SBS experience also becomes slightly lower at home than in office. Working hours and habits will be considered later to further analyze data. Lastly but not least, previous research focused more on thermal comfort and indoor air quality because better control of thermal comfort and indoor air quality can not only create a comfortable work environment but also save energy. Through the data analysis, this study found that ocular symptoms remain the most frequently experienced symptoms when both working in office and working from home, which indicates that visual comfort is of great importance from the health perspective. Therefore, it is essential to develop advanced technologies to help improve visual comfort.

# 6  Conclusion

This sudden global crisis has made many people work or study from home. Companies also started to consider the feasibility of long-term home-based working or studying. Therefore, there is an urgent need to explore whether the home environment can provide occupants a comfortable place to work and study. To this end, a nationwide survey was designed with identified measurement factors and indicators, and distributed to professionals and students to collect data regarding their satisfaction of office work environment and home-based work environment, and their SBS experience in office and at home. Because of the characters of home-based working (e.g., single occupancy, flexible schedule, etc.), satisfaction showed a slight increase from office work environment to home-based work environment, and the frequency of SBS experience showed a slight decrease from office to home. However, ocular symptoms remained the top concern whenever working in office or from home. With the identified problem, this study sheds lights on what area, such as visual comfort, that technologies should focus on to improve home-based work environment, and then improve well-being and health. More importantly, this study can also contribute to the improvement of new working style, working from home, from an indoor environment design perspective.

# References

1. Mervosh, S., Lu, D., Swalse, V.: See which states and cities have told residents to stay at home, New York Times (2020). https://www.nytimes.com/interactive/2020/us/coronavirus-stay-at-home-order.html. Accessed 13 Jun 2020
2. Takeda, M., Saijo, Y., Yuasa, M., Kanazawa, A., Araki, A., Kishi, R.: Relationship between sick building syndrome and indoor environmental factors in newly built Japanese dwellings. Int. Arch. Occup. Environ. Health **82**(5), 583–593 (2009)
3. Wong, S.K., et al.: Sick building syndrome and perceived indoor environmental quality: a survey of apartment buildings in Hong Kong. Habitat Int. **33**(4), 463–471 (2009)
4. Haynes, B.P.: The impact of office comfort on productivity. J. Facil. Manag. **6**(1), 37–51 (2008)
5. Mak, C.M., Lui, Y.P.: The effect of sound on office productivity. Build. Serv. Eng. Res. Technol. **33**(3), 339–345 (2012)
6. Dhungana, P., Chalise, M.: Prevalence of sick building syndrome symptoms and its associated factors among bank employees in Pokhara Metropolitan, Nepal. Indoor Air **30**, 244–250 (2019)
7. Ghaffarianhoseini, A.A., et al.: Sick building syndrome: are we doing enough? Archit. Sci. Rev. **61**(3), 99–121 (2018)

8. Crook, B., Burton, N.C.: Indoor moulds, sick building syndrome and building related illness. Fungal Biol. Rev. **24**(3–4), 106–113 (2010)
9. Singh, J.: Health, comfort and productivity in the indoor environment. Indoor Built Environ. **5**(1), 22–33 (1996)
10. Lan, L., Wargocki, P., Wyon, D.P., Lian, Z.: Effects of thermal discomfort in an office on perceived air quality, SBS symptoms, physiological responses, and human performance. Indoor Air **21**(5), 376–390 (2011)
11. Fang, L., Wyon, D.P., Clausen, G., Fanger, P.O.: Impact of indoor air temperature and humidity in an office on perceived air quality, SBS symptoms and performance. Indoor Air, Suppl. **14**(SUPPL. 7), 74–81 (2004)
12. Dickerson, E.C., Alam, H.B., Brown, R.K.J., Stojanovska, J., Davenport, M.S.: In-person communication between radiologists and acute care surgeons leads to significant alterations in surgical decision making. J. Am. Coll. Radiol. **13**(8), 943–949 (2016)
13. Rock, B.A.: Thermal zoning for HVAC design. ASHRAE J. **60**(12), 20–30 (2018)
14. Li, D., Menassa, C.C., Kamat, V.R.: Non-intrusive interpretation of human thermal comfort through analysis of facial infrared thermography. Energy Build. **176**, 246–261 (2018)
15. Tsai, D.H., Lin, J.S., Chan, C.C.: Office workers' sick building syndrome and indoor carbon dioxide concentrations. J. Occup. Environ. Hyg. **9**(5), 345–351 (2012)
16. Lai, A.C.K., Mui, K.W., Wong, L.T., Law, L.Y.: An evaluation model for indoor environmental quality (IEQ) acceptance in residential buildings. Energy Build. **41**(9), 930–936 (2009)
17. Hwang, T., Jeong, T.K.: Effects of indoor lighting on occupants' visual comfort and eye health in a green building. Indoor and Built Environment **20**(1), 75–90 (2011)
18. Mui, K.W., Wong, L.T., Cheung, C.T., Yu, H.C.: An application-based indoor environmental quality (ieq) calculator for residential buildings. World Acad. Sci. Eng. Technol. Int. J. Archit. Environ. Eng. **9**(7), 822–825 (2015)
19. Choi, J.H., Loftness, V., Aziz, A.: Post-occupancy evaluation of 20 office buildings as basis for future IEQ standards and guidelines. Energy Build. **46**, 167–175 (2012)
20. Kang, S., Ou, D., Mak, C.M.: The impact of indoor environmental quality on work productivity in university open-plan research offices. Build. Environ. **124**, 78–89 (2017)
21. Day, J.K., Futrell, B., Cox, R., Ruiz, S.N.: Blinded by the light: occupant perceptions and visual comfort assessments of three dynamic daylight control systems and shading strategies. Build. Environ. **154**, 107–121 (2019)
22. Al horr, Y., Arif, M., Katafygiotou, M., Mazroei, A., Kaushik, A., Elsarrag, E.: Impact of indoor environmental quality on occupant well-being and comfort: a review of the literature. Int. J. Sustain. Built Environ. **5**(1), 1–11 (2016)
23. La Roche, P., Milne, M.: Effects of window size and thermal mass on building comfort using an intelligent ventilation controller. Sol. Energy **77**(4), 421–434 (2004). SPEC. ISS
24. Dahlan, N.D., Jones, P.J., Alexander, D.K., Salleh, E., Alias, J.: Daylight ratio, luminance, and visual comfort assessments in typical malaysian hostels. Indoor Built Environ. **18**(4), 319–335 (2009)
25. Li, D., Menassa, C., Kamat, V.: Robust non-intrusive interpretation of occupant thermal comfort in built environments with low-cost networked thermal cameras. Appl. Energy **251**, 113336 (2019)
26. Frontczak, M., Andersen, R.V., Wargocki, P.: Questionnaire survey on factors influencing comfort with indoor environmental quality in danish housing. Build. Environ. **50**, 56–64 (2012)
27. Ren, L., Qiu, H., Wang, P., Lin, P.M.C.: Exploring customer experience with budget hotels: Dimensionality and satisfaction. Int. J. Hosp. Manag. **52**, 13–23 (2016)

28. Day, J., Theodorson, J., Van Den Wymelenberg, K.: Understanding controls, behaviors and satisfaction in the daylit perimeter office: a daylight design case study. J. Inter. Des. **37**(1), 17–34 (2012)
29. Kim, J., de Dear, R., Cândido, C., Zhang, H., Arens, E.: Gender differences in office occupant perception of indoor environmental quality (IEQ). Build. Environ. **70**, 245–256 (2013)
30. Li, D., Menassa, C.C., Kamat, V.R.: Personalized human comfort in indoor building environments under diverse conditioning modes. Build. Environ. **126**, 304–317 (2017)
31. Marmot, A.F., Eley, J., Stafford, M., Stansfeld, S.A., Warwick, E., Marmot, M.G.: Building health: an epidemiological study of 'sick building syndrome' in the Whitehall II study. Occup. Environ. Med. **63**(4), 283–289 (2006)
32. Lan, L., Lian, Z., Pan, L.: The effects of air temperature on office workers' well-being, workload and productivity-evaluated with subjective ratings. Appl. Ergon. **42**(1), 29–36 (2010)
33. Beutell, N.J.: Work schedule, work schedule control and satisfaction in relation to work-family conflict, work-family synergy, and domain satisfaction. Career Dev. Int. **15**(5), 501–518 (2010)
34. Tietjen, M.A., Myers, R.M.: Motivation and job satisfaction. Manag. Decis. **36**(4), 226–231 (1998)
35. Sherman, L.E., Michikyan, M., Greenfield, P.M.: The effects of text, audio, video, and in-person communication on bonding between friends. Cyberpsychology: J. Psychosoc. Res. Cyberspace **7**(2) (2013)
36. Bergmo, T.S., Kummervold, P.E., Gammon, D., Dahl, L.B.: Electronic patient-provider communication: Will it offset office visits and telephone consultations in primary care? Int. J. Med. Inform. **74**(9), 705–710 (2005)
37. Kim, K., Lim, J.H., Proctor, R.W., Salvendy, G.: User satisfaction with tablet PC features. Hum. Factors Ergon. Manuf. **26**(2), 149–158 (2016)
38. Chu, S.K.W., Kennedy, D.M.: Using online collaborative tools for groups to co-construct knowledge. Online Inf. Rev. **35**(4), 581–597 (2011)
39. Goetz, K., Kleine-Budde, K., Bramesfeld, A., Stegbauer, C.: Working atmosphere, job satisfaction and individual characteristics of community mental health professionals in integrated care. Heal. Soc. Care Community **26**(2), 176–181 (2018)
40. Farr, J.L.: Incentive schedules, productivity, and satisfaction in work groups: a laboratory study. Organ. Behav. Hum. Perform. **17**(1), 159–170 (1976)
41. Shikdar, A.A., Das, B.: The relationship between worker satisfaction and productivity in a repetitive industrial task. Appl. Ergon. **34**(6), 603–610 (2003)
42. Lee, Y.S.: Office layout affecting privacy, interaction, and acoustic quality in LEED-certified buildings. Build. Environ. **45**(7), 1594–1600 (2010)
43. Kim, J., Candido, C., Thomas, L., de Dear, R.: Desk ownership in the workplace: the effect of non-territorial working on employee workplace satisfaction, perceived productivity and health. Build. Environ. **103**, 203–214 (2016)
44. Roxburgh, S.: Exploring the work and family relationship: gender differences in the influence of parenthood and social support on job satisfaction. J. Fam. Issues **20**(6), 771–788 (1999)
45. Mathieu, F.: Specialist, "transforming compassion fatigue into compassion satisfaction : top 12 self-care tips for helpers developing an early warning system for yourself top 12 self-care tips for helpers", March, 2007
46. Runeson-Broberg, R., Norbäck, D.: Sick building syndrome (SBS) and sick house syndrome (SHS) in relation to psychosocial stress at work in the Swedish workforce. Int. Arch. Occup. Environ. Health **86**(8), 915–922 (2012). https://doi.org/10.1007/s00420-012-0827-8

47. Wright, T.A., Cropanzano, R.: Psychological well-being and job satisfaction as predictors of job performance. J. Occup. Health Psychol. **5**(1), 84–94 (2000)
48. Liaw, S.S., Huang, H.M.: Perceived satisfaction, perceived usefulness and interactive learning environments as predictors to self-regulation in e-learning environments. Comput. Educ. **60**(1), 14–24 (2013)
49. Kinman, G., Jones, F.: A life beyond work? Job demands, work-life balance, and wellbeing in UK academics. J. Hum. Behav. Soc. Environ. **17**(1–2), 41–60 (2008)
50. Portello, J.K., Rosenfield, M., Bababekova, Y., Estrada, J.M., Leon, A.: Health, comfort and productivity in the indoor environment. Ophthalmic Physiol. Opt. **32**(5), 375–382 (2012)
51. Tham, K.W., Wargocki, P., Tan, Y.F.: Indoor environmental quality, occupant perception, prevalence of sick building syndrome symptoms, and sick leave in a green mark platinum-rated versus a non-green mark-rated building: a case study. Sci. Technol. Built Environ. **21** (1), 35–44 (2015)
52. Jung, C.C., Liang, H.H., Lee, H.L., Hsu, N.Y., Su, H.J.: Allostatic load model associated with indoor environmental quality and sick building syndrome among office workers. PLoS One **9**(4), e95791 (2014)
53. Jung W., Jazizadeh F.: Multi-occupancy indoor thermal condition optimization in consideration of thermal sensitivity. In: Smith, I., Domer, B. (eds.) Advanced Computing Strategies for Engineering. EG-ICE 2018. LNCS, vol 10864. Springer, Cham. (2018). https://doi.org/10.1007/978-3-319-91638-5_12
54. Despenic, M., Chraibi, S., Lashina, T., Rosemann, A.: Lighting preference profiles of users in an open office environment. Build. Environ. **116**, 89–107 (2017)
55. Kojima, T., et al.: The impact of contact lens wear and visual display terminal work on ocular surface and tear functions in office workers. Am. J. Ophthalmol. **152**(6), 933–940.e2 (2011)
56. Rosenfield, M.: Computer vision syndrome: A review of ocular causes and potential treatments. Ophthalmic Physiol. Opt. **31**(5), 502–515 (2011)
57. Takigawa, T., et al.: A longitudinal study of aldehydes and volatile organic compounds associated with subjective symptoms related to sick building syndrome in new dwellings in Japan. Sci. Total Environ. **417–418**, 61–67 (2012)

# Research of Comfort Model of Eye Massager During Siesta in the Office

Qi Huang[✉] and Hongmiao Liu

Zhejiang University, Hangzhou, Zhejiang Province, China
kylehq@163.com, 1343567237@qq.com

**Abstract.** This article conducted a series of studies on the comfort of eye massager product during siesta in the office, and obtained the key influencing factors that affect the comfort in this scene, that is, the "shading effect", "heat temperature", "massage force", "breathability", "pressure on eye area", "cost", and "eye fatigue after wearing". On the basis of theoretical research and extraction analysis of comfort influencing factors, combined with statistical methods, this article establishes the comfort model of eye massager product during siesta in the office, and evaluates and verifies the rationality and effectiveness of the model.

Compared with previous comfort or discomfort perception models, the comfort model established in this paper can make a relatively quantitative evaluation of the comfort of massage eye mask products in specific scenarios, providing a basis and ideas for the product development process.

**Keywords:** Eye massager · Comfort model · Siesta in the office

## 1 Introduction

The problem of insufficient rest or excessive use of eyes has become a common problem in the world. In China alone, more than 300 million people have problems with sleep disorders; more and more consumers are showing strong desire to consume sleep products. There is a huge and continuously growing market; at the same time, people also need to spend more and more time on electronic screens every day, which inevitably has an impact on people's eye health. Based on the above situation, many companies have launched massage eye mask products to improve the quality of the user's rest and relieve the user's eye fatigue. However, for the emerging product form such as eye massager product, there is still a lack of targeted comfort research work. At present, the academic research on comfort is relatively rich, mainly concentrated in the fields of climate, environment, architecture, seat design and hand tool products. [1] Research on the new product form of eye massage is still relatively lacking, leading to the lack of guidance of relevant theoretical models and unified evaluation methods for the development of eye massager product.

This article will try to explore the key factors affecting the comfort of the massage eye mask experience based on comfort theory and research methods, and establish a model suitable for describing and evaluating the comfort of the massage eye mask product during siesta in the office to provide product developers in related industries available design tools.

© Springer Nature Switzerland AG 2020
C. Stephanidis et al. (Eds.): HCII 2020, LNCS 12429, pp. 495–508, 2020.
https://doi.org/10.1007/978-3-030-59987-4_35

## 2    Research Ideas

The research on comfort has started from the first half of the last century, and has gradually become a hot topic in human factors engineering and other disciplines, especially in the fields of climate, seat design and medical rehabilitation. Designers and manufacturers of products such as seats, cars, beds, hand tools, and factory lines are also trying to find ways to improve the comfort of the product experience or reduce the discomfort during the use of the product, but the academic community has not been able to Form a clear and unified definition of the concept of comfort.

This article draws on the relevant achievements or methods of seat comfort research, starting with specific comfort influencing factors, researching and collecting the significant factors that affect the quality of nap and eye comfort which provides the basis for the extraction and analysis of key factors; later, the main comfort factors are extracted to discuss the relationship between each key impact factor and the relationship with the product experience, so as to establish a more targeted and a comfort model for quantifying evaluation capabilities. After that, the comfort model is further verified. According to observations and product sales data, the typical use scenario of eye massager products is office siesta, and office white-collar workers are their typical users. Therefore, this study focuses on the specific scene of office siesta, taking office white-collar workers aged 21–40 The main target group.

## 3    Comfort Factor Collection

This chapter refers to the research of Zhang or Kuijt-Evers et al. in seat comfort [2] and hand tool comfort research [3]. First, user interview and expert interview were combined to collect comfort influencing factors.

**Research Progress**
At this stage, 30 office white-collar workers with physical and mental health, experience and habits in using eye massager were recruited to participate in the interview, 15 males and 15 females, aged 21–40 years old. Ergonomics experts, industrial design experts and staff with personal care product development experience were invited to form an 8-person expert team to participate in the study.

(1)    Respondents were requested to recall, introduce and evaluate factors related to the comfort of using eye massager during siesta in the office as much as possible. Users are prompted to select factors from product characteristics, personal factors, environmental factors, emotions and operation method. The dialogue content of the interview participants was recorded in detail and each interview conducts an independent interview to reduce the interference between the participants. Certain remuneration was paid to the interviewees after the interview.

(2)    The interview records of the participants were summarized and four expert team members were asked to participate in the collation of the interview content and the extraction of factors affecting the comfort.

(3) Referring to the "Delphi Method", and the potential factor list was obtained by the above steps will be divided into three rounds of anonymous screening, improvement and evaluation by 4 experts who did not participate in the above interviews. No further deletions or additions were made by experts, and the resulting list of comfort influencing factors could be considered relatively complete.

## Research Results

According to the classification of factors by Naddeo et al. [4], the factors of eye massager comfort during siesta in the office were classified as shown in Table 1:

**Table 1.** List of potential comfort factors

| Classification | Number | Factors | Classification | Number | Factors |
|---|---|---|---|---|---|
| Product Characteristics | 1 | Shading effect | Usage | 35 | Wear convenience |
| | 2 | Heat temperature | | 36 | Charge convenience |
| | 3 | Hot zone | | 37 | Switch convenience |
| | 4 | Temperature rise speed | | 38 | Temperature adjustment convenience |
| | 5 | Massage Force | | 39 | Massage mode adjustment convenience |
| | 6 | Massage frequency | | 40 | Portability |
| | 7 | Massage zone | | 41 | Single wear time |
| | 8 | Product noise | | 42 | Bluetooth convenience |
| | 9 | Breathability | Personal Factors | 43 | Nap posture |
| | 10 | Product weight | | 44 | Duration of nap |
| | 11 | Product volume | | 45 | Eye fatigue before wearing |
| | 12 | Pressure on eye area | | 46 | Eye fatigue after wearing |
| | 13 | Strap pressure on the head | | 47 | Body fatigue state before wearing |
| | 14 | Firmness | | 48 | (Evening) Sleep quality |
| | 15 | Battery capacity | | 49 | (Evening) Sleep quality |
| | 16 | Shape | Working Environment | 50 | Environment temperature |
| | 17 | Outer surface material | | 51 | Environment sound |
| | 18 | Outer surface color | | 52 | Environment humidity |
| | 19 | Internal surface material | | 53 | Environment wind speed |
| | 20 | Internal surface color | | 54 | Environment smell |
| | 21 | Massage contact material | | 55 | Seat comfort |
| | 22 | Band material | | 56 | Weather condition |
| | 23 | Band color | Gratification Level and Emotions | 57 | Mood when wearing |
| | 24 | Smell | | 58 | Work before lunch break |
| | 25 | Sleep aid music | | 59 | Work before lunch break |
| | 26 | Product removable and washable | | 60 | Work arrangements after lunch break |
| | 27 | Cleanliness of outer surface | | | |
| | 28 | Cleanliness of inner surface | | | |
| | 29 | Product used time | | | |
| | 30 | Product wear or loss | | | |
| | 31 | Product gifts/accessories | | | |
| | 32 | Packaging | | | |
| | 33 | Cost | | | |
| | 34 | Brand | | | |

At this stage, methods such as user interviews and expert interviews were used, referring to the classification and description of comfort factors by Naddeo and others, and a total of 60 comfort factors for massage eye mask products in the office lunch break scene were extracted (as shown in Table 1). According to the source, the factors are summarized into five categories: product characteristics, usage, personal factors, working environment and gratification level and emotion. After multiple rounds of compound evaluation, it could be considered that the above potential factors basically comprehensively cover all aspects of the product using scenario.

## 4 Extraction of Key Impact Factors

Based on the study of the comfort factors, this section uses psychological questionnaires and interviews to extract the key factors affecting the comfort of eye massager during siesta in the office, and analyzes the impact of each key factor on the overall product experience.

### 4.1 Experiment Preparation

A total of 180 office white-collar workers with the habit of using eye massager product during siesta in the office and physical and mental health were recruited as the participants in this research, and the experimenters were informed in advance of the approximate experiment purpose and experiment form. A certain amount of experimental remuneration was provided to the users.

Based on the 60 potential factors extracted in the previous article, a psychological questionnaire was prepared. The eleven-point psychological scale used in the design of this questionnaire, the scale is set from "−5" (very dissatisfied) to "5" (very satisfied) to form an eleven-level score (as shown in Fig. 1), which is convenient to judge the tendency (positive or negative) of the subject's evaluation.

Very Dissatisfied                      Ordinary                    Very Satisfied

−5                          0                      5

**Fig. 1.** Eleven-point psychology scale

Since users cannot make a clear distinction between comfort and discomfort, and the purpose of this experiment is to extract and analyze key impact factors rather than distinguish the relationship between comfort and discomfort, the term "overall experience" is used to represent comfort or discomfort. The formed comprehensive feelings are evaluated by the subjects using psychology scales. From a logical point of view, the "overall experience" evaluation can be regarded as the dependent variable in the product use process, and the user's evaluation of many impact factors can be regarded as the independent variable in the product experience. In addition to personal information topics, the questionnaire includes 60 potential factor items and a overall experience evaluation item.

## 4.2   Experiment

The subjects were reminded and asked one day in advance to prepare their own eye massager on the day of the experiment (working day), use personal eye massager to relax during lunch break in accordance with personal habits in the noon and the subjects were allowed to adjust the usage of product and other conditions. Before the end of the lunch break, the experimenters and related objects should avoid direct contact with the subjects to avoid affecting the user's product experience process Fig. 2 [4].

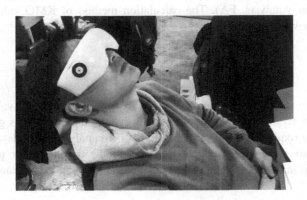

**Fig. 2.** A subject was wearing the product during siesta in the office

## 4.3   Data Analysis

A total of 162 questionnaires were finally recovered. First of all, the questionnaire is preliminarily screened, and the questionnaires with too short filling time (less than 150 s), incomplete filling, and the occurrence rate of the same option exceeding 70% are judged as invalid questionnaires; and the box chart is used to check the outliers and extreme values in the remaining questionnaire. After screening, finally 150 question-naires remained.

(1)   Reliability and validity test of data samples

Before the analysis, the reliability of the obtained data samples is first tested using the Cronbach's alpha [5]. The calculation method of Cronbach's alpha (non-standardized) is shown in formula (1):

$$\alpha = \frac{k}{k-1}\left(1 - \frac{\sum_{i=1}^{k}\sigma_{Y_i}^2}{\sigma_X^2}\right) \tag{1}$$

Based on the analysis result showed in Table 2, it is comprehensively demonstrated that the reliability of the data is high and can be used for further analysis.

**Table 2.** Result of Cronbach's alpha inspection

| Cronbach's alpha | Cronbach's alpha (standardized) | Amount |
|---|---|---|
| 0.951 | 0.957 | 61 |

After the check of reliability of the data sample, the validity of the sample data is analyzed by the KMO value and the Bartlett sphericity test [6], and it is determined whether the data sample is suitable for Principal Component Analysis (PCA) or factor analysis (Factor Analysis, FA). The calculation method of KMO value is shown as formula (as shown in formula 2):

$$KMO = \frac{\sum\sum_{i \neq j} r_{ij}^2}{\sum\sum_{i \neq j} r_{ij}^2 + \sum\sum_{i \neq j} r_{ij \cdot 1,2 \cdots k}^2} \tag{2}$$

The validity calculation results are shown in Table 3. The KMO value of this data sample is 0.849 (> 0.6), which initially proves that the data validity is good and meets the prerequisite requirements of principal component analysis or factor analysis. While the sample also passes the Bartlett's test (p < 0.05) which further proves that the research data is suitable for principal component analysis or factor analysis.

**Table 3.** Result of KMO and Bartlett's test

| KMO and Bartlett's test | | |
|---|---|---|
| KMO | | 0.849 |
| Bartlett's test | Approx. Chi-Square | 5337.363 |
| | df | 1770 |
| | p | 0.000 |

Afterwards, the principal component analysis and factor analysis have not achieved a relatively ideal analysis effect. The number of factors after dimensionality reduction is large, and the corresponding relationship with the research items is not ideal enough. In this sample data, there are multiple independent variables corresponding to one dependent variable, so we try to use the stepwise regression method to deal with it.

(2)  Stepwise regression analysis

The stepwise regression method can ensure that the regression equation can retain the variables that affect significantly, and eliminate the non-significant variables. At this stage, a stepwise regression analysis was performed on the data sample, with "overall experience" as the dependent variable, 60 potential comfort factors as independent variables, with VIF (Variance Inflation Factor) test using to check the multicollinearity of the model. The calculation method of VIF is shown in formula (3) and the DW

(Durbin-Watson) value was calculated to test the model's autocorrelation. The results of stepwise regression analysis are shown in Table 4.

$$VIF = \frac{1}{1-R_i^2} \qquad (3)$$

**Table 4.** Result of stepwise regression analysis

| | Unstandardized regression coefficient | | Standardized regression coefficient | t | p | VIF | $R^2$ | Adjusted $R^2$ | F |
|---|---|---|---|---|---|---|---|---|---|
| | B | Standard deviation | Beta | | | | | | |
| Constant | 0.024 | 0.165 | – | 0.143 | 0.886 | – | 0.748 | 0.735 | F(7,142) = 60.145 |
| Shading effect | 0.198 | 0.049 | 0.223 | 4.038 | 0.000** | 1.723 | | | P = 0.000** |
| Heat temperature | 0.124 | 0.05 | 0.129 | 2.507 | 0.013* | 1.492 | | | |
| Massage force | 0.225 | 0.05 | 0.237 | 4.479 | 0.000** | 1.579 | | | |
| Breathability | 0.105 | 0.04 | 0.133 | 2.599 | 0.010* | 1.477 | | | |
| Pressure on eye area | 0.135 | 0.049 | 0.17 | 2.738 | 0.007** | 2.165 | | | |
| Cost | 0.125 | 0.046 | 0.143 | 2.719 | 0.007** | 1.558 | | | |
| Eye fatigue after wearing | 0.138 | 0.046 | 0.166 | 3.013 | 0.003** | 1.71 | | | |
| Dependent variable: overall experience | | | | | | | | | |
| D-W:2.068 | | | | | | | | | |

* p < 0.05 ** p < 0.01

Finally, 7 variables (impact factors) of "shading effect", "heat temperature", "massage force", "breathability", "pressure on eye area", "cost", and "eye fatigue after wearing" are retained in the regression model. Each variable showed a significance of 0.01 level. $R^2$ is 0.748, which means that the above 7 independent variables can explain the 74.8% change of the dependent variable (overall experience), and the explanation effect is acceptable. The model passes the F test (F = 60.145, P < 0.05), indicating that the model is effective. In the multicollinearity test, the VIF values of all variables in the model are all less than 5, which means that the model does not have collinearity problems. The D-W value is near the number 2, which means that the model does not have autocorrelation. Because the dimensions or units in the data sample are the same (all are user evaluation scores), the relative size relationship between the unstandardized coefficients and standardized coefficients of each variable is relatively close, so this paper selects the unstandardized coefficients as regression coefficients to establish a regression model.

Finally, the residuals in the regression analysis are tested by normal graph and P-P graph which confirms that the normality of the residual value of this regression model is good. And the seven items extracted by the regression model are also in line with psychological expectations. In summary, it can be preliminarily considered that the model established by this stepwise regression has statistical significance.

### 4.4 Analysis Conclusions

In this experiment, through the processing and analysis of the sample data, the regression model shown in formula (4) established:

$$Y = 0.198 \times X_s + 0.124 \times X_t + 0.225 \times X_f + 0.105 \times X_b + 0.135 \times X_p + 0.125 \times X_c + 0.138 \times X_e + 0.024 \tag{4}$$

In which:

$X_s$——evaluation of "shading effect"
$X_t$——evaluation of "heat temperature"
$X_f$——evaluation of "massage force"
$X_b$——evaluation of "breathability"
$X_p$——evaluation of "pressure on eye area"
$X_c$——evaluation of "cost"
$X_e$——evaluation of "eye fatigue after wearing"
$Y$—— evaluation of product overall experience evaluation (which represents a comprehensive feeling of comfort and discomfort)

The significance of this regression model is:

(1) There are 7 variables entered into the final model, and all have good significance. This is equivalent to extracting 7 key factors from the 60 comfort factors in the office nap scene that are more critical and will affect the overall experience. Evaluation of key factors that have a significant impact. Through the examination of the seven key factors, the overall use experience of the product can be evaluated and predicted more effectively, which has certain reference value for researchers and product developers.

(2) By observing the regression coefficients of each variable, the relative importance relationship of these 7 key impact factors can be judged. In the specific product development practice, the seven factors in the experience of this massage goggles product should be examined. R&D team should pay more attention to relevant work with significantly higher coefficients and invest more resources appropriately. For example, the coefficients of "shading effect" and "massage force" are significantly larger, which proves that these two aspects have a greater impact on the evaluation of the overall experience of the product.

(3) For the sample data in this study, the regression model has a good ability of inductive interpretation. On this basis, after subsequent verification and processing, the comfort model of the massage eye mask in the office nap scene can be established accordingly, which is of great significance for the evaluation of the comfort of the massage eye mask and the product development practice.

# 5   Validation of Comfort Model

Based on the previous regression analysis, it is necessary to verify the regression model shown in formula (4) from the prediction effect and physiological index measurement experiments for auxiliary verification.

## 5.1   Predicted Performance Verification

10 users with eye massager product experience and 10 users without product use experience to participate in the verification test were selected and invited. The users are 21–40 years old office white collars with physically and mentally health. The relationship between the user experience evaluation and the predicted value calculated by the regression model is used to test the prediction ability of the regression model.

**Table 5.** Evaluation from users with product experience

| Key factors | $X_s$ | $X_t$ | $X_f$ | $X_b$ | $X_p$ | $X_c$ | $X_e$ | Overall experience evaluation | $Y$ (Predicted value) | Absolute value of difference |
|---|---|---|---|---|---|---|---|---|---|---|
| Regression coefficients | 0.198 | 0.124 | 0.225 | 0.105 | 0.135 | 0.125 | 0.138 | | | |
| | 3 | 3 | 3 | 2 | 3 | 3 | 4 | 3 | 3.207 | 0.207 |
| | 2 | 3 | 2 | 1 | 2 | 2 | 1 | 2 | 2.005 | 0.005 |
| | 3 | 3 | 4 | 2 | 4 | 2 | 3 | 3 | 3.304 | 0.304 |
| | 2 | 2 | 3 | 2 | 2 | 3 | 2 | 3 | 2.474 | 0.526 |
| | 4 | 4 | 3 | 3 | 5 | 2 | 4 | 3 | 3.779 | 0.779 |
| | 5 | 4 | 4 | 2 | 3 | 2 | 3 | 3 | 3.689 | 0.689 |
| | 2 | 3 | 2 | 1 | 3 | 4 | 2 | 3 | 2.528 | 0.472 |
| | 2 | 3 | 2 | 1 | 2 | 2 | 2 | 2 | 2.143 | 0.143 |
| | 4 | 4 | 2 | 2 | 4 | 2 | 1 | 3 | 2.9 | 0.1 |
| | −1 | 1 | 1 | 0 | −2 | 0 | 1 | 0 | 0.043 | 0.043 |
| Average | | | | | | | | 2.5 | 2.6072 | 0.3268 |

In this experiment, it is necessary to select and purchase 5 eye massager products with different brands, different price, similar functions and certain brand awareness. The experiment content and product prices, product usage methods were briefly introduced to the subjects during 10: 00–11: 00 on weekdays. The users were required to wear a eye massager during siesta. Experimenters and related objects avoid direct contact with the subject.

Within half an hour of the end of the lunch break, two types of users are invited to fill in a psychological questionnaire which contains 7 key factors evaluation items and a overall experience evaluation item according to their product experience during the siesta in the office.

A total of 20 valid questionnaires were finally recovered, and the calculation was carried out by substituting the questionnaire scale filled in by the user into the regression model to compare the actual overall evaluation of the user with the predicted value of the regression model as shown in Table 5 and Table 6.

**Table 6.** Evaluation from users without product experience

| Key factors | $X_s$ | $X_t$ | $X_f$ | $X_b$ | $X_p$ | $X_c$ | $X_e$ | Overall experience evaluation | Y (Predicted value) | Absolute value of difference |
|---|---|---|---|---|---|---|---|---|---|---|
| Regression coefficients | 0.198 | 0.124 | 0.225 | 0.105 | 0.135 | 0.125 | 0.138 | | | |
| | 4 | 5 | 3 | 1 | 1 | 2 | 1 | 2 | 2.739 | 0.739 |
| | 4 | 4 | 2 | 4 | 3 | 2 | 3 | 3 | 3.251 | 0.251 |
| | 3 | 2 | 2 | 1 | 2 | 2 | 2 | 2 | 2.217 | 0.217 |
| | 2 | 0 | 2 | 1 | 2 | 1 | 2 | 1 | 1.646 | 0.646 |
| | 3 | 2 | 3 | 2 | 2 | 2 | 1 | 2 | 2.409 | 0.409 |
| | 5 | 4 | 4 | 2 | 4 | 3 | 3 | 4 | 3.949 | 0.051 |
| | −1 | −1 | 1 | −3 | −4 | −3 | 0 | −2 | −1.303 | 0.697 |
| | 2 | 3 | 2 | 1 | 2 | 3 | 4 | 3 | 2.544 | 0.456 |
| | 2 | 4 | 3 | 1 | 3 | 2 | 2 | 3 | 2.627 | 0.373 |
| | 3 | 3 | 2 | −1 | 1 | 3 | 0 | 2 | 1.845 | 0.155 |
| Average | | | | | | | | 2 | 2.1924 | 0.3944 |

From Tables 5 and 6, we can see that the average difference (absolute value) between the predicted value of the regression model and the actual evaluation of the overall product experience of the two groups of people is 0.3268 and 0.3944, which are within the acceptable range. And the maximum of the absolute value of difference basically does not exceed 1.

Above all, it is preliminarily believed that the prediction effect of the regression model can be used in the evaluation of product comfort.

## 5.2    Physiological Measurement

According to the related research, the use of physiological measurement can make up for the bias of research results of subjective evaluation due to personal factors.

The factor "eye fatigue after wearing" is directly related to the physiological indexes of the human body. The correlation test between the "overall experience" and "eye fatigue after wearing" in the 150 sample data obtained in the previous experiment was tested. Since the original data sample does not have obvious normal distribution characteristics, Spearman's rank correlation coefficient was used for analysis, the results are shown in the Table 7:

**Table 7.** Results of Spearman's rank correlation coefficient

| | | | Overall experience evaluation | Eye fatigue after wearing |
|---|---|---|---|---|
| Spearman's rho | Overall experience evaluation | Correlation coefficient | 1 | 0.545** |
| | | Sig. (2-tailed) | | 0.000 |
| | | N | 150 | 150 |
| | Eye fatigue after wearing | Correlation coefficient | 0.545** | 1 |
| | | Sig. (2-tailed) | 0.000 | |
| | | N | 150 | 150 |

* p < 0.05 ** p < 0.01

It can be seen from the table that in this data sample, the correlation coefficient value between "overall experience" and "eye fatigue after wearing" is 0.545, and it shows a significance of 0.01 level, which implies there is a significant positive correlation between "overall experience" and "eye fatigue after wearing". It can be speculated that the overall experience evaluation of the product is more likely to increase with the improvement of satisfaction of the factor "eye fatigue after wearing".

Based on the above analysis and speculation, by measuring the physiological indicator of the user's eye fatigue state after the product experience, it can assist the evaluation of the overall product experience. After using the eye massager product, the lower the user's eye fatigue, the better the fatigue relief effect of the product, and the more likely it is to give a positive evaluation of the experience process. Here, the critical flicker frequency test is used to detect the user's eye fatigue state to prove the above inference and indirectly verify the rationality of the regression model in formula (4).

(1) Experiment preparation

The flash fusion frequency meter (as shown in Fig. 3) to test eye fatigue by detecting the highest light source flicker frequency that the subject can visually distinguish, which is the critical flicker frequency (CFF). In general, when the CFF value is relatively large, it's indicated that the subject's eye fatigue is relatively low.

**Fig. 3.** The flash fusion frequency meter

Due to individual differences among subjects, such as innate vision level and current physical state, this leads to different CFF values for each subject under ideal conditions. Therefore, the CFF value of each subject cannot be directly used for horizontal comparison. The CFF value of the same user after using different products should be measured, and the change of each CFF value measurement result should be compared with the user's subjective evaluation. The result would be used to verify the speculation: the user's evaluation of the factor of "eye fatigue after wearing" reflects the physiological index of the user's eye fatigue. By comparing the user's eye fatigue after the product is used, the comfort of different products can be evaluated to a certain extent.

Ten participants in the prediction effect experiment were recruited (5 people were selected and invited from each group) to participate in the experiment. The participants were physically and mentally healthy, without color blindness and color weakness. Before the experiment, the subjects were informed of the approximate experiment purpose and experiment form and reminded that the experiment may involve the task of observing the flickering light source. selected in the prediction effect experiment The five samples purchased in the prediction experiment were marked as sample 01-sample 05 for this CFF experiment.

(2) Experiment

Participants would use a total of five products from Sample 01 to Sample 05 in a two-week experiment period. Participants will wear a sample eye mask during siesta in the office. Within a few moment after the subjects awake to remove the device, the user will be tested for eye fatigue using the flash fusion frequency meter.

In the experiment, the minimum change method was used to measure the user's CFF value; during the test, the power of the flash fusion frequency meter was turned on, and the subject's eyes were guided to the instrument observation window, and the blinking bright spot appearing in the center of the instrument was watched. The initial bright spot flashing frequency defaulted to 10 Hz, and the subject slowly adjusted the frequency knob (slowly adjusted with a gradient of 0.1 Hz), gradually increasing the flashing frequency of the bright spot, until the subjects could not observe the flashing of the bright spot. Subjects should immediately pause the frequency adjustment and report, at this time the subjects were required to repeatedly adjust the knob around the possible critical flicker frequency until the bright light flicker cannot be observed and report, and the value on the frequency count display screen at this time would be recorded as the CFF value of the subject in this experiment.

Each product experience experiment was carried out 1–2 days apart, until the subject completed the experience of the five sample products and the CFF measurement experiment. In order to avoid mutual interference between the products, the subjects' eye fatigue state should be ensured to have returned to the normal state before the next experience. After each CFF test, it was also necessary to ensure that the subjects had got more complete relaxation and rest to avoid permanent damage to the user's eyesight caused by the flash fusion frequency meter. Subjects would be paid for participation.

(3) Analysis of results

The results of this experiment were summarized and a series of line charts was drawn as shown in the Fig. 4:

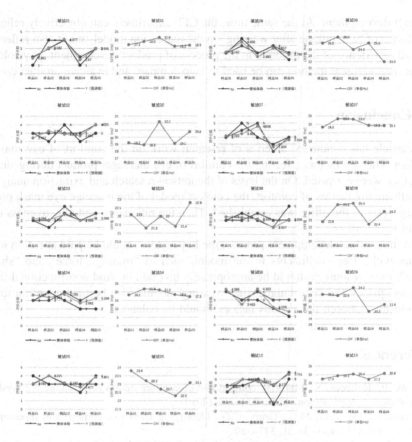

**Fig. 4.** The result of CFF test

By observing the experimental results in Fig. 4 especially for the same subject's $X_e$ (evaluation of "eye fatigue after wearing"), overall experience evaluation and CFF By comparing and analyzing the relationship between the values, we can clearly find that:

When the CFF value is high, the subject's score for $X_e$ is also often high, and the change trend of the two variables is almost the same, which can prove that the subject's description of the physiological state of eye fatigue is relatively accurate and objective.

For the cases in the sample, when the CFF value is high, the participant's evaluation of the overall product experience would not be too low, so in some cases, the user's eye fatigue after product usage can be used to an initial evaluation and prediction of the overall product experience. And the result also indirectly verified the rationality of the regression model in formula (4).

## 5.3    Conclusion of Verification

Through the prediction effect experiment and the flash fusion critical frequency experiment, the effectiveness of the comfort model in formula (4) is verified to a certain extent, and it is initially believed that the model can be used for products to guide product development. At the same time, the CFF experiment can objectively reflect the key factor of "eye fatigue after wearing" in the regression model, and it also reflects the overall experience of the product. In the process of product development, physiological index measurement method can be used to help compare and evaluate product comfort.

## 6  Conclusion

This article has conducted a series of research work on the comfort of eye massager product. The key factors affecting the comfort of eye massager product during siesta in the office were extracted. On the basis of theoretical research and extraction analysis of the influencing factors of comfort, the comfort model of the massage eye mask product during siesta in the office was established. Then the rationality and effectiveness of the model was verified.

In the product development process, the key factors should be paid attention to. For factors with large coefficients in the model, such as "massage force" and "shading effect", more resources should be appropriately invested in. And non-functional factors such as "price" and "eye fatigue after wearing" should also be paid attention to. The relationship between the various factors should be balanced.

## References

1. Vink, P., Hallbeck, S.: Editorial: comfort and discomfort studies demonstrate the need for a new model. Appl. Ergon. **43**(2), 271–276 (2012)
2. Zhang, L., Helander, M.G., Drury, C.G.: Identifying factors of comfort and discomfort in sitting. Hum. Factors, **38**(3), 377–389
3. Kuijt-Evers, L.F.M., Groenesteijn, L., de Looze, M.P., Vink, P.: Identifying factors of comfort in using hand tools. Appl. Ergon. **35**(5), 453 (2004)
4. Naddeo, A., Cappetti, N., D'Oria, C.: Proposal of a new quantitative method for postural comfort evaluation. Int. J. Ind. Ergon. **48**, 25–35 (2015)
5. Tavakol, M., Dennick, R.: Making sense of Cronbach's alpha. Int. J. Med. Educ. **2**, 53 (2011)
6. Gim Chung, R.H., Kim, B.S.K., Abreu, J.M.: Asian American multidimensional acculturation scale: development, factor analysis, reliability, and validity. Cult. Divers. Ethnic Minor. Psychol. **10**(1), 66–80 (2004)

# Extracting and Structuring Latent Knowledge for Risk Recognition from Eyes and Utterances of Field Overseers

Noriyuki Kushiro[(✉)], Yusuke Aoyama, and Toshihiro Mega

Kyushu Institute of Technology, 820-8501 Iizuka Fukuoka, Japan
kushiro@mx1.ttcn.ne.jp

**Abstract.** A tool for promoting verbalization of latent field overseers' knowledge for risk recognition with eyes and an algorithm for visualizing logic structure in risk knowledge as propositional network are proposed in the paper. The tool was applied to eliciting risk knowledge from actual field overseers and the algorithm was also applied to visualizing logical structures of risk knowledge included in their utterances. As a result, we find out noticeable structure in experts' knowledge for risk recognition and significant differences between risk knowledge used by the field overseers and knowledge described in work procedure manual.

**Keywords:** Tool for promoting verbalization of latent knowledge · Algorithm for structuring knowledge · Differences of risk recognition knowledge in manual and knowledge used by field overseers

## 1   Introduction

In 2019, 127,329 workers were injured and/or killed by industrial accidents in Japan. Most Companies, e.g., construction, manufacturing, and transportation industries, provide work procedures manuals to prevent the accidents. Furthermore, all the workers in the industries, are obliged to take risk recognition trainings on the manuals. The KYT (Kiken Yochi Training) [1] is one of the most popular risk recognition trainings in Japan. The KYT is conducted on the following 4 procedures:

1. Prepare an illustration of typical work scene included in work procedure manual
2. Detect risks from the illustration through brainstorming among workers
3. Select one serious risk from the detected risks
4. Discuss proper work procedure to avoid the risk

However, the risks extracted from the KYT are limited to just obvious ones, which are easily detected in the illustration, and the KYT often fails to improve workers' proficiency of risk recognition. Unfortunately, the number of the industrial accidents is increasing.

We set the following research questions as reasons why the existing risk recognition trainings (based both on the manual and the KYT) fail to improve workers' proficiency of risk recognition:

© Springer Nature Switzerland AG 2020
C. Stephanidis et al. (Eds.): HCII 2020, LNCS 12429, pp. 509–528, 2020.
https://doi.org/10.1007/978-3-030-59987-4_36

1. Illustration omits indispensable information required for workers' risk recognition due to its limitation on expression
2. Practical knowledge for risk recognition is not included in the work procedures manual

For answering these questions, a tool for promoting verbalization of latent field overseers' knowledge for risk recognition and an algorithm for visualizing structure of risk knowledge as propositional network are proposed in the paper. The tool was applied to eliciting risk knowledge from 22 field overseers with different years of experience and the algorithm was utilized to visualize logical structures of risk knowledge in their utterances. The rest of paper is organized as follows: Sect. 2 explains outlines of the tool and the algorithm proposed in the paper. In Sect. 3, results of experiments, in which the tool and the algorithm were applied to risk recognition training, were described. Section 4 concludes the paper.

## 2    Outline of Tool and Algorithm

The tool for promoting verbalization of latent field overseers' knowledge for risk recognition with utterances and eyes, and the algorithm for structuring risk knowledge as propositional network are explained in the section.

### 2.1    Tool for Eliciting Risk Recognition Knowledge

Interview is one of the most popular methods to elicit knowledge from experts. However, the interview can not work well in this context. Because, the risk recognition has difficulty to be verbalized, it requires tacit dimension of knowledge [2], e.g., perceiving latent dynamics in the risk scene and postulating risk scenarios from these dynamics. Nyi [3] and Dreyfus [4] insisted the following issues to utilize the interviews as methods for retrieving knowledge from experts:

- Experts often express general or mediocre remarks, which was never used in their actual work
- Experts are able to talk their knowledge only by specifying a scene concretely

On these informations, we decided to introduce a video based tool with eye tracking sensor for extracting risk recognition knowledge from field overseers. The videos can express surroundings and dynamics in the work scene, and the eyes promote verbalizing field overseers' knowledge for risk recognition. Figure 1 illustrates overview of the tool. The tool consists of a PC, a monitor, an eye tracking sensor (Eye Tribe Tracker ® [5]) and a motion sensor (Kinnect ®).

A cluster of 8 PCs helps the tool analyze the eyes and the utterances as backend of the tool. The eye tracking device identifies positions of trainee's intention look at every scene and the motion sensor records the trainee's utterances and behaviors during the training. The PC provides videos to the trainee, and records trainees' all the utterances and behaviors (including eyes) during the training. The PC also identifies objects included in the video with DNN technologies [7]

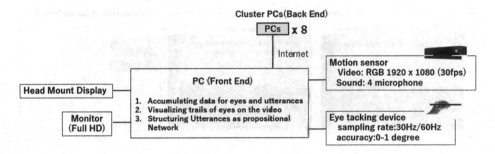

**Fig. 1.** Video based risk training tool

for analyzing transitions for the trainee's objects of interest. For a working scene in narrow space, e.g., constructions in indoor, the tool can be enhanced to handle a panoramic moving picture of 360° view by utilizing VR technologies (Head mounted display) [6]. Prior to the study, the accuracy of the eye tracking device was evaluated by 6 subjects. The subjects gazed 21 points dispersed in the monitor (resolution of the monitor: 1920 × 1080), and differences between true and measured positions were evaluated. As a result, the average errors were within 63 pixels for all the points. We confirmed that the errors are allowable for the application. The tool provides the following major functions: visualizing eyes and structuring trainees' utterances (Table 1).

**Table 1.** Functions of tool

| Categories | Outline |
|---|---|
| Eyes | Visualize present positions of eyes on videos |
| | Visualize trails of eyes around present position as heat map |
| | Analyzing transitions of gazed object |
| Utterances | Converting utterances to semiformal descriptions and structuring logical relations as propositional network |

Figure 2 is examples of the tool's output. Figure 2 (1) and (2) provide trainees their present positions of eyes on videos. Figure 2 (3) gives trainees transitions for gazed objects and intention ratio for each object. By presenting these results for each trainee and inquiring "Why do you gaze it?", we expect that it promotes verbalization of latent knowledge for risk recognition.

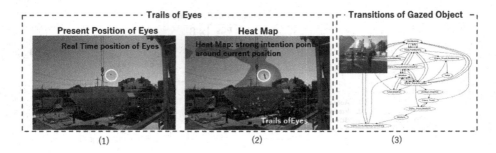

**Fig. 2.** Examples for outputs of tool

## 2.2    Algorithm for Visualizing Logic Structure in Knowledge

The processes for converting trainees' utterances to propositional network are shown in Fig. 3. At the first step, the trainees' utterances are converted into texts with the voice-to-text features in Google Document. Then, the texts are converted into semiformal description [10] by an algorithm called "semiformalizer". The "semiformalizer" also identifies logical relations among atomic propositions, e.g., And, Or, Not, Imply, etc. [12]. At the last step, an algorithm called "proponent" draws semiformal descriptions as propositional network for visualizing the logical structure of the utterances. The detail algorithm of "semiformalizer" is shown in Algorithm 1.

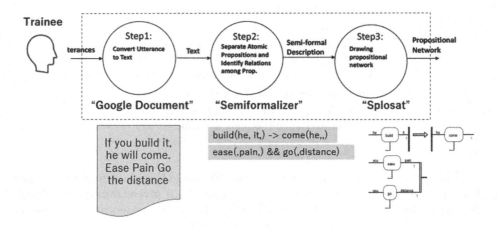

**Fig. 3.** Process for logic visualization in utterances

**Algorithm 1.** Convert Sentences to Semiformal Descriptions

**Definition:**
    children($b$) is a list of *clauses* that modify a *clause* $b$.
    push($l, e$) appends an element $e$ to a list $l$.
    pop($l$) removes the last element $e$ from a list $l$ and return $e$.
    last($l$) is the last element of a list $l$.
    reversed($l$) is a list in the reverse order of a list $l$.
    apply($c, e$) applies an operator $c$ to a semiformal description $d$ in a tuple $e$ ($e = (d, B)$ where $B$ is a list of *clause* that is associated to $d$) and returns a tuple of a semiformal description $d'$ that is the result of application of $c$ and a list of *clauses* that is associated to $d'$.
    NewSemiElement($b$) converts a *clause* $b$ to an element of the semiformal description.
    NewOperator($s_t, s_s$) returns a new operator from two elements of the semiformal description. $s_t = (d_t, B_t)$ and $s_s = (d_s, B_s)$. $d_t$ and $d_s$ are a semiformal description $d_t$ modifies $d_s$. $B_t$ and $B_s$ are lists of *clauses* that are associated to $d_t$ and $d_s$ respectively.

**Input:**
    $b$: a terminal *clause*
**Output:**
    $s$: converted semiformal description

```
1:  procedure CONVERT(b)
2:      stack ← ()
3:      C ← children(b)
4:      s_t ← (NEWSEMIELEMENT(b), (b))                          ▷ Rule 1
5:      s_c ← nil
6:      while true do
7:          if s_c = nil then
8:              if |C| = 0 then
9:                  break
10:             end if
11:             c ← pop(C)
12:             s_c ← (CONVERT(c), (c))
13:         end if
14:         comb_{s_c} ← NEWOPERATOR(s_t, s_c)                  ▷ Rule 2
15:         if |stack| = 0 ∨ comb_{s_c} is prior to last(stack) then
16:             push(stack, comb_{s_c})
17:             s_c ← nil
18:             continue
19:         end if
20:         comb_last ← last(stack)
21:         if comb_last can apply to s_c then
22:             s_c ← apply(comb_last, s_c)                     ▷ Conversion 1
23:             continue
24:         end if
25:         s_t ← apply(comb_last, s_t)                         ▷ Conversion 2
26:         s_c ← nil
27:     end while
28:     for all comb in reversed(stack) do
29:         s_t ← apply(comb, s_t)                              ▷ Conversion 3
30:     end for
31:     return s_t
32: end procedure
```

The algorithm is composed of 2 kinds of rules: association rules for clause and phrase, and assignment rules for semiformal description. The conversion algorithm utilizes "cases" as a grammatical information [16], which provide informations about the role of each word in a sentence, e.g. subject, object, relation, and constraints. Figure 4 shows an example of semiformal descriptions generated by the "semiformalizer". Words in a sentence are assigned as elements in an atomic proposition according to their own "cases". The "cases" are obtained from results of syntactic parsers, e.g., Stanza [17] for English, and KNP [11] for Japanese.

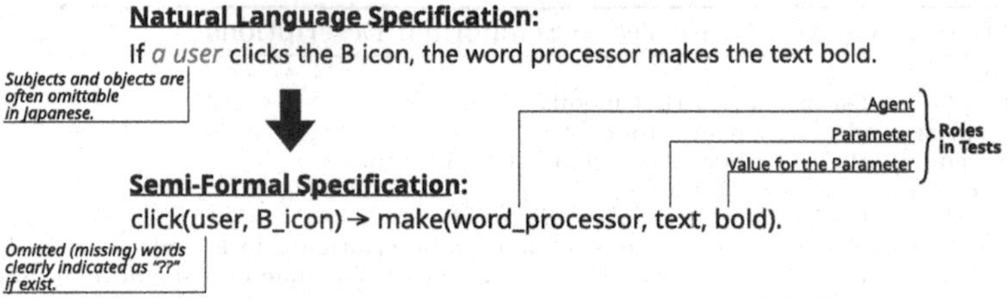

**Natural Language Specification:**

If *a user* clicks the B icon, the word processor makes the text bold.

*Subjects and objects are often omittable in Japanese.*

Agent

Parameter

Value for the Parameter

Roles in Tests

**Semi-Formal Specification:**

click(user, B_icon) → make(word_processor, text, bold).

*Omitted (missing) words clearly indicated as "??" if exist.*

**Fig. 4.** Example of semiformal description

Logical relations among the atomic propositions [12] are described with the fundamental logical symbols: "Not(!)", "And(&)", "Or(—)" and "Imply(→)". Furthermore, the following four symbols: "One", "Exclusive", "Inclusive" and "Require", are supplemented to express complex conditions among the atomic propositions. These relations are expressed by using "p_constraint" on the notation syntax shown in Fig. 5. The order of precedence among logical symbols is based on general mathematical order.

```
/* Written in Extended Backus–Naur Format (EBNF) */
statement = expression, "." ;
expression = "(", expression, ")",
    [ "<", p_constraint, { ",", p_constraint }, ">" ] |
    expression, "&", expression |   /* and */
    expression, "|", expression |   /* or */
    expression, "->", expression |  /* imply */
    "!", expression |               /* not */
    clause ;
/* the operator precedence is "!" > "&" > "|" > "->" */
clause = verb, "(", subject, ",", object,
    { ",", verb_constraint }, ")",
    [ "<", p_constraint, { ",", p_constraint }, ">" ] ;
p_constraint =
    [ "!" ], "O", "<", group_name, ">" /* One */ |
    [ "!" ], "E", "<", group_name, ">" /* Exclusive */ |
    [ "!" ], "I", "<", group_name, ">" /* Inclusive */ |
    [ "!" ], "R", "<", direction, ",",
    group_name, ">"                    /* Require */ ;
direction = "s" | "d"; /* Source or Destination */
group_name = ident;
verb = ident;
subject = ident;
object = ident;
verb_constraint = ident;
ident = /* Japanese and English Letters */;
```

**Fig. 5.** Notation rules for semiformal description

Semiformal descriptions illustrate logical relations explicitly, however, it remain still difficulty to grasp complex logical relations because of their textual notation. The "proponet" visualizes logical relations among semiformal descriptions as a propositional network (Fig. 6). In the propositional network, each atomic primitive is illustrated as an element of the network (the part encircled with broken line in Fig. 6), and logical relation among the atomic primitives, e.g. "&", "|" and "→", are depicted with structural expression defined in Fig. 6.

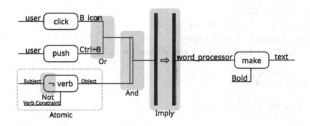

**Fig. 6.** Propositional network

The risk knowledge in the utterances is regarded as a set of statements referring to "antecedents" and "consequents" for each risk. The "semiformalizer" extracts "antecedents" and "consequents" as atomic propositions and the "proponet" expresses their relations among atomic propositions with the implication "→". The "proponet" emphasizes a boarder between "antecedents" and "consequences" as bold bars (Fig. 6). The "proponet" also provides a function to find out similar atomic propositions, and to reconfigure them as one propositional network (Algorithm 2). Figure 7 is an example of the propositional network merged on the Algorithm 2. Two antecedents "if user clicks B icon" and "if user click I icon", which result the same consequence "word processor makes text" are combined as one.

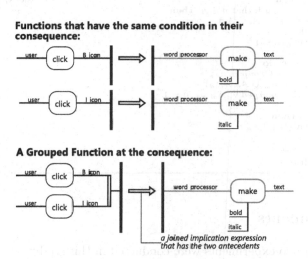

**Fig. 7.** Example for merging atomic propositions on their similarities

---

**Algorithm 2.** Combine Similar Atomic Propositions

---

**Definition:**
    $T$: a set of node types;
        $T = \{Atomic, And, Or, Imply\}$
    $n$: a node; $n = (t, A), t \in T$
    $A$: the arguments of a node;

$$A = \begin{cases} (s, o, r, C) & (t = Atomic) \\ \text{a set of nodes} & (t \neq Atomic) \end{cases}$$

    $s$: subject, $o$: object, $r$: relation, $C$: a set of constraints

**Input:**
    $n_l$: a node; $n_l = (t_l, A_l)$
    $n_r$: a node; $n_r = (t_r, A_r)$

**Output:**
    $N_m$: a set of merged nodes

1:  **procedure** Group($n_l, n_r$)
2:     $A_{new} \leftarrow \{\}$
3:     $merged \leftarrow false$
4:     **if** $t_l = t_r = Atomic$ **then**
5:         define $s_l$, $o_l$, $r_l$, and $C_l$ where $A_l = (s_l, o_l, r_l, C_l)$
6:         define $s_r$, $o_r$, $r_r$, and $C_r$ where $A_r = (s_r, o_r, r_r, C_r)$
7:         **if** $s_l = s_r \wedge o_l = o_r \wedge r_l = r_r$ **then**
8:             **return** $\{(t_l, (s_l, o_l, r_l, C_l \cup C_r))\}$
9:         **end if**
10:       **return** $\{n_l, n_r\}$                                      ▷ not merged
11:     **else if** $t_l = Atomic \vee t_r = Atomic$ **then**
12:         define $t_k$ and $A_k$ where $t_k \in \{t_l, t_r\}$, $A_k \in \{A_l, A_r\}$, and $t_k \neq Atomic$
13:         define $n_k$ where $n_k = (t_k, A_k)$
14:         **for all** $n \in A_k$ **do**
15:             $A_{merged} \leftarrow Group(n, n_k)$
16:             $A_{new} \leftarrow A_{new} \cup A_{merged}$
17:             $merged \leftarrow merged \vee |A_{merged}| = 1$
18:         **end for**
19:         **if** merged **then**
20:             **return** $\{(t_k, A_{new})\}$
21:         **end if**
22:         **return** $\{n_l, n_r\}$                             ▷ not merged
23:     **end if**
24:     **if** $t_l = t_r$ **then**                       ▷ neither $t_l$ nor $t_r$ is Atomic
25:         **if** $\exists n \in A_r$ such that $n \in A_l$ **then**
26:             **return** $(t_l, A_l \cup A_r)$
27:         **end if**
28:         **return** $\{n_l, n_r\}$                             ▷ not merged
29:     **end if**
30:     **for all** $n \in A_l$ **do**
31:         $A_{merged} \leftarrow Group(n, n_r)$
32:         $A_{new} \leftarrow A_{new} \cup A_{merged})$
33:         $merged \leftarrow merged \vee |A_{merged}| = 1$
34:     **end for**
35:     **if** $merged$ **then**
36:         **return** $\{(t_l, A_{new})\}$
37:     **end if**
38:     **return** $\{n_l, n_r\}$                                 ▷ not merged
39: **end procedure**

---

# 3   Experiments

The following two experiments were conducted in this study:

1. Eliciting risk recognition knowledge from field overseers with the tool
2. Clarifying differences of knowledge between used in the field and described in the manual

## 3.1 Experiment 1: Eliciting Risk Recognition Knowledge

We applied the tool to the risk recognition training for 12 field overseers in a construction company and collected data for their eyes and utterances during the training. The trainees were composed of 4 experts (over 20 years carriers), 4 novices (within 3 years experiences) and 4 middle_rank field overseers. The experiments were conducted on the following two steps:

1. Each trainee watched three movies, while taking memos of risks his/her noticed
2. Each trainee supplemented his/her annotations about the reasons why heshe looked the portions on the screen, referring to the trails of eyes

Three videos contained typical work scenes for the company were applied to the training. The outlines of each video are described in Fig. 8.

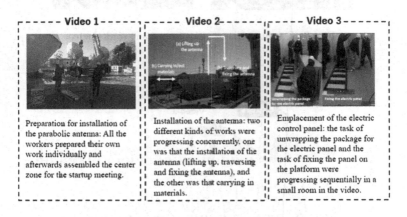

**Fig. 8.** Videos for task recognition training

**Features of Experts' Eyes and Utterances.** The differences in risk recognition between experts and novices were analyzed on the data. As the results, big differences among experts and novices both for eyes and utterances were observed [9]. The following were features for the experts:

1. Experts surveyed screen widely to grasp risks in each scene.
2. Experts perceived more than one risk and payed their attention to every risk concurrently
3. Experts not only payed their attention to immediate risks, but also care for future risks anticipated on their knowledge
4. Experts checked latent risks, e.g. hazard of weather (wind, rain, cloud), intrusion of persons not concerned the construction, effect of the workers' motivation, from the surroundings in each scene on their knowledge

Figure 9 are examples of eyes both for the expert and the novice at the same time passed 25 s from the start of the video 2. The eyes for the expert spread widely in the scenes (Fig. 9), in contrast, the novice's eyes remain in the small area relatively. Figure 10 shows the area of eyes movements in every 3 s for the expert and the novice. The expert observed larger areas in each scene, and frequently repeated extensive observations and gazes to small area more than the novice did.

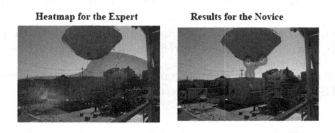

**Fig. 9.** Results of heat map for expert and novice

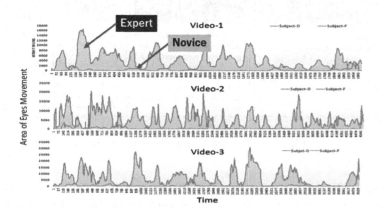

**Fig. 10.** Fluctuations of eyes for expert and novice

The video 2 contained two tasks: lifting, traversing and fixing the antenna, and carrying in/out materials. The screen was partitioned into areas [13,14] to analyze the shift of trainees' focal tasks in each scene. In case of Fig. 11, the tasks for lifting and fixing the antenna were fulfilled mainly on the areas 3, 4, 5 and 6. The task for carrying in/out materials was on the areas 2 and 4. The novices payed strong attentions (67%) to the area 3 and 4 at the scene of the lifting the antenna. On the other hand, the experts payed their attentions (33%) to the area 6, where the antenna would be fixed. At the scene of fixing the antenna, the experts shared their attentions both to the area 2 and 3 (46%) and to the area 6 (43%). The experts recognized two risk scenarios in the video and paid their attentions to these tasks concurrently. The experts also tended to predict future risks along the scenario which they perceived in the video. On the other hands, the novices kept their attentions to the area 6 (68%) and hardly payed attentions to the area 2 and 3.

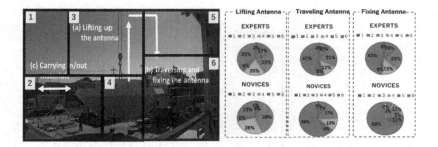

**Fig. 11.** Results for attention area in the video 2

Figure 12 is results of visualizing transition of gazed objects for expert and novice for the video 1. The expert managed his intentions on procedural knowledge [15] (Fig. 12(a)). The expert dispatched his attentions to significant objects for risk recognitions and all the objects, which he observed intentionally, were appeared in his utterances. On the other hand, the novice observed each scene exploratory on declarative knowledge [15] obtained from the manual (Fig. 12(b)). Many objects were not appeared in the novice's utterances.

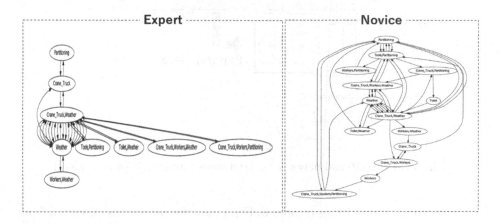

**Fig. 12.** Transitions of gazed object in the video 1

**Features of Structure of Risk Knowledge.** The logical structure of the utterances extracted from all the trainees for video 1 is drawn in Fig. 13. For example, a portion of propositional network in Fig. 13 is interpreted as the followings: (I observe weather_forecast) and (I observed distant view (tree, upper part of crane, cloud, electric wire)) imply (I recognize wind) imply (I care for weather).

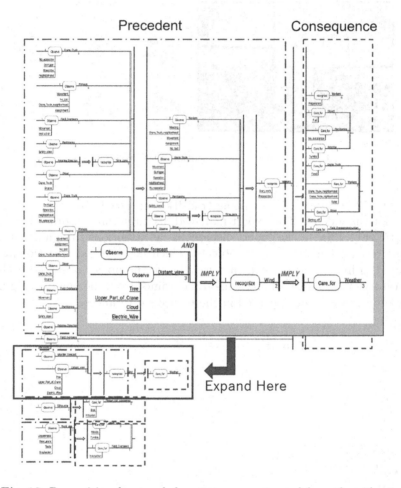

**Fig. 13.** Propositional network for utterances extracted from the video 1

The atomic propositions colored in Fig. 14 are the utterances extracted from each category of field overseers (expert, middle and novice) for the video 1. 81% propositions in the whole utterances are included in the experts' utterances (Fig. 14(a)). The omissions of the experts' utterances are concerning to the risks for objects' falling and for antenna's tumbling. These risks are too obvious to point them out for the experts in this case. 52% propositions are included in the middles' utterances (Fig. 14(b)). Almost obvious risks are pointed out in the middles' utterances. However, the latent risks for hazard of weather, effect of field overseer's skill and the workers' motivation are omitted. 32% proposition are included in the novices' utterances (Fig. 14(c)). Plenty of the obvious risks and the latent risks are omitted in the novices'.

We confirmed that the experts grasp the risk scenarios on detailed informations in the video. Most experts' propositions connect to the serious risks, which should be cared by, and contain various former propositions, which are useful to notice the serious risks. On the other hand, the propositions obtained by middles and novices contain less former proposition and the probability of noticing the serious risks relatively becomes low.

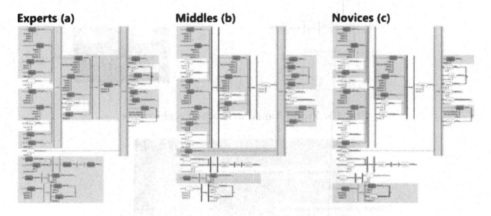

**Fig. 14.** Propositional network of each category for the video 1

The utterances for each trainee were also analyzed with the algorithm. Figure 15 is an example of the propositional network both for the traineeA (expert) and for the traineeL (novice). The novice payed his attention just to prominent objects in the video like crane and stepladder. On the other hand, the expert payed his attention to more detail objects and surroundings, like various symptoms of weather, assignment of worker, silhouette of person not concerned the construction, by utilizing his obtained knowledge as a guide line for postulating the risk scenario.

Risks were perceived on the following processes:

1. Perceive two parallel tasks (installation of antenna and carrying in materials) by observing working site widely
2. Recall risk knowledge for each tasks (sideswipe accidents between antenna and workers, intrusion of workers into prohibited area) described in the work procedure manuals

3. Suppose precedents 1 (antenna's vibration by wind, defect of partition for work area) to increase probabilities of risk occurrence
4. Recall measures to avoid risks (rope to lead antenna, standby area for workers)
5. Suppose precedent 2 to invalidate the risk avoidances (shortage of rope's length, absence of supervisor)

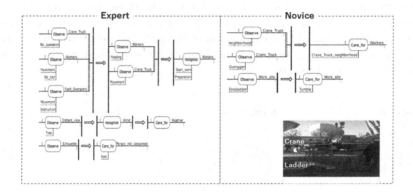

**Fig. 15.** Propositional network of each trainee

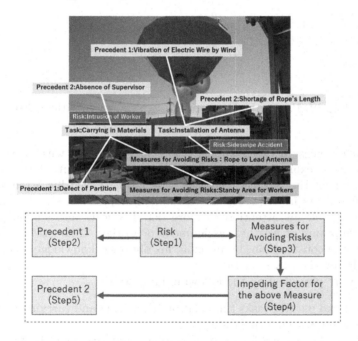

**Fig. 16.** Expert's risk recognition process

## 3.2   Experiment 2: Clarifying Differences of Knowledge Between Used in the Field and Described in the Manual

We tried to clarify differences of knowledge between used in actual field and described in a manual. The differences were explained by comparing propositional networks obtained from utterances of actual field overseers and from the manual.

**Setups for Experiment 2.** At the first step of the experiment 2, the risk recognition knowledge in the work procedures manual (Table 2) was structured as the following steps:

**Step 1:** Make a noise word dictionary, which contains nouns appearing frequently in the manual, e.g., demonstrative pronoun. "lifting" is set as initial keyword
**Step 2:** Extract all nouns, which appear in the same sentence with the key word
**Step 3:** Remove words included in the noise word dictionary from the extracted nouns in Step 2 and store them as candidates of co-occurred nouns
**Step 4:** Select a word from the candidates of co-occurred nouns and set the word as the new key words
**Step 5:** Repeat from **Step 2** to **Step 4** during new nouns being discovered or until predetermined number of repeat times
**Step 6:** Extract sentences which include the candidates of co-occurred nouns from the manual
**Step 7:** Analyze all the sentences extracted in **Step 6**, with the proposed algorithm

Table 2. Targeted work procedure manual for experiment 2

| Items | Contents |
| --- | --- |
| Targeted task | Lifting (lifting heavy load to roof) |
| Targeted Manual | Work Procedure Manual of a construction company for building facilities |
| Number of Pages | 81 pages (3 sections), 8466 morphemes |

At the second step, the utterances were elicited through the following steps from the trainees shown in Table 3

**Step 1:** Each trainee watched panoramic moving picture of 360° view with the VR headsets (Fig. 17 left)
**Step 2:** Each trainee supplemented annotations about the reasons why he/she looked the portions (Fig. 17 right)

As a result, **794 atomic propositions** are obtained as risk recognition knowledges for "Lifting heavy load to roof" from the manual, and **228 atomic propositions** are obtained through the interview on the tool.

**Table 3.** Extracting risk knowledge from field overseers

| Items | Contents |
|---|---|
| Targeted Video | Panoramic moving picture of 360° view for "lifting" |
| Trainees | 10 field overseers in a construction company<br>2 novices within 3 years experiments and 8 experts from<br>10 to 30 years experiments |
| Required time for Exam. | 30 min for each trainee<br>Step1: 10 min, Step2: 20 min |

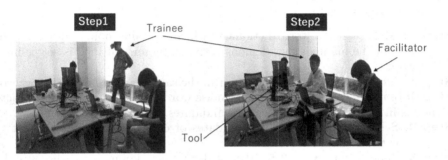

**Fig. 17.** Extracting risk recognition knowledge from field overseers

**Clarifying Differences of Knowledge Between Used in the Field and Described in the Manual.** The risk recognition knowledge both extracted from the work procedures manual and the utterances of field overseers were merged on the algorithm, after correcting orthographical variants. As a result, total of **984 atomic propositions** are obtained through the examination 2 (Fig. 18).

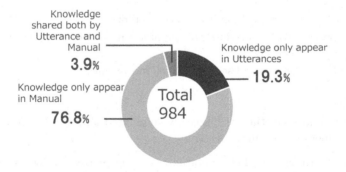

**Fig. 18.** Risk recognition knowledge from manual and utterances

Greater part of the risk recognition knowledge (**76.8%**) is obtained from the manual, slight few knowledge (**3.9%**) are shared with the knowledge obtained from the utterances and from field overseers. The proportion of the shared knowledge between the manual and the field overseers was quite small, even it takes consideration that the targeted video may not contain risk scenes described in the manual. **19.3%** of the risk recognition knowledge is only appeared in the utterances of the field overseers. The knowledge only appeared in the utterance of the field overseers is mainly regarded as portents, which increase probability of serious risks, e.g. weather conditions (wind, rain condition), traffic condition around construction site, workers' assignment, preparation of equipment required for the task, workers' moral in the site, etc.

Whole propositional network generated both from the manual and the utterances of the field overseers is shown in Fig. 19. The colored atomic propositions in Fig. 19 depict the risk recognition knowledge elicited from the utterances. Most of the knowledge only appeared in the utterances are assigned as precedents in the propositional network. Since the order of the propositional network is regarded as causeeffect relations, the knowledge located in the former position is regarded as precedents, which lead risks located in the later position.

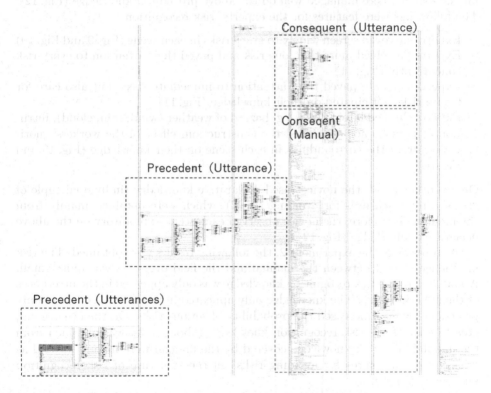

**Fig. 19.** Propositional network of risk recognition knowledge from manual and utterances

# 4    Conclusions

In this paper, the tool for promoting verbalization of latent field overseers' knowledge for risk recognition with eyes, and the algorithm for visualizing logic structure in risk knowledge as propositional network are proposed. The tool and the algorithm were applied to the risk recognition trainings for 22 actual field overseers. The following two experiments were conducted in this study:

**Experiment 1** Eliciting risk recognition knowledge from field overseers with the tool

**Experiment 2** Clarifying differences of knowledge between used in the field and described in the manual

As a result of the experiment 1, the following results were obtained. The experts utilized the structured knowledge, which is composed of 5 elements (Fig. 16), as procedural knowledge for perceiving risks and precedents. The eyes for the experts were managed well on the above procedural knowledge (Fig. 12). The followings were features for the experts' risk recognition:

- Experts surveyed screen widely to grasp risks in each scene (Fig. 9 and Fig. 10)
- Experts perceived more than one risk and payed their attention to every risk concurrently (Fig. 11)
- Experts not only payed their attention to immediate risks, but also care for future risks anticipated on their knowledge (Fig. 11)
- Experts checked latent risks, e.g. hazard of weather (wind, rain, cloud), intrusion of persons not concerned the construction, effect of the workers' motivation, from the surroundings in each scene on their knowledge (Fig. 15 and Fig. 16)

On the other hand, the novices used declarative knowledge (individual tuple of "risks" and "measures for avoiding risks"), which were obtained mainly from the manual. Therefore, the novice observed each scene exploratory on the above declarative knowledge (Fig. 12).

As a result of the experiment 2, the following results were obtained. The risk knowledge shared between the manual and the field overseers was quite small. About 20% of the risk recognition knowledge was only appeared in the utterances of the field overseers. The knowledge only appeared in the utterance was mainly precedents, which increased the probability of serious risks. On the other hand, greater part of the risk recognition knowledge (about 80%) was obtained from the manual. The risk knowledge covered by the manual were mainly located as "risks" and "measures for avoiding risks" in the structure of risk recognition knowledge (Fig. 16).

Most field overseers, both experts and novices, had obtained sufficient declarative knowledge, tuple of "risks" and "measures for avoiding risks", from the manuals. However, the procedural knowledge for perceiving precedents by utilizing the declarative knowledge, was not enough for the novices. The procedural knowledge should be disciplined through the risk recognition trainings.

Finally, we would like to answer the research questions.

1. Illustration omits indispensable information required for workers' risk recognition due to its limitation on expression:
   Yes, material for the training had better to contain surroundings and time-series changes, which is useful for obtaining procedural knowledge, in the risk recognition training. Video or panoramic moving picture of 360° are suitable for the training.
2. Practical knowledge for risk recognition is not included in the work procedures manual:
   Greater part of the risk recognition knowledge was covered by the manual. However, the knowledge of precedents for leading risks, and the procedural knowledge required for reasoning, were omitted in the manual. Parallel to the education using the work procedure manual, the risk recognition trainings is indispensable.

We will enhance the experiments so as to collect risk recognition knowledge for the other tasks appeared in the manual, and realize a practical training tool with the VR technologies. We hope our study and the risk recognition training tool developed here, will contribute to reduce industrial accidents.

# References

1. http://www.jisha.or.jp/zerosai/kyt/index.html
2. Palanyi, M.: Tacit Dimension, University of Chicago Press, Reissue edition (2009)
3. Edward, F., McCorduck, P., Penny Nyi, H.: The Rise of the Expert Company. New York Brockman Associates Inc., New York (1988)
4. Dreyfus, H.L.: Mind Over Machine: The Power of Human Intuition and Expertise in the Era of the Computer. The Free Press, New York (1986)
5. https://s3.eu-central1.mazonaws.com/theeyetribe.com/index.h
6. Kushiro, N., Nishinaga, K., Aoyama, Y., Mega, T.: Difference of risk knowledge described in work procedure manual and that used in real field by field overseers. In: 23rd International Conference on Knowledge based and Intelligent Information & Engineering Systems. Procedia Computer Science, vol. 159, pp. 1928–1937 (2019). https://doi.org/10.1016j.procs.2019.09.365
7. https://pjreddie.com/darknet/
8. https://www.graphviz.org/doc/info/lang.html
9. Kushiro, N., Fujita, Y., Aoyama, Y.: Extracting field oversees' features in risk recognition from data of eyes and utterances video based risk recognition training tool. In: IEEE International Conference on Data Mining Workshop (ICDMW) (2017)
10. Rolland, C., Achour, C.B.: Guiding the construction of textual use case specifications. Data Knowl. Eng. **25**(12), 125–160 (1998). ELSEVIR
11. Kawahara, D., Kurohashi, S.: A fully-lexicalized probabilistic model for Japanese syntactic and case structure analysis. In: Proceedings of the Human Language Technology Conference of the North American Chapter of the Association for Computational Linguistics (HLT-NAACL2006), pp. 176–183 (2006)
12. Myers, G.J., Sandler, C., Badgett, T.: The Art of Software Testing, 2nd edn., pp. 65–84. John Wiley & Sons, Hoboken (2004)

13. Horiguchi, Y.: Comparison of train driver's eye-gaze movement patterns using sequence alignment. SICE J. Control, Meas. Syst. Integr. **8**(2), 114–121 (2015)
14. Zhang, Z.: A classification method between novice and experienced drivers using eye tracking data and Gaussian process classifier. In: SICE Annual Conference 2015, vol. 2830, July 2015
15. Winograd T.: Frame Representations and the Declarative procedural Controversy, In. Bobrow and Collins (eds.) 1978
16. Maxarweh, S.: Fillmore Case Grammar: Introduction to the Theory. Grin Publishing, Munich (2010)
17. Manning, C.D., Surdeanu, M., Bauer, J., Finkel, J., Bethard, S.J., McClosky, D.: The Stanford CoreNLP natural language processing toolkit. In: Association for Computational Linguistics (ACL) System Demonstrations, pp. 55–60. http://www.aclweb.org/anthology/P/P14/P14-5010.2014

# Design and Evaluation of a Prototype
## of an Airbag-Based Wearable Safety Jacket
## for Fall Accidents in Construction
## Working Environments

Byung Cheol Lee[1]([✉]) and Byoung-Chul Ji[2]

[1] Texas A&M University Corpus Christi, 78412 Corpus Christi, TX, USA
byungcheol.lee@tamucc.edu
[2] Kyungbook National University, Daegu, South Korea
bcji@knu.ac.kr

**Abstract.** Construction workspace is identified as aggressive work environments. The number of fatalities from falls is growing continuously due to dynamic heavy objects, dangers approaching from multiple directions, trip hazards, challenging surroundings, blind spots, and irregular walk surfaces, which pose severe risks to workers' safety. Although safety training and organizational monitoring systems are required and are worked as layered protection to the workers, these are often insufficiently effective and lack of body protection systems. This study introduced a prototype of a wearable safety jacket using airbag system developed by advanced weaving technology and optimal sensor and inflator manufacturing technology. The jacket was designed to protect the human body from fall from less than the heights of 5 m without sacrificing productivity and user convenience. The fall shock absorption can be achieved by the advanced inflator system using precision sensors, and by the novel airbag design to minimize air leakage and to manufacture high durability air bag fabric against external impact. The free fall tests were conducted to evaluate the feasibility of the airbag-based wearable safety jacket and assessed the expandability and shock absorption performance among three prototypes. The test results suggested optimum airbag volume and minimum airbag expansion trigger timing to minimize impact and protect human body from falls.

**Keywords:** Fall prevention · Airbag · Construction workers · Fall detection

## 1 Introduction

Construction workspace is often considered as hazardous work environments, resulting in higher number of fatalities. Many work components such as equipment, personnel, and materials are usually moving around, and there are higher chances of falls. The largest number of casualties were caused by falling accidents in various industrial working environments. The mortality rate of the fall accidents is much higher than that of other disasters. Falls are the leading cause of both fatal and non-fatal injuries in construction workers. The high number of incidences, long-term effects, and significant

© Springer Nature Switzerland AG 2020
C. Stephanidis et al. (Eds.): HCII 2020, LNCS 12429, pp. 529–542, 2020.
https://doi.org/10.1007/978-3-030-59987-4_37

costs associated with fall-related injuries present a significant burden to our health care system and social welfare. 20% of falls result in serious injuries that may require prolonged medical care including hospitalization and rehabilitative services.

In 2015, 96% of fall fatality were attributed to falls to a lower level [1]. The number of this incidents increased 36% from 260 deaths in 2011 to 353 deaths in 2015. The rate of such deaths also increased from 3.0 to 3.6 deaths per 100,000 full-time equivalent workers during the same period. Overall, 4,439 construction workers were dead by the falls to a lower level between 2003 and 2015, about 341 deaths annually. The number of days away from work from fall injuries increased 21% from 2011 to 2015, accounting for 30% of the nonfatal injuries in construction in 2015. Falls on the same level increased faster than any other nonfatal fall injury, reaching 8,120 in 2015, a 49% increase over the 2011 level.

Effective human body protection from falls is crucial to reduce fall injuries. Occupational Safety and Health Administration (OSHA) requires employers to provide fall protection before any work that necessitates the use of fall protection begins [2]. Although safety training and instructions and organizational monitoring systems are provided as layered protection to the workers, these are often insufficiently effective. In order to prevent fall accidents, it is crucial to not only evaluate the fall risk for construction workers in a quantifiable and systematical manner but safety device minimizing harm from the fall [3]. A study based on the National Institute for Occu-pational Safety and Health (NIOSH) indicates that a large number of construction workers were dead by falls did not have access to personal wearable safety gears when the incident occurred [4]. In order to prevent disasters and deaths caused by falling accidents, there is an urgent need for the development and dissemination of effective safety gears that can be directly worn by workers while reducing the burden on additional facilities at construction sites.

As an innovative safety gear from fall accidents, an airbag-based wearable safety jacket can be suggested as a viable solution [5]. The wearable safety jacket using airbag system operates in similar processes in automotive airbags. When a fall occurs, the sensors, accelerometer or gyroscope, recognizes the fall, and the sensor send a signal to generate currents to ignite an inflating device. The time it takes is only a hundredth of a second. When ignited, a small explosion occurs in the nitrogen generator, which is quickly pushed through the filter into the airbag. It takes about 0.5 s for the airbag to fully inflate after ignition.

In this study, this paper aims to introduce a novel approach to develop a prototype of an airbag-based wearable safety jacket by an optimal inflator manufacturing and airbag design process. The joining technology of these textile and advanced sensor technology enables to make an airbag-based wearable safety jacket as a final safety layer for construction workers. This study conducted free fall tests as a feasibility test for the jacket to assess the expandability and shock absorption performance in the event of fall accidents.

## 2 Research Background

### 2.1 Current Gaps in Fall-Prevention Techniques in Construction

Occupational Safety and Health Administration (OSHA) has reported falls as the major hazard resulting in a significant number of fatalities in the construction industry [6]. Because of the prevalence of fall risks such as fatigue or worker exhaustion on constructional workplaces, OSHA regulations specifically specified these risks [7]. However, while these regulations have been helpful in reducing some fall accidents, Johnson et al. [8] found that OSHA's requirements are not enough to address fall risks for a wide range of trades that work in dangerous environments. According to Dzeng et al. [9], due to the heavy physical demands of construction works, the workers in construction industry are more prone to drowsiness, fatigue, muscle pain, distraction, and loss of balance; these factors easily lead to impaired performance, increased safety hazards, and fall accidents.

Several investigative research about fall accidents in the construction domain showed that there are viable solutions for combating and reducing fall hazards. Evidence from Im et al. [10] suggested that the importance of safety training on body balance and the physiological status of the workers can decrease the risk of loss of balance and falls. The implementation of fall protection training programs is proposed to reduce the occurrences of construction falls. Kaskutas et al. [11] identified that many novice workers are easily exposed to fall hazards and are not prepared to handle these situations. They also mentioned that fall protection procedures in work sites are inconsistently instructed and safety mentorship from experienced workers is often insufficient. A training program emphasizing the importance of communication about fall hazards was suggested, and it effectively supported to use fall protection devices or procedures, improving safety behaviors, and enhancing on-the-job training and safety communication as well as in aiding mentorship skills for prevention of construction falls [11]. Figure 1 shows the number of articles in PubMed based on the fall related keywords.

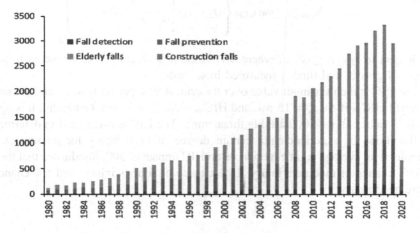

**Fig. 1.** The number of fall related articles in PubMed

The classification of fall risk by different worker group and different work environments can be suggested as an important step toward preventing fall accidents. Some people tend to fall more often than others, even in the same environment, and individuals do have different levels of fall risks [12]. A worker or a task with a high fall risk profile would be identified to implement effective fall prevention measures. However, there is still lack of objective method to evaluate the fall risks and current fall risk assessment techniques in construction mostly rely on experts' judgment or qualitative means [13]. Several assessment tools to measure the fall risk by the gait stability have been introduced and particularly used in clinical applications, including Detrended Fluctuation Analysis [14], Stride Interval Dynamics [15], Maximum Lyapunov exponents [16], and Maximum Floquet Multipliers [17]. While these approaches have proven useful in clinical settings, their feasibility for characterizing fall risks in a dynamic construction environment has not been demonstrated enough. It is necessary to develop a direct means of measuring the construction workers' fall risks.

## 2.2  Head Injury Criterion (HIC) and Injury Risk in the Airbag Evaluation

Head Injury Criterion (HIC) is a one of major metrics developed for assessing automotive safety. It quantifies the potential for head injury by a function of magnitude and time duration of head acceleration [18]. The HIC, one of injury assessment values, is calculated from measurements, such as forces or accelerations, taken on human subjects or crash test dummies. Experiments must be performed to validate and calibrate the relationship between an injury index and the risk of an injury of a specified severity under certain test conditions. The HIC metric was originally developed for automotive applications to measure the safety performance of airbags, but recently applied to other domains such as sports equipment manufacturing and human-robot interaction. The HIC can be computed as follows:

$$\text{HIC } (\Delta t_{max}) = max_{t1,t2}\left\{ (t_2 - t_1)\left[\frac{1}{t_2 - t_1}\int_{t_1}^{t_2} a(t)dt\right]^{2.5}\right\},$$

Subject to $t_2 - t_1 \leq \Delta t_{max}$, where $a(t)$ is the head acceleration measured in acceleration of gravity and time is measured in seconds.

The HIC is the maximum value over the critical time period $t_1$ to $t_2$, and the results are called $\text{HIC}_{15}$ if $\Delta t_{max} = 15$ ms, and $\text{HIC}_{36}$ if $\Delta t_{max} = 36$ ms. Generally, it is agreed that HIC values above 1000 are life threatening. The HIC is often used in determining the likelihood of experiencing a certain degree of head injury for an impact. For example, if an average adult experiences an HIC impact of 500, it indicates that there is an 45% chance of moderate injury, 15% chance of serious injury, and 5% chance of severe head injury

The HIC values can be more comprehensible correlating to the abbreviated injury scale (AIS), which classify the severity of injuries by the body regions. The AIS ranges from AIS 0, meaning "no injury," to AIS 6, meaning "virtually unsurvivable injury." The HIC has been validated as a predictor for skull fracture and brain injury of certain severities. HIC is an injury index that correlates to the risk of AIS $\geq$ 2 skull fracture and AIS $\geq$ 4 brain injury [19]. Mertz et al. [19] suggested the conversion from HIC to a risk estimate, which is based on experiments that recorded of the presence or absence of skull fracture and brain hemorrhage. However, since it is unclear what data has been used to justify the expanded classification curves between AIS and HIC values, the conversion of HIC to a risk of minor injury (AIS = 1) or virtually unsurvivable injury (AIS = 6) may lack experimental verification. Due to the uncertainties involved, it is standard practice in automotive safety assessment to round HIC to the nearest integer [20].

## 2.3 Airbag System for Human Body Protection

Airbag systems have become an essential safety device for guaranteeing the physical well-being of drivers and their passengers. Unlike other safety devices, airbags are used as the final layer in a collision, and because they are directly linked to the life of the driver and passengers, the proper functioning of the system is a critical to protect human body in collision accidents. Airbag systems are not only applicable in vehicle safety but also other industrial sites to protect human body or life from various collision and fall accidents.

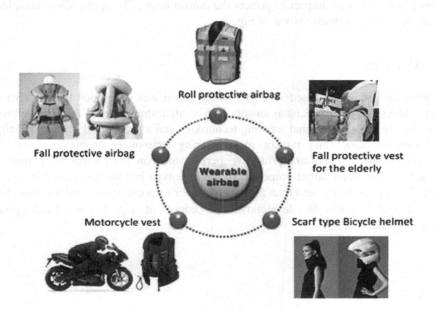

**Fig. 2.** Applications of wearable airbag systems

The research on the air bag system for the protection of the human body is continuously progressed beyond the application of vehicle airbag products. Among them, an airbag-inner protective vest composed of a polyurethane tube with a compressed air cylinder was developed using an air distribution structure to protect human body from the fall accidents [21]. A motorcycle driver's airbag has been recommended, and all riders in the professional motorcycle racing are now required to wear a protective suit equipped with a functioning airbag system. The motorcycle driver's protective suit is made up of nylon material that protects the driver by expanding the suit with the same principle as an aircraft life vest while pulling the straps connected to the motorcycle. An advanced model has been developed to adopt an autonomous system without straps or cables connected to the motorcycle, and it includes an electronic system detecting a fall and triggering the inflation of the nitrogen airbags to protect the rider's upper body [22].

The wearable safety device using airbag system can be divided by its types of impact: collision detection and fall detection. A collision detection wearable air bag works similar to vehicle air bag. This air bag is mainly used for two-wheeled vehicles and instantly expands automatically when the occupants are bounced off from the two-wheeler in case of an accident, protecting the human body from external impacts. A fall detection air bag protects the human body by inflating momentarily when the worker working in high altitude of construction site or shipbuilding. A fall detection air bag also can absorb fall impacts causing fractures and protect the elderly or horse riders. A fall detection air bag requires an algorithm to classify various human behaviors and to detect fall from other human body movements. These air bag systems function that airbags are expanded through instant injection of air by the inflator when necessary to absorb the temporary impact to protect the human body. The application examples of wearable airbag systems shown in Fig. 2.

## 3 Methods

A prototype of airbag-based wearable safety jacket was developed by the advanced textile technology and precision sensors with an algorithm to detect falls and rollovers. Specifically, a 3-dimensional weaving technology and a specialized coating technique, and optimal sensor and inflator manufacturing technology enable to detect falls accurately and to maximize protective performance on the human body from fall accidents. The major target properties of the prototype include less than 0.07 cc/cm$^2$/min of air permeability, less than 200 ms of sensor response speed, and less than 1,000 HIC. Figure 3 shows the development procedures of a prototype of airbag-based wearable safety jacket.

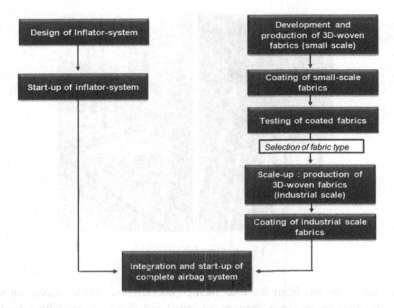

**Fig. 3.** Development procedures of a prototype of airbag-based wearable safety jacket

The main function the jacket is to expand an airbag in the jacket before the worker's body hitting the ground. The jacket needs to react after about 1 m of free fall and to expand the airbag after 1.5 meters. At least from 2 meters of the height, the jacket should be fully inflated to exert its full protective effect. The response time was calculated with a scenario of falling a person with a weight of 85 kg, and basic design properties of the prototype were analyzed to satisfy the minimum deployment condition of the airbag expansion. According to the calculation, it takes about 680 ms for a person with falling at a height of 2.3 m, and the target response time of the sensor was determined at 200 ms. The target response time is computed to reach adequate air pressure in the airbag, which can sufficiently dampen the impact energy generated from the fall to the ground. This impact energy can be decreased by the negative acceleration obtained by the airbag, and HIC value indicates the hazards of the deceleration process. In general, it is evaluated that the HIC value should not exceed 1000, so as not to cause fatal damage to the body.

For the evaluation of the airbag system performance, the free fall test was conducted at a test bench. The free fall test is commonly used for assessing human body protective performance of airbags from fall impact. The test was conducted at the tested bench that is shown in Fig. 4. In the test, an airbag is placed in the center of the floor, and air is injected through the air inlet of the airbag through a pipe. After the test, HIC is calculated based on the acceleration of falling the plate when the integrated value of the acceleration is maximized.

**Fig. 4.**  Free fall test facility

The data collected from the tests include deceleration due to impact on inflated textile structure, air pressure changes by initial inflation volume, falling height and volume as well as shape of textile structure, and damage of textile structure. The fall tests were carried out at three different initial air pressures, 0.2 bar, 0.4 bar and 0.6 bar, in the inflated textile structure. The deceleration values were used to determine the HIC. Basic physical properties for the falling test are shown in Table 1.

**Table 1.**  Basic physical properties for airbag design

| Physical Property | | |
|---|---|---|
| Load (kg) | 85 | |
| Height (m) | 2.30 | 5.00 |
| Drop time (sec) | 0.68 | 1.01 |
| Velocity at impact (m/s) | 6.7 | 9.9 |
| Kinetic energy (J) | 1918 | 4170 |
| Braking time at bearable acceleration (a*) (ms) | 17 | 25 |
| Deformation distance (cm) | 5.75 | 12.5 |
| Force at impact (N) | 33,350 | |
| Fabric area of impact | 0.01 | |
| Momentary airbag pressure (bar) | 33 | |

\* Maximum bearable acceleration, $a_{3ms,Head} = 80\,g$, $a_{3ms,Breast} = 60\,g$

Based on above physical properties, HIC is calculated and represents the level of impacting damage on human body. Generally, the standard HIC value that can protect the human body from fall impact should be maintained less than 1000, which means that the airbag system can protect a human body without significant damages. Since physical property requirements related to inflation characteristics such as the actual expansion volume, pressure (gas cylinder pressure, maximum airbag pressure, etc.), and expansion retention time are very difficult to control through actual test conditions, they were determined based on the basic values through theoretical calculations. Therefore, basic design specifications for the form factor or volume of the airbag could not be optimized by the data collected from the tests and were determined by try and error approach.

## 4  Results and Discussion

### 4.1  Fall Detection Sensor-Based Inflator

We developed a prototype of the airbag-based safety jacket using a fall detection sensor-based inflator and high-pressure resistant airbag textile. The inflator includes a fall detection sensor detecting a fall above a predetermined height, a compressed air cartridge that can instantly inflate the airbag, and a trigger sensor that activates the inflator through a signal from the fall detection sensor. Figure 5 shows components of the inflator.

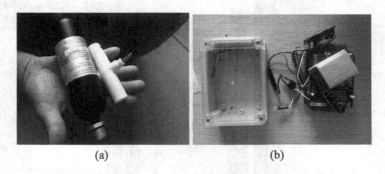

(a)                                          (b)

**Fig. 5.** (a) Compressed air cartridge and (b) fall detection sensor unit

The fall detection sensor was developed using the Arduino® platform system and the 9-axis kinematic sensor. It was designed to be responded by the signal within 200 ms. The inflator detects the signals from the fall detection sensor, and the signals were generated when the wearer falls at a predetermined height and when an accelerometer was reached at the trigger set value. The electric signal opened the compressed air gas cylinder to expand the airbag. The calculated level of acceleration and deceleration and the timing of the airbag expansion significantly affect to secure a safe HIC value to protect human body from falls. They also provide the specification of the airbag volume and the physical properties of the jacket.

## 4.2    Airbag Internal Pressure and Airbag Volume

Considering the overall functions of the airbag-based safety jacket, the internal air pressure in the airbag has a critical effect on the HIC. Basically, HIC can be decreased by the integrated value of acceleration by the degree of acceleration and/or deceleration within the airbag inflating period during a fall. The internal air pressure is an important metric to inflate airbag enough to protect the falling human body. As the inlet of the high-pressure gas bottle is opened by the electric signal detected by the sensor, and the adiabatic expanded high-pressure air enters the air bag through designed paths, and then the internal pressure of the airbag can be reached and maintained at an appropriate constant pressure. Since the airbag pressure is determined by the ratio of the volume of the high-pressure gas in the bottle to the volume of the air bag, the volume is one of the most important dimensioning specifications for determining HIC value. In addition, the smaller the volume of the airbag can reduce the weight of the gas bottle, so the overall weight can be reduced and the wearability will be improved. The minimum volume of the airbag can be limited by the deformation caused by a fall which is about 12.5 cm from 5 m fall with estimated acceleration of 40 g ($392.4$ m/sec$^2$). The HIC value in this case can be maintained at less than 700, and the airbag can be safely recovered by 99%. Figure 6 shows exemplary designs of airbags that were considered in developing the prototypes of the safety jacket.

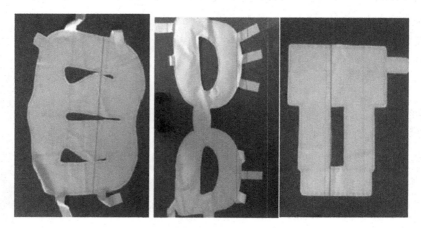

**Fig. 6.** Airbag design samples for Airbag based safety jacket

## 4.3    Free Fall Test

The free fall tests were conducted for two airbags for airbag-based safety jacket. Table 2 shows the designs and 3D models for two airbags. Among several potential designs, we choose the scaffold bag, and the volume of the airbags were determined to 32 L and 16 L.

**Table 2.** Two airbags for airbag-based safety jacket for free fall test

| Model | P1 | P2 |
|---|---|---|
| Volume (liter) | 32 | 16 |
| Design | | |
| 3D Model | | |

Figure 7 shows the results of free fall test for airbags prototypes. The HIC value decreased as the volume of the airbag increased, but the impact of airbag overpressure was not significant in all three prototypes. Except overpressure of 0.2 bar with 4 m fall, HIC values of P1 airbag prototype were maintained less than 1000, which is the criterion for safe human body protection. The P2 prototype was effective only less than 3 m falls. Instead of tightness of the airbag, overall volume would be more critical design aspect. The free fall results apparently demonstrated the performance of the airbag jacket highly depends on fall heights, and the HIC values are significantly different by fall heights. More investigation on effective fall heights are required as a future study.

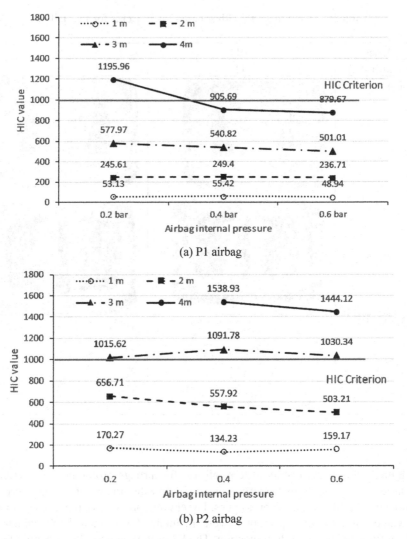

**Fig. 7.** Free fall test results for airbags: (a) P1 airbag (32 $\ell$) and (b) P2 airbag (16 $\ell$)

## 5  Conclusions

This study introduced a prototype of a wearable safety jacket using airbag system developed by advanced weaving technology and optimal sensor and inflator manu-facturing technology. The safety jacket was designed to protect the human body from fall from less than the heights of 5 m with an airbag that is expanded by an algorithm developed by precision sensor signals. The algorithm enables fall detection sensor to be responded by the signal within 200 ms. The response time to inflate the airbag and its volume are critical design metrics. The airbag was designed to deform the airbag less than 12.5 cm by the 5 m fall with estimated acceleration of 40 g. The fall shock absorption can be achieved by the novel airbag design, and it minimized air leakage and is manufactured by high durable fabric against external impact. The free fall tests were conducted to evaluate the feasibility of the airbag-based wearable safety jacket and assessed the expandability and shock absorption performance among three prototypes. A 32-liter volume airbag prototype showed enough safety performance in less than 4 m fall, but a 16-liter airbag showed insufficient HIC values (less than 1,000). The test results suggested optimum airbag volume and minimum airbag expansion trigger timing to minimize impact and protect human body from falls.

# References

1. Trauner, T.J., Lowe, S., Nagata, M.F., Manginelli, W.A.: Construction Delays. Elsevier (2017)
2. Kang, Y., Siddiqui, S., Suk, S.J., Chi, S., Kim, C.: Trends of fall accidents in the US construction industry. J. Constr. Eng. Manag. **143**(8), 04017043 (2017)
3. Sousa, V., Almeida, N.M., Dias, L.A.: Risk-based management of occupational safety and health in the construction industry–Part 1: Background knowledge. Saf. Sci. **66**, 75–86 (2014)
4. Dong, X.S., Largay, J.A., Choi, S.D., Wang, X., Cain, C.T., Romano, N.: Fatal falls and PFAS use in the construction industry: findings from the NIOSH FACE reports. Accid. Anal. Prev. **102**, 136–143 (2017)
5. Teizer, J., Allread, B.S., Fullerton, C.E., Hinze, J.: Autonomous pro-active real-time construction worker and equipment operator proximity safety alert system. Automat. Constr. **19**(5), 630–640 (2010)
6. Jebelli, H., Ahn, C.R., Stentz, T.L.: Fall risk analysis of construction workers using inertial measurement units: validating the usefulness of the postural stability metrics in construction. Saf. Sci. **84**, 161–170 (2016)
7. Jebelli, H.: Assessing gait and postural stability of construction workers using wearable wireless sensor networks (2015)
8. Johnson, H.M., Singh, A., Young, R.H.: Fall protection analysis for workers on residential roofs. J. Constr. Eng. Manag. **124**(5), 418–428 (1998)
9. Dzeng, R.-J., Fang, Y.-C., Chen, I.-C.: A feasibility study of using smartphone built-in accelerometers to detect fall portents. Automat. Constr. **38**, 74–86 (2014)
10. Im, H.-J., Kwon, Y.-J., Kim, S.-G., Kim, Y.-K., Ju, Y.-S., Lee, H.-P.: The characteristics of fatal occupational injuries in Korea's construction industry, 1997–2004. Saf. Sci. **47**(8), 1159–1162 (2009)
11. Kaskutas, V., Dale, A.M., Lipscomb, H., Evanoff, B.: Fall prevention and safety communication training for foremen: report of a pilot project designed to improve residential construction safety. J. Safety Res. **44**, 111–118 (2013)
12. Liu, J., Zhang, X., Lockhart, T.E.: Fall risk assessments based on postural and dynamic stability using inertial measurement unit. Safety Health Work **3**(3), 192–198 (2012)
13. Helander, M.G.: Safety hazards and motivation for safe work in the construction industry. Int. J. Ind. Ergon. **8**(3), 205–223 (1991)
14. Herman, T., Giladi, N., Gurevich, T., Hausdorff, J.M.: Gait instability and fractal dynamics of older adults with a "cautious" gait: why do certain older adults walk fearfully? Gait Posture **21**(2), 178–185 (2005)
15. Jordan, K., Challis, J.H., Newell, K.M.: Walking speed influences on gait cycle variability. Gait Posture **26**(1), 128–134 (2007)

16. Chang, M.D., Sejdić, E., Wright, V., Chau, T.: Measures of dynamic stability: detecting differences between walking overground and on a compliant surface. Hum. Mov. Sci. **29**(6), 977–986 (2010)
17. Bruijn, S.M., Bregman, D.J., Meijer, O.G., Beek, P.J., Van Dieen, J.H.: The validity of stability measures: a modelling approach. J. Biomech. **44**(13), 2401–2408 (2011)
18. Gao, D., Wampler, C.W.: Head injury criterion. IEEE Robot. Autom. Mag. **16**(4), 71–74 (2009)
19. Mertz, H.J., Prasad, P., Irwin, A.L.: Injury risk curves for children and adults in frontal and rear collisions. SAE Trans. 3563–3580 (1997)
20. Simoni, P., Ostendorf, R., Cox, A.J.: Effect of air bags and restraining devices on the pattern of facial fractures in motor vehicle crashes. Archives Facial Plastic Surgery **5**(1), 113–115 (2003)
21. Fukaya, K., Uchida, M.: Protection against impact with the ground using wearable airbags. Ind. Health **46**(1), 59–65 (2008)
22. McKeegan, N.: Dainese tests electronically operated airbag system for motorcycle racing. https://newatlas.com/dainese-d-air-motorcycle-airbag/8710/. Accessed 06 March 2020

# The Effect of Break on Discomfort and Variation in EMG Activities While Using a Smartphone: A Preliminary Study in a Chinese University Population

Peilin Li[1], Yi Wang[1], Yi Ding[1,2(✉)], Yaqin Cao[1,2],
and Vincent G. Duffy[2]

[1] School of Management Engineering, Anhui Polytechnic University,
Wuhu, People's Republic of China
fengdulpl@163.com, caoyaqin.2007@163.com,
xxr0912@gmail.com, emiledy@sina.com
[2] School of Industrial Engineering, Purdue University, West Lafayette, IN, USA
duffy@purdue.edu

**Abstract.** (1) Background: Despite the substantial increase in the number of adolescent smartphone users, few studies have investigated the behavioral effects of smartphone use on adolescent students as it relates to musculoskeletal discomfort; (2) Methods: The aim of our study was to estimate the prevalence of musculoskeletal symptoms in university students and determine the relationship between smartphone use and musculoskeletal symptoms among this population through an online survey. Considering the dynamic and cumulative characteristics of muscle activities, the most common body parts reported discomfort in the survey were selected to gauging muscle activities during smartphone use by collecting surface EMG signals. Then, according to the changing of muscle activities, a comparison experiment was conducted to give an intervention to eliminate the probability of occurrence of muscle discomfort; (3) Results: Neck/shoulder, arms, upper back, wrist/hand, and low back were the most commonly reported muscle locations with discomfort/pain; in the EMG experiment, a 10-min rest after 30-min smartphone usage was effective to keep the EMG activity at a relatively stable state; (4) Conclusions: This study offers the possibility of being applied to smartphone users and provides preliminary data support and theoretical exploration for follow-up early muscle fatigue detection system.

**Keywords:** Musculoskeletal discomfort · Surface EMG · Smartphone use · Adolescent · Intervention

## 1 Introduction

The smartphone has been one of the most used devices in our daily life. People can read news, play games, shop online, and chat with each other with social networks and so forth with just a smartphone. Smartphones have become the first things people reach for after waking up in the morning [1, 2]. However, along with this rise of mobile handheld device use, there is a growing concern about the potential adverse effects on

© Springer Nature Switzerland AG 2020
C. Stephanidis et al. (Eds.): HCII 2020, LNCS 12429, pp. 543–556, 2020.
https://doi.org/10.1007/978-3-030-59987-4_38

mental and physical health for prolonged mobile hand-held use [3–7]. Phrases have been coined such as "Cellular phone neck" for smartphone overuse and lots of studies explored the factors causing overuse behavior. The use of a mobile hand-held device has been linked with muscle disorders, although causal relationships between mobile use and muscle disorders have not yet been established [5, 7–9].

Many studies have investigated the risk factors associated with sedentary behavior or VDTs (visual display terminals) work for about three decades. Three major psychosocial factors related to musculoskeletal symptoms are divided into task difficulty, psychological stress, and lack of social support [9–11]. Punnett and Bergqvist [12] reviewed the epidemiological studies of muscle disorders among computer workers, and reported that computer work indicated higher risk of neck, shoulder, arm, wrist, and hand musculoskeletal illness than non-computer work. People have paid considerable attention to the possibility of musculoskeletal symptoms working with VDTs or sedentary behavior. Similar to computer work, mobile hand-held device use may contribute to the risk of muscle fatigue and pain in neck and shoulders [8]. Compared with computer work, people usually need less force when typing on a touchscreen keyboard [13]. Moreover, people can use a mobile hand-held device anywhere even walking. In this condition, people need to hold their hands in a static posture and look sharply downwards when using smartphones. People may perceive cervical extensor muscle strain with a lower display location [14–16]. With the popularization of mobile hand-held devices, more attention should be paid to the risk of musculoskeletal symptoms for prolonged mobile hand-held devices use.

Recently, a few epidemiological studies have investigated the prevalence rate of muscle disorders associated with mobile hand-held devices use [17]. Cohen [18] reported the prevalence rates of nearly 50% in some degree of neck symptoms in both children and adults. A Canada study has reported that 84% of university students reported pain in at least one body part [19]. Kwok et al. [20] investigated the perceived outcomes related to smart device use from 960 adolescents, and they reported that the one-week prevalence of perceived musculoskeletal disorders was nearly 40%. To the best of our knowledge, a handful of studies have quantitatively investigated muscle activities when using different mobile hand-held devices with various screen sizes. Xie et al. [17, 21] compared muscle activities in using smartphones between people with neck-shoulder pain and people without neck-shoulder pain by analyzing surface EMG (electromyography) signals. They reported that higher activities in neck extensor and thumb muscles were obtained in smartphone texting. Guan et al. [16] investigated the gender difference of head and neck flexion when young adults using mobile phones. They found that male participants had a significantly larger head and neck flexions than females. The other two studies from Lee, Kang and Shin [22] and Ning et al. [9] explored the neck flexion when participants operating smartphones, and they found that significantly deeper head flexion in texting messages. Gustafsson et al. [23] compared the thumb kinematics and upper limb muscle activities when texting on a keypad and a touchscreen smartphone by using 3D motion analysis and surface EMG. Significantly lower activities (50th and 90th percentile) of the thumb and forearm muscles and less thumb flexion were obtained when users using a touchscreen smartphone compared to a keypad phone. However, how does the muscle activity change with the smartphone time continuing? And what should the users do to prevent muscle symptoms? These problems have not been thoroughly investigated either.

Therefore, our study aimed to estimate the prevalence of musculoskeletal symptoms in China university students and determine the relationship between smartphone use and musculoskeletal symptoms among this population. Considering the dynamic and cumulative characteristics of the muscle activity, the most common body parts were selected to gauging muscle activities during the process of touchscreen smartphone use. Then, according to changes in muscle activities, a comparison experiment was conducted to give an intervention to eliminate the probability of occurrence of muscle discomfort. The hypotheses of this study are: (1) Higher muscle activity will be obtained with the device use continuing; (2) The muscle activity will significantly decrease after intervention.

## 2 Preliminary Study

A preliminary study with an internet-based questionnaire was conducted to collect self-report musculoskeletal symptoms in upper extremity, neck, upper back, and visual symptoms from 489 students (235 females and 254 males, aging from 17–35 years, Mage = 23.9 years, SDage = 5.8) at a Chinese university between April 10 and May 7 in 2018. Then 47 questionnaires were deleted for the completion time less than 120 s and outliers of the data via the boxplot [24]. At last, the data was from 442 students and faculty (230 males and 212 females, aging from 17–35 years, Mage = 25.7 years, SDage = 6.8).

The general characteristics of the participants were presented in Table 1. The results showed that 86.02% of users continuously use a smartphone for 1–2 h in a weekday. Therefore, the experiment duration was set for 2 h. Most of the users use a smartphone with a sitting posture. Hence, the task duration was set 2 h in the EMG measurement experiment and users use a smartphone with a sitting posture (Sect. 3.3). Also, the three most commonly used purpose of smartphone were chatting, news browsing and video watching, which were selected as the tasks in the EMG experiment.

The survey results showed that neck, shoulder, back and upper extremity are the most common locations of perceived pain or discomfort (Fig. 1). Hence, the upper trapezius and the latissimus dorsi were chosen to record the EMG activities during smartphones use.

Also, we analyzed the relationship between items in Table 2. The results showed that there was no relationship between the screen size of smartphones and perceived muscle discomfort. Therefore, participants used their own smartphones to do tasks in the EMG experiment. Perceived muscle discomfort was significantly correlated with smartphone use hours, and 30 min was set as the intervention time when subjects using smartphones.

**Table 1.** The general characteristics of the subjects

| Characteristics | Categories | n | % |
|---|---|---|---|
| Height | M ± SD | 168.6 ± 8.69 | |
| Weight | M ± SD | 61.8 ± 12.78 | |
| BMI | <18.5 | 13.8% | |
| | [18.5, 24) | 68.8% | |
| | ≥ 24 | 17.4% | |
| The duration of continuous smartphone use | <30 min | 34 | 7.8% |
| | 30−60 min | 53 | 12.1% |
| | 60−90 min | 136 | 30.69% |
| | 90−120 min | 157 | 35.43% |
| | ≥ 120 min | 62 | 13.98% |
| Smartphone screen size (inch) | 4 inches | 17 | 3.8% |
| | 4.5 inches | 88 | 19.9% |
| | 5 inches | 132 | 29.9% |
| | 5.5 inches | 158 | 35.7% |
| | more than 5.5 inches | 47 | 10.6% |
| Posture of Smartphone use | Sitting | 324 | 73.3% |
| | Standing | 25 | 5.7% |
| | Laying on the back | 38 | 8.6% |
| | Laying on the face | 9 | 2.0% |
| | others | 46 | 10.4% |
| Purpose of Smartphone use | News browsing | 301 | 68.1% |
| | Listening to music | 250 | 56.6% |
| | Playing games | 170 | 38.5% |
| | Chatting | 355 | 80.3% |
| | Purchasing | 207 | 46.8% |
| | Document processing | 120 | 27.1% |
| | Watching video | 280 | 63.3% |
| | others | 112 | 25.3% |

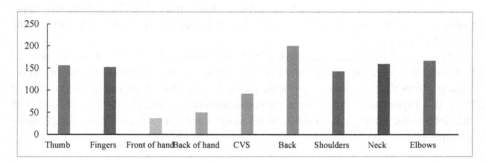

**Fig. 1.** Reports of muscle discomfort from smartphone users.

**Table 2.** Correlation coefficients between multiple measures

| Indexes | Hand | Neck | Back | Shoulder | Elbow | Eyes | Use hours | LCD size | BMI | Age |
|---|---|---|---|---|---|---|---|---|---|---|
| Hand | 1 | | | | | | | | | |
| Neck | .286** | 1 | | | | | | | | |
| Back | .443** | .244** | 1 | | | | | | | |
| Shoulder | .282** | .652** | .249** | 1 | | | | | | |
| Elbow | .519** | .145** | .616** | .179** | 1 | | | | | |
| Eyes | .040 | −.014 | .057 | .007 | .088 | 1 | | | | |
| Use hours | .118** | .094* | .143** | .078 | .106* | .048 | 1 | | | |
| LCD size | −.021 | .079 | -.003 | .029 | −.025 | −.130** | .153** | 1 | | |
| BMI | .105* | 0.011 | −.014 | −.023 | 0.013 | -.057 | −.022 | .116* | 1 | |
| Age | .068 | 0.011 | .073 | .002 | .066 | .105* | −.280** | −.042 | .214** | 1 |

Note: *p < 0.05, **p < 0.01.

## 3 EMG Measurement and Muscle Discomfort

### 3.1 Participants

We recruited 16 university students (half men, 20 to 25 years old, Mage = 23.25 years, SDage = 1.18) to participate the EMG signals measurement experiment. They are all right-handed, healthy individuals with normal or corrected-to-normal vision, without a history of musculoskeletal, neurological, or vascular problems that hinder the ability to perform phubbing for more than 2 h. None of the participants were allergic to the electrodes used in the experiment. They all had a good rest and had no strenuous exercise before the experiment. The participants' mean height and weight (±SD) were 168.2 (±8.1) cm and 61.0 (±9.8) kg, respectively. Here, the difference between groups was not investigated, so participants who use a smartphone per weekday for only lower than 3 h were selected. All participants provided written informed consent forms before the experiment and received a gift as compensation.

### 3.2 Experimental Design

Firstly, participants were asked to sit in a quiet room with normal light. The environmental conditions were also controlled with soft light (125LX ± 5 LX) to eliminate the impact of light on participants' subjective perception. The microclimatic environment was set at a comfortable level with a temperature of 24 ± 0.9°C and a relative humidity of 30.2 ± 2%. Some physiological measures concerning workload measurement or prediction are sensitive to temperature, e.g., humidity, age, sex, time of day, and season [25]. Therefore, the environmental conditions during the experiment were remained constant to eliminate the impact of the task environment as much as possible. One of the most popular posture in smartphone use is siting, and most users use smartphones with a continuous using time of 1 ~ 2 h from the preliminary survey. Hence, the surface EMG signals were collected from participants in a sitting posture for using smartphone in 2 h.

Then electrodes were put on the subject's skin and the experiment was introduced to the subjects. They were asked to browsing Wechat moments, watching entertaining videos and reading news. Each kind of task lasted for half an hour, and after each task, the participant had a 10 min rest. The participants were not required to have substantial body shaking during the smartphone use. The participant's muscle discomfort was measured with Borg's CR-10 scale [26] every 30 min (marked as T0, T1, T2, and T3) and had a break for about 10 min (marked as B1, B2, and B3). The screen size had nothing to do with the muscle discomfort from the preliminary survey, so participants used their own smartphones in the experiment. The experiment was conducted between May and July 2019.

### 3.3    EMG Signals Recording and Analysis

EMG signals were recorded by using the ErgoLAB man-machine-environment synchronization platform (Beijing Kingfar technology co. LTD, China). EMG signals were collected by non-invasive wearable sensors from the latissimus dorsi muscle and the trapezius muscle based on the preliminary survey. Three Kangren® pre-gelled disposable AgCl electrodes with an active area of 6.15 mm$^2$ (Type: CH3236TD) were placed on the right and left upper trapezius muscles with a distance of 20 mm between the center of the middle electrode and the center of each of the two lateral (active) electrodes. And three electrodes were placed along the muscle fiber of the latissimus dorsi muscle. The reference electrode was placed at the center of the two active electrodes. The sample rate of EMG was 1024 Hz with a band-pass filter of $5 \sim 500$ Hz and a noise level of 1.6 μV. The root mean square (RMS) of the signal was determined

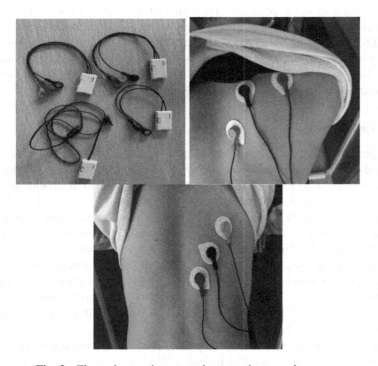

**Fig. 2.** Electrodes, equipment and posture in smartphone use.

using a time constant of 120 ms. All electrode impedances were maintained below 5 kΩ during the experiment. Skin was prepared to reduce impedance by using scrubbing cream and cotton swab (Fig. 2).

Raw EMG signals were recorded during the experiment as well as 5 min before the experiment. The recorded raw data were processed with electrocardiography (ECG) reduction and full-wave rectification. They were then averaged within 200 ms to determine RMS marked by Yrms. In spectrum frequency analysis, the fast Fourier transform was used to estimate the MF. The signal processing was conducted by using ErgoLAB man-machine-environment synchronization platform (Beijing Kingfar technology co. LTD, China). Then, repeated-measures analysis of variance (ANOVA) was used to examine the effects of time-varying on subjective ratings and physiological parameters. Violation of sphericity was handled with a Greenhouse–Geisser correction and the effect size (eta squared $\eta^2$) is reported for all ANOVAs. A paired t-test was used to analyze the pairwise comparisons. The data analysis was carried out using SPSS version 24.0 (IBM Corporation, Armonk, NY, USA). Pearson's correlation was calculated to identify the relationships between different measures. Statistical significance for all tests was set at $p < 0.05$. Data outliers were deleted using boxplots [24].

## 4   Results

### 4.1   Perceived Muscle Discomfort

We collected the subjective ratings of perceived discomfort every 30 min. The result was showed in Fig. 3. The subjective ratings of muscle discomfort were 5.15 (SD = 1.17), 6.30 (SD = 1.15) and 7.50 (SD = 2.01) for varied time. The repeat ANOVA result showed that time had the main effect on the subjective rating of muscle discomfort with $F(2,30) = 156.24$, $p < 0.001$, $\eta2 = 0.912$. The post hoc analysis showed higher ratings with smartphone use for $d = -2.19$, $p < 0.001$ and $d = -4.44$, $p < 0.001$. Hence, from the subjective ratings, we can see that the break after 30 min of smartphone use did not affect users' subjective perception of muscle discomfort.

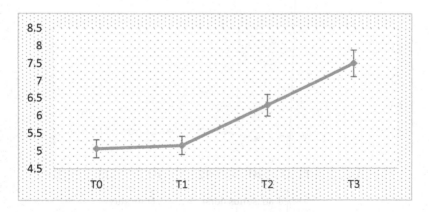

**Fig. 3.** The subjective rating of muscle discomfort with time-varying.

## 4.2    EMG Variation During Smartphone Use and Break

EMG activities were continuously recorded during the experiment to identify whether there was a significant effect of break on participants' EMG activities. The EMG signals were pre-amplified at the source (gain of 100) and bandpass filtered (5–500 Hz). The RMS of the muscle amplitude was determined using a time constant of 125 ms. The bandstop filter was used to eliminate 50 Hz power frequency interference. The amplitude and median frequency (MF) are the most commonly used indicators in EMG studies [27]. As the physical load increases, the muscular amplitude becomes larger and MF decreases [27, 28]. The repeated-measures ANOVA results of $Y_{rms}$ showed that there was no main effect of break with $F(1,15) = 1.453$, $p = 0.247$, $\eta^2 = 0.088$ but there was main effect of time with $F(2,30) = 8.870$, $p = 0.001$, $\eta^2 = 0.372$ for the trapezius muscle. The post-hoc analysis showed that the muscle was more active in T3 than T1 and T2 with $t(15) = 2.981$, $p = 0.009$ and $t(15) = 3.224$, $p = 0.006$, but there was no significant difference between T1 and T2 with $t(15) = 1.417$, $p = 0.177$. There were no main effects of break and time with $F(1,15) = 3.822$, $p = 0.069$, $\eta^2 = 0.203$ and $F(2,30) = 2.369$, $p = 0.118$, $\eta^2 = 0.136$ for the latissimus dorsi muscle.

Moreover, repeated-measures ANOVA results of MF showed that there were no main effects of break and time with $F(1,15) = 2.967$, $p = 0.106$, $\eta^2 = 0.165$ and $F(2,30) = 0.252$, $p = 0.779$, $\eta^2 = 0.017$ for the trapezius muscle. There was no main effect of time with $F(2,30) = 0.243$, $p = 0.786$, $\eta^2 = 0.016$ but there was main effect of break with $F(1,15) = 7.564$, $p = 0.015$, $\eta^2 = 0.335$ for the latissimus dorsi muscle. The post-hoc analysis showed that MF was higher in the break than the smartphone use with $t(15) = 2.355$, $p = 0.033$.

We also compared the muscle activities from smartphone use and pre-experiment, and the result showed that there were significant differences between T0 and T2 with $t(15) = -2.107$, $p = 0.05$, and between T0 and T3 with $t(15) = -3.484$, $p = 0.003$ for the trapezius muscle in $Y_{rms}$ but no significant difference in the latissimus dorsi muscle. For the MF, there were no significant differences between them with $p_s > 0.05$ for latissimus dorsi muscle and trapezius muscle, respectively. The variation of EMG was shown in Fig. 4 and Fig. 5 for $Y_{rms}$ and MF, respectively.

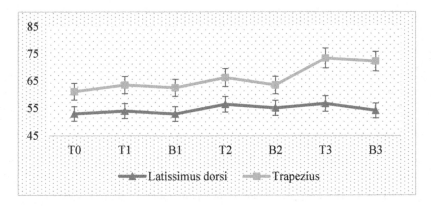

**Fig. 4.** The variation of Yrms.

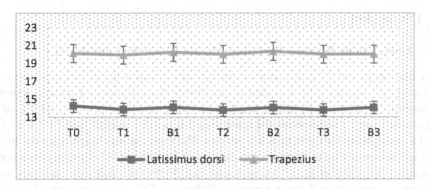

**Fig. 5.** The variation of MF.

## 4.3 Correlations Between Perceived Muscle Discomfort and EMG

We also analyzed the correlations between subjective ratings (SRs) of muscle discomfort and EMG indexes ($Y_{rms}$ and MF), which were showed in Table 3. The results showed that there were no significant relationships between perceived muscle discomfort and EMG indexes. There was only a positive correlation between the $Y_{rms}$ and MF of the trapezius muscle.

**Table 3.** Pearson correlations between different kinds of measures.

|          |             | SR | $Y_{rms1}$ | MF1   | $Y_{rms2}$ | MF2    |
|----------|-------------|-----|-----------|-------|-----------|--------|
| SR       | Correlation | 1   | 0.092     | 0.064 | −0.277    | 0.103  |
|          | Sig.        | –   | 0.536     | 0.667 | 0.057     | 0.486  |
|          | N           | 16  | 16        | 16    | 16        | 16     |
| $Y_{rms1}$ | Correlation |     | 1         | .454** | −0.089   | −0.127 |
|          | Sig.        |     | -         | 0.001 | 0.547     | 0.390  |
|          | N           |     | 16        | 16    | 16        | 16     |
| MF       | Correlation |     |           | 1     | 0.211     | −0.137 |
|          | Sig.        |     |           | –     | 0.149     | 0.352  |
|          | N           |     |           | 16    | 16        | 16     |
| $Y_{rms2}$ | Correlation |     |           |       | 1         | −0.216 |
|          | Sig.        |     |           |       | -         | 0.140  |
|          | N           |     |           |       | 16        | 16     |
| MF2      | Correlation |     |           |       |           | 1      |
|          | Sig.        |     |           |       |           | -      |
|          | N           |     |           |       |           | 16     |

**Correlation is significant at the 0.01 level (2-tailed)

# 5  Discussion

## 5.1  Correlations Between Perceived Muscle Discomfort and EMG

This study explored the prevalence of smartphone use and negative outcomes, and then surface EMG signals were recorded to investigate the variations of muscle activities. A majority of adolescence use a smartphone every day. In this study, 91.2% of the respondents used a smartphone for more than 2 h per day overall, and 51.7% of them used a smartphone for more than 4 h per day. The duration was longer than the limited time recommended by the American Academy of Pediatrics [29]. Similarly, in a survey conducted by Yang et al. [7], they found that 56.6% of adolescent students use a smartphone more than 3 h per weekday. Toh et al. [30] also investigate the mobile touch screen devices' use and associations with musculoskeletal symptoms of Singaporean adolescents. They found that 95.1% of respondents use a smartphone and the adolescents use a smartphone per weekday for 474 min. They all showed that a greater amount of h/day smartphone use was associated with musculoskeletal symptoms (i.e., especially in neck/shoulder, arms, upper back, wrist/hand, and low back). The prevalence of smartphone use has been a concern in many fields. In this study, neck/shoulder, back, arm, hand/wrist were the most common locations reported with muscle discomfort/pain. Also, the correlations showed that discomfort/pain of all the locations was significantly positively associated with smartphone use hours per weekday.

## 5.2  The Effect of Intervention on Muscle Discomfort

There are amount of studies exploring the antecedents and consequences of musculoskeletal symptoms for smartphone use [31–34]. However, the EMG variations of common locations with musculoskeletal symptoms during the smartphone use were rarely concerned. The EMG measurement experiment was designed and EMG activities during a 2-h smartphone use were collected based on the preliminary survey in this study, and 30 min was set as the intervention time based on studies about muscle activities [35–37]. In the EMG experiment, participants perceived higher muscle discomfort with smartphone use continuing (Fig. 3). The EMG results showed that EMG amplitudes were more active in T3 than T2 and T1, but there was no difference between T1 and T2 for the trapezius muscle. For the latissimus dorsi muscle, there was no difference in the amplitudes evoked from smartphone use and break, and there were no significant EMG variations with smartphone use continuing. Moreover, there were no differences between break and smartphone use in MF for the trapezius muscle, but higher MF was obtained in the intervention than smartphone use for the latissimus dorsi muscle. In a study conducted by Choi et al. [38], the normalized EMG of the lumbar erector spinae muscles was greater when using a smartphone while walking than when walking without using a smartphone. Similarly, our study found that higher muscle activity was obtained in the trapezius muscle than without smartphone use. However, in a study conducted by Park et al. [39], they found higher activities in the bilateral cervical erector spinae at 5–6, 10–11, and 15–16 min of usage than at the start of usage when using smartphone, but decreased EMG activation of the lower trapezius at 5–6, 10–11, and 15–16 min of usage. The smartphone-using time and intervention may contribute to this disparity. The EMG activities evoked during smartphone usage and intervention showed that a 10 min rest after 30 min of smartphone usage could effectively release the muscular load. An intervention about smartphone usage found that shoulder taping can reduce neck discomfort but does not affect muscle activity while subjects conducted 30 min texting task [40]. In this study, have a 10 min rest can keep the muscle activity at a level for 90 min, but it will increase after 2 h of smartphone usage for the upper trapezius muscle. There was no significant change during the 2 h experiment for the latissimus dorsi muscle, but subjects' perceived discomfort significantly increased during smartphone usage. The tasks' differences and duration of the experiment may lead to this difference.

## 6 Conclusions

The purpose of this study was to estimate the prevalence of musculoskeletal symptoms in university students and determine the relationship between smartphone use and musculoskeletal symptoms among this population. Neck/shoulder, arms, upper back, wrist/hand, and low back were the most commonly reported muscle locations with discomfort/pain. The EMG variation during smartphone usage was investigated. The perceived muscle discomfort increased as smartphone use continuing. The intervention results showed that a 10-min rest after 30-min smartphone usage could restrain the EMG activity in a relatively stable state. However, the correlations did not show any relation between subjective ratings and EMG activities. Overall, this study showed the prevalence of muscle discomfort for smartphone use and the findings provide preliminary data for the muscle discomfort measurement.

Our study did not investigate the behavioral difference in smartphone users and the antecedents of musculoskeletal symptoms, in which the effects of gender, experience, and addiction should be considered in the future. Also, the survey data was from a limited number of universities, a wider range of smartphone users may be helpful for understanding the associations between smartphone use and perceived physical and psychosocial outcomes. Moreover, in the EMG study, a 2-h smartphone usage experiment was conducted to collect the EMG signals and analyze the EMG variation with intervention, while this experiment was not a longitudinal population-based cohort study. Hence, the effect of intervention on muscle discomfort in the long-term should be considered. We investigated the EMG activity in sitting posture but no other postures were considered such as walking while using a smartphone with a single hand or both hands. Additional studies are needed to address the above shortcomings and help achieve the ultimate goal of this research, namely to develop a real-time system with EMG measurement that can be used to identify the muscle states.

# References

1. Perlow, L.A.: Sleeping with your Smartphone: How to Break the 24/7 Habit and Change the way you Work. Harvard Business Press, Brighton (2012)
2. Chotpitayasunondh, V., Douglas, K.M.: How "phubbing" becomes the norm: the antecedents and consequences of snubbing via smartphone. Comput. Hum. Behav. **63**, 9–18 (2016)
3. Berolo, S., Wells, R.P., Amick III, B.C.: Musculoskeletal symptoms among mobile hand-held device users and their relationship to device use: a preliminary study in a Canadian university population. Appl. Ergon. **42**(2), 371–378 (2011)
4. Ming, Z., Pietikainen, S., Hänninen, O.: Excessive texting in pathophysiology of first carpometacarpal joint arthritis. Pathophysiology **13**(4), 269–370 (2006)
5. Namwongsa, S., Puntumetakul, R., Neubert, M.S., Boucaut, R.: Effect of neck flexion angles on neck muscle activity among smartphone users with and without neck pain. Ergonomics **62**(12), 1524–1533 (2019)
6. Xie, Y., Szeto, G.P., Dai, J., Madeleine, P.: A comparison of muscle activity in using touchscreen smartphone among young people with and without chronic neck–shoulder pain. Ergonomics **59**(1), 61–72 (2016)
7. Yang, S.Y., Chen, M.D., Huang, Y.C., Lin, C.Y., Chang, J.H.: Association between smartphone use and musculoskeletal discomfort in adolescent students. J. Community Health **42**(3), 423–430 (2017)
8. Yang, G., et al.: Association between internet addiction and the risk of musculoskeletal pain among chinese college freshmen—a cross-sectional study. Frontiers Psychol. **10**, 1959 (2019)
9. Ning, X., Huang, Y., Hu, B., Nimbarte, A.D.: Neck kinematics and muscle activity during mobile device operations. Int. J. Ind. Ergon. **48**, 10–15 (2015)
10. Ariëns, G.A., Bongers, P.M., Hoogendoorn, W.E., Houtman, I.L., van der Wal, G., van Mechelen, W.: High quantitative job demands and low coworker support as risk factors for neck pain: results of a prospective cohort study. Spine **26**(17), 1896–1901 (2001)
11. Eltayeb, S., Staal, J.B., Hassan, A., De Bie, R.A.: Work related risk factors for neck, shoulder and arms complaints: a cohort study among Dutch computer office workers. J. Occup. Rehabil. **19**(4), 315 (2009)
12. Punnett, L., Bergqvist, U.: Visual display unit work and upper extremity musculoskeletal disorders. Stockholm: National Institute for Working Life, vol. 997 (1997)
13. Kim, J.H., Aulck, L., Bartha, M.C., Harper, C.A., Johnson, P.W.: Are there differences in force exposures and typing productivity between touchscreen and conventional keyboard? In: Proceedings of the Human Factors and Ergonomics Society Annual Meeting, Sage CA: Los Angeles, CA: SAGE Publications, vol. 56, 1, pp. 1104–1108, September 2012
14. Straker, L., Skoss, R., Burnett, A., Burgess-Limerick, R.: Effect of visual display height on modelled upper and lower cervical gravitational moment, muscle capacity and relative strain. Ergonomics **52**(2), 204–221 (2009)
15. Young, J.G., Trudeau, M., Odell, D., Marinelli, K., Dennerlein, J.T.: Touch-screen tablet user configurations and case-supported tilt affect head and neck flexion angles. Work **41**(1), 81–91 (2012)
16. Guan, X., et al.: Gender difference in mobile phone use and the impact of digital device exposure on neck posture. Ergonomics **59**(11), 1453–1461 (2016)
17. Xie, Y., Szeto, G., Dai, J.: Prevalence and risk factors associated with musculoskeletal complaints among users of mobile handheld devices: a systematic review. Appl. Ergon. **59**, 132–142 (2017)

18. Cohen, S.P.: Epidemiology, diagnosis, and treatment of neck pain. In: Mayo Clinic Proceedings, vol. 90, 2, pp. 284–299. Elsevier, 1 February 2015
19. Berolo, S., Wells, R.P., Amick III, B.C.: Musculoskeletal symptoms among mobile hand-held device users and their relationship to device use: a preliminary study in a Canadian university population. Appl. Ergon. 42(2), 371–378 (2011)
20. Kwok, S., Lee, P., Lee, R.: Smart device use and perceived physical and psychosocial outcomes among Hong Kong adolescents. Int. J. Environ. Res. Public Health 14(2), 205 (2017)
21. Xie, Y.F., Szeto, G., Madeleine, P., Tsang, S.: Spinal kinematics during smartphone texting– A comparison between young adults with and without chronic neck-shoulder pain. Appl. Ergon. 68, 160–168 (2018)
22. Lee, S., Kang, H., Shin, G.: Head flexion angle while using a smartphone. Ergonomics 58(2), 220–226 (2015)
23. Gustafsson, E., Coenen, P., Campbell, A., Straker, L.: Texting with touchscreen and keypad phones-a comparison of thumb kinematics, upper limb muscle activity, exertion, discomfort, and performance. Appl. Ergon. 70, 232–239 (2018)
24. Charles, R.L., Nixon, J.: Measuring mental workload using physiological measures: a systematic review. Appl. Ergon. 74, 221–232 (2019)
25. Nakphet, N., Chaikumarn, M., Janwantanakul, P.: Effect of different types of rest-break interventions on neck and shoulder muscle activity, perceived discomfort and productivity in symptomatic VDU operators: a randomized controlled trial. Int. J. Occup. Saf. Ergon. JOSE 20(2), 339–353 (2014)
26. Cao, Y., Qu, Q., Duffy, V.G., Ding, Y.: Attention for web directory advertisements: a top-down or bottom-up process? Int. J. Hum.-Comput. Interact. 35(1), 89–98 (2019)
27. Halder, A., Gao, C., Miller, M., Kuklane, K.: Oxygen uptake and muscle activity limitations during stepping on a stair machine at three different climbing speeds. Ergonomics 61(10), 1382–1394 (2018)
28. Viitasalo, J.H., Komi, P.V.: Signal characteristics of EMG during fatigue. Eur. J. Appl. Physiol. Occup. Physiol. 37(2), 111–121 (1977)
29. American Academy of Pediatrics.: American Academy of Pediatrics: children, adolescents, and television. Pediatrics, 107(2), 423, February 2001
30. Toh, S,H., Coenen, P., Howie, E.K., Mukherjee, S., Mackey, D.A., Straker, L.M.: Mobile touch screen device use and associations with musculoskeletal symptoms and visual health in a nationally representative sample of Singaporean adolescents. Ergonomics 17, 1–6 (2019)
31. Ahmed, S., Akter, R., Pokhrel, N., Samuel, A.J.: Prevalence of text neck syndrome and SMS thumb among smartphone users in college-going students: a cross-sectional survey study. J. Public Health 6, 1–6 (2019)
32. Korpinen, L., Pääkkönen, R., Gobba, F.: Self-reported wrist and finger symptoms associated with other physical/mental symptoms and use of computers/mobile phones. Int. J. Occup. Saf. Ergon. 24(1), 82–90 (2018)
33. Yang, G., et al.: Association between internet addiction and the risk of musculoskeletal pain among chinese college freshmen—a cross-sectional study. Front. Psychol. 10, 1959 (2019)
34. Areeudomwong, P., Oapdunsalam, K., Havicha, Y., Tantai, S., Buttagat, V.: Effects of shoulder taping on discomfort and electromyographic responses of the neck while texting on a touchscreen smartphone. Saf.Health Work 9(3), 319–325 (2018)
35. Balci, R., Aghazadeh, F.: Effects of exercise breaks on performance, muscular load, and perceived discomfort in data entry and cognitive tasks. Comput. Ind. Eng. 46(3), 399–411 (2004)

36. Davis, K.G., Kotowski, S.E.: Postural variability: an effective way to reduce musculoskeletal discomfort in office work. Hum. Factors **56**(7), 1249–1261 (2014)
37. Sheahan, P.J., Diesbourg, T.L., Fischer, S.L.: The effect of rest break schedule on acute low back pain development in pain and non-pain developers during seated work. Appl. Ergon. **53**, 64–70 (2016)
38. Choi, S., Kim, M., Kim, E., Shin, G.: Low back muscle activity when using a smartphone while walking. In: Proceedings of the Human Factors and Ergonomics Society Annual Meeting, Sage CA: Los Angeles, CA: SAGE Publications, vol. 63, 1, pp. 1099–1102, November 2019
39. Park, J.H., Kang, S.Y., Lee, S.G., Jeon, H.S.: The effects of smart phone gaming duration on muscle activation and spinal posture: Pilot study. Physiotherapy Theor. Pract. **33**(8), 661–669 (2017)
40. Areeudomwong, P., Oapdunsalam, K., Havicha, Y., Tantai, S., Buttagat, V.: Effects of shoulder taping on discomfort and electromyographic responses of the neck while texting on a touchscreen smartphone. Saf. Health Work. **9**(3), 319–325 (2018)

# Proactive Analysis of Complex Systems Through DHM: Paradigmatic Application of an Innovative Ergonomic Cumulative Index to Large Retail Stores

Carlo Emilio Standoli[1] , Nicola Francesco Lopomo[2] ,
Stefano Elio Lenzi[2] , and Giuseppe Andreoni[1,3](✉) 

[1] Department of Design, Politecnico di Milano, Milan, Italy
giuseppe.andreoni@polimi.it
[2] Information Engineering Department, University of Brescia, Brescia, Italy
[3] National Research Council - Bioimaging and Molecular Physiology Institute,
Segrate, Milan, Italy

**Abstract.** This paper describes a specific methodological approach focused on workplace ergonomics, by considering the most actual scientific knowledge and integrating in a coherent and complementary way both the validation of the binding regulatory and technical standards, and the testing of novel method-ologies applied to the shops, logistics and production sites present in large scale retail companies. Nowadays, this working condition represents a common sit-uation in which are carried out not only simple and separated assignments, but mixed tasks and shifts defining in a very complex scenario. Thus, a compre-hensive approach is needed. This study integrated ethnographic observations, task analysis and wearable technologies, within the definition of a novel Ergonomic Cumulative Index (ECI), which was designed to assess the risk exposure to musculoskeletal disorders by considering three different factors, namely kinematics/posture, muscular fatigue and joints overload. A specific multi-body digital human model was implemented for this purpose. Main findings of this work highlighted the need for an integrated and multi-parametric perspective addressing workers' activities, tasks management and environment organization. ECI specifically provided useful information in order to define the working day and to assess risk exposure by focusing on a holistic approach, which considers the body as a whole, but can highlight the contribution of each joint and muscle.

**Keywords:** Workplace assessment · Ergonomic index · Digital human modeling · Integrated cumulative approach

## 1 Introduction

Ergonomics is a system science, integrating human-product-environment-process-task requirements and features into a global approach aiming at maximizing safety and efficiency of the system as a whole. Humans are the central and key point, though not the only ones, in the design of good workplaces and tasks.

© Springer Nature Switzerland AG 2020
C. Stephanidis et al. (Eds.): HCII 2020, LNCS 12429, pp. 557–567, 2020.
https://doi.org/10.1007/978-3-030-59987-4_39

Today simulation tools and techniques allow for a new vision and perspective. Ergonomics must intervene not only *ex post* to correct or assess existing situation but, thanks to proactive ergonomic methods, it represents an early challenge to design, virtually assess and choose the optimal solutions.

In the frame of nowadays complex working activities, a single task or posture or place is not enough to determine the exposition to specific risk factors for developing Work-Related Musculoskeletal Diseases (WRMSDs) but, as ergonomics requires, a global approach results to be mandatory to define the optimal work design, in terms of place, tasks and shifts [1].

If standard indexes, such as OCRA [2, 3], NIOSH Lifting Equation [4], MAPO [5], LUBA [6], MMGA [7], Snook-Ciriello [8], are task-specific and prescription/assessment-oriented, a new multi-parametric perspective is required, specifically addressing workers' health and wellbeing.

This global perspective should include an integrated approach that has to consider each single performed task within the complete working day, keeping into account the whole set of different conditions present within the working environment. For example, nowadays many tasks that involve loads handling are characterized by working rotation on multiple activities, which can actually be very different from each other, concerning musculoskeletal biomechanics.

In this perspective, we aimed to propose a novel approach based on the definition of an integrated index, namely the Ergonomic Cumulative Index (ECI). The proposed method was applied on an actual case study; we specifically analyzed exposure to WRMSDs in large retail chain, where risk factors are associated with repetitive lifting and overloading tasks, further including several task-shifts and different procedures. Indeed, in this context a multifactorial and cumulative analysis is strictly required.

## 2 Materials and Methods

### 2.1 Methodological Approach

In this very complex scenario of several tasks integrated in a single working activity, the standard methodology offers spot assessments whose general application is then obtained by means of coefficient and factors describing repetitions and frequencies.

In our view the recent availability of wearable systems for measuring body kinematics and muscular activation can become an extraordinary opportunity for a direct, ecological and objective measurement of the actual working conditions. Furthermore, the continuous recording makes possible to consider all the working time and not only to interpolate it from spot measures. This approach aims to be more respondent to the true condition.

From all the above, in order to develop the ECI, the working hypotheses were the following ones:

- measurements and assessments must be objective and quantitative in order to eliminate any ambiguity on the outputs (i.e. operator-independent procedures with methodologically validated instruments that provide 3D joint angles and not video-based 2D estimations);

- the method must be simple, effective and reliable;
- the results must be intelligible and easily interpretable;
- the index must highlight and summarize the overload to the different districts (i.e. upper limbs and lumbar spine) with a single numerical value, overcoming the distinction proposed in the three parts of ISO 11228 [1];
- the approach should comply with the use of non-invasive wearable equipment that allow continuous recording of the activity (i.e. collection of body kinematics in real setting and ecological conditions to the best reliability);
- the index can be used both to evaluate the activity during the work planning phase and for risk mapping by assessing the existing situation.

These requirements were tested in a dedicated ethnographic observation that verified the technical feasibility of the proposed approach and allowed - through task analysis - to identify the different macro- and micro-activities executed during a "prototypical" day considering all the analyzed tasks.

## 2.2   ECI Definition

The proposed ECI was designed to be an absolute cumulative index based on the "the lower the better" approach. ECI was specifically computed as the weighted sum of the risk indexes calculated for each activity carried out by the operator for his/her specific task/s during a complete working day. Starting from the detailed, descriptive task analysis and from a study of the optimal approach in biomechanics and DHM, the ECI was hence developed focusing on three different factors that can expose the workers to the risk of developing WMSDs:

- **Kinematics/Posture Discomfort:** based on the Method for Movement and Gesture Analysis (MMGA index [7]), starting from the total body kinematics, but analyzing both the body and each anatomical district, by weighting the single district contribution to the ergonomic index according to the different mass of each body part.
- **Muscular Fatigue (MF):** based on physiological studies that are oriented to the identification of the Residual Muscular Capacity, including also a specific coefficient for cumulative activities.
- **Joint Overload (MMC):** this part of the index is based on Joint Moment/Forces computation starting from body kinematics and including dynamics parameters.

From the above the ECI is structured as a weighted sum (in time, i.e. considering the whole working day) of a product of the three sub-indexes related to the three biomechanical components:

$$ECI = \sum_{i=1}^{N} t_i \times \sum_{j=1}^{M} \left[ MMGA_j \times MF_j \times MMC_j \right]_i \qquad (1)$$

where:

- N is the number of the activities in the working day,
- $i$ is the $i$-th activity,

- $t_i$ is the coefficient weighting the duration of the $i$-th activity with respect to the total working time in the day $t_i = \frac{duration_i}{duration_{TOT}}$ so that $0 \le t_i \le 1$,
- M is the number of joints,
- $j$ is the j-th joint of the biomechanical model of the human body,
- MMGA is the index describing postural and movement effort driven by joint kinematics, so that with $MMGA_j \ge 1$,
- $MF_j$ is the coefficient related to muscular activity (maximum fatiguing during the i-th activity) for the $j$-th joint, computed for the mainly involved muscle group and the duration of the activity with $MF_j \ge 1$,
- $MMC_j$ is the coefficient describing the level of possible overload for the $j$-th joint during the $i$-th activity according to the reference posture is $MMC_j \ge 1$.

In this definition, the index compute a cumulative value for time and joint describing the overall workload but also having the possibility to consider the single components both for typology of load (e.g. postural or muscular fatigue or joint load) and for each single joint.

Muscular activation and joint loads were estimated by using DHM, specifically realized through multi-body modelling. More in detail, the general model was developed in OpenSim (OpenSim 4.0, Simbios, Stanford, CA, USA), an open source simulating software [9], by integrating two different models available in literature [10, 11] and updating the models at the basis of the muscular actuators and considering different virtual marker sets (one for the marker-based optoelectronic acquisitions and one for the tracking realized via wearable inertial sensors); the overall model included 29 different bodies, 303 muscles and 39 degrees of freedom. An inverse kinematics approach was used to estimate joint movements, whereas static optimization was applied to identify the activation state of each muscle. Muscular fatigue was thence estimated by using a three compartments model [12], whereas joint overload was computed by top-down inverse dynamics approach.

In order to make outcomes reliable and comparable, each component of the ECI was normalized with respect to «standard» postures, i.e. sitting or standing postures (Fig. 1) so that $MMGA_j \ge 1$.

## 2.3    Experimental Setup

The wearable kinematics recording system was selected and validated in specific sessions reproducing in a laboratory setting the operative conditions and related tasks and comparing data with the goal standard data set collected by means of a marker-based optoelectronic system, (Vicon M460, Vicon Motion Systems Limited).

In this preliminary setup, simultaneous recordings of typical activities and kinematic data from the different wearable mocap systems (including the Awinda system by XSens Technology, the Wearnotch by Notch Interfaces Inc. and the WaveTrack by Cometa Systems) were compared to the reference movement acquired by the optoelectronic motion analysis system to verify reliability and usability (Fig. 2).

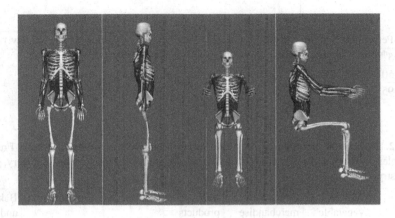

**Fig. 1.** The Digital human model (skeleton and muscles) and reference postures.

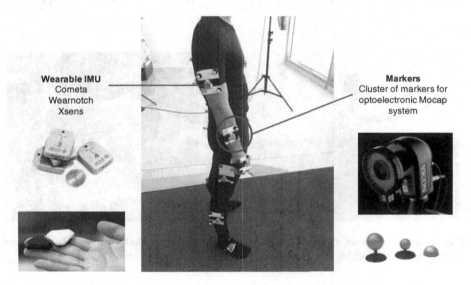

**Fig. 2.** Wearable motion capture comparison and validation with respect to optoelectronic Mocap (reference).

This activity led to the choice of the XSens Awinda system for the measurement of the workers in ecological setting, due to the overall reliability of the system itself and the available analysis software (MVN Analyse).

In our validation context, kinematics was directly acquired on 52 workers, who performed very different tasks in their departments, by means of a wearable system. The sample population was structured by sex, stature (Table 1) and department (Table 2). This court is representative of the subject working in each large retail stores and each task was repeated three times to have not only a wider data set but also the possibility to exclude possible outliers (Fig. 3).

**Table 1.** Population description by clustering in percentile of stature.

| Percentile | Stature – males (avg ± std.dev.) | Stature – females (avg ± std.dev.) |
|---|---|---|
| 5th | 159 ± 2,5 cm | 148 ± 2,5 cm |
| 50th | 175 ± 2,5 cm | 163 ± 2,5 cm |
| 95th | 192 ± 2,5 cm | 177 ± 2,5 cm |

**Table 2.** Population description by store department and activity/task, where Fruit and vegetables, Grocery and general merchandising, Milk products, Delicatessen, Buthcery, Bakery and Pastry

| Dept. | Fruit & vegetable | General merchandise | Milk products | Delicatessen | Butchery | Bakery and pastry |
|---|---|---|---|---|---|---|
| Subjects | 5 | 12 | 3 | 11 | 8 | 13 |

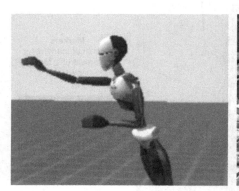

**Fig. 3.** An example of the data measurement during normal daily activity. The acquired kinematics of the working task (right) is represented with a digital manikin (left).

As shown in Fig. 3, the subject is wearing the wearable system under his standard uniform (image on the right). Contextual video recording allows for the computation of standard indexes (such as OCRA or NIOSH Lifting equation for specific tasks and for direct comparison). In fact, each working task is actually composed by several tasks as usual ergonomic approaches are considering them separately.

The complete dataset was processed to compute the ECI index for each structured activity and by combining the different activities according to the day scheduling for each worker, the complete working day assessment is then obtained.

## 3 Results

The method was applied to a defined set of tasks to provide a complete assessment of the activities in a large retail store. Two paradigmatic examples are presented here.

The first use case concerns the task of preparing the good for shelves refueling in the back side of the store; this task includes repetitive manual handling of loads, lifting and push-pull of the trolley (Fig. 4).

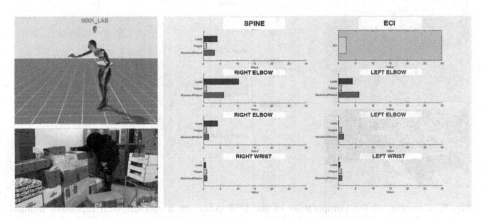

**Fig. 4.** Example of the computation of the ECI index in a task of preparing the good for shelves refueling in the back side of the store, with repetitive manual handling of loads, lifting and push-pull of the trolley. The representation of the movement kinematics with a DHM (on the left upper side) and the corresponding video recording (on the left lower side) allow for an intuitive understanding of the current value of the aggregated ECI index and also joint-by-joint and component by component. Data on the upper body are presented. (Color figure online)

In this first situation, the standard analysis would have recommended the application of the NIOSH lifting equation to assess the risk. Anyhow, this approach would have represented only a partial analysis of a small portion of the task and focused only on the lumbar spinal load. The availability of the body kinematics and of the estimated muscular forces and joint loads the forces helps in considering the different contribution to the workload and its implication. The horizontal histograms in the Fig. 4 present the contribution of the three factors (MMGA – in blue, MF – in green, MMC – in red) for each selected joint at the current instant of time. These histograms are time-varying so as offering a dynamic visual representation of the risk index. Thus, second by second it is possible to verify the specific risk for each body part in order to have not only an assessment value but also a proactive effect to redesign tools and environments thus to improve the working condition and reduce the WRMSD risks. In the presented situation, at the identified instant of time the shoulders are the joints specifically loaded as clearly shown in the figure. Then, and as expected to the forward trunk flexion, the spine is the third most solicited compartment even if under the lifting threshold - in perfect accordance to the fact that no goods are handled in that temporal frame.

The second example is the cashier activity (Fig. 5). In this case, in the selected time frame, ECI global value is lower as expected, with a reduced load on the spine but greater and distributed loads (in terms of movement and loads on the joints) on the upper limbs are measured. This is coherent with the task and the handling of small loads and high frequency. Due to the relatively low task frequency and the actual good weights, muscular fatigue is indeed low.

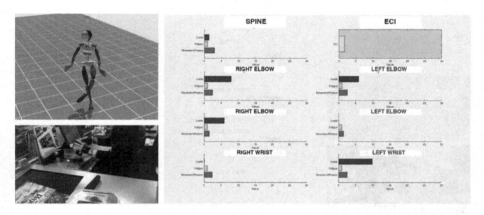

**Fig. 5.** Example of the computation of the ECI index for a cashier, with repetitive manual handling of little loads at high frequency. The representation of the movement kinematics with a DHM (on the left upper side) and the corresponding video recording (on the left lower side) allow for an intuitive understanding of the current value of the aggregated ECI index and also joint-by-joint and component by component. Focus on the upper body is presented.

In this case, the standard method to be used for the ergonomic analysis of the task is OCRA. A comparative analysis shows a general coherence of data between ECI and OCRA index, with a supposed overestimation or the WRMSD risk for this last one.

In order to obtain a comprehensive index but specifically to define a correct interpretation criterion and related thresholds, we competed all the value for each subject, every task or complex working activity identified by a complete operative sequence, and each trial or repetition of these activities to implement a dataset of ECI values. These values have been analyzed in term of statistical distribution (Fig. 6) and according to a percentile analysis of the task in parallel ISO methods and in particular OCRA index, NIOSH Lifing equation and push-pull index from Snook-Ciriello, we have identified the following classification criterion for assessing the exposure to WRMSD risk:

- ECI value ≤ 10: low risk exposure, no action required (green area),
- 10.1 ≤ ECI value ≤ 16: Possible exposure risk, monitoring required (yellow area),
- ECI value ≥ 16.1: Presence of exposure risk, corrective actions required (red area).

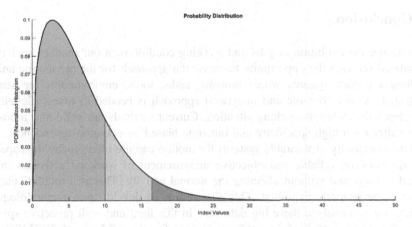

**Fig. 6.** The distribution of the ECI values of activities in large retail stores and the identification of the WRMSD risk thresholds for low risk exposure (green area), shift to be monitored (yellow area) and operations/shifts that require attention and intervention (red area). (Color figure online)

By applying these thresholds, through the composition of the kinematic recordings of the different activities in accordance with the working day scheduling of the different categories of worker it is possible to analyze the complete working shift.

The following Fig. 7 shows the computation of the WRMSD exposure index through the ECI values of different phases and for the complete shift for a male subject belonging the 50th percentile in stature and whose activities are cashier and shelves refueling, with changes to avoid prolonged seated and fixed posture issues.

| | OP1 | P | OP1 | OP2 | P | OP2 | OP1 | SHIFT END |
|---|---|---|---|---|---|---|---|---|
| Task | CASH DESK | PAUSE | CASH DESK | REPLENISHMENT | TASK CHANGE | REPLENISHMENT | CASH DESK | CLOSING |
| Time Duration [s] | 1188 | 528 | 1848 | 3696 | 528 | 2508 | 2640 | 264 |
| ECI/Task | 1.351 | 1.000 | 1.351 | 8.271 | 1.000 | 4.806 | 1.351 | 1.000 |
| Percentage/Shift | 9% | 4% | 14% | 28% | 4% | 19% | 20% | 2% |
| ECI | 3.910 | | | | | | | |

**Fig. 7.** Example of the analysis of a working shift for a male 50th percentile operator and computation of ECI values for activities and for the complete working day.

This representation is very useful to provide a comprehensive overview of the workers activities and related effort or exposure/risk. Single insights and detailed analysis is available on the three different factors (movement and posture, muscular fatigue and articular loads), thus to have not only a simple assessment or post-hoc significance but even a proactive capability to identify the most appropriate solutions (i.e. introduction of tools, redesign of environments, redesign of products) to intervene in specific cases and situations.

# 4   Conclusion

Considering the evolution of jobs and working conditions in our modern society, we considered relevant the opportunity to revise the approach for the ergonomic analysis of these complex systems where humans, tasks, tools, environments are strongly integrated. A more organic and integrated approach is needed to assess globally but with depth the different working situation. Current methods are valid and robust but often suffer from high specificity and outcome biased by operator-dependency.

The availability of wearable systems for motion capture offers today the capability of a quantitative, reliable and objective measurement of workers' activities in ecological settings and without affecting the normal activity. This is a revolutionary situation to be properly exploited. This also means to develop new methodologies to collect, use and analyze these big data sets. In this light and with proactive spirit we faced the development of an integrated view for the analysis of WRMSDs risk exposure for complex working activities. Thus, the proposed approach allowed a complete and comprehensive but detailed description of the working activity, with specific insights but also in line with the definition of Ergonomics as system science. The selected case study was the analysis of large retails stores because of the variety and complexity of activities involving several single but integrated risk factors.

Facing the new era of new jobs and workplaces, and of wearable tools in ergonomics, a methodological rethinking and update is needed. In this perspective, we developed a novel integrated approach based on a multi-parametric analysis. Preliminary applications to the large retail stores provided us with very interesting and promising results; ECI specifically provided useful information in order to define the working day and to assess risk exposure by considering an holistic approach, which considers the body as a whole, but that can focus also on the contribution of each single joint and muscle. Furthermore, the comparison with respect to epidemiological data is ongoing to follow the methodological validation in full.

Furthermore, ECI could not be used only in the assessment i.e. post-hoc conditions; surely the possibility to use of ECI even in a proactive ergonomics approach, i.e. predictively with respect to several factors like, gender, percentile, single or complex tasks or activities, design of tools and environments, design of processes, duration of these activity/ies, and/or duration of shift, will be a very relevant and next future perspective.

# References

1. International Organization for Standardization: ISO-TR 12295—Ergonomics—Application document for ISO standards on manual handling (ISO 11228-1, ISO 11228-2 and ISO 11228-3) and evaluation of static working postures (ISO 11226) (2014)
2. Occhipinti, E.: OCRA: a concise index for the assessment of exposure to repetitive movements of the upper limbs. Ergonomics **41**(9), 1290–1311 (1998)
3. Occhipinti, E., Colombini, D.: The occupational repetitive action (OCRA) methods: OCRA index and OCRA checklist. Handb. Hum. Factors Ergon. Methods 1–14 (2005)

4. Health. Division of Biomedical, & Behavioral Science: Work practices guide for manual lifting (No. 81-122). US Dept. of Health and Human Services, Public Health Service, Centers for Disease Control, National Institute for Occupational Safety and Health, Division of Biomedical and Behavioral Science (1981)

5. Battevi, N., Menoni, O., Ricci, M.G., Cairoli, S.: MAPO index for risk assessment of patient manual handling in hospital wards: a validation study. Ergonomics 49(7), 671–687 (2006)

6. Kee, D., Karwowski, W.: LUBA: an assessment technique for postural loading on the upper body based on joint motion discomfort and maximum holding time. Appl. Ergon. 32(4), 357–366 (2001)

7. Andreoni, G., et al.: Method for movement and gesture assessment (MMGA) in ergonomics. In: Duffy, V.G. (ed.) ICDHM 2009. LNCS, vol. 5620, pp. 591–598. Springer, Heidelberg (2009). https://doi.org/10.1007/978-3-642-02809-0_62

8. Snook, S.H., Ciriello, V.M.: The design of manual handling tasks: revised tables of maximum acceptable weights and forces. Ergonomics 34(9), 1197–1213 (1991)

9. Delp, S.L., et al.: OpenSim: open-source software to create and analyze dynamic simulations of movement. IEEE Trans. Biomed. Eng. 54, 1940–1950 (2007)

10. Beaucage-Gauvreau, E., et al.: Validation of an OpenSim full-body model with detailed lumbar spine for estimating lower lumbar spine loads during symmetric and asymmetric lifting tasks. Comput. Methods Biomech. Biomed. Eng. 22, 451–464 (2019)

11. Saul, K.R., et al.: Benchmarking of dynamic simulation predictions in two software platforms using an upper limb musculoskeletal model. Comput. Methods Biomech. Biomed. Eng. 2015(18), 1445–1458 (2015). https://doi.org/10.1080/10255842.2014.916698

12. Looft, J.M., Herkert, N., Frey-Law, L.: Modification of a three-compartment muscle fatigue model to predict peak torque decline during intermittent tasks. J. Biomech. 77, 16–25 (2018). https://doi.org/10.1016/j.jbiomech.2018.06.005

# A Bibliometric Analysis and Social Network Analysis on Ergonomics Studies of Emergency Equipment

Hao Tan[1], Yuyue Hao[2], Aobo Sun[2], Xiuyuan Guo[1(✉)], and Dongdong Guo[2]

[1] Key Laboratory of Advance Design and Simulation Technology for Special Equipments, Ministry of Education, Changsha, China
guo529@purdue.edu
[2] School of Design, Hunan University, Changsha, China

**Abstract.** This study aims to make a quantitative analysis of the current research in the field of emergency equipment ergonomics. Based on 1125 papers obtained with keywords related to Emergency Equipment Ergonomics and Human Factors from Elsevier Scopus database, the core research themes and cooperation in this field are discussed by using BibExcel and Gephi. The further study analyzed keywords, core themes, co-word networks, author's influence and collaborations patterns by utilizing method of bibliometrics and social network analysis. The results show that ergonomics researches in field of emergency equipment are relatively scattered and less relevant. The key research domains were identified to be "medical safety", "safety standards and system", "human error" and "usability". The results of social network analysis show that the overall density of the literature network is at a low level, and the academic cooperation between developed countries in Europe and the United States is closer.

**Keywords:** Bibliometrics · Social network analysis · Emergency equipment · Ergonomics

## 1 Introduction

Emergency management, as the integrated discipline of engineering science and social management, shows incredible value after series of disasters like Chernobyl Disaster, 911 attack, Fukushima Nuclear Leak and Hurricane Sandy aroused concerns and acts globally, such as international organization TIEMS, FEMA of the USA and official agencies in Japan and Europe [1–3]. Hazards in 21 Century evidenced those agencies have the strength in dealing with an emergency, but also exposed the weakness and vulnerability as a lacking of the integrated emergency management system for disaster prevention and mitigation system [4]. With the serious impact of COVID-19 has caused great damage to the world during 2020, the public emergency response has also aroused attention around the world. The improvement of emergency response ability depends on the development of science and technology manufacturing, and the research and design of emergency equipment is the core to support the improvement of national and local emergency response power.

© Springer Nature Switzerland AG 2020
C. Stephanidis et al. (Eds.): HCII 2020, LNCS 12429, pp. 568–583, 2020.
https://doi.org/10.1007/978-3-030-59987-4_40

Emergency equipment for emergency response mainly includes searching, detection, jacking, demolition, power, lighting, communication, transportation, emergency medical care and personal protection [5], involving various emergency rescue scenarios like natural hazards, disasters and public emergencies. In the scenario of emergency response, the emergency equipment needs to meet the ability to deal with complex and high-risk tasks such as high-pressure operation, life rescue and response to the harsh environment with high temperature, high humidity and high radiation. In emergencies, human factors in the complex system are more likely to induce accidents or increase the severity of accidents, which require emergency equipment to be more usable, reliable and friendly to use [6]. These devices play an important role in emergency conditions and protect the safety and interests of relevant people. However, the ergonomics and human factors should be honored to ensure emergency equipments work more efficiently and safer under harsh situations. Ways to optimize the human factors/ergonomics of emergency equipment, improve operational efficiency, and ensure the safety of life is an important problem and challenge of emergency equipment design. As a scientific systematic method, bibliometrics has been applied in many research fields. However, systematic quantitative research is still scarce in the field of emergency equipment design, especially for human factors/ergonomics of emergency equipment design. Therefore, this paper uses bibliometrics to make a comprehensive study on the ergonomics of emergency equipment.

This paper aims to analyze and conclude the research of emergency equipment ergonomics in the past 20 years. The current research status of ergonomics of emergency equipment is discussed through empirical analysis of keywords, core themes, co-word networks, author's influence and collaborations patterns.

## 2  Methodology

Based on bibliometrics, this paper explores the hot topics in the field of ergonomics for emergency equipment. Bibliometric analysis can analyze the basic conditions of related research areas from the correlation between the needs of target research and the quantity and quality of papers. Therefore, the beginning of scientific research [7] is constantly developing along with the development of bibliometrics. In recent years, common methods mainly include co-occurrence analysis [8], social network analysis [9], multivariate statistical analysis, and information visualization. Based on previous studies, this paper combines bibliometrics and social network analysis techniques to analyze the field of ergonomics in emergency equipment abroad. In the bibliometric part, BibExcel is used to provide relevant statistical data such as keywords, authors, countries, and regions for subsequent analysis. Combined with Gephi, the content of network analysis is completed. The reasons for using the two tools of BibExcel and Gephi are as follows:

(1) BibExcel is highly flexible in modifying and/or adjusting input data imported from various databases including Scopus, and it is compatible with different computer applications including social science statistical software package (SPSS), Excel, Unicet, and Gephi. BibExcel is also used to prepare input data for detailed network

analysis to provide comprehensive data analysis for a range of network analysis tools including Gephi, VOSviewer, and Pajek [10].

(2) Gephi is used for interactive visualization and detection of various networks and complex systems, dynamic and stratified maps, and is widely used for exploratory data analysis, link analysis, social network analysis, and biological network analysis [11] chooses Gephi to complete further analysis and visualization of data in this field.

## 2.1   Initial Data Statistics

Bibliometric analysis of ergonomics in emergency equipment is carried out in this paper. Based on the data analysis of bibliometrics, the high-frequency research objects of ergonomics of emergency equipment are emergency control and management, system cognitive decision, human error, and Emergency medical treatment.

In this study, we choose the Elsevier Scopus academic database as the initial data. Because the Elsevier Scopus academic database has a higher coverage rate than WOS in the four fields of natural science and Engineering (NSE), biomedical research (BR), Social Sciences (SS), and arts and Humanities (AH). This study has imported "("emergency" AND ("product" OR "software" OR "system") AND ("human-factors" OR "ergonomics"))"a total of 1125 papers on ergonomics related to emergency equipment were obtained as the initial literature data. The research trend and hot spot for the field of emergency equipment ergonomics in the past 1994–2020 years are shown in Fig. 1. In general, the number of papers per year is increasing.

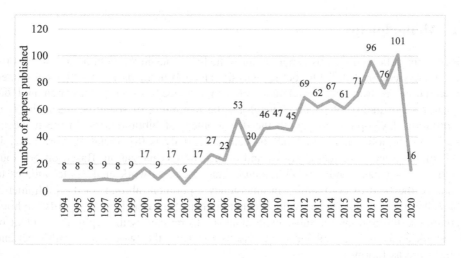

**Fig. 1.** −2020 trend chart of published literature *when data was collected, the year 2020 had not yet finished.

## 2.2   Bibliometric Analysis

Namkyung et al. [12] noted that scholars in the field of emergency management (EM) have accumulated a large number of papers for decades. Knowledge synthesis using a large number of papers provides a huge opportunity for the further development of EM theory and strategy. Here we use the bibliometric technology to measure the emergency equipment of human-machine engineering. In this paper, we use the keyword frequency analysis, Co-word analysis, and word frequency analysis, and co-word analysis to study the current research status of ergonomics in emergency equipment. Through the above research, we can get the current situation and trend of emergency equipment ergonomics research and the top 20 authors with a large number of papers, great contributions, and high quality of academic achievements and their relevant information. The authors and their related information on the high quality of academic achievements are further explained in terms of word frequency analysis and co-word analysis.

Keyword frequency analysis is the quantitative statistics of keywords in scientific documents in related fields. Word frequency analysis establishes a dictionary of word frequency for the related fields, and effectively displays the concentrated areas and dispersed regions, which lays the foundation for subsequent directional analysis and internal connection as well as social network analysis.

Co-word analysis is to study the co-occurrence and frequency [10] among each word and another word, which needs to be analyzed based on word frequency analysis. The co-word analysis explores the relationship between words and effectively establishes the internal and external links of the research topic [13]. The centrality, centrality, and density of the whole research network have been obtained, providing systematic data support for this research.

## 2.3   Social Network Analysis

Wasserman [14] proposed that social network analysis helps to establish an analytical method system for mathematical analysis network structure. Because the network composed of a large number of nodes will cause confusion, social network analysis can be visualized and supplemented by mathematical models to quantify the relationship between network attributes to relieve the confusion caused by a large number of nodes in the network. In general, the word co-occurrence matrix can be regarded as a network. Social network analysis is an easy method of visualization and quantification for network system t. This research adopts a network analysis method such as centrality, density, strategy map, and so on. The following three ways are introduced respectively.

Centrality is used to measure the dominant position of nodes in the social network. Therefore, the keywords or themes with high centrality can be defined as the center and important position in the cluster or the center of the whole research field. The research on the emergency management man-machine field shows high centrality of safety, ergonomics, patient safety, medical and safety culture. It is an important area of research.

Density refers to the intensity of association between nodes in a social network in the same research topic. Density is a measure of the connectivity of a network and varies between 0 and 1 [15]. It is an indicator of network connectivity. If the density is 0, there is no correlation between nodes in the network, and if the density reaches 1, it shows that all nodes in the network are paired in pairs.

Based on centrality and density, a scatter graph known as a strategic diagram [16] was built to describe the internal relations within a cluster, as well as the interactions among different fields.

The strategy diagram is used to describe the relationship within the cluster and the interactions among different domains. In the strategy chart, the X-axis represents the centrality, the Y-axis represents the density, and the origin of the strategic chart is the median value of each axis. When different clusters of research topics are distributed in different positions in the two-dimensional coordinate system, different positions show different situations in the research field. For example, when the research object is in the first quadrant, the research cluster has high centrality and density, and is relatively mature and concentrated in the whole research field. In the second quadrant, it means that the research direction is not the center, but develops well. In the third quadrant, the research direction is on the edge and underdeveloped. In the fourth quadrant, due to the low density and centrality, the research direction is not only undeveloped and immature, or may tend to mature fields [16, 17].

## 3    Results

### 3.1    Keyword Analysis

The keywords for an article can express its main content, and the keyword frequency of academic journal articles can measure the importance of related themes in a specific field. In this study, the records of 1125 articles were selected for subsequent analysis. With the aid of BibExcel, 3296 keywords were extracted from these article records (2.93 keywords per article).

It was noted that not all of the keywords provided by authors were normalized; thus, the extracted keywords were normalized using affinity propagation, according to the method noted by Brendan J in 2007. This algorithm takes the similarity matrix of the data set as the input. At the initial stage of the algorithm, all samples are regarded as potential clustering centre points [8]. The standardization of these keywords is to ensure consistent handling of singular and plural words, the unification of synonyms, and the unification of abbreviations and non-abbreviations. For example, replace "human errors" with "human error"; replace "systems safety" with "safety systems"; "CPR" with "cardiopulmonary resuscitation", etc. Before keyword replacement, we first treated the keyword case in a unified way. This is mainly to avoid the interference of capitalization. Removed general terms and addresses, such as model, China, Beijing, etc. The entire process of normalization helped to determine the final keywords for the analysis, with the aid of two professors specializing in this field and discussion within the research team.

After the standardization was completed, keywords with a frequency of more than 4 were selected, and 113 keywords were finally determined, with a total frequency of 835 (approximately 25.6% of all keyword frequencies). These keywords represent the main content of ergonomic research on emergency equipment. Using BibExcel to count the frequency of keywords fields in the original text, the top 20 keywords and frequencies are shown in Table 1.

**Table 1.** The top 20 keywords of ergonomic research in emergency equipment

| No. | Keyword | Frequency | No. | Keyword | Frequency |
|-----|---------|-----------|-----|---------|-----------|
| 1 | Patient safety | 37 | 11 | Situation awareness | 15 |
| 2 | Safety | 32 | 12 | Health care | 14 |
| 3 | Emergency medical service | 21 | 13 | communication | 13 |
| 4 | Human error | 21 | 14 | Training | 13 |
| 5 | Simulation | 21 | 15 | Decision making | 13 |
| 6 | Safety culture | 18 | 16 | Quality improvement | 13 |
| 7 | Usability | 17 | 17 | Nurse | 11 |
| 8 | Emergency department | 16 | 18 | Emergency management | 10 |
| 9 | Medical error | 15 | 19 | Human factor engineering | 10 |
| 10 | Emergency response | 15 | 20 | Virtual reality | 9 |

It can be seen from the table that the top 10 keywords with the highest keywords are patient safety, safety, emergency medical service, human error, simulation, safety culture, usability, emergency department, medical error, and emergency response. It can be seen from this that ergonomic research on emergency equipment focuses more on medical, safety, and human factors-related research.

According to keywords frequency and co-word frequency, the overall attributes of keywords or topics can be made more clear. The top 10 keywords with the highest co-word frequency are shown in Table 2.

**Table 2.** The top 10 keywords with high co-word data of emergency equipment ergonomics research

| No. | Keyword | Total co-word frequency |
|-----|---------|-------------------------|
| 1 | Safety | 78 |
| 2 | Patient safety | 74 |
| 3 | Safety culture | 62 |
| 4 | Emergency response | 47 |
| 5 | Safety systems | 47 |
| 6 | Ergonomics | 46 |
| 7 | Common cause failures | 44 |
| 8 | Functional safety management system | 44 |
| 9 | Independent protection layers | 44 |
| 10 | Risk reduction | 44 |

Each of the top ten keywords listed in Table 2 can represent the focus of ergonomic research on emergency equipment to varying degrees. The keywords "safety", "patient safety", and "safety culture" are frequently used, indicating that they are at the core of the high-frequency keyword network and are representative of the research field of ergonomics of emergency equipment. The theme has the most direct and extensive connection.

## 3.2  Core Themes

Using the modularity clustering method in Gephi, with the clustering step being set up at one level, 11 clusters (named Cluster 1 to Cluster 11) were obtained. Each of these clusters could be regarded as a research theme. The 113 keywords from the normalization process were divided into 11 theme-clusters. If keywords are grouped into a cluster, they are more likely to have an identical research theme. In this study, between 5 and 30 keywords with top frequencies and co-word data were selected to represent each theme-cluster, because these keywords were most likely to be chosen and used by researchers in each cluster. Table 3 shows the representative keywords within each theme-cluster.

**Table 3.** 11 clusters of emergency equipment ergonomics gathered

| Cluster | Cluster name | Keywords |
|---|---|---|
| 1 | Emergency control and management | Accident; control; emergency situation; nuclear power plant; reliability; design; management; training; crisis management; performance; leadership; main control room |
| 2 | System cognitive decision | Adaptation; collaboration; coordination; decision making; naturalistic decision making; resilience engineering; topics; cognitive systems engineering |
| 3 | Human error | Simulation; adverse event; medical error; patient safety; quality improvement; aviation; communication; crew resource management; emergency medicine; cause of error; classification of error; risk management; non-technical skills; workflow; crisis resource management |
| 4 | Emergency medical treatment | Ergonomics; teamwork; emergency medical service; paramedic; cardiac arrest; cardiopulmonary resuscitation; musculoskeletal disorders; firefighter; intervention; low-back disorders; workload; health |
| 5 | Safety standard system | Safety; common cause failures; functional safety management system; independent protection layers; risk reduction; safety systems; third party certification |
| 6 | Cognitive decision making | Accimap; sociotechnical systems; AHP; cognitive model; emergency management; human behavior; human error; automation; decision support system; human computer interaction; risk assessment; human reliability analysis; command and control; decision support; emergency services; situation awareness; resilience |
| 7 | Medical aid | Injury; nurse; ambulance; trauma; emergency department; electronic health records; human factor engineering |
| 8 | Design of emergency medical system | Pediatric; resuscitation; checklist; health care; user-computer interface; emergency evacuation; system design |
| 9 | Safety supervision | safety culture; emergency response; incidents; offshore; permit to work; process safety management; regulatory regime |
| 10 | Emergency system engineering | Alarm; control room; emergencies; human-systems integration; validation; virtual reality; evacuation; egress; systems engineering |
| 11 | Human machine interface design | Disaster; risk; stress; usability; user interface; user centered design; interface design; mass casualty incident; security; product design |

It can be seen from Table 3 that there are 11 research clusters or themes for ergonomic research of emergency equipment. Through consultation with experts in the field of ergonomics, we believe that the above clustering is a good representation of the current status of ergonomic research in emergency equipment. At the same time, according to the keywords under each cluster, we will summarize the cluster content, through Fig. 2 you can intuitively see the current status of research in related fields. In general, the research directions of 11 categories are relatively uniform. Emergency medical research has the most research, accounting for 17.72%; ergonomics and human factors research are also relatively important research directions; cognitive decision-making and emergency medical system design are relatively least focused on research and account for 4.90%.

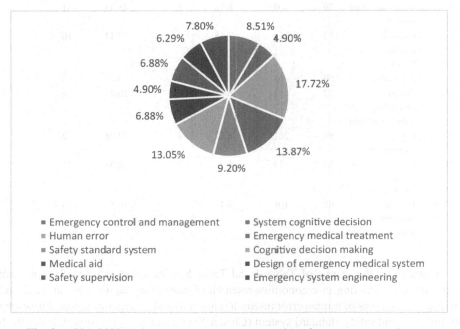

**Fig. 2.** 1994–2020 Emergency management ergonomics focuses on research areas

In this study, the co-word data includes the total frequency and total co-word frequency and their average values (shown in Table 4), and can more explicitly demonstrate the characteristics of each research theme-cluster. The comprehensive and proportional average values of co-word data can be designated as very specific indicators for distinguishing each research theme. To obtain an accurate and explicit comparison among these 11 theme-clusters, the rankings of their respective average frequency and average co-word frequency are listed in Table 4. The rankings show the relative positions and statuses of related themes emergency equipment ergonomics research.

**Table 4.** The frequency and co-word data of each theme-cluster

| Cluster | Cluster name | Total frequency | Total co-word frequency | Average frequency | Ranking of average frequency | Average co-word frequency | Ranking of average co-word frequency |
|---|---|---|---|---|---|---|---|
| 1 | Emergency control and management | 73 | 89 | 6.08 | 8 | 7.42 | 9 |
| 2 | System cognitive decision | 42 | 79 | 5.25 | 11 | 9.87 | 7 |
| 3 | Human error | 152 | 289 | 10.13 | 1 | 19.27 | 3 |
| 4 | Emergency medical treatment | 119 | 175 | 9.91 | 2 | 14.58 | 4 |
| 5 | Safety standard system | 79 | 409 | 8.78 | 3 | 45.44 | 1 |
| 6 | Cognitive decision making | 112 | 121 | 7.18 | 6 | 7.11 | 10 |
| 7 | Medical aid | 59 | 68 | 8.42 | 4 | 9.71 | 8 |
| 8 | Design of emergency medical system | 42 | 71 | 6 | 9 | 10.42 | 6 |
| 9 | Safety supervision | 59 | 261 | 8.42 | 4 | 37.28 | 2 |
| 10 | Emergency system engineering | 54 | 57 | 6 | 9 | 6.33 | 11 |
| 11 | Human machine interface design | 67 | 105 | 6.7 | 7 | 10.5 | 5 |

Combining the results of Table 4 and Table 5, several larger research topics and sub-directions existing in ergonomics research of emergency equipment can be found, which are the areas of human error research (cluster 3) and emergency medical treatment (Cluster 4) and safety standard system (Cluster 5) and safety supervision (Cluster 9). In contrast, the relevant indicators for emergency control and management (clustering 1), system cognitive decision-making (clustering 2), and emergency systems engineering (clustering 10) are relatively low and are not the focus of research. In addition, human factors research, emergency medical treatment, and cognitive decision-making (cluster 6) have a relatively high total frequency and total co-word frequency, indicating that research in this field has received considerable attention in the field of emergency equipment ergonomics and is a research hotspot. In addition, the safety standards system has a high total co-word frequency, indicating that safety standards have played a central role in the study of ergonomics of emergency equipment. However, the total co-word frequency of cluster system cognitive decision-making, medical rescue (cluster 7), emergency medical system design (cluster 8), and emergency system engineering is relatively low, and it has not received much attention in the field.

## 3.3    Co-word Network Analysis

Table 5 lists the density and centrality of keyword clusters. Density indicates the strength of association between keywords within each cluster in the entire network structure. The greater the value of density, the stronger the correlation. Centrality measures the dominant position of each cluster in the entire network structure. The greater the centrality, the cluster is located in the center or an important position in all clusters, or the center of the entire research field.

**Table 5.** The top 10 keywords with high centrality

| Cluster | Cluster name | Density | Centrality |
|---|---|---|---|
| 1 | Emergency control and management | 0.258 | 2.833 |
| 2 | System cognitive decision | 0.607 | 4.25 |
| 3 | Human error | 0.419 | 5.867 |
| 4 | Emergency medical treatment | 0.424 | 4.667 |
| 5 | Safety standard system | 1 | 8 |
| 6 | Cognitive decision making | 0.162 | 2.588 |
| 7 | Medical aid | 0.429 | 2.571 |
| 8 | Design of emergency medical system | 0.476 | 2.857 |
| 9 | Safety supervision | 1 | 6 |
| 10 | Emergency system engineering | 0.278 | 2.222 |
| 11 | Human machine interface design | 0.467 | 4.2 |

As can be seen from the above table, the clusters 2, 5, and 9 are relatively density in the literature, and the links between the keywords within the respective clusters are the closest. Clusters 2, 3, 4, 5, 9, and 11 have relatively large centrality, indicating that these fields have extensive connections with others.

On the basis of the above, the density of the overall research network was calculated. The density of the network with all keywords is 0.076, which is a relatively low level and indicates that emergency equipment ergonomics research is decentralized. Then, the centrality is taken as the horizontal, and the density is taken as the vertical. The average degree and the average value of the density are used as the origin to draw the strategic diagram, as shown in Fig. 5. The strategic diagram divides the 11 clusters into four quadrants, which can reveal the current status or trends of ergonomic research on emergency equipment.

The cluster density and centrality in quadrant I are relatively large, indicating that the cluster in the quadrant has a high internal correlation and is closely related to the external. The clustering theme in quadrant I is the focus of scholars in this field [18]. It can be seen from this that the field of safety standards represented by cluster 5 and cluster 9 has matured, and is at the core of ergonomic research on emergency equipment.

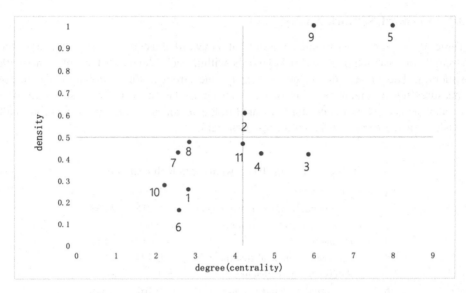

**Fig. 3.** Strategic diagram of 11 theme clusters of emergency equipment ergonomics research

The clustering density in quadrant II is high and the centrality is low, indicating that the topics in the quadrant are relatively mature, but they are not strongly related to other topics and are not in the center of the field. There is no clustering group with high density and low centrality in quadrant II, which shows that the current research topics are relatively concentrated, and there are few research topics that are on the edge and are concerned.

Cognitive decision-making represented by clusters 1, 6, 7, 8, and 10, research in the field of emergency medical system design and emergency system engineering is located in quadrant III, which is an unpopular and immature research field. This also echoes the results in Table 7, indicating that there are still many marginal and immature studies in the field of emergency equipment ergonomics. Among them, cluster 8 is closer to the horizontal, which shows that the research topic of cluster 8 has great potential to develop into a more mature field.

The quadrant IV shows several different types of clustering. The density of these clusters is low and the centrality is high. In other words, clustering in the fourth quadrant is the core of ergonomics research on emergency equipment, but it is not yet mature. For example, clusters 3 and 4 represent human errors and emergency medical care. In addition, we can also find that cluster 11 is very close to the origin, which shows that the research topic of cluster 11 has great potential for development.

## 3.4    Author's Influence

In line with the previous research of Behnam et al. [19], an author's influence in a field is measured by the number of papers they publish. Based on this, to investigate an author's influence, BibExcel was used to calculate the frequency of the appearance of authors, to represent the number of the author's publications. Because the author's name in the Scopus database is abbreviated, and the name of the Chinese author in the extracted literature is easy to repeat, it is not suitable to directly extract the author field for analysis. Notably, Scopus provides an author identifier (Author ID) field for distinguishing between ambiguous names, by assigning each author in Scopus a unique number. Therefore, we extracted the Author ID in the CSV file, and saved it as a TXT format file which can be processed in BibExcel for subsequent analysis Table (6).

**Table 6.** The top 10 authors based on number of publications

| No. | Name | Publications |
|---|---|---|
| 1. | FAIRBANKS, R.J. | 14 |
| 2 | WEARS, R.L. | 12 |
| 3 | PERRY, S.J. | 9 |
| 4 | LI, Z. | 9 |
| 5. | LAVENDER, S.A. | 7 |
| 6 | SIMS, V.K. | 7 |
| 7 | REICHELT, P.A. | 7 |
| 8 | CONRAD, K.M. | 7 |
| 9. | KRYWONOS, M. | 6 |
| 10. | CHAMBERLAIN, J.M. | 6 |

As can be seen from the table, FAIRBANKS, R.J is the most prolific author and published 14 articles. WEARS R.L published 12 articles, second only to FAIRBANKS, R.J. For the authors with the high volume of the above articles, query their units. The top ten authors are the University of Rochester, Imperial College London, University of Florida, University of Florida, Columbus Ohio Lextant, University of Florida, Ohio State, Washington Children's National Medical Center, and Sam Houston State University. This shows that the United States and the United Kingdom have achieved relatively large academic achievements in the field of emergency equipment ergonomics, and have had a relatively large impact on the research of emergency equipment ergonomics.

## 3.5 Collaboration Patterns

Based on the graph density tool in Gephi, the total density of the entire network is calculated to be 0.011, which belongs to a lower level. As mentioned in the SNA section above, the density of the network, which varies between 0 and 1, is a measure of the connectivity of a network. Low density means the co-authorship network of emergency equipment ergonomics research is not very well-connected, and low network density is typical in co-authorship networks with large numbers of authors [15]. Nevertheless, the mean degree of centrality of the entire network is 4.613, meaning that on average every author has approximately 3 or 4 co-authors.

Besides the global network statistics, we then switch to node-level centrality measures to identify the central actors in our network with high levels of social and intellectual capital. Typically, central nodes in a network are important, insofar as they are able to influence the rest of the network [20]. These central actors may also become gatekeepers of the research community, and thus sought-after collaborators. It follows that identifying these actors is important for understanding the overall network structure. In this study, we employ two distinct centrality measures, i.e. degree and betweenness centrality.

**Table 7.** Degree and betweenness centrality, top 10 authors

| No. | Name | Degree | No. | Name | Betweenness |
|-----|------|--------|-----|------|-------------|
| 1 | SUN, L. | 18 | 1 | WEARS, R.L. | 0.022177 |
| 2 | FAIRBANKS, R.J. | 17 | 2 | SHI, J. | 0.016897 |
| 3 | WEARS, R.L. | 17 | 3 | LI, Z. | 0.016868 |
| 4 | LIN, L. | 14 | 4 | LI, Y. | 0.015941 |
| 5 | PERRY, S.J. | 14 | 5 | CARAYON, P. | 0.015332 |
| 6 | LI, Z. | 14 | 6 | FAIRBANKS, R.J. | 0.011207 |
| 7 | BISANTZ, A.M. | 13 | 7 | SUN, L. | 0.008608 |
| 8 | WIEGMANN, D. | 13 | 8 | WIEGMANN, D. | 0.008608 |
| 9 | BENDA, N.C. | 12 | 9 | PATTERSON, E.S. | 0.005999 |
| 10 | CLARK, L.N. | 12 | 10 | PERRY, S.J. | 0.005841 |

Table 7 shows the degree and normalized betweenness centrality measures for the top 10 authors for the entire network, along with the mean values for these measures. It can be seen from Table 7 that Sun, L, Fairbanks, R.J, Wears, R.L are ranked higher in the ranking of degree of centrality. Among the top ten authors, Fairbanks, RJ, Wears, and RL also ranked first and second, respectively. This shows that Fairbanks, RJ, and Wears, RL are not only active in the research of emergency equipment ergonomics, And the cooperation is more extensive.

For the above authors, we also collected data about their research interests and working institutions through Scopus. It was found that these authors mainly concentrated in the fields of medicine, safety science, psychology, engineering, computer science, neuroscience, and so on.

In addition to the cooperation between scholars, it is also necessary to understand the situation of emergency equipment ergonomic research between countries. To this end, we use BibExcel to extract the affiliation of the authors in the literature, and calculate the co-occurrence of the authors' institutions, and analyze the collaboration between countries and regions. Table 8 is the result of the frequency analysis of the co-occurrence of author countries and regions. It can be seen from the table that the three countries of the United States, the United Kingdom, and Italy are the central countries, and they have more connections with other countries. Among them, the United States has the closest cooperation with researchers in Brazil, Australia, and the United Kingdom, and has published more than 9 papers. As can be seen from the top ten countries and regions listed in the table, most of them are developed countries and regions.

**Table 8.** Collaborations between countries and regions

| No. | Countries and regions collaborated | Frequency |
|-----|-----------------------------------|-----------|
| 1 | Brazil and United States | 10 |
| 2 | Australia and United Kingdom | 9 |
| 3 | United Kingdom and United States | 8 |
| 4 | Canada and United States | 8 |
| 5 | Australia and New Zealand | 5 |
| 6 | Germany and United Kingdom | 4 |
| 7 | Germany and United States | 4 |
| 8 | Greece and Italy | 3 |
| 9 | Austria and Italy | 3 |
| 10 | France and Italy | 3 |

# 4 Conclusion

Based on the methods of bibliometrics and social network analysis, this paper analyzes the keywords and authors of 1125 articles of emergency equipment ergonomics from 1994 to 2020, and summarizes the current situation of emergency equipment ergonomics by quantitative methods. Through the quantitative analysis of bibliometrics, the study clarifies the research status and cooperation relationship in the field of emergency equipment ergonomics and determines the hot topics and key areas of research. The specific conclusions are as follows:

Firstly, by using the keyword analysis and co-word analysis, 114 keywords with a threshold value greater than 4 are selected in keyword analysis, accounting for 26.4% of the total number of keywords. Among them, the keywords with the highest frequency are "Safety", "Emergency response" and "Human error", indicating the key issues in the field of emergency equipment ergonomics. It is revealed that emergency equipment ergonomics research is still in its early stages and comes with kinds of opportunities and direction worldwide. According to keyword analysis and co-word analysis, it is revealed that the research on human factors of emergency equipment focuses on "medical safety", "safety standard", "human error" and "usability", indicating that the research in these areas is relatively high, which can be used as a representative of the field of emergency equipment Ergonomics research, while other topics and research points are relatively low.

Secondly, by using the social network analysis method to cluster the keywords, keywords are divided into 11 clusters, these keywords are divided into 11 clusters, by doing so, the theme groups of emergency equipment ergonomics are determined. These clusters are divided into high-level clusters and low-level clusters according to the measurement of their average frequency and average co-word frequency. High-level clusters with high keyword and co-word frequency mainly include "Emergency medical treatment", "Human error", "Safety standard system", "Safety supervision", which shows that these topics are the center of ergonomics research in the field of emergency equipment. According to the strategic map analysis, the clusters of keyword have been divided into four quadrants by density and centrality of the cluster, to reveal the current status and trend of the research of emergency equipment ergonomics. Researches on "Safety supervision", "Safety system" and "System cognitive decision" is relatively mature and at the core of the field of emergency equipment; researches on "Emergency medical treatment", "Human error" and "Human-machine interface design" is at the core of this field, but lack of mature development. It should be paid attention to continuously and considered to be the future direction of this field. Researches on "Emergency control", "Emergency medical system design" and "Emergency system engineering" are not popular and mature, which means they are on the edge of the field. The distribution of clusters in quadrants also shows that the research topic distribution in this field presents a trend of polarization, which means that there exist themes with high degrees of attention and development, and also themes with immature and marginalized development. This result also means that the field of emergency equipment ergonomics needs to have a balanced development of multi-polarization in the future.

The next, based on the analysis of the influence and cooperation mode of researchers in the field of emergency equipment ergonomics, it is found that the majority of authors are from the University of Rochester in the United States, Imperial College London in the United Kingdom and the University of Florida in the United States. In addition, there is no significant cooperative relationship between the authors, which shows that there are not many cooperative research phenomena between institutions. From the perspective of nations, the cooperation between developed countries in Europe and America is more frequent, mainly concentrated in the cooperation between the United States and the United Kingdom, Canada, Brazil, Germany, as well as the cooperation between Italy and Greece, Austria, France. Brazil makes the greatest contribution in developing countries and has close cooperation with the United States.

Nevertheless, analysis in this paper is far from being perfect, and these results need to be verified and recognized in further studies. On the one hand, the accuracy of this study is affected by the integrity of the literature contained in the scientific database network, because the literature contained in the database may be incomplete. On the other hand, the diversity of keywords and choosing keyword processing algorithms also affect the accuracy of bibliometric analysis. For instance, this study uses the affinity propagation method for keyword normalization, and the modularity clustering method provided by Gephi for keyword clustering, which results may be different from other methods of keyword normalization and modularity clustering. Moreover, this paper discussed the ergonomics and human factor researched the whole kinds of emergency equipment. Future studies could focus on specific emergency equipment such as medical equipment, personal protective equipment or hazard rescue equipment.

**Acknowledgement.** The research was supported by National Key Technologies R&D Program of China (2015BAH22F01).

# References

1. EMI Strategic Plan 2018–2022 (2018). https://training.fema.gov/strategicplan.aspx
2. Cabinet Office, Government of Japan. http://www.bousai.go.jp/kaigirep/chuobou/index.html
3. EURANOS: European approach to nuclear and radiological emergency management and rehabilitation strategies (2004). http://www.euranos.fzk.de
4. Liu, B., Zhao, X., Li, Y.: Review and prospect of studies on emergency management. Proc. Eng. **145**, 1501–1508 (2016)
5. Weijian, H., et al.: The demand study of the technological equipments for disposal to the emergency rescue of a great earthquake in China. Acta Scientiarum Naturalium Universitatis Pekinens, **46**(05), 844–850 (2010)
6. Yang, P., Liu, Y., Wang, Y., et al.: Qualitative and quantitative analysis on human factors under emergency state. Chem. Eng. Trans. **77**, 721–726 (2019)
7. Meho, L.I., Rogers, Y.: Citation counting, citation ranking, and h-index of human-computer interaction researchers: a comparison of scopus and web of science. J. Assoc. Inf. Sci. Technol. **59**(11), 1711–1726 (2008)
8. Gan, C., Wang, W.: Research characteristics and status on social media in China: a bibliometric and co-word analysis. Scientometrics **105**(2), 1167–1182 (2015)
9. Persson, O., Rickard, D., Wiborg Schneider, J.: How to use bibexcel for various types of bibliometric analysis. Celebrating Sch. Commun. Stud. Festschrift Olle Persson 60th Birthday **5**, 9–24 (2009)
10. Okubo Y.: Bibliometric indicators and analysis of research systems. Oecd Sci. Technol. Ind. Work. Pap. 649–655 (1997)
11. Guan, Y., Xiang, Y., Chen, K.: Research and application of visual analysis method based on Gephi. Telecommun. Sci. **29**(S1), 112–119 (2013)
12. Oh, N., Lee, J.: Changing landscape of emergency management research: a systematic review with bibliometric analysis. Int. J. Disaster Risk Reduct. 155–159 (2020)
13. Corrales-Reyes, I.E., Reyes-Pérez, J.J., Fornaris-Cedeño, Y.: Bibliometric analysis of the journal of oral research. J. Oral Res. **5**(5), 188–193 (2016)
14. Wasserman, S., Faust, K.: Social Network Analysis: Methods and Applications, vol. 8. Cambridge University Press, Cambridge (1994)
15. Ilhan Ali, O., Murat, C.: Oguz.: collaboration in design research: an analysis of co authorship in 13 design research journals. Des. J. **22**(1), 5–27 (2019)
16. Callon, M., Courtial, J.P., Laville, F.: Co-word analysis as a tool for describing the network of interactions between basic and technological research: the case of polymer chemistry. Scientometrics **22**(1), 155–205 (1991)
17. Muñoz-Leiva, F., et al.: An application of co-word analysis and bibliometric maps for detecting the most highlighting themes in the consumer behaviour research from a longitudinal perspective. Qual. Quant. **46**(4), 1077–1095 (2012)
18. Tang T., Xiao-Lan, H.E.: Research topics in the field of knowledge management in national fund projects based on strategic coordinate diagram. Inf. Sci. 2018, 36(02), 71 − 76 + 124 (2018)
19. Fahimnia, B., Tang, C.S., Davarzani, H., Sarkis, J.: Quantitative models for managing supply chain risks: a review. Euro. J. Oper. Res. **247**(1), 1–15 (2015)
20. Knoke, D., Burt, RS.: Prominence. Appl. Netw. Anal. 195–222 (1983)

# A Task Simulation and Ergonomics Analysis Method Based on JACK

Hongjun Xue[1], Jiayu Chen[1], and Xiaoyan Zhang[2(✉)]

[1] School of Aeronautics, Northwestern Polytechnical University,
Xi'an 710072, China
[2] School of Marine Science and Technology, Northwestern Polytechnical
University, Xi'an 710072, China
zxyliuyan@163.com

**Abstract.** Human errors are caused by unreasonable ergonomics design mostly. There are various ergonomics design and evaluation methods. However, traditional ergonomics evaluation methods are the absence of efficiency and convenience. This paper focuses on building a novel ergonomics method for system design and evaluation. This method enables to establish virtual circumstances, create a manikin model, assign the manikin to complete relevant tasks and perform man-machine ergonomic analysis in the process of task execution based on the software JACK. The ergonomic analysis includes dynamic spatial accessibility analysis, visibility analysis, working posture analysis and predicted time of completing tasks. This method has been vitrificated and validated by the task of rotating the left and right handles in the working scenario. Also, this method can be typically used to analyze and judge whether the human, machine and environment system is harmonious. In comparison to traditional methods, this method is given access to shorten the design cycle, reduce the research cost and improve the research efficiency.

**Keywords:** Ergonomic analysis · Task simulation · Dynamic spatial accessibility · Working posture analysis · JACK

## 1 Introduction

There is an association among operational errors and ergonomic design of man-machine interaction interface, such as display and operation system in the working environment. These are the exposure and embodiment of the weakness of man-machine interaction ability in the working environment [1]. In order to verify the display and operation system are reasonable, there is a need to build ergonomic evaluation methods to carry out man-machine ergonomic analysis. The ergonomic analysis should be executed to ensure the efficiency and health of workers [2, 3].

Currently, the methods used in ergonomic analysis had been developed rapidly including drawing inspection, solid model ergonomic analysis, simulator ergonomic analysis and computer-aided ergonomic analysis. The traditional methods have their range and area. The drawing inspection method can only provide the analysis data of initial design. The solid model ergonomic analysis requires real size environmental

© Springer Nature Switzerland AG 2020
C. Stephanidis et al. (Eds.): HCII 2020, LNCS 12429, pp. 584–594, 2020.
https://doi.org/10.1007/978-3-030-59987-4_41

model and a large number of subjects with different anthropometric data. Above all, these methods always need a long time to build and induced uneconomical and inefficient. Besides, authenticity of the simulated environment, number of subjects and individual differences will affect the accuracy of the analysis results in somehow [4]. Simulator ergonomic analysis requires the use of computer test equipment, which is the best tool for evaluation analysis to display the real size of the graphics. However, this method also needs a long time to construct model [5]. Computer-aided ergonomic analysis can utilize the information technology for ergonomic analysis, so that the product design cycle can be shortened, the productivity can be improved and the development cost can be reduced [6, 7]. Thus, these methods had been promoted rapidly to evaluate the product.

As far as we know, there are plenty of computer aided ergonomic analysis systems. For example, Dayton University established COMBIMAN for the U.S. Air Force in 1973 for flight attendants' vision analysis and hand accessibility analysis. Job Evaluator Toolbox [8] was an ergonomic analysis software based on network interface designed by Ergoweb. Company EASE [9] developed ErgoEase which is a manufacturing-oriented ergonomics analysis software. Sun [9] from Zhejiang University developed a prototype system called ZJU-ERGOMAN for man-machine simulation analysis. Liu [10] established a manikin modeling prototype system which reflects Chinese human body size characteristics in UGII environment. Yan [11] from Harbin Engineering University built a virtual manikin modeling system called OPEHM for ergonomic design and evaluation of automobiles under UG secondary development environment. Compared with traditional methods of ergonomics, computer-aided ergonomic analysis methods can evaluate the product scheme and model in advance in the design stage. It can be seen that computer-aided ergonomic analysis methods have been more and more concerned and applied.

In summary, in order to assist the efficient ergonomic evaluation, this paper proposes a task simulation and ergonomic evaluation analysis method based on the JACK. JACK is a software which can perform dynamic ergonomic analysis on the workers in the process of man-machine interaction. This method can not only focus on a single posture ergonomic, but also emphasize the dynamic ergonomic analysis on the process of the task. This computer-aided analysis method can simulate the actual working scenarios, which ensure that the analysis results are more accurate. Because of the efficiency of computer-aided evaluation, the method is of great significance to shorten the design cycle, reduce development costs and improve the development efficiency.

## 2   Method

### 2.1   Ergonomics Analysis Model

**The Modeling Platform JACK Software.** JACK is a software which includes different manikin modeling simulation and various ergonomic evaluation tools of Siemens industrial software company. It has intuitional operation interface, rich anthropometric database, complete ergonomic evaluation kit and powerful human motion simulation capability. Therefore in the demonstration and project stages of display and operation system, JACK can take human factors into comprehensive consideration by building different manikin models for ergonomic use. Meanwhile, JACK provides the ability to regard human, machine and environment as an organic whole to perform task simulation and ergonomic analysis. In the process of ergonomic analysis, JACK can simulate the manikin model dynamically, test the relationship among human, machine and environment more realistically and effectively and then optimize the display and operation system design. This paper selects JACK 8.0 as the platform of task simulation and ergonomic analysis.

**The Ergonomic Analysis Procedure.** To carry out task simulation and ergonomic analysis in JACK, we need to establish a virtual environment and a manikin model and put the manikin model into the environment with corresponding tasks. Through Task Analysis Toolkit, we can analyze the human factors of manikin model under the specific working environment [12], which includes spatial accessibility analysis, visibility analysis, working posture analysis and predicted time of corresponding tasks according to the work process. The procedure of task simulation and ergonomic analysis is presented in Fig. 1.

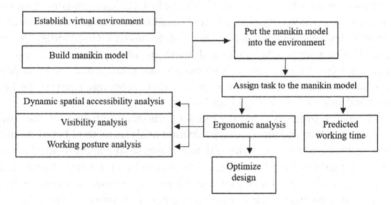

**Fig. 1.** The procedure of task simulation and ergonomic analysis

To create 3D simulation environment in JACK, we import two-dimensional figure data into simulated environment. After reading the data, we need to assemble the parts according to the requirements in the task process, and establish the environment model of the task process.

**The Manikin Modeling Method.** The steps followed is to show how to build manikin modeling in Fig. 2

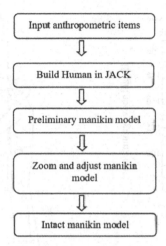

**Fig. 2.** The process of the build manikin modeling

Firstly, import 26 anthropometric items required in JACK from GB10000-88. And then input these 26 measured data into Build Human to create a preliminary manikin model. The zoom window of manikin model is shown in Fig. 3 The height and weight percentiles of male and female workers are respectively 99, 95, 50, 5 and 1.

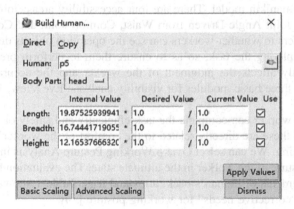

**Fig. 3.** The zoom window of manikin model

**The Evaluation Indicators.** The evaluation indicators in JACK include: dynamic spatial accessibility analysis, visibility analysis, working posture analysis and predicted time of completing tasks. Spatial accessibility means the static and dynamic dimensions of the range of the worker's limbs. The range of the close-up working space is constrained by the functional arm length. In order to maintain body balance, the work space of upper body and arms must be limited. Figure 4 shows the close-up working space of standing posture with a single arm and both arms based on the body size of the fifth percentile male [13].

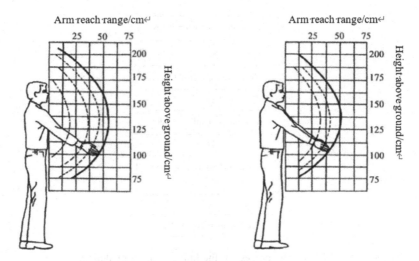

**Fig. 4.** Close-up working space of standing posture with a single arm and both arms

Accessibility affects not only the time and quality of task, but also the psychological state of workers. Therefore, if the worker cannot control the operation objects accurately, the task will not be completed safely and efficiently. By using the Reach Zones in JACK, we can generate a zone that maps out the maximum accessible range for specific size of manikin model. There are four accessibility areas: Joint Angle Driven from Shoulder, Joint Angle Driven from Waist, Comfort solid and Constraint Drive.

Visibility refers to whether workers can see the operation objects during the normal process of completing the task, so as to ensure them to perform precise operations. Visibility directly affects the judgment of the worker and the accuracy of the task. JACK provides three basic modules for visibility analysis: Eye View, View Cones and Visual Fields

Whether the worker can complete the task efficiently and safely or they are easy to feel tired, all of these are directly related to the comfort of the worker's posture in the process of working. We can select Ovako Working Posture Analysis in JACK to check the working posture of the worker in the ultimate state. The evaluation level is based on the load requirements of human's back, arms and legs. Table 1 shows the grades and corresponding "corrective needs" for working posture [14].

**Table 1.** The grades and corresponding "corrective needs" to working posture

| Level | "corrective needs" for working posture |
|---|---|
| 1 | The working posture is normal and there is no need to correct |
| 2 | The working posture may have some negative effects, it does not require immediate action, but should be adjusted in the near future |
| 3 | The working posture has negative effects, and it should be corrected as soon as possible |
| 4 | The working posture will do great harm, and it must be corrected immediately |

By using MTM-1 method to predict time of completing the task, the work process is divided accurately according to the basic action (therbligs). Working time analysis tools through application of MTM -1 therbligs as shown in Table 2. As a result, when we analyze working time, we need to divide a job into multiple parts at first and determine the working way and the influence of working equipment. Through the Predetermined Time Standard we can analyze the time needed to complete each part of the task and obtain the whole time of performing the task.

**Table 2.** Therbligs in JACK

| Number | Name | Logogram |
|--------|------|----------|
| 1 | Reach | R |
| 2 | Move | M |
| 3 | Turn | T |
| 4 | Apply Press | AP |
| 5 | Grasp | G |
| 6 | Positioning | P |
| 7 | Release | RL |
| 8 | Disengaging | D |
| 9 | Crank | C |
| 10 | Eye Track/Focus | ET |
| 11 | Foot/Leg Motion | FM |
| 12 | Side Step | SS |
| 13 | Walk | W |
| 14 | Kneel | K |
| 15 | Sit/Stand/Bend/Twist | SIT |

## 2.2 Ergonomics Analysis Example

**The Tasks.** In the operating environment, we can take the worker rotating the left and right handles respectively as an example. This task is generally applied to the operating environment of workers in aerospace, ship, railway and other industries. The workers have to operate objects with the standing posture and do subsequent actions including lifting the arms to grasp the handles, gripping the handles, and rotating the handles.

**The Analysis Process.** While establishing the task environment, the CATIA model is converted into format of ".jt" through ANSYS SCDM, which is suitable for JACK to read. During the transformation process, internal parts which have no effect on analysis results in the original model will be removed to improve the efficiency of ergonomic analysis.

We will take the Chinese male worker as an example for the establishment of the manikin model in JACK. In ergonomics, when using anthropometric dimensions to design or optimize a work platform, 5th manikin model is usually used. The 5th percentile model ensures that the design can meet the requirements of most workers. Therefore, the manikin model of the 5th Chinese male is selected in this case. The zoomed and adjusted manikin data of the 5th percentile of the Chinese male is shown in Fig. 5.

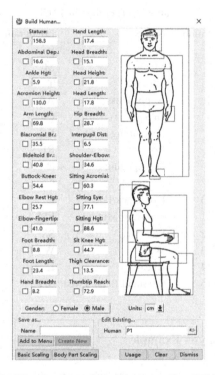

**Fig. 5.** Manikin size data of the 5th percentile of Chinese male

Assign the worker to finish the task in the task. Figure 6 shows that the worker faces handles. Figure 7 shows that the worker looks up at the handle while holding the right handle with his right hand.

**Fig. 6.** The worker faces rotate handles

**Fig. 7.** The worker looks up at the handle while holding the right handle with his right hand

To carry out spatial accessibility analysis under the working posture of the worker, we can use the Reach Zones and select the palm as the analysis benchmark of the maximum accessibility field. Then we can obtain the maximum accessibility field of the left and right hands. Spatial accessibility analysis is shown in Fig. 8.

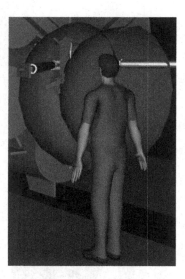

**Fig. 8.** Spatial accessibility analysis in working posture

When the workers need to rotate the left and right handles respectively, we can use the Eye View to analyze the worker's field of vision. The Fig. 9 shows the visuality analysis of the right eye when the worker uses his right hand to rotate the right handle.

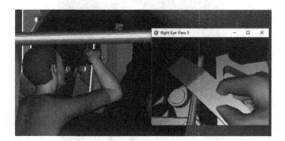

**Fig. 9.** Visuality analysis of the right eye in working posture

We can use Ovako Working Posture Analysis to check the worker's working posture when he is rotating the left and right handles respectively. Figure 10 shows the analysis result of the worker's working posture when the worker lifts his right arm to rotate the right handle.

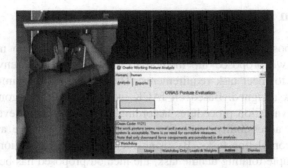

**Fig. 10.** Working posture analysis in working posture

According to the requirements of therbligs to decompose the task of rotating left and right handles respectively, we use the Predetermined Time Standards to calculate time. The results of the working time analysis are shown in Table 3.

**Table 3.** Time analysis according to therbligs decomposition

| Therbligs decomposition | Predicted time(s) |
| --- | --- |
| Left hand grasps the left handle (pose) | 0.634 |
| Adjust the posture of gripping left handle (get) | 0.504 |
| Rotate left handle (put) | 0.252 |
| Restore the standing posture (pose) | 0.634 |
| Right hand grasps the right handle (pose) | 0.634 |
| Adjust the posture of gripping right handle (get) | 0.504 |
| Rotate right handle (put) | 0.252 |
| Restore the standing posture (pose) | 0.634 |

## 3   Result

In this paper, Chinese male model in the 5th percentile has been built and assigned in the virtual working environment. The simulated human was required to perform the task of rotating the left and right handles respectively. By the ergonomic evaluation method built here, the results suggested that the left and right handles are accessible by the worker which meet the accessibility requirements in ergonomics, when the handles are rotated, the operating object locates in the visual range of the worker which meets the requirements of visuality field design in ergonomics and there is no need to correct when the working posture of rotating handles while the posture meets the requirements of ergonomics and reaches higher level. The predicted working time that required to complete the rotation of the left and right handles is 4.048 s. In the man-machine interaction task of rotating the handles, the results of ergonomic analysis meet the requirements of ergonomics. The worker can finish the assigned task safely and efficiently, which verifies the rationality of the original device design laterally.

## 4 Discussion and Conclusion

This paper proposes a task simulation and ergonomic evaluation method based on JACK. Firstly, we proposed the method to establish a virtual environment and a manikin model to meet task requirements. Then we make the simulated human to perform the task assigned. Based on JACK, we proposed the ergonomic evaluation indicators and evaluation procedures accordingly. To be specific, evaluations include dynamic spatial accessibility, visibility analysis, working posture analysis and predicted time of completing tasks. By using Jack to do the simulation and ergonomic analysis of a simple rotating handle task, the method proposed has been validated and verified.

The task simulation and ergonomic evaluation method based on JACK enable the designers to simulate actual work scenarios and take the emphasis on ergonomic analysis to optimize the system design. The results can serve to optimize the design to be safer, more efficient and more comfortable. Besides, the method can shorten the design cycle, reduce the research cost and improve the research efficiency to the maximum extent.

## References

1. Xue, H., Zhang, X: Ergonomic design and evaluation method in civil aircraft cockpit. Northwestern Polytechnical University, Xi'an (2012)
2. Zhang, X: Modeling and simulation of pilot dynamic vision and operation characteristics in cockpit. Northwestern Polytechnical University, Xi'an (2016)
3. Luo, J., Sun, S., Tang, M: Research on computer aided ergonomic design. J. Zhejiang Univ. (Eng. Sci.), 805–809 (2005)
4. Zhang, K., Hui, C., Shang, L.: Application of comprehensive evaluation method in ship cockpit design. J. Wuhan Univ. Technol. 35(5), 1077–1080 (2011)
5. Zhang, X: Research on ergonomic evaluation method in civil aircraft cockpit. Northwestern Polytechnical University, Xi'an (2010)
6. Feyen, R., Liu, Y., Chaffin, D.: Computer-aided ergonomics: a case study of incorporating ergonomics analyses into workplace design. Appl. Ergon. 31(3), 291–300 (2000)
7. Wilson, J.R., Corlett, E.N.: Evaluation of Human Work: a Practical Ergonomics Methodology. Taylor & Francis, London (1995)
8. Ergoweb Homepage, http://ergoweb.com/software/jet/
9. Xu, M: Human biomechanical model for ergonomic simulation analysis. Zhejiang University, Hangzhou (2006)
10. Liu, C: Human body modeling system for automotive ergonomic design and its key technologies. Wuhan University of Technology, Wuhan (2002)
11. Song, F.: Research on Virtual Human Body Model Based on Automotive Ergonomics. Harbin Engineering University, Harbin (2007)
12. Tan, Z., Xue, H., Su, R.: Research on evaluation of cockpit visibility of civil aircraft based on JACK. Aeronaut. Comput. Technol. 40(5), 79–82 (2010)
13. Ding, Y.: Ergonomics. Beijing Institute of Technology Press, Beijing (2011)
14. Niu, J: Human factors engineering foundation and application examples based on JACK. Electronic Industry Press, Beijing (2012)

# Classification of Human Posture with RGBD Camera: Is Deep Learning Necessary?

Hongbo Zhang[1]($\boxtimes$) ⓘ, Denis Gračanin[2] ⓘ, and Mohamed Eltoweissy[1] ⓘ

[1] Virginia Military Institute, Lexington 24450, USA
{zhangh,eltoweissymy}@vmi.edu
[2] Virginia Tech, Blacksburg 24060, USA
gracanin@vt.edu

**Abstract.** We describe an approach to human posture classification using RGBD camera (Kinect V2 sensor) data. We compared deep learning methods for human posture classification versus classical data classification methods. We conducted a user study where participants assumed various postures, including whole body, upper and lower body, as well as body transition motion. Several classical data classification methods, such as support vector machine, random forest, neural network, and Adaboost, were used for posture classification. Results show that the posture classification accuracy for the classical data classification methods is between 75% an 99%. The accuracy of the classical data classification methods is comparable to the accuracy of the long-short-term-memory (LSTM) deep learning method which is between 86% and 99%. Our findings suggest that the use of the classical data classification methods on the RGBD camera data is likely sufficient for posture classification, at least for certain task scenarios without incurring the overhead of deep learning.

**Keywords:** Computer vision · Human posture · Deep learning · Machine learning

## 1 Introduction

Classical human posture classification methods use reflective markers for capturing human motion [17,21–23]. However, portable RGBD camera (e.g., Kinect V2 sensor) do not require markers and support 3D tracking [9]. Kinect sensor was used for various tasks including gait cycle detection [20], motion pattern quantification for Parkinson's disease [6], detection of foot posture [12], kinematics measurement in workspace [4], sport training [24], human metabolic rate determination [13], hand motion recognition [16], and senior health monitor [15]. These studies suggest that the accuracy of Kinect sensor for evaluation of human motion tasks is acceptable [2].

© Springer Nature Switzerland AG 2020
C. Stephanidis et al. (Eds.): HCII 2020, LNCS 12429, pp. 595–607, 2020.
https://doi.org/10.1007/978-3-030-59987-4_42

Some recent classification approaches use deep learning methods to address various challenges, such as cluttered backgrounds, occlusions, viewpoint variation, execution rate, and camera motion [19]. The examples include measurement of upper extremity motion [11], human action recognition [1], and geometry based learning strategy for action recognition [14], person identification [8], and people counting (using deep residual learning framework) [5].

Deep learning methods are computationally expensive and require hardware such as graphic processing unit (GPU) for training. They also need large datasets for training (e.g., ImageNet [3]). The training and fine tuning costs are also extensive. The classical data classification methods, such as support vector machine, random forest, have the advantage that they can work on inexpensive hardware and with limited training resources. However, these classical methods often have lower accuracy compared to the deep learning methods [10].

Therefore, the question is whether the classical data classification methods can be used on RGBD camera data to accurately classify various postures. To answer this question, we have designed the following study to collect human posture data and apply both classical machine learning and deep learning methods for classification of the posture. The study can contribute to the selection of effective method for posture classification.

## 2    Method

We conducted a preliminary user study where five participants assumed various postures, including whole body, upper and lower body, as well as body transition motion. All participants have signed the consent form. At the beginning of the study, participants were asked to warm up first to get themselves familiar with the experimental setup. Each participant performed indoor posture tasks in a random order. The tasks required completion of whole body, upper body, lower body, and body transition motion, as shown in Table 1.

The postures are shown in Fig. 1. The experiment is conducted in a general indoor environment, where no particular setting requirement is imposed.

Figure 1 shows the joint centers (layered over the participant) connected by the green lines, as provided by the Kinect V2 sensor SDK. Evidently, the missing markers or redundant markers persist through some trials of the experiment. These data were subsequently removed manually by screening the markers data prior to data processing step.

Following data collection, the image classification label was made by using our customized image labeler. The collected raw images were processed through Kinect V2 camera SDK, where 3D kinematics data $(x, y, z)$ coordinates of body poses were obtained. That includes foot, ankle, knee, hip, spine, shoulder, elbow, wrist, and hand. The 3D coordinates of both left and right joints are considered.

**Table 1.** The summary of investigated body postures.

| Whole Body Motion | Lower Body Motion | Body Transition Motion |
|---|---|---|
| *Jumping posture* Participants perform intermittent jumps in the frontal plane. One image is taken when participants jump off from the ground. Another image is taken during the landing phase. | *Sit to stand posture* Participants raise their left/right leg intermittently in the sagittal plane. One image is taken when participants either raise their left or right leg. Another image is taken when participants lower their their left or right leg. | *Leg raising/lowering posture* Participants perform the transition of sit to stand posture in the sagittal plane. One image is taken while participants are in the sitting posture and another image is taken for standing posture. |
| **Upper Body Motion** | | |
| *Bending posture* Participants bend forward intermittently in the sagittal plane. One image is taken while participants assume the upright posture. Another image is taken while participants bend forward in the sagittal plane. | *Turning posture* Participants turn their body intermittently in the transverse plane. One image is taken while body turns in the transverse plane with both arms held horizontally in front of their chests at left side of the body. Another image is taken at the right side of body. | |

The 3D coordinates of joint center are concatenated to serve as the training input for the classification. Each posture is also associated with a numerical label to serve as the ground truth of the classification. The Hyper parameters of the classifiers are shown in Table 2. The train-and-test split ratio is set at 60% to 40%. In order to address the over-fitting, the random integer noises of zero or one are applied to the labels of the data prior to the processing step by classifiers.

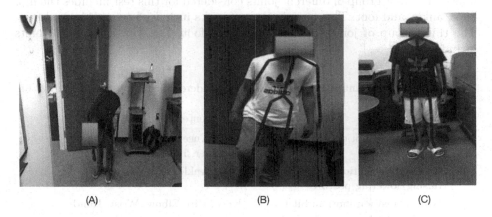

(A)                    (B)                    (C)

**Fig. 1.** The postures assumed by the participants: (**A**) bending posture; (**B**) leg raising and lowering; and (**C**) upright standing.

All the images were taken using one Kinect V2 sensor (Microsoft, Inc.). Each posture is repeated 2,000 times with the intermittent time interval between two consecutive motions at the comfortable pace for the participants to ensure the completion of postures and also allow the postures to be recorded by the RGBD camera.

We removed some redundant data (insignificant joint motion data) during the classification process to reduce the confounding variables as well as to improve the efficiency of training of the classification, as shown in Table 3. For example, during the upper body motion, the lower body motion is limited and thus could be ignored. Similarly, the upper body motion is limited during the lower body motion thus the upper body motion was not included in the analysis.

**Table 2.** The summary of hyper-parameters of classification methods.

| Method name | Hyper parameters |
|---|---|
| Support vector machine | Linear kernel |
| Gaussian Naive Bayesian (NB) | Largest variance of the features $= 10^{-9}$ |
| Random forest | The number of trees in the forest $= 10$ |
| | Minimum samples split $= 2$ |
| AdaBoost | Maximum number of estimators where boosting is terminated $= 50$ |
| | Learning rate $= 1$ |
| Neural network | 9 hidden units (3 layers in total) |

More specifically, the different number of joints involved for determining the classification accuracy of leg raising and lowering motion has also been determined. The first group of different joints considered for this test includes the hip, knee, ankle, and foot. The second group of joints includes knee, ankle, and foot. The third group of joints includes ankle and foot. The fourth group of joints includes foot.

**Table 3.** The significant motion joint centers considered for the posture classification.

| Body motion | Joint center |
|---|---|
| Whole body motion: Jumping posture | Foot, Knee, Hip, Spine, Head, Shoulder, Elbow, Wrist, Hand |
| Lower body motion: Leg raising/lowering posture | Foot, Ankle, Knee |
| Body transition motion: Sit to stand posture | Knee, Hip, Elbow, Wrist, Hand |
| Upper body motion | Bend posture: Spine, Hip, Head, Shoulder, Elbow, Wrist, Hand |
| | Turn posture: Knee, Hip, Shoulder, Elbow, Wrist, Hand |

The impact of noise on the classification accuracy has also been analyzed. Different noise levels were applied on the labels of the data. The noise levels chosen as the percentage of the labels respectively at the following ratios of all labels: 1.5/100, 4.5/100, 8/100, 15/100, 20/100, and 30/100.

A comparison of the classical classification methods with deep learning methods is done using the long-short-term-memory (LSTM) deep learning method [7], as shown in Fig. 2. The left side shows the input, where the $(x, y, z)$ coordinates are used. For the LSTM method, it further shows the cell state and (C) the hidden state (H).

In total, there are five sequential layers of LSTM modules, where the modules are interconnected through the cell state for achieving the long term dependency cell state memorizing effect. The five layers of LSTM modules are further processed through fully connected layers as the output for classifying the posture. Within the LSTM method, the cross entropy is used as the loss function. It is well known that learning rate is one of the most important hyper-parameter of the LSTM method. For ensuring the continuous decrease of the loss function and improvement of the accuracy, the cyclic learning rate is employed to fine tune the learning rate [18].

For the cyclic learning rate, the key idea is to alter the learning rate rather than keeping it at a fixed value or simply monotonically decreasing the learning rate. More specifically, we adopted the cos function as the changes of the learning rate through the training process. Experiments show that the adoption of the cyclic learning rate is effective to keep the loss function decrease while ensuring the improvement of the accuracy. Early stopping is utilized to avoid over-fitting.

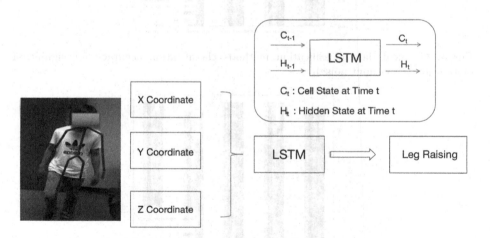

**Fig. 2.** The diagram of the long short term memory (LSTM) method used for posture classification.

## 3  Results

The results of classification for different postures using different classifiers are provided in Figs. 3, 4, and 5. Figure 3 shows the classification accuracy when only the relevant joints are considered. Figure 4 shows the classification accuracy when only the relevant joints are considered with Gaussian input noises added. Figure 5 shows the classification accuracy for all joint centers considered.

The impact of noise on the classification accuracy is shown in Fig. 6 for the different noise levels applied to leg raising and lowering motion. Specifically, for the leg raising and lowering motion we used six different level ratios, 1.5/100, 4.5/100, 8/100, 15/100, 20/100, and 30/100 of all labels are contaminated with noises.

Features extracted from different groups of joints and how they influence the leg raising and lowering motion classification accuracy are shown in Fig. 7. The choices of these different joint groups for posture classification are driven by the principles that for leg raising and lowering motion, the upper body does not

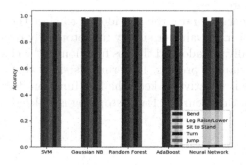

**Fig. 3.** Classical data classification methods classification accuracy for significant motion joints (without noise).

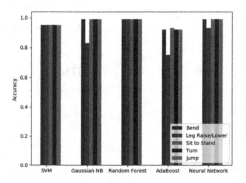

**Fig. 4.** Classical data classification methods classification accuracy for significant motion joints (with random noise, zero or one, added).

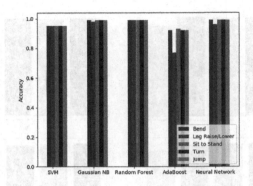

**Fig. 5.** Classical data classification methods classification accuracy for all joints (without noise).

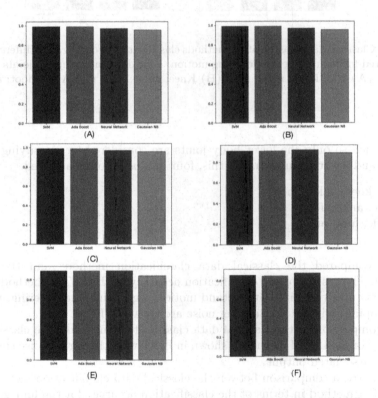

**Fig. 6.** Classical data classification methods classification accuracy with different noises applied on the label of leg raising and lowering motion. Six different level ratios of all labels contaminated with noise: **(A)** 1.5/100; **(B)** 4.5/100; **(C)** 8/100; **(D)** 15/100; **(E)** 20/100; and **(F)** 30/100.

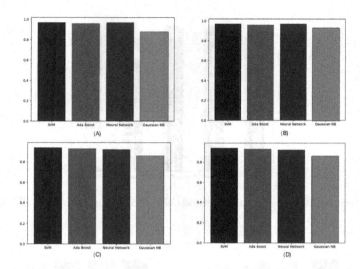

**Fig. 7.** Classical data classification methods classification accuracy with different joints considered for leg raising and lowering motion. Four different groups of joints are considered: **(A)** Hip, knee, ankle, foot; **(B)** Knee, ankle, foot; **(C)** Ankle, foot; and **(D)** Foot.

move much so only the lower body joints are considered for classifying the leg raising and lowering motion. For this, four groups of joints are used:

1. Hip, knee, ankle, foot;
2. Knee, ankle, foot;
3. Ankle, foot; and
4. Foot

We compared the classical data classification methods and the LSTM method. The results of the classification accuracy of the LSTM method for different postures (bending, sit to stand motion, leg raising and lowering, turning, and jumping) without considering noise are shown in Fig. 8.

In comparison to the classical data classification methods, the classification accuracy of the LSTM method is shown in Fig. 9 with the varied noise conditions and the associated output.

Similarly, a comparison betwen the classical data classification methods and the LSTM method in terms of the classification accuracy for the four groups of joints is shown in Fig. 10.

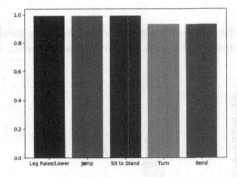

**Fig. 8.** The LSTM method classification accuracy for different postures (without noise).

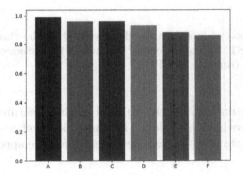

**Fig. 9.** The LSTM method classification accuracy with different types of noise applied on the label of leg raising and lowering motion. Six different ratios of all labels contaminated with noise: **A)** 1.5/100; **B)** 4.5/100; **C)** 8/100; **D)** 15/100; **E)** 20/100; and **F)** 30/100.

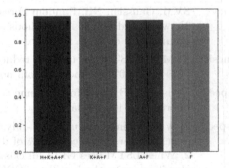

**Fig. 10.** The LSTM method classification accuracy with different joints considered for leg raising and lowering motion. Four different groups of joints (**H**ip, **K**nee, **A**nkle, and **F**oot) are considered (without noise).

A comparison between the classical machine learning methods and the LSTM method in terms of inference speed (40% of data) is shown in Fig. 11.

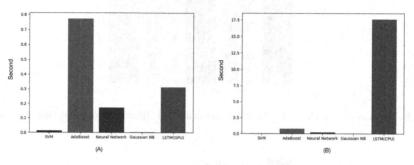

**Fig. 11.** A comparison of inference speed between: **(A)** the classical data classification methods and LSTM (running on GPU); and **(B)** the classical data classification methods and LSTM (running on CPU).

A brief comparison between the classical machine learning methods and the LSTM method is provided in Table 4. The comparison metrics include the highest accuracy, most resistant to noises, the fastest inference speed, and the slowest inference speed.

**Table 4.** A brief comparison between the classical data classification methods and the LSTM method

| Metric | Superior method(s) |
| --- | --- |
| The highest accuracy | SVM, Gaussian NB, Random Forest, Neural Network, and LSTM All methods achieved 99% of accuracy for different scenarios |
| Most resistant to nosie | SVM and LSTM Accuracy is reduced from 99% to 86% when 30% of labels contain noise |
| Fastest inference speed | Gaussian NB The inference time is 0.0024 s for inference of 40% of data |
| Slowest inference speed | 1. When all methods use CPU only, LSTM is the slowest (17.6 s for inference of 40% of data) 2. When LSTM uses GPU, all classical data classification methods still use CPU AdaBoost is the slowest (0.77 second for inference of 40% of data) |

# 4    Conclusion

We explored the posture classification performance when using classical data classification methods on RGBD camera data. Results have shown that the classical data classification methods are able to classify the posture with accuracy ranging between 75% and 99% (mostly >95%). We have also examined the use of relevant joint centers as well as the complete joint centers and compared their posture classification performance.

Interestingly, the results have shown that the use of only the significant motion joints is sufficient for classifying the posture in comparison to the use of all joints for classification. We have also varied the number of joints involved in the classification process for leg raising and lowering motion. The reduced number of joints does induce the reduction of the classification accuracy from over 90% to over 84%. However, the majority of the classification accuracy is still over 90%. It only drops to over 85% only when a single motion joint (foot) is considered.

The introduction of noise to address the over-fitting demonstrates that the performance of the classifier does not decreases significantly even when random integer noise for the labels is added. Following the introduction of six noise levels, the classical data classification methods accuracy drops from over 90% to over 80%. The classification accuracy however only starts to fall below 80% when there are at least 20% of labels contain noise.

We have also compared the classical data classification methods with the LSTM method. The results show that the LSTM method is able to achieve on-par or slightly better classification accuracy.

The classification accuracy of classical data classification methods is between 75% and 99%, where the LSTM method has accuracy between 86% and 99%. Indeed, the LSTM method does seem to yield better performance in terms of the worst classification performance, but for the majority of the conditions, classical data classification methods do provide sufficient accuracy.

Results also show that the inference speed of the classical data classification methods is not inferior to the LSTM method. As a matter of fact, the Gaussian NB method has the highest inference speed, even when the LSTM method uses GPU. The LSTM method is up to 20 times slower compared to the slowest classical data classification methods, when GPU is not used.

Our findings can help guide the choice of different classifiers for different posture classification tasks. The research has practical implications for motion related applications such as health and safety monitoring.

# References

1. Chang, M.J., Hsieh, J.T., Fang, C.Y., Chen, S.W.: A vision-based human action recognition system for moving cameras through deep learning. In: Proceedings of the 2019 2nd International Conference on Signal Processing and Machine Learning, pp. 85–91. ACM, New York (2019)
2. Clark, R.A., Pua, Y.H., Bryant, A.L., Hunt, M.A.: Validity of the Microsoft Kinect for providing lateral trunk lean feedback during gait retraining. Gait Posture **38**(4), 1064–1066 (2013)
3. Deng, J., Dong, W., Socher, R., Li, L.J., Li, K., Fei-Fei, L.: ImageNet: a large-scale hierarchical image database. In: Proceedings of the 2009 IEEE Conference on Computer Vision and Pattern Recognition, 20–25 June, pp. 248–255. IEEE (2009)
4. Dutta, T.: Evaluation of the Kinect$^{TM}$ sensor for 3-D kinematic measurement in the workplace. Appl. Ergon. **43**(4), 645–649 (2012)
5. Fuentes-Jimenez, D., et al.: DPDnet: a robust people detector using deep learning with an overhead depth camera. Expert Syst. Appl. **146**, 113168 (2020)
6. Galna, B., Barry, G., Jackson, D., Mhiripiri, D., Olivier, P., Rochester, L.: Accuracy of the Microsoft Kinect sensor for measuring movement in people with Parkinson's disease. Gait Posture **39**(4), 1062–1068 (2014)
7. Hochreiter, S., Schmidhuber, J.: Long short-term memory. Neural Comput. **9**(8), 1735–1780 (1997)
8. Huynh-The, T., Hua, C.H., Tu, N.A., Kim, D.S.: Learning 3D spatiotemporal gait feature by convolutional network for person identification. Neurocomputing **397**, 192–202 (2020)
9. Kaenchan, S., Mongkolnam, P., Watanapa, B., Sathienpong, S.: Automatic multiple Kinect cameras setting for simple walking posture analysis. In: Proceedings of the 2013 International Computer Science and Engineering Conference (ICSEC), pp. 245–249 (2013)
10. Krizhevsky, A., Sutskever, I., Hinton, G.E.: ImageNet classification with deep convolutional neural networks. Commun. ACM **60**(6), 84–90 (2017)
11. Ma, Y., Liu, D., Cai, L.: Deep learning-based upper limb functional assessment using a single Kinect v2 sensor. Sensors **20**(7), 1903 (2020)
12. Mentiplay, B.F., Clark, R.A., Mullins, A., Bryant, A.L., Bartold, S., Paterson, K.: Reliability and validity of the Microsoft Kinect for evaluating static foot posture. J. Foot Ankle Res. **6**(14), 10 (2013)
13. Na, H., Choi, J.H., Kim, H., Kim, T.: Development of a human metabolic rate prediction model based on the use of Kinect-camera generated visual data-driven approaches. Build. Environ. **160**, 106216 (2019)
14. Papadakis, A., Mathe, E., Spyrou, E., Mylonas, P.: A geometric approach for cross-view human action recognition using deep learning. In: Proceedings of the 11th International Symposium on Image and Signal Processing and Analysis (ISPA), 23–25 September 2019, pp. 258–263. IEEE
15. Parajuli, M., Tran, D., Ma, W., Sharma, D.: Senior health monitoring using Kinect. In: Proceedings of the 2012 Fourth International Conference on Communications and Electronics (ICCE), 1–2 August 2012, pp. 309–312. IEEE
16. Pedersoli, F., Adami, N., Benini, S., Leonardi, R.: XKin -: extendable hand pose and gesture recognition library for Kinect. In: Proceedings of the 20th ACM International Conference on Multimedia, pp. 1465–1468. ACM, New York (2012)
17. Qu, X., Xie, Y., Hu, X., Zhang, H.: Effects of fatigue on balance recovery from unexpected trips. Hum. Factors **62**(6), 919–927 (2020)

18. Smith, L.N.: Cyclical learning rates for training neural networks. In: Proceedings of the 2017 IEEE Winter Conference on Applications of Computer Vision (WACV), 24–31 March 2017, pp. 464–472. IEEE
19. Wu, D., Sharma, N., Blumenstein, M.: Recent advances in video-based human action recognition using deep learning: a review. In: Proceedings of the 2017 International Joint Conference on Neural Networks (IJCNN), 14–19 May 2017, pp. 2865–2872. IEEE
20. Xu, X., McGorry, R.W., Chou, L.S., Lin, J.H., Chang, C.C.: Accuracy of the Microsoft Kinect$^{TM}$ for measuring gait parameters during treadmill walking. Gait Posture **42**(2), 145–51 (2015)
21. Zhang, H.: A comparison of critical time interval between young and old subjects. In: Rau, P.-L.P. (ed.) HCII 2019. LNCS, vol. 11577, pp. 270–278. Springer, Cham (2019). https://doi.org/10.1007/978-3-030-22580-3_20
22. Zhang, H., Nussbaum, M., Agnew, M.: A time–frequency approach to estimate critical time intervals in postural control. Comput. Methods Biomech. Biomed. Eng. **8**(15), 1693–1703 (2015)
23. Zhang, H., Nussbaum, M.A., Agnew, M.J.: Use of wavelet coherence to assess two-joint coordination during quiet upright stance. J. Electromyogr. Kinesiol. **24**(5), 607–613 (2014)
24. Zhang, L., Chien Hsieh, J., Wang, J.: A Kinect-based golf swing classification system using HMM and neuro-fuzzy. In: Proceedings of the 2012 International Conference on Computer Science and Information Processing (CSIP), 24–26 August 2012, pp. 1163–1166. IEEE

# Author Index

Printed in the United States
By Bookmasters